The Clinical Practice of Educational Therapy

Despite the wide array of services offered to students with learning disabilities, attention-deficit disorder, and a variety of comorbid conditions, large numbers of students are caught in the struggle of surviving school. Unfortunate school experiences may impact their sense of self and the degree of tenacity with which they pursue further training or challenging opportunities in the workplace. These are the people for whom educational therapy provides relief, enlightenment, and the coveted prize of success.

This is the first book to provide a comprehensive review of the interdisciplinary profession and practice of educational therapy as it exists today. It describes the scope and practice of educational therapy from its European roots to its growing presence in the United States and provides case studies to illustrate the work of educational therapists.

Interdisciplinary Perspective—Other books focus on either educational or therapeutic interventions but rarely discuss the blend and synergy of disciplines (e.g., special education, neuropsychology, assessment, and social work) that are the hallmark of this unique profession.

Illustrative Cases—The text draws heavily on case studies as a means of understanding the practice of educational therapy, especially the dynamic relationship that exists between therapist and client.

Expertise—The editors are both highly visible educational therapists. Chapter authors are either experienced educational therapists or allied professionals who have made scholarly contributions to the profession, such as Dorothy Ungerleider, Patricia Waters, Roslyn Arnold, and George McCloskey.

This book is appropriate for not only educational therapists, but also for professionals who work in related fields such as special education, regular education, school and educational psychology, school counseling, psychology, speech and language pathology, occupational therapy, social work as well as in medicine and psychiatry.

Maxine Ficksman, M.A., a board certified educational therapist, has worked in regular and special education for the past forty years, specializing in guiding students with learning difficulties and their families through the educational process as well as developing, coordinating, and teaching graduate level training programs and courses in educational therapy.

Jane Utley Adelizzi, Ph.D., a board certified educational therapist and published author whose work focuses on the impact of psychological trauma and its impact on learning and functioning, has worked in higher education for over twenty-five years. She has developed programs for older adolescents and adults who live with the fear and memories of school failure and the emotional impact of these struggles.

The Clinical Practice of Educational Therapy

A Teaching Model

Edited by
Maxine Ficksman
Jane Utley Adelizzi

Routledge
Taylor & Francis Group

NEW YORK AND LONDON

First published 2010
by Routledge
270 Madison Avenue, New York, NY 10016

Simultaneously published in the UK
by Routledge
2 Park Square, Milton Park, Abingdon, Oxon OX14 4RN

Routledge is an imprint of the Taylor & Francis Group, an informa business

Typeset in Minion by EvS Communication Networx, Inc.
Printed and bound by TJ International Ltd, Padstow, Cornwall

Library of Congress Cataloging-in-Publication Data
Ficksman, Maxine.
The clinical practice of educational therapy : a teaching model / by Maxine Ficksman and Jane Utley Adelizzi.
p. cm.
Includes bibliographical references and index.
1. Educational psychology. 2. Educational psychologists—In-service training. I. Adelizzi, Jane Utley. II. Title.
LB1051.F45 2010
371.7'13—dc22
2009040391

ISBN 10: 0-415-99856-5 (hbk)
ISBN 10: 0-415-99857-3 (pbk)
ISBN 10: 0-203-85549-3 (ebk)

ISBN 13: 978-0-415-99856-7 (hbk)
ISBN 13: 978-0-415-99857-4 (pbk)
ISBN 13: 978-0-203-85549-2 (ebk)

To the family I cherish:
my husband, David, daughter, Caroline, and son, Eric,
for their love, humor and inspiration.

MF

Thank you, Gene, for nudging me forward with this project.
Thank you Loryn, Brandon, Jodi, and Lily for your presence in my life.

JUA

There are no extra pieces in the universe.
Everyone is here because he or she has a place to fill,
and every piece must fit itself into the big jigsaw puzzle.

~Deepak Chopra~

Every worthwhile accomplishment, big or little,
has its stages of drudgery and triumph;
a beginning, a struggle, and a victory.

~Ghandi~

CONTENTS

FOREWORD

ALBERT M. GALABURDA, MD

What a cardiologist is to a person with coronary artery disease, or a psychiatrist to a person with obsessive–compulsive disorder, an educational therapist is to an individual with a learning disability. Just as the patient with angina, or heart failure, depends on the medical specialist for her knowledge, experience, and dedication, so does the student with school difficulties depend on the educational specialist's unique abilities and training.

A learning disability is not very different from a heart ailment, after all. Both have innate and environmental components, or, stated in another way, in both a part of the problem is inherited, while the rest is learned (Is it a compensation or a response to a hostile environment?). Some people inherit a propensity to develop heart disease, but the lives they lead can help worsen or ameliorate the consequences of this inheritance. Smoking, for instance, which damages the inside of blood vessels, is a well-known sociocultural habit that brings out the worst in someone's inherited tendency to develop coronary artery disease. The same is true with learning disabilities. An individual who has inherited genes for dyslexia, for instance, may engage in self-destructive behaviors that worsen the deficits and hamper the ability of special educators to treat them. But also, an individual with learning disabilities may simply fall prey to the demeaning effects of his failures and become depressed, anxious, angry, or even worse—apathetic.

There exist genes—more of them being identified every year—that predispose to one or another learning disability. But, everyone with these genes does not go on to manifest the disability to the same degree. Some children are protected by other genes they may harbor, to be sure, but many are also protected by sociocultural factors, such as the nature of the language tasks they need to master (the language they speak), the quality of the school system to which they have access, and, I daresay, the state of their mental health. As with anything, the mental health of a patient with genetic and learned cognitive and behavioral deficits plays an important role in the severity of the clinical manifestations and in their treatment. A depressed or angry patient following a heart attack will be much less likely to stick to a program of cardiac rehabilitation, for sure. Moreover, they will be more likely to engage in self-damage. Of course, if one believes that learning disabilities are just another example of a medical condition, by virtue of the presence of special genes and unique brains underlying the dysfunction, together with sometimes toxic learned behaviors, one would be correct in thinking of educational therapists as important members of the team of allied medical/educational professionals trusted to improve the health and quality of life of these particular fellow human beings.

The present book defines the field of educational therapy, presents case studies that illustrate challenges and successes, as well as possibilities for failure, and harps on the importance of the relationship that is established between a failing student and her educational therapist. The book clearly establishes that an educational therapist specializes in the emotional complications of educational failure, a welcome member of the team with a role that usefully complements the work of special educators and medical professionals. The reader who did not previously know about this specialized contribution will learn a great deal, and the initiated will be able to hone his and her skills.

PREFACE

In the mid-1960s Maxine attended Boston University, the front doors of which opened onto Commonwealth Avenue. This young woman from New York was not daunted by the city of Boston, but rather embraced the urbanity of the hub and voguish Kenmore Square, enjoying her undergraduate studies in education. During the same period of time, Jane, a native of the area, was attending the Art Institute of Boston on Beacon Street, the back windows of which faced the front doors of Boston University on Commonwealth Avenue. Maxine may have been interning at a school in the area while Jane was sketching in Boston's North End. Both young women surely bumped elbows at mixers, or crossed paths on Newbury Street, unbeknownst to the fact that they would be coediting a book together many years later.

Time passed, and both women married and had families. Maxine received her first master's degree in secondary education and taught reading in the New York City schools. After moving across the country to Tarzana, California, she prepared for a career in educational therapy by seeking a special education credential, a second master's in reading and involvement in the Association of Educational Therapists (AET), founded in the Los Angeles area. Jane remained in the Canton, Massachusetts area, taught in higher education in New England for many years, eventually pursuing her doctoral degree in education, the focus of which was the impact of psychological trauma on learning and functioning. She went on to research and write about the practice of educational therapy, and became a member of AET in the 1980s, not knowing that Maxine was the president of this professional organization!

While Maxine was developing multiple post-masters training and certificate programs in educational therapy in California, Jane was developing the first AET study group in the Greater Boston area, eventually offering post-master's courses in educational therapy at a local college. Both women worked with clients across the life span, understanding the experience of children who struggled with the culture of school and the academic tasks that comprise their individual profiles. Similar to many ETs, these women developed a keen insight into how and why these experiences impact the lives of adults as they transition from one stage of human development to the next.

Both Jane and Maxine envisioned a book about the unique and interdisciplinary practice of educational therapy for a very long time, knowing full well what an undertaking this project would be. During the summer of 2007 Maxine called Jane and asked her if she was interested in coediting a book with her about the unique profession which had helped to define their individual and collective work. Predictably, Jane responded with an unhesitating "yes!" For a 2 year period both women recruited, invited, and collaborated with authors, exploring the many aspects of the practice that would be most useful to both veteran and novice ETs.

ACKNOWLEDGMENTS

As the coeditors we wish to thank the contributing authors for their hard work, their perseverance, and the spirit they bring to the profession of educational therapy. Their patience and endurance has been deeply appreciated since the book's neophyte stage. Thank you to each and every one of you!

We are grateful for the support and encouragement of Risa Graff, the Association of Educational Therapists' (AET's) current president, and Deborah Doyle, AET's most recent former president. All of the former AET presidents and members laid the groundwork for the realization of this book, which will contribute to the professional training of educational therapists, and create a place among the ranks of other licensed, professional models in the fields of education, psychology, and sociology.

Without the grass-roots efforts of the following professionals, the practice of educational therapy would not be the burgeoning field it is today: Dorothy Ungerleider, who employed the methods developed by her predecessors such as Maryanne Frostig and Selma Sapir, established the Association of Educational Therapy in California; Gertrude Webb, an innovative educator and interventionist for students with learning disabilities, developed the first mainstreamed program in the nation to assist college students with learning disabilities, while Charles Drake was opening the doors to the Landmark School at Prides Crossing; and Irene Caspari, a principal psychologist at the Tavistock Clinic in London, whose efforts led to the creation of the Caspari Foundation, a charitable organization for children who experience difficulty with learning. We are honored to continue their work.

We wish to thank our clients across the lifespan who have permitted us to witness their struggles as well as their achievements in life.

A special thank you to:

The editorial staff at Routledge, especially Lane Akers for understanding our vision, and to Alex Sharp for her support and patience.

David Ficksman for his legal counsel. Kathryn Francis for her technological expertise.

When he took time to help the man up the mountain, lo, he scaled it himself.

(Tibetan Proverb)

I

Theoretical and Historical Framework of Educational Therapy

1

THE DYNAMIC OF EDUCATIONAL THERAPY
Theoretical Framework and Model

MAXINE FICKSMAN AND JANE UTLEY ADELIZZI

I've learned that people will forget what you said, people will forget what you did, but people will never forget how you made them feel.
(**Maya Angelou cited in Haffner & Hutchinson, 2009, p. 70**)

The words of Maya Angelou describe the heart and soul of the practice of educational therapy, whether it takes place in a library, an office, by the bedside of a sick child, or in a waiting room with an adult client. The approach to the work may always share the common element of caring, a hope for the restoration of a client's dignity. While an educational therapist's (ET's) ultimate goal is for her client to experience success, the individual outcomes in educational therapy are unpredictable as not everyone is able to actualize his or her dream. The positive aspect of what Angelou implied is that despite whether or not a client experiences a sense of accomplishment in educational therapy, the outstanding feature is that "people will never forget how you made them feel."

ABOUT THE BOOK

The theoretical underpinnings of the book include the evolution of the practice of educational therapy from its native Europe to the United States, withstanding the test of time over many decades. One author from the United Kingdom describes a reading program she developed, bringing parents and children together in a team effort to address literacy skills, targeting not only reading but the emotional aspects of the learning process. Another author from Tasmania shares her very comprehensive research on empathy, the soul of insight which resides in one degree or another in most human beings, providing the cohesiveness of the relational aspect of educational therapy. Another contributing author, George McCloskey, a school psychologist and an advocate for the work of ETs, offers his perspective on the clientele whose underlying difficulties often reside in executive functioning. Comorbid diagnoses are discussed in some chapters, reminding readers that difficulties in learning do not necessarily exist alone, but rather in the company of other disabilities, disorders, or conditions, encompassing not only the cognitive and academic aspects of functioning and performance, but also the emotional, social, neurobiological, and cultural features as well.

Almost all of the chapters either include, or are centered around, case studies which illustrate how and why ETs work in a variety of settings, revealing the uniqueness of the practice as well as its very practical application in the classroom, in private settings, clinics, hospitals, schools, and colleges. The Association of Educational Therapists' (AET's) first formal research project is included, a study by two esteemed colleagues, Dorothy Ungerleider, AET's founding president, and Phyllis Maslow, an AET fellow and advisory board member. This brought Maxine and Jane to the future trends of the practice, inviting the exploration of assistive technology, the future training of professionals in the field, and the projection of the impediments that clients with a range of learning disabilities may face in the years ahead.

While this book is not written for or about AET, many of the authors are members of the organization and have been doing the work of educational therapy for many years. All of the authors, despite how their specific expertise contributes to their own work and to the profession in general, acknowledge the human condition. Through carefully cultivated professional relationships the human condition is nurtured, reconsidered, and sometimes transformed.

The intended audience for this book was to be only those interested in educational therapy and professional training. However, as Maxine and Jane began working with authors they realized the book encompassed much more than what they anticipated. Yes, allied professionals as well as experienced educational therapists would be interested. They sensed that many clients and parents would want this book and that they might recognize their own experiences emerge within the text. Special education teachers and administrators would find this book helpful as they grappled with an increasing number of students whose learning profiles were increasing in complexity. On a grander scale, with implications for the entire field of education, this text promised to demonstrate the significance of the dynamic approach of educational therapy: how to reach and teach to the individual with optimism, respect, and dignity.

THE THEORETICAL FOUNDATIONS OF THE BOOK

During the development of the "Principles of Educational Therapy" course for graduate training programs, Maxine Ficksman created a mnemonic structure in order to guide students through the complex material they were required to absorb and synthesize. She coined the "3 P's of the Principles of Educational Therapy" in order to illustrate the relationship among theory, research, and practice within the treatment alliance, mindful of the relationship and interplay of learning and emotions in the work of educational therapy. The elements of the 3 P's continue to emerge in this text, creating a unifying link amongst all the chapters.

Plasticity (Neuroplasticity)

Plasticity, or neuroplasticity as it is known today, implies that there is malleability in the brain. According to Marilee Sprenger (2008), neuroscience encompasses two crucial components, one of which is plasticity. The interplay of mental and physical activity prods new connections in the brain; new knowledge will be gained or lost dependent upon this interplay in conjunction with environmental and genetic influences. According to Maryanne Wolf (2007),

> ... the generative capacity of reading parallels the fundamental plasticity in the circuit wiring of our brains: both permit us to go beyond the particulars of the given. The rich associations, inferences, and insights emerging from this capacity allow, and indeed invite, us to reach beyond the specific content of what we read to form new thoughts. In this sense reading both reflects and reenacts the brain's capacity for cognitive breakthroughs. (p. 17)

Current neurological research suggests our brains, throughout the lifespan, are not hardwired. Human brains adapt and improve (a concept unheard of in the 1960's but now universally accepted) as ETs skillfully and optimistically employ developmentally appropriate remediation methods, utilizing task analysis and scaffolding techniques as a means of intervention. Relaying this optimistic view can be a powerful tool for effective collaboration within the treatment alliance.

Perception

Perception permeates every aspect of the educational therapy process. How ETs perceive the child, parents, and the ecocultural contexts of that child's life may differ from the manner in which the client and/or school perceives a specific situation or meeting. Therefore, ETs continually reassess their perceptions of the process in order to ensure effective communication and outcomes through collaboration, helping to reframe perceptions in a more positive light when necessary. Additionally, clients and other team members may misperceive the information and the manner in which ETs present the process-oriented work of educational therapy. For example, the concurrence of an ET at pivotal moments during an individualized education program (IEP) meeting often enhances the collaborative process by allowing all parties to share information as equals. Demystification of information and diagnoses that are laden with technical jargon assists the child and parents in gaining a deeper understanding of the implications of the assessment in relation to the client's strengths and weaknesses, making it possible subsequently to design and implement appropriate interventions. This process increases the likelihood that the client's self-awareness, self-confidence, self-advocacy, and level of autonomy will increase.

Perception affects the client's sense of self throughout the lifespan. Whether in the school setting when the client is attempting to learn the process of long division or in the workplace when he or she is trying to master a task or a social situation, a client may perceive the task at hand as too difficult, even if it is within his or her intellectual ability. Clients may employ avoidance skills in order to protect themselves, thereby bypassing the revisitation of shame that derived from past experiences. Within the treatment alliance, ETs listen deeply to their clients' stories while cheering, modeling, and role playing with them in order to encourage their perseverance and motivation, ultimately heightening their self-esteem.

Professionalism

Professionalism implies that ETs consistently demonstrate ethical, dignified, and respectful behavior toward clients, families, and other professionals who are included in the treatment alliance during the educational therapy process. Educational therapists avoid the counter-productiveness of the "savior syndrome," or regarding their work as heroic, thereby creating an imbalance in the ET's/client relationship and/or with other members in the treatment alliance. Another aspect of professionalism involves the ET's pursuance of professional development and lifelong learning through workshops, conferences, publications, and courses that assist in the accrual of cutting edge research which informs the implementation of techniques. Participation in study groups, self-assessment, and supervision, arranged through professional organizations such as AET, provides ETs with necessary collegial support. Educational therapists' inherent and laudable multi-tasking skills may lead to intense practices that leave these clinicians vulnerable to their work impacting the more personal aspects of their daily lives. Self-reflection contributes to the harmony ETs seek amid their involvement in work, family, and play. To maintain confidentiality and appropriate boundaries, ETs adhere to professional ethical standards and practices as promulgated by AET through its Code of Ethics (http://www.aetonline.org/about/ethics.php).

During Jane Adelizzi's earlier work in teaching learning and developmental theories to graduate students, and the subsequent establishment of the first post-master's certificate in educational therapy on the East Coast, she created a model of self in order to assist her students in identifying and articulating perceptions of themselves in relation to others within the multi-contexts of life. This model considers the conscious and unconscious manners in which people learn and function, regardless of their intellectual gifts or challenges. The components, while listed separately, are considered as parts which contribute to one's entire sense of self: the cognitive self; the social self; the emotional self; the neurobiological self; the cultural self; and the spiritual self.

Cognitive Aspect of Self

The cognitive aspect of self implies that there is a fundamental awareness of one's intellectual acumen and/or potential. The thinking self may be unconscious, considering the automaticity with which human beings respond to one another out of necessity in order to survive, or because they are responding to the needs of others with the natural flow of empathy. This aspect may also be conscious as one deliberately moves through a problem-solving process, or the meta-analysis of single or multiple concepts and systems.

Social Aspect of Self

The social aspect of self implies that each person has some degree of interaction with other people, either willingly or because it is an expected norm in many situations and settings (e.g., school, the workplace). There is an expectation of mutuality to this aspect of self with the addition of geniality. When human beings are not able to fully develop this aspect of self they may suffer a sense of impoverishment in their lives, which for some is not a hardship, but for others is a tragedy.

The Emotional Aspect of Self

The emotional aspect of self is a fluctuating state, recognizable as a result of one's subjective response to a thought, situation, or person. The emotional aspect of self ranges from the manifestation of behaviors that are unconscious responses to thoughts, situations, and people, to the conscious and explicit awareness of sadness, joy, or longing, providing a means of interpreting and communicating the needs of others when they are witnessed, and gauging one's own needs when they are experienced.

The Neurobiological Aspect of Self

The neurobiological aspect of self considers both the neurological and biological disciplines of human learning and functioning. Neurological aspects of this subset include one's mental status, and the motor and sensory systems. The interface of neurology and biology addresses brain function in relation to one's ability to learn, function, feel, and relate to others, analogous to the plasticity to which Maxine referred in the 3 P's.

The Cultural Aspect of Self

The cultural aspect of self takes into consideration the family and societal norms in which one lives, and how the contribution of both these discrete and integrated cultures impact the ways in which one feels, thinks, behaves, and communicates in a variety of contexts, and in the process of acculturation. This aspect of self influences one's expectations of self and that of others in the ET/client relationship as well as within the broader treatment alliance.

The Spiritual Aspect of Self

The spiritual aspect of self implies a subjective and holistically-oriented perspective for some people, as well as a sense of devotion to a tenet of thought or doctrine to others. This aspect of the self is personally defined and communicated through one's response to others in an explicit way, or by way of quiet reverence. For some, it's it is almost an unconscious sense, and like empathy, is akin to the soul of insight.

Together, The 3 P's of the Principles of Educational Therapy and The Model of Self present a synergistic relationship that is present in the work of educational therapy, neither model operating without the other's energy, spirit, and fundamental understanding of the practice, which ultimately creates a fluid and self-propelling process of teaching and learning.

Maxine and Jane want to engage you as you read this text. Their wish is to propel you into each setting, develop a familiarity with the ETs, the clients, and the passion of the work. They want to share with you the multi-disciplinary field of educational therapy and its promise for the future of education in a global sense.

THE RELATIONAL ASPECT OF EDUCATIONAL THERAPY

> The dichotomy between selfishness and unselfishness disappears altogether in healthy people because in principle every act is both selfish and unselfish.
> **(Abraham Maslow quoted in Maslow & Maslow, 1993, p. 19)**

Most of an ET's work takes place in a one-to-one dyad, just as it does for many other types of therapies. In this case, there is an ET and a client, who may be a young child, adolescent, or adult. The reason why clients seek the services of ETs is because they are experiencing some kind of dissonance in their learning and functioning beyond that which Paula Fuqua (Field, Kaufman, & Saltzman, 1993) has described as "a disruption" in the learning of something new, which may cause undue stress for some children as they attempt to accommodate a new skill. For children with learning disabilities, the process of disruption may take place for a more extended period of time, not be resolved completely if the skill has not been accommodated, and will return like an ill wind when the child is again confronted with trying to learn the same skill. The continued repetition of this process may precipitate a wide range of symptoms and behaviors, ranging from fatigue to carefully crafted avoidance, all of which contribute to a loss of self-esteem with each episode and perception of failure. In essence, the child who enters educational therapy brings with her an invisible suitcase full of both partially learned and un-learned skills, which seem to bury the learned skills and talents at the bottom of the pile.

The practice of educational therapy employs a psychodynamic approach, as it addresses not simply the conscious and very obvious behaviors and levels of achievement that are accessible to us through a variety of assessments. Diagnostic implications assist in the preparation of an individualized educational therapy treatment plan, offering a place to begin the work, with room to make note of both hallmarks and pitfalls in the process in order to re-design and re-negotiate each goal. What also contributes its fair share to this work is the more informal process of assessment, or the ET's astute observations of a client's behaviors, the choice of language used to describe early learning experiences, and the manner in which the client engages or disengages in the developing alliance. Some practitioners feel that they are intuitively meeting the needs of their clients and may not be aware that they are responding to unconscious behaviors exhibited as a result of expectations imposed by self or others. And, the dance continues....

Much of the work of educational therapy relates to some of the earliest learning experiences of a client. In conscious reflection, ETs can reach back to those earlier memories the client has disclosed, and at salient points during the process of educational therapy, point out the similarities in present behaviors and responses to those of the past. Additionally, there may be traits in teachers or other people in the life of that person which are reminiscent of those who in some way contribute to current fear and anxiety.

If we look at the definition of "classroom trauma" (Adelizzi, 1995, 1998, 2001) and the similarities of the responses of this phenomenon to posttraumatic stress symptoms, there is a striking resemblance in the ways that previous, and sometimes unconscious feelings and motives, manifest themselves in clients across the life span. Individual survival tactics are not based solely on the ability to call forth executive functioning skills, but also on the primitive coping and adapting skills that are learned early in life. If a client was repeatedly humiliated in the classroom, then the sights, sounds, smells, and emotional responses that are related to those experiences are again packed in the invisible luggage that arrives with the client at the threshold of the ET's office.

Selma Sapir (1985) stated that "The therapist, teacher and diagnostician become one" (Sapir, 1985, p. 24). Reyes-Simpson (2004) described Bion's thoughts about the mother–child attachment, which resonates with Sapir's perspective, stating that ".... thinking is not an abstract mental process, but the result of a relationship, a human link" (p. 123). Attachments of this nature may survive for a long period of time, taking a respite now and then, depending on the developmental factors involved in the process of surviving school, or in the case of adult clients, the workplace.

Clients may stay with educational therapy for years at a time, and some drift through with an immediate need, not leaving ample time to create an enduring alliance, but developing sufficient trust to allow the ET to impart her knowledge and assist in decision-making. The ET participates in the relationship by employing listening skills that enable her to glean valuable information that is embedded in the language the client selects to describe a situation or perception. This kind of engagement places the client in the position of the provider of information, while the ET becomes the recipient, listening without preconceived notions, acknowledging the client as the knower. There are subtle shifts in roles in the relationship, which may occur smoothly, or with a series of disruptions or dissonance.

THEORETICAL FRAMEWORK OF EDUCATIONAL THERAPY

The theorists who contributed to the model and the practice of educational therapy are many, and are outlined in a chapter on the migration of the profession from its European roots to the United States. The ancestry of the practice extends beyond geographical locations and into the carefully honed practices of professionals, who in turn, share their techniques and informal research with those who follow in their footsteps. This trail of practice is created in part by individual experience and intuition borne from necessity and delivered with spontaneity, as well as through the contributions of theorists and researchers in education, psychology, and sociology who provide educational therapy with the foundational support that makes this dearth of knowledge coalesce to form its own theory. These foundational theorists are as follows:

John Dewey's theory of the child centered curriculum (Fraser & Gestwicki, 2001) contributes to the practice of educational therapy, supporting the notion that the client is the focus of the work and the more active participant in the dyad. This places the ET in a secondary role as the knower, and the client in the more active role in of constructing knowledge and understanding.

Jerome Bruner, a forerunner in the development and recognition of constructivist theory and the concept of meta-analysis, introduced the concepts and utilization of scaffolding and the spiral curriculum, supporting the approach of establishing basic principles and concepts unique to each learner, revisiting and expanding upon them until they are learned and able to withstand the pliability of being recognized in multiple contexts. This lays the groundwork for introducing and strengthening the ability to make intuitive or cognitive leaps in thinking and problem-solving. In other words, ETs model for their clients how they can actually use new information in relation to other information, particularly in relation to concepts in reading comprehension, mathematics, science, and the social sciences. This concept also applies to the ET's role in more fully developing literacy skills with clients, specifically written expression in clients who have not grasped the versatility of written language across the curriculum of life. Most importantly, encouraging intuitive leaps enhances our clients' motivation, curiosity, and love of learning.

In her work at Bank Street, Selma Sapir integrated the concepts from the best of the psychological theorists to create her clinical teaching model, the basis for how educational therapists work today. She described her model as "interactive, integrated, and developmental in its perspective" (Sapir, 1985 p. xiii). Diagnosis is an ongoing process allowing for the adjustments in treatment to reflect changes in temperamental, emotional, social, and cognitive development (based on a strong understanding of normal child development) and an individualized approach to intervention.

The sociocultural view of development created by Urie Bronfenbrenner and certainly influenced by Lev Vygotsky's sociocultural perspective, provides the educational therapist with a model for viewing the child's context or environment. From the microsystem of the child's family, school, peers, and neighborhood, to the macrosystem that includes a broad ideology of laws and cultural customs, and then to the chronosystem that includes life's unexpected events such as illness, divorce, and natural disasters, ETs help families and clients deal with the impact of these events as they affect the child's learning. For example, after the California earthquake in Los Angeles in 1994, the level of anxiety was extremely high in the general population, and as a result some children had difficulty sleeping and remained in their parents' beds for months. This created very unusual sleeping patterns and certainly affected many children's academic performance. Some of the more severe cases were referred for counseling. Most ETs provided extra support for their clients during this time, and expanded their services to include relaxation techniques as well as more opportunities for art projects and puppetry to encourage meaningful conversations with these anxious children. During this time, ETs communicated with parents and teachers in order to monitor the progress of these students.

THE MULTI-DIMENSIONAL MODEL OF EDUCATIONAL THERAPY

In 1998 two models of educational therapy were developed by Ann Kaganoff and Maxine Ficksman. Both models were published in *The Educational Therapist* and included in formal training materials as both visual and conceptual representations of the core elements of the practice. The current model (Figure 1.1) defines domains of responsibilities for the ET and educates the public about the profession, bringing attention to how it differs from the work of allied professionals and capturing more of the multi-disciplinary and comprehensive nature of the practice. Additionally, the current model illustrates to allied professionals how some of the elements of educational therapy are present in their work, inviting them to seek further information about the field and the potential for reciprocity and alliance within a treatment alliance.

The authors selected interlocking puzzle pieces to represent the emerging model's elements. The treatment alliance, the relational dyad between a client and ET in conjunction with the other members of the team, is placed as the locus of the model, the point from which other components reciprocally converge and interact, and in which all components are embodied. Within the treatment alliance, ETs consecutively and simultaneously encounter and contend with all these elements as they impact the client and the client's context in the process of educational therapy.

THE TREATMENT ALLIANCE

The treatment alliance is the conceptual cornerstone of this model, and is illustrated as the central piece of the puzzle. It is comprised of the client, who is the focus of the alliance; the client's family as a functioning unit and its ability and willingness to adhere to an agreed upon treatment plan; and, the allied professionals who contribute their expertise. This partnership is key in moving the client from one level of learning and functioning to the

The Multi-Dimensional Model of Educational Therapy

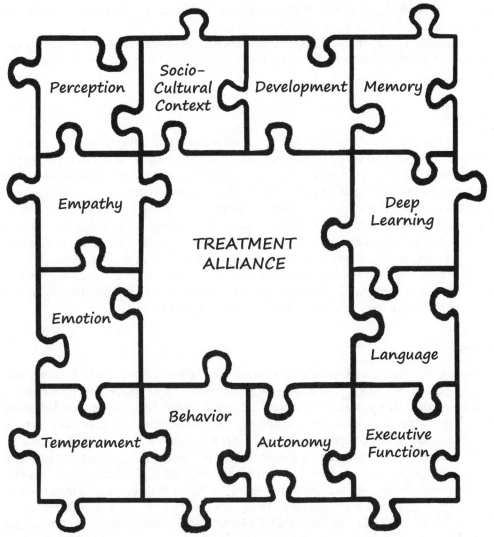

Figure 1.1 The multi-dimensional model. Copyright © 2009, Ficksman & Adelizzi.

next, while maintaining a stability that allows the client to experience incremental positive changes and successes that will provide the enthusiasm to approach the next challenge.

Gavin et al. (1999), in their research article, "Treatment Alliance and Its Association with Family Functioning, Adherence, and Medical Outcome in Adolescents with Severe, Chronic Asthma," stated that the "Treatment alliance affords a sense of shared goals and mutual positive regard, as well as a lack of negative behavior that potentially could undermine the relationship and the treatment" (p. 355). The research went on to say that similar studies have been completed in the field of psychotherapy, indicating that the strength of the alliance is related to more successful outcomes in treatment. By using the medical and mental health models of the treatment alliance to illustrate the structure and function of a treatment alliance in educational therapy, it becomes clear that the quality of the relationships within the alliance is a motivating factor for positive outcomes in clients who experience difficulty in school, the workplace, and in relationships that permeate the arenas of life.

The following components represent the attributes necessary for an ET to model and employ in her work in order for her client to develop into a well adjusted and autonomous person:

Autonomy

The ET strives to create an adequate level of autonomy in her clients in order to move them from a dependent state to a more self-governing approach to daily tasks. The instill-ment or fostering of autonomy is an incremental process, and not one that can be rushed or infused. Some clients exhibit greater levels of autonomy in some aspects of their lives, usually those in which they demonstrate more confidence in their performance and ability. The ET/client relationship often exhibits a reciprocal teaching-and-learning approach, so that at any given time each member of the dyad takes on the role of the "knower", which allows the other member to become the learner. When the role of the knower is played by the client he or she is engaging in an unconscious autonomous state. Later, upon reflection of the behaviors experienced, it can be revealed to the client when and how that individual demonstrated autonomy in a task, a decision, or in an effort.

Behavior

Observing behavior in a client's learning process by the trained eye of an ET is a key ele-ment in assessment, and a contribution to the development of appropriate intervention. Children, adolescents, and adults with learning and attentional disorders exhibit behaviors that point to both their conscious and unconscious fears. For example, an adolescent in educational therapy may negotiate a task in order to circumvent aspects of that task that she knows will be difficult for her to maneuver. Some clients will begin negotiations with a conscious, prepared plan, ready for arguments, rebuttals, and evidence that supports their proposal. Others will unconsciously sense the threat that comes with the arrival of specific tasks, and lapse into a practiced avoidance strategy. The ET listens carefully to a client, the family, and allied professionals to understand the reasons why contentious and conflicting behaviors occur, and what measures can be taken to remediate the behaviors. Educational therapists teach their clients self-regulation and self-monitoring strategies to encourage independent behavior.

Deep Learning

Although an ET may begin a task with mere surface coverage, it is a way to introduce a new word, idea, or plan. Once dialogue has begun and the discussion begins to move to the periphery of the surface, it may be time to introduce a more analytical perspective of the task, relating one aspect of the task to that of another, requiring that the client broaden his or her thinking about the original idea. The process of gliding with a client through a task or concept, and then moving on to a deeper level of knowing through investiga-tion, analysis, and establishing hypotheses can occur through a process akin to a Socratic method of teaching, or occur through a mentoring relationship, the likeness of which is found in the work of an ET.

Mentors give us the magic that allows us to enter the darkness; a talisman to protect us from evil spells, a gem of wise advice, a map, and sometimes simply courage. But always the mentor appears near the outset of the journey as a helper … a midwife to our dreams. (Daloz, 1986, p. 17)

Development

While human development encompasses many theories which apply to virtually every task, context, and situation, the ET concerns herself with how each client performs within each level of learning, determining the "readiness" of the individual to move to another level. At that juncture, she can estimate the degree of ease in which her client keeps up in the classroom, in relationships, or in the workplace. One area of a client's life may be very advanced, possibly in social development, while another area is lacking in maturity, possibly in emotional regulation. The difference of a year in the life of a child or adolescent can exhibit a leap in maturity, impacting the ability to master new tasks and material.

Emotions

An individual's emotions are often associated with temperament, an indicator of mood, which in turn can predict a level of motivation in approaching a task. Emotions and learning do not occur in turn, but rather simultaneously and subjectively. ".… emotional engagement must be a part of the learning process. The recognition that passion is central to learning and the capacity to provide emotional support when it is needed … are required of the mentor" (Daloz, 1986, p. 33). The ET often uses reflective periods in sessions to talk about the emotional responses clients have to specific tasks that are reminiscent of earlier, unpleasant learning experiences, pointing out that emotional responses are "to be expected, rather than rejected." Each small success heightens a client's self-esteem and leads the client away from the shame of failure.

Empathy

The ET enters into each new relationship with a client by modeling an understanding of a client's range of feelings and fears. Genuine and reciprocal empathy is a strong agent in maintaining a cohesive ET/client relationship. Some ETs find that the modeling (or apprenticeship) of empathy helps younger clients more easily enter in discussion about understanding the feelings and perspectives of others. With adolescent and adult clients ETs can engage in both subjective and objective discussions about these skills, citing examples of behaviors, and applying these skills to role playing situations.

Executive Function

A child in educational therapy often experiences difficulty with specific executive functions because his skills do not always develop at the same time. It is the work of the ET to provide opportunities to practice these skills, similar to an apprenticeship model which exists at the Howard Gardner School for Discovery in Scranton, PA. Gardner "identifies apprenticeships as a model for 21st century schools because of the practical nature of learning beside someone who has a working knowledge of a subject or craft. Allowing a master to pass on that knowledge is both a gift and a practical way to scaffold the learning process" (http://howardgardnerschool.com). In this case, the master may be an adult (e.g., the ET or a parent) who models executive functioning skills in a variety of contexts, explaining her process and rationale as she moves from one task to the next. Like working new muscles, executive functioning skills grow stronger with practice, and eventually can flex themselves in order to address a range of issues that require emotional regulation, decision-making, wise choices, and a host of other skills that are age-appropriate.

Language

In most educational therapy sessions spoken language is the prime means of communication. Students with hearing impairments may communicate through American Sign Language (ASL), finger-spelling, gesturing, or by using language/communication boards for the deaf and blind. Language communication within the ET/client dyad offers rich opportunities for practicing vocabulary; the typical 6-year-old has stored between 10,000 and 13,000 words, although their ocular development and working memories are still maturing. Six and 7-year-olds still love to be read to, which serves as a means to discussion about characters, plots, values, and beliefs. Their language development has brought them to a level where they are able to listen, and understand how to solve age-appropriate problems (Sprenger, 2008). According to Selma Sapir (1985), "Language is one of the major contributions to ego strength and readiness for academic learning" (Sapir, 1985, p. 40). Educational therapists skillfully remediate weaknesses in written expression beginning with the development of a topic sentence, to the elements of a creative story, and then to a five paragraph essay. These professionals role play with clients to address the nonverbal aspects of language, while simultaneously emphasizing the relevancy of writing, reading, listening, and speaking.

Memory

Clients experience a wide range of memory problems in educational therapy, the amelioration of which begins with both formal and informal assessments. Bringing the client into the planning of an intervention also serves to open up discussion which reveals the nature of memory in relation to a range of tasks. The information processing model introduces encoding, storage, and retrieval, a process that invites conversation in relation to many academic and daily tasks. Time-sensitive and chronological processing of memory present the same opportunities for discussion: sensory memory, short term- and long long-term memory. According to Harvard Professor of Psychology, Daniel Schacter (1996), memories are not merely pieces of information, they are "composed of a variety of distinct and dissociable processes and systems" (p. 4).

Perception

The concept of perception is included in the fields of education, psychology, and philosophy to name a few. The study of perception focuses on developing an awareness of one's sensory system in relation to learning, the negotiation of space, time, and other functions. One person's perception of an idea is not always the same as another's; and, likewise, one person's visual perception of a piece of artwork does not elicit the same emotional response in everyone. An ET and her client work through perceptual problems in math, science, and other disciplines that hypothesize solutions to a plethora of problems.

Socio-Cultural Context

In educational therapy there exists an underlying awareness of both the social and cultural contexts in the lives of clients; the social context meaning the series and combinations of relationships which require participation in communication, as well as the expression of empathy and insight in the lives of others; the cultural context meaning the influence of family, ethnic, and religious cultures, as well as other groups which define their own unique culture and purpose in the lives of people. A client's treatment alliance is comprised of multi-cultures which help to shape and influence the life of the client, and is communicated with the use of spoken and written language in addition to the music and art which are common to each group's socialization. Project CHILD, a longitudinal research study at the University of California, Los Angeles, revealed that assessments and interventions which match a client's contexts, routines, beliefs, goals, and values, are more likely to be effective (Keogh,1995). Thus, ETs tailor their advice to fit the family's specific socio-cultural systems.

Temperament

Part of what comprises personality is temperament, which has both a genetic and biological bases. Certain temperaments are more compatible to change, while others struggle with both large and small adjustments in life. Temperament affects school and job performance, relationships, and family life, all of the contexts in which the ET works with her clientele. Developmental psychologists such as Jerome Kagan have added to the bodies of research contributed earlier by Thomas's and Chess's Nine Characteristics of Temperament in Children. Assessments for temperament are helpful in establishing comfortable zones in which to dialogue about one's strengths and foibles, for both the client and the ET in their work together.

Collectively, the elements in this model characterize the range and depth of the educational therapy process throughout the lifespan. It is the authors' intent that the reader utilizes the model as a scaffold from which to identify commonalities, patterns, and trends that emerge in the chapters of this book.

DISTINCTIONS BETWEEN EDUCATIONAL THERAPISTS AND ALLIED PROFESSIONALS

The ET maintains the position in the dyad as the "juggler" of tasks, and the person responsible for tempering potentially volatile or disheartening situations; and, also as the individual who knows when, how, and if to begin the actual work of organizing a plan to complete a train of thought, a homework assignment, or a long division problem. Most importantly, the ET's juggling act includes the responsibility of always making sure that the door is left open for discussion of the emotional fallout that ensues when a client is faced with entering a new situation, or one that brings with it some haunting memories of previous fears or failures.

The ET's work is not confined to the work of a content tutor, although a focus on academic success is indeed a goal for many clients. Nor is the work of an ET likened to that of a psychoanalyst, although the conscious and unconscious processes with which all humans function in daily life are certainly worthy of consideration when regarding the frailty of ego many individuals cope with in their lives as a result of their self-perceived failures. Psychotherapists work with their clients or patients in changing behaviors and thoughts through the process of adaptation. Educational therapists have a background in developmental psychology in order to identify when and how a client is functioning within expected norms in a variety of areas of learning and functioning (e.g., language, reading, and memory development). Their work includes a psychodynamic approach which seeks to create change in an individual's perception of self as well as the skill levels at which they perform. The change is not brought about necessarily as a result of adaptation to a specific environment and the people therein, but rather adaptation from the view of Piaget's concept of adaptation, which indicates that clients may need assistance in assimilating and accommodating new information. The wide range of skills and knowledge employed by ETs as a result of their professional training in contextual analysis, assessment, intervention, collaboration, advocacy, and case management distinguishes them from many of their allied professionals.

It is often difficult for a client or a family to understand the difference between the function of an ET and a tutor. A tutor assists with homework and/or specific subject matter, possibly remediating a set of skills in math, reading, or writing with the goal of achieving a higher score on an exam, final, or a standardized test such as the ISEE and SAT. The ET's primary goal for the client is an increased level of autonomy. If a client has particular difficulty in a subject such as geometry or chemistry, an ET may refer that person to a tutor, someone who will isolate and then address the skills or tasks. Unlike most tutors, ETs are trained to serve as a resource for parents. Educational therapists offer the benefit of consultation to parents regarding modifications to home routines, socialization, and appropriate interventions and referrals. They also assist families in interpreting reports written by allied professionals, and provide them with current information and research in the fields of educational therapy and learning disabilities in order to build a greater understanding of the ET's recommendations for intervention and school placement. Additionally, the ET steps in to provide advocacy services for families at team meetings as the treatment alliance builds a case for fair and appropriate services for the client. School psychologists usually work within a school system assessing students for designated services and developing plans to improve students' academic and social performance. Educational therapists work with individual clients as part of a treatment alliance comprised of school psychologists, teachers, parents, special education department members, and often speech therapists, occupational therapists, psychiatrists, psychotherapists, and sometimes criminal justice system personnel. The chart below details (Table 1.1) the distinguishing characteristics of ETs as compared with the various allied professionals involved in the collaborative process.

In order to further distinguish the services of an ET, Sandra Mosk, a past president of AET, authored an article, "Refining the Definition of Educational Therapy," which appeared in a 2004 issue of the journal, *The Educational Therapist*. She wrote, "… educational therapy is an educational, not a psychological service. The therapeutic component of educational therapy refers to the non-academic interventions necessary to facilitate the remediation of learning disabilities and problems, such as improving metacognition, organizational skills, attention, and self-esteem" (Mosk, 2004, p. 4).

Table 1.1 Distinguishing Characteristis of an Educational Therapist and Allied Professionals

Practitioner	Characteristics of Practice
EDUCATIONAL THERAPIST (ET)	1. ETs provide individualized intensive intervention, formal and informal assessment, and case management for clients who present a wide range of learning disabilities and learning differences, including: dyslexia, AD/HD, academic difficulties, or failure. Additionally, ETs provide assessment and intervention in language processing, motivation, self-esteem, social skills, and overall executive functioning. 2. ETs provide clients with: appropriate school placement or workplace support; ongoing consultation and communication with members of the educational therapy treatment alliance. 3. ETs require extensive backgrounds in learning disabilities, special education, and/or other specific genres of learning difficulties, in addition to their training in educational therapy. 4. Goals of the educational therapy treatment plan include: developing clients' strategic use of strengths in order to foster learning, developing a sense of autonomy, and understanding the interrelationship between learning and social/emotional functioning.
Audiologist	An audiologist is a professional who administers diagnostic testing in order to determine an individual's hearing deficit in conjunction with its origin and develops an appropriate treatment plan which may include surgery and/or an amplification system.
Clinical Psychologist	Clinical psychologists evaluate and diagnose mental and emotional disorders of individuals and administer therapeutic programs of treatment in a variety of settings such as clinics and rehabilitation centers.
Developmental Optometrist	A development optometrist examines and prescribes corrective lenses as well as detects eye diseases. These professionals are trained in the developmental aspects of vision in conjunction with the impact of environmental factors. They often recommend vision therapy as a means of improving a patient's reading and visual proficiency.
Developmental Pediatrician	Developmental pediatricians have specialized training in developmental and behavioral pediatrics. These professionals generally are experts in diagnosing and making appropriate educational/training recommendations for patients with traumatic brain injuries and/or autistic spectrum disorders.
Educational Psychologist	Educational psychologists investigate the pedagogically sound principles in education and psychology which are directly related to a client's ability to learn. These professionals may be involved in formal research or may concentrate in an area of psychoeducational assessment in order to diagnose learning disabilities.
Marriage & Family Therapist; Licensed Social Worker	Marriage and family therapists generally are licensed mental health care professionals or social workers who provide counseling and psychotherapy services relative to individual and family problems, or dysfunctions. These professionals may recognize a learning or educational problem as an anomaly to be addressed within the family dynamic, but are generally not trained to formally identify, diagnose, or treat these problems.
Neurologist	A neurologist is a medical doctor who has specialized training in human nervous system disorders and conditions as well as diseases of the brain and spinal cord. These professionals administer diagnostic testing that evaluate mental, motor, and sensory functions.
Neuropsychologist	A neuropsychologist receives professional training in psychology and generally earns the credential of Ph.D. or Psy.D., the focus of which is on cognitive functioning, especially as it impacts learning. These professionals do not prescribe medication, although they do administer diagnostic testing for brain dysfunction.
Nurse Practitioner	A nurse practitioner is a registered nurse who has completed an advanced degree in a specialized area such as psychiatry, cardiology, or gynecology. They may function independently from other medical professionals, diagnose and prescribe medication, counsel patients, and perform minor surgery, depending upon the state in which the NP is licensed.
Occupational Therapist	Occupational therapists provide sensory motor integration assessment and training to patients who are seeking to achieve independence in response to the external physical demands which shape the life of an individual.

(continued)

Table 1.1 Continued

Practitioner	Characteristics of Practice
Osteopath	An osteopath is a physician whose training focuses on the musculoskeletal system. These professionals approach treatment from a holistic perspective, considering the physical as well as the mental well being of each patient.
Pediatric Opthamologist	A pediatric opthamologist examines and prescribes corrective lenses and treats diseases of the eyes in children. These professionals receive specialized training in performing eye surgery for individuals who have sustained eye injuries or who suffer from diseases and conditions of the eyes.
Physician's Assistant	A physician's assistant is a healthcare professional who practices medicine under the supervision of a medical doctor. These professionals can diagnose illnesses and prescribe medication under the auspices of the supervising physician; and they make recommendations for preventive healthcare as well as referrals for specialized care (e.g., psychiatry).
Primary Care Physician	A primary care physician is a medical doctor who is generally a patient's ongoing physician as well as the major source for referring them to other medical, neurological, psychological, or mental health professionals for specialized services. These professionals collect data about a patient from a variety of sources in order to determine a diagnosis and create an effective treatment plan.
Psychiatrist	A psychiatrist is a medical doctor whose specialized training is in mental health/psychiatry. and who is eligible to diagnose psychiatric disorders, provide appropriate treatment, and prescribe medication. These professionals work in diverse settings such as hospitals, clinics, programs, research centers, the criminal justice system, and in private practice.
Speech & Language Therapist	A speech and language therapist is generally involved in the assessment, diagnosis, and treatment of clients with speech and language problems, developmental delays, or disorders. These professionals are often found working within a public school system.
Subject Matter Tutor	A tutor generally provides assistance with homework assignments and teaches and/or reviews subject matter material. A tutor's background generally does not include training in learning disabilities, specific syndromes, case management, the applicability of executive functioning to social intelligence, and the overall academic and emotional survival of the formal classroom experience.
School Psychologist	A school psychologist receives training in both psychology and education and is licensed by the state in which they practice. They generally work in public school systems and administer psychoeducational diagnostic testing in order to determine the source of a student's academic difficulty. They may work in collaboration with other school professionals in developing an individualized education plan (IEP).

This origins of this chart were developed by Maxine Ficksman and Ann Kaganoff in 1995 as part of the curriculum for educational therapy training courses. The chart has been modified since that time, and updated for its inclusion in Chapter One of this book by Maxine Ficksman and Jane Utley Adelizzi (2009). Copyright © 2009, Ficksman & Adelizzi.

In this article, the author refers to a list of "Do's and Don'ts" that Maxine Ficksman developed for the educational therapy training courses, which were subsequently shared with all national training programs. They are as follows:

Educational therapists do not:

- Diagnose, assess, or prescribe medication for any medical conditions including Tourette syndrome, ADD/ADHD, and co-morbid conditions such as depression.
- Administer intelligence or other psychological tests.
- Practice psychotherapy.

Educational therapists do:

- Refer clients to allied professionals for assessments for the above conditions.
- Describe behaviors to parents and allied professionals regarding conditions such as Tourette syndrome, ADD/ADHD, and co-morbid conditions such as depression.
- Interpret intelligence tests and assessment reports from allied professionals. (Ficksman, quoted in Mosk, 2004)

It should be noted that some states allow professionals, other than licensed psychologists, to administer intelligence tests, and that "educational therapists should not give any test (including, but not limited to intelligence tests) unless trained and certified according to the guidelines in the test manuals and as set by the publishing houses that sell such tests" (Mosk, 2004, p.4). However, some ETs are also licensed in other disciplines such as family therapy, speech and language therapy, and educational psychology, and administer assessments and guidelines mandated by those professions.

DEFINING THE EDUCATIONAL THERAPIST IN PRACTICE

According to Katrina de Hirsch (1977, p. 100), there are two goals in education: (1) learning how to learn, and (2) being excited about the learning. Learning how to learn requires that an ET guides an individual to a level of metacognitive awareness. Excitement about learning means "being actively involved in the process." It may result from repeated successes that offer a degree of relief, gradually lessening the anxiety which has historically been linked to production overload and the mismatch of curriculum to student. Each student or client arrives at a comfort zone in his or her own way, with a different time table, and with different hopes and expectations.

The ET approach is psychodynamic as it is the aim of the work to create change by alleviating fears, and boosting self-esteem by providing opportunities for incremental successes, thereby improving the attitude and behaviors related to learning and functioning in school, the workplace, and in the broader social-intellectual contexts of life. Within the context of the clinical setting of educational therapy, the client and ET discuss the expectations of each context, collaboratively designing ways in which to cope, adapt, and experience a sense of accomplishment and pride. The actual anatomy, or clinical practice, in individual sessions is a task analysis approach, identifying the area(s) requiring attention (e.g., un-mastered academic or social skills) through informal and formal assessment, and then applying appropriate interventions within the zone of proximal development (Miller, 2002), allowing the client to experience success which prepares her to take yet another step in her journey. The ET/client relationship, the consideration of the client-in-context in everyday life, the ET's psychodynamic approach, and the task-analysis of the sessions all contribute to the goal of elevating a client's self-esteem while simultaneously decreasing feelings of hopelessness. An educational therapist, as defined by the Association of Educational Therapists (AET), "is a professional who combines educational and therapeutic approaches for evaluation, remediation, case management, and communication/advocacy on behalf of children, adolescents, and adults with learning disabilities or learning problems" (Association of Educational Therapists By-laws, 1979).

Some educational therapists may more strongly embrace one or more of the aforementioned functions as a focus in their work (e.g., advocacy and/or assessment). What remains a constant in the process of educational therapy is the relationship, which over time, may survive the many shifts and changes precipitated by the undertaking of a new task, or the revisitation of a previous situation or assignment that was unclear. The ET simultaneously employs both cognitive and therapeutic principles in her work, a reciprocal process which invites each member of the alliance to become both the knower and the learner. The emotional aspect of this work is ever-present in the relationship, and may be infused in the language or behavior of the dyad, often setting the stage for reflection. While the aforementioned characteristics and processes are inherent in how an educational therapist is defined by AET, they are shared by many professionals who do the work of educational therapists but identify themselves as learning specialists or therapeutic teachers. The rudiments of the practice of educational therapy can be applied to a wide range of settings (e.g., classrooms, programs that assist college students, training, or vocational sites).

A reasonable mastery of developmental theories provides the ET with a comprehensive picture of what is expected and what is a realistic possibility for a client across a wide range of skills and functions. Developmental stage theories such as Jean Piaget's stages of cognitive development, Erik Erikson's stages of psychosocial development, and Maria Montessori's stages of child development, just to name a few, provide concrete levels of expectations, some of which operate on the belief that one skill may not be acquired without the mastery of the previous one. Other theories, more psychologically and/or psychoanalytically oriented, such as Sigmund Freud's psychoanalytic theory, which while still a stage theory, present more of a cause and effect relationship between libidinal desires and later developmental behaviors. John Bowlby was one of the earlier theorists who posited that the establishment of early human relationships (e.g., psychological attachment) shaped an individual's ability to form healthy relationships in life, a theory that supports the development of healthy connections between the ET and client.

With a solid foundation in development, the ET attempts to target a skill which appears to be either delayed or unaccomplished in classroom learning or in relation to high stakes testing, without the consideration and basic understanding of the developmental level at which the client is operating. The client, of course, can be operating on a variety of levels depending upon the skill or task in question. Often the ET works with teachers and other school staff in modifying assignments to match the student's developmental level. For example, many children at age 10 lack the executive functioning skills to organize a report and need assistance in creating a structure comprised of identifiable steps. In this format, the student can view the assignment as achievable within a designated period of time. Educational therapists collaborate with teachers to determine which modifications would best serve a child's needs based on his specific learning profile, while also helping parents to understand the significance of these developmental milestones.

A quality which contributes to positive outcomes for clients includes the presence and awareness of empathy in an ET, a foundational element in any relationship, and one that is germane in the practice of educational therapy. When clients present themselves with the inability to imagine and/or predict the experiences and subsequent emotional responses and behaviors of others, the opportunity to both model and objectively discuss these phenomena becomes the aha! moment in teaching, coaching, and mentoring. Additionally, an ET's genuine sense of empathy provides a plethora of opportunities to observe, analyze, and interpret the level of self-esteem at which the client functions, and the degree of responsibility, and sometimes guilt, parents may experience regarding their child's plight.

By modeling a sense of respect for a client, the ET is able to then observe how and if the client responds to what Rogers referred to as an unconditional positive regard (Rogers & Freiberg, 1994). By maintaining comprehensive clinical notes following each session, the ET provides herself with the opportunity to track changes in language and behaviors that reflect reciprocity, respect, and the presence or lack of empathy. A sense of humor, a welcome respite during a session, has the potential to provide a client with an opportunity to reflect on the ET's perspectives as well as his or her own. Humor also serves as an informal assessment in determining if limited social perception impacts a client's ability to identify, understand, and respond (Semrud-Clikeman & Teeter-Elllison, 2009, p. 306).

Clients in educational therapy often have language-based disabilities, written expression being one of the more common impediments across the life span. These clients require the assistance of a professional who can work with them in developing skills that enhance the ability to learn more advanced material across the curriculum, an incremental and integrative process. Commonly, clients will regard their writing assignments in isolation, as an individual task to be completed within a specific amount of time. An ET has the ability to broaden and integrate that task with others, creating an opportunity for the client to recognize writing as a skill to be learned, honed, individualized, and consistently nurtured in order to recognize and appreciate its relevancy in other areas of learning, as well as within the mandated curriculum. This may be accomplished by asking a client to keep a learning-journal for a weaker subject such as math, literature, or science. The entries can be shared and then built upon in order to nudge the next entry, asking for more in in-depth responses which require more written language. The quality and process of the development of language may then be compared by both the ET and client to written responses expected on homework assignments to note taking, e-mailing, or responses written on the white board during a session. Eventually, the ET and client are able to recognize how language has become more than an isolated task, broadening its use to a means of communication, and a way of building connections among disciplines, thoughts, and ideas. The possibilities are endless, but can be more successfully executed if the ET has strong language and communication skills, which not only contribute to guiding a student in written language development, but also become a necessary tool for the ET in writing clear and accurate reports for parents, teachers, and other members of the treatment alliance.

Flexibility is a necessary skill for the ET as the dynamic of a session and task analysis can change without warning, informing the ET to prepare to shift to another paradigm, approach, or strategy in order to accommodate a presenting need. To say that it is not only helpful, but also necessary for the ET to be secure in his level of executive functioning is an understatement. The ability to think on the spot, be ready to stop in the middle of a task in order to address a symptom, behavior, or misperception, and then redirect the session again, are compulsory skills for the ET. In order to assist a client in scaffolding techniques that are useful in the process of grappling with either an academic task, or a social concern that pervades the session, let alone the life of the client, an ET must maintain an awareness of how she manages these skills herself.

In summary, the ET's executive functioning skills are fundamental tools and attributes in her profession, and provide the ability to manage a session, bring it to satisfactory closure, and complete clinical notes that will ultimately inform the following session and simultaneously contribute to the overall progress of the treatment. These notes also provide the ET with qualitative data that is useful in the ongoing process of reflection, and the subsequent need to re-assess a client's progress, or the methods and approach employed with that person. It is then fair to say that even without having a conscious awareness of it, the ET is a teacher, a mentor, a conduit for emotional expression in relation to the task at hand and the impediments thereof, and a researcher, mindful of the ever-fluctuating relationship of the dyad as a contributing factor in the intellectual and emotional growth that takes place over a course of time.

RANGE AND SCOPE OF THE EDUCATIONAL THERAPY PRACTICE

Educational therapists are typically drawn to the profession from fields including special and regular education, child development, psychology, speech and language, marriage and family counseling, and parent and professional advocacy. Some do make second and third career changes from professions including business and law, in which case a shift in careers is often a personal one, possibly influenced by a family member who experiences difficulty in learning and functioning.

Clients who are typically served by ETs range from pre-school aged children to adults who exhibit learning disabilities. They may suffer from low self-esteem, school related anxiety, and inhibited motivation as a result of difficulties in auditory, visual, and language processing which impact their reading, writing, math, and executive function skills. These clients may present with comorbid profiles such as ADHD, Tourette Syndrome, Asperger Syndrome, nonverbal learning disabilities, depression, and post traumatic symptoms. Some ETs do choose to specialize in a particular age range, while others prefer working with clients across the lifespan. Educational therapists work in a variety of settings, some in a combination of educational or clinical environments. Most ETs are in private practice, either alone or with a group of colleagues, at an office, home, clinic, public agency, learning center, public or private school, hospital, university, college, or a vocational school. No matter where or with whom the ET practices, the underlying goal is to help instill a sense of confidence and motivation in the client.

Educational therapists engage in an ongoing synergistic balance of remediation and a watchfulness of a client's affect. ETs often address clients' fluctuating self-esteem, which may interfere with a wide range of skills and functions in life. The acquisition of fundamental skills such as reading, writing, and math are vulnerable to being under-developed and overlooked as a result of low self self-esteem, as the child and adolescent in question may be skilled at invisibility and over-compliance in other areas.

While ETs cannot infuse self-esteem into a client, it remains a palpable presence in a session, driving the outcome for a wide range of externally imposed expectations. This is a painful and sometimes lonely undertaking for some clients, although ETs can ease some of this discomfort with reminders of what a client can do and what she can reasonably expect of herself. Marcel Proust stated: "We don't receive wisdom; we must discover it for ourselves after a journey that no one can take for us or spare us from." Educational therapists may feel a sense of empathy for a client and be witness to the emergence of increased self-esteem following a series of incremental successes, but the client ultimately is alone in his work, experiencing the familiar fears and need for avoidance that comes with each new task or expectation.

DISTINGUISHING CHARACTERISTICS OF THE EDUCATIONAL THERAPIST

The population of clients with whom an ET works does not have difficulty just learning a skill, but often experiences difficulty learning how to learn. Educational therapists offer opportunities to learn through mirroring or modeling a technique or behavior with a client. They role play situations with clients, enhancing their ability to become self-advocates; they offer a range of techniques that invite clients to make choices based on their understanding of their ability and confidence level; and, they demystify their clients' learning strengths and weaknesses, providing a learning profile for the specific individual which strives to stretch the client to his or her maximum potential. In order to accomplish these goals an ET employs the distinguishing characteristic of interpreting the vernacular of allied professionals in order to communicate and collaborate with those who are involved in a treatment alliance.

Educational therapists may address an under-developed math or reading skill, but they do not adhere exclusively to a specific program or method; rather, they acknowledge the range of emotional symptoms that often emerge as a result of a client's perception of self, the fear of failure, and embarrassment related to previous experiences, as well as the development of a treatment plan that offers a range of ways to revisit or re-learn a skill or task. Ongoing dialogue occurs between the ET and client regarding the emotional response precipitated by returning to a task that was previously unattainable, serving as both a therapeutic measure as well as a means of exercising language and thought.

Selecting techniques from a variety of sources depends on the individual client's needs and the comprehensiveness of the ET's training. For example, if 10 educational therapists were surveyed about how they teach the recognition of the main idea in a paragraph to a specific client-profile, all 10 ET's would probably report utilizing different materials, with some commonality, in order to reach that goal. In questioning them about their reasoning for their choices, their rationales might include a preference for what has proven to be successful in the past and what is compatible for the client's learning profile. What remains a constant in this process, is the relationship that, over time, provides the comfort zone where new strategies and techniques can be attempted. When the threat of failure emerges in a session the comfort zone provides a place to examine the level of anxiety it precipitates, thereby opening up the dialogue for reflection, re-defining goals and priorities, and making the decision to re-enter the task in a new way, or to abandon it until the next session.

Similar to other types of clinical professionals, ETs are case managers, trained and supervised in developing a treatment alliance with other specialists, and in maintaining clinical data that contributes to both research and treatment purposes. Case management in this profession is necessary for the ET who meets clients on a regular basis in her office for one-to-one sessions; for the ET who tends to offer more advocacy or consultation services to clients and their families; and, to the ET who tends to offer more educational diagnostic services in conjunction with consultation.

Unique to the profession of educational therapy is the formal training and expected skill in administering both formal and informal assessments which are appropriate to the level of experience and background of the ET. In conjunction with varying levels of expertise in administering assessments is the need to be able to interpret data, as well as understand the interpretation of other evaluators in order to create and implement effective educational therapy treatment plans, consistently monitoring and evaluating a client's progress while simultaneously fostering motivation. While the mastery of a skill is important in the work of an ET, it remains only a piece of the overall puzzle of effective learning. The characteristic psychoeducational goals the ET may choose for a client include:

1. An augmentation of self-esteem by creating opportunities for success and the recognition of one's unique islands of competency (Brooks, & Goldstein, 2004);
2 A self-awareness of resiliency and an elevated level of coping skills when recovering from a disappointment or self-perceived failure;
3. A decrease in anxiety related to academic and social demands;
4. A self-awareness and strengthening of executive functioning skills;
5. An increase of self-advocacy skills;
6. An expansion of autonomy in meeting academic and social demands.

THE DETECTION AND ANALYSIS OF VITAL CLUES IN EDUCATIONAL THERAPY: DEVELOPING A CASE STUDY WITH FORENSIC EVIDENCE

As is evident from the cover of this book, the work of an educational therapist requires that she regards the practice, especially the scrutiny of individual case studies, as puzzles to be solved. The puzzle is a work-in-progress, always in motion, and never "perfect." The vigilance this process requires is akin to good detective work, and like the work of a forensic artist, the face of the individual may be revealed enough for recognition and assumptions about the person's functioning, but the mysterious layers of behaviors and emotional responses remain ongoing, keeping time with human development in a way that is not always obvious, but is often recognized after-the-fact.

The contexts, or settings, of this detective work change continually, although the initial meetings and subsequent interpretation of data may occur behind the table in the office with only the company of a lamp and possibly some background music, reminiscent of earlier books and films that place us on the shoulders of famous detectives. Educational therapists are information-gatherers, accruing data like Jane Marple collects tiny little facts about her list of suspects, categorizing and re-developing her suppositions in order to build a solid case that supports her hunches. Hercule Poirot, another astute observer of human behavior, uncovers his data from sources that are not always obvious to others. It might be as a result of noticing a client's handedness, or habits and characteristics that are rather subtle, but nevertheless of great importance in building a case that speaks to human learning and functioning, with or without the additional evidence that is provided by formal assessment.

According to Linda Siegel and Connie Bagshaw from the University of British Columbia (1997), the creator of these famous detectives, Agatha Christie, was home-schooled and allegedly had a learning disability which manifested as a difficulty with numbers and spelling, and bore a similar profile to that of many other extraordinarily talented people. Her analytic and detection skills were unsurpassed in her field, and she shared her talents with younger students for whom she edited essays. What amazing educational therapy skills she possessed: a deep understanding for the struggles of a student who exhibited difficulty with traditional teaching and learning; an analytical mind that accrued the details of an individual's behaviors and temperament; and, an empathic spirit that provided us all with a way to look into the experience of others in their plight.

The ET of today generally works with a treatment alliance, comprised of individuals who contribute evidence that assists in solving, or reworking the puzzle in order to provide the best possible outcome for a client. Some allied professionals play a larger role than others in this forensic-like work, offering evidence that comes from their experience in living or working with a client. Others contribute a single source of quantitative data that supports a theory or an alleged truth. The evidence that is useful in building a client-profile may be biological in nature (e.g., genetic predispositions to learning disabilities and attentional disorders); or it may of a more qualitative nature as a result of ongoing informal questions and interviewing, providing the ET with a developmental perspective of a client's executive functioning skills in a wide range of contexts. The development of a client's profile then leads to a careful choice of techniques which directly address the continued growth of individual talents, while confronting the nemesis of personal weaknesses in learning and functioning.

In 2001, the quintessential ET and educational psychologist, the character Evah Nellsom, made an appearance in the book, *Parenting Children with Learning Disabilities* (Adelizzi & Goss, 2001), demonstrating her detective skills as she observed the behaviors of her clients in their own settings, gathering evidence-based details from previous data in order to build a developmental profile of her clients. She allowed the accrued data to germinate in her thinking, regarding the client from a variety of perspectives, dependent upon the nature of the evidence. She took the time to explain the multi-faceted process of learning to clients and their families, providing them with an opportunity to share in solving the puzzle which keeps us all detecting …, analyzing …, and searching for the answers.

REFERENCES

Adelizzi, J. (1995). *Shades of trauma*. Plymouth, MA: Riverside Press.

Adelizzi, J. (1998). *A closer look: Perspective and reflections on college students with learning disabilities*. Milton, MA: Curry College.

Adelizzi, J. (2001). *Parenting children with learning disabilities*. Waterford, CT: Bergin & Garvey.

Association of Educational Therapist By-Laws. (1979). http://www.aetonline.org/fils/pulbic/AETBylawsRev08.pdf

Brooks, R., & Goldstein, S. (2004). *The power of resilience: Achieving balance, confidence, and personal strength in your life*. New York: McGraw-Hill.

Daloz, Laurent L. A. (1986). *Effective teaching and mentoring*. San Francisco: Jossey-Bass.

De Hirsch, K. (1977). Interactions between educational therapist and child. *Bulletin of the Orton Society, XXVII*, 87–101.

Field, K., Kaufman, E., & Saltzman, C. (1993). *Emotions and learning reconsidered: International perspectives*. New York: Gardner Press.

Fraser, S., & Gestwicki, C. (2001). *Authentic childhood: Exploring Reggio Emilia in the classroom*. Florence, KY: Cengage Learning.

Gavin, L. A., Wamboldt, M. Z., Levy, S. Y., & Wamboldt, F. S. (1999). Treatment alliance and its association with family functitoning, adherence, and medical outcome in adolescents with severe, chronic asthma. *Journal of Pediatric Psychiartry, 24*, 355–365 .

Haffner, C., & Hutchinson, G. (2009). *Better because of you*. Seattle: Washington Bending Corners Press.

Kaganoff, A., & Ficksman, M. (1998). The AET graphic model of educational therapy. *The Educational Therapist, California: The Association of Educational Therapists, 19*(2), 3–5.

Keogh, B. (1995). Why interventions don't work. *The Educational Therapist, California: The Association of Educational Therapists, 16*(2), 15.

Maslow, A., & Maslow, B. (1993). *The farther reaches of human nature*. New York: Penguin.

Meltzer, L. (Ed.). (2007). *Executive function in education*. New York: Guilford Press.

Miller, P. (2002). *Theories of developmental psychology* (4th ed.). New York: Worth Publishers.

Mosk, S. (2004). Redefining the definition of educational therapy. *The Educational Therapist, California: The Association of Educational Therapists, 25*(3–4), 4–5.

Reyes-Simpson, E. (2004). When there is too much to take in: Some factors that restrict the capacity to think. In

D. Simpson & L. Miller (Eds.), *Unexpected gains: Psychotherapy with people with learning disabilities.* (The Tavistock Clinic Series) (pp. 122–132). London: H. Karnac Books Ltd.

Rogers, C., & Freiberg, H. J. (1994). *Freedom to learn* (3rd ed.). Upper Saddle River, NJ: Prentice Hall.

Sapir, S. (1985). *The clinical teaching model.* New York: Brunner/Mazel.

Schacter, D. L. (1996). *Searching for memory.* New York: Basic Books.

Semrud-Clikeman, M., & Teeter-Ellison, P. A. (2009). *Child neuropsychology: Assessment and intervention for neurodevelopmental disorders* (2nd ed.). New York: Springer.

Siegel, L. L., & Bagshaw, C. C. (1997). *Reconsidering normal: Learning disabilities in the classroom.* Lecture at the University of British Columbia. http://www.publicaffairs.ubc.ca/media/releases/1997/mr-97-15.html

Simpson, D., & Miller, L. (Eds.). (2004). *Unexpected gains: Psychotherapy with people with learning disabilities.* (The Tavistock Clinic Series). London: H. Karnac Books Ltd.

Sprenger, M. (2008). *The developing brain: Birth to age eight.* Thousand Oaks, CA: Corwin Press.

Wolf, M. M. (2007). *Proust and the squid: The story and science of the reading brain.* New York: Harper.

2

DEVELOPMENTAL STAGES OF THE EDUCATIONAL THERAPY PROCESS

KAREN A. KASS

Educational therapy (ET) is a process in which two people, therapist and client, join in a connected relationship and proceed on a journey. Relationships do not just happen; they develop over time and follow a somewhat predictable path. In the beginning, the relationship focuses on getting to know one another. It then proceeds into familiarity and joint purpose. Social relationships may perhaps continue on a permanent basis, deepening in connection and value. However, the educational therapy relationship is contractual, and it eventually ends. Because of this, to enable the process of termination to proceed in a more genial way the relationship enters a stage of gentle disconnection in its final weeks. The stages in a relationship are developmental; one stage is preparation for the next.

The stages of the educational therapy process are not unlike the stages an actor experiences when landing a part in a play and performing the role until the play closes. Each of the stages has its unique characteristics and requires diverse expertise from the actor and the ET. The following process is written in a similar format to that of a live theater production.

Stage I, the Initial Contact, begins when the parent of the child calls the ET. There is the possibility of a job! For the actor, Stage I occurs when the agent calls with the possibility of a part in a play. Both the parent and the actor's agent briefly state what the work will entail, resulting, it is hoped in *Stage II*, an *Intake* session for the ET and parent, which is not unlike the audition for the actor. When the ET meets the parents and the client for the first time, she is, in a sense, auditioning for them, as the actor auditions for the part in a play. Each is making a decision about whether there is a good match, a good fit, between the requirements of the play and the personalities of the people being considered for the role. Assuming all goes well with the initial meeting and audition, the ET lands the job of working with the client and the actor earns the part in the play. The ET describes the policies which guide the business part of the relationship; the actor's agent negotiates the terms under which the actor will participate in the play. At this point, *Stage III, Developing the Working Relationship*, begins for the ET and rehearsal commences for the actor. This stage requires the establishment of the structure or the ambiance of the work; each participant taking cues from the other, collaborating on the best way in which to proceed. The comfort zone is *Stage IV, Case Management*, where the therapeutic process is full speed underway, and the actor participates in the run of the show. There is a level of calm and familiarity between the therapist and the client; the therapist is in continuous contact with the parents, the school, and any allied professionals with whom the client works. Since the ET and the actor are contracted for a period of time. *Stage V, Termination*, at some point, becomes a reality. The client reaches goals or it is time to move on; the play has had its run and it closes. Occasionally, the therapist and client may work together in the future, where they enter *Stage VI, Encore*; the actor is asked to perform in the revival of the play. But for now, their therapeutic relationship comes to an end.

The ET must possess various skill sets during each of the stages and present an engaging, warm, reliant personality in order to get the job. So too, the actor calls upon her many character traits when auditioning and rehearsing for the play. Just as the actor gathers information about the character, setting, and design of the play, at the outset, a great deal of individual and shared information is gathered by the ET about the client, the family, and the many contexts in which the client participates. The ET must be a good interviewer, and be able to both ask questions and develop a schema within which the answers begin to fit. The actor develops a relationship with the other actors and the audience; the ET develops a relationship with the client, the family, and allied professionals. Knowledge of interpersonal dynamics and the ability to sense internal affective responses from the audience—the client—are critical components of the relationship and therapeutic work.

The ensuing sections of this chapter further delineate the developmental stages of the educational therapy process. Case examples are presented to facilitate understanding of the requirements and nuances of each stage. Additionally, questions are presented which encourage the ET to continually hypothesize not only about the needs of the client but also about the best ways in which to help the client feel understood and experience success along the journey.

STAGE I: THE INITIAL CONTACT (THE PHONE RINGS)

The educational therapy process typically begins with a phone call from a parent wanting help for her child. As with any new undertaking, a level of anxiety is frequently experienced in both parties. The parent—often the mother if only one parent attends the initial meeting—no doubt feels somewhat anxious because she wants help and hopes the person on the other end of the phone, the ET, will be the answer. Similarly the ET may experience some anxiety for several reasons, two of which may have to do with the origin of the referral, and whether or not the person on the other end of the phone will, indeed, become a client. A colleague, allied professional, school administrator or counselor, classroom teacher, or a current (or former) client gives the ET's name and number to a prospective client. The ET has come highly recommended; the referring individual has endorsed her or his qualifications and competency. Will the ET live up to the advance press? Will the ET be successful with this client? Will the ET get the job? Will the ET communicate well enough over the phone to be perceived as a good fit with the client? If there is time in the practice to schedule a new client, and the presenting issues seem to be within the ET's scope of practice, the next considerations are reflections of individual differences in psychological makeup and personality.

Successful maneuvering through this stage depends upon several professional and personal competencies. First, the ET must return the phone call promptly and at a time when he or she can spend enough time to talk so that initial information may be gathered and the parent feels as though she is being heard. Timeliness in returning a phone call can be an important factor. How many times has an ET returned a call only to hear that the parent had already chosen to see another ET who called back first! The ET's voice must contain qualities of warmth, engagement, and empathy. Decisions about whether or not this relationship has a chance at succeeding are frequently based on the first 10 minute phone call. Additionally, the ET must have the ability to gather information in a short period of time, set a time for an appointment, and be able to end the conversation without the parent feeling rushed or cut off. This is no easy task. The parent probably feels a sense of desperation, she or he wants to be heard and emotionally responded to. The phone call could continue for quite a bit of time if the ET does not bring it to a close.

Other more practical considerations at this stage involve business materials. The ET has to create a system whereby information is recorded. Some ETs simply take basic factual information (name and phone number) and set an initial appointment time. Others have developed phone intake forms requiring more extensive information regarding the client (e.g., current school, recent assessments, presenting issue). The time spent on the phone and the preliminary information gathered during the initial contact depends upon the individual ET.

Mrs. Tucker left a brief message about needing someone to work with her 13-year-old 8th grade son Ted who attended a private Catholic middle school. When we spoke she apologized for missing my earlier call, and proceeded to tell me that she was on the phone with her son's teacher. The teacher had called to say that Ted was even more distracted than usual, and, in fact, she had to move Ted's seat to the other side of the room so that he would be sitting right in front of her. She thought she would go the route of educational therapy; she got my number from searching the Internet, probably through the AET. In response to my asking a little bit about Ted's school history, Mrs. Tucker said that for the last 3 years Ted's been doing mediocre work in school, but now was just barely skating by. Sometimes Ted was also hostile or defiant. I asked if Ted exhibited the same behavior with his father. She said less so, but Ted talks back to his dad as well. Her daughter, the "nonproblem" child, was up North in college and doing very well. I thought about some of the typical factors which might explain a change in this middle schooler's behavior at home and in school—substance use, some medical condition, emotional problems, or perhaps problems at home. Going out on a limb, I asked about drug usage as a possibility. Mrs. Tucker said that there were no drugs involved so far as she knew. She said that she and Ted's father had been divorced for over 5 years. She had Ted in therapy years ago, but it didn't seem to work with the woman who saw him, and after a time, the therapist recommended that Ted see a male therapist. Mrs. Tucker wasn't sure how productive that therapy experience was either and thought that the therapist just took Ted's side and said that Ted was really okay, doing fine.

I ascertained that Ted had not had any neuropsychological or academic testing. I summarized the options for Mrs. Tucker as follows. We could set up an appointment to meet, then I could meet with Ted, then I could determine the next steps which probably would require an assessment or she could begin with the assessment and I would give her a referral. She asked my fee and felt she could handle that. Mrs. Tucker wanted to meet with me first, and have me see Ted later. I asked how she thought Ted would respond to meeting with me, and that, if she wanted, I could meet with them both and then tell Ted what I thought about his school performance challenges and the next step to be taken; it was sometimes easier for a child to hear something from a third person. She thought Ted would do best without her in the room. We set two appointments for the following week.

Factors to Consider in Stage I

There are many factors, and a great deal of information gathered from both sides, which come into play when an ET is in private practice and a prospective client phones. Initially, there are practical considerations such as whether or not there is time for a new client, whether the fee charged is acceptable, whether or not the presenting issue seems to be within the scope of practice, and available personal resources and resiliency to take on another client with presenting issues that are similar to others in the ET's practice. I had room in my practice for more clients at the time when Ted's mother phoned me. The available appointment time worked for both Ted and Mrs. Tucker. Additionally Mrs. Tucker let me know my fee was acceptable. I needed to meet Mrs. Tucker and Ted to determine exactly how Ted's issues manifested themselves and whether or not I had the personal resilience to take on another client like Ted—I have worked with many clients with issues similar to those of Ted.

The ET learns a great deal about the client and his or her family during the initial phone contact. Educationally, I learned that Ted was distracted and that this distractibility was not new. Ted had earned poor grades over the last 3 years, the beginning of middle school, and now his performance in school was getting worse. Questions I asked myself concerned whether Ted's academic struggles were related to his abilities, the difficulty of the academic requirements, and I guessed that it was some combination of both. Emotionally, I thought about Ted's sense of himself given his poor school performance. I wondered whether avoidance and denial were part of Ted's defensive coping mechanisms. His parents were divorced when Ted was about 5 years old, not an easy age to have a parent move from the home. Mrs. Tucker mentioned her "nonproblem" child, her daughter. How much did Ted feel in competition with his sister? How much of his sense of failure was a reflection he saw when looking at his sister's successes? What were the subtle messages Ted "heard" and integrated into a sense of who he was as a learner, a son, a sibling?

When a child experiences learning challenges, the professionals frequently look within the child to determine the causes of the challenge and their concomitant possible remedial implications. Neuropsychological and academic assessments focus on how the child processes information and achieves on cognitive, performance, and academic tasks. The professional who administers assessment typically suggests a number of possible recommendations and interventions to either ameliorate or compensate for the child's learning challenges. In this case, Ted would need a thorough evaluation to determine his learning style, cognitive functioning, processing ability, problem solving strategies, and the like. However, the ET must evaluate the recommendations and interventions with respect to the context of the client and the family.

It is extremely important to hear all the information gathered at this stage and subsequent stages through the lens of context, which has been defined as the physical, social, and psychological environments of home and school (Keogh, 2005). Context relates to the variety of communities within which the client and family live, such as family life, school, and classroom environment (Levine, 2003; Ungerleider, 1997). I had a brief peek at the context within which Ted functions. He is an adolescent who lives at home with his mother. He sees his father outside of the home. I wondered about the dynamic between mom and dad. Were they friendly or hostile? After a visit with dad, did Ted's behavior change in school or at home with his mother? What impact did Ted's learning challenges have on his parents? Did either parent exhibit similar challenges during their school years? Did either parent feel a sense of guilt at "passing along" the challenges to Ted? How much understanding did the parents have? Which parent is responsible for communicating with the school? What was the school and classroom environment? Was the administration or teacher educationally prepared to deal with Ted's learning challenges? Were there resources in the school to provide Ted with additional academic support? Was mom available when Ted got home from school to help with homework, keep him focused? What personal and professional demands were placed on mom? Did she have the resources necessary to help Ted? I looked forward to my meeting with Mrs. Tucker and Ted as we progressed to the next stage.

STAGE II A & B: INITIAL MEETING WITH THE PARENT AND CLIENT (THE AUDITION)

Typically the ET sets up separate appointments with the parent and the child. Whom the ET meets first, how much information is obtained from an assessment prior to meeting the child is again an individual preference. Regardless of whom the ET meets first, parent or child, the ET is auditioning for the job. Assuming all things being equal and the therapist is competent to deal with the client's particular issue(s), the primary factor regarding whether or not the ET works with the client will be the therapist's personality, sensitivity to the issues faced by the parent and child, and the ET's ability to build initial rapport with both parent and child. The ET must also provide an interesting, engaging, welcoming, and comfortable environment. Both parent and child need to feel as though the environment can facilitate the learning tasks as well as support a developing relationship. A setting which includes areas for relaxed conversation as well as for learning tasks appeals to both parent and child. The ambiance of the setting also depends upon the age of the client. Young children want to play; teenagers do not want to be infantilized.

Part A: Meeting with the Parent(s)

It didn't take long before Mrs. Sanders started tearing up and Mr. Sanders began to pat her knee. "My wife gets so upset," said Mr. Sanders. "Alex will be fine, he just needs to grow up." However, school had not come easy to Alex, even in grade school. Alex's parents were called to school many times because he just wasn't working "up to his potential," and sometimes didn't seem to try. After such meetings, there would be a plan, a commitment from Alex to do better, and then, things would fall apart again. He was a bright boy, all his teachers said so, and his teachers liked Alex. However, 7th grade Alex was not doing so well in school. He procrastinated with homework, and when he did do his homework, he frequently forgot to turn it in. School policy was that late or missing homework affected grades, so Alex's grades were poor. He seemed to be distracted, didn't read for pleasure, frequently felt tired, and said school was boring. When Alex was asked about school, he didn't engage in much conversation, and said he didn't know why he didn't do better. He liked playing guitar. Both parents reported that Alex liked something, became obsessive about it, then a few months later he would drop it. They worried that he had no goals or motivation; he didn't stick with things when they were challenging. He avoided rather than confronted difficult situations.

Mom and dad both worked full time. Alex had after school activities, mostly sports, which he was good at. Homework time was after dinner, when the family tried to get together. The meal frequently ended in disaster; one question about school led the family down a dismal road which ended with Alex leaving the table and slamming his bedroom door. If and when homework was started, it was typically mom who helped. She said that Alex's written work was very disorganized. He had good thoughts, but no one could appreciate his thoughts since the writing was so confusing. There was no academic subject that Alex liked, according to his parents, though he did enjoy his pottery class and said that it relaxed him. Alex's parents were not thrilled that pottery was a favorite subject—you couldn't amount to much with pottery. Alex had friends. He hung out with them on weekends. Alex's parents had met some of the friends, but not all of them. They were not crazy about one or two and thought they might be a bad influence on Alex. There were two other siblings in the home—an older brother who did well in school, and a younger sister in 4th grade who did "OK." Alex had chores to do at home, but never remembered to do them without being prompted. He always said he'd do them after being reminded, but somehow forgot. At the request of the family, Alex was scheduled to begin a neuropsych assessment in 2 weeks. The school referred Alex to the ET.

Who is this parent who sits in front of the ET for an initial meeting? What are the experiences and history which accompany this first visit (Lawrence-Lightfoot, 2003). Hallowell (2007a) presents a realistic, albeit painful, portrait of the parent of the learning challenged child. The parent wants help, not only for the child, but also for the family. Frequently parents feel that they are to blame for their child's difficulties, there was something that could have, should have been done differently. Moreover, learning challenges are typically found in families so the affected child may be one of several family members with similar difficulties (Muenke, n.d.). The parent may feel as though the child inherited the problem. During the initial audition, the parent is in need of validation for their frustrations and their attempts to help, as well as some understanding about their child's learning issues.

The importance of gathering further information concerning the context of the child and family during this stage in the process cannot be stressed enough (Ungerleider, 2005). Simply asking about a typical day in the family's life can elicit a wealth of critical information in working with the child and his family. The recommendations for interventions can result in failure if the context cannot support their implementation. The child's family life, peer group, community, and educational environments may all impact the achievement of goals.

Initially, the ET has to present a welcoming and engaging persona. Like the actor, the ET must be charismatic, charming, and yet maintain a professional approach. During the preliminary session, the ET must make the parent feel both heard and understood. The ET must communicate to the parent that frustration and anxiety are normal; having a child with learning difficulties presents parenting challenges. It is also important to commend the parents' efforts in trying to help their child. The course of demystification begins at this stage, "a process in which a child's plight is described so that it contains as little myth, fantasy, and mystery as possible" (Levine, 2001, p. 568). Parents need to frame and appreciate their child's challenges. As a result of helping to demystify the situation, the ET is presenting herself as a person who is knowledgeable, experienced, helpful, and empathic. By the end of the initial meeting, the parent has to consider the ET to be a willing helpmate and resource for the family as well as the child.

During the audition, the parent determines whether the ET is, in fact, *the* person. On what basis does the parent make this decision? Is this the first attempt at getting help for his or her child? Has the child worked with other therapists or allied professionals? Why is the parent seeking help from someone else? Has the child just been identified by the school as needing some outside help? Has the child been assessed? What has the parent been told about the child's educational challenges? On what basis is the parent determining whether or not his or her son or daughter would be a good fit with the ET? Qualities such as a dynamic personality, the ability to tolerate difficult feelings, a sense of humor, strength, and "togetherness" are critical for the audition stage.

The ET also needs to ask the right questions in order to formulate several possible hypotheses about the child and the family. At the very least, the ET must obtain information about the presenting problem, school history and intervention history, the social context of the child and the family, and a sense of the parents' ability to partner with the ET.

At some point during the initial meeting with the parents, the ET needs to check in with the parent to see if the process will proceed. Assuming that the parent indicates that she or he would like to proceed, the ET must then get down to the business part of the relationship. The ET needs to have forms and prepared materials to gather and relate information. An appointment schedule is developed that indicates the day and time of sessions. The ET needs to describe his or her background and qualifications and role; this is frequently reiterated in a prepared statement of qualifications which the parent can take home and review. Typically, there is discussion about the nature of the sessions and length of time required for the process—will it be months or years? In addition to the need for identifying and qualitative information, at this point the ET begins to set the boundaries so necessary to the educational therapy contract (Chidekel, 2003). Parents are informed about what to expect in terms of the frequency of phone or in person parental contact (i.e., on a regularly scheduled basis or as the need arises). Policies must be stated regarding confidentiality, fees and billing procedures, and cancellations. Information forms are usually given to complete and return regarding general information, policy agreements, release of information forms, and school contact information (e.g., teacher's name, phone number, e-mail address, and subject area taught). The length and nature of information required on these forms varies from ET to ET. Some ETs use the developmental history information taken from the formal assessment. Alternately, ETs may require parents to complete a detailed developmental history specific to the ET's need for information.

Part B: Meeting with the Client—The Audition with the Child

When I went into the waiting room to get Molly for our initial session, she was sitting slumped in a chair with her eyes closed; her mother silently mouthed, "She doesn't want to be here!" Immediately, my anxiety went up a notch, and I could feel myself getting a bit annoyed. Many thoughts went through my head: I didn't feel like engaging in battle; how was I going to win this kid over; over the course of many years of practice, like any ET I'd encountered reluctance and I'd been ok; perhaps there will be some divine intervention, and we'll begin the journey together. Molly slumped her 5th grade self onto my couch and put her head back, staring at the ceiling. "You don't want to be here, right?" I said, a reasonable thing to say to let her know I got the message. "I don't blame you," I continued, "Why would you?" She looked at me and nodded. "Did your mom tell you why she brought you?" Molly nodded again and said, "Yeah, school." I confirmed that she was right, and that I help kids who have difficulties in school. I explained that this session was about us getting to know one another, and that no decision had been made about our working together; she and I would have to determine that. Molly sat up a bit when I mentioned her role in this. I told her that I wanted to get to know her a bit, and maybe she had questions for me as well. She shook her head. I asked about what kind of music she liked, what movies she had seen recently,, who her best friend(s) was, whether she had pets, and what she liked to do when she wasn't in school. The questions seemed to take Molly by surprise. She answered eagerly, and gave me the information with embellished details. We both relaxed. Eventually, we talked about school. Molly told me she had trouble understanding what she read, she could repeat what happened in a story, but she couldn't answer some of the harder questions. "You mean questions like 'what's the main idea' or 'the author's purpose'?" Her face lit up, and she said, "Yeah, exactly!" I assured her that those kinds of questions were not easy, but that if we worked together, I could help her in that area. In response to some additional probing about life at school, Molly said her desk was usually a mess, the teacher gave so many papers, and she didn't have time to get them organized. She also pointed to her backpack, which she brought with her, and said, "That's a mess as well. My mother always wants to help me organize it, but then she gets mad when I don't keep it organized." I acknowledged that organization was a challenge for lots of kids, and that I could be helpful with that as well. I told her that an organized brain, desk, backpack, or room, was like an organized closet; it's easier to find what you're looking for. I asked if it would be OK to look in the backpack, and whether anything was going to bite me or was there an old sandwich which might be yucky if I touched it. Molly laughed and said not to worry. Together we sorted through papers, I showed her interesting folders I had in the office and she chose ones she liked. I brought out the label maker, and I think that sealed the deal! Molly made labels for all the folders. I told her that if we continued to meet she and I could try to keep up the organization together. Moreover, I said that we would be partners on working out the school challenges; I would rely on her to let me know how I was doing and if what we did was something she thought helpful. After a bit more organizing, chatting, and asking if Molly had any questions, we agreed to a trial period for us to work together. She couldn't wait to show her mother her neatly organized backpack. When Molly and her mother, now smiling when she saw her daughter smiling, left the office, I noticed that my initial dread had lifted and that I was looking forward to working with Molly.

The most important skills an ET can have during this stage are the ability to develop rapport with a young person, the flexibility to be spontaneous and fluid, the empathy to join with the child about the agony of needing to come to sessions at all, and the personality to let the child/client know that she, the ET, is actually an okay person! The ET must communicate, or demonstrate sensitivity to the emotional state of the child, and be engaging enough to elicit an initial agreement to partner in the journey toward school success rather than failure.

Several questions should come to mind when preparing for meeting a new (child) client. Who is the child sitting on the other side of the room or next to you? How does the child approach the world temperamentally (Child Development Institute, 1998a, 1998b)? How long has the child been struggling in silence or out loud? How is that child feeling about him- or herself, school, coming to an ET (what's that!), facing another adult who will let the child know that he or she is not "doing school well?"

Again, Hallowell (2007b) provides a poignant, yet at times, comical glimpse into the mind of a child with ADHD. However, more often than not, the child does not recognize the ET as a helpful person until well into the process. At the initial meeting, he just expects to be reminded of his shortcomings. Continued failure experiences over time increase the chances that the child who sits before you for the first time feels defeated, deflated, and helpless (Gordon & Gordon, 2006; Gorman, 1999).

Occasionally, a child will come in with a somewhat encouraging attitude. Perhaps the child sees the ET as a person who can, indeed, turn things around. This child appears ready to engage quite quickly, tell you all about her school experiences, her favorite subjects and educational challenges, who she eats lunch with, and who she avoids on the playground!

> Sydney's mother said that Sydney, her 4th grader, was somewhat hesitant about coming to see me since it would focus on her learning challenges, and Sydney was all about a high level of performance. Within minutes of our first session, Sydney and I were chatting away about her troubles at school. After listening to her a bit, we talked about how people's brains work differently. I told her that I needed quiet when I read, and that my son could work better if music was playing. I could tell by the look on her face that she was interested in what I was saying and seemed calmer. The next time I saw Sydney, our first work session, she stated what she wanted to work on and in what order. Our work had begun almost immediately. Sydney was ready to engage in the process of change. She responded to a positive approach that focused on her strengths; there were many identified in that first session.

Some children who come to an ET do not have a clue about why they are not doing well in school. They just don't seem to understand what is expected. One fact doesn't compute in the brain, then the next, until finally they are lost in a sea of bewilderment. The defense mechanism of avoidance works wonders. They don't want homework, so they forget they have it. When questioned about school, answers are short and vague. If only people would leave them alone, things would be fine. The only positive experiences in school are those which are considered outside the classroom learning environment (Hallowell, 2007b).

> William was a very nice adolescent young man. He did not present any behavior problems at home or in school. In fact, everyone liked William, including his teachers, even though he was not doing well in school. He was an enigma. He was bright, but just did not play the game of school. When asked about why his mother brought him to treatment, he said that he didn't do well last year in 9th grade. In response to being asked about his thoughts regarding the situation, he said that he didn't focus and spent time on other things. He was not sure what the problem was and certainly not sure that he could be helped. The school put him on academic probation and suggested he see an ET. He was currently taking medication for a diagnosed attention deficit disorder. I got the feeling that William just went along in life. He would show up for appointments, do whatever was asked, make promises to use the Web sites available to study, even when he didn't have homework!

A successful initial interview with a child is the beginning of the working relationship. The ET needs to be aware of the nuances in a child's affective responses, and the differences in approaches based upon the age of the child being seen. Beginning the interview with unexpected questions related to the child's current interests, rather than the failures and challenges of school, often facilitates his or her willingness to give the therapist a chance

(Edgette, 2002). The ET wants the child to respond positively and indicate a level of openness to working together. It would be nice if the child felt as Renée Zellweger did in the movie Jerry Mcguire when she said to Jerry, "You had me at hello." However, the reality of the progression through the ET process is sometimes fraught with bumps along the road.

The practical business concerns at this point relate to having forms available to record information from your interview with the child. ETs vary in the information they want and the ways in which information is recorded. For example, ETs may create an intake packet for the child including questionnaires regarding likes and dislikes, executive functioning skills, writing samples, how well the game of school is played, and the like (Dawson & Guare, 2004; Heacox, 1991; Kaganoff, 2002, 2003). Other ETs may make take notes as sessions unfold regarding such skills and interests. In any case, the ET has to be flexible enough to forego the formal interview if the client needs to go in a different direction during the first meeting.

STAGE III: DEVELOPING A WORKING RELATIONSHIP (REHEARSAL)

Both ET and client get down to business during Stage III in the educational therapy process. Reports have been read, school work has been reviewed, academic skills have been informally assessed during the sessions, the client has been observed during learning tasks, and the ET must begin to pave the road to successful accomplishment of the tasks at hand. It is during this stage that the therapist's knowledge of the child's learning style, remedial programs, and remedial interventions permit her to discover what works best for the particular client. All the data from the neuropsychological assessment, the parents, the classroom teacher, and, most importantly, the child is synthesized. At this point, the ET and client are engaged in a process akin to rehearsal. Materials are used, approaches attempted until there is synchronicity. The student and therapist begin to understand how each works best; they develop a nonverbal (as well as verbal) communication system, a joining of metaphorical hands as they proceed on their journey together.

However, just as an actor can be adept at learning the lines of the play, there is no meaningful performance without engagement and emotional connection with the audience. So too, the relationship, the tacit alliance between therapist and client, provides the foundation of process to move forward. deHirsch (1997) notes,

> As does psychotherapy, remedial work rests on a treatment alliance between the child and the adult, on a pact—spoken or unspoken—that the two will work together towards a common goal, that in spite of inevitable frustrations, occasional anger, worse, boredom, they will stick together in the service of learning. (p. 89)

> After several months of working with Susie, I wanted to quit. Nothing was happening. I never looked forward to her twice weekly appointments; in fact, I dreaded them. Her father brought her to the appointments and barely acknowledged me when I went to the waiting room to get Susie—maybe a no-eye-contact "hi." I felt as though Susie's father did not like me and that I had done something to offend him, although I could think of nothing that I had done. Susie's teachers and other people who had worked with Susie said she was funny and bright; I didn't see it. Susie would show up, look blankly at me as she did whatever I asked her to do. She came; she left. On occasion, Susie would say something that I thought was so off the wall, I had to comment; her

logic was just so faulty and rigid. Nothing I said made a difference. I was upset every time she left the office because I felt empty, like a failure. I knew I was not the right ET for her. And, Susie was certainly not the right client for me. Finally, I had had enough. I asked the parents to meet me at a local coffee shop, my treat. I was breaking up with this family—how could I have them pay for a regularly scheduled session. To say that I was anxious was an understatement. How was I to tell these parents that Susie and I were not a good match; I would be happy to refer the family to a (more competent!) colleague. At some point in my talking with Susie's parents, but before I broke up with the family, they said that Susie liked coming to sessions; she thought they were help-ing. I said that I was surprised; I did not think that anything much was happening. I then said that I was thinking of not working with her anymore, "I just don't have a relationship with Susie, there's no connection." I did not realize until then what had been bothering me so much in my work with Susie. The parents replied that they had heard that before from others who had worked with Susie. I also admitted that it felt as though dad was always mad at me, and that it felt really bad to work with a child whose parent didn't like me! Mom looked at dad, then at me, and said not to worry, many of her friends have felt the same way. Dad smiled an apology, and said it wasn't me, I had done nothing wrong. I began to feel relieved—in fact, I was beginning to like Susie's parents. Mom then spearheaded the conversation and suggested that Susie and I continue working together and focus on a few very specific goals; I agreed. Need-less to say, after several more sessions, Susie and I started developing a relationship. I responded to (and enjoyed!) her cleverness and quirky sense of humor. At one point, Susie reacted to something I had said, using a displeased tone, by saying, "I don't want you to be mad at me." Her concern and comment took me by surprise because I wasn't mad at her. Moreover, at that moment, I realized that we were connected and had formed a relationship; we both mattered to each other.

How do you develop a relationship with someone? Only when someone feels comfort-able and emotionally safe can he or she relax into the ease and comfort zone in which a relationship can take place. Students who come to an ET have frequently experienced repeated failure and its concomitant sadness and anxiety. These students sit in classrooms not feeling quite up to snuff! All too frequently, learning becomes a stressful situation, and trauma results with repeated failure. Consequences of traumatic learning failure in-clude diminished value of the self, externalization of blame for failure to protect the self, and withdrawal from learning activities which may actually result in positive results—all learning situations are viewed as potential arenas for failure (Orenstein & Levin, 2003). To build a relationship with a child who has experienced repeated learning failure, the ET must be knowledgeable about the emotional aspects of learning disabilities, and focus on islands of competence (Brooks, 2006) and the client's resiliency (Spekman, Goldberg, & Herman, 1993). It is crucial for the ET to provide positive learning situations from the first working session.

Charlie came in for his first session with a look of doom and gloom. This immediately made me feel anxious. I was under pressure! I had to turn that gloom and doom into a smile and instill in Charlie a sense of hopefulness and a willingness to move forward. Charlie came to the session needing to write a short paragraph about a story which had been read in class. I asked if he thought he was one of those kids who could come up with great ideas, but then had some challenges in the organization of the ideas. Or, was he great at organizing once he had the ideas. He said that he had the ideas, the organizing was difficult. A big smile came across my face, and I sighed in relief. I told Charlie that organizing was the easy part—thank goodness he was one of those bright, creative kids with lots of ideas! Organizing was so much more fixable than lack of creativity. He looked at me wearily, wanting to believe what I said, but having no experience with trusting me. After a brief time, Charlie had typed out several sentences. I told him just to get his ideas down and not to worry about spelling, grammar, or organization. When he completed his sentences, I copied and pasted them so we could edit together. In fact, Charlie's sentences were quite good. As we edited, he recognized grammatical and syntax errors. As we read, we highlighted the sentences using the same color for sentences related to the same topics. We noticed that we had a red sentence, then a yellow, another yellow, and another red, a blue, and so on. Then through the magic of cut and paste, we put all the sentences of the same color together, used some transitional words when necessary, and voila! A well organized paragraph based on Charlie's ideas. Charlie grinned from ear to ear. For his next appointment, Charlie came in ready to work on a big writing project he had in social studies, "We have to do that color thing," he said. "It made writing so easy!"

If only all clients would respond as well as Charlie to a simple little intervention like color coding sentences. It wasn't the specifics of the intervention, per se, but the fact that Charlie experienced something he could do which was positive. All was not lost. He could exercise his creativity and utilize a strategy that made sense to him. I was seen as someone who could help, who tried to understand his difficulty and move him a bit further along.

I sat at the desk with Max, a bright 10th grader, to begin some of his homework. It was a packet of grammar pages. Max had not only to make the necessary corrections but also rewrite every sentence in his own handwriting! I looked at Max and said with all true empathy, "This is painful." He looked at me and nodded in agreement. Later, as we worked together, I was able to run interference for him with the teacher and ultimately the school district so that he did not have to spend countless hours doing busy work.

During our very first session, Jeffrey talked about what school was like for him. An extremely bright boy, who months later I referred to as "the professor," Jeffrey had his problems. At one point, he revealed that sometimes he missed things the teacher said and wasn't getting the grades teachers expected him to earn. "And then, they say…" and he choked up, I added, "That you're not trying hard enough?" The tears rolled down from his big brown eyes as he nodded.

With both Max and Jeffrey, it was extremely important for me to indicate to each boy that I knew what their emotional experience was like. In those first initial moments I created for them a safe place to feel their pain; I became their ally in helping them positively alter their school experiences. It was as if I helped them experience a sense of relief from some of their misery and previous learning trauma. Metcalf (1994) states that there are two main phenomena that she continually encounters in her remedial work with children: a natural impetus to learn and its counterpart, resistance to change. Furthermore, she posits four main tenets: All people can be affected by favorable influences; one of the important factors in change is a secure base from which to explore and learn which takes time to establish; the nature of interpersonal relationships can be altered through corrective experiences with a new important figure; and change, itself, can seem threatening and can provoke resistance. In discussing the tenets, Metcalf incorporates the concepts of attachment, temperament, knowledge of remedial techniques, creation of a consistent, safe, encouraging, and resourceful base, and resistance as being a normal phenomenon.

Sussman (2005a, 2005b) elaborates on the role that attachment plays in developing an alliance and working relationship in the educational therapy setting. She suggests that the ET has a dual function as a facilitator of school-related learning, and as a provider of an optimal, supportive, safe environment. Moreover, she conjectures that children need to have an attachment relationship that satisfies basic needs for contact and closeness before they can be ready for learning.

Educational therapists need to be flexible in approach. As shifts in affect occur, ETs need to be acutely aware of the nuances of affect responses, feel confident enough to acknowledge the shift, and elicit elaboration from the child about the affect shift. This is not to suggest that ETs become psychotherapists or cross the lines between the two disciplines. However, when the client comes to session with tears after losing a beloved pet, or with angst having just had a fight with mom in the car, or with anxiety about an upcoming test, the educational learning takes a back seat to the emotional needs of the child. The ET plays a critical role in helping with the client's emotional regulation. A few minutes of conversation as feelings get sorted out removes the clutter which stands in the way of moving forward to the academic tasks at hand.

This discussion about relationship between client and therapist cannot be completed without mention, albeit brief, of unconscious processes (Adelizzi, 2006), transference, and countertransference as they impact the therapeutic relationship. "During the establishment, maintenance, and termination of the relationship, unconscious processes are operating which play a role in the destiny of the student's personal and academic growth" (Adelizzi, 1994, p. 3). The unconscious is that part of the mind which is not necessarily in awareness yet impacts our experience and sometimes action. In every encounter, there is the reality of encounter—the overt actions and verbalizations—and the unconscious reality of the encounter—the covert feelings and thoughts. The covert or unspoken feelings about the person are referred to as *transference.*

> One day, Molly came into the session and started taking off her shoes. She stopped herself, and recognizing the unusualness of this action she commented, "I can't believe I was taking off my shoes; it felt like I was home."

I think Molly feeling like she was at home spoke to the ease and comfort she felt with me. These feelings were not overtly expressed but nonetheless impacted the development of our working alliance. Clients will frequently *transfer* feelings of authority onto the ET. This may negatively impact the relationship depending upon the client's experience with authority figures. Not only the client, but also the client's parents can transfer feelings onto the ET. Again, this can positively or negatively impact the relationship depending upon one's personal history. Lawrence-Lightfoot (2003) exquisitely describes transference phenomena between teacher and parents, and parents and their children.

Countertransference refers to the feelings the therapist has about the client, or parent, or classroom teacher, or school administrator, or allied professional: whatever the ET feels during a session or encounters with a client or someone in the client's world. When I am in session and experience a feeling that seems to come from outside myself, I engage in a bit of inner self-talk. I try to identify or name the feeling and then wonder what is going on for my client. Perhaps they are lost or bored, feel overwhelmed, have mentally left the session for some reason—something seems to be communicated. I will stop whatever activity and engage in a brief conversation about what I sense. The client will usually respond to my gentle probe and explore their thinking/feeling with me. The time-out to explore the unspoken typically removes obstacles to forward movement with the task at hand. Sometimes countertransference is negatively experienced.

> I dreaded my sessions with Mitchell. Sessions with Mitch seemed endless in anticipation and in reality. There was not positive reinforcement from him for anything I tried. In fact, I just felt like a failure and thought I knew nothing about being an ET; I wondered why I was in the profession!

My feelings were so negative that I consulted a colleague. During our consultations, I was able to understand the interplay between my countertransference feelings and Mitch's *transference* feelings. In the end, my work with Mitch taught me quite a bit about myself and the therapeutic part of the educational therapy process. Gordon (2001) suggests a number of questions an ET can ask herself to determine the presence and impact of countertransference with any given client.

A word must be said about the working relationship between the therapist and the child's parents. As previously stated, parents want to feel heard and understood regarding the trials and tribulations of their experiences with the child and his or her classroom and school. You are not only the child's ally but also the parents' in attempting to create a more positive learning environment for the child. Parents are usually very appreciative and acknowledge the central role played by the ET, and therapists do need to spend time developing a positive relationship with the parents. In addition to more frequent contact via phone and e-mail in the early stages of working with a child, I usually meet with the parents after 6 weeks to 2 months, to touch base and talk about how things are proceeding. This meeting also permits me to extend myself as a resource to the family. I will frequently assist parents in setting up boundaries at home regarding family dynamics around homework completion, cell phone and computer use, television viewing, and general routines. Periodic meetings with parents support the collaborative relationship.

The practical business concerns during this stage relate to having ready and obtaining necessary remedial resources (e.g., games, programs, workbooks, story books, software, manipulatives, and the like). Additionally, session notes should be recorded as well as income documented. Storage of materials and access to them should be considered during this stage.

STAGE IV: CASE MANAGEMENT (RUN OF THE SHOW)

Rehearsals are over. The scenes have been blocked. The actors have a good understanding of their roles and the show proceeds with a life of its own. So too, this stage in the educational therapy proceeds comfortably for the most part. Therapist and client join in humor, gentle teasing, and easy banter which indicate their knowledge of each other, the limits to push against, and the coaxing necessary for forward movement. The educational therapy as case manager ensures that things run smoothly. Aspects of this stage begin earlier. When an ET begins to work with a child, the therapist usually will contact the classroom teacher and others working with the child. During stage IV, the team is solidified and collaborates in the agreed upon method of meeting the child's needs. Foster (1995) elaborates on the value of professional collaboration as an integral part of the ET's work and the means by which the treatment of a learning challenged child is most fully realized. She suggests ways in which collaboration can be effectively achieved.

Kaganoff (2001) describes the role of case management with words such as *liaison* (for family and school), *mediator* (of differences), *educator* (in explaining the child's learning style, temperament, strengths, and challenges), *evaluator* and *advisor* (regarding actions taken by allied professionals), *diplomat* (in securing what's best for the child), and *negotiator* (for programmatic modifications). Ungerleider (1991. p. 17) uses the term *Ombudsman* when describing the ET as case manager.

After the first few sessions of working with a child, I write a letter of introduction to the teachers and other school administrators that the parent has identified. The letter is given to the teacher and administrator(s) by the parents, or I e-mail it, with a copy to the parent. The letter alerts the teacher to the fact that I am working with a particular child and outlines the general academic areas the work will be addressing. The letter suggests that I work collaboratively with the teacher and that information from the teacher is very much appreciated. Additionally, I ask to be alerted to upcoming assignments, quizzes and tests, future reading materials, and long term projects so that I may assist the child as needed. Having knowledge about the classroom requirements gives me a better understanding of what tasks are demanded and permits me to have information when the child "forgets" to bring something to a session or "fails to mention" something about an upcoming academic task. I also inform the teacher that I am there to work on learning tasks identified by the teacher, and hope that she or he will regard me as a useful resource. In some cases, classroom teachers do not respond. However, most teachers are happy to collaborate and maintain frequent e-mail contact.

Although an "expert" in helping children with learning challenges, the ET must take into account the context of the classroom, the training and attitude of the classroom teacher, and the knowledge base of the school administration when proposing curriculum and behavioral accommodations (Brooks, 2004). She must take care not to come across as the "expert" who knows the best way to help the challenged learner become successful! In all collaboration, the ET must maintain an attitude of respect for the professional knowledge of the classroom teacher, administrator, and allied professional. The ET has a unique perspective in working one-on-one with a child. She has access to the child's world through his or her eyes. If the ET exhibits some humility, openness to hearing other perspectives, and appreciation of the expertise of other professionals it goes a long way in facilitating collaboration.

After just a few sessions with Max and his grammar packet, I spoke with Max's special education teacher. She expressed concern about my wanting to alter the work she had given Max; she did not know me, and was under the mandate of the public school. I acknowledged the position she was in. I empathized with the demands placed on her to provide a home school curriculum for Max while being responsible for the class of students she met with on a daily basis. She and I eventually developed a system whereby I provided extended instruction in grammar and punctuation by having Max write original stories (rather than rewrite sentences with corrected grammar). She and I became co-teachers in Max's education. Eventually, the school district actually "hired" me as an outside consultant (since I had my teaching credential) to teach Max a literature course over the summer; this arrangement was quite unusual for the district. However, I attended several IEP meetings for Max with school and district personnel, in addition to having a relationship with Max's teacher and school counselor. At all encounters, I was part of the team, and all of us demonstrated mutual respect for each other, collaborating on the recommendations for Max rather than seeking to control the situation as individuals: we were a team working for Max's benefit.

I cannot emphasize enough the need for political savvy during the case management stage. Roth (2005) cautions the private practitioner as he discusses the public school ambivalence about the role of the private practitioner in the IEP process. I think his cautions extend far beyond the IEP process into the entire collaboration process. Roth suggests three areas in which obstacles to successful public school and private practitioner collaboration can arise. The first relates to a lack of shared understanding concerning the legal responsibilities of school districts. This results from the ambiguity of the legal language used regarding setting, "appropriate," "least restrictive," and the definition of "special education" itself. Second, there is inadequate understanding and implementation of the law, which can result in parental frustration and alienation from the school district. Finally, school professionals are ambivalent concerning collaboration with private practitioners due to insensitivity to the teacher and public school. Roth lists careless scheduling requests, inaccurate communication, shotgun approaches to recommendations, and inappropriate referral and service recommendations as areas in which collaborative efforts can be negatively impacted. It behooves the ET to be up-to-date in knowing the law and the public school obligations and constraints regarding program design and implementation. An invaluable resource for keeping up-to-date with the laws and regulations regarding eligibility and treatment for children with learning disabilities is the LD Web site (http://ldonline.org/). The business practices at this stage relate to ethical issues regarding information sharing and the role of the ET as a referral resource. The ET must have a supply of authorizations to release and obtain information from other professionals with whom the client is working. Additionally, ETs should develop a form letter of introduction, which is adapted to specific clients, to disseminate as the need arises, and ETs should develop a resource file for parents. The file should include contact information for a variety of allied professionals across a number of disciplines (e.g., psychotherapists, neurophysiologists, developmental optometrists, speech therapists, content tutors, and homework helpers). Additionally, a parent education resource file should be maintained with relevant professional information such as suggested books and copies of articles to distribute as the need arises.

STAGE V: TERMINATION (THE SHOW CLOSES)

The educational therapy relationship must come to an end, just as the show must run its course and close. The ET's goal is an eventual termination, when the clients assume responsibility for their own learning, identify with their unique learning style, and are proud of their personal participation in making this termination possible (Metcalf, 2005, p. 8).

It is interesting to think about the process of termination. Two people join in an intense relationship, journey together on a course with ups and downs, both in need of the other (yes, the ET also has needs to save, instruct, make a difference). When the relationship is initially entered into it is known that it will eventually end. The ET must take care that the end of the relationship is handled with as much care and professionalism as characterizes the entire relationship. No doubt, there are ETs who experience great difficulty in terminating a relationship with a client. Not only is there an emotional loss, but also a financial one as well. Therapists should pay attention to whose needs are being served by prolonging a relationship with a client. At such times, consultation with a trusted colleague should be considered.

From the beginning, the ET, parent, and client must address the time limitations of the relationship. Frequently, parents will ask how long the process will take as if the process is a canned package with an expiration date! Likewise, suggesting a time frame for the work may encourage a reluctant learner's participation in the process—"Let's work together for two months and see how it goes." Frequent discussion about goal setting and goal achievement should occur throughout the process.

In the psychotherapy field, stirrings about termination typically come from the client. There is less to say during a session; life is manageable, even good! Similarly, if the ET and client are paying attention to the signs and listen, they can sense when independence is near. Those of us in the helping professions need people to help! There are always areas in which we perceive the need for our assistance. However, the parent grooms the child to leave home and make a life for himself; the ET must develop in the child a sense of autonomy and mastery. The last session should be calendared and anticipated. Feelings of separation for both therapist and client should be acknowledged and expressed. Acknowledgment and great regard for the work that has been done must be part of the last session; Metcalf (2005) talks about "tokens of termination." For example, ETs write a summary or letter to the child about the child's accomplishments during their work together. Others give the child a keepsake or have a special treat. Regardless of the nature of the terminating session, therapist and client need to share words of mutual admiration and respect.

POSSIBLY A STAGE VI: CLIENT RETURNS (SHOW REVIVAL)

Occasionally a client will contact you for issues that have come up since last you worked together. When clients move up in grades or enter college, there are novel demands imposed on them which may be experienced as challenging enough to once again seek your assistance. This is frequently a delightful experience! It gives you a chance to see how your client has grown and developed, blossomed into a teenager or young adult. The two of you resume your working alliance and focus on the current challenges. Your time together at this stage is typically short lived; there is only need for a refresher course or the application of skills to new materials.

PROLOGUE

One enters the theater, locates the assigned seat, and gives oneself over to the experience provided by the actors, and, one hopes, emerges at the end of the performance, impacted or transformed in some way. The educational therapy process is a developmental progression. People meet, engage in dynamic, insightful, knowledgeable, and often trial-and-error activity pursuits as they journey together in a transformative endeavor. The field of educational therapy presents a unique opportunity for combining the disciplines of both education and psychology. The educational therapy relationship evolves over time into a dynamic duo.

With psychological understanding and sensitivities to the developing child on the part of the ET, along with her knowledge and expertise of remedial interventions, the process of educational therapy is transformative, the impact is lifelong. Enjoy the journey!

P.S. Just as one enjoys watching a movie or attending a play for a second time, so too the educational therapy process may be revisited. Be prepared for a client to unexpectedly call again in the future—always welcome, always embraced, the relationship revived.

REFERENCES

Adelizzi, J. U. (1994). The unconscious process in the teacher-student relationship within the models of education and therapy. *The Educational Therapist, 15,* 3–8.

Adelizzi, J. U. (2006). Revisiting the unconscious process. *The Educational Therapist, 27,* 6–10.

Brooks, R. B. (2004). To touch the hearts and minds of students with learning disabilities: The power of mindsets and expectations. *Learning Disabilities: A Contemporary Journal, 2,* 9–18.

Brooks, R. B. (2006).The search for islands of competence: A metaphor of hope and strength. *The Educational Therapist, 27,* 1–3.

Child Development Institute. (1998a). Temperament and your child's personality. *LD OnLine.* Retrieved from http:/www.childdevelopmentinfo.com

Child Development Institute. (1998b). The 9 temperament traits. *LD OnLine.* Retrieved from http:/www.child-developmentinfo.com

Chidekel, D. (2003). The place of boundaries. *The Educational Therapist, 24,* 5–11.

Dawson, P., & Guare, R. (2004). *Executive skills in children and adolescents: A practical guide to assessment and intervention.* New York: Guilford Press.

deHirsch, K. (1997). Interaction between educational therapist and child. *Bulletin of the Orton Society, 23,* 88–101.

Edgette, J. S. (2002). *Candor, connection, and enterprise in adolescent therapy.* New York: Norton.

Foster, J. A. (1995). Professional collaboration. *The Educational Therapist, 16,* 19–21.

Gordon, A. (2001). Some thoughts on the role of countertransference in educational therapy. *The Educational Therapist, 22,* 4–8.

Gordon, R., & Gordon, M. (2006). The turned off child. *The Educational Therapist, 27,* 12–14.

Gorman, J. C. (1999). Understanding children's hearts and minds: Emotional functioning and learning disabilities. *LD OnLine.* Retrieved from http://www.ldonline.org

Hallowell, N. (2007a, October). *The parent's soliloquy.* Talk presented at the Association of Educational Therapists Conference, San Francisco.

Hallowell, N. (2007b, October). *A young man's soliloquy.* Talk presented at the Association of Educational Therapists Conference, San Francisco.

Heacox, D. (1991). *Up from underachievement.* Minneapolis, MN: Free Spirit Press.

Kaganoff, A. (2001). Educational therapy defined. *The Educational Therapist, 22,* 17–20.

Kaganoff, A. (2002). Study skills and homework survey: A diagnostic tool for assessing study strategies. *The Educational Therapist, 24,* 15–17.

Kaganoff, A. (2003). Have you ever tried? Kaganoff interest inventory. *The Educational Therapist, 23,* 18–20.

Keogh, B. (2005). A different perspective on differences. *The Educational Therapist, 26*(2), 16–19.

Lawrence-Lightfoot, S. (2003). *The essential conversation: What parents and teachers can learn from each other.* New York: Ballantine Books.

Levine, M. (2001). Approaches to management. In *Developmental variations and learning disorders* (pp. 566–603). Toronto, Canada: Educators Publishing Service.

Levine, M. (2003). Output's inputs. In *The myth of laziness* (pp. 145–168). New York: Simon & Schuster.

Metcalf, B. (1994). Psychoeducational perspectives: Effecting change. *The Educational Therapist, 15,* 15–17.

Metcalf, B. (2005). Thoughts about the termination phase of educational therapy. *The Educational Therapist, 26,* 8–10.

Muenke, M. (n.d.). The ADHD Genetic Research Study at the National Institutes of Health and the National Human Genome Research Institute. The National Institutes of Health. Retrieved from http://www.genome.gov

Orenstein, M., & Levin, F. (2003). Thoughts on traumatic learning failure. *The Educational Therapist, 24,* 11–14.

Roth, D. (2005). Public school ambivalence about the role of the private practitioner in the IEP process: Advice to educational therapists from a director of special education. *The Educational Therapist, 26,* 4–6.

Spekman, N. J., Goldberg, R. J., & Herman, K. L. (1993). An exploration of risk and resilience in the lives of individuals with learning disabilities. *Learning Disabilities Research & Practice, 8,* 11–18.

Sussman, R. P. (2005a). Creating a therapeutic relationship with the child in educational therapy, part I. *The Educational Therapist, 26,* 6–10.

Sussman, R. P. (2005b). Creating a therapeutic relationship with the child in educational therapy, The attachment relationship. *The Educational Therapist, 26,* 4–8.

Ungerleider, D. (1991). An educational therapist is... *Psychoeducational Perspectives.* Los Angeles: Association of Educational Therapists.

Ungerleider, D. (1997). Context: The missing piece in our assessment. *The Educational Therapist, 18,* 8–12.

Ungerleider, D. (2005). A different perspective on differences. *The Educational Therapist, 26,* 10–16.

3

EDUCATIONAL THERAPY'S ANCESTRY AND MIGRATION

GAIL WERBACH, BARBARA KORNBLAU, AND CAROLE SLUCKI

HISTORY

The educational therapist of the 21st century has a rich endowment of techniques based on the practice, writings, and scientifically sound methods of professionals who have worked with children and adults with learning problems for the last hundred years. Practitioners and therapists in the fields of special and remedial education, psychiatry, psychology, and sociology have contributed their narratives to develop the guidelines of this burgeoning profession in the United States and Europe. While these professionals "all expressed consensus that educational therapy referred to a melding of the clinical and psychotherapeutic with the pedagogical and educational ... their operational definitions of professional practice and the titles they gave themselves were as varied as their geographic locations" (Ungerleider, 1986, p. 3).

The term *educational therapist* has replaced the terms *therapeutic tutor, psychopedagogist, special teacher, reinforcement therapist, clinical teacher, remedial therapist, language therapist, multidisciplinary teacher*, and *learning therapist* as the person who remediates learning problems. Several detailed accounts of this history have previously appeared in print in articles and publications such as *The Educational Therapist* (1985, 1986), *Journal of Learning Disabilities* (1984), and *Psychoeducational Perspectives* (1991). The authors acknowledge books and articles by Field (1993), Hellmuth (1966, 1969), Johnston (1984), Ungerleider (1985, 1986) and Werbach (1998) for their work which has contributed greatly to this publication.

Beginning in the 1940s, parallel development of the field took place in Europe and the United States. The earliest documentation of these roots followed the scientific prominence gained with the publication of Itard's clinical observations done in the 1800s based on *The Wild Boy of Aveyron* (Itard, 1932). When Itard's first scientific account of a child with serious motivational, neurological, and emotional handicaps was presented to clinicians it gave impetus to the treatment of exceptional children. In the 1800s, Edward Seguin organized the first educational system for mentally retarded children. Itard, Seguin, and Humphrey provided many ideas for Maria Montessori who developed the first formal educational program to facilitate the cognitive and emotional tendencies of culturally deprived children. Montessori encouraged the use of free movement to develop mastery over the physical environment thereby developing control over inner mental functions (Montessori, 1964/1912).

In the 1920s, in Vienna, the field of child psychology was influenced by the Freudian school comprised of Anna Freud, Alfred Adler, and others who contributed to the roots of therapeutic education. "Leaders in the field of child psychology were concerned with the establishment of a psychological milieu in schools for normal and emotionally disturbed children where an appropriate balance between educational goals and therapeutic intervention could be used to maximize the individual's emotional and intellectual potential" (Johnston, 1984, pp. 200–204). Another follower of the Freudian school, August Aichorn, created a combined educational and therapeutic environment developed mainly for delinquents, which he called *heilpedagogie*, meaning social therapy, or the helping teacher. Recent work in Belgium uses the terminology of *heilpedagogie* as well.

Aichorn's book, *Wayward Youth* (1935/1925), dealt with the antisocial nature of troubled adolescents. He believed that disturbances in early child–parent relationships and subsequent arrested development in youth were precursors to antisocial behavior. Katrina DeHirsch, another pioneer in the field, was influenced by Aichorn's work with troubled adolescents. She left her native Germany in the 1940s to study speech therapy and Gestalt psychology in England. She migrated to New York and in her early work in a language disorders clinic was introduced to the theories of Samuel T. Orton. She later became one of the founders of the Orton Society (Jansky, 1984). DeHirsch became convinced that the child's milieu and psychological makeup played a role in the eventual resolution of problems. In 1977, DeHirsch wrote her seminal article on the "treatment alliance" between the educational therapist and child, in which she defined the professional role and desirable personal traits of an educational therapist (DeHirsch, 1977). According to Ungerleider, of note is DeHirsch's differentiation between the roles of the educational therapist involved with "the pathology of learning" whose goals were educational and "concerned with the psychic organization that deals with reality" and the psychotherapist, whose commitment was to the resolution of "unconscious conflict and inner fears that interfere with functioning" (cited in Ungerleider, 1986, p. 4). Her definition stressed the difference between the educational therapist and the psychotherapist. DeHirsch warned, "The educational therapist who sees himself as a psychotherapist is bound to fail in both roles" (cited in Ungerleider, 1986, p. 4). Ungerleider notes that DeHirsch's warning may have retrospectively explained the slow acceptance of the notion of "educational therapy" in the 1940s.

While the term *therapy* itself was not in general use until post-World War II, an attitude prevailed that did not recognize the teacher as any kind of therapist. However, therapeutic teaching was becoming more understood by some therapists because of the nature of the work being accomplished in schools. Anna Freud directed a Montessori school in the 1920s and 1930s. Consultants to the school included prominent psychoanalysts such as Bettelheim, Blos, Erikson, and Redl, just to name a few. In the United States, educators such as Margaret Rawson and Ray Barsch began to acknowledge therapeutic teaching of the whole child. Dorothy Ungerleider published *The History of Educational Therapy Reconsidered* in the 1990s (Ungerleider, 1995). There are many differing interpretations of educational therapy by individual proponents in different geographic locations of the United States and Europe. The order of presentation is roughly chronological, generally by decade rather than by year, moving among the descriptors of "therapeutic education" to "educational therapy" as practitioners began to diverge in their philosophical allegiances from the early psychoanalytic influences to new theoretical constructs arising from research in learning disabilities and neurologically based specialties. There was little standardization in practice or theoretical framework, even in the same general geographic locales, due to the lack of uniform training standards. The forbearers were questioners and individualists, applying foundations from past models and then revising or rejecting content, theory, and methodology as they observed what seemed to work for their clients.

Carl Fenichel began to question the appropriateness of earlier psychoanalytic models for the highly disturbed youngsters with whom he worked (Hellmuth, 1966). In 1953, as Director of the League School for Seriously Disturbed Children in Brooklyn, New York Fenichel described the budding realization by therapeutic educators that the children they were seeing didn't fit into neat clinical packages, that each needed an ongoing psychoeducational assessment of his or her unique patterns of behavior and functioning. He began, along with others, to believe that there were many reasons for the disorganization, withdrawal, disorientation, and confusion of clients, and heretically suggested that the overwhelming problems may in fact be "more closely related to serious learning disorders and language handicaps than to repression of traumatic childhood memories or unresolved intrapsychic conflicts" (Fenichel, 1966, p. 213), and that disturbed behavior may not be the cause but rather the result of these disorders. He even suggested that the disturbed behavior may be caused by some constitutional, neurological, or biochemical disorders.

Marianne Frostig was primarily known for research, test development, and training in visual perception (Hellmuth, 1969). After working with Belle Dubnoff in the 1940s and 1950s, she established The Marianne Frostig Center in the Los Angeles area (1951), which provided broader training in all aspects of educational therapy (Frostig & Maslow, 1973). Through writing and training, Frostig urged educational therapists to disregard labels and provide specific training programs for amelioration in four broad areas: (1) specific developmental lags; (2) academic progress through teaching of subject matter; (3) emotional and social development through the therapeutic relationship; and (4) global, pervasive disturbances, such as disorganization, impulsivity, attention, hyperactivity, and sequential difficulties. Taken from psychoanalytic terminology, the fourth area is described as defects in ego development affecting all ego functions—motility, perception, language, thought, social behavior, and emotional reaction. Her prescriptive approach to clients, refined in the 1960s, was similar to that of Ruth Mallison.

Belle Dubnoff used an integrated approach based on the work of Erikson, Hebb, Kephart, J. McV. Hunt, Piaget, Strauss, and Lehtinen in addressing the child's needs for competence on all levels of functioning from sensorimotor to cognitive, social, and emotional (Hellmuth, 1966). There was an underlying concern in regard to the ego and its role in the socialization of the individual. Dubnoff and Frostig collaborated in the late 1940s and 1950s, and each eventually created her own center. Established in 1948 as a private school for elementary aged children with special and learning and developmental needs, the Dubnoff Center pioneered the development of educational programs and curricula which enabled the child with atypical development to learn and develop as normally as possible within a personalized, structured, and therapeutic learning environment. Barbara Biber formulated the developmental-interaction theory at Bank Street College in the 1950s, emphasizing the interaction of the cognitive, affective, and social systems (Sapir, 1985).

Ruth Mallison wrote *Education as Therapy* (Mallison, 1968), which was based on a series of seminars on educational therapy for neurologically impaired children. She distinguished educational therapy from therapeutic education but acknowledged that in either case, the skill and sensitivity of the teacher are of utmost importance. Mallison included parents in joint sessions with or without the child when indicated, and advocated the importance of listening to both their viewpoints and cares while remaining neutral, serving as a "… bridge over which they can talk to each other and begin to hear each other" (Mallison, 1968 p. 154). Mallison defined educational therapy as "… a prescriptive approach to instruction wherein highly specialized skills are utilized to reduce or modify various learning disabilities" (Hensley, 1966, p. 130). She said educational therapy consists of assessment of the total child and formulation of a dynamic program that "will include areas of functioning, behavior, and social behavior, as well as academic work." She added, "there is no rote approach, no standardized system…. Every child seems again new at every session" (Mallison, 1968, p. 161). She warned that "The educational therapist cannot really divide teaching and therapy when dealing with a neurologically impaired child. Therefore, we must look at the child in a practical way which will give us a working idea of what the child can and cannot do, what kind of person he is, what has happened to him along the way, and where we are going to start work with him" (Mallison, 1968, p. 13).

Bessie Sperry, who worked at the Judge Baker Guidance Center in Boston in the 1950s and the 1960s, defined "…therapeutic tutoring" as "a kind of educational practice in which the knowledge available about the child's educational and emotional problems can be used in the interaction between the tutor and the child for the alleviation of the psychogenic learning problem" (quoted in Hellmuth, 1969). The therapeutic tutor adapts his knowledge of the child's dynamics to manipulate certain aspects of the relationship including the transference. She also uses her knowledge of the child's level of cognitive, emotional, and educational development to shape his style of communication… "utilizes two important aspects of the traditional psychotherapeutic process: 1.) the personal relationship with its transference quality, and 2.) the educative aspects in their broader meanings" (Sperry & Templeton, 1969, p. 176). Sperry advocated combined psychotherapeutic and "theraeducational" interventions but suggested there were times when learning problems could be reasonably well handled by therapeutic tutoring alone, such as when psychotherapy has already been employed to resolve major psychological issues, or when either parent or child is too resistant to traditional psychotherapy to achieve an effective alliance.

Harold Esterson, Mattie Cook, Muriel Mendlowitz, and Charles Solomon established an experimental program with educationally retarded and emotionally disturbed children from troubled homes in a New York housing project through Manhattanville Community Centers in the 1960s (Hellmuth, 1969). These educators were interested in training "therapeutic teachers" as part of a multidisciplinary team to do management, behavior modification, education, and the understanding of behavior and motivation. They noted that, in their attempts to train teachers, "only a very few seemed willing and able to take on the responsibility of teaching and treating" (Esterson, Cook, Mendlowitz, & Solomon, 1969, p. 317).

W. W. Lewis designed Project Re-Ed, a research project in Nashville, Tennessee. He used mental health professionals to train experienced elementary school teachers who exhibited natural skills in relating to troubled children to be "teacher-counselors" (Hellmuth, 1966). Lewis challenged the central assumption of the medical model that "emotional disturbance reflects an underlying pathology within a child," operating instead on the premise that emotional disturbance is "a disruption between a child and his primary socializing systems (family, school, peer groups, etc.) rather than a pathological process within the child himself" (Lewis, 1966, p. 307). He theorized that educational techniques, broadly construed in a carefully constructed educational milieu, might be preferred over more time-consuming psychotherapeutic interventions, adding psychotherapy only for those cases that did not respond.

Roslyn Cohen defined therapeutic education as "… the incorporation of clinical understanding of emotional disorders of childhood into educational practice," combining the knowledge of "theoretical concepts and therapeutic techniques from the professions of psychiatry, social work, psychology, and teaching" (Cohen, 1966, p. 139). She was influenced by the writings of Bettelheim, Ekstein, Ginott, Leton, Motto, and Redl. Cohen challenged the need to perpetuate the "teacher or therapist" debate, urging collaboration of all related disciplines to do whatever is necessary by whoever is capable of effecting change in behavior and adaptation of emotionally disturbed children (Hellmuth, 1966).

Mary Kunst worked with Kay Field using "educational therapy" to describe Kunst's work as tutor/psychologist and as a form of psychotherapy combining educational, psychological, and psychiatric skills at Michael Reese Hospital in Chicago. Kunst focused on fostering communication through play and conversation (Field, 1993), and defined educational therapy as an integration of the tutoring and healing processes, recognizing teachers as "psychological tacticians of the learning process." In 1965 in Chicago, she founded the Teacher Education Program (TEP) with Field under the auspices of the Institute for Psychoanalysis.

George Devereaux and Edward French wrote about therapeutic education (Devereaux, 1965), defining theory and practice in a residential treatment center for emotionally disturbed adolescents (Hellmuth, 1966). "Education becomes part of a total therapy program when, in addition to imparting knowledge, skill acquisition is consciously utilized for ego-building purposes" (French, 1966, p. 430). They utilized reality situations as complementary on the conscious level to the interpretation of emotional reactions at the unconscious level in psychotherapy. Devereaux and French appreciated the special educator's contribution to the total therapy program through his or her unique knowledge of educational principles and understanding of psychodynamic principles. The interventions employed included: individualized and flexible programming and scheduling, controlled competition, athletics, and rehabilitative student–staff relationships. The aforementioned attributes are akin to the principles of practice and approach developed by August Aichorn in his guidance clinics in Austria during the early 1900s, efforts which were later joined by Anna Freud.

Peter Knoblock (1969) trained special education teachers at Syracuse University in the 1960s. He noted a major distinguishing characteristic of psychoeducationally oriented teachers: "The belief that they are in a position to effect changes in the attitudes and behavior of children via (the teacher-child) relationship" (Knoblock, p. 396). Knoblock advocated the importance of the therapeutic teacher/child relationship, the interdisciplinary team, and diagnosis through observation (Hellmuth, 1969). Knoblock suggested the personal characteristics (accurate empathy, nonpossessive warmth, and authenticity) necessary for the therapeutic relationship and the creation of a total psychoeducational environment. He advocated a focus directly on behavior, a coordination of clinical and educational data, facilitation of successful group experience, and collaborative interdisciplinary team functioning.

Betty Osman authored several books including *Learning Disabilities: A Family Affair* (1980) and *No One to Play With: The Social Side of Learning Disabilities* (1982), which spoke to the practice of educational therapy. At the same time in New York, the active Orton Society chapter provided professional training to practitioners working with individuals with learning disabilities. In 1950 Loretta Bender authored the paper, "Research Studies from Bellevue Hospital on Specific Reading Disabilities," which was presented at the First Annual Program Meeting of the Orton Society in New York City. This seminal paper described the work of early researchers in the field of learning disabilities and mentioned Silver's work in neurological and perceptual deviations in children with reading disabilities.

Selma Sapir described her "clinical diagnostic teaching model" based on the developmental-interaction approach of Biber, in her book, *The Clinical Teaching Model* (1985). The model encourages the teacher to integrate knowledge of social, temperamental, emotional, and cognitive development with treatment based on significant knowledge and observations of the individual and Sapir noted that "The therapist, teacher, and diagnostician become one" (p. 24). She defined the model as a dynamic one because assessment is a continuous, holistic process, and interventions must respond according to the constant growth and change in the child. Treatment strategies integrate "... cognitive and academic issues, even while they attend to the child's social and emotional needs" (p. xiii).

Dorothy Ungerleider (1985, 1986, 1991, 1995) was the founding President of the Association of Educational Therapists (AET) in 1979. This was the first professional association of its kind in the United States, and its purpose was to define "educational therapy" as a distinct profession. She contributed to the development of the principles, ethics, and standards of practice, which related to the multifaceted role of the practitioner. This, in turn, led to the development of interdisciplinary training requirements for educational therapists.

Through her writings Ungerleider envisioned a more eclectic practice than had been previously articulated by her predecessors, suggesting that today's educational therapist had to be a generalist in a world of increasing specialization, integrating multiple roles as an evaluator, remedial teacher, case manager, communicator, and interpreter among and between those involved with the child (school, family, and other helping professionals). She professed that the therapeutic relationship between educational therapist and client, distinguished educational therapy from remedial tutoring, and needed to remain the foundation upon which all else was built in order to address (in conjunction with learning/processing remediation), the social/emotional aspects affecting the learning process. In addition, a broad range of factors within the multicontexts of the client's life had to be considered and addressed in order to determine the goals and direction of the intervention, so that appropriate alterations and accommodations could be made. Thus, a holistic, interactive, and collaborative role emerged as one that acknowledged the social and emotional aspects of educational therapy.

EARLY PROGRAMS/CENTERS

California

The Raskob Learning Institute (RLI) in Oakland, California, was founded in 1953 by Sister Eileen Cronin as a clinic that provided one-to-one remedial education to students with learning disabilities, as well as training for teachers in the center's innovative approaches. Now located at Holy Names University, Oakland, RLI is one of the oldest programs in the United States for individuals with learning disabilities, and its educational therapy services provide individualized diagnostic-prescriptive teaching. Students receive remediation in a variety of literacy disciplines in conjunction with study and organization skills. Other pioneering centers included A Learning Place, led by Jim Harris and Gerald Block in the mid-1960s, which was joined by Eva Newbrun in 1975, and in current collaboration with the Ann Martin Center, Reach for Learning in the East Bay directed by Corrine Gustafson, and The Bay Center, founded by Vivian Hershen.

The following educators in the Los Angeles area had a significant influence during the initial stages of private practice in the field. Marianne Frostig was among the therapists who studied with August Aichorn, and brought his theories to the United States: "Frostig praised Aichorn's remarkable capacity to gain trust from his students and to seek causes of behavior" (Ungerleider, 1986, p. 4). When Frostig came to America in 1939, she used the term educational therapy to explain the combined educational and therapeutic environment she had utilized with Aichorn in Vienna. She was a pioneer in the study, diagnosis, and treatment of children with learning disabilities, and in 1951 she founded The Frostig Center, which remains a nonprofit organization dedicated to the mission of: conducting research regarding the causes and effects of learning disabilities; providing parent, tutor, and educator training and consultation in how to work with children who struggle to learn; and, offering direct instructional services to children with learning disabilities. Frostig's teaching and mentoring of new educational therapists (1950s through 1970s) established Los Angeles as one of the pioneer centers of educational therapy.

In the 1940s Belle Dubnoff established one of the first preschool early intervention programs for high risk children from birth to 5 years of age. In 1948 she founded a private school for children with special learning and developmental needs called the Dubnoff Center in North Hollywood, California. The school grew into the current concept as a comprehensive community service setting, integrating special education, clinical treatment, residential care, vocational training, and related support services.

Barbara Cull is an educator who became frustrated with the inability of the public school system in the 1970s to adequately assist special needs children. By 1980 she started the Educational Resource and Services Center (ERAS; currently known as the Kayne-ERAS Center). The center emphasizes a multidisciplinary educational model, stressing innovative educational strategies to meet the unique needs of each child and family, providing useful training for educational therapists who work at the center. In the 1990s Sandra Mosk, an educational therapist supervisor at the ERAS Center, and Maxine Ficksman, the Coordinator of the Educational Therapy Certificate Program at the University of California at Los Angeles Extension (UCLAX), developed a three-tiered educational therapy training and supervision program in order to provide internship opportunities for students. This training was useful as well for aspiring educational therapists from other professions.

In 1967 Bill Coggins became the director of a center in the Los Angeles area, the Kaiser Permanente Watts Counseling and Learning Center, which provided counseling and educational services to Kaiser Permanente members and nonmembers. Coggins served as executive director of the center for 32 years. Jean E. Virtue currently serves as the Manager of Educational Therapy and Educational Outreach Programs at the center, and provides support, collaboration, and leadership to the eight staff members in their implementation of over 15 different programs conducted either at the center or within the underserved community of Watts. They are one of the facilities in the United States that offers free educational therapy, advocacy training, and support to parents, and individual educational assessments.

Janet Switzer was an early pioneer in the training of educational therapists at the Switzer Center in Southern California which opened in 1966. At the time, the only students with learning problems who were being served in public schools were preschoolers. She stressed the need for individualized work with students, parent education, and a focus on cognitive development. Switzer's center became a training center in the 1970s for educational therapists. From Frostig to Switzer, the programs that were developed, the teaching methods that were implemented, and the encouragement of these pioneers helped to provide the framework that led to the establishment of the Association of Educational Therapists in 1979.

New York

In the New York area in the 1960s many educational therapists began their training at Teachers College, Columbia-Presbyterian Medical Center University which awarded a master's degree in special education in minimal brain dysfunction. Carla Horowitz, Francis Connor, Elizabeth Freidus, Judy Reibel, and Margaret Shepherd were among those mentors who focused on considering the whole child, encouraging the experts to collaboratively formulate a plan of treatment for their clients with learning disorders. Katrina DeHirsch and Jeannette Jansky evaluated children with learning disorders in the early1960s and taught courses at Columbia-Presbyterian for people who were already working as educational therapists. In 1965 Elizabeth Freidus, a visionary educator, collaborated with a parent, Claire Flom, in establishing the Gateway School to provide assistance to students with learning disabilities. At the time, educational therapists were also working at the Stephen Gaynor School which was developed in 1964 in company with the Brearley and Midtown School of Ethical Culture which provided services for special education students at that time.

Anna Gillingham, a consultant at the Ethical Culture School, was an educator and psychologist who worked with Samuel T. Orton. She trained teachers and published reading instruction materials which contributed to the production of the Orton–Gillingham approach. In collaboration with Bessie Stillman Gillingham she wrote what has become the Orton–Gillingham manual: *Remedial Training for Children with Specific Disability in Reading, Spelling and Penmanship*, first published in 1935–1936, and updated and republished regularly.

Massachusetts

Charles Drake founded the country's largest educational program for students with dyslexia on the East Coast. Drake himself came to learn that his own dyslexia did not relate to, or impact intelligence. After earning a doctorate in education from Harvard University, in 1971 he established the first Landmark School at Prides Crossing, Massachusetts. The curriculum emphasized bolstering the confidence of students in classes with small student–teacher ratios in conjunction with intensive one-to-one teaching provided by learning disability specialists, many of whom were doing the work of educational therapists. In 1983 the program expanded to offer a one-year college preparatory program, and then in 1984 evolved into Landmark College, located in Putney, Vermont. In the 1980s Landmark School's second campus was established in Los Angeles, California, supported by the efforts of parents in the local area whose children were boarding at the Massachusetts school, known then as Landmark West, and today as Westmark. The school's teaching and learning environment provided training opportunities for many educational therapists. In 1979 Drake founded the Landmark East School in Wolfville, Nova Scotia, modeling it after the schools he developed in the United States. Landmark East presently has no affiliation with the U.S. schools, and is governed by the Landmark East Association in Canada, a charitable organization that supports the needs of students with learning disabilities. However, the missions of the Landmark schools are aligned in their goal to assist individuals who struggle with learning.

In 1957 the Riverview School was established by William Janse on Cape Cod, Massachusetts, serving the educational needs of children with complex learning disabilities. During the 1960s Riverview established a long term relationship with the Learning Clinic at the Massachusetts General Hospital, where language and reading disability studies were conducted and then field-tested at the school. In 1990 Richard Lavoie was appointed as the Executive Director of Riverview until 2001 when Ms. Maureen Brenner assumed the post. Under her direction the postsecondary program, "Getting Ready for the Outside World" (GROW), was instituted, serving the needs of young adults who integrate their educational experience with the skills required to live independent lives. In 1967 Dr. Edwin Cole and a group of community members established the Carroll School in Lincoln, Massachusetts, designed to address the needs of students with language-based learning disabilities. The school continues to provide a diagnostic and highly structured approach to learning, and the Carroll Center provides parent support and teacher training.

In the 1960s Gertrude Webb was teaching in the education department and the lab school for children with learning disabilities at Curry College in Milton, Massachusetts, and during that time founded the Massachusetts Association for Children with Learning Disabilities. Webb went on to develop and direct the Program for the Advancement in Learning (PAL) at Curry College, the first program in the United States to offer a mainstreamed assistance program for college students with diagnosed learning disabilities. In the early 1980s Webb developed the first graduate degree program in education at Curry College, where many of her ideas about both general and special education were integrated into the curriculum, including the work of Reuven Feuerstein with whom she spent time in professional collaboration during the 1980s in Israel. In 1990 Jane Adelizzi founded Women Involved in Lifelong Learning (WILL), a unique support group and nonprofit organization for women with learning disabilities who were gathering the courage to either begin or return to a postsecondary setting. In 1994 WILL was integrated into Curry College and is currently known as The Adult Center at the Program for Advancement in Learning (PAL). In 1995 Grace Rooney developed the Program for Advancement in Learning/ English as a Second Language (PAL/ESOL) program. In 2002, under the direction of Pat Mytkowicz, this effort became known as PAL for Multilingual Students, serving the needs of international students with learning disabilities. These programs were unique to New England during their development and integration into a liberal arts college.

Nancy Ratey, author of *The Disorganized Mind* (2008), began the first grassroots effort to familiarize Harvard University's faculty and administration with the needs of students with learning disabilities. From 1984 to 1992 Nancy coordinated The Harvard Dyslexia Awareness Group and Speakers' Series, supported by the university, and widely attended by parents, students, faculty, and nationally recognized professionals. Ratey's work eventually became a model for other universities, a step forward in the recognition and acknowledgment of the needs of individuals with learning disabilities across the lifespan, and the subsequent support programs that were developed.

TRAINING

As a result of the work of early pioneers in the field, training programs began to emerge in the United States and Europe. In Chicago in the 1940s and 1950s, psychologist Mary Kunst was among the first in the Midwest to use the term *educational therapy* to describe her work as a tutor of children with learning impairments within the milieu of a psychiatric hospital. She stated, "Educational therapy may be thought of as a form of psychotherapy involving a combination of educational, psychological and psychiatric skills. The educational therapist integrates the tutoring with the healing process whenever the child is psychologically ready" (quoted in Field, 1993, p. xxvi). In 1965 Kunst's work at the Teacher Education Institute (TEP) at the Institute for Psychoanalysis in Chicago applied many of the basic developmental/psychodynamic concepts and remedial techniques of educational therapy to teacher training. In 1983, Kunst and Field developed the Clinical School Services Program in order to train some much-beleaguered public school teachers in the clinical skills of listening, observing, communicating, and empathizing. This training focused more specifically on mental health tasks essential for effective teaching and how the cognitive/affective modes of learning could be integrated with the teaching/learning process. Unique to this program was the recognition of the emotional impact that the behavior and learning outcomes of these children had on their teachers. This may be referred to by some theorists, clinicians, and practitioners as unconscious responses in the therapeutic relationship.

Kunst and Field's Clinical School Services Program aimed to develop professionals who could: (1) identify high risk children; (2) help children with learning, behavioral, and emotional disorders; and (3) provide classroom teachers with needed assistance. They focused on the totality of the troubled child and created "…a cadre of professionals who can study the developmental and psychological factors affecting children and teachers relative to the larger context of the modern school" (Field, 1993, p. xxxv).

In 1983 the Clinical School Services Program was instituted in Chicago, the goal of which was to train a new category of leadership personnel in special education, known as educational therapists, or consultants in special education: "It was designed to bring an integrated, developmental approach to the multiple dimensions of human learning in the home, the classroom, and the consulting room" (Field, 1993 p. xxxv). In 1991 a new master's program at the DePaul University School of Education prepared educators, administrators, and mental and physical health professionals to work in diverse settings.

Philip Hansen was a professor and chairperson of the department of Special Education at California State University, Northridge (CSUN). He developed curricula for the master's in special education/learning and reading disorders in the 1970s, and was a guiding force in the formation of AET, serving as chairperson of the first advisory board. His work integrated psychoeducational concepts and assessment, as well as reading instruction. The practicum he developed was a precursor for current training programs AET has established. Ray Barsch was a professor of special education at CSUN who promoted the idea that there was a vital connection between movement and cognition, which he called "movigenics" (Barsch, 1968). He was a supporter of interdisciplinary approaches to assessment and teaching in special education. Barsch contributed to the early development of professional training in the field, and served on the first advisory board of AET.

During the 1960s at the Bellevue Clinic in New York, Archie Silver and Rosa Hagin were involved in research that addressed the specific needs of children with learning disabilities, which eventually contributed to the work of educational therapists from NILD, currently based in Virginia. The National Institute for Learning Development (NILD)

Educational Therapy program was first conceived in the 1960s by Deborah Zimmerman, a nurse and educator, who studied in New York at Bellevue Hospital with Archie Silver and Rosa Hagin. She referred to the individuals she trained as educational therapists. In 1982 Zimmerman and Grace Mutzabaugh, a nurse/educator from Virginia, developed an intervention program which became known as the Norfolk Institute for Learning Disabilities. Zimmerman's methods were based on the work of Silver and Hagin, Wechsler, Orton, Gillingham, and others. In 2007 the program became known as the National Institute for Learning Development (NILD), the mission of which continues to be the training of qualified teachers as educational therapists. The NILD's method of educational therapy is employed as a way for children and adolescents to overcome specific cognitive vulnerabilities. The organization's leading professionals have been trained to utilize Feuerstein's Instrumental Enrichment (FIE), and have studied in Israel with Reuven Feuerstein at the International Center for the Enhancement of Learning Potential.

In the 1950s and 1960s, significant progress was made in several European countries to expand the role of educators in dealing with children with learning problems. In 1952 the Child Psychiatric Institute in Oslo, Norway charged Anna-Marit Sletten Duve, a public school teacher of children with mental retardation, to help rethink and redesign educational methods for assessing the learning problems these children experienced. The clinic's efforts were led by child psychoanalyst Nic Waal, who received his clinical training in the United States, and felt that suitable techniques were lacking in the field of educational testing. Following this collaboration, Duve designed an observational diagnostic instrument for teachers working with emotionally disturbed children with comorbid learning problems.

In 2002 The Barents Health and Social Programme, a partner to the Euroarctic Council in Norway, offered its 11th annual conference in educational therapy, the focus of which was "the resilient child," a reminder that the practice of educational therapy maintains an ongoing international presence. The 1960s recognized the development of the terminology and practice of educational therapy in the United Kingdom following the first training program in the field developed by Irene Caspari (1978), an educational psychologist at the Tavistock Clinic. Caspari stressed the importance of the therapeutic value of remedial teaching, and established a part-time evening course for teachers: "Psychological Aspects in the Treatment of Severe Reading Disability." Over time she broadened the educational therapy perspective to include working with families. While Caspari stressed that her approach did not exclude other etiological factors such as inadequate teaching or neurological dysfunction, she stated, "Educational therapy is based on empirical evidence suggesting that some emotional disturbance is present in most cases. The problem of treatment is, therefore, approached with particular regard to the child's emotional needs and great importance is attached to the understanding of the child's feelings, and of his emotional reactions" (Field, 1993, p. xxix). Key elements of her courses in professional practice included clinical training and individual supervision of the teachers. In 1974, Caspari presented a paper in Philadelphia describing the treatment of reading disability using a family approach, thus bringing her ideas to the attention of therapists in the United States. She worked with Muriel Barrett, David Campbell, and Dorothy Heard to include the psychiatric and psychological disciplines in her multidisciplinary training. In 1973, Caspari established the Forum for the Advancement of Educational Therapy (FAET). While no formal training program in educational therapy was established in the United Kingdom, the 1980s was a time of continued growth in this field. Barrett and Trevitt (1991) note that,

"The educational therapist seeks to reawaken the child's capacity for play and learning to rediscover the skills he does not possess" (Field, 1993, p. xxxi). International meetings focusing on educational therapy were held during the 1980s, and in 1989 the Fifth International Conference of Educational Therapy was held in Chicago. Over 300 educators and therapists from the United Kingdom, Norway, Israel, South America, Central America, and many cities in the United States were in attendance. The educational therapists in the United Kingdom recently renamed their work *educational psychotherapy.*

The Association of Educational Therapists began training educational therapists in the 1980s, beginning with professional development for its members, and then followed by training programs including master's and post-master's programs in colleges and universities. New students arrived with professional backgrounds in many fields including general and special education, psychology, early childhood education, and speech and language therapy. During the earlier stages of training programs AET recognized it was imperative to implement established guidelines into program policies and curricula, the results of which evolved from the professional expertise of those who worked in the field and understood the developmental roots and theoretical principles of the practice.

The following are the colleges and universities in California where AET established training programs, and the professionals who contributed to the development of them: California State University Northridge, developed by Susan Fogelson, Dorothy Ungerleider, and Gail Werbach; the University of California Extension at Los Angeles, developed by Maxine Ficksman, Dorothy Ungerleider, and Phyllis Maslow; the University of California Extension at Berkeley, developed by Beverly Metcalf and Nancy Cushen White; the College for Developmental Studies, developed by Karen Kass; the University of California Extension at San Diego, developed by Victoria Knotsman and Victoria Martin; and San Francisco State University, developed by Arlee Maier.

Currently there are master's and post-master's courses at University of California Extension at Riverside, developed by Maxine Ficksman and Ann Kaganoff; the University of California Extension at Santa Cruz, developed by Phyllis Maslow and Beverly Metcalf; California State University Northridge, developed by Maxine Ficksman, Dorothy Ungerleider; and Marcy Dann; and Holy Names College, developed by Arlee Maier. Maxine Ficksman, coordinator of the University of California Extension program in educational therapy for 10 years beginning in 1992, was instrumental in the development and establishment of the program's curriculum, which subsequently influenced UCBX, Holy Names, and Curry College, which was developed and coordinated by Jane Adelizzi, and CSUN. In 2008, the newly revised master's in educational therapy and post-master's certificate in educational therapy at CSUN were approved. This exemplary program now includes an internship as well as clinical work with students in a multidisciplinary setting serving a diverse student population, the Learning Center at CSUN. The Massachusetts School of Professional Psychology in Boston, MA will be offering an elective in their Doctor of School Psychology program in 2010: "Pedagogical Perspectives and Dynamics in Educational Therapy," designed by Jane Adelizzi, and open to educational therapists and allied professionals who may benefit from a deeper exploration of this interdisciplinary profession.

The last few years have seen the initiation of the Educational Therapy Institute (ETI) developed by AET, and coordinated by Maxine Ficksman, providing post-master's courses across the United States. There is a two-tiered system of courses to appeal to educational therapists of varying experience and background. As of 2009, four courses have been offered in Chicago, and the program has recognized its first graduating class. The Association of

Educational Therapists will soon be making online courses in educational therapy available. Thus, there are now numerous ways in which professional development and training is offered, which contributes to the sustainability of ET in the United States, and beyond our borders into Canada and South America as well as into other countries. Professional training in this area is now more accessible in many countries, particularly to those in outlying areas where conventional courses may not be readily available.

PRIVATE PRACTICE

The late 1950s on into the 1960s and 1970s saw the beginning of the private practice of educational therapy in the United States. While most practitioners did not call themselves educational therapists, they were aware that their function went beyond the typical duties usually performed by academic tutors. Many of these professionals completed graduate courses and degrees, and worked with mentors who assisted them in developing a conceptual framework through which to develop an educational therapy treatment plan. Early in the development of the practice educational therapists regarded an individual in a comprehensive and holistic manner, within the contexts of family, school, and other settings and relationships. Private practice resulted from professionals who worked in clinics, centers, programs, schools, and colleges nationwide.

THE ESTABLISHMENT OF STUDY GROUPS

The most apt definition of a study group is a group of individuals who meet in order to share their common interests, their shared fields of study, and their general and specific inquisitiveness about the relationship of their work to the work of others. Educational therapists have been coming together for this purpose since the inception of the practice in the United States, beginning in the living room of Dorothy Ungerleider. Since that time, study groups define their individual missions according to their location (someone's home, a clinic, or a school) and the consensus of the group. While the group is certainly a place for camaraderie, it also provides the time and place to feel a sense of affirmation about one's work. Much of the work of an ET, especially in private practice, occurs in isolation, and the study group provides a forum for professional exchange, and the sharing of common concerns and problem solving. Within the group sessions new techniques are shared; opinions are voiced; visiting allied professionals are welcomed; and case studies are reviewed as a means of informal training through the consistent process of reiteration, reflection, synthesis, and analysis. Some study groups are comprised of members who have been together for a long period of time. Some groups may have a core membership, but also recognize a more transient group of visitors who are curious about the practice. A Virtual Study Group has been developed by AET which offers regular, online meetings for professionals who are not able to attend group meetings, thereby welcoming members who are located nationwide as well as in other countries.

Southern California

In the 1970s a small group of practitioners in the Los Angeles area began meeting in the home of AET founder, Dorothy Ungerleider, for professional networking, sharing their concerns about private practice, and exploring techniques appropriate for their clientele, acknowledging the ET/client relationship as the foundation for this work. Guest speakers were invited to provide information which was deemed valuable in practice, such as educational and psychological testing, perspectives on child development, the practice of speech and language therapy, and reading and math remediation. This became the model for study groups, the heart and soul of AET, providing support, networking, and lifelong learning for this emerging profession.

As a result of the professional collaboration which had been taking place in the early years of the evolution of the profession these early practitioners were encouraged to submit articles on the theory and practice of educational therapy. This newsletter became a widely recognized professional journal, *The Educational Therapist,* published by AET. In 1985 Dorothy Ungerleider published an in-depth case study, *Reading, Writing and Rage;* in 1996 the book's second edition was published. In 1991 she also published a compilation of her articles from *The Educational Therapist, Psychoeducational Perspectives.* Both publications remain seminal resources in professional training in educational therapy.

Northern California

In the early 1980s in San Francisco Dorothy Ungerleider encouraged a group of practitioners from Northern California to share their thoughts and ideas about their clinical practices. Several of these professionals received special education training at the University of the Pacific and San Francisco State University, and had been in practice for many years. This core group, led by Beverly Metcalf, added yet more practitioners who were resource specialists and special education school personnel, all of whom contributed to the interdisciplinary practice and perspectives of educational therapy. Beverly Metcalf holds the distinction of being the first president of AET elected outside of the Los Angeles area.

New York

In the New York area a small group of educational therapists began meeting in the early 1970s at the home of Linda Dunn to discuss cases and share intervention techniques. Several years ago Jackie Levine developed and led a study group, a core group of professionals who contributed to the subsequent development of a study group in New York City led by Susan Micari. Study groups in New York and Massachusetts developed and maintain a collegial relationship which encourages the sharing of experiences, new theories that speak to the practice of educational therapy, and a vision for expanded growth on the East Coast.

Chicago

In the 1990s a study group, similar in mission to that of early study groups in California, was established in Chicago. These members were often mentored by psychologists and clinical social workers such as Rita Sussman, adding yet another perspective to the professional work of existing members such as Nan Freund, former president of AET, and Risa Graff, AET's current president. Professionals in special education and social work in Chicago, including Arthur Neyhus, Steffa Miral, Joe Palombo, and Pearl Rieger then began to use the term *educational therapy.* Joe Palombo remains a friend and mentor to educational therapists with his book, *Nonverbal Learning Disabilities: A Clinical Perspective* (2006), relied upon by ETs nationwide.

Massachusetts

Although the practice of educational therapy existed in numerous schools and programs in New England, one of the first graduate courses to speak directly to the conceptual underpinnings of the work was presented in a PhD program at Lesley University in 1990 by George Hein in his class "The Interface of Teaching and Therapy." Hein's work was influential in the development of the first AET Massachusetts study group comprised of several members of the PAL/Curry College faculty as well as professionals from other schools and colleges. These efforts took place in the late 1990s, led by Jane Adelizzi and Patty Kean, with the support of Sandra Mosk, AET's president during that time. In 2004 Adelizzi was the invited speaker at Lesley University's George Hein Lecture Series. Her topic was "The Interface of Teaching and Therapy: Educational Therapy," delivered to an audience of faculty, alumni, and students from Lesley's PhD program in educational studies, in a consciousness-raising effort. Currently there is an active study group at Curry College led by Laurie Fox. There are numerous educational therapists in private practice throughout New England, as well as in private schools, programs, and colleges.

THE ESTABLISHMENT OF THE ASSOCIATION OF EDUCATIONAL THERAPISTS (AET)

As the national professional association in the field of educational therapy AET defined its practitioners in the following manner: "An educational therapist is a professional who combines educational and therapeutic approaches for evaluation, remediation, case management, and communication/advocacy on behalf of children, adolescents and adults with learning disabilities or learning problems" (Educational Therapy Defined, p. 1). Professional standards were established including continuing education requirements for professional development and training. Educational therapists were encouraged to communicate with parents, teachers, and allied professionals such as physicians, psychologists, psychiatrists, and speech and language therapists in order to create a treatment alliance that encompassed the comprehensive learning needs of the client. In order to communicate with members, a newsletter was established which later became the journal, *The Educational Therapist*. Educational therapists were encouraged to submit articles on the theory and practice of educational therapy, and as a result it quickly became apparent to the early leaders of AET that a certification process was central to the very definition of the profession. In order to establish the credibility of the professional organization, a mechanism was needed to demonstrate that individual members were able to meet the highest goals and objectives of the profession. During the formative administration, headed by Dorothy Ungerleider from 1979 to 1981, the application procedure, including a case study format, was designed by a committee including Shelby Holley, Paul Klinger, Barbara Kornblau, Dorothy Ungerleider, and Gail Werbach. In 2002, a separate board was established, delineating the higher standards, and the existing certified members were grandfathered as Board Certified Educational Therapists (BCET). This organization currently provides mentors for the purpose of training new educational therapists across the country.

1990s

The 1990s recognized the national expansion of the Association of Educational Therapists as well as its relationship with other organizations and allied professionals with similar missions. The organizations included, but were not limited to: American Speech-Language-Hearing Association, California Association of School Psychologists, Council for Learning Disabilities, International Reading Association, Learning Disabilities Association(s), National Institute for Learning Development, the Orton Dyslexia Society, and The Network. Educational therapists networked with psychiatrists, psychologists, speech and language therapists, physicians, teachers, and developmental optometrists. The Association held conferences and members taught seminars to help its colleagues understand how to collaborate with other helping professionals. Training programs and graduate courses were instrumental in helping AET gain international recognition, creating a national familiarity of the practice of educational therapy.

2000–2008

In an effort to expand the efficacy of educational therapists and collaborate on a national level, AET, guided by the efforts of Phyllis Maslow, Dorothy Ungerleider, and Sandra Mosk, was accepted as a contributing member of the National Joint Committee on Learning Disabilities (NJCLD). Jane Adelizzi, Dale Carberry, and Jeanette Rivera eventually became AET's representatives in this nationally recognized organization, which facilitates communication among its member organizations in order to identify research and appropriate services in the field of learning disabilities. The member organizations include: American Speech–Language–Hearing Association, Association for Higher Education and Disability, Council for Learning Disabilities, Division for Communicative Disabilities and Deafness, Council for Exceptional Children-Division of Learning Disabilities, International Dyslexia Association, International Reading Association, Learning Disabilities Association of America, National Association for the Education of African American Children with Learning Disabilities, National Association of School Psychologists and National Center for Learning Disabilities. Educational therapy became a part of the IDEA revision in 2004, which has implications for the inclusion of educational therapy services to those with learning disabilities.

An AET research team led by Phyllis Maslow and Dorothy Ungerleider, and guided by Barbara Keogh, designed a study of treatment efficacy (Maslow & Ungerleider, 2007), demonstrating the perceived accountability held by ETs in relation to their clients. In addition, the study provided useful information for the continued growth of AET's specialized training programs, master's and post-master's level certificate programs, workshops, seminars, and conferences. Following a pilot study, Board Certified Educational Therapists (BCETs) were asked to submit the survey to the parents of clients who had terminated educational therapy within the last 2 years. Of the surveys returned by the parents of these clients, 90% of the respondents reported that educational therapy had provided them with needed support; 88.6% of the respondents felt that educational therapy helped their children function more effectively; and, 74.2% of respondents perceived educational therapy as helping their families function more effectively. The authors state, "A further study of the family and environmental perspectives of the treatment is needed, with an increased awareness of the importance of collaboration among parents, teachers, and all other family members and professionals concerned with the academic, social, and emotional development of the client" (p. 20).

The evolutionary roots of educational therapy developed during the 1800s in Europe, as professionals relied upon their clinical observations and treatment of exceptional children. In the 1900s schools that stressed a balance between educational goals and therapeutic interventions were developed in order to help those who could not learn successfully in traditional settings. Numerous universities, colleges, private clinics, and mentors provided guidelines for the early stages of the private practice of educational therapy. Textbooks and research journals were valuable tools that informed educational therapists about many areas in the fields of psychology, sociologically, language development, and teaching methodology. Additionally, collaboration with allied associations and colleagues was important to the development of the field because their individual and collective expertise and theoretical foundations contributed to the comprehensiveness of the practice of educational therapy.

EDUCATIONAL THERAPY TODAY

In the latter part of the 20th century, AET and NILD developed standards of practice for ETs, the former defining their work as an interdisciplinary approach and practice, and the latter defining its work as specific methodology. The developmental roots of the practice provided by August Aichorn in Vienna many years ago currently echoes in New York City at the August Aichorn Center, directed by Dr. Michael Pawel. Educational therapists in Britain continue their work at the Tavistock Clinic and in schools throughout the country, their work integrating the task to be mastered with the acknowledgment of the unconscious processes that reside in each child as well as in the therapeutic relationship which ushers clients' progress to successful outcomes. Whether we regard the work of ETs as an approach or a methodology, the goal remains the same; offering remediation, relief, and a cohesive sense of self to individuals whose progress, production, and learning have been compromised.

REFERENCES

Aichorn, A. (1935). *Wayward youth*. New York: Viking. (Original Work published 1925)

Barrett, M., & Trevitt, J. (1991). *Attachment behavior and the school child: An introduction to educational therapy*. London: Tavistock/Routledge.

Barsch, R. (1968). *Enriching perception and cognition*. Seattle, WA: Special Child.

Caspari, I. (1978). Educational therapy. In V. Varma (Ed.), *Psychotherapy today* (pp. 215–232). London: Constable.

Cohen, R. (1966). Clinical principles of curriculum selection. In J. Hellmuth (Ed.), *Educational therapy* (Vol. 1, pp. 137–154). Seattle, WA: Special Child.

DeHirsch, K. (1977). Interactions between educational therapist and child. *Bulletin of the Orton Society, 27*, 88–101.

Devereaux, G. (1965). *Therapeutic education*. New York: Harper.

Educational Therapy Defined. (2000). [Pamphlet]. Los Angeles: Association of Educational Therapists.

Esterson, H., Cook, M., Mendlowitz, M., & Solomon, C. (1969). The team approach in therapeutic education: Successes and failures. In J. Hellmuth (Ed.), *Educational therapy* (Vol. 2, pp. 311–320). Seattle, WA: Special Child.

Fenichel, C. (1966). Psycho-educational approaches for seriously disturbed children in the classroom. In J. Hellmuth (Ed.), *Educational Therapy* (Vol. 1, pp. 207–221). Seattle, WA: Special Child.

Field, K. (1993). A selective history of educational therapy: 1940–1991. In K. Field, E. Kaufman, & C. Saltzman (Eds.), *Emotions and learning reconsidered: An international perspective* (pp. xxiii–xli). New York: Gardner Press.

French, E. L. (1966). Therapeutic education: Theory and practice in a residential treatment center for emotionally disturbed adolescents. In J. Hellmuth (Ed.), *Educational therapy* (Vol. 1, pp. 425–437). Seattle, WA: Special Child.

Frostig, M., & Maslow, P. (1973). *Learning problems in the classroom*. New York: Grune & Stratton.

Gillingham, A., & Stillman, B. (1935). *Remedial training for children with specific disability in reading, spelling and penmanship*. Cambridge, MA: Educators Publishing Service.

Hellmuth, J. (Ed.). (1966). *Educational therapy* (Vol. 1). Seattle, WA: Special Child.
Hellmuth, J. (Ed.). (1969). *Educational therapy* (Vol. 2). Seattle, WA: Special Child.
Hensley, G. (1966). Therapeutic teachers of exceptional children. In J. Hellmuth (Ed.), *Educational therapy* (Vol. 1, pp. 119–136). Seattle, WA: Special Child.
Itard, J-M-G. (1932). *The wild boy of Aveyron*. M. Humphrey (trans.). New York: Century.
Jansky, J. (1984). Foreword. In K. DeHirsch, *Language and the developing child* (pp. ix–xi). Baltimore, MD: Orton Dyslexia Society.
Johnston, C. L. (1984). Educational therapy: Past perspectives, current practices and a proposal for change. *Journal of Learning Disabilities, 17*(4). 200–204.
Knoblock, P. (1969). Teacher-child relationships in psychoeducational programming for emotionally disturbed children. In J. Hellmuth (Ed.), *Educational therapy* (Vol. 2, pp. 391–412). Seattle, WA: Special Child.
Lewis, W. (1966). Project Re-Ed: Educational intervention in emotional disturbance. In J. Hellmuth (Ed.), *Educational therapy* (Vol. 1, pp. 295–315). Seattle, WA: Special Child.
Mallison, R. (1968). *Education as therapy*. Seattle, WA: Special Child.
Maslow, P., & Ungerleider, D. (2007). The efficacy of educational therapy, Part 2. *The Educational Therapist, 28*(3), 16–21.
Montessori, M. (1964). *The Montessori method*. New York: Schocken. (Original work published 1912)
Osman, B. (1980). *Learning disabilities: A family affair*. New York: Warner Books.
Osman, B. (1982). *No one to play with: The social side of learning disabilities*. New York: Random House.
Palombo, J. (2006). *Nonverbal learning disabilities: A clinical perspective*. New York: W.W. Norton.
Ratey, N. (2008). *The disorganized mind: Coaching your ADHD brain to take control of your time, tasks, and talents*. New York: St. Martin's Press.
Sapir, S. (1985). *The clinical teaching model: Clinical insight and strategies for the learning-disabled child*. New York: Brunner/Mazel.
Sperry, B., & Templeton, R. (1969). The principles and dynamics of therapeutic tutoring. In J. Hellmuth (Ed.), *Educational therapy* (Vol.2, pp. 173–194). Seattle, WA: Special Child.
Ungerleider, D. (1985). *Reading, writing and rage: The terrible price paid by victims of school failure*. Rolling Hills Estates, CA: Jalmar Press.
Ungerleider, D. (1986). History of educational therapy: The profession, the association. *The Educational Therapist, 8*(1), 3–9.
Ungerleider, D. (1991). *Psychoeducational perspectives*. Los Angeles: Association of Educational Therapists.
Ungerleider, D. (1995). The history of educational therapy reconsidered in the '90s. *The Educational Therapist, 16*(3), 3–11.
Werbach, G. (1998). Special education therapy. In S. Eth & S. Harrison (Eds.), J. Noshpitz (Editor-in-chief), *Handbook of child and adolescent psychiatry* (pp. 581–588). New York: Wiley.

II

Perspectives on the Clinical Practice of Educational Therapy

4

EMPATHIC INTELLIGENCE IN EDUCATIONAL THERAPY

An International Perspective

ROSLYN ARNOLD

Therapists and educators attuned to the needs of students share much in common. They recognize the influence of students' emotional states and inner world on their sense of well-being and readiness to learn. They also recognize the powerful influence of relationships on their intellectual and emotional development. For the best and fullest human consciousness, education and therapy require that we understand and respect the inner world of individuals wherein thought and feeling are complementary psychic processes. It is equally important to understand how individuals interact with others, and how they derive significance from such interactions. In exploring those phenomena, possibilities become as important as probabilities, and those engaged in seeking to explore those phenomena are themselves changed by the quest, with all their resolutions and ineffable ambiguities.

Empathic intelligence is a concept developed to articulate the practice of teachers and therapists who are attuned to the interface between cognitive and affective development, and mindful of the power of relatedness in learning, teaching, and self-development. It is a concept which reflects many of the practices of teachers and educational therapists who seek to mobilize students' tacit abilities in the service of their development into informed, well-integrated, resourceful individuals. The phenomenon of learning defies easy explanation, but when people attune to each other, something significant can happen in the space between them. Arguably, empathic intelligence supports the development of partnerships between teachers and therapists whereby within their different contexts of practice there can be complementarities in theoretical approach, in the service of those in their care.

Empathic intelligence (Arnold, 1993, 1994, 1998, 2004, 2005) was formulated to articulate some complex qualities of effective pedagogy (teaching and learning) and to mobilize those practitioners who demonstrate its characteristics and gain affirmation from its articulation. They can use the theory of empathic intelligence to deepen their self-understanding as practitioners and through observation and introspection, shape its elaborations to enliven their practices.

In this chapter, empathic intelligence will be explained along with those characteristics of its practice which relate to the work of both teachers and therapists in educational settings. These characteristics include attunement to self and others, the ability to generate a dynamic between thinking and feeling, the ability to create positive relationships, to model attitudes conducive to positive effects, to mirror students' feelings, and to understand the nature of inter/intrasubjectivity.

EMPATHY

The cornerstone of empathic intelligence is empathy, defined here as an ability to understand the thoughts and feelings of self and others. It is a sophisticated ability involving attunement, decentering, and introspection: an act of thoughtful, heartfelt imagination.

This is a convergent definition which gives equal weight to thought and feeling. In this definition, empathy is a process of observing the phenomena of intersubjective and intrasubjective engagements to collect data to inform decision making or interventions in phenomenological moments. In order to achieve the necessary objectivity, self-understanding and complex cognitive and affective functioning are required.

DEFINITION OF EMPATHIC INTELLIGENCE

Empathic intelligence is a theoretical concept (Arnold, 2005) underpinned by an argument that effective pedagogy and educational therapy happen when a practitioner is able to create a dynamic or energy between thinking and feeling, in a context which is perceived as intelligently caring. Empathic intelligence is a sophisticated form of empathy in action. It is a sustained system of psychic, cognitive, affective, social, and ethical functioning derived from an ability to: differentiate self-states from others' states; mobilize a dynamic between thinking and feeling in self and others; engage in imaginative, reflective, and analogic processes to understand dynamics; work creatively in tacitly felt, but yet unrealized ways, guided by resilience and adaptive capacity; commit to the well-being and development of self and others; and, generate a climate of care in contexts of practice.

Empathically intelligent practitioners demonstrate a number of qualities, attributes, predispositions, and abilities, in particular those which contribute to enthusiasm, capacity to engage others, expertise, and empathy. Such practitioners are sensitive to the function of attunement and mirroring as affirmation and a means of modulating response.

Empathic intelligence defines a complex system of psychic functioning developed through affective sensitivity, a habit of self-reflection, knowledge about the ways humans learn and process experiences, and certain philosophical predispositions about human values and human potential. In this definition, precursors to the development of full empathic intelligence are both affective, such as a capacity for sympathy and compassion, and cognitive, such as a capacity for analytic thought, for imagination, for reflection, and for analogic processing whereby the significance of connections between disparate phenomena are recognized.

Skilled practitioners working in this model can draw on a complex repertoire of abilities and attitudes appropriate to the needs of the client/student. Empathic intelligence is a well structured, mature, patterned, and consistent way of functioning cognitively, socially, ethically, and emotionally. It seeks to understand rather than to judge and it is imbued with the morality of caring.

Underpinning the theory of empathic intelligence is a philosophy that believes in the inherently person-centered nature of effective pedagogy, and a psychology which understands human development as dynamic, experiential, interdependent, self-driven, and self-enhancing. The development of the theory of empathic intelligence has been influenced by scholars, researchers, and practitioners in cross-disciplinary fields of human interaction (Bruner, 1972, 1986, 1990; Dewey, 1916, 1939/1963, 1964, 1971; Gardner, 1983, 1985, 1993, 1997; Polanyi, 1959, 1969, 1974, 1983; Rogers, 1959, 1962, 1975; Vygotsky, 1978, 1987, 1988). Education therapists and teachers who share these beliefs and professional orientations might find empathic intelligence resonates with their practice. The value of working within a framework or theoretical orientation is that it provides a structure which can support reflective practitioners as they introspect on their engagements with clients/students. Ideally, such a theoretical orientation works best when it is liberating, supportive, enhances practice, and enables clients/students to transform their own lives, which is an ideal of both therapy and pedagogy. When it is that, it grows in complexity and usefulness, enlivening all parties and offering hope that the complexities of human mind, thought, and feeling can be harnessed in the service of human development.

DYNAMISM

Dynamism as it is theorized in empathic intelligence refers to the sense of energy, tension, or movement present when we relate with deep thought and feeling to a situation. Empathic attunement to self, others, and the world of experience underpins that process. It is a psychic and recursive energy which moves both outwards and inwards propelled by the human capacity to learn from experience. Interpersonal relationships, work, and play can involve dynamic experiences, alongside energy generated by our own mental and physical states.

It is inherent in life that things change constantly. Reflective people monitor closely their own internal dynamics. For them, it is second nature to observe, reflect, and analyze their own thoughts and feelings, and their interactions with others and the environment. Such people tend to develop a rich inner life, the product of that recursive, dynamic process of intersubjective and intrasubjective engagements.

Dynamism functions to fuel deep learning, insight, and psychic development. Even within the concept of dynamism as outlined here, there is a role for stillness and for attuned listening to self and to others. Dynamism in the case of poise or stillness might be thought of metaphorically as potential, rather than actual energy.

Educational therapists and teachers skilled in attuning to the needs of others can recognize this suspended energy within themselves and use it to fuel the psychic activity of reflecting upon both their thoughts and the feelings prior to responding to the other. In responding, they might choose to amplify the other's feelings or suggest a strategy. A common statement made by students in classrooms is "I hate math." A teacher can reply "You will need math when you grow up so you must persevere" or "It's frustrating when you can't quite remember the formula, isn't it? Let's go through the steps again." It is easy to see which response is likely to mobilize the student. In their interactions with students, education therapists and teachers have multiple opportunities for judicious choices in empathic responses.

EMPATHY AND BRAIN-BASED RESEARCH

One of the promising developments in science at the beginning of this new century is the increasing interest in the nature and function of the emotions in humans. Under the influence of scientific research into human consciousness, much of it in the 1990s (Damasio, 1994, 2000, 2003; LeDoux, 1996, 2003; Rose, 1993, 1998), attitudes to human thinking and the nature of intellectual maturity are changing. The concept of rational thought, associated particularly with the work of the 18th century philosopher René Descartes (1637), is being reconceptualized because brain neural imaging and research on the development of consciousness illuminates the synergies between the cognitive and emotional parts of human brains (Carpenter, 2002; Damasio, 1994, 2000, 2003; Davia, 2002; LeDoux, 1992, 1996, 2003; Williams, 2001).

The work of Antonio Damasio (1994, 2000, 2003) provides scientific evidence to inform an understanding of inter- and intrasubjective experiences. He argues that human consciousness is actually consciousness of the feeling and experiencing of self. His case studies make compelling reading and offer deep reassurance to those who believe in complementarity in intellectual development of emotion and cognition. He argues that emotion and feeling "provide the bridge between rational and non-rational processes, between cortical and subcortical structures" (Damasio, 1994, p. 128).

Based on the evidence of his research with brain-damaged patients, Damasio (1994) concludes:

> My investigation of neurological patients in whom brain lesions impaired the experience of feelings has led me to think that feelings are not as intangible as they have been presumed to be.... Contrary to traditional scientific opinion, feelings are just as cognitive as other percepts.... Feelings form the base for what humans have described for millennia as the human soul or spirit. (pp. xvi-xviii)

EMPATHY IN INFANCY

The work of Daniel Stern (1985) on the role of empathy in infancy illuminates the importance of empathic attunement in early learning, emotional development, and socialization. Stern writes about the development of "intersubjective relatedness," that ability to experience one's self as a separate being from others, but as a dependent being too. The process by which the mother's empathic responsiveness evokes, stimulates, validates, and maybe names the infant's emotional and physical state, ensures that her underlying affective response is encoded in the baby's brain.

According to Stern, the degree to which the major affect states (interest, joy, surprise, anger, distress, fear, contempt, disgust, and shame) are encoded in the baby's brain influences the development of their core relatedness. That sense of core relatedness forms the basis for the development of intersubjective relatedness. Stern argues that in the preverbal stage infants seek to share joint attention, intentions, and affect states with significant others. The process of organizing the affect responses of the mother to the infant, and indeed, possibly the infant's own physiological responses also, Stern refers to as the laying down of templates into "Representations of Interactions that have been Generalized" (RIGS) (Stern, 1985, p. 97). It is the mother's (and others') empathic responsiveness to the infant which influences the integrations of "agency, coherence, and affectivity" to provide the infant with a unified sense of a core self and a core other: "the existential bedrock of interpersonal relations" (Stern, 1985, p. 125).

ORIGINS OF THE CONCEPT OF EMPATHY

Apart from a reference in Aristotle's *Rhetoric* to "empathiea," as Susan Verducci (2000a) points out empathy first appears in 19th-century German aesthetics in the work of Friedrich Vischer (1807–1887) and his son Robert Vischer (1847–1933), and following them, Martin Buber and Theodore Lipps. Friedrich Vischer called empathy a process of "symbolic interjection of emotions into objective forms," such as engaged in by viewers of works of art. Verducci (2000a, p. 67) notes that Vischer's son Robert named this process "Einfuhlung," which Titchener later translated as empathy. Robert Vischer described the process as projecting one's own life into the lifeless form: "Only ostensibly do I keep my own identity...I am mysteriously transformed into this Other" (F. Vischer, 1994, pp. 19–20). The philosopher Martin Buber (1965) describes the experience of feeling strong connectedness with subjects or objects:

> ... to glide with one's own feeling into the dynamic structure of an object..., understanding the formation and motoriality of the object with the perceptions of one's own muscles; it means to "transpose" oneself over there and in there. (p. 97)

Lipps (1851–1914) went further than the Vischers and Buber, saying: "empathy is the fact here established, that the object is myself and by the very same token this self of mine is the object ... the antithesis between myself and the object disappears, or rather does not yet exist" (quoted in Mallgrave & Ikonomou cited in Verducci, 2000a, p. 68). He saw the phenomenon as projective, imaginative, and primarily affective. Susan Verducci (2000a) notes that in these early ideas of empathy, "the seed of this process lies in the imagination, the flower in the viewer's affective life. The imagined mental representation of an object and the viewer's feelings become inseparable" (p. 67). Arguably, in these rudimentary views of empathy, concentration and a capacity for absorption are functioning too. What is not mentioned yet is a capacity for cognitive distancing or awareness of a self engaging in the experience. The experience as described by these philosophers is aesthetically pleasing though no judgment or cognition is involved. As Verducci notes (2000a), "empathy as sole grounding for the aesthetic experience cannot account for the phenomenon of aesthetic judgment" (p. 69).

CONCEPTS OF EMPATHY

Research and scholarship on the nature of empathy highlights its theoretical complexity (Barnes & Thagard, 1997; Barnett, 1987; Barnett & Thompson, 1984, quoted in Berliner & Calfee, 1996, p. 280; Eisenberg & Strayer, 1996; Feshbach & Feshbach, 1987; Kohut, 1959, 1971, 1979, 1982, 1985; Verducci, 2000a). A recent study in Australia (Nicolson, 2009) outlines some of the contentions about definitions of empathy, including whether or not it is a necessary condition of prosocial behavior (Ellis, 1982; Hoffman, 1982, 1984b), its relationship with behavior (Bush, Mullis, & Mullis, 2000; Eisenberg & Fabes, 1998), whether there is increased risk or predictability of antisocial behavior with restricted or delayed empathic development (Bradford & Lyddon, 1994; Bush et al., 2000; Ellis, 1982; Hoffman, 1975; Pecukonis, 1990), and whether or not it involves both cognitive and affective components (Eisenberg & Fabes, 1998; Hoffman, 1977).

Nicolson (2009) explores three different constructs of empathy: the cognitive or perspective-taking view (Gladstein, 1983, p. 468; Mead, 1934); the affective view which regards empathy as a concordant emotional response emerging from another's emotional state (Gladstein, 1983, p. 468); and the view that empathy is either cognitive or affective depending on the situation (Duan & Hill, 1996, p. 263; Gladstein, 1983). Nicolson (2009) also explores whether or not empathy is a personality trait, a general ability bestowed by nature, or developed through experience (Davis, 1983; Feshbach, 1975; Kestenbaum, Farber, & Sroufe, 1989; Mead, 1934), or a vicarious response to others' experiences (Duan & Hill, 1996, p. 262).

In her recent research, a self-study of a teacher's empathic attunement, Nicolson (2009) used a developmental construct of empathy comprised of both cognitive and affective components (Bower, 1983, cited in Duan & Hill, 1996; Feshbach 1975; Greenberg, Rice, & Elliott, 1993; Greenson, 1960; Isen, 1984; Katz, 1963; Schafer, 1959; Strayer, 1987). While acknowledging that defining empathy is a complex task, Nicolson (2009) argues that empathy exists where individuals can "perceive the internal frame of reference of another with accuracy and with the emotional components and means which pertain as if one were the other person, but without ever losing the 'as if condition' (Rogers, 1959, p. 210) [which] Kohut (1959) describes … as 'vicarious introspection.'" Nicolson's (2009, p. 70) study highlights some of the positive and long-lasting effects on students of empathically attuned practices (She gives permission for contact at Susan.Nicolson@kidsguardian.nsw.gov.au).

Verducci (2000a) comments that an "unusually diverse group of American educational thinkers are calling for cultivating empathy in schools for the purpose of moral education" (p. 63). She cites the work of educators Thomas Lickons, William Bennett, and Maxine Greene, care theorist Nel Noddings, and moral philosophers John Deigh, Deborah Meier, and Martha Nussbaum, noting that despite their different ideologies, they "understand empathy as connected to morality" (2000a, p. 63). Verducci (2000a) further notes that "When educational discourse focuses on cultivating empathy for moral education, theorists are referring to very different phenomena" (p. 64). She cites the work of Lorraine Code (1995), who suggests empathy is an epistemological experience, Deigh (1995), who requires that the empathizer consciously recognize the other as a separate entity, and Reed (1984) who argues that empathy has been delineated as either active or passive, rational or mystical, artistic or scientific, and a symbol of projection or reception. Noddings regards empathy as a quality necessary in times of distress or emotional turmoil (Noddings, 1993) and argues (1988, 1993, 1998) that an ethic of caring is significant in pedagogy and the development of imagination. Hoffman (2000) establishes the links between empathy and moral development, identifying their implications for caring and justice.

INTROSPECTION AND EMPATHY

The psychoanalyst Heinz Kohut's (1959) definition of empathy as "vicarious introspection" includes both affective attunement and the cognitive capacity to judge how best to respond sensitively to another's emotional and cognitive state. Importantly, the notion of "vicarious" in Kohut's definition cautions that it should not be assumed we can know what another is thinking or feeling based solely on identifications, projections, or hypotheses. Through introspection and dialogue with the other, some approximation of another's reality can be gleaned.

The work of Tansey and Burke (1989) is helpful in understanding how empathy, projective identification, and countertransference can be theoretically integrated. They demonstrate that these phenomena, "often thought to be disparate, are actually elements of one overall sequence through which a therapist can use his (sic) emotional responsiveness to achieve an empathic outcome" (Tansey & Burke, 1989, p. 37). They define empathy as,

the optimal outcome that results from the successful processing of an identification and leads to emotional knowledge of the patient's experience. Empathy is a process, not just an identification. In building on the traditional view of empathy as a two-step process, we are extending the usual conceptualization of empathy to include complementary as well as concordant identifications in the empathic process. (p. 58)

Further, they comment that empathy,

is often described as an intrapsychic rather than an interpersonal phenomenon. Not only does it seem to be conceptualized as though the patient has nothing to do with the therapist's singlehanded acquisition of empathic insights, empathy is sometimes viewed as ending with what the therapist understands internally. In contrast, we would propose that the empathic process not only involves taking in the patient's influence (Reception), followed by analyzing and arriving at tentative understandings of this material (Internal Processing), but also entails the process of "giving back" to the patient. (p. 99)

Pigman (1995) argues,

Empathy (Einfühllung) ... plays a greater role in Freud's thinking than readers of the *Standard Edition* realise ... Although ... (it) never translates Einfühlung as 'empathy' in a clinical context, Freud regards it as essential for establishing the rapport between patient and analyst that makes interpretation possible. (p. 237)

Arguably, Freud meant regarded empathy as an ability to decenter and to recognize differences between one's self and others. Earlier followers of Freud such as Theodor Reik and Robert Fliess regarded empathy as essentially a cognitive process of identifying the feelings of their therapy patients while attempting to maintain an emotionally distanced relationship with them.

HOW EMPATHIC INTELLIGENCE SUBSUMES EMOTIONAL INTELLIGENCE

Empathic intelligence is not the same as emotional intelligence (Goldman, 1995, 1998). While emotional intelligence is a necessary part of empathic intelligence, there are important differences between them. One is that empathic intelligence relies for its functioning on the creation of a dynamic between both cognitive and emotional intelligence and seeks to understand how each contributes meaning to a situation. Empathic intelligence is the application of cognitive and emotional intelligences to beneficial effect. It has an underpinning of ethical intention within a climate of care which gives it a distinctive quality.

By modeling that quality in practice, therapists and teachers provide a rationale for the development of conscience as the ideal of "just relationships." Behavior which damages just relationships becomes unconscionable. Learning in classrooms and working with a therapist can be emotionally perilous in the absence of "just relations." For those unable to understand the source of their discomfort in an unjust relationship, the peril is exacerbated. The ethical and insightful practitioner determines in a disinterested way, "who" is responsible for "what" in interpersonal engagements. Such practitioners tolerate emotionally discomforting insights in the best interests of their clients/students.

Mayer and Salovey (1997, p. 5) argue that emotional intelligence should refer to heightened emotional and mental abilities, as opposed to simple emotional awareness or responsiveness. They define emotional intelligence as "the ability to perceive emotions, to access and generate emotions so as to assist thought, to understand emotions and emotional knowledge, and to reflectively regulate emotions so as to promote emotional and intellectual growth." Mayer and Salovey (1997) point out that this definition "combines the ideas that emotion makes thinking more intelligent and that one thinks intelligently about emotions. Both (ideas) connect intelligence and emotion" (p. 5).

INTER/INTRASUBJECTIVITY

Empathic intelligence is a complex concept which attempts to articulate those aspects of intersubjective (dynamics between subjects) and intrasubjective (dynamics experienced within subjects) engagements which influence learning. It acknowledges the fluidity of human engagements in its focus on dynamics but proposes that enthusiasm, expertise, a capacity to engage others, and, of course, a capacity to act empathically, are foregrounded behaviors and attitudes exemplified by those who are empathically intelligent practitioners.

Embedded in expertise is the capacity to mirror others, to attune to them and to be self-reflective. While empathic intelligence attempts to capture something of the resonance of human engagements, it acknowledges the necessity for participants themselves to observe, feel, intuit, think, introspect, imagine, and test their own data gathering of phenomenological moments, mindful that in adopting a stance of engaged and subjective objectivity, that attitude itself will influence the phenomena of engagement. That is, the nature of an engagement is influenced by all the dynamics in play. Phenomenological moments arise without warning but often as the result of careful attunement, preparation, and sensitivity to dynamics. They are moments of high emotional impact which result in a significant shift in thinking and awareness. They can be pleasant (surprising, exciting, exhilarating) or unpleasant (shocking, distressing), but their lasting impact upon thinking and feeling depends very much on how well they are understood and integrated by individuals.

Charles Darwin (1872/1965) noted the expression of universally recognizable affects in human beings. He argued that while there are idiosyncratic variations in the physiological expressions of those feelings, it is possible to recognize in humans the expression of basic affects such as fear, anger, surprise, anguish, shame, excitement, disgust, and joy.

In an empathic model of learning and therapy, attention needs to be given to the function of facial expression in intersubjective experiences (Ekman, 2003). The expressiveness of the face can mobilize engagements between people or it can thwart such engagements. While we rarely see our own expressions as we connect with others, their responses to us tell us who we are and signal how encounters can be modulated. Along with voice and body language, facial expressions can convey significant information to even severely brain-damaged people (Damasio, 2000) or those suffering from Alzheimer's disease (Crisp, 2000; Kitwood, 1997).

Given the many emotional, cognitive, and social disorders from which students can suffer, including autism and nonverbal learning disorder, education therapists and teachers can profitably share their professional expertise in the management of these students.

THE RATIONALE FOR EMPATHICALLY INTELLIGENT PRACTICE

Empathic intelligence creates the possibility that the ineffable might well become the visible and tangible, given the potential of imaginative minds to create and explore psychic new worlds. At its best, empathically intelligent practice can be transformative. It can mobilize tacit abilities, create affirming emotional templates for learning, and support the development of higher-order cognitive abilities through scaffolding and mirroring.

The positive influence of teacher quality upon pedagogy is well established through research. Hattie (2003) studied America's very best teachers to determine the attributes of excellence. His research shows that the student brings to the school context about 50% of the variance influencing student achievement, teachers account for approximately 30% variance, and factors such as peer effects, school principals, schools, and home account for 5 to 10% of the achievement variance. He argues that while resources are deployed to reducing class sizes, introducing new testing methods, encouraging parental assistance in the school, and focusing on problem students, "the greatest source of variance that can make the difference" (Hattie, 2003, p. 3) is the classroom teacher. Hattie argues "We need to ensure that the greatest influence is optimized to have powerful and sensationally positive effects on the learner (directing) attention at higher quality teaching, and higher expectations that students can meet appropriate challenges" (Hattie, 2003, p. 3). To that end, we need to "identify, esteem, and grow those who have powerful influences on student learning" (Hattie, 2003, p. 4).

INTELLIGENT CARING

It is argued here that part of understanding the phenomenon of intersubjective engagement is to recognize that learning is best achieved in a climate of care and mutual respect. Such care is offered, not imposed, and respects the human need for autonomy, self-determination, and challenge, as well as their need for security and safety in making mistakes.

Care involves more than a feeling or attitude of warmth toward a person or an experience. Intelligent caring embodies within it attention, engagement, and an assessment of the consequences of care. The intelligent carer is mindful of the context in which the need for care arises, and mindful of the need to offer support which mobilizes the other's coping strategies to circumvent the development of codependency. For example, engrossment in another's issues can swamp one's critical faculties and run counter to intelligent caring. Nonetheless, a capacity to engage with experience in an attuned, mindful way is necessary if one is to gather data and learn from experience. Without attention, engagement, and the application of intelligent caring intersubjective experiences are perfunctory. Intelligent caring can harness the psychic energy emanating from intersubjective warmth, attention, and engagement to modulate decision making in functional ways. It positions intersubjective and intrasubjective engagement as the foundation for transformative experience because it involves a considered modulation of both thought and feeling. Self-understanding is a precursor to empathic intelligence. In this model, care is modulated by intelligence and imagination which can anticipate consequences while recognizing the limitations of anticipation. Such intelligent caring can consider options within a context of multiple responsibilities; intelligent caring models self-reliance and mutuality.

Arguably, applied empathic intelligence and imagination not only liberates, it also humanizes. The American educational philosopher Martha Nussbaum (1995, 1997) argues that three capacities, above all, are essential for the cultivation of humanity in today's world:

First is the capacity for critical examination of oneself and one's traditions for living what, following Socrates, we may call "the examined life" … [Second] Citizens who cultivate their humanity need … an ability to see themselves not simply as citizens of some local region or group but also, and above all, as human beings bound to all other human beings by ties of recognition and concern…. The third ability of the citizen, closely related to the other two, can be called the narrative imagination. This means the ability to think what it might be like to be in the shoes of a person different from oneself, to be an intelligent reader of that person's story, and to understand the emotions and wishes and desires that someone so placed might have. (Nussbaum, 1997, pp. 9–11)

According to Nussbaum (1997), the cultivation of humanity means "learning how to be a human being capable of love and imagination" (p. 14). Further, she argues that when a child and a parent learn to tell stories together, sharing a sense of wonder,

the child is acquiring essential moral capacities … stories interact with (children's) own attempts to explain the world and their own actions in it. A child deprived of stories is deprived, as well, of certain ways of viewing other people. For the insides of people, like the insides of stars, are not open to view. (p. 89)

The habits of wonder promoted by storytelling thus define the other person as spacious and deep, with qualitative differences from oneself and hidden places worthy of respect. (p. 90)

Foucault (2000) posits a connection between care and curiosity:

I like the word [curiosity]; it suggests something quite different to me. It evokes "care"; it evokes the care one takes of what exists and what might exist: a sharpened sense of reality, but one that is never immobilized before it; a readiness to find what surrounds us strange and odd; … a passion for seizing what is happening now and what is disappearing; … I dream of a new age of curiosity. (p. 325)

Foucault suggests something of the attention, focus, and preparedness for risk-taking which can characterize the empathic stance. In that stance there is a heightened awareness to possibilities and a willingness to move beyond the known. In that sense, too, the empathic stance is both self-caring and other-caring, since both parties are crucial to the dynamic. The curious practitioner is likely to evoke students' curiosity, in both the attuned and caring sense of the word as it is elaborated here. Further, it requires something of an imaginative and poetic frame of mind to accept the crossing of boundaries evoked by this discussion of care and curiosity; a suspension of literal meaning in favor of a creative meaning.

THE ROLE OF MIRRORING IN THERAPY AND EDUCATION

Mirroring is a powerful form of self/other modulating. It is a means by which we develop identity, manage our relations with others and with our intersubjective world. Self psychologists such as Kohut (1982, 1985) and child development theorists such as Stern (1985) talk about mirroring as the process by which infants develop their sense of self, modulated by the feel of the mother's touch, sounds of her voice, and sight of her facial expressions. Mirroring is a dynamic intersubjective process by which we develop a sense of self as individuals and in relationship with others. It can occur in multiple social and emotional experiences such as viewing art, listening to music, reading novels, conversing with friends; wherever our thoughts and feelings are engaged in experiencing, and reinforced or modulated through the processes of experience. Self psychologists Rowe and Mac Isaac (1991) explore deeply the nature of empathic attunement as a technique of psychoanalytic self psychology, identifying the therapeutic effects of attuned engagements between therapists and clients. Allowing for the different purposes and settings of clinical and educational practice, the value of empathic attunement in both kinds of practice can be acknowledged.

Mirroring can function as an expression of bonding between individuals, and it can act as a form of unconscious or conscious reinforcement. Through tone of voice, gestures, silence, and facial expressions, therapists and teachers constantly mirror back to their clients and students how attuned they are and how they feel about them. Depending on the quality of engagement between the teacher or therapist and the student/client, mirroring processes will be powerful to positive or negative effect.

THE FUNCTION OF HOPE IN THERAPY AND EDUCATION

Of particular importance in mobilizing positive effects in students and clients is the function of hope. It is an emotion which exerts a powerful effect on students' and clients' capacity to mobilize coping and learning strategies. Hope has a natural affinity with empathic intelligence because it functions best as both a quality of feeling and thinking. In its feeling capacity it acknowledges the depth of another's aspirations, disappointments and efforts, in its thinking capacity it recognizes the function of denial, the value of introspection and insight, and the limits of rationality in mobilizing change. In its integrated capacity synthesizing both feeling and thought, it conveys a belief in the enduring nature of human growth, the persistence of psychic evolution, and belief in the tacit abilities of humans to mobilize internal resources in the service of survival and the search for meaning.

Even as I write this I recall my own adolescent dramas and my mother's reminder, "Life is very long and changes all the time. You never know what's around the corner." Even as I reminded her I had looked around that corner and didn't like what I saw, the robust part of me wanted to believe her, albeit I didn't admit that.

The mere presence of an attentive, attuned therapist or teacher with a deep-seated belief in the enduring nature of the human spirit, can mobilize hope. The therapist or teacher who can then model ways of thinking and feeling which build confidence and competence can be truly transformative. Elsewhere (Arnold, 2005) I have written about the role of narrative and the arts in developing imagination and opening our eyes to possibilities beyond the familiar. Likewise, therapists and teachers with imagination and flexibility can open their clients' eyes to possibilities beyond the known.

THE VALUES AND ETHICAL POSITION OF EMPATHIC INTELLIGENCE

Empathic intelligence is fundamentally a concept which values those human processes and systems designed to nourish high levels of human, social, intellectual, emotional, creative, and transformative experience. Inevitably, such transformative processes involve trust, mutual respect, participation in community life, tolerance of difference, equity, and transparency in the management of resources, respect for human dignity. and congruence between espoused values and behavior. Such values are affirmed to the extent that they enable humans to recognize and develop their potential to enhance their own lives and to contribute to the well-being of others as members of democratic communities. Such dialogues can have a cast of several characters as we reimagine the voices of those who have influenced us in the past, or we recall incidents which have been affecting. The processes involved in making the connections involved the kind of intra- and interpersonal intelligence that is of interest here. Empathic intelligence can work to maximize the benefits of both affectivity and rationality. It can guide therapists and educators in making decisions about mobilizing clients' or students' resources through appropriate interventions.

IN CONCLUSION

Empathically intelligent practice is a dynamic, democratic process engaging both the past and the present, the felt and the known, the tacit and the visible, kinetic and potential energy. Such practice harnesses complex intellectual, affective, and interpersonal skills, primarily for the benefit of students and others for whom its practitioners are responsible, and secondarily for the creative self-affirmation which can occur in the service of meeting others' needs.

Sustained achievement in intellectual and emotional development is enhanced by the informed encouragement, persistence, positive relationships, and mentoring offered by therapists and educators. It requires mental agility to be empathically intelligent; not unlike the mental agility needed to tell stories and to engage with them. Logic alone will not explain the most complex phenomena of life or the concept of empathic intelligence; rationality and emotion have to cooperate in the quest, along with self-understanding and complex cognitive and affective functioning.

Empathic intelligence is grounded in practice and intrinsically mobilized by speculation and imagination, It can be, therefore, both a defining and an enabling theory when practiced by deeply reflective professionals. The complexities of intersubjective and intra-subjective engagement affirm belief in the power of relationships to mobilize tacit abilities for deep learning. Such engagement draws on charity, or intelligent caring, as a principled strategy, and hope as an enabling affect in transformative learning.

REFERENCES

Arnold, R. (1993). The nature and role of empathy in human development and in drama in education. In W. Michaels, (Ed.), *Drama in education: The state of the art* (Vol. 2). Sydney, Australia: Educational Drama Association.

Arnold, R. (1994, November). The theory and principles of psychodynamic pedagogy. *Forum of Education, 49*(2), 21–33.

Arnold, R. (1998, December). The role of empathy in teaching and learning. *The Education Network, 14.*

Arnold, R. (2004). *Empathic intelligence: The phenomenon of inter-subjective engagement.* Paper presented at annual conference of Australian Association for Research in Education. Retrieved from http://www.aare.edu.au/04pap/arn04242.pdf

Arnold, R. (2005). *Empathic intelligence: Teaching, learning, relating.* Sydney, Australia: University of New South Wales Press.

Barnes, A., & Thagard, P. (1997). Empathy and analogy. *Dialogue: Canadian Philosophical Review, 36*(4), 705–720.

Barnett, M. A. (1987). Empathy and related responses in children. In N. Eisenberg & N. Strayer (Eds.), *Empathy and its development* (pp. 146–162). Cambridge, England: Cambridge University Press.

Berliner, D., & Calfee, R (Eds.). (1996). *Handbook of educational psychology.* New York: Simon & Schuster.

Bradford , E., & Lyddon W. J. (1994). Assessing adolescent and adult attachment: An update. *Journal of Counselling & Development, 73*(2), 215.

Bruner, J. S. (1972). *The relevance of education.* Harmondsworth, England: Penguin.

Bruner, J. S. (1986). *Actual minds, possible worlds.* Cambridge, MA: Harvard University Press.

Bruner, J. S. (1990). *Acts of meaning.* Cambridge, MA: Harvard University Press.

Buber, M. (1965). *Between man and man* (R. G. Smith Trans.). New York: Macmillan.

Bush, C., Mullis, R., & Mullis, A. (2000). Differences in empathy between offender and non-offender youth. *Journal of Youth and Adolescence, 29*(4), 467–478.

Carpenter, P. (2002). *Evidence of perception, cognition and individual differences.* Paper presented at Learning and the Brain Conference, Boston.

Code, L. (1995). I know just how you feel: Empathy and the problem of epistemic authority. In *Rhetorical spaces: Essays on gendered locations* (pp. 120–143). London: Routledge.

Crisp, J. (2000). *Keeping in touch with someone who has Alzheimer's.* Melbourne, Australia: Ausmed.

Damasio, A. (1994). *Descartes' error: Emotion, reason and the human brain.* New York: Grosset/Putnam.

Damasio, A. (2000). *The feeling of what happens: Body, emotion and the making of consciousness.* London: Vintage.

Damasio, A. (2003). *Looking for Spinoza: Joy, sorrow and the feeling brain.* Orlando, FL: Harcourt Books.

Darwin, C. (1965). *The expression of the emotions in man and animals.* Chicago: University of Chicago Press. (Original work published 1872)

Davia, C. (2002). *Minds, brains, chaos and catalysis: An ontological approach to the mind/brain problem.* Paper presented at Learning and the Brain Conference, Boston.

Davis, M. (1983). Measuring individual differences in empathy: Evidence for a multidimensional approach. *Journal of Personality and Social Psychology, 44*(1), 113–126.

Deigh, J. (1995) Empathy and universalization. *Ethics, 105,* 743–763.

Dewey, J. (1916). *Democracy and education: An introduction to the philosophy of education.* New York: Macmillan.

Dewey, J. (1963). *Freedom and culture.* New York: Capricorn Books. (Original work published 1939)

Dewey, J. (1964). *John Dewey: Selected writings.* (R. Archambault, Ed.). New York: Modern Library.

Dewey, J. (1971). *The child and the curriculum and the school and society.* Chicago: University of Chicago Press.

Duan, C., & Hill, D (1996). The current state of empathy research. *Journal of Counselling Psychology, 43*(3), 261–274.

Eisenberg, N., & Fabes, R.A. (1998). *Prosocial development: Handbook of child psychology* (5th ed., Vol. 3, pp. 701–778). New York: Wiley.

Eisenberg, N., & Strayer, J. (Eds.). (1996). *Empathy and its development.* Cambridge, England: Cambridge University Press.

Ekman, P. (2003). *Emotions revealed: Recognizing faces and feelings to improve communication and emotional life.* New York: Henry Holt.

Ellis, P. L. (1982). Empathy: A factor in antisocial behavior. *Journal of Abnormal Child Psychology, 10*(1), 123–134.

Feshbach, N. D. (1975). Empathy in children: Some theoretical and empirical considerations. *The Counseling Psychologist, 5*(2), 25–30.

Feshbach, N. D., & S. Feshbach (1987). Affective processes and academic achievement. *Child Development, 58,* 1335–1347.

Foucault, M. (2000). *Ethics: Subjectivity and truth* (Vol. 1). London: Penguin.

Gardner, H. (1983). *Frames of mind: The theory of multiple intelligences.* New York: Basic Books.

Gardner, H. (1985). *Leading minds: An anatomy of leadership* London: HarperCollins.

Gardner, H. (1993). *Creating minds.* New York: Basic Books.

Gardner, H. (1997). *Extraordinary minds.* London: HarperCollins.

Gladstein, G. (1983). Understanding empathy: Integrating counseling, developmental, and social psychology perspectives. *Journal of Counseling Psychology, 30*(4), 467–482.

Goldman, D. (1995). *Emotional intelligence: It can matter more than IQ.* London: Bloomsbury.

Goldman, D. (1998). *Working with emotional intelligence.* New York: Bantam Books.

Greenberg, L. S., Rice, L. N., & Elliott, R. (1993). *Facilitating emotional change: The moment-by-moment process.* New York: Guilford.

Greene, M (1995). *Releasing the imagination:Essays on education, the arts and social change.* San Francisco: Jossey-Bass.

Greene, M (1998). *A light in dark times and the unfinished conversation.* New York: Teachers College Press.

Greenson, R.R. (1960). Empathy and its vicissitudes. *International Journal of Psycho-Analysis, 41,* 418–424.

Hattie, J. (2003). *Teachers make a difference: What is the research evidence?* Australian Council for Educational Research. Retrieved from http://www.ecer.edu.au/documents

Hoffman, M. L. (1975). Children; discipline; interaction process analysis; moral development; parent child relationship; parent influence. *Developmental Psychology, 11*(2), 228–239.

Hoffman, M. L. (1977). Empathy: Its development and pro-social implications. In C. B. Keasly (Ed.), *Nebraska Symposium on Motivation* (Vol. 25, 169–218). Lincoln: University of Nebraska Press.

Hoffman, M. L. (1982). Development of pro-social motivation: Empathy and guilt. In N. Eisenberg (Ed.), *The development of pro-social behavior* (pp. 281–313). New York: Academic Press.

Hoffman, M. L. (1984a). The contribution of empathy to justice and moral judgment. In N. Eisenberg & J. Strayer, (Eds.), *Empathy and its development* (pp. 47–80). New York: Cambridge University Press.

Hoffman, M. L. (1984b). Interaction of affect and cognition in empathy. In C. E. Izard, J. Kagan, & R. B. Zajonc (Eds.), *Emotion, cognition, and behavior* (pp. 103–131). Cambridge, England: Cambridge University Press.

Hoffman, M. L. (2000). *Empathy and moral development: Implications for caring and justice.* New York: Cambridge University Press.

Isen, A. (1984). Towards understanding the role of affect in cognition. In R. Wyer & T. Srull (Eds.), *Handbook of social cognition* (pp. 179–237). Hillsdale, NJ: Erlbaum.

Katz, R. L. (1963). *Empathy: Its nature and uses.* London: Free Press of Glencoe.

Kestenbaum, R., Farber, E., & Sroufe, L. A. (1989). Individual differences in empathy among preschoolers: Concurrent and predictive validity. In N. Eisenberg (Ed.), *Empathy and related emotional responses: New directions for child development* (pp. 51–56). San Francisco: Jossey-Bass.

Kitwood, T. (1997). *Dementia revisited.* Buckingham, England: Open University Press.

Kohut, H. (1959). Introspection, empathy and psychoanalysis: An examination of the relationship between mode of observation and theory. *Journal of the American Psychoanalytic Association, 7*(3), 459–483.

Kohut, H (1971). *The analysis of the self.* New York: International Universities Press.

Kohut, H. (1979). The two analyses of Mr Z, Part 1. *The International Journal of Psycho-Analysis, 60,* 3–27.

Kohut, H. (1982). Introspection, empathy, and the semi-circle of mental health. *International Journal of Psycho-Analysis, 63,* 395–407.

Kohut, H. (1985). *Self psychology and the humanities.* New York: Norton.

LeDoux, J. (1992). Emotion and the amygdala. In A. P. Agglington (Ed.), *The amygdala: Neurobiological aspects of emotion, memory and emotional dysfunction* (pp. 339–351). New York: Wiley-Liss.

LeDoux, J. (1996). *The emotional brain: The mysterious underpinnings of emotional life.* New York: Simon & Schuster.

LeDoux, J. (2003). *Synaptic self: How our brains become who we are.* New York: Penguin Books.

Mayer, J., & Salovey, P. (1997). What is emotional intelligence? In P. Salovey & D. Sluyter. (Eds.), *Emotional development and emotional intelligence: Educational implications* (pp. 3–31). New York: Basic Books.

Mead, G. H. (1934). *Mind, self and society: From the standpoint of a social behaviorist.* Chicago: University of Chicago Press.

Mendes, E. (2003). What empathy can do. *Educational Leadership, 61*(1), 56–59.

Nicolson, S. (2009). *A self study of a teacher's empathic attunement* (Doctoral thesis, University of Sydney, Australia).

Noddings, N. (1988). An ethic of caring and its implications for instructional arrangements. *American Journal of Education, 96*(2), 215–230.

Noddings, N. (1993). *Educating for intelligent belief or unbelief.* New York: Teachers College Press.

Noddings, N. (1998). Ethics and the imagination. In W. Ayers & J. L. Miller (Eds.), *A light in dark times and the unfinished conversation: Maxine Greene (pp.* 159–169). New York: Teachers College Press.

Noddings, N. (2005, June). Identifying and responding to needs in education. *Cambridge Journal of Education, 35*(2), 147–159.

Nussbaum, M. (1995). *Poetic justice: The literary imagination and public life.* Boston: Beacon Press.

Nussbaum, M. (1997). *Cultivating humanity: A classical defense of reform in liberal education,* Cambridge, MA: Harvard University Press.

Pecukonis, E V. (1990). A cognitive/affective empathy training program as a function of ego development in aggressive adolescent females. *Adolescence, 25*(7), 59–76.

Pigman, G. W. (1995). Freud and the history of empathy. *International Journal of Psychoanalysis, 76*(Pt 2), 237–256.

Polanyi, M. (1959). *The study of man.* Chicago: University of Chicago Press.

Polanyi, M. (1969). *Knowing and being—Essays by Michael Polanyi* (M. Greene, Ed.). Chicago: University of Chicago Press.

Polanyi, M. (1974). *Personal knowledge: Towards a post-critical philosophy.* Chicago: University of Chicago Press.

Polanyi, M. (1983). *The tacit dimension.* Gloucester, MA: Peter Smith.

Reed, G. S. (1984). *Empathy.* Hillsdale, NJ: Erlbaum.

Rogers, C. R. (1959). A theory of therapy, personality and interpersonal relationships as developed in the client-centered framework. In S. Koch (Ed.), *Psychology: A study of a science. Study 1. Conceptual and systematic: Vol. 3. Formulations of the person and the social context* (pp. 184–256). New York: McGraw-Hill.

Rogers, C.R. (1962). The interpersonal relationship: The core of guidance. *Harvard Educational Review, 32,* 416–429.

Rogers, C. R. (1975). Empathy: An unappreciated way of being. *The Counseling Psychologist, 5,* 2–10.

Rose, S. (1993). *The making of memory.* Toronto, Canada: Bantam Books.

Rose, S. (Ed.). (1998). *From brains to consciousness: Essays on the new science of the mind.* Princeton, NJ: Princeton University Press.

Rowe, C. E., & Mac Isaac, D. S. (1991). *Empathic attunement: The technique of psychoanalytic self psychology.* London: Jason Aronson.

Schafer, R. (1959). Generative empathy in the treatment situation. *Psychoanalytic Quarterly, 28,* 342–373.

Stern, D. (1985). *The interpersonal world of the infant.* New York: Basic Books.

Strayer, J. (1987). Affective and cognitive perspectives on empathy. In N. Eisenberg & J. Strayer (Eds.), *Empathy and its development* (pp. 218–244). New York: Cambridge University Press.

Tansey, M. J., & Burke, W. (1989). *Understanding counter-transference: From projective identification to empathy.* London: Analytic Press.

Verducci, S. (2000a). A conceptual history of empathy and a question it raises for moral education. *Educational Theory, 50*(1), 63–79.

Verducci, S. (2000b). A moral method? Thoughts on cultivating empathy through Method acting. *Journal of Moral Education, 29*(1), 87–99.

Vischer, F. (1994). *Empathy, form and space: Problems in German aesthetics 1873–1893* (H. F. Mallgrave & E. Ikonomou, Eds.). Los Angeles: The Getty Center for the History of Art and the Humanities.

Vygotsky, L. (1978). *Mind in society: The development of higher psychological processes.* Cambridge, MA: Harvard University Press.

Vygotsky, L. S. (1987). *The collected works of L. S. Vygotsky* (Vol. 1). New York: Plenum.

Vygotsky, L. S. (1988). *Thought and language.* Cambridge, MA: Harvard University Press

Williams, L. (2001, April 4). *The emotional brain.* Address to Science Forum, University of Sydney, Australia.

5

EDUCATIONAL THERAPY ACROSS THE LIFESPAN
The Case of Amy

MAXINE FICKSMAN

Far away in the sunshine are my highest aspirations. I may not reach them, but I can look up and see the beauty, believe in them and try to follow where they lead.

(Louisa May Alcott, 1994, p. 42)

INTRODUCTION

The dynamic profession of educational therapy cultivates life-altering experiences for both the client and educational therapist. Helping others reach their potential engenders profound satisfaction and joy for everyone. Educational therapists possess keen intuitive and empathic skills. Through the years, these skills become deeper, integrating into their daily lives.

At times I have been accused of being overly optimistic about a student. Some may consider this a negative comment, but it is a great compliment; children have unrealized potential that educational therapists can help nurture and develop. Self-confidence, resiliency (Brooks & Goldstein, 2001), curiosity, motivation, self-advocacy, and active learning are long-range psychoeducational goals that educational therapists strive for with their clients. We have the luxury of working with our students over a span of time often from a few months to several years. Sometimes our relationship with a student and family is so special in that we have the good fortune to view their growth throughout their lifespan. We guide our clients as they take on their role of independent learners, transitioning into junior and senior high school and preparing for college. By sharing that long range perspective with other clients' parents, we help them feel more comfortable in setting realistic yet optimistic long range goals for their children.

Through our collaborative efforts, ETs often assist allied professionals, teachers, and other school personnel in viewing these students as perhaps developmentally delayed, certainly not lazy, and likely to be more capable than they seem at that moment in time. By helping to lessen the math, reading, and writing anxiety, morning and evening bedlam, disorganization disasters, and other similar issues, we provide solutions to match or fit the individual student, family, home, and school situations. Barbara Keogh (1995) notes that, "Professional advice is effective when it is congruent with the child's characteristics, meaningful to the family, and easily incorporated into the family daily routine" (p. 15).

Each case is unique. Like an ocean voyage, there are storms and lulls. While our clients encourage us to pursue the shortest route, the most direct path is often met with resistance as a result of unexpected life and environmental circumstances. The passage can be tumultuous and then calm; it ebbs and flows. Change is inherent in the process, and is organic and dynamic like the sea. But at the end of the journey, in most cases, students become autonomous learners who are proactive and ready for life's challenges.

While I began my clinical educational therapy experiences simultaneously working with clients in a clinical psychologist's office, a speech and language clinic, and as a volunteer with at risk adolescents in the juvenile justice system, it was apparent to me that as a self-starter I particularly enjoyed working in private practice. Initially, working with students in their home environment gave me great insight into the family dynamic, which allowed me to provide parents with firsthand advice for structuring their child's homework time and space. Unfortunately, there was often not a quiet place for us. Siblings, curious about our work, would find excuses for interrupting us. Sometimes parents would try to use our time as their opportunity to leave—a convenient babysitting service. More importantly, the inability to predict how a session might progress, along with the space limitations of my car, forced me to compromise my selection of materials for each student. I soon realized that I could better serve my clients with an office in my home. For me, my home office is ideal. My environment is inviting, safe, and quiet. Bookshelves lining my office walls convey my love of reading while my colorful puppets and a wide assortment of games for every skill level contribute to my aphorism that learning is exciting. In lieu of working in the student's house, home visits for my students are incorporated into the study skills component of my practice.

THE CASE OF AMY

The following is the case study of Amy, beginning with my initial meeting with her parents. My work with her as an educational therapist commenced in fourth grade and continued, sometimes sporadically, through high school, allowing me to observe her growth, her challenges, and her successes through her lifelong journey. Identities have been changed to maintain confidentiality.

Meeting Amy's Parents

When Amy's mother called me to discuss the possibility of working with her child, she impressed me with her understanding of educational therapy. Amy had already worked with an excellent educational therapist who moved to another state. According to Mother, Amy was a late reader, but reportedly blossomed more than any other student her teacher ever had in second grade. Amy's parents, who were both professionals, came to our meeting, as per my instructions, well-prepared with a copy of the recent neuropsychological evaluation, the previous end-of-year standardized test results, and samples of Amy's current writing, reading, and math classroom achievement.

Both parents spoke candidly of their daughter's strengths as well as weaknesses. They knew she was smart, empathic, and intuitive and were hoping I could help make her life in school a bit easier. They saw her vulnerabilities as being unsophisticated and clumsy, and her stronger suits as loving fantasy play, art, and reading. The strength and support of family was very important to them all.

Amy had been on medication for ADHD for one year; the medication had been updated recently. Mother selected a psychiatrist, who in addition to overseeing the medication, would be someone Amy could feel comfortable discussing issues with even as an adult. This would prove to be a wise decision later in Amy's development. Amy was the oldest child in the family, and had two younger siblings, one with some learning issues and another who seemed to sail through school with ease. Her parents seemed very open and willing to accept suggestions. They reported Amy had been tested in second grade in her neighborhood public elementary school and the individual education plan (IEP) indicated that she met criteria for a specific learning disability due to the significant discrepancy between her cognitive functioning and her achievement in written language, reading recognition, and math. According to both parents, her fourth grade teacher reported Amy had difficulty with following directions, sequencing information, computing and analyzing math problems, spelling, synthesizing information, recognizing and determining saliency, taking timed tests, copying from the board and paper, as well as reading social cues. Her writing pace was slower than average. We discussed these issues and my background and experience in handling students with these types of weaknesses.

The parents agreed to have me work with their child (once a week due to their financial situation), and we discussed ways to assure they would feel communication between us would be effective. This initial meeting allowed the parents to tell their story and begin the first step of building the important bridges between us (Briggs, 1998). Please note here that I do not add to my practice more than one new client every few weeks so that I can focus completely on this new client, family, school, and environment. Each time educational therapists begin working with a new student, additional hours are required for us to listen with our third ear (Reik, 1948) to parents, teachers, and allied professionals' remarks, read reports, and then synthesize all the information to create an educational therapy plan. This plan is continually reevaluated by discussions and meetings with parents and client, teachers, and allied professionals, as well as school and home visits (Bronfenbrenner, 1979).

Meeting Amy

Cherubic Amy threw open my front door, and exuberantly yelled, "Hi." I had just completed my previous session with another student who was waiting for his parent to return. It was apparent that my student was puzzled by this unusual girl. I introduced them to each other by first name, and told my previous student that he could read while he was waiting for his parent and led Amy to my office. As we walked into my office, I told her how pleased I was to meet her. Once in my office and not within earshot of my other student, I gently suggested that next time she arrives, to close the door behind her. After all, I was sure she didn't want any of the lizards or rabbits coming into the house. We giggled together. Amy was special. She had an unsophisticated optimism about her that was so refreshing to me but not quite so appealing to her fourth grade classmates.

Amy had blonde curls, sparkling blue eyes, and a peaches and cream complexion with deep dimples. She walked clumsily, slightly tilting her head to one side. Amy talked incessantly and had difficulty giving eye contact when she talked, although her verbal ability was exceptional. Immediately I was drawn to her and I secretly hoped she would become a poet. At 10 years of age, during our initial session, Amy wrote her three wishes: This is how her work appeared unedited: (*"What will you wish for?" the genie with a voice like booming thunder asked again. I paused once more and then after thinking told it.*)

My wishes:

I wish for world peace, so that no one will get hurt and people can talk things out sensabley

I wish away pollution and global warming so the earth and all its creatures may survive.

And now one wish for myself I would like to do something no one has ever done, not something that people think of like living on the moon but something nobody has ever thought of.

Amy titled her paper *The Green Dense Mist.* It took her about 10 minutes to do this project and, during that time, she verbalized to help herself stay on task.

Amy chose pencil rather than markers for her drawing of her family. She preferred the texture of the pencil. I didn't ask her to draw everyone doing something so she drew her family standing in a row in order from right to left: Mom, Dad, Amy, and two siblings. Everyone had long necks, developed bodies, including specific clothing and shoes, fingers, hair, and facial features. Her parents had their arms around each other and everyone else was almost touching. Amy had a lovely short dress on with a bow at the neckline and short slightly ruffled sleeves. She drew Dad wearing a belt and two pockets on his pants and Mom had a design on her shirt and pants. The facial features of all the family members were very simple: dots for eyes and nose, and a curved line for the smiling mouths. The ears were hidden by the long hair she drew on each of them. Everyone's hair and clothing looked different. An enormous fish tank filled with several different types of fish and plants sat on a table nearby. She drew her other pets at the top of the page. Amy's drawing depicted her as bright, developmentally mature, and secure in her loving family.

In addition to the aforementioned activities, my first session with students also includes an interest inventory and additional academic activities to highlight their strengths and weaknesses. The 3 Wishes activity gave me great insight into Amy's expressive strengths and weak mechanics. She also completed a few computational problems and word problems so I could view her approach to the tasks. Amy appeared tentative in her multiplication and division skills and she seemed reluctant to employ her verbal skills when calculating word problems. Throughout our session, Amy appeared focused and motivated. My sessions typically end with a game of the student's choice. Providing students with opportunities to make decisions helps build our trusting relationship. Before leaving, I asked Amy if she would like to continue our work together, and she agreed to return.

The Neuropsychological Report

According to the neuropsychologist's report completed when Amy was in the third grade, Mother reported bleeding during the first six months of her pregnancy. Amy was born with the cord around her neck, but with no apparent complications. She weighed 8 pounds, and was reported as having the usual childhood illnesses. She did not have high fevers or traumatic incidents. Her developmental milestones were reported as age appropriate. Before the age of 2 Amy became easily frustrated, with a low threshold for crying. Both parents completed graduate degrees with no indication of learning issues. Assessments reported that Amy had a significant 28-point discrepancy between her very superior verbal

IQ and her average performance IQ. Her visual sequencing, visual-motor integration, pencil paper skills, and visual memory were areas of weakness. Amy also demonstrated difficulty in following multistep directions in a variety of modalities. Her assessment revealed that her specific weaknesses impacted her spelling, mathematical reasoning, and numerical operation skills. There was considerable discussion of Amy's highly developed language skills and sweet personality obscuring her learning differences in the classroom. Educational therapy and a medical evaluation for ADHD were recommended. Today, Amy would be classified as a gifted student with learning issues, twice exceptional (Baum & Owen, 2004). There was no mention in the report of executive function as we know it today, but as she progressed in school, Amy exhibited obvious weaknesses in the areas of initiation, planning, and organization.

After my first session with Amy, I asked her parents for approval to speak with the neuropsychologist who tested her. They had already provided the written report to me at our initial parent meeting. In speaking with the neuropsychologist, it became apparent he did not share my optimism about this case. The examiner felt Amy's prognosis was grim. He envisioned her continually needing support throughout life and experiencing difficulty recognizing social cues. I felt as though we had seen two different Amy's. I worked with students who had been assessed by this neuropsychologist in the past and remembered that he tended to be overly pessimistic about students who were diagnosed with nonverbal learning disabilities. These were the students with significant discrepancies between verbal and performance modes. They exhibited weaknesses in saliency determination, visual/motor performance, and recognizing social cues (Palombo, 2006). Perhaps the neuropsychologist's less optimistic prognosis was a result of his tendency to focus on Amy's weak test scores. Educational therapists tend to look at the strengths, weaknesses, and beyond to the contextual elements of the particular case. Amy's supportive family bolstered her strong verbal abilities and motivation. I continued my positive attitude with this case and reserved judgment on the neuropsychologist's confidential opinion for our periodic reevaluations.

The Dynamic of our Sessions

In the framework of our one-hour weekly session, it was particularly important to prioritize our goals. When I first began working with Amy, we addressed what I refer to as daily skills. Amy had not yet mastered the months of the year, seasons, her address, and phone numbers. Reaching this goal was important to Amy and her parents. We discussed how some people just have great memories and don't have to work hard to learn these things while others do need to actively work on these skills. I told Amy that while it seems that people who memorize these facts seem very smart, it was more important to have a brain like hers that thinks on a very high level. I added that in college her brain would be the one most appreciated. She smiled. I assured her she would be able to learn this within the next month, and she was agreeable.

Providing a goal within a structured period of time helped motivate Amy. We devoted about 10 minutes per session for the first month of our work on these items, using all the senses to help her master this information. For the months and seasons, we sang a song and she drew a picture of the salient points of each season with the specific months included. For example, for summer, she drew people swimming in the ocean with the sun shining; and, for winter, she drew people skiing on a snowy mountain with hats, scarves, and snowsuits. She loved songs that described the months of the year and number of days in the months. To learn her address and phone number, she pictured it in her head, wrote it in the air, and then on the whiteboard, simultaneously verbalizing the information. By the 4th week, she had learned all these important facts and was very proud of her accomplishments. Of course, we continued to review these concepts periodically for several months to verify mastery.

Addressing Amy's writing issues, mechanical as well as expressive, was another top priority for our work together. Amy's spelling weaknesses were a result of her developmental writing and reading lag. To remediate Amy's spelling skills we concentrated on syllables, word origins, and meanings. Amy's spelling test scores were adequate so we did not address the weekly spelling words. Usually a conceptual leap occurs around sixth grade after writing and reading more often and for longer periods, improving spelling proficiency and automaticity. As Amy wrote longer stories, became an avid reader, and focused on her poetry, her spelling did improve.

While Amy verbalized complicated stories, her writing pace was so slow that she tended to shorten her writing to meet classroom time limits. My greatest concern for this type of student is that she loses her self-confidence and feels she is a poor writer. Once this occurs, it is difficult to overcome the pain and potential shame. We continually discussed how she was a gifted writer who had some difficulty with her pace, and that she would overcome that by the end of the year. Providing a timeframe helped Amy feel this goal was achievable. We worked on speed writing exercises to improve her pace. Since she also had difficulty copying from the board and paper, Amy practiced holding at least four letters in her head at once and then looking back at the board or paper to complete the word. Often, these children copy one letter at a time greatly slowing their production and giving them a headache with the constant head-turning. This activity also improves the student's visual memory. Additionally, I introduced her to webs, Venn diagrams, and other graphic organizers to help her plan and structure her thoughts for longer assignments. She also learned how to write a brief outline in the margin of her paper as a reminder of the different ideas she wanted to write about in her essay. These strategies helped Amy lessen her anxiety and feel more self-confident about her writing. By the end of the school year, Amy's writing pace improved, and she was able to write lengthy stories and essays in class with some additional time accommodations agreed upon and provided by her teacher.

Throughout our work together, saliency determination skills were addressed. Children with nonverbal learning disabilities exhibit difficulty distinguishing between incidental details and main ideas in all aspects of their lives. I helped Amy employ a multiprong metacognitive approach to address saliency in reading comprehension (including math and content areas), receptive and expressive language, written expression, as well as social interaction and organization.

Screening for irrelevant information became one of our main goals. For example, in the area of reading comprehension for various genres and subjects, activities involving determining the main idea were utilized; in the area of receptive language, activities involving note taking and chunking strategies were employed; in the area of written language, graphic organizers, and strategies comparing creative and expository writing were explored; in the areas of expressive oral language and social interaction, role playing was utilized; and in the area of organization, techniques using charts, timelines, and calendars were introduced. Taking this global approach helped Amy realize the impact of saliency determination on so many aspects of her life. Increasing her self-awareness helped Amy proactively apply these metacognitive strategies. To ascertain the effectiveness of the generalization of our work to both home and school, regular check-ins with the teacher and parents were scheduled through phone calls with me.

For most of fourth grade, we addressed Amy's weaker visual spatial issues, which affected her math skills relating to time, fractions, and measurement. According to her teacher and parents, Amy seemed very anxious when working on math problems of all kinds. I explained that since Amy was so creative, mathematics did not come as naturally to her. However, through her strong verbal and thinking skills, we decreased Amy's math anxiety and heightened her self-confidence. By previewing math concepts and the vocabulary required for math, Amy was more willing to participate in class. Increased self-confidence in class also helped her maintain focus for longer periods of time. Amy had particular difficulty with part-to-whole geometric problems. For example, when attempting to compute the area of part of a shaded geometric figure, she could not "see" why she needed to subtract the area of the smaller geometric shape from the area of the larger one. We created similar shapes on a blank piece of paper and cut the smaller shape from the larger so she could see how they could be separated and then put back together to create the larger figure. We simplified the process by using rectangular shapes and then progressed to the more complicated. I also taught her additional strategies including how to break down multistep word problems by substituting two and three digit numbers with simple one digit numbers, utilizing mnemonic acronyms such as DMSB for division steps, and identifying and then circling key words in word problems to determine which process or processes needed to be employed for solving the problems. Amy particularly enjoyed assuming the role of the teacher, and enjoyed teaching a recently learned concept to me. We giggled when she found my errors and corrected me.

For time concepts, we created word problems that used her name and her daily activities so they would be more relevant for her. We addressed borrowing in subtraction using measurement and time outside the 10 base system, an aspect of subtraction that usually was not given proper attention for our students. For example, when subtracting in feet and inches, she learned how to borrow 1 foot and convert that to 12 inches and then subtract. Using her strong verbal skills, Amy vocalized the steps and practiced retrieving them in subsequent sessions.

Having several methods and strategies on hand for solving a specific problem helped Amy feel less anxious when confronted with a test. Employing her high level verbal skills, Amy learned strategies to help her cope when she would "get stuck." Some teachers felt her cognitive inflexibility was a stubborn quality. In fact, her parents had reported that Amy's first grade teacher unkindly nicknamed her "Donkey." But, sweet Amy was misunderstood. She had difficulty with cognitive shifting, often a behavior of children with ADHD and weakness in executive functioning (Meltzer, 2007).

Getting stuck was particularly noticeable when Amy perceived an assignment as difficult. One day, in fifth grade, we were working on long division, a challenge for many students. Amy's weakness in sequencing caused her to make many errors. While computing a two-place long division problem, Amy mistakenly wrote the answer in the subtraction part of the problem. When I tried to help her understand why it was incorrect, she became quite obstinate. Although Amy's parents had described this behavior they observed at home, it was the first time I had personally experienced it. So, I sat back, paused for about a minute and said, "Amy, how long do you think I have been working with students in math?"

She thought and said, "I don't know but I'm sure it's several years."

I replied, "More than 20 years. I think right now you are getting stuck. Do you know what that means?"

Amy thought about it and said she didn't. I told her I wanted her to really think about how she was feeling. I suggested that we review what had just happened. She was computing a problem and I was trying to help her with it so that she could find the answer. The way she was computing the problem, the answer would not be correct. I showed her, after we did the problem together correctly, how she could check the problem using multiplication. But I stressed how important this session had become because now she would know when she was getting stuck so she could "unstick" herself. This was an epiphany for her, and for me. Amy could use her well-developed verbal skills to navigate the cognitive shifts and she would be in charge of this demystification!

The next session, we reviewed the sequence for division utilizing the DMSB acronym as well as encouraging Amy to verbalize the steps aloud. Additionally, we worked on strategies Amy could utilize to evaluate her performance on the math tests. My students are encouraged to learn from their mistakes by reviewing the types of errors they make and finding strategies to avoid committing the same type of errors on subsequent tests. In Amy's case as with many others, she wrote the numbers so small and on top of a line, that careless errors were inevitable. I showed her how to space the numbers between the lines on the page or the boxes of the graph paper so they are very large and easily read. We also carefully read all the directions and reviewed how she should circle the key words and signs for the next test. The next session, Amy proudly showed me her math test with a grade of B! Amy continued to have moments of difficulty with cognitive shifts, but the intensity and duration gradually lessened.

After a year of working on developing math strategies, Amy accepted that she could be a strong math student. When the teacher introduced a new concept, Amy was able to feel confident enough to focus on it, and grasp the idea with enthusiasm. At our next meeting, Amy's parents expressed their satisfaction with her progress and appreciation for our work together. Although I would have liked to continue working with Amy, they decided to take a break mid-fifth grade. In the beginning of sixth grade, I received a note from Amy's mom telling me everything seemed to be going well and thanking me for the work we had accomplished. Mom took on the role of case manager during this time.

Organizational Turbulence

A call came from Mother in the middle of sixth grade; Amy seemed to have more difficulty with organization. We discussed how some teachers have organizational styles that match specific students, the reverse being true as well. Adapting to the teacher's learning style could be a learning experience for Amy, and with my help, she would become better organized. In a telephone conversation with her teacher, I learned Amy was not handing in some of her math assignments. Mother described it as going into a "tailspin for some unknown reason." When Mother asked Amy's teacher what she was having a problem with, the teacher's reply was "everything." The teacher, according to the Mother, said that Amy seems "totally baffled and cannot seem to focus on the concepts." She seemed to have improved for a while and then regressed to forgetting work, losing assignments, and bringing the wrong books to class. It was obvious the teacher was frustrated with Amy, and Amy was frustrated with herself. The teacher and I planned a time when I could make a classroom visit. This was also a time for me to reconnect with the psychiatrist to discuss school behaviors and the efficacy of Amy's medication. In the doctor's opinion, the medication was working effectively so we approached the organizational issues from an educational therapy perspective.

Amy and I resumed weekly educational therapy sessions. During the first meeting, I asked Amy for her interpretation of what was and was not working in school. She told me that in the last 2 weeks she misunderstood some of the teacher's directions so she did not hand in some of her homework. She was having difficulty with all of her papers. Sometimes she would leave them in her desk at school and then would not have them for her work at home and vice versa. At one of our sessions, she confided to me: "I wish I could do all my work, and then go into a time warp and go back in time and hand the work to myself all finished so I could have all the leisure time I want."

Amy and I discussed how important it was for her to be better organized so she could have the wished-for leisure time, and also so she could have a smooth transition to middle school. This is about the time when the curriculum advances in conceptual thinking—layers and layers of thought. We met with Amy's mother and devised a plan. They color coded her books and binders by subject. Amy agreed to clean out her desk and binders every week. She stored tests and papers in file folders, arranged by subject. With my help, Amy came up with a checklist for her materials and homework, organized by subject, and then placed in her backpack for school the next day. Amy was in charge of arranging everything she needed for school in her backpack the night before, and placed it by the door where she would exit in the morning. Mother could easily see the backpack at the door as a check before retiring for the night.

Amy said, "My desk stays neat for a week then it looks like a hurricane came through." During one of the sessions, Amy brainstormed about "Ways to keep my desk more orderly". Her "Solutions," as she named them, were (unedited):

Sort out the papers and books and throw away things I don't want

Arrange magazines and books on my empty shelves

Once a week I will clean my desk

Often I just slump things onto my desk. I need to put it back where it belongs.

Some of the stuff belongs to my brother so I should tell him not to leave stuff in my room.

All of the above (Just kidding)

Organization was frustratingly difficult for Amy and she still managed to keep her sense of humor! Each week, Mother, Amy, and I had a conversation about her work getting to and from home and these strategies seemed to work. Amy was now in charge of her work and successfully handling it.

Fostering Relationships

Amy and I had developed a trusting relationship so she felt comfortable discussing her social issues with me. She confided that sometimes she felt "out of the group." When I spoke with her teacher, she told me Amy was showing improvement but sometimes she would hold back and have difficulty initiating conversation. Students who have fewer play dates find they have fewer reasons to connect and converse with their classmates.

In addition to our conversational work and role playing activities, I usually suggest to parents of children who have difficulty initiating conversations that they select or create a group activity their child will embrace. Often this can foster new or renewed friendships as students will meet other classmates who share similar interests. Amy's mother decided to form a book club for Amy and some of her friends. It was a wonderful idea and seemed to help Amy strengthen friendships with some of the other students in her class. Having Mom available and willing to support my suggestions was integral to the success of this case.

In sixth grade, students who apply to secondary private schools, take the ISEE exam. While I do not coach students to take the exam, I help demystify the exam, review the format, and guide them through the essay process. Amy's parents were eager for her to attend a specific academically competitive secondary school. Having a personal relationship with the educational therapist on staff, I agreed to talk with her about Amy. While this particular school always prided itself in taking children with some differences, I had the distinct impression from my colleague that, upon her interview, Amy was not viewed as a student who would fit in. It was surprising since she had scored extremely well on her ISEE: 99% in verbal, 98% in verbal comprehension, 92% in quantitative ability, and 69% in math achievement. While Amy's scores were certainly high enough for her to be easily accepted into this school, it was apparent that at this point in time, Amy appeared, from the faculty's perspective, "socially different" from the other students on campus. Amy and her parents chose another competitive school with a middle/high school combination. Amy and her family planned an extended holiday that summer and looked forward to Amy attending this new school in the fall.

Since Amy continued to make significant progress with her math and organizational skills and her teacher reported strong progress across all areas, Amy's parents decided she could take a break at the end of sixth grade and begin seventh grade at this new school without my assistance. I try to help parents understand that the transition from elementary to middle school can be quite challenging for most of my students. Parents often do not realize how traumatic school transitions can be for individuals with learning issues. Over the years while working as an educational therapist, my understanding of parents' feelings and needs has become more realistic. I suggest options to my parents and then they decide whether to continue educational therapy. We need to help our parents perceive our resource role as nonjudgmental so they will continue to feel comfortable asking for advice. If the child needs additional help at a later time, the ongoing trusting relationship may permit parents to reach out to their educational therapist. In this case, Amy and her parents decided to let Amy try to handle this new experience on her own. Of course, I hoped Amy would feel strong enough to handle the demands of middle school. Mother kept in close contact with me and Amy seemed to manage the beginning of seventh grade well.

A Distress Call

During the second semester of seventh grade, often a turbulent time, I received another call from Amy's parents. She was becoming overwhelmed and not performing as well in school as everyone had hoped. Of course I agreed to see Amy again. While Amy had grown tall and I almost did not recognize this lovely young lady, our trusting relationship appeared intact. We discussed which aspects of school Amy felt were and were not successful. At the end of the session, we planned a home visit so I could observe Amy's homework environment and make some suggestions for improvement.

Amy worked upstairs in her bedroom. Her room was well lit except for her desk area. She worked on a lovely antique desk but Mother and she agreed it didn't work well with the computer equipment she needed. So, Mother offered to find another desk for the computer and a better arrangement with a lamp that could provide better light as well as containers for her materials and a cabinet for her files. Then we tackled Amy's shelves and other areas where she kept many interesting collections. We discussed how she could better store them so they were out of her sight when she was working. I left feeling Amy would take my advice and quickly make effective changes.

In the next few weeks, Amy reported her progress. Amy boxed her collections and odds and ends that she did not need on a daily basis and set up a filing cabinet with her tests and papers that could remain at home. A new large desk and two new lamps had arrived and Amy now had plenty of room for her computer and materials with proper lighting. She even took pictures to show me how wonderful everything looked.

At this time, Amy's younger sibling was exhibiting difficulty with learning. The parents had their child tested and so asked if I would take the child on as a client as well. We discussed my policy—I do not work with siblings of my clients. I have found this policy important for me, and especially so for the family and my client. As educational therapists, we establish a trusting relationship with our clients, and if we work with a sibling, that relationship can be compromised. Our first allegiance is to our current client. Often, there are hidden issues that wouldn't even surface as long as we refer the sibling to another educational therapist. I told the parents I appreciated their request but it is my policy not to work with siblings. We discussed other educational therapists in the area that I thought might be a good match for their child. While it may be more difficult for the parents to transport their children to two different educational therapists, parents generally report being pleased with the outcomes.

At the end of seventh grade, Amy confided that she was learning about the music her schoolmates enjoyed. She played an instrument in the orchestra and loved classical music. Amy decided that by finding out about the kind of music her classmates preferred, she would have another topic of conversation with them. She told me sometimes it was difficult for her to feel that she belonged in the group when they discussed their favorite music and bands because she did not have anything to contribute. I told her how proud I was that she was being proactive in finding ways to improve herself. Our work in initiating and sustaining conversations with others who may not share the same interests gave her the confidence she needed. Here again, her verbal intelligence helped her navigate the social environment more effectively.

In eighth grade, Amy's parents decided to again apply to other secondary schools that might nurture her writing prowess beginning in ninth grade. This was a particularly difficult year for Amy because her English teacher was frustrated by what she perceived as Amy's lack of attention in following directions and proofreading. Amy was unable to attain a grade of A in English. She received a perfect score for her content, but not for spelling or following directions. For example, Amy had to complete a journal in which she composed original poems and writings as well as critical reviews of assigned literature, for which she received a grade of A for her content. She misspelled a word in the title of one of the short stories she reviewed, and lost further points for each of the eight times she misspelled the same word. The teacher directed the students to scotch tape their papers in a specific way. Unfortunately, Amy forgot this and stapled her pages together which led to a grade of D for the mechanics section and a B for the entire project. This scenario repeated itself many times over the course of years at this school and frustrated all of us, particularly Amy. Rather than judged on her writing, she was judged on her weak executive functioning skills.

In seventh grade science class Amy adored her teacher, and throughout the year, she maintained the highest grade in the class. Unfortunately, the eighth grade science teacher was more inconsistent in her methods and Amy had great difficulty following the format. She assigned more multiple choice tests and fewer projects, so that memorization was emphasized instead of conceptual understanding. All the teachers in this school graded on a point system. If more than two homework assignments were missing this could lower a grade considerably. Amy had been ill for a few days and her science teacher would not allow her a few extra days to make up her work. Amy's self-advocacy skills were unsuccessful, so I suggested to Mother that she needed to intervene. I consider myself the third level of advocacy when both student's and parent's pleas are ignored. At Mother's request, I spoke with the science teacher but she seemed unwilling to accept my pleas as well.

By the end of the semester, Amy received a B in the science and English courses. For ninth grade, Amy's parents (with Amy in agreement) transferred her to a public magnet school where she could receive 504 accommodations such as untimed tests and allowances for her spelling and clerical miscues. Amy thrived at this school. She loved playing in the large school orchestra. Several of her writings were sent to children's magazines and published. The larger number of students in ninth grade gave her more choices, thus extending her circle of friends. For Amy, public school was a better choice than private.

At this point, I became more of a resource and advisor for Amy and her family. In the 10th grade, I helped Amy with some of her math issues for the SAT and then referred her to a specialized SAT math tutor. When Mother called to tell me she had scored in the 600s for Math and a perfect 800 for the Verbal, I was so very proud of Amy!

Self-Realization

Amy and her parents decided on a small liberal arts college in the Midwest, a perfect choice for her. She made many new friends and enjoyed the college atmosphere. By now, Amy could organize and follow her schedule, self-advocate, and even find a part-time job. I continued to keep in contact with Amy and her mother. After graduation, Amy returned home, and a few months later, we made plans to have lunch together.

Meeting Amy renewed my optimistic outlook for my students. The head tilt and slightly nervous mannerisms had faded. Amy talked with authority and yet the sweetness in her voice remained. From our discussion, I learned that Amy had decided to remain at home while she was interviewing with different companies in the publishing business and saving some money. She was still in contact with college friends all over the country and had a fairly large social group from high school and college in her immediate geographic area. With these friends, she enjoyed classical music, attending a concert at the Hollywood Bowl during the summer, as well as going to movies and parties. Amy also shared that she was dating a fine young man she had known since high school. She seemed very mature as she described their relationship and how well-suited they were for each other.

Then we started reminiscing about our work together. She remembered our conversations about "getting stuck." Amy told me she still finds herself getting stuck at times but they were simple things that happen to us all. For example, Amy said sometimes when she worked on footnoting for a historical document in the college library, she would get stuck on persisting to search for information that really did not pertain to the document. She found herself wandering into "side facts." She realizes this mimics the way she thinks— "connected terms, not linear that create a logical narrative." She "goes off on tangents because it makes sense to her." It was gratifying to learn how she remembered working on her organizational skills and still applies them.

Amy also reminisced about our working on math problems from different angles, solving the same problems in different ways. She remembered gaining confidence in her math ability because if she forgot how to solve a problem, she had several other ways to approach it. Also, she felt this multitiered approach helped improve her math sense and lessen her math anxiety. She remembered we "talked a lot." I agreed and reiterated that her highly developed verbal skills helped her improve in all areas.

The conversation shifted to her job interviews. Amy told me how she worked in the university library and received some experience in editing. We began discussing the interview process, and it was refreshing to hear her perspective on the process. I find often that when a student graduates from college, trying to navigate the real job market can be a major disappointment. If a job is not secured almost immediately, students become depressed and easily lose their self-confidence. Amy had a different slant on this. With her optimistic attitude, she viewed this as an adventure, learning about people and new experiences. Amy did not express any disappointment because she was not hired on the spot. Some of her interviews gave us the giggles. As an example, one man spoke gruffly with lots of off-color language. I asked her if she was offended. She said she just thought this was the man's culture and he was not trying to offend her. She was not sure she would accept a job even if it was offered. Amy's mature attitude toward her job interviews assured me she would find a job soon. As we left, I told her how proud I was of the fine young woman she has become.

Today, Amy presents very differently from that moment in time when the neuropsychologist tested her in the third grade. She refined many of her skills beginning in elementary school until the present. Currently, Amy seems average in most areas that were diagnosed as weak more than 10 years ago. While her exceptional language skills continue to be her dominant strength, Amy developed strong empathic and intuitive skills. She may still need reminders with organization, but her self-awareness helps her define her needs and stay focused. Her self-advocacy skills and willingness to ask for help add to her resourcefulness. From my viewpoint, Amy's only area of continued weakness is spatial. Dr. Mel Levine, in his text, *Educational Care* (Levine, 1994), correctly points out that, in school, children need to be proficient in all areas while in adult life, one is sufficient. I view Amy as proficient and competitive in many areas. She has a circle of friends with whom she is comfortable and feels nurtured. Growing up in a functional family with continued educational therapy and psychological support and the necessary integration of modeling and role playing gave Amy the necessary boosts to her interpersonal skills.

As noted previously, all cases are unique. Amy's case, in many ways, had an outcome probably more positive than most. However, if we review her past storms, beginning with the name of "donkey" in first grade, the bleak neuropsychologist report in third grade, the turbulence in fourth, fifth, sixth, seventh, and eighth grades, it is apparent that Amy's outcome might have been very different if her parents had not sought the necessary therapies.

A few weeks later, I learned Amy was hired as an assistant editor. Amy's mother and I met to reminisce and talk about Amy. Mother reminded me how she has always felt Amy "sees the glass not only as half full but it is a really pretty crystal glass." She is very proud of Amy as an "authentic" person who does not suppress or hide her true self—she celebrates who she is even though she knows she does not fit into every group. She emphasized how important it is for a gifted child with a learning disability to have parental, educational therapy, school, and psychological support in order to "embrace" the difficulties, remaining proud of being a little quirky and eccentric. According to Mother, Amy expressed some misgivings because her job is boring, but she found a way to help herself by decorating her cubicle with whimsical desk accessories shaped as butterflies, snails, and alligators that have an interactive quality to them. She agreed to work with a coach for a few sessions to help her better organize her daily schedule and work on graduate school applications. When she feels the need she can visit with her psychiatrist who she has continued to see sporadically, a long term connection that has been helpful for her.

About a month later, Amy and I talked again. She had already been working for several weeks as an assistant editor for a market research magazine. Amy had bought a car and was proudly making her car payments. She decided to live at home for a while to save some money. How ironic, she thought, that she had applied for 36 jobs, participated in six interviews, and the job she accepted was not a result of the process; she was called by the company because they had read her resume on Monster.com. But Amy felt those six interviews gave her lots of practice so she could understand how to interview and negotiate a decent first salary. While her job is not that creative, she feels it will give her a year of technical resume information. She will probably take the GREs for graduate school. We talked about her finding some help for the math portion as well as to demystify the application and testing process.

Amy has met many of her immediate goals, finding a good job that matches her skills and temperament, living at home to save money, as well as buying her first car and using her salary to make the monthly payments. She told me another immediate goal is to be more aggressive in keeping social contacts all over the country as well as in her immediate area. Amy shared that while she was shy in high school, she found wonderful friends in college and plans to continue nurturing those relationships. She knows it will be difficult and will take some effort on her part. Of course free long distance phones and the Internet help that process quite a bit. Amy and several of her out-of-state friends are busy planning visits with each other. Applying to graduate school and determining the specific graduate program will be Amy's current long term goal. It seems she will pursue employment in the writing area but she is also drawn to teaching.

Six months later, Amy and I spoke again. As a result of her professional network, she learned of an employment opportunity developing creative programs for children. She interviewed and was hired! How fortunate she was to find another job that matched her interests and strengths.

Whatever journeys Amy embarks upon, she will be successful as a result of her work ethic, self-motivation, self-advocacy skills, resiliency, curiosity for and love of learning, and empathy and compassion for others. I look forward to hearing about her future progress.

REFERENCES

Alcott, L. M. (1994). *Work: A story of experience.* New York: Penguin Books.

Baum, S., & Owen, S. V. (2004). *To be gifted and learning disabled: Strategies for helping bright students with LD, ADHD, and more.* Mansfield Center, CT: Creative Learning Press.

Briggs, M. (1998). Families talk: Building partnerships for communicative change. *Topics in Language Disorders, 18,* 3, 71–84.

Bronfenbrenner, U. (1979). *Ecology of human development: Experiments by design.* Cambridge, MA: Harvard University Press.

Brooks, R., & Goldstein, S. (2001). *Raising resilient children.* Chicago: Contemporary Books.

Keogh, B. (1995). Why interventions don't work. *The Educational Therapist, 16*(2), 15.

Levine, M. D. (1994). *Educational care.* Cambridge, MA: Educators Publishing Service.

Meltzer, L., (Ed.). (2007). *Executive function in education from theory to practice.* New York: Guilford Press.

Palombo, J. (2006). *Nonverbal learning disabilities.* New York: Norton.

Reik, T. (1948). *Listening with the third ear: The inner experience of a psychoanalyst.* New York: Grove Press.

6

SITTING AT THE TABLE

Accommodating Diagnoses and Approach in Educational Therapy

JANE UTLEY ADELIZZI

INTRODUCTION
Sitting at the Table—The ET and Client Alliance

Most of my work as an educational therapist (ET) occurs while sitting at a table with a client. The Table might be located in a home office, a school, or a clinic where there are tables, chairs, paper, notebooks, colored markers, pens, pencils, and all the paraphernalia usually found in a classroom. It's not important to me what the client's feet are doing under the table, and whether the person is draped over the arm of the chair, or sitting up straight. Most clients I see are glad to find some security on their side of the table. It becomes their territory. We might share the middle of the table with a cup of pencils and pens, or some cookies. I'm not privy to all their body language, and I provide them with a way to "hide" most of themselves from me. They can fold their hands, doodle on some paper, shuffle index cards, and it's all legitimate and appropriate behavior in this setting. The conscious and unconscious behaviors as a result of the exposure from sitting in a chair facing another person without something to lean on or hide behind belongs in another setting with another type of therapist. My aim, as the ET, is to create our own person-in-context setting so that I can assist in assuaging my client's distress by providing her with a place to "put" her books and papers, as well as the emotional responses that come with acknowledging the grief and stress related to learning and functioning in daily life.

Johnson and Blasco (1997) reported that children begin developing their language and social skills around the table. For many families across a range of cultures the kitchen or dining room table is a place where people gather, not only to sit and share a meal, but also to converse and to listen to others, often leaving the table with a sense of being "fed" either by a shared meal, or by a modicum of sage advice from a family member. The clinical setting of The Table offers a similar opportunity by being not only a place to sit with materials that symbolize a pending task, but also a place to talk about the work that like a vapor may loom heavily over a client.

The Table becomes the clinical setting where it's safe to reveal the many facets of oneself, such as sliding down into the chair when it feels as if an embarrassing moment is imminent. My job is to assure the client sitting on the other side that it's okay to reveal the layers of oneself which feel safe to share, to let things "slip" in conversation without feeling embarrassed or self-conscious. That allows me, as the ET, to understand how the cognitive, biological, psychological, emotional, and cultural aspects of self serendipitously contribute to the gestalt of a learning profile, and ultimately, to our work together as a team.

In all the years I have been assisting adolescents and adults with suspected or diagnosed learning and attentional disorders, I have never seen a learning profile that is as neat and crispy clean as it appears in the *Diagnostic and Statistical Manual of Mental Disorders* (*DSM-IV-TR*; American Psychiatric Association, 2000). No one is ever "just dyslexic," or simply suffers from the inability to read at their expected level of development, or to organize and write a research paper. These are often difficulties that relate to one another and manifest their symptoms in the process of learning and functioning in the office of an ET, in the classroom, at home, in a wide range of relationships, as well as in the office of a psychotherapist. Rarely have I seen an individual sitting with me at The Table who has not suffered repetitive blows to his or her self-esteem as a result of the sweat the person breaks in class while attempting to deliver the correct answer to a question, or to effectively hide behind his or her desk in an attempt at invisibility. The degree to which low self-esteem causes lasting damage is dependent upon the client's typical response and sensitivity to external stimuli, mental stability, and the degree of resiliency evidenced. Like fingerprints and palm prints, the impact of a compromised ego manifests itself in the unique profiles that unfold before me in our unique table-and-chair setting.

I, like many of my colleagues, regard my work as being holarchical as well as interdisciplinary, meaning that the work accomplished in alliance between myself and the client functions much as in Bronfenbrenner's nesting structure (Sugarman, 2001), enveloped or surrounded by the variety of theories and contexts in which that person functions: the specific tasks required within each of these contexts, some of which call for mediation, remediation, or relearning a behavior in order to master a specific task. This is akin to McCloskey's holarchical model of executive functioning (McCloskey, Perkins, & Van Diviner, 2008), and to a psychodynamic approach I employ as together my client and I strive to change behaviors and attitudes that contribute to the development of self-esteem, self-efficacy, and the flexibility to consider and ultimately employ new ways of functioning. These hoped-for changes may occur as a result of learned behavior (Miller, 2001), developmental readiness, a burning desire to succeed for personal reasons (the restoration of one's dignity), or as a result of steady engagement in cognitive behavioral therapy, specifically designed to meet the needs of the working alliance between the ET and client. Often the incremental steps to changes are the result of a culmination of these shifts and changes in behaviors, presenting themselves as both qualitative and quantitative outcomes. These changes may be apparent through clients' self-reports, or qualitative data; or, they may become apparent through the quantitative data resulting from sources such as diagnostic assessments, and tests and quizzes.

The precarious balance of comorbid diagnoses or conditions ebb and flow in response to my client's functioning at any given time and according to the task at hand. While regarding the holarchical model as comprised of both crystal and fluid functions, characteristics, and idiosyncracies, its nature may be regarded as systemic, one in which the multicontextual lives of the client in relation to the ability to experience success and a sense of well-being in learning and functioning are considered. With all that said, I will offer a case study that will exemplify the practice of educational therapy with a client who bears the burden of comorbid disorders or conditions, followed by two brief case vignettes, all of which are regarded in a systemic kind of analysis. These cases are concerned with young adults in college, each of which illustrates the uniqueness of the individual student's comorbid profile as well as the fluid and holarichical characteristics of the practice of educational therapy.

THE CASE OF PRESIJA

The Ritual

Presija, a young woman of 22, on the surface did not appear to suffer from low self-esteem as a result of her significant language-based learning disability. Despite her challenges in academic skills, she sailed through elementary and middle school with adequate grades. She was recognized as "a good kid" (even when considering her history with emotionally noteworthy meltdowns) and was an accomplished and competitive athlete. She frequently reminded me of her talents, and pointed out on a regular basis that her outlook was healthy, her way of compensating for the academic skills with which she experienced difficulty. And, after all, she would remind me, it was genetic anyway. Not her fault, so therefore not her responsibility. We had many conversations about her father's family and the wide range of abilities and disabilities that each member exhibited, some of which she praised, but most of which she criticized with regularity. She made valiant efforts to place the blame and responsibility for her specific difficulties in life on her family, some of which allowed her to shed excess guilt as she attempted to cross the threshold into adulthood, and the remainder of which allowed her to deny responsibility for her attitude and choices. We often discussed how much responsibility was hers when it came to finishing a paper, considering the difficulties she exhibited in executive functioning, and within the confinements of guidelines imposed by her professors.

It took me some time to understand that what I observed as Presija's range of emotion bore unambiguous facial and body expressions, none of which melded or transformed into another with any degree of fluidity, but rather manifested themselves as distinct shifts from a smile to a frown, and then back again. At times she exhibited a very deliberate pensive look, complete with furrowed brow and a pose like Rodin's *The Thinker*. Each expression was carefully matched with something she had learned as a behavior, and presented itself somewhat as a work of art. Social learning theory was a tool of the trade for her survival as she negotiated the daily struggle of pleasing those who mattered, and scorning those who could not serve her well.

During many of our sessions as I sat on my side of The Table, I was amazed at Presija's practicality, her short-lived satisfaction with the successes she experienced, and in what appeared on the surface to be her respect for self and others. However, on the days we would sit down together at The Table, aware that a deadline for a major paper was breathing down her neck, her entire being changed. Not a flicker of a smile, genuine or feigned, would cross her face. Her remarks were curt. It was a deadly charge, this paper, for both of us. In her chosen field of political science she needed to push her thinking like a boulder uphill, in order to synthesize and then translate the internal and external world of her thoughts and ideas into writing.

As I came to recognize the tides of Presija's personality as it was impacted by the academic demands of a college curriculum, I also came to know the psychiatric diagnosis which, like a heavy blanket, engulfed her from time to time, especially when the expectations of a system of learning made little acknowledgment of the degree of angst she experienced at any given time. The understanding of the biological aspects of her mood fluctuation brought my comprehensive understanding of her profile to a new level, broadening my view of symptomatology and its direct impact on the ability to learn and function. In the case of this client, The Table was a comfort zone during the worst of times, providing her with a place on which to rest her head when the sight of her books and papers became too much to bear. Those were the times when I would sit patiently, sipping a cup of tea, possibly making notes to myself or reading my e-mail, waiting for her to ready herself for the task. Sometimes, after 20 minutes or longer, she would raise her head, look me in the eye, and announce, "Okay, I'm ready."

Red Alert! The books came out of the bag, slammed on the table with a sense of purpose, possibly even resentment, and I would position myself at the whiteboard, often taking on a secretarial role, mapping her random thoughts and perspectives on material over which she was attempting to gain a sense of mastery. Once the whiteboard was filled with what often looked like notes from a mad scientist, she would begin reorganizing the material into some semblance of an outline in order to move another step forward with the paper. At that point, I always knew we were making progress. The transition into the task, and the initial process of shedding the old familiar fears that smothered her efforts, seemed to elicit the most angst in her. Once her interpretation of the material was spoken aloud like some kind of confession, and then discussed, organized, and reorganized, she experienced a sense of relief, a thin sliver of light through the same old dark tunnel. It was then that she took complete control, and moved forward in her work. With the pending doom of each new paper, I prayed that we could move to the point of our ritual: me at the whiteboard, and she at The Table rearranging and sequencing her thoughts into an outline. Sometimes our roles shifted, and it was she at the whiteboard, and me at The Table, often nudging, questioning, and encouraging her to share her brilliant thoughts and interpretations. On a good day she would engage in a discussion about her spelling and her difficulty in sequencing language in order to express a coherent thought. These discussions always seemed to be about someone else, and not her. When she used the pronoun *I*, it was as if that referred to another person, *not herself.*

At the point in each session when our collaborative efforts came to an adequate close, even if just partially, the sense of relief and accomplishment became an excuse for idle chatter, deliberate smiles, and plans for upcoming events. I knew that maybe tomorrow, or maybe next week, we would begin the same process all over again. It was a ritual.

Presija's Case Analysis

Close Encounters and What's in the File?   Very often when a new student was expected to become part of my teaching load I chose not to read the file before our first meeting, preferring to meet the student first without outside opinions or assessment scores influencing my expectations during the initial stages of our relationship. Presija's file lay unopened on a pile with several others on my desk. The first time she entered my office she stood in my doorway, staring at me, trying to size me up, I assumed.

"Hi. I'm Presija, and I'm from Arizona. Are you Jane?" she asked as she stared hard at the schedule in her hand.

"Yes, I am, and please come in and sit down."

She dropped her book bag with a thud and plopped down on a chair, her head immediately swiveling in order to take in as much as she could about the office, although I suspected it was an immediate and spontaneous reaction to a new surrounding, and not because she was trying to analyze me within the context of my environment.

"So, Jane, how old *are* you?"

"I'm pretty old compared to you."

"So how old is *that*?"

"I could be your grandmother—almost."

She nodded her head thoughtfully with not a trace of a smile.

"Presija, would you like a cup of tea? Some water?"

"Tea's good. I'll have it with honey."

"I don't have honey, but you can have sugar." For some reason many students expect you have a kitchen like the one at home.

"Okay."

She got up and followed me into the narrow corridor where we kept the electric teakettle and usually a stray cookie or two. She watched every move I made, and then carried her own mug back to the office. We sipped silently.

"So, why don't you let me see your schedule?" I asked.

She handed it over, and watched me over the rim of her mug.

I slid two sheets of paper in front of her which contained several questions about how she perceived herself as a learner, her contact information, and a request for two wishes for herself during our work together. I placed a pen next to the sheet, and announced that I would be back in a minute after a trip to the copy machine. When I returned with a copy of her schedule in my hand, she looked up at me, and said,

"What kind of a question is that—*'my wishes'*? Should I click my ruby slippers together?" She rolled her eyes in exasperation. I knew my work would be uphill from there.

"What is it that you would like to see happen for you at the Learning Center?"

"I want to pass my courses. What do you *think*?" she snorted softly, appearing to lose her patience with me.

"Anything else?"

She played with the pencils and pens on The Table, and then looked up at me.

"I want to feel better about myself. I'm sick and tired of feeling stupid! Because I'm *not* stupid. I think I'm actually pretty brilliant in some respects." Silence. She had said what she needed to say.

"Okay, now I have an idea what it is you would like to accomplish. Can we consider that a wish list?"

"Sure—think you can deliver?" Her sarcasm felt like a paper cut.

"No, but *you* will, and I'll help you to learn how to do that yourself."

From there we worked together on a personal checklist which covered her family, educational, and medical histories. She disclosed her family's psychiatric history, and her own fairly recent diagnosis of bipolar disorder. She had been hospitalized briefly on two occasions over the last 12 months. When I told her that other than her learning or attentional disorder, it wasn't necessary for her to talk about her diagnoses, she pointed her finger at me she said, "Yes, it *is* necessary. If this is going to work, then you have to know it *all*, okay?"

I nodded in agreement, and asked her not to point her finger at me anymore. She agreed. When she left my office we shook hands. I saw her turning back to look at me as she headed out the door to the parking lot. She made an attempt to turn the corners of her mouth up into a smile.

That evening I took Presija's file home with me. She had received three psychoeducational assessments in her life, the most recent of which suggested she seek the services of a new psychiatrist because her current medications no longer seemed to be working (I always felt that the word *working* was nebulous when considering the effects of medications on life's daily struggles). I knew that Presija's current diagnosis of bipolar disorder might make some twists and turns at this pivotal point in her development, and on my faithful spiral notepad I reminded myself to ask her to fill out a consent form so that I could speak with her therapist, primary care physician, and her psychiatrist should I notice any radical changes in her behaviors or moods. I also discovered that she bore the diagnosis of attention deficit hyperactivity disorder (ADHD) as a child, the symptoms of which seemed to have a major impact on her ability to actually *be* in a classroom when she was young, let alone engage in her work and then meet imposed deadlines.

As I spread the assessment results in front of me at home, I noticed that other than her diagnosis of ADHD, things did not look too alarming during childhood; there was not an enormous discrepancy between her verbal and performance IQs on the Wechsler, although there was an intratest roller-coaster effect with a weak ACID profile, indicated by the examiner as the appearance of dyslexia at that stage in her development.

She struggled during the early stages of reading, but then became proficient, and according to her parents was a precocious reader—another parental perception to add to my own notes. The most recent Wechsler, a WAIS-III, revealed a more prominent spike in the verbal mode, and a noticeably lower score in the performance mode than on the WISC-IV. When I studied the WAIS-III indexes I noted that her perceptual organization was almost 30 points lower than her verbal comprehension, an abnormal spread, or "wingspan" as I affectionately named it in order to sound less clinical during conversations with clients and their families.

My first impression of Presija was that she exhibited some of the behaviors and affect common to a nonverbal learning disability (NLD), although this was not a diagnosis which appeared on her most recent evaluation (Palombo, 2006). I was always very careful with my first impressions, although I never put them aside. Most often I added them to the growing list of observations and impressions I amassed. I based my first impression of her on what seemed to be her less than animated affect, tactless remarks, and the bare bones responses I received from her, delivered often with an angry sting. Her first two assessments mentioned that Presija experienced "temper flare-ups" at frequent intervals at home, with less frequency at school, but they were nevertheless noted by her teachers who otherwise appreciated her as a student.

I knew that Byron Rourke reported that he did not think the incidence of bipolar disorder was any higher for individuals with nonverbal learning disorders than it was for any other population, but I perused other research in order to gain further insight. In a (2002) study by DelBello, it was reported that children and adolescents who were diagnosed with bipolar disorder also demonstrated clinically significant scores across all domains on the Behavior Rating Inventory of Executive Function, a finding familiar to me in the course of my work with adolescents and adults with both already diagnosed and suspected NLD. This often led to a diagnosis of ADHD for adolescents and young adults, especially if they exhibited a restless and risk-taking nature. Presija's most recent evaluation offered the comorbid diagnosis of attention deficit hyperactivity disorder and a learning disability, not otherwise specified. Her psychiatric diagnosis was not included in this report but existed on a separate report from the hospital, diagnosed as a result of a psychosocial interview in an outpatient unit, and an initial visit with a psychiatrist following admittance. The psychoeducational examiner did not see the psychiatric diagnosis, and the psychiatrist did not ask to see her psychoeducational evaluation.

I recalled Presija's conversation style during our first encounter, and then I focused on what sounded like a heartfelt plea for understanding: "I want to feel better about myself. I'm sick and tired of feeling stupid! Because I'm not stupid. I think I'm actually pretty brilliant in some respects." Joseph Palombo (2006) reported the following:

> Clinical data support the view that many children with NLD have negative feelings about themselves that are the product of low self-esteem. Some respond defensively, believing themselves to be special or superior to others, demeaning or denigrating others. Some appear oblivious to these issues, displaying a curious lack of awareness of their status, and apparently taking no ownership of their condition. (p. 113)

While ruminating on Palombo's findings, I kept returning to my first encounter with Presija. I was not looking through my microscope to identify a new and more interesting diagnosis. However, I was looking for further clues to explain Presija's social behaviors, at least my impressions of them upon our first encounter, and her previous academic performance which exhibited a similar rollercoaster effect to what appeared on her subtests. We would have to see what unfolded as the semester progressed.

Task Analysis within Context

At the Table   Within the context of our sessions, sitting at The Table, Presija began to relax after the first two or three sessions. She didn't abuse her telephone privileges, and she discovered that it was helpful for her to e-mail me her thoughts almost daily. I wasn't expected to respond all the time, but I was expected to read. She liked to review some of her thoughts when she arrived for her one-to-one sessions, using that as a way to decide when we should move the conversation on to her academic work. When I can trust that a student has the judgment skills to know that we really do have to monitor their academic tasks, then I encourage their orchestration of our work together. One day she admitted to me that on her walks up the hill to the Learning Center she rehearsed how she wanted the session to unfold: 10 minutes of discussion about her thoughts and experiences in the dorm, and then on to academic work. She looked forward to the cups of tea we shared and decided we would save that for the last 15 minutes of the session, making it a social-intellectual event. Eventually, I learned that this was a good time for me to talk about social interactions, and we agreed that we would talk about her favorite soap opera, which became a virtual theater where from a safe distance she could observe the behavior of others in a variety of situations.

Several weeks into the semester I brought in an article about modern social learning theory (Miller, 2001) and she immediately identified the tenets of the theory as a means of identifying behaviors and their cause and effect within each situation. This format provided a safe way to make mistakes in judgment, leaving her the flexibility to change her mind. The soap opera became part of our work together in order to unravel the mystery of predictable outcomes that were the direct result of behaviors she witnessed on the screen. Together we charted her observations of each character in a situation, creating a triad of characteristics, such as biological, cognitive, and environmental, with subsequent questions that addressed the social conduct, sense of justice, and empathic responses of each. Often we disagreed, but the active engagement in the analyses of characters and their behaviors led to discussions about Presija's ability to introspect, imagine, or match a particular behavior with a predictable outcome. Eventually, we broadened our perspectives, and expanded the triad to a model of self which I presented to her as: the cognitive, biological, neurological, psychological, emotional, social, and cultural aspects of an individual.

In the Dormitory   Presija's life occurred in a variety of contexts, and our clinical setting, The Table, was just one. Although I was not a proponent of visiting students' dorm rooms, I do like to see where they live, even if it's just a peek inside the foyer. Presija lived in an "over-21" dorm. Although she was registered for her first semester at the college, she had transferred from another college in the Midwest because she was failing most of her courses as a junior. She chose to be a political science major, and while this suited her nicely in some respects, there came a time when she was expected to move beyond "reporting the facts" to interpreting them, often with the additional burden of using some imagination, or the flexibility that is required in conceptual thinking which sometimes involves predicting an outcome with a degree of spontaneity.

The over-21 dorm was relatively quiet on the Wednesday night when I visited with one of my colleagues. We both met our students in the foyer and asked how they liked their living conditions. I found Presija very quiet, allowing the other student to do most of the talking. The other young woman was very animated, excited about the weekend, and about her major in sociology. When I prodded Presija, she shot me a dirty look which I interpreted as, "Don't ask me questions. Just leave me alone."

My colleague invited both students to have supper with us in the cafeteria. Her student awkwardly explained how she was ordering pizza with her friends, and then politely excused herself. Presija looked up at me from her perch on the arm of a chair, and said, "I'll go. I'm starved." At first I was surprised, figuring that I had been dismissed after the dirty look, but as I thought it over I knew that she preferred the company of adults whose conversation she could listen to, join in if she felt so inclined—or not. She instinctively knew we would be more forgiving of faux pas, and less demanding of her than her peers.

In the cafeteria, two or three students said hello to Presija. She mumbled a response, keeping her head down and eyes averted. She filled her tray first and informed my colleague and I that she would find a table for us, which turned out to be in a corner by a window, as far away as possible from the laughter of other groups who were clearly there for social as well as dining purposes. My hunch was that earlier in life she had learned that a degree of isolation was a safe choice.

As my colleague and I began some small talk Presija listened carefully as she sat hunched over her plate of salad, pulling her baseball cap down so far I wondered how she could see her food. The presidential election came up and immediately Presija's interest peeked. She interrupted us several times to let us know the recent poll results, the opinions of the analysts, and very carefully, what her opinion was, looking us both in the eye. We listened, and then responded. For a while we were able to have a balanced conversation on a controversial topic, much like watching a game at Wimbledon. No fighting. Just serving and returning.

Later, on the ride home I became aware of how my colleague and I provided a safe forum from which my client could air her opinions without fear of being chastised, something which is often a risk in a younger peer group. We let her "practice" the game, and pretend we were at Wimbledon, when in fact we were really on stage, a move up the cognitive-social ladder from our discussions about soap operas. While this was clearly a step beyond her position as a "lurker" to becoming a "player," I wasn't sure when or if she would be ready to handle herself well in a peer group. This became the topic for our next discussion over tea, another example of our task analysis within a social-intellectual context.

The Context of Family   The third context was very helpful to me in determining how Presija's assessment and my subsequent decisions about appropriate interventions converged in order to create a meaningful educational therapy treatment plan. Mrs. M, Presija's mother, called me a few weeks into the semester and asked if she could come for a visit, not an unusual request for parents if they are making a trip to visit with their child in college. She said she notified her daughter and that we could all meet in the coffee shop on campus, an idea I liked better than meeting in my own setting. I wanted to observe the family on neutral ground.

As I entered the coffee shop I immediately noticed Presija in a corner table (again), her yellow baseball cap pulled down to hide her eyes. She pointed at me, and her mother and father stood up. We shook hands, and I noticed that Mr. M's handshake was like his daughter's; there was no grip, no muscle tension, and an inability to know when to withdraw his hand. Mrs. M touched his shoulder and edged him over to his chair, a routine I guessed that was employed often. He smiled at me, and it was genuine, fluid, and not a learned response similar to what I observed in his daughter. I remembered that Presija labeled her father as being socially inept, a topic that she returned to many times during our work together, defining his bouts of depression as a weakness. She professed she would never allow herself to be as dependent on anyone as he was on her mother.

Mrs. M was very engaging, an attractive woman, who kept trying to push Presija's baseball cap up and away from her eyes, an effort which was greatly unappreciated by her 22-year-old daughter. Being a parent, I completely understood the consistent, albeit inappropriate, gestures that mothers make in order to make their children "presentable" to the public, no matter how old they are. Again, we were on stage. Mrs. M exhibited quick, darting movements, her head either on a constant swivel or leaned in as close to mine as possible when speaking directly to me. I recalled reviewing the initial intake sheet at home, and remembered that Presija identified her mother as a "control freak" whose moods ranged from the intensity of a tsunami to the depressed calm of shallow water on a cloudy day. I was hopeful that today I was observing something in the midrange of what my student described.

As we struggled through 20 minutes of small talk, Mr. M invited his daughter to take him on a visit to her dorm room. She hedged for a while, and then finally consented, probably just to escape the situation of sitting at a table with her ET and her parents. This gave Mrs. M and me a chance to talk and I knew that she had something to say or she would not have requested a meeting. Mr. M did not seem like a spontaneous kind of person who would off-handedly suggest a tour of the dormitory. I suspected he would rather pick up the newspaper and sit on one of the couches, devouring the news of the day, paragraph by paragraph, page by page, hoping not to be interrupted. Presija turned to look back as she headed out the door with her father, reminding me of our first encounter.

Mrs. M launched into conversation immediately, probably trying to time how much ground we could cover within a limited timeframe. She leaned over, close to my face. I backed up a few inches. She advanced closer.

"I am desperate to know how Pressie is doing. She is our only child." Her eyes teared. "We waited a long time for her. And what a smart little thing she was! Always traveling around with her books under her arm."

I remembered the comments on Presija's assessment. Mrs. M reported her daughter as being a precocious reader. I responded, "And, she's still smart! She really knows her way around politics, Mrs. M." I paused for a few seconds as she dabbed at her eyes with a tissue. "Mrs. M, how old was your daughter when she learned to read?" This was often a key question I asked either my client or a parent about her child.

"Oh, she had a time catching on, but she always loved books, and if she didn't know what a word was she would make it up. She memorized a lot of what we read to her. She talked a little late I think. Probably when she was around 3 or so. But, she did talk by the time she was in kindergarten, and it was like all the language came pouring out of her like an endless stream." She laughed nervously, and I noted how her hands trembled as she patted her hair.

"So how old do you think she actually was when it appeared as if she had some kind of mastery of reading? I think you reported that she was a precocious reader."

"Yes, yes! She was probably in the third grade when I think she was actually reading and *understanding* the words, or at least I *think* she understood. And then, once she started there was no stopping her. It was like when she learned to talk. It all just rolled out! I had to literally pull her books away so that she would go outside and play with the kids in the neighborhood. We had terrible disagreements when I told her she had to attend a social event. She wanted to bring her books!" She shook her head as if still surprised by her daughter's behaviors.

"As she got older what kinds of books did she like to read?"

"Ah, well she did move through the world of Harry Potter with breakneck speed, and then it was on to *Watership Down*, which she liked well enough but she then avoided similar books. Oh, but that was in high school I think. I can't remember. By middle school she was hooked on biographies, and I mean really hooked! She talked about these people like she knew them."

Palombo danced through my head. "… although the verbal language of children with NLD appears advanced or even sophisticated, closer scrutiny of the content reveals limitations in their capacity to process abstract and complex material" (2006, p. 99).

I suspected that during a period of time Presija found the anthropomorphism of *Watership Down* entertaining, especially when the rabbits faced both human and animal encounters. However, as she transitioned through adolescent development she found she had difficulty navigating relationships, especially in uncovering, understanding, and then predicting the outcomes of social cues as they concerned *her*. I reminded myself of how accurately she felt she diagnosed her parents' shortcomings, yet did not seem to recognize any similarities to her own difficulties.

"What happened that made her transfer here? I was not on campus, so someone from admissions met with her. I always feel as though I've missed an important part of my work by not being the interviewer."

"Well, she came alone, and we don't really know how the interview went. She insisted we not come with her because she was an adult. We only know that she was accepted here conditionally, and we are genuinely grateful for that! She completed two years at the other college, and began a major in political science during her third year, something Mr. M and I thought was a good idea considering how dedicated and widely read she is in those realms. However, her adequate grades declined rapidly, and then she began failing everything. It was as if she gave up. I think there were some dormitory incidents…."

"What kind of incidents?" I asked.

"I'm not sure, and the dean did not want to discuss it. He wanted Pressie to leave on her own without being asked to go." Mrs. M began to cry. "I think I didn't pursue the matter any further because I really didn't want to know. I just wanted a fresh start for her. And, now she has *you*! She never had anyone before that she could talk to. I *know* she talks to you. She tells me!"

This was always a part of my work which I entered into with trepidation.

"You know it's always my privilege to be a witness to someone's growth, and I am always grateful for my role in some of those developmental spurts our young adults experience. But, I have to tell you that I cannot engage in the kind of therapy that Presija requires at this stage of her life. She needs a psychotherapist who understands how she learns and functions, and most importantly, how she deals with the painful disappointments that relationships present her with. I can still be her ET, and we will continue to make progress. But, she does need another player on our team."

Mrs. M nodded. *I* was grateful.

Even though my work with Presija took place within the confines of the college campus I was able to glean information for my own interpretations about her in several contexts: The Table, our clinical setting, the dormitory, the cafeteria, and her presence and behaviors within the family context, albeit briefly. Each flicker of a smile, even though it might have disappeared before it fully materialized; each sidelong glance as she attempted to guess what I was about to do next; each near-flare up she experienced in her frustration with my ability to move at her speed, to anticipate her mood, to be at peace with her, helped me to create the most helpful educational therapy treatment plan I could manage. My aim was for her to feel understood, and to encourage her to enter the social world with a degree of confidence that would allow her to recognize and then take advantage of the affordances within each context of her life. My concern was that she would not recognize those affordances as something that might enhance her experience, or the ability to match that affordance with the benefit it would provide in her own world.

The Psychodynamic Approach

There is a delicate interplay of emotions that occur in any relationship, often with one person experiencing a greater level of response than the other. Everyone's emotional gauge as a means of understanding the feelings of self and others is different, as if the mercury on each thermometer operates in accordance with the fluidity of awareness in each person. The role of an ET is not a model that usually takes place within the sole context of the clinical setting, and is rather more of a multicontextual model than that of many other types of therapies. As a result of the ET's interest in knowing as much as possible about the client in a variety of contexts in order to design the most appropriate and comprehensive educational therapy treatment plan, she is at risk for becoming more involved in the life of that person, stepping in and out of a variety of contexts, thereby creating greater vulnerability for herself.

I had become an attachment figure for Presija while she continued her coursework at our college. I could be depended upon as a reliable partner in uncovering the layers of resistance which magically appeared as an invisible wall when we approached the deadline for a major paper. We dissected the directions and then developed her ideas, with Presja eventually taking the role of orchestrator in the process, bringing her closer every day to an autonomous approach in her academic work.

She depended on what she perceived as my innate ability to understand her, and had to be reminded that other people in her life required the same kind of regard from her.

Because she was intellectually able to engage in conversations about facts and theory we were able to discuss how some of those applied more to certain situations and behaviors than did others. What she was identifying in me was empathy, and what concerned me was that while she learned to feign a sympathetic stance in some situations, she did not move into action, being *with* someone in their experience, or imagining what their experience might feel like.

The Balance of Comorbidity

During many of our sessions Presija experienced a hyperactive quality while at The Table, and then often by the end of the session she was emotionally and mentally exhausted, literally dragging her book bag out the door to the parking lot. This range in energy was especially evident when we were involved in "getting ready" to write a paper, exemplifying her difficulty with executive functioning skills, a contributing factor to her present psychoeducational diagnosis of ADHD. Her moods matched her energy levels, and it was sometimes unpredictable how she would be feeling on any given day, or even hour.

We had many conversations about how difficult it was for her to control her emotional responses to people and situations, and how less able she was to mask those feelings when she was younger. She said that her "meltdowns" were interpreted by her teachers as temper tantrums, but she saw and experienced them as biological and emotional responses to a set of circumstances and environmental factors that became intolerable to her. When we discussed social learning theory we spent some time applying Bandura's three types of environments: imposed, selected, and created (Blakemore, Berenbaum, & Liben, 2008). She found her moods and responses much more difficult to control when her environment was uncomfortable as a result of it being imposed on her, the classroom being a perfect example because it encompassed the characteristics of both confinement and exposure. Presija was aware that as she moved into later stages of adolescence that life became somewhat easier when it came to controlling her emotions, as she could select specific kinds of classes and activities that felt less threatening to her. Actually, what had occurred was a respite from unrealistic expectations, which presented her with less challenge or threat, thereby experiencing fewer emotional meltdowns. Together, she and I created a learning environment as we watched a soap opera, and then analyzed the behaviors of the characters, discussing them as if they were lab rats behind a two-way mirror. Her created environment did not include choosing to interact with her peer group. This she did only when forced into the situation, such as a meal in the cafeteria, group work as part of her course assignments (a grueling experience for her), and casual conversation in the corridor. We watched the soap opera; we analyzed the behaviors; and then we practiced the skills.

As I documented our sessions together I tried to look objectively at Presija's response to others. I wasn't expecting to learn what actually happened in her previous college setting, but I knew from experience that young adults who were burdened with comorbid conditions similar to Presija's were often at risk for emotional meltdowns that occurred as the result of frustration in trying to understand their role within a social context; their inability to maintain a sense of organization in their living quarters; their emotional response and often intolerance of the behavior of others; and, the need for isolation in order to complete academic work in a timely way.

The trust that Presija developed in our relationship was most apparent when we had discussions about the soap opera characters and how she would have handled the situation differently. At first she was not tolerant of my disagreeing with her on any point, which led to a series of conversations where we discussed the concept and actual practice of reciprocity in intellectual discourse. I pointed out that in this process there is not an absolute truth, nor an imbalance of power. We then practiced the process in order to develop turn-taking in discussion, an interesting task to undertake and then later analyze together.

The actual subject of the triad of identified conditions (LDNOS, ADHD, and bipolar disorder) that impacted her learning and functioning became infused into the model of self that we had expanded upon earlier in our work when discussing social learning theory. It was often difficult for her to distinguish between which symptoms in her daily life directly impacted a specific task or situation, but I did encourage her to begin documenting what she either knew or intuited as the connections so that she could later reflect on her own perceptions of cause and effect.

THE CASE OF CYD: A SNAPSHOT

If I could take a snapshot, a freeze-frame of a session with Cyd, it would be the day when he arrived at my office during another student's scheduled session, head turned aside, eyes closed, and arm extended as if begging me to remove a poisonous object from his grasp. I rose from my seat, and walked slowly toward him.

"Cyd, what's wrong? Are you okay?" I asked.

He mumbled something unintelligible. My other student, Randy, stood up from The Table and walked over to him. Carefully, he extracted the paper that Cyd held, and then handed it to me. Together, Randy and I studied the red F that stood out like a flashing red neon sign. Cyd's posture had not changed, and I noted with some interest that Randy had shifted his role from being my student to becoming my cohort, a coconspirator of sorts. He kicked my office door shut to give the three of us some privacy, and led Cyd by his extended arm to our table. We all sat in silence for a few minutes, Randy's hands outspread on my table as if he were considering something important to say. With a degree of dread, I noted that he had begun to take control of the situation, an increasingly troubling behavior.

Cyd turned to face me, his eyes filled with tears.

"I worked my butt off on this paper!"

Randy leaned in closer, clearly fascinated with my student's demise. I leaned in closer as well, and looked Randy square in the eye.

"Randy, you have to leave now. Cyd and I have to talk."

He looked puzzled. "Why?"

"Because Cyd and I need to talk. Alone. This is about *Cyd*."

"I can help," mouthing the words slowly as if I might not understand his intent.

I felt myself becoming exasperated, and tried to remain calm for Cyd's sake, noticing one lonely tear that zig-zagged its way down his cheek.

"You know what, I know you can help. But, maybe later on today, okay? Maybe Cyd will call you and ask for help."

Randy didn't move. He not only had significant difficulty picking up the nuances of social communication, but when he made a decision about something, anything, it was nearly impossible to convince him to consider other options, even if the other options might actually benefit people other than himself. Part of me always began the mental conversation I had with myself in times like these by accusing Randy of being passive-aggressive, of just digging his heels in and persevering to the point where I wanted to scream. But, then I would elevate my thinking to a point beyond the buttons he pushed in me to a more extensive and professional understanding of his behaviors.

I tried to stare him down, but it wasn't working. Cyd sat between us, staring at his lap, seeming not to care that another situation, beyond his own, was unfolding at the table. I stood up, grabbed Randy's book bag, and began packing his materials. He stood up, pulled the bag out of my hands, and unpacked his bag. After about 30 seconds of silence, he repacked his bag and stomped out of the office, slamming the door behind him. I knew he would come back to The Table later in the day, even if it was only out of curiosity about Cyd's situation.

Cyd sniffled loudly, so I provided him with our communal box of tissues. He mumbled a thank you, always showing his manners, always grateful for attention. He worked very hard to keep his emotions under control, but today the situation was clearly *out* of his control.

Cautiously, I leaned further into the table. "Cyd, what happened? You were prepared for the politics and history class. You knew the information cold."

"I know I did! But, he gave more multiple choice questions than he said he would. He said he would give around 12, and he gave 20 of them! Twenty is not near 12, not even close to it! It's almost twice the amount if you consider that 'around 12' might mean around 10. How fair is that?"

"Well, Professor Danke possibly found more items that needed to be presented in that mode, rather than in an essay question."

Cyd blew his nose into the tissue noisily, and then reached for another, placing the used one in front of me, as if he expected me to discard it for him.

"No. No, that's not the case because he could have taken some of the items and put them into fill-ins or matching. He didn't have to do so many of the questions in multiple choice, especially the way he writes. He's so complex. Nothing is simple. There's always a twist like he's trying to screw me up or confuse me."

He looked me square in the eye. "If I didn't know better I'd think he wants me to fail."

"I don't think he wants you to fail, Cyd."

"You don't know that. He calls on me and doesn't wait for me to raise my hand. And, when I raise my hand, he ignores me. It's like he only wants to hear me when he knows I'll have to admit I don't know the answer."

"Let's put that aside for now, and concentrate on the test. How many essay questions were there?"

"Two."

"Well, as I recall he said that's how many he was going to ask, right?"

"Right. But, he didn't say that the other questions would all be multiple choice, my weakness by the way, as if he didn't know that." He snorted indignantly.

"And how did you do on the essay questions?"

"Huh! Not very well considering he didn't phrase them the way he indicated he would when we did a review session."

"But did you know enough of the material to write something?"

At that point Cyd decided he wasn't going to answer any more of my questions. He stood up and walked over to the computer and pulled up his e-mail.

"Cyd, does this mean we are through talking, or are you going to show me the study guide so that we can talk about what might have happened when you took the test?" He knew that my method of working backwards in order to gain a deeper understanding of what might have happened to affect his performance was about to unfold. He wasn't ready.

"Neither. I'm getting my e-mail. Then I'll show you the study guide."

"Okay, but I think you have a rude tone to your voice right now."

He turned around and looked at me. "No. I am not being rude."

It was often at this point that I would announce I was going to get my mail and would be back in about 5 minutes. That gave me time to rethink my strategy for the remainder of the session, and offer Cyd an opportunity to rethink his behaviors. On my way out the door I asked if I could get him a cup of tea. No response.

When I returned to the room he was sitting at the table with a copy of the study guide and his test, side-by-side, aligned perfectly. I sat down with my tea and my mail.

"I see you have tea."

"Yes, I asked if you wanted something."

"I didn't hear you."

I ignored him. "So how does the study guide look? Do you think you misinterpreted the questions on the test, or the material in the study guide?"

His eyes filled up with tears. "I just didn't study hard enough."

"Maybe you did, but you might have misinterpreted something. Let's take a look."

Cyd and I often had sessions like this, which began with his interrupting another student's session, progressing with a parade of rude and negative comments, and sometimes ending with his willingness to listen and talk, not necessarily in that order, but in a way that would reveal to both of us where exactly he had strayed from his original plan when preparing for a test or exam. Often he became distracted by a secondary point covered in the material, and enthusiastically investigated it further, disregarding the clues he initially picked up from his reading and discussion. If I noticed that this was the case—and I couldn't be his watchdog for everything he did—I would redirect him to the question and to the primary points or concepts which required his attention. His distractibility and subsequent pursuit of interesting information, which was not necessarily relevant, seeped into his social life. Friends like Randy could be depended upon to stick around and either watch Cyd sabotage an interpersonal encounter or on a good day, stop Cyd from doing or saying something that would cause him to be regarded as a troublemaker, or simply a socially inept person, neither of which is helpful in college life.

As a child Cyd was diagnosed with attention deficit disorder based on his significant distractibility in the classroom. However, he did not experience difficulty in his social life, even as a child, solely because he was distractible. He found it difficult to read people, and to pick up on social cues in both individual and group encounters. His basic comprehension of most reading material was very literate, and the richness of a piece of literature could only be discussed once he was prodded to look for it—which he was able to do. His intellectual perspective on all things great and small was immense, but he did require a roadmap of sorts, a blueprint of how the unpredictable range of social situations in life might be approached, much as the twists and turns in a piece of literature that requires reading and rereading in order to experience the nuances, the emotional foundation that invites the language speak to each one of us.

In high school, just as Cyd was applying to colleges, his guidance counselor pointed out to his family that he was getting himself into considerable trouble with both his peers and teachers. If someone sitting nearby in homeroom reportedly failed a test or a class, Cyd offered unsolicited advice and opinions. His delivery was sometimes caustic depending upon the level of his need to point out what he recognized as being faulty or lacking in intellectual acumen. Twice in his junior year of high school he embarrassed teachers as he pointed out their errors in spelling and historical data in their presentation materials, resulting in uncomfortable conversations between Cyd's parents, the guidance counselor, and teachers.

It was at that time that Cyd received his second psychoeducational evaluation, followed by a visit to a psychiatrist who worked primarily with spectrum disorders. The evaluation demonstrated that his skills in reading comprehension and concept formation were weak. However, if someone worked one-to-one with Cyd he could be prompted to move beyond the concrete and into the world of ideas that magically seemed to connect with one another on a variety of levels. Cyd regarded this process as akin to fantasy games, regarding himself not as a character, but as the person responsible for bringing the characters to life, making them interact with one another, and then reducing their animation to stagnation, ending the relationship.

THE CASE OF RANDY

Randy had perfect attendance for his scheduled sessions in educational therapy, even better than his friend Cyd. Twice each week I counted on seeing him hovering in my doorway either on time or maybe a little early. I was not perceived to be busy if I was on the phone, at the computer, or with pen in hand. I was only perceived to be busy when I was engaged in conversation with *him*. Interrupters were interlopers to Randy, and were frowned upon. On the occasions when Cyd interrupted his session he was more apt to be forgiven, as Randy was Cyd's self-designated keeper.

When Randy was about 5 years old he was the survivor in an automobile accident that took the life of his father. He sat in the car with his dying father until the police arrived, which was only about a 10-minute period, but when Randy revisits some of his fragmented memories, that period of time seems like hours. Although he was quickly whisked away from the scene the imprint of the trauma in his memory and the impact on his exteroceptive senses will remain with him throughout his life. As a result of this experience and the tortuous symptoms that followed, Randy was diagnosed with posttraumatic stress disorder (PTSD), which for a young child manifests itself in ways which are not always discernable by family members, educators, or even psychotherapists who are not well versed in the subtleties of the manifestations of time skewing and omen formation (Hamblen, 2001).

For many years Randy related the events leading to the ride in the car with his father in a variety of ways, not accurately remembering or interpreting the sequence of events that led up to the ride, the actual accident, or the ensuing feelings he experienced. The police report stated that when they arrived at the scene of the accident Randy was hugging his father, and that it took two officers to unpry his small hands in order to determine the man's condition. As a result of Randy's internalization of time skewing, he continued to experience difficulty with placing events, expectations, and details in order, yet put enormous effort into controlling tasks that helped him move from one day to the next, and even from one hour to the next. That's why he was always on time for his sessions, but also why he checked and rechecked his next move. For example, we took 10 minutes before the close of a session to plan out the next part of the day. What building would he go to next? What would be the best route? Which assignment should he tackle first? Should he take a shower before or after supper? Without his overthinking the expectations of the hourly chunks of the day and night, he would spin out of control—or, at least that was his perception, and possibly mine as well. As an ET I consistently struggled with the boundaries of enablement.

Omen formation brought Randy to not only overthink the possible consequences of his every choice during the day, it also led him to do the same for the people with whom he has formed attachments, Cyd being one of those people. He was alternately vigilant of Cyd and his well-being, and then unkind to him, sometimes to his own surprise. He reminded Cyd every day of the things he needed to do, and the rituals he needed to adhere to in order to make his day as mishap-free as possible. When the opportunity presented itself I reminded Randy to let Cyd make his own decisions.

During a typical session Randy brought in his time management book (TMb), one which he chose himself, not one that I suggested. This, of course, was after much discussion and debate, not to mention the shopping for it. On one particular day he sat by my side—he did not like to sit across or at a right angle to me, but only next to me—and read the events of the day from his TMb to me, one by one. We had narrowed down the list of appropriate items (I knew he wanted to talk about his pending dentist appointment) to address in our session to just two: (1) reading a chapter from his history class and taking notes so that he could take part in the classroom discussion, and (2) writing a one page reflection paper for his communication class. I suggested that we begin with the reflection paper as I knew it might only involve a brief discussion with a map or outline, probably completed on the computer. That way I knew he was able to continue the momentum we developed and complete the paper on time—unless he became bogged down by a decision. His language skills were excellent, and he could "imagine." He could conceptualize. Surprisingly, he agreed with me, which made my day. I wondered where his stubborn streak was hiding, and when it would reappear. His stubborn streak was of course the oppositional stance he assumed as a means of buying extra time to rethink a previous decision, or a pivotal point in that moment.

He took out his history book and began automatically highlighting what he perceived as valuable information for class discussion. I knew Randy required little guidance in this task, but would require input for how he might enter into, or exit from, group discussion. When he was finished I asked him to make a list of the specific topics (he always checked the subheadings as a guide) he thought he might like to contribute to in discussion. Quickly he rattled off two topics and stood up at the whiteboard, an automatic response for him. With blue marker in hand, he drew a circle, erased it, and drew it again, only larger. He wrote the topic in the circle. He erased it again and drew a rectangle which he seemed to prefer, after stepping back to judge its appeal. Despite the repetitiousness of his entry into the task, I knew from prior experience that he would need to complete the visual, discuss it, and then leave in order to find a quiet space to transition the conceptual stages of his work to written form.

THE GROUP ENCOUNTER

I placed Presija, Cyd, and Randy in a small group together several times during the course of a semester so that they could identify ways for them to better understand how and why they interacted with others the way they did. I did not have any expectations beyond offering them a peer group in order to share experiences. Our first group was scheduled to run for 55 minutes. We met in my office at The Table, our clinical setting.

Randy arrived first, and rearranged the way I had laid out pads of paper and a bowl of candy.

"Are you having cookies tonight? Last semester you had cookies."

"Yes, later when we have coffee." I responded distractedly.

"You seem to be very late tonight. Are you feeling okay?"

"Yes, thank you. Just a little rushed."

Presija walked in, a disgusted look on her face. She took her usual seat at The Table, sighing heavily as she slunk down in her chair, pulling her baseball cap down tighter. Luckily Randy had chosen another chair, facing the door. He regarded her with some interest and attempted a smile, but she turned away and started text messaging.

"Sorry Presija. Ground rule one: no text messaging and no laptops." I said quietly.

"Well you could have told me before I sat down! Anything else I should know?"

Randy looked a little taken back at the razor-sharp caliber of her response.

"No. Not yet. I can't promise I won't surprise you now and then." I continued what I was doing, making hot water, opening a new box of cookies.

Cyd walked in looking a little flustered, but no less so than usual. He sat next to Randy and stared at Presija who turned completely around this time, but had nothing to busy herself with in order to make herself invisible. I sat down next to Presija and as I looked at The Table it appeared as if two females were facing off against two males. I made an effort to smile and felt oddly uncomfortable because I sensed the overall uneasiness of our little group.

I folded my hands because I wasn't sure what to do with them at that point in time. "So, let's get acquainted." They just stared at me. I went on to just say who I was (like they didn't know) and talked a little about my background. I nodded to Cyd.

"Can you tell the group a little about yourself?"

He stared at me for a moment, probably tempted to offer a flip remark, but decided against it.

"This is my second year here. I really don't like my classes much, and I think the professors are totally ridiculous! I got screwed on a few essay exams and still don't know why, but I think it'll get better. I hope. And, I think I have seen you in my politics class." With a raised eyebrow he looked at Presija.

She nodded. "Yup. I saw you. Isn't that Professor Raines a dork-and-a-half?"

"Yes, he's the one who screwed me!"

Randy and I watched the conversational tennis match with some amusement. He got up and helped me make the tea and serve the cookies, Cyd and Presija continuing their splaying of the professor and his carefully planned syllabus. I knew that at some point I needed to move us on to other conversation, although for the moment I was content that some kind of connection had been established between Presija and Cyd, despite the negative commentary.

"Randy, would you like to share something about who you are?"

"Sure. I've been here for three years, and I am a good friend of Cyd's." He needed to establish the boundary. Cyd nodded. Presija looked unimpressed. "I'm a communications major and am thinking of a career in advertising. I like most of my professors and my grades are pretty good."

"Then why are you here?" asked Presija.

Randy looked puzzled for a moment. "Well, because I do have memory problems, and need to check in with someone to make sure that everything is under control."

Presija pressed him for more details. "So what kind of memory problems? Short term? Long term? Can't remember your name?"

I gave her a stare, the kind that mothers give their children when they have been rude to another person. Cyd laughed with a little snort, and I transferred my stare to him. It was clear that an interesting group dynamic was taking shape.

Randy cleared his throat and continued. "I was in an accident when I was very young, and sustained significant damage to my memory."

Presija leaned into the table, much as I remember her mother doing when we met. "Do you have *brain damage*?"

He was hesitant, but said, "Yes, I think so."

I turned to Presija. "So tell the group who *you* are."

She expelled her usual heavy sigh, rolling her eyes. "This is my first semester here. I transferred from another college because I was failing in my junior year, and…"

There was a brief silence. Then Cyd leaned into the table.

"And what? What else happened? Did you *do* something?"

Presija put her feet on the rungs of my chair, and cocked her head to one side.

"Well, let's say the dean did not appreciate it when I repeatedly locked my roommate out of our room. I changed the locks."

Both young men looked captivated. She had removed her baseball cap and pulled her hair into a ponytail. In unison they asked, "And then what?"

"Well, I refused to stop doing this unless the dean's office made everyone behave with some kind of moral aptitude. They behaved like animals and never did their work!"

"Oh my God!" exclaimed Cyd. "They kicked you out, didn't they!"

They all snickered, their somewhat immature behaviors surfacing within just a 15 minute period of time. I knew I would have to work hard to keep the conversation productive and respectful to one another, as well as to the other people who walked in and out of their lives. The group session brought me into yet another context of their lives, one in which they recognized the value as well as the vulnerability in others. And, while there was some humor, I would have to work hard to see that it was contained within a socially appropriate and kind-hearted context.

Before me the theatrical perspective of human behavior unfolded. The interplay of intellect and emotions presented themselves in the unique characters who moved from knowing their scripts to improvising, inadvertently creating a social microcosm at The Table. The complexity of their profiles became the richness of their encounter. I, again, was the privileged onlooker.

REFERENCES

American Psychiatric Association. (2000). *Diagnostic and statistical manual of mental disorders* (text revision). Washington, DC: Author.

Bandura, A. (1999). Social cognitive theory: An agentic perspective. *Asian Journal of Social Psychology, 2*(1).

Blakemore, J., Berenbaum. S., & Liben, L. (2008). *Gender development.* New York: Psychology Press.

DelBello, M. P. (2002). *Twelve month outcome of adolescents with bipolar disorder following first-hospitalization for a manic or mixed episode.* University of Cincinnatti, Medicine: Epidemiology (Environmental Health), 2006.

Hamblen, J. (2001). Fact sheet. National Center on Post Traumatic Stress Disorder (NCPTSD). Retrieved from http://www.ncptsd.org

Johnson, C. P., & Blasco, P. A. (1997). Infant growth and development. *Pediatrics in Review, 120*(5), 1183–1215.

McCloskey, G., Perkins, L., & Van Diviner, R. (2008). *Assessment and intervention for executive function difficulties.* New York: Routledge

Miller, P. (2001). *Theories of developmental psychology* (4th ed.). New York: Worth.

Polombo, J. (2006). *Nonverbal learning disabilities: A clinical perspective.* New York: Norton.

Rourke, B. (2009, June). Are persons with NLD prone to develop bipolar disorder? Retrieved from http://www.nld-brourke.ca/BPRA38.html

Sugarman, L. (2001). *Lifespan development: Frameworks, accounts, and strategies.* New York: Psychology Press.

7

MULTILINGUAL COLLEGE STUDENTS WITH LEARNING DISABILITIES

PATRICIA MYTKOWICZ

BEGINNINGS

Krysta's application for admission to the Program for Advancement of Learning for Multilingual Students (PML) at Curry College touched my heart. An Eastern European native and orphanage survivor, she was adopted at the age of 10 by an American family, and she earnestly asked for a chance: she said she was capable of academic achievement if she was given an opportunity and was provided the kind of support she needed. Her vulnerability was apparent. "I know that I am not stupid. In some ways, I really am smart. I wish there were a way for it to be easier."

On the other hand, Luis, a South American immigrant, entered his interview session with bravado and swaggering self-confidence, and I knew he would be a tough nut to crack if he entered the program. "No problem," was his standard answer when I queried his reading and writing abilities. Mei, guarded, apprehensive, and somewhat sullen, appeared on my doorstep because her Asian family was well able to afford to send her to an American university where there was recognition of and support for students with dyslexia. "I am here for my father, not me," this international student from Asia told me during our first meeting.

Perhaps the most challenging student to apply to PML was John, who had spent most of his life in a refugee camp after he was forced to separate from his family and flee his troubled African nation. He was lucky enough to attend a competitive high school in the United States after his arrival, but would this sparse, 4-year background make up for years of trauma and lack of formal education? "I know I cannot help my people without an education." John's sincerity was tough to ignore, and despite my reservations, I took a chance, not only on John, but on Luis, Krysta, and Mei as well. All of these students entered the Program for Advancement of Learning for Multilingual Students at Curry College and each brought unique, yet somewhat typical issues to the educational therapy table. This chapter looks at the challenges of working with college students whose native language is not English, who have learning disabilities, who cope with longstanding cultural and personal shame, and who have very different histories compared to most of the students we encounter in our traditional work. While this chapter focuses on postsecondary students and issues, many of the lessons learned can be applied to other settings.

BACKGROUND

There are a number of nonnative English speakers who enroll in American postsecondary institutions each year. Some students are immigrants, or the children of immigrants; others come as U.S. citizens from multilingual Caribbean islands to practice English in a native setting; and another group consists of international students who choose to study in the United States. While second language speakers are on the rise at many postsecondary settings (Abel, 2002), both international and multilingual learners encounter a number of challenges. Problems include language proficiency, unfamiliar teaching practices, and sociocultural differences (Bodycott & Walker, 2000).

Some multilingual students may be at even greater risk due to learning disabilities (LDs). In some cases, the student is well aware of the disability; in other cases, the concept of an LD may be unrecognized in the student's home culture, may have been ignored, not diagnosed, or not previously encountered in native language learning (Gallardo, 1999; McLoughlin, Beard, Ryan, & Kirk, 2000; Schwarz, 2000). For any English speaker of other languages (ESOL), the task of becoming proficient in academic English is daunting. Add a learning disability to the ESOL student's profile and the situation becomes overwhelming at best, particularly for those students whose cultures or educational backgrounds do not recognize or accept LDs (Gallardo, 1999; Preece, Rice, Beecher, Roberts, & Stearns, 2003; Sunderland, Klein, Savinson, & Partridge, 1997). Because of these complexities, cognitive, cultural, emotional, and linguistic, this population presents a range of challenges to the educational therapist.

CHALLENGES

One of the first difficulties that the educational therapist faces in dealing with nonnative speakers who may be experiencing academic problems is trying to determine whether an LD may be part of the presenting problem. Accurately identifying LDs in nonnative speakers is not only problematic, but may, in fact, be impossible due to overlapping characteristics of second language acquisition and LDs, current testing procedures and norms, and cultural issues.

DIAGNOSIS AND LANGUAGE ACQUISITION

Learning difficulties are often not diagnosed because problems are attributed to normal stages in second language acquisition (SLA) (Deponio, Landon, & Reid, 2000; Levine, 2002; Ortiz, 1997; Rooney & Schwarz, 1999; Schwarz, 2000). When students fail to progress as English learners, LDs may be overlooked, and instead, causes can be erroneously attributed to multiple factors like low intelligence, lack of motivation, and poor assessments that are not culturally/linguistically sensitive (Ortiz, 1997, 2002; Rooney, 2002; Schwarz, 2000). A number of studies suggest that when proficiency has not been achieved in a first language, particularly in reading and writing, learning a second language can be even more difficult (Levine, 2002; McLoughlin et al., 2000); thus first language literacy must be examined thoroughly as one of the first steps in gathering relevant diagnostic information when an educational therapist begins to work with a nonnative English speaker who may be having difficulty with English language learning.

For educational therapists who suspect that an ESOL student's failure to achieve English language literacy and academic language proficiency may be due to an LD, Rooney and Schwarz (1999) suggest the importance of a multifaceted assessment. This kind of evaluation should include (1) a comprehensive educational history; (2) a cognitive profile, but they caution that "analysis of the results of [any cognitive testing] should take into consideration differences in language, culture and norming population" (p. 11); (3) a nonverbal test like the Comprehensive Test of Nonverbal Intelligence (C-TONI); (4) a writing sample; and (5) dynamic testing that can assess whether the student can apply strategy instruction and mediation to a specific cognitive or academic task (Feuerstein & Feuerstein, 2001). Often, an educational therapist can glean the most useful information from qualitative data gathered from the student, parents, and educators to assess prior linguistic performance. In some very difficult cases, the therapist may need to work with a native speaker in order to assess whether the student exhibits similar mistakes in the first language (Woodman, 2001).

One of the most difficult aspects of working with these students can be convincing them to be evaluated. Schwarz (2000) says, "… some students refused to be tested, fearing adverse family reactions; others balked at the cost; still others were simply not convinced of the need" (p. 200). For many students, fear of disability prevents them from moving forward and facing an LD diagnosis. The stigma that many students and their families attach to a diagnosis that points to a disability can be significant, depending on cultural norms and expectations. In describing the viewpoints of a number of minorities, Dr. Sam Chin, a professor at California Polytechnic Institute, states, "disability of any kind is viewed often with a significant amount of stigma and because of that, many parents of children with learning disabilities will associate that disability with a sense of shame, a need to keep that disability private or hidden within the family" (as cited In Gallardo, 1999). Because of the desire to "hide" the disability, lack of awareness of LDs in many countries, and the difficulty with diagnosis, many ESOL and culturally diverse students are not diagnosed until they reach postsecondary settings. By this point, shame and low self-esteem are an integral part of the student's identity and it takes a skilled educational therapist to address these feelings if any academic progress is to be made.

ENGLISH LANGUAGE SKILLS

Educational therapists also need to be aware of the "embedded curriculum" which is the role of language skills as a determinant of success in the classroom; this curriculum, often unrecognized by many teachers and university professors, can be a deterrent to the ESOL student with an LD (Olivier, Hecker, Klucken, & Westby, 2000). College classrooms, in particular, show an increased "language load" that is difficult for the typical ESOL student, but even more so for the language impaired student to manage. Olivier and others (2000) describe increased "language load" as:

> Reading assignments are longer, and teachers speak for longer periods of time for different purposes, using different forms of discourse. Students are expected to write and speak with increasing accuracy, completeness, and sophistication. The demand for simultaneous performance of language skills increases, as students must take notes while listening to a lecture, or reading a textbook, or apply spelling, capitalization,

punctuation, organization, and handwriting skills simultaneously while composing the response to an essay test (pp. 6–7)

Students who manage two or more linguistics systems and who also have language processing difficulties have great difficulty with language load, and it is the educational therapist's job to help the student to find strategies that will assist in effective management of the multiple language-oriented tasks presented in the classroom.

Many professors mistakenly believe that if a student's basic or automatic communication skills appear intact, then they are able to handle the more complex academic language demands of the classroom (Cummins, 1984; Levine, 2002). Cummins estimates that, on average, ESOL students achieve conversational ability in 1 to 2 years but need 5 to 7 years to achieve academic language proficiency (1984). Fluent basic interpersonal communication skills often mask difficulties in second language acquisition and possible learning problems, which are more likely to surface as a student encounters increasingly complex academic language and literacy demands. Cummins also points out, however, that limited academic language is not an automatic indication of an LD, a common misdiagnosis, and that students must be given adequate time to develop this level of English proficiency before being labeled LD.

Since it takes a great deal of time to develop academic language, ESOL students with LDs are at a disadvantage and professors may not understand their unique struggle. The educational therapist will benefit from constant awareness of how challenging it is for nonnative speakers with LDs to cope with heavily language laden courses, particularly if these students are still working in the translation stage of processing language.

CASE STUDIES

It appears that some of the very pedagogy that supports students with learning disabilities is similar to that which is foundational to the success of second language learners (Ijiri & Rooney, 1995; Rooney, 2002; Rooney & Schwarz, 1999). Yet few studies examine the relationship between these two educational philosophies. Several researchers point out the need for educational supports and strategies that address the duality of SLA and LD (Cloud, 1988; Ortiz, 2002), yet it appears that few service providers combine pedagogy from the two fields to address the specialized needs of this population. Ortiz (2002) suggests, "English language learners who need special education services are further disadvantaged by the shortage of special educators who are trained to address their language- and disability-related needs simultaneously" (p. 1).

PML Background

Curry College's long-standing Program for Advancement of Learning (PAL) began to address the needs of this distinctive population in 1995 through PAL for Multilingual Students (PML). Like PAL, PML's underlying philosophy is strength-based and metacognitive in nature, and the program relies on the relationship that students develop with their professors who serve in the role of educational therapists. Ricardo Stanton-Salazar (as cited in Nieto, 1999) believes that multicultural college students, in particular, need "institutional agents, that is individuals who help negotiate institutional resources and opportunities, including information about academic programs, career decision making … role modeling, and emotional and moral support" (p. 97). Educational therapists will benefit if they are able to function in the role of an institutional agent as they work with all college students, but particularly when they work with international and immigrant students.

Four case studies follow. Each represents a type of multilingual student with an LD that an educational therapist might encounter: an adult immigrant, an international student, an adoptee from another country, and a refugee. These cases are composites of the types of students who have gone through the program at Curry College. Problems associated with assessment as well as complex cultural, linguistic, psychological, and learning issues are addressed.

Luis

Luis, an adult immigrant from a South American country, embodies many of the risks associated with this population. He was diagnosed with dyslexia and attention deficit disorder after he enrolled in ESOL classes in the United States. His story unfolded slowly: he struggled with Spanish literacy in his native culture, had great difficulties paying attention in school, and was often in trouble because of his uncontrolled anger and frustration. By the time I met him, he was coping with deep-seated shame, difficulty with cultural transition, unresolved emotional difficulties, self-doubt, and anger.

As I slowly learned more about Luis, I understood that writing a paper required hours as he struggled not just to find and but also to spell the English words that he needed to express his thoughts. Microsoft Word's automatic red lines appearing under his misspelled words frustrated and paralyzed him, and it was easier not to write at all than to cope with the "blood" as he described it. We quickly moved to my scribing his words, and this strategy enabled him to devote his attention and energy to generating ideas and the language needed to express those ideas. Scribing became a comfortable and effective way for us to work: I asked him questions, forced him to explain his ideas logically and coherently, and taught him grammar and vocabulary as I recorded his ideas. At the beginning, our work was slow and exhausting for him. Thinking in two linguistic systems simultaneously requires a tremendous amount of cognitive focus and energy. But as he witnessed his words appear on the screen, he grew more confident, his use of language improved, and he felt more successful as a learner.

I found that the best way to help him comprehend his reading assignments was to read to him, so I could explain the English words he had not yet acquired. Reading aloud also gave us the opportunity to discuss ideas, and through our discussions I learned more about Luis's strong conceptual ability as well as his troubled past. One of the most important sessions that I had with Luis was after I had already known him for over a year. He had progressed to the point that he could struggle on his own through many of his reading assignments with the aid of a Spanish-English dictionary, followed by discussion of the reading material with me. I had asked him to read a psychology chapter, and I was annoyed when he admitted he had not done the reading. As I began to read the section on the effects of child abuse on later adult functioning, I looked at Luis to see if he needed any vocabulary explication. His head was down and tears were falling. I stopped and waited. "You just read a description of my life," he whispered. Luis admitted he had read the passage the night before but wanted the chance to share and reveal why he had had so many difficulties in his life. He didn't know how to begin, so my reading the section aloud allowed an entry into Luis's shame and failure.

Hearing me read the words in the text unleashed his story. Luis described not living up to his educated and accomplished father's expectations. He talked about the misery of not being able to read and trying to hide it. He admitted the years of beatings when he couldn't "get it." And it was almost as though he understood for the first time what those years of failure and beatings had cost him. As he heard the words that I read from the page, that child abuse can cause problems like failed marriages, substance abuse, and uncontrollable anger in later life, he said he was starting to see why his marriage had failed, why he struggled with drinking, and why he was still facing difficulties staying out of fights. Luis had been to therapy before, but our discussion allowed me to broach the idea again. He began to see a psychologist and as his self-esteem slowly grew, his confidence in himself as a learner progressed as well.

One of the most important lessons that an educational therapist can take from Luis's story is the need to make a strong connection with the client so that the work that needs to take place can happen in a safe and trusting relationship. While it is imperative to make such a connection with any student with whom one works, it is even more important to do so with a student who may be coping with the alienation and isolation that coexist with culture shock. Boyer and Sedlacek (as cited in Stoynoff, 1996) assert that the "strongest predictor of non native students' GPAs was the availability of a strong support person" (p. 333). Positive connections and personal relationships with students are important factors in establishing "a climate for learning, that … cannot be separated from a climate in which care, concern and love are central … love is at the core of good teaching because it is predicated on high standards, rigorous demands, and respect for students, their identities, and their families" (Nieto, 1999, p. 100). It had taken over a year of work together before Luis trusted me enough to reveal his story, yet it wasn't until his story was able to be told that Luis was able to take control of his educational future and subsequent success.

Additionally, the educational therapist will benefit from being culturally aware and sensitive. Reflective practitioners can examine their own teaching/communication styles to determine whether they are creating climates conducive to respect and care for their students as well as affirming students' cultural and personal differences, important considerations in working with diverse populations (Talbert-Johnson & Beran, 1999). In Luis's case, a great deal of his difficulty in accepting his failure was a result of cultural expectations. For a Latino male, any perceived diminishing of masculine power is shameful. Without an understanding of Luis's reality, it would have been far more difficult for me to gain his trust. Ultimately, my work with Luis was not centered on improving his English; instead, my work was helping him to understand how the humiliation he had suffered because of his LD, his parents' and society's expectations, and the lack of awareness of dyslexia in his native school system had damaged his self-perception and functioning.

It was not an easy road, but Luis graduated from Curry College. Luis knows that, ultimately, he was the sole driver on his road to a college degree; but he also knows it was the partnership, collaboration, and mutual respect that he and his educational therapist as navigator developed, that empowered him to take control of his journey. Once he was able to trust me, he was able to reveal and face what was getting in the way of his progress. Knowing that I believed in him helped him to believe in himself and that was the beginning of his path to success.

Mei

Mei was one of the lucky ones. While she had encountered years of frustration and academic difficulties in her native Asian country where there was little recognition or awareness of

LDs, she was eventually diagnosed with dyslexia while she was in high school. Mei's difficulties began with native language learning, and research suggests an increasing awareness that dyslexia can be cross-lingual. Yin and Weekes (2003) suggest that while "little is known about the prevalence of dyslexia in Mainland China … the data from Hong Kong show that dyslexia is as much of a concern for Chinese speakers as it is for English speakers" (p. 272). Mei was a classic example of cross-cultural dyslexia, struggling for years in both her native language and English acquisitions. Yin and Weeks (2003) also correlate a higher incidence of dyslexia with left-handedness. Mei was forced to change her dominant left-handedness by her mother when she was a young child.

And that fact is a very telling one because it hints of a long, arduous, and usually unsuccessful attempt on Mei's part to please her parents, in particular, her mother. Mei's story is an important one for educational therapists because it illustrates the need for cultural awareness, shows the importance of looking at first language literacy in diagnosis, and underscores the traumatic effects of unmet expectations.

Certainly, an ethnic stereotype suggests that Asian parents hold exceptionally high expectations and standards for their children; yet a body of research suggests the stereotype is, in fact, verifiable and points out that many Asian children feel the need to conform to their parents' wishes, particularly to their academic demands (Chen & Lan, 1998; Sunmin, Hee-soon, Martinez, Robinson, Bawa, & Grace, 2009). Without understanding both Mei's difficulties with first language literacy and the intense, culturally acceptable pressure to achieve which was part of her life, I would have missed a very significant threat to Mei's very existence.

Her difficulties began early on in learning Cantonese. She recalled difficulty in learning how to write in Cantonese in her early grades. "Writing in Chinese was really a problem. In reading Chinese, I'm really, really slow. I could not remember how to write words because [in] Chinese there are a lot of characters. We don't use an alphabet, we use characters and some of the words have the same meaning but you write them differently."

Mei's early difficulties with Cantonese were most likely related to her then undiagnosed dyslexia. Yin and Weekes (2003) report that many Chinese dyslexics have difficulty learning the "visual configuration of characters" (p. 272); and this is a problem that Mei described when she discussed her native language learning difficulties. Mei had demonstrated an inability to remember Cantonese characters well before her problems with English began in middle school. "One Chinese word needs, I don't know how many lines. There are thousands of characters. So I was having trouble even before English."

As she was exposed to English instruction in middle school, her learning problems became more and more apparent. "I started to have trouble in eight grade or seven grade. But I didn't know I have a learning disability, I just know that I was having trouble because I always failed my English subjects. I didn't get the word, and I spelled every word wrong. If you get grammar wrong, the whole thing's wrong, and in my country, you're expected to do well in school. A lot of kids' moms compare your grade to other genius kids. They say, 'Why that person get that excellent grade and you get a 0 or 10 grade?' A lot of moms do that; compare your grade to other kids in your class. My mom did that and I felt really stupid." Mei told me that academic achievement is a cultural expectation and source of parental pride. "They expect you to get A in every single subject." Mei was fortunate to be diagnosed and finished high school in the United States at a secondary school that specializes in helping students with dyslexia. When I met her, she was still trying to please her parents, so she enrolled in college, having no interest in furthering her studies. Thus, it became really important to try to help Mei learn more about herself, her strengths, and her own learning style as a means to assist her in becoming an autonomous, self-reflecting adult.

Mei needed to learn how to learn and to focus on the areas in which she excelled. Strength-based learning helps students develop strategies that go beyond a specific learning circumstance to generalize an ability to monitor and modify their own learning in other situations (Chamot & O'Malley, 1994; O'Malley & Chamot, 1990; Oxford, 1990; Pennini & Peltz, 1995). Metacognitive strategies, those that are related to executive functions: planning, reflecting, monitoring and evaluating (Brown, 2000), can be effectively integrated into educational therapy to support success for all learners (Brown, 2000; Downey & Snyder, 2001; Ganschow, Schneider, & Evers, 2000; Ijiri & Rooney, 1995; Leons, 2002; Levine, 2002; O'Malley & Chamot, 1990; Oxford, 1990; Pennini & Peltz, 1995). The goal of metacognitive instruction is not a short-term one meant merely to support current academic needs; instead, its main purpose is to assist students in life-long goal setting, planning, and reevaluation. Riley (1998) reports the significance of self-learning and awareness in a student's words: "The metacognition doesn't just help with school; it comes up all through my life" (p. 114). For both students with learning disabilities and students whose first language is not English, metacognitive strategy instruction can be a crucial educational intervention.

For Mei, strategy instruction was critical, as was a strength-based approach to her success. When I asked her what she was good at, she impishly replied, "Math—like all Asians!" Of course, Mei would still need to take language-laden courses like psychology, sociology, and philosophy, but the first thing we did was to use her math ability both for short term purposes and also for long term goals. When we discussed why she was good at math, we discovered that she thought in sequential, logical steps. We began to break all her assignments into a hierarchy of tasks that she could approach much like she did a math problem. For longer term success, I assisted her with planning an individually designed major in applied mathematics and accounting, so she could use her strong calculation skills as the basis for a successful course of study. Reading continued to be problematic, so I encouraged her to use the Kurzweil scanner, an assistive technology tool that digitizes and reads back text. Using this assistive technology never improved her dislike for reading, but it made her reading assignments more manageable. Sometimes, the best intervention is actually supplied by the student; Mei gave me this advice when we first began working together. "I think you need to understand the student first and ask the student what they need to help themselves, so you can then help or figure out with the student what works." Despite her own advice, however, Mei was unable to define what it was that would help her, until, ironically, she started to think metacognitively. Much later in our work together, as she understood more about her own learning strengths, she began to provide her own solutions to academic challenges.

Despite this progress that became more tangible in a number of Dean's List semesters, however, Mei did not seem happy or satisfied or any better able to talk about her own feelings. One warm day she entered my office dressed in a heavy, long-sleeved sweat shirt. She slammed a book down on the table, and for the first time, she let me see inside her incredible pain. She had just received her grades, and while she had well over a 3.0 GPA, her mother had asked her why it was not higher. She began to cry as she pulled the heavy sweat shirt over her head, revealing a series of old scars with a few new, freshly cut lines on her arms. That's when I began to understand the deep effects of Mei's frustration and shame. In an attempt to gain control over her emotional pain, Mei had been cutting herself, a practice that is on the rise, particularly in adolescent girls. "Prevalence studies report rates of 5–47% in community adolescent samples, 12–35% among college students, and 4% in general adult populations…" (Dyl, 2008, p. 1). Hinshaw and Kranz (2009) directly attribute parental pressure as a contributing factor in this disturbing trend of self-mutilation.

I'd like to say that Mei got better immediately after I insisted that she begin to see a therapist, but improvement came slowly and arduously. At last, however, the unrealistic academic pressure, the shame of her many failures and resulting pain were at least on the table and the devastating consequences could be addressed. I could now ask openly about whether she was cutting, and surprisingly, while she didn't continue therapy for very long, she seemed able to move past that destructive practice, to manage her feelings, and to cope in a more productive way. I was able to convince her father to have her see a therapist when she was home during the summer, and again, while she did not continue the therapy for a long period, she seemed better able to handle frustration and stress. During her last semester, much of our work centered on how she would live her life when she returned to her home country, and we developed many strategies that she could use in her daily life, employment, and relationships.

Krysta

Krysta's story is an important one to tell because it shows the educational therapist that despite good intentions and solid interventions, comorbid conditions can conspire to block success. Krysta, a petite young woman from an impoverished Eastern European country, was adopted by an American couple when she was 10 years old. Born to and raised by an alcoholic mother and an alcoholic maternal grandmother, Krysta spent her final years in her native country in an orphanage after being removed from her birth family because of neglect and abuse. Krysta's mother was working as a prostitute during the time of her conception. Her mother reportedly drank heavily throughout her pregnancy and Krysta herself suggested that she may, in fact, have suffered from fetal alcohol syndrome (FAS).

Krysta had few memories of her traumatic former life. Although she told me that education was compulsory in her native country, she also said, "I don't remember if I went. I don't know much about schools there because none of my family went to school. I learned to read when I came to America, and I didn't even know how to speak my own language. Well, I knew, but I had the vocabulary of a 5-year-old even though I was 10." She did remember angry and defiant reactions at being taken from the only home she had ever known. "I was 10 years old and very scared because I did not speak English. I was brought to America on a long plane ride that I didn't want to make. I was a very angry and confused little girl."

Initially, Krysta did not transition easily to her new American home. Her first response to her adoptive parents and her new home was violent according to her personal recollections of the move. Krysta admitted her abusive, explosive behavior focused on her adoptive mother during her first few years in America. "I never let her touch me. I used to beat her." Rage and aggressive behavior characterized her early years in her adoptive home with interventions that included attachment therapy, family and individual counseling, and therapeutic summer camps.

Krysta's profile embodies the complexity involved in evaluating multilingual students, particularly those from impoverished backgrounds. In Krysta's case, it is difficult to assess whether her learning difficulties are organic, emotional, psychiatric, and environmental or a combination of these contributing factors. With multilingual students like Krysta, the diagnosis of an LD is difficult at best and not verifiable in reality. Schwarz (2000) suggests that diagnosis may be "no more than an accurate guess" (p. 194), and Rance-Raney (2000) believes an accurate diagnosis may, in fact, be impossible in many cases.

Academic concerns first emerged with difficulties in reading, understanding complex instructions and learning new concepts after Krysta had been in an English-speaking school for one year. Many second language learners exhibit characteristics of LD in the normal stages of language development until they become more proficient (Carrasquillo & Reyes Bonilla, 1990; Willig, 1986). However, Krysta continued to display increasing difficulty in the classroom which did not appear to be related to normal language acquisition. Krysta's scores on early administrations of the Wechsler Intelligence Scales for Children (WISC–III), followed by later evaluations using the Wechsler Adult Intelligence Scales (WAIS-III), reflected low average overall IQ with better nonverbal than verbal processing abilities. Unfortunately, there was no documentation of her native language learning to assess whether similar issues existed prior to her challenging English language learning. To complicate matters, Krysta had been diagnosed with bipolar disorder in the middle of her high school years.

Without a doubt, Krysta presented as an at-risk student with multiple challenges. She needed an incredible amount of support if she were to have any chance at success. Ultimately, my desired outcome was that Krysta would experience academic success for the first time in her life, helping her to begin to believe in herself. However, I was aware that this goal could not happen without extensive therapeutic support, both from me educationally and from her psychotherapist, with possible additional on-campus counseling.

As an educational therapist, my role was to design a plan to support Krysta as she began her first year at Curry College. It was important for me to develop a relationship with Krysta that established boundaries and encouraged trust. This was particularly difficult because Krysta admitted, "I have a lot of trust and attachment issues because of my background." Equally essential was my support of Krysta's continued participation in psychotherapy to help her deal with the emotional overlay and trauma from her past as well as the mood swings associated with her bipolar disorder.

Krysta's first year at Curry College was riddled with short bursts of academic interest, and punctured by emotional crises, difficult social relationships, substance abuse and erratic use of antidepressants. While the fall semester was not easy, she committed to regular work with me and finished all her courses with a respectable grade point average. But then disaster struck in the form of her birth mother's continued difficulty and its intrusion in Krysta's life.

During late adolescence, Krysta insisted on reconnecting with her birth mother, and she traveled to her native country where she met the woman who had given birth to her. Despite years of physical separation, Krysta's emotional health was still directly impacted by her birth mother's actions. When Krysta's birth mother abruptly left a detoxification facility and went missing for several weeks, Krysta's academic work and emotional health suffered a serious setback; she stopped attending classes and refused to answer phone calls from me. Because of her fragility and emotional link to her dysfunctional birth mother, Krysta's personal downward spiral continued after her birth mother reappeared and continued her own destructive cycle. Krysta was attached by an invisible bungee cord that allowed occasional detachment followed by a sharp yank back into her birth mother's painful and destructive choices. Krysta was drinking heavily herself and engaging in promiscuous relationships. She was inexorably connected to the woman who had given her life as well as to the destructive patterns that had preceded her own birth, even when this link threatened Krysta's own ability to succeed.

Ultimately, Krysta had to withdraw from two classes during her second semester. Her attendance in the remaining classes was erratic and her work with me was sparse at best. She admitted she frequently avoided seeing me because I confronted her with the reality of missed classes and assignments. At this point as the academic year came to a close, Krysta's future at Curry College was in jeopardy, and as an educational therapist, my job was to help her see that she could not summon the energy that she needed to succeed academically unless she was willing to face her demons through continued psychotherapy and medical treatment.

I tried everything: daily phone calls; long conversations with her therapist to help me find ways to get her into my office; sessions spent tackling the untouched assignments; assistive technologies to help make the work more manageable; heart-to-heart conversations in which I tried to get Krysta to accept responsibility for the bad choices she was making. Ultimately, Krysta failed and had to drop out of college. The last I heard she was expecting her second child, was unmarried and unemployed. In some cases, educational therapy cannot heal or minimize the damage that has occurred in a student's past life. For Krysta, the cycle of her birth mother's destructive behavior, coupled with her own mental health issues, proved too strong for her to break free at that time in her life. I think back to the first words I heard from Krysta: "I know that I am not stupid. In some ways, I really am smart. I wish there were a way for it to be easier." From our work together, I saw that Krysta, indeed, was smart in many ways. I only wish that I could have found the way for it to be easier for her.

John

When I met John, I was immediately charmed by his flashing smile and humble demeanor. He explained that he had been given a Christian name because his village had been converted to Christianity by missionaries years ago, but he proudly carried his African family name as well. As I reviewed John's testing, I found his WAIS-III profile alarming for a prospective college student. His nonverbal processing score was far below average, but I had worked with nonnative speakers of English long enough to know that the scores were not reliable, and in fact, were invalid since the normative sample did not include a single person like John. Despite his difficulty pronouncing some of the English sounds that are not present in his African language, he was able to convince me that his language skills were strong enough that he might be able to survive with a lot of support.

I didn't know it then, but his language skills, though challenging, would be the least of my trials in working with John. In some ways, those low nonverbal scores were accurate predictors of the kinds of difficulties John would encounter as someone who would have problems understanding social situations and interpreting nonverbal language, facial expressions, and gestures. But was it really his low performance scores, his tribal village upbringing, or the consequences of losing his family at a young age and struggling for survival in a refugee camp that was the more important factor in his difficult transition to living and studying in an American postsecondary environment?

Additionally, John had great difficulty with a number of executive functions, particularly those that relate to working memory and recall. A number of researchers (Emdad, Sondergaard, &Tores, 2005; Gilbertson, Gurvits, Lasko, Orr, & Pitman, 2001; Koso & Hansen, 2006) have positively correlated impaired memory and executive functions with posttraumatic stress disorder (PTSD), and John had been diagnosed with PTSD not long after his arrival in the United States. John would be a challenge, and often over the next few years, I was reminded that "it takes a village" because more than once I needed the support of others on campus to help John succeed.

John illustrates how important it is to teach direct expectations to a nonnative speaker with an LD. So many things that educators take for granted in their work with students cannot be assumed when working with a student like John. He had spent 4 years in an American high school, and during that time he had countless people wanting to support him: peers, teachers, and compassionate community members who all fell in love with the lovable John. But John was now in college where he knew no one and where he had to be responsible for himself after having been in the United States for only 5 years. We had a long journey ahead of us.

I felt it was important to see John more frequently than I see many of my new students. I scheduled sessions every day I was on campus; an effective strategy for assuring that John had an agenda and a to-do list every day. As I began working with him, I saw that I needed to help him practice something very simple: eye contact. I knew that in his culture, making eye contact with older people is not acceptable, and it took some time with John sitting next to me and facing in the opposite direction before I felt he was ready to be instructed that this behavior was not appropriate in American culture. Clearly, however, looking me directly in the eye was uncomfortable for John, and even after months of working with him, he often looked away as we conversed. His inability to maintain eye contact went beyond his cultural discomfort, though, and it could also signal shame or regret about something that may have happened on campus: a fight, a drinking episode, or not having completed an assignment. I found that his looking away during conversation was often linked to his comfort level regarding what was being discussed, and each time he entered my office and did not look at me, I knew something was up, usually not good.

I found that I needed to be explicit in all my dealings with John. I needed to directly instruct what a syllabus was and how to use it. It didn't matter how many times I helped John organize his syllabi and other papers, I still needed to do a weekly backpack check with him to reorganize and reprioritize his work. John seemed incapable of holding onto things and often lost work that we had completed. We used every possible organization system known to man: binders, agendas, sticky notes, calendars, color-coded schedules, cell phone reminders, but organization continued to be one of John's greatest challenges, not only in his academic life, but also in his personal one. I made copies of all completed work, either in hard copy or in a digital file on my hard drive.

One day when John came to tell me had lost yet another assignment we had completed, I was exasperated, and even more so when he said we could just do the work again. I proposed an imaginary situation to him: "Okay, John, you are a supervisor who has spent several hours working with one of your employees to complete a project. He comes to work the next day and tells you he has lost the notes you worked on together." John's eyes widened and it was as though he finally recognized that his actions were disrespectful because they did not take my time and effort into account. I'd like to say that it never happened again, but it wouldn't have been John if it hadn't. And even if he lost important documents after that, he at least seemed to understand that it was a bigger deal than he had previously acknowledged.

John was also a great head nodder, and educational therapists will benefit from understanding that English language learners often use this technique either because they think they understand what they have heard, or because they do not want to admit that they do not. Very quickly, I discovered that I needed to have John repeat back to me his understanding of what I had said. This was an excellent way for me to check his comprehension, but it also gave John practice in short term memory, synthesizing, and interpreting more complex language.

Far more important, however, than John's linguistic misunderstandings, was his harrowing past and its intrusion on his current life. John rarely spoke of fleeing his burning village, losing his family, and living in a refugee camp, but the past trauma often surfaced, and it was important for me to understand that when it did, John needed to deal with it before any kind of educational progress could continue. John's charismatic smile usually brightened the room when he entered, so I'll never forget the day that John entered my office with a heavy scowl on his face. For a brief moment his eyes met mine, and I saw rage like I had never witnessed in my life. Once again, John had run into a disciplinary issue within the residence hall and that morning had had to attend a hearing; he had not told me about this latest transgression. I usually accompanied John to his hearings because he often had difficulty understanding why he was being sanctioned, so my job was to help him to process how he had gotten into trouble, what steps he could take in the future to avoid these types of problems, and to understand why the "punishment" was appropriate. John began to rant about how the disciplinary officer had been unfair, how the sanction was not called for, how he was not responsible for any of the problem. And then he stopped and said, "It reminds me of the camp, especially the day I was beaten to within an inch of my life." I said nothing. John described a day when he waited interminably in an impossibly long line with hundreds of other refugees under a blazing sun. "You would not believe how thin I was, how thirsty, how hungry, how many people were in front of me, and the camp officials were so slow that I thought I was going to die before I reached the front of the line. My heart was beating out of my chest and I got out of line and started to stagger forward."

Camp police grabbed John and beat him mercilessly. John's experience in his disciplinary hearing that morning had returned him to a place and a time when he had almost died, and clearly we would make no progress on his latest assignment. I immediately called the college psychologist who had also been working with him. John left my office to meet with the counselor. When he returned a few hours later, his usual bright smile had returned, and he was ready to work.

John and I have navigated a number of challenging courses over the last few years, and he is close to completing his degree. I still joke with him about his being on African time, but he has become more aware of fast-paced American responsibilities. He still needs many reminders of what he needs to do, but he has developed better organizational strategies to help him with his impaired memory functions. He has confirmed my belief that he had the potential to succeed in college and it is rewarding working with someone who had so few opportunities early in life and who is so grateful now for the chances he has been given. I know John will use his education to improve the lives of his extended family who continue to live in impossibly difficult conditions in his African village.

LESSONS LEARNED: INTERVENTIONS

While there is no "one size fits all" intervention when it comes to working with ESOL students with LDs, there are a number of strategies that can be employed to assist this group. Each student's needs, of course, are unique, but educational therapists should understand the importance of the following:

- Establishing a Mentoring Relationship;
- Introducing students to on-campus support systems (like counseling);
- Assisting students in understanding and using personal learning strengths;
- Exposing students to assistive technologies such as the Kurzweil scanner to assist reading fluency, comprehension, and academic language development;
- Supporting development of English language skills in both oral and written formats;
- Encouraging accountability, self-advocacy, and independence;
- Helping students connect the relationship between commitment, personal responsibility, and results.

IMPORTANCE OF PERSONAL CONNECTION

Educational therapists are important support providers and may, in fact, make the difference between success and failure for ESOL students with LDs. The case studies, however, show that educational therapists need far more than academic preparation and a laundry list of teaching strategies to instruct students with LDs, particularly when those students come from linguistically and culturally diverse backgrounds. These types of students need to make strong associations with service providers and need to feel that the educational therapist knows them personally and cares about them (Adelizzi, 1995; Corey, 2003; Finn, 1999; Pennini & Peltz, 1995; Preece et al., 2003). Research suggests that the LD support practitioner is a major factor in students' perceptions and ultimate success (Finn, 1999; Ijiri & Rooney, 1995; Vogel, Leyser, Wyland, & Brulie, 1999), but it is the relationship that students develop with the educational therapist that appears to be more critical than any metacognitive or study strategy instruction that occurs (Ijiri, Carroll, Fletcher, Manchester, & VonSomeren, 1998; Ijiri & Rooney, 1995; Pennini & Peltz, 1995). Research also indicates that multilingual students, too, need a supportive practitioner. Rooney and Schwarz (1999) suggest that multilingual students:

> appreciate learning strategies for time management, organization, spatial orientation, reading, writing, listening, speaking, and note taking, but having "their own person" to listen to, encourage, and understand them, helps them develop a sense of self-worth and self-confidence that can carry them to independence and success. (p. 14)

For educational therapists to work successfully with culturally diverse populations, they need to examine their own cultural assumptions to be sure they are open and unbiased, so they can establish a critical level of trust necessary for working with this kind of client. They must be able to affirm cultural and personal differences by learning as much as possible about each student's script and culture. Teachers in general, and educational therapists in particular, who take the time to get to know their students as people; who show respect, particularly for different cultures and learning styles; and who demonstrate an ethic of care can positively impact student learning (Collinson & Killeavy, 1999; Peart & Campbell, 1999; Talbert-Johnson & Beran, 1999; Tebben, 1995). Dr. Robert Brooks (2003), a well-known researcher and practitioner in the LD field refers to the importance of what Dr. Julius Segal called the "charismatic adult" in people's lives. The "charismatic adult" can assist others in recognizing and developing what Brooks terms their individual "islands of competence." Educational therapists who can become "charismatic adults" in the lives of ESOL students with LDs can help these clients to discover their own unique "islands of competence." When asked what had made the difference for her as she completed her bachelor's degree at Curry College, one of my former PML students described the importance of having such a person in her life. "Well, I always think that when someone believes in you and encourages you that always overcomes everything. That's very, very important. That makes you feel important and that makes you feel like you'll succeed and overcome challenges."

REFERENCES

Abel, C. F. (2002). Academic success and the international student: Research and recommendations. In B. H. Carmical & B. W. Speck (Eds.), *Internationalizing higher education: Building vital programs on campuses* (pp. 13–20). San Francisco, CA: Jossey-Bass.

Adelizzi, J. U. (1995). The unconscious process in the teacher–student relationship within the models of education and therapy. In J. U Adelizzi & D. B. Goss (Eds.), *A closer look: Perspectives and reflections on college students with learning disabilities*. Boston, MA: Curry College.

Bodycott, P., & Walker, A. (2000). Teaching abroad: Lessons learned about inter-cultural understanding for teachers in higher education. *Teaching in Higher Education, 5*(1), 79–95. Retrieved June 5, 2000, from http://www.epnet.com/ehost/login.html

Brooks, R. (2003). *The power of mindsets: Nurturing resilience in our children and ourselves.* Opening Plenary Session presented at the 15th annual meeting of the Children and Adults with Attention-Deficit/Hyperactivity Disorder (CHADD) International Conference, Denver, CO.

Brown, H. D. (2000). *Principles of language learning and teaching* (4th ed.). White Plains, NY: Addison, Wesley, Longman.

Carrasquillo, A. L., & Reyes Bonilla, M. A. (1990). Teaching a second language to limited-English-proficient learning disabled students. In A. L. Carresquillo & R. E. Baecher (Eds.), *Teaching the bilingual special education student* (pp. 67–89). Norwood, NJ: Ablex.

Chamot, A. U., & O'Malley, J. M. (1994). *The CALLA handbook: Implementing the cognitive academic language learning approach.* Reading, MA: Addison-Wesley.

Chen, H. & Lan, W. (1998). *Adolescents' perceptions of their parents' academic expectations: Comparison of American, Chinese-American, and Chinese high school students.*

Cloud, N. (1988). *ESL in special education.* Washington, DC: ERIC Clearinghouse on Languages and Linguistics. (ERIC Document Reproductive Service ED 303044)

Collinson, V., & Killeavy, M. (1999). Exemplary teachers: Practicing an ethic of care in England, Ireland and the United States. *Journal for a Just and Caring Education, 5*(4), 349–367. Retrieved March 9, 2002, from http://www.epnet.com/ehost/login.html

Corey, R. (2003, July). *Listening to student voices: Best practices in disability services.* Paper presented at the annual meeting of the Association on Higher Education and Disabilities (AHEAD), Dallas, TX.

Cummins, J. (1984). *Bilingualism and special education: Issues in assessment and pedagogy.* Austin, TX: Pro-Ed.

Deponio, P., Landon, J., & Reid, G. (2000). Dyslexia and bilingualism—Implications for assessment, teaching and learning. In L. Peer & G. Reid (Eds.), *Multilingualism, literacy and dyslexia: A challenge for educators* (pp. 52–60). Trowbridge, England: Cromwell Press.

Downey, D. M., & Snyder, L. S. (2001) Curricular accommodations for college students with language learning disabilities. *Topics in Language Disorders, 21*(2), 55–67.

Dyl, J. (2008). Understanding cutting in adolescents: Prevalence, prevention and intervention. *The Brown University Child and Adolescent Behavior Letter, 24*(3), 1–8.

Emdad, R., Sondergaard, H. P., & Tores, T. (2005). Learning problems, impaired short-term memory and general intelligence in relation to severity and duration of disease in posttraumatic stress disorder patients. *Stress, Trauma, and Crisis, 8*(1), 25–43.

Feuerstein, R., & Feuerstein, R. S. (2001). Is dynamic assessment compatible with the psychometric model? In A. S. Kaufman & N. L. Kaufman (Eds.), *Specific learning disabilities and difficulties in children and adolescents: Psychological assessment and evaluation* (pp. 218–246). New York: Cambridge University Press.

Finn, L. L. (1999). Learning disabilities programs at community colleges and four-year colleges and universities. *Community College Journal of Research & Practice, 23*(7), 629–640.

Gallardo, M. (1999). *A culture undiscovered: Racial and ethnic minority college students with learning disabilities.* Boston, MA: Association for Higher Education and Disabilities (AHEAD).

Ganschow, L. Schneider, E., & Evers, T. (2000). Difficulties of English as a foreign language (EFL) for students with language-learning disabilities (dyslexia). In L. Peer & G. Reid (Eds.), *Multilingualism, literacy and dyslexia: A challenge for educators* (pp. 182–191). Trowbridge, England: Cromwell Press.

Gilbertson, M., Gurvits, T., Lasko, N., Orr, S., & Pitman, R. (2001). Multivariate Assessment of Explicit Memory Function in Combat Veterans with Posttraumatic Stress Disorder. *Journal of Traumatic Stress 14*(2), 413–432.

Hinshaw, S., & Kranz, R. (2009). *The triple bind: Saving our teenage girls from today's pressures.* New York: Random House.

Ijiri, L., Carroll, J., Fletcher, S., Manchester, J., & VanSomeren, D. (1998). *A comprehensive model of a post-secondary learning disabilities program: The program for the advancement of learning (PAL) at Curry College.* Washington, DC: ERIC Clearinghouse on Languages and Linguistics. (ERIC Document Reproductive Service-ED420124)

Ijiri, L., & Rooney, G. (1995). Learning disabilities in speakers of English as a second language. In J. Adelizzi & D. Goss (Eds.), *A closer look: Practitioners' perspectives and reflections on college students with learning disabilities* (pp. 208–224). Milton, MA: Curry College.

Koso, M., & Hansen, S. (2006). Executive function and memory in posttraumatic stress disorder: A study of Bosnian war veterans. *European Psychiatry, 21*(3), 167–173.

Leons, E. (2002). *Meeting the needs of students with language based learning disabilities in the world language classroom.* Poster session presented at the Multilingual and Cross-Cultural Perspectives on Dyslexia Conference, Washington, DC.

Levine, M. (2002). *A mind at a time.* New York: Simon & Schuster.

Lucas, K. (2004, April 23). Success Asian style. *CQ Researcher, 14,* 345–372. Retrieved from http://library.cqpress.com/cqresearcher/cqresrre2004042300.

McLoughlin, D., Beard, J., Ryan, A., & Kirk, J. (2000). Dyslexia support in a multilingual university environment. In L. Peer & G. Reid, (Eds.), *Multilingualism, literacy and dyslexia: A challenge for educators* (pp. 161–181). Trowbridge, England: Cromwell Press.

Nieto, S. (1999). *The light in their eyes: Creating multicultural learning communities.* New York: Teachers College Press.

Olivier, C., Hecker, L., Klucken, J., & Westby, C. (2000). Language: The embedded curriculum in postsecondary education. *Topics in Language Disorders, 21*(1), 15–29.

O'Malley, J. M., & Chamot, A.V. (1990). *Learning strategies in second language acquisition.* Cambridge, England: Cambridge University Press.

Ortiz, A. (1997). Learning disabilities occurring concomitantly with linguistic differences. *Journal of Learning Disabilities, 30*(3), 321–333. Retrieved from http://www.epnet.com/ehost/login.html

Ortiz, A. (2002). *English language learners with special needs: Effective instructional strategies.* Washington, DC: ERIC Clearinghouse on Languages and Linguistics. (ERIC Document Reproductive Service EDO-FL-01-08)

Oxford, R. L. (1990). *Language learning strategies.* Boston, MA: Heinle & Heinle.

Peart, N., & Campbell, N. (1999). At-risk students' perceptions of teacher effectiveness. *Journal for a Just and Caring Education, 5*(3), 269–284.

Pennini, S., & Peltz, E. (1995). Mentoring college students with learning disabilities: Facilitating metacognitive development. In J. U Adelizzi & D. B. Goss (Eds.), *A closer look: Perspectives and reflections on college students with learning disabilities.* (pp. 52–73). Boston, MA: Curry College.

Preece, J., Rice, M., Beecher, M., Roberts, N., & Stearns, L. (2003, July). *Thirteen years on—Where are we, where are we going—Student perspectives.* Paper presented at the annual meeting of the Association on Higher Education and Disabilities (AHEAD), Dallas, TX.

Rance-Raney, J. (2000). *Unlocking the mysteries of learning problems with ESL adults: ESL at Lehigh.* Bethlehem, PA: Lehigh University.

Riley, M. K. (1998). Leveling the playing field: Students with learning disabilities enjoying their competence, working hard and having fun in college. In T. Citro (Ed.), *The experts speak to parents of students with learning disabilities* (pp. 101–129). Boston, MA: Learning Disabilities Association of Massachusetts.

Rooney, G. (2002). *Providing support services for college students with learning disabilities who are not native English speakers: The challenge of the LD/ESOL student.* Washington, DC: ERIC Clearinghouse on Higher Education. (ERIC Document Reproductive Service ED469337)

Rooney, G., & Schwarz, R. (1999). Identifying and accommodating learning disabled students. *The Advising Quarterly for Professionals in International Education, 50*, 9–15.

Schwarz, R. L. (1999). The first international multilingualism and dyslexia conference. *Learning disabilities on-line: LD in depth.* Retrieved November 13, 2002, from http://www.ldonline.org/ld_indepth/foreign_lang/multi-culturalism_conf699.html

Schwarz, R. L. (2000). Identifying and helping learning-disabled English as a second language (ESL) students in a college intensive English programme. In L. Peer & G. Reid (Eds.), *Multilingualism, literacy and dyslexia: A challenge for educators* (pp. 192–202). Trowbridge, England: Cromwell Press.

Stoynoff, S. (1996). Self-regulated learning strategies of international students: A study of high and low achievers. *College Student Journal 30*(3), 329–336.

Sunderland, H., Klein, C., Savinson, R., & Partridge, T. (1997). *Dyslexia and the bilingual learner: Assessing and teaching adults and young people who speak English as an additional language.* London: London Language and Literacy Unit.

Sunmin, J., Hee-soon, J., Martinez, G., Robinson, E. S., Bawa, J., & Grace, M. X. (2009). Model minority at risk: Expressed needs of mental health by Asian American young adults. *Journal of Community Health, 34*(2), 144–152. Retrieved May 10, 2002, from http://www.epnet.com/ehost/login.html

Talbert-Johnson, C., & Beran, D. (1999, October). Higher education and teacher immediacy: Creating dialogue for effective intercultural communication. *Journal for a Just & Caring Education, 5*(4), 430. Retrieved from "http://www.epnet.com/ehost/login.html"

Tebben, S. (1995). Community and caring in a college classroom. *Journal for a Just and Caring Education, 1*(3), 335–345. Retrieved from http://www.epnet.com/ehost/login.html

Vogel, S. A., Leyser, Y., Wyland, S., & Brulie, A. (1999). Students with learning disabilities in higher education. *Learning Disabilities Research & Practice 14*(3), 173–187.

Willig, A. C. (1986). Special education and the culturally and linguistically different child: An overview of issues and challenges. *Reading, Writing and Learning Disabilities, 2*, 161–173.

Woodman, K. (February, 2001). *Learning disabilities: What can teachers do?* Paper presented at TESOL 2001 Conference, St. Louis, MO.

Yin, G. F., & Weekes, B. S. (2003). Dyslexia in Chinese: Clues from cognitive neuropsychology. *Annals of Dyslexia, 53*, 255–279. Retrieved from http://www.epnet.com/ehost/login.html

8

ADULTS IN EDUCATIONAL THERAPY
A Triage Approach

LINDA CLOW LAWTON

INTRODUCTION

The educational therapist who is best equipped to treat adult clients possesses analytical and interpersonal skills different from those required in the remediation of problems of academic learning in the school-age child. The accumulated history and complexity of adult functioning call for insight from the ET that extends into the worlds of family and relationship dynamics, business acumen and knowledge of work demands, and a fundamental grounding in scientific knowledge which contributes to the interpretation of the dynamic interplay of cognitive deficits in the many roles that are assumed by adults in a multicontextual society. Executive dysfunctions are often primary problems in the lives of adults with learning and attentional difficulties, impact their lives globally, and are expressed in the myriad routines that range from independently getting to work on time, managing the responsibilities of home and family, to attending college, being vigilant about long term cardiovascular health, and saving for retirement (Barkley, Murphy, & Fischer, 2008).

The popular concept of "lifelong learning" describes a situation that calls for "lifelong support for learning" for those clients who suffer from executive dysfunction possibly in conjunction with a learning disability or an attention deficit. Women who must master unfamiliar job skills after divorce, new fathers who are learning to balance work and family demands, workers who must retrain in a changing economy and who bear the burden of discouraging academic histories, those who advance in their careers only to hit the bottom of complexity without margin, aging folk whose resources are compromised by health conditions that push them into territory where they no longer can compensate enough—these are the adult clients who may seek the guidance of educational therapists. The treatment of executive dysfunction in adults is a complex and rewarding experience for the educational therapist. Though there are significant differences in presentation, the issues of the mature client are analogous to those of the younger client in many ways. The maturational delay of youngsters with executive dysfunction may perplex parents, but it has been accumulating much longer in the adult client. Is it any wonder that benchmarks of adulthood such as college graduation, financial independence, successful committed relationships, or career advancement are likely to be reached later than expected or not at all?

Abandoned dreams and recurring mistakes can render the "chronic underachiever" perennially apologetic or defensive. Parental confusion at the mismatch between perceived potential and realistic expectations for the child may have been replaced by the disappointment or anger of a partner or spouse. The fear and frustration felt by the young student trying to complete homework assignments may grow into despair in adulthood; the accompanying stress which that insecurity and chaos can produce over years of repeated output failure can be debilitating. The adult, just like the child, tries to understand how such a thing could happen to a person who has the best of intentions.

Fortunately, the adult who independently seeks treatment is often a person whose self-narrative assumes an internal locus of control and is not in denial of her problems, which often presents a highly motivated client who experiences immediate and dramatic progress when the real source of her difficulties is clarified. The adult client often has fewer members of the treatment team and less support, both financial and social, than children do. The course of therapy may be lengthy and could be expensive. The ultimate goal of optimal independence guides the treatment plan and leads to fundamental practical and social–emotional benefits. Establishing priorities in treatment is a mutual process, but the insight of the clinician is paramount in directing this process so that it leads to synergistic, incremental progress.

THE CONCEPT OF TRIAGE DEFINING TREATMENT

The client often presents herself at the intake interview as being overwhelmed. There may be so many areas of her life that are in need of reorganization that she may perceive it as "a disaster." *Triage* is the term used in the medical management of disasters, and here it is a useful concept for the educational therapist. The word *triage* (from the French *trier,* to separate, sort, or select) suggests that the clinician consider the comprehensive picture of the client, and flexibly seek available resources. The model simple triage and rapid treatment (START) developed by Hoag Hospital and the Newport Beach, CA Fire Department for trauma management following an earthquake, provides a simple algorithm (http://www.citmt.org/start) that works well in developing an educational therapy treatment plan. The problems can be categorized into four groups: (1) those that cannot be treated, or whose treatment falls outside your expertise (analogous to the deceased—"dead issues"); (2) those whose treatment can be delayed; (3) urgent or threatening conditions; and (4) quick fixes that will simplify the environment, at least temporarily. The START model includes the idea of "the Golden Hour," which posits that those who receive treatment for acute trauma within an hour stand the best chance for recovery. It could be postulated that in this "disaster," the Golden Hour is that first hour with the educational therapist. If the ET can help the client see hope for success and the promise of relief, she will return to do the longer-term work of the treatment plan.

If a client is mourning a failed marriage, neglecting her health, about to lose her job for repeated tardiness, and loses her keys frequently, the order of operations is clear. Establishing a "launch pad" by the front door for essentials such as keys, phone, and purse is a relatively simple innovation that will make a fundamental difference on a daily basis, a success that may serve as motivation for more ambitious projects. The ET can propose this near the conclusion of the intake interview, to engage the client in a positive experience that heralds the changes available through educational therapy

At the first session, the ET might record an analysis of the steps involved in the journey to work, a precise plan that measures the length of time involved in each action. This activity functions on multiple levels, as worthwhile interventions often do. It is:

An exercise in perspective taking and planning
    A practical intervention
    A rehearsal of a realistic action plan
    A rubric for process analysis
    A framework for anticipating obstacles
    An opportunity to formulate alternative courses of action
    A practical tool to use for independent practice

The complexity of the process of getting somewhere on time is often a revelation to the client. Once she has achieved some level of mastery and put in place the supports, such as checklists, alarms, and timers, other threats to immediate stability can be addressed. When pressing needs have been met, the longer-term issues can be addressed, one-by-one, as time permits. The ET should keep in mind that new compelling issues will continue to arise. As they do, each issue and strategy can be used as a platform to demystify the client's disorder and refine the ET's approach to the therapy. Eventually, the benefit of greater structure and effective routines will free the client's time to take care of health, leisure, and goals for the future. Depending on the severity of her grief over the failed marriage, referral to a psychotherapist would be appropriate at the point when the threat of job loss has been passed or following the point where greater equilibrium has been established between work and leisure. Every client's needs are different.

Jean Piaget's theories that so elegantly explain the development of the child's ability to make sense of the world are aptly applied to the adult client who is delayed or deficient in the development of executive functions. Piaget's stages of cognitive development are a useful analytical tool for the ET working with adults. The adult client with executive dysfunction experiences age-*in*appropriate developmental challenges and may exhibit characteristics of earlier stages of operation when in "cognitive distress." Though many who seek educational therapy possess the intellectual capacity for formal operations, when engaged in activities that place too high a demand upon the capacity for executive function, clients often revert to behaviors characteristic of the concrete operational or even preoperational stages. For example, difficulty in dividing attention may result in the preoperational behavior of centration (focusing on only one perceptual aspect at a time). Some clients may adapt by using egocentric monologue to mediate challenging tasks, just as small children do and for the same reason, because the capacity for internal self-talk is limited, but in the adult it may be attributable to a deficit of working memory or attention. The educational therapist is responsible for helping clients to adjust a host of failing assimilations involving flawed schemata that are causing them to live in a constant state of Piagetian disequilibrium (Wadsworth, 2004).

The goal of treatment is the equilibration of both the client's potential and intention with the demand and expectation in the environment. This takes place at the *interface* where the client's condition meets the societal norm. Just as students who fail to meet the "normal" demands embedded in the educational institutions of our society are under constant stress due to their invisible compromises, so are adults the victims of "support failure" when the normal work, family, or social expectations present difficulty at every turn. Similar to working with children, the ET guides the adult client through the process of accommodation using Vygotsky's concepts of scaffolding in the zone of proximal development (Berk & Winsler, 1995). The interactive relationship is an opportunity for the ET to model positive self-talk scripts and an opportunity to encourage the client to use private speech to strengthen self-regulation. Fortunately, the use of our technologically advanced cultural tools can be taught prospectively to help the client adapt more successfully. The work of the therapist is accomplished through a variety of means, with techniques drawn from all the stages development. Sensorimotor activities such as imitation or establishing reflexive habits can help a client who has trouble establishing routines. For some clients, "out of sight, out of mind" is a troublesome sensorimotor-stage characteristic that can be addressed with external memory supports easily accessed through computers or Post-It notes. Preoperational activities such as "thinking aloud" or role play can allow those who struggle with social issues to develop perspective and insight. The ET will often find herself working at the whiteboard, diagramming complex projects at the concrete operational level. Demystification, accommodation, compensation, motivation, adaptation, and well-structured communication are all required to redistribute the cognitive load (Ahern & Marshall, 2005), the cumulative demand of intellectual processing which reflects cognitive strengths and weaknesses and the conditions that determine the effort that goes into a task given the neuropsychological functions involved (Sweller, 1988). The scope of treatment includes the client's past, present, and future, personal, interpersonal, and professional roles. The assessment of pretreatment condition and posttreatment gains is a functional tool of intervention and provides useful information for both therapist and client. The measure of success is a relatively comfortable fit between a resilient client and the world.

Effective treatment produces practical gains and should result in a shift in identity that includes a positive revision of the personal narrative (Palombo, 2001). This begins with the client's education about the nature, scope, and impact of executive dysfunction, and is accomplished both indirectly through the client's improved effectiveness, and directly through the educational therapist's gentle shaping of the client's stories. The information that the client may use to redefine the self is contained in the ET's persistent reminders to describe the source of difficulties correctly, as ED rather than character flaws, recognition of the client's accomplishments, and a regular and generous dose of positive regard.

Though our culture allows an extended moratorium on the development of adult identity (Erikson, 1980), executive dysfunction often misdirects this process and delays it further (Palombo, 2001). In the adult client, disruption may have occurred at every stage of Erikson's progression of psychosocial development, giving the appearance of an individual whose developmental profile is "uneven" and sometimes delayed. The Table 8.1 suggests how some symptoms of executive dysfunction might confuse an adult's successful construction of identity.

Joseph Palombo in *Learning Disorders and Disorders of the Self In Children and Adolescents* (2001) and Russell Barkley, Kevin Murphy, and Maryellen Fischer's seminal work *ADHD in Adults, What the Science Says* (2008) were the fundamental inspiration for this diagram and are essential reading for the clinician who will work with adults suffering from any of the disorders whose expression compromises executive functions. The ET should bear in mind that some clients immediately begin to independently integrate the information and results into the self-narrative with enthusiasm and growing confidence, and may still benefit from some psychotherapeutic work. Others have been damaged so deeply that they cannot even take advantage of educational therapy without first easing

Table 8.1 Possible Impairments Attributable to Executive Dysfuntion in Eric Erickson's Stages of Psycholsocial Development

Stage	Symptom	Impairment
Trust v. Mistrust 0–18 months	Parents may have EFD, ineffectual or unresponsive to infant's needs	Still suffers from underlying feelings of insecurity
Autonomy v. Shame 18 mos–3 years	Disinhibition or inability to split attention may delay toilet training	Lingering feeling of low self-worth, self-esteem
Initiative v. Guilt 3–6 years	Impulsivity, difficulty with modulation of effort, poor planning yield disappointing results or mistakes	Weak self-confidence and possibility of school trauma
Industry v. Inferiority 6–12 years	Inability to sustain focus, plan and persevere leads to output failure	Slower rate of knowledge and skills acquisition leads to diminished competence and perceived potential; reduced academic opportunities
Identity v. Role Confusion Adolescence	Perspective-taking and social skills deficits create problems being accepted by peers	Foreclosure or diffusion in identity formation; inauthentic personality, rebellion, negative peer relationships, being an "outsider", loneliness, dangerous decision-making strategies
Intimacy v. Isolation Young Adulthood	Executive dysfunction impacts success in higher education/work and life balance	Identity issues plus diminished capacity for adult responsibilities make it difficult to succeed at developing committed relationships and career
Generativity v. Stagnation Middle Adulthood	Adult version of "failure to thrive"	Secondary psychological symptoms and consequences of long-term problems may be debilitating; diminished achievement and effectiveness has monetary cost
Ego Integrity v. Despair Late Adulthood	Biological echoes of long term and poor life balance	Health problems from cumulative stress and neglect in self-care

enough of their emotional pain and psychological maladjustment in the care of a mental health professional who is aware of, and alert to the significance of the neuropsychological deficit (Ratey, 2001).

Adults who seek treatment in educational therapy are usually in chronic or acute distress. Some may be numb to their condition, having endured its consequences for a lifetime. Their suffering, however, has usually led them through many attempts at relief. Given the state of science and the lag in professional training in this area, well-meaning practitioners may have misdiagnosed the symptoms, often without benefit of objective measures of executive or cognitive function. Misdirected treatment may have exacerbated secondary consequences, such as diminished self-esteem, and given ammunition to others, such as partners or parents, who play important roles in the social ecology of the client. It is not unusual to hear a narrative during the intake interview that organizes the history in justification of an older diagnosis that is psychologically based, or a self-constructed theory of personality that was built upon the assumption of fundamental character flaws. Ironically, these same aspects of character can actually be highly developed, and often motivate and support an aggressive desire for implementation of therapeutic measures in the adult client, as illustrated in the case study that follows.

This case study illustrates the broad range of skills and information that are brought into play in adult educational therapy. The client's determination to succeed in life took her on a long path of exploration that finally led to educational therapy. The practical interventions and demystification of her cognitive challenges gave her tools she could use to realistically adjust her expectations and creatively adapt to the demands of her work and personal life.

THE CASE OF SAM

Sam was referred to me by a therapist with whom I had previously shared a case. She suggested that I might be able to help Sam with time management issues. Our first conversation took place in early March, and we set up an intake interview for the last week of the month. Sam thought we might consult a few times before the end of her school year, possibly leading to a steady relationship in the fall. My diagnostic antennae began to quiver with the slow and careful approach Sam took to planning our encounter. Most clients are in a rush to get started, once they have made the decision to see me for educational therapy.

Seven years earlier Sam had been diagnosed with AD/HD, inattentive type. She returned to graduate school for a master's degree in reading remediation and found that despite her aptitude, intelligence, and best efforts, she struggled to meet academic expectations. Her diagnosis and treatment included a neuropsychological assessment, a prescription for Ritalin, and psychotherapy. With that plus accommodations and generous understanding coming from her department, Sam successfully completed her studies. She went on to obtain an appointment to the faculty of a local college where she taught remedial courses in reading and writing. Wisely, given the protections of her union, she sought accommodations on her job under The Americans with Disabilities Act (ADA), and was given an adjusted course schedule for her teaching responsibilities. It wasn't enough, and now in the second semester of her second year, Sam was near despair and in a state of panic much of the time. Her daily living routines were in chaos. She was severely sleep-deprived because she was constantly struggling to keep up, and losing weight because she couldn't manage her time in order to shop for food. Sam didn't have the time or appetite to get lunch during her teaching day. She feared losing her personal relationship in the fray. Her life was all work and no play.

In advance of our meeting, Sam sent me a copy of the neuropsychological assessment report, written by a neuropsychologist from her HMO. Her diagnosis: axis I, 294.9 cognitive disorder not otherwise specified (NOS), associated with 314.01, attention-deficit/hyperactivity disorder, predominantly inattentive type; and, axis II 301.9, personality disorder NOS with avoidant, and dysthymic features. According to the *Diagnostic and Statistical Manual of Mental Disorders* (2000) 294.9, cognitive disorder NOS may include an "impairment in cognitive functioning as evidenced by neuropsychological testing or quantified clinical assessment" (American Psychiatric Association, 2000, p. 98).

A sampling of her significant formal assessment results:

WAIS-III
FSIQ: 126
Verbal IQ: 125
Performance IQ: 121
Verbal Comprehension Index: 129
Working Memory Index: 117
Perceptual Organization Index: 114
Processing Speed Index: 108
(VC > 15 points than PO); (VC > 20 points than PO); (VC > 12 points than WM)

Sam's performance on nonverbal tasks and manipulation of nonmeaningful stimuli, though still respectably average, did not approach her superior performance on verbal measures. According to Sam's examiner her learning and memory functions were in the superior range; on tests of executive functioning, her scores were variable. Verbal abstract reasoning was in the high average range and social judgment in the superior range. However, in visual organization she performed in the average range, again in contrast to her Verbal Comprehension ability.

The model that was emerging in my mind as a result of the examiner's report was that Sam "sees slowly." In other words, and for whatever reason, she makes sense of her visual environment with difficulty, in contrast to performing a similar function using her strength in language, leaving her vulnerable for functioning efficiently on a daily basis.

This diagnostic picture suggested to me that Sam's complaints about the difficulty in execution of the complex tasks of her life had a basis that was distinct from any psychological problem. This was a young woman of considerable intellectual power who had an inadequate cognitive capacity to meet the demands of many tasks, placing her at risk for an ongoing assault of her sense of self. Her disequilibrium motivated her to pursue an acceptable explanation. Years of psychotherapy had produced little improvement in the conditions of her life, though according to Sam, she reaped some benefit, especially in perspective-taking and decision-making techniques that helped her modify some of her ineffective behaviors.

The neuropsychologist summed up the assessment in the following way:

> Ms. ____ is a 29-year-old woman who was referred for evaluation of attention deficit disorder. Current neuropsychological assessment reveals that she is functioning in the superior range of intellectual ability (96th percentile) and memory functioning (99th percentile). There is clear evidence that she in fact has an attention deficit disorder in that her sustained attentional ability is only in the low average range (29th percentile). All of her executive functioning measures were also only in the average range (60th to 80th percentile). Personality assessment reveals that she is mildly depressed and has a number of personality issues that may also contribute to her attentional difficulties.

After reviewing the evaluation I wondered how might this young college instructor's already fragile self-concept have been affected when she discussed it with the neuropsychologist, and then later when she read it alone? What intrigued me was how much of her personality assessment related to her cognitive difficulties, and how her attribution of her difficulty in output and coping mechanisms to a failure of will, self-discipline, or volitional self-control might compound her problems. It could lead to ineffective strategies, counterproductive efforts, consequent frustration, and confusing conclusions about her self.

Many of the findings in the personality report were confirmed by the history I had collected, and it led me to postulate a host of connections between the assessment descriptions and the cognitive breakdowns. One of Sam's most important objectives for our work together was to understand the contents of this report from my perspective as an educational therapist. I knew that the manner in which I explicated the neuropsychologist's findings could have a profound impact on Sam's self-narrative, for better or for worse, and that her future comfort with her life choices might hinge on the sense of power and control she could derive from my interpretation of these findings, and my ability to communicate this accurately considering my position as the educational therapist, and not the examiner (Palombo, 2001). My goal was to help her develop a realistic assessment of her strengths and weaknesses and a resilient problem-solving approach that was built upon acceptance of her legitimate vulnerabilities and appreciation of her obvious talents.

The Intake

Three weeks later, an attractive, well-groomed young woman presented herself in my office for the intake interview, 20 minutes later than the appointed time. She apologized profusely, expressing concern that I might read her actions as disrespect for my time (and demonstrating empathy in the process). I introduced Sam to the "No Shame Time Zone" which I developed for my clients. I make sure that my office represents temporal *reality* to my clients, virtually all of whom are challenged by time. It is an island where their *disability* is recognized for what it is. No more than you would shame someone who cannot see for bumping into the furniture in your office the first time they visit, people who arrive late to their appointments with me are assured of compassion for their struggle to reach an unfamiliar destination under time pressure. It frees them to stop apologizing, covering up, and feeling terrible about something they haven't been able to change. It never fails to move me how powerfully therapeutic this small gesture is—most clients have never felt anything but disapproval from others when they are in the very uncomfortable emotional state that accompanies being late when one is confused: hyperaroused, disoriented, anxious, and fearful of the response that awaits one. Her very professional demeanor crumpled at this small gesture of generosity and tears spilled out. She thanked me genuinely, and professed that no one had ever treated her quite like that when she had been late in the past.

She set down her things and sat, with just a whisper of physical awkwardness. Looking at me openly and with a wry smile, she regained her composure, and let me know that she had an agenda for our meeting. Though the neuropsychologist had explained the report to her, she was hoping I would be able to clarify some points that confused her now. I let her know that I wouldn't really be ready to do so until I had a chance to collect my own observations during today's interview and reflect on the report in light of them. She seemed a little agitated at that, looking away and frowning, then looked at me directly and pressed me with a polite demand, "So, we will be able to do that next time?" I reassured her that we would. I have come to recognize this constellation of behaviors as a state Sam identifies as "cranky." When she questions what we're doing or worries about the time passing and tends toward agitation in her demeanor she often apologizes for "getting cranky."

Sam had come prepared with a typed document, "Questions to Discuss with Linda Lawton." It was unusual in my experience for clients to prepare so elaborately. Her insightful organizing question, "What is the most strategic way for me to contribute to the Department and College in the long term?" was followed by bulleted points revealing that my client was a very talented thinker, yet another clue that she needed an extraordinary degree of orientation.

Together, we decided that to fulfill her intention she also needed help understanding how to accomplish:

- Being a skillful team player on the faculty of her college
- Handling the day-to-day demands of her job
- Realistically assessing her responsibilities
- Developing a strategy for long term career growth

- Keeping her room and closet clean
- Maintaining her relationship
- Shopping for food, clothing, and sundries
- Making plans for eating during the work day
- Planning her recreation, social life, and vacations
- Balancing her time between work and play
- Building a routine to support her health
- Understanding her disorder and its implications
- Managing her medications appropriately

The conversation took a long time, but Sam asked that we schedule long sessions since she was traveling far to see me. This tall order was our first collaborative experience; a marriage of my protocol, knowledge, and intuition, directed by Sam's thoughtful, intelligent agenda and her willingness to be transparent and coachable.

The 90-minute interview culminated in a touching revelation that belied the trust Sam was willing to invest in the process of reconstructing her life for our collaborative analysis. Trying to choke back tears, Sam sobbed that all she really wanted was "to do something besides struggle every day." This was the most poignant moment in the therapeutic process. The seed of the most inspiring moment was in her organizing question for our agenda: "What is the most strategic way for me to contribute to the Department and College in the long term?" Despite all her setbacks and frustrations, still, this woman lived to make a contribution in life. The human spirit is so remarkable.

TREATMENT

We addressed the findings in the report in our first therapy session, at last clarifying for Sam what the dominant issues seemed to be, and validating the seriousness of her challenges in working memory, perceptual organization, and processing speed, and her superior strength in verbal comprehension. Sam's deep brown eyes, evenly set in her face, met my gaze steadily:

"Is this why I always forget where I park my car? Last weekend I spent 45 minutes wandering around my neighborhood searching for it and my roommate who came out to help saw it from my front door!" Her eyes filled with tears.

This was a perfect illustration of her deficits in real life situations. Sam had trouble recognizing her own car. She had no memory of where it was, had no strategy to encode it, searched without a pattern or plan, and had a strong emotional reaction, severe enough to compound her confusion and motivate her to ask for help despite her embarrassment. Was the cognitive load of looking and searching, simultaneously, too great for her brain to coordinate the functions of her perceptual organization, working memory, and processing speed? Had she forgotten to look for the car as she tried to orient herself for the search? Was finding her way taxing all her working memory capacity?

I explained that these aspects of her cognitive functioning, independent of her superior intelligence, governed all of her visual interface with her environment and could be understood as "seeing slowly, or a little at a time." Her weaknesses could add to the cognitive load and give her too little visual information too late. The implications could extend to her life choices and social decisions. Misunderstandings, and other peoples' attributions regarding this invisible, practically unimaginable confusion she experiences, could be a secondary cost of great magnitude.

We discussed the possible impact on her driving of attention, working memory, processing speed, and perceptual organization. I recommended that she use Google Earth to familiarize herself with landmarks before beginning a new journey, and Google Maps to verbally mediate and rehearse her route. I emphasized that driving is a potentially dangerous activity for which she needs to be responsibly prepared. I suggested that Sam might benefit from an evaluation of her visual efficiency at UC Berkeley's Binocular Vision Clinic. This might lead to some new perspectives relating to her diagnostic conclusions and successful treatment, all of which might contribute to Sam's positive outcome.

Sam helped me to understand how she experiences visual vulnerability in real life. The most important information came from two personal vignettes she told that day, related to shopping. She shared how she dreaded shopping for food, and that it was a great challenge to her because she couldn't choose quickly among many options and often left the store out of sheer frustration without making a purchase. She would get angry at having to start all over again, and often simply wouldn't eat or would eat out at the closest restaurant and spend too much money. Once she went along with a friend to The Container Store. This store is merchandised in patterns that are quite pleasing to most spectators, an attractive physical catalog of vessels in a dizzy array of colors, which are nonmeaningful to a person who can't *image*-ine what would go inside them. They spent about 40 minutes in the store. When Sam reached the car, she put down her head and wept, for about 10 minutes, sobbing so hard she couldn't speak. Her friend, mystified, asked what was wrong. Not sad, not angry, Sam couldn't say why, but knew that she felt overwhelmed. She hadn't even been attempting to purchase something from the kaleidoscope which was displayed all around her. The unrelenting flood of demand for visual pattern recognition and identification of function exhausted Sam's capacity for categorization, to the point that her social–emotional regulation collapsed and her coping mechanisms broke down outside the store. This was a real life situation that called on specific visual-spatial-orienting skills from her formal assessment, and confirmed Sam's impairment in making sense out of what she sees.

This clue led us to discuss how to make visual decisions in greater detail. Sam cannot decode tax forms, but instead has her very simple tax return professionally prepared, an expense she willingly bears. She feels it is ridiculously difficult for her to copy and collate the papers she prepares for her classes. It's a time-consuming, exhausting production. Her closet has no organization, she doesn't know where to put away her clothes and the resultant mess in her room distracts and confuses her. Her backlog of chores included the disposition of many pounds of paper from her graduate studies, and the organization of her desk in her new shared office at the college. She suffered shame each day when she had to contemplate the messy trunk and backseat of her car.

These were all visual–spatial tasks, whose disposition required executive function; Sam had no idea how to approach them efficiently. They threatened to eat up what little time she had to restore herself in preparation for the next task. I recommended a professional organizer who understood AD/HD and is very gentle and sensitive. Thankfully, Sam earns a good salary and doesn't own a house or have any dependents. She could afford to work with the organizer to set up systems and help her dig her way out of the backlog. Sam decided that my recommendation to schedule monthly maintenance after the initial organization was a good preventative measure and an investment in her health and sanity.

She next appeared in my office on April 18th, just after filing an extension for her tax return, and was frustrated with herself for being late, a fresh opportunity to provide a reality check with her strengths and weaknesses. Tax forms are hard for most people, and are remarkably hard for people with challenges similar to those of Sam. She shared the accomplishments of the preceding 3 weeks, and realized that she was proud of them. She decided that the tax extension wasn't such a bad thing after all. I asked her to share her immediate concerns. Sam expressed her puzzlement with all the many people she interacts with at work. She was clearly experiencing the elements of this social system in a state of uncertainty, and it was causing her a great deal of confusion and anxiety about how she should behave in her professional relationships (Ahern, 2008). I attempted to establish some familiarity in these elements for Sam in order to reduce her cognitive load, according to the principles recommended by Ahern.

Using the large whiteboard in my office, Sam and I constructed a map of the professional arenas in which she is expected to perform, the purpose and personality of each group, the objective she has for her social relationships, and her concerns about disclosing her weaknesses in each one of them. We named the office staff and characterized the relationship: she needs their cooperation, she wants to express her appreciation for their help, which she can expect as a faculty member, and she is friendly, though not necessarily "friends with them." Then Sam did it for her relationship with her tenure committee beginning with the question, "How do you want them to think of you?" Sam thought they should think of her as "one of us," reliable, ready to contribute, and responsibly innovative. (This led Sam to develop a grant proposal and position paper about her instructional technique.) The groups of key words made a stark graphic, a verbal mind map, easy enough for Sam to decode when she had collaborated in building the form. I was careful to keep the number of elements in the graphic to a manageable five, and checked in with Sam regarding the visual complexity. This, like my treatment of tardiness, was a new experience for her, establishing a healthy respect for her challenges, and modeling the vocabulary of what I hoped would soon be her own comfortable self-advocacy in this crucial area. Inside that therapeutic tone, rather than struggling to exhaustion or breakdown, Sam told me when the board was growing too complex for her visual comfort, so we stopped. As I got to know Sam better, her frequent states of distress and some of the vignettes she shared confirmed my suspicions that we were not dealing with an "ordinary" case of executive dysfunction associated with inattentive ADHD.

At our next meeting 2 weeks later, we started down another channel entirely, one that twisted and turned and took courage to navigate. First, Sam checked in with good news. She and the organizer had made great headway and were enjoying a comfortable camaraderie. They had set up a schedule to alternate weeks with me, moving Sam ahead in her project quickly, triage for her peace of mind with practical benefits for her chronic time deficit. The bad news was that she was concerned about her stimulant medication. She probed my thinking. Part of the job of the ET is to provide the facts, refer the client to competent specialists, and help those who take medication to work out practical strategies for managing them. I had to tread very delicately in the confusing scenario she constructed for me. Sam had been seeing a psychiatrist for 7 years who prescribed stimulant medication in a way that Sam judged was very off-hand.

"She just asks me 'How are you doing?' and I say 'Okay' and she writes me another prescription. I'm out of there in 10 minutes. Seven years ago she prescribed 10 mg of Ritalin three times a day, and no more than four pills in a day. I always run out before I'm supposed to and she always writes the scrip and just says, 'Remember, no more than four in one day.' She's never asked me or told me anything else!"

I knew Sam had some guilt and misgivings about her medication, so, to gauge the reality of her concern, I asked her how much she was taking. I didn't gasp when she said, "Oh, sometimes I take eight pills in a day. I'll even go home at lunch to get more."

I could tell she was really worried from her knitted brows, and the fact that she was attempting to control her supply. I strongly urged her to consult her doctor, and perhaps enlist the neuropsychologist in exploring the problem, since she lacked confidence in the doctor. I was clear that we were moving out of my area of expertise and into a referral. I told her that she would have to work with a medical doctor on this problem. She had reservations about working with her health plan psychiatrist but didn't want to pay out-of-pocket. She asked me what I thought a doctor who knew more about AD/HD might do.

Careful of my boundaries and her vulnerability, I outlined several possibilities, after reissuing my disclaimer that I am not a medical professional and this is a medical problem. I knew she was scared, and this might ease her mind enough to consult a very competent psychiatrist. I had someone in mind who had worked with adult AD/HD for many years and stays current on medication research. I outlined some options for her, all predicated on a visit with a medical doctor.

"I think a careful psychopharmacologist, who understands AD/HD and the cognitive profile you have, would probably want to find out why the medications aren't working well. It would begin with a history and symptom inventory. He or she might try other formulations that have less potential for abuse. You would be interviewed regarding the effects of each trial and the dose would be gradually titrated to your response. The doctor would monitor your consumption with you."

During this point in our work together, it was noteworthy that I considered the following line of thinking: Executive dysfunction renders the client less effective in the patient–physician relationship. Clients are frequently confused by the information presented by their doctors. Their confusion makes it difficult for them to formulate questions and previous negative experiences inhibit or intimidate them from expressing themselves. They may hold back important information and concerns, the revelation of which can improve their own treatment. The ET's experience, clinical distance, and professional standing give her power to act as an ombudsman with the client's physician. This can be a therapeutic event on an emotional level, distinct from an improved medical outcome. A collegial relationship with referring doctors is a very important element in the treatment of executive dysfunction in the adult.

I gave Sam the names of three psychiatrists whom I trust, having sent them some complicated cases that had turned out well. As soon as she left, I faxed her release to one of them and called him. When I told him the quantity of Ritalin that Sam consumed he confirmed what she and I both already knew, that this could be endangering her health. I called Sam and transmitted the information, urging her to make an appointment as soon as possible.

A month later at our last session and before her summer vacation, I asked how much medication she had taken lately and she told me that she had taken so much one day during the last week of school that she had felt sick. Sam declared that she planned to take a drug holiday all summer long. She would wait and see if it was still a problem when she started meds again in the fall. I believed her, since I had no other recourse. Temporarily relieved, we attended to some concerns about her upcoming road trip and made plans to continue our work over the phone next year, weekly for half an hour, with a long face-to-face meeting once a month.

As soon as we resumed our work together we began with schedules and systems for grading papers, prepping lessons, and keeping a healthy balance between work and play. Sam felt much better about her work and the insight she got from our discussions of her concerns and priorities, giving her some perspective on time management and maintaining a balance in her life. However, by the third week of school she expressed that her medication use was again "out of control." I asked her which doctor she would like to call, determined to take decisive action on the spot. Hesitantly, she confessed her fear that she would be met with disapproval. I was able to reassure her that the doctor I had called last spring, though concerned, had regarded the situation as a medical problem, not a failure of character. She promised me she would make an appointment with him.

The same doctor worked her into his schedule the following week. They worked out a plan for Sam to cleanse her system of all medication. It was one of the accomplishments she cited when I saw her in person a month later. They tried another medication. "It was like somebody turned the lights on in my head, instead of just revving the engine!" Indeed, the new medication worked better, and Sam was no longer taking more and more, like washing the car to change the tire, trying to get results. She felt safely medicated now, and was no longer actively worrying about the issue, though Sam, and the doctor and I were still carefully monitoring her use. Her sleep and her appetite improved rapidly. I suggested that she bring up her debilitating PMS with him. He referred her to another specialist who was able to help her manage one more area of her life that had been a chronic drain on her time. These effects were added to our gains.

OUTCOME

With the added presence of mind she was enjoying, Sam felt confident to take the lead at work in writing a grant for her department, a timely and necessary move in her strategy for tenure and career growth. In preparing the proposal, she researched and wrote a position paper that validated her innovative instructional techniques. She often said that she felt proud of her accomplishments, her contribution to her students, and the order that she brought to her life with her judicious decisions and purposeful actions. We moved through the demystification of her disorder, always coming back to her acceptance of her strengths and weaknesses. The establishment of supportive routines, a structure for regular perspective-taking, prioritization, and schedules for work, gave her the freedom to turn her attention to her quality of life. She experimented with adding a yoga class to her weekly routine. She planned several social events with me, and the rehearsal and anticipation of outcomes gave her the opportunity to enjoy herself instead of fretting away the event, worrying about what would happen next (Barkley, 1997).

Sam wept when she told me how gratified she was that she was able to dance, happily, for the first time in her life when she enrolled in a dramatic dance class. High school social dances had been a form of torture that she had quickly learned to avoid. From watching others, she had never been able to infer the rules, map the movements, and capture the unwritten social code of dancing. The learning of that information puts a simultaneous and high demand on visual memory and working memory, pattern recognition, processing speed, and careful attention; the "perfect storm" for Sam. The mediation of verbal instruction, chained and overlearned kinetic melodies, lists of suggested elements for costumes, and a light-hearted, encouraging, and fun approach were the perfect recipe for Sam's success. This experience, rich in accessible multisensory content and emotional weight, seemed to crystallize Sam's acceptance of the validity of her struggle.

Perhaps the most important work I have been doing with Sam over the last year has been to help her see that her difficulty in making sense of visual information in the environment in conjunction with her fragile attention impacts her ability to function. This alleviates her feelings of failure. The strategies are working and the good effects are accumulating. She is less "cranky" and more reflective, and she is in the habit now of appreciating her accomplishments. She hears when she is unfairly critical of herself as she talks to me in our weekly phone call. She tears up easily still, but she doesn't need to have a good cry before we can begin work, and often the tears are tears of relief instead of frustration.

CONCLUSION

I often wonder about the origin of Sam's condition. Was it inherited? Was the abuse she suffered from her alcoholic father a contributing factor? Did her father self-medicate because he, too, was "cranky" too much of the time. Were her psychological problems a maladaptive response? Fortunately, I don't need answers to all my questions in order to help her. We perform lots of experiments, based on her concerns, with solutions designed from our understanding of her cognitive deficits. We continue to revise the goals and approach to her treatment. She still has the visual efficiency evaluation on her to-do list. She continues to work with her new psychopharmacologist to optimize her medication. She recently hired a TA to help her grade papers. We just concluded that our face-to-face meetings are more successful than phone work because it's difficult for Sam to "keep me in mind" when she doesn't have an immediate visual cue to color her understanding of our relationship. She has difficulty reimaging my face and imagining my affect and has to fight to keep me from becoming a kind of disembodied voice over the phone. Her visual–perceptual weaknesses may explain why she finds the phone work much more stressful. Once again, I have taken her through the process of evaluating a scheme that won't bend to the environmental demands (she's trying to save travel time by working on the phone and *should be able to do it*) and helped her understand and justify an accommodation that doesn't make sense in that old equation. We have balanced it by decreasing the frequency of our visits out of appreciation for her very real and chronic time deficit.

The tools of direct, explicit, sequential multisensory instruction, interpretation of assessment, judicious analysis of narrative evidence, careful adjustment of cognitive load, interdisciplinary knowledge, and sensitive case management have brought greater and greater resolution to a blurry diagnostic picture. More may yet be revealed. This case has been fascinating and challenging. Sam is generous with her enthusiasm for the work we do and I expect that with her strong drive to make a difference for her students she will continue to move toward, and soon will enjoy a life that includes more grace and ease. It's been a privilege to be instrumental in the journey.

NOTE

1. Numerosity, according to Ahern (2008), is a variable that increases cognitive load. In a state of numerosity, stimuli are not well-learned, require conscious attention and demand mental energy. They are not organized into recognizable groups but instead occur as discrete units of information. Sam had no organizing structure for mentally manipulating the social information about her colleagues. They all occurred as individuals and she struggled to organize appropriate responses to them. Because there were so many people, in several social categories, she was not able to think critically and choose appropriate behaviors around them. Her apprehension about making social mistakes was well-founded. In creating a pattern where the individuals were grouped by function and explicitly expressing her strategy for each relationship we lightened her cognitive load, through chunking and rules. This allowed her to free up mental energy to make decisions about how to relate to them in real time as she encountered them in the course of her work.

REFERENCES

Ahern, C. A. (2008, November). *The learning zone: Understanding brain-based principles of learning.* Keynote address presented at the 30th Annual Conference of the Association of Educational Therapists, San Francisco, CA.

Ahern, C. A., & Marshall, M. (2005). Understanding inconsistent academic performance in students: Integrating educational and neuropsychological perspectives. *The Educational Therapist, 26*(1), 12–17.

American Psychiatric Association. (2000). *Diagnostic and statistical manual of mental disorders* (text revision). Washington, D.C: Author.

Barkley, R. A. (1997). *ADHD and the nature of self-control.* New York: Guilford Press.

Barkley, R. A., Murphy, K. R., & Fischer, M. (2008). *ADHD in adults: What the science says.* New York: Guilford Press.

Berk, L. E., & Winsler, A. (2004). *Scaffolding children's learning: Vygotsky and early childhood education.* Boston: Pearson Education,

Erikson, E. H. (1980). *Identity and the life cycle.* New York: Norton.

Palombo, J. (2001). *Learning disorders & disorders of the self, in children and adolescents.* New York: Norton.

Palombo, J. (2006). *Nonverbal learning disabilities: A clinical perspective.* New York: Norton.

Ratey, J. J. (2001). *A user's guide to the brain; perception, attention, and the four theaters of the brain.* New York: Vintage Books.

Sweller, J. (1988). Cognitive load during problem solving: Effects on learning. *Cognitive Science, 12,* 257–285.

Wadsworth, B., J. (2004). *Piaget's theory of cognitive and affective development* (5th ed.). Boston: Pearson Education.

III

Perspectives on Assessment and Intervention in Educational Therapy

9

APPLYING AN EXECUTIVE FUNCTION FRAMEWORK IN EDUCATIONAL THERAPY

GEORGE MCCLOSKEY AND LORI LENNON

OVERVIEW

Educational therapists (ETs) work with many clients whose academic and social problems are directly or indirectly related to one or more executive function difficulties. It is therefore critical that ETs have a good understanding of executive functions and their role in learning and production (love this word). This chapter will provide ETs with a broad overview of a comprehensive model of executive functions, assessment methods, and intervention approaches for identifying and dealing with executive function deficits. A more detailed discussion of these issues is provided in *Assessment and Intervention for Executive Function Difficulties* (McCloskey, Perkins, & VanDivner, 2009).

A COMPREHENSIVE MODEL OF EXECUTIVE FUNCTIONS

Although the term *executive functions* is becoming more readily recognized by both professionals and laypeople, adequate understanding of the term is somewhat problematic. Well-intentioned but oversimplified definitions offer metaphorical comparisons that view executive functions as a singular directive capacity, such as the CEO of the brain or the conductor of the brain's orchestra (Brown, 2006; Gioia, Isquith, & Guy, 2001; Goldberg, 2001; Wasserstein & Lynn, 2001). Describing executive functions as a kind of global capacity of the brain threatens to reduce the clinical utility of the construct and greatly increases the likelihood that it will join the ranks of other popular but inaccurate neurospeak clichés.

The term *executive functions* refers to a very broad neuropsychological construct that encompasses multiple mental capacities that appear to be responsible for cueing, directing, and coordinating multiple aspects of perception, emotion, cognition, and action (Gioia, Isquith, Guy, & Kenworthy, 1996; McCloskey et al., 2009). This perspective uses six interrelated concepts to describe the nature of executive functions:

1. Executive functions are multiple in nature rather than a single, unitary capacity.
2. Executive functions are directive capacities, that is, they are responsible for cueing and directing the engagement of other mental capacities.
3. Executive functions differentially cue and direct other mental capacities within four broad functional domains: perception, emotion, cognition, and action.
4. Executive functions can vary greatly in their use across four arenas of involvement: intrapersonal, interpersonal, environment, and symbol system use.
5. Executive functions begin development near birth and continue to develop well into the adult years.
6. Executive function use involves the activation of neural networks within some portion of the frontal lobes.

Consistent with these six concepts, executive functions can be defined as a set of directive capacities that are responsible for a person's ability to engage in purposeful, self-regulated, self-aware, goal-directed processing of perceptions, emotions, thoughts, and actions. As a collection of directive capacities, executive functions cue and coordinate the use of other mental capacities such as reasoning, language, visuospatial representation, and memory time frames. Nearly all of the clients encountered by educational therapists are likely to manifest difficulties with one or more of these directive executive functions.

The six concepts stated above have been used as the basis for constructing the McCloskey model of executive functions, a comprehensive, developmentally oriented holarchical model of executive functions (McCloskey et al., 2009). This model is visually represented in Figures 9.1 and 9.2, and builds on conceptual and empirical work from multiple disciplines in an attempt to integrate neurobiological findings with psychological and psychospiritual traditions of thought (Assagioli, 1976; Barkley, 1997/2005; Denckla, 1996; Freeman, 2000; Maslow, 1962, 1970; Miller, 2001; Stuss & Alexander, 2000; Wilber, 1977, 1979, 1995, 2000). The model is offered as a way to conceptualize and organize the interplay of the multiple executive capacities that involve frontal lobe neural functions. As shown in Figures 9.1 and 9.2, the model is structured into five holarchically organized tiers representing different levels of specificity of executive function capacity. Each of the tiers is discussed briefly below. The holarchical model enables the ET to appreciate the overlapping, multidimensional nature of executive function development and the problems associated with developmental lags at one or more levels. The development of executive functions will be discussed in more detail later in this chapter.

Self-Activation

The *self-activation* tier represents the neural processes involved in the awakening or "ramping up" of executive function capacities after sleep or other prolonged nonconscious states (Balkin et al., 2002). During the self-activation process, a less than optimal state of perceiving, feeling, thinking, and acting is experienced; this suboptimal state of consciousness is referred to as sleep inertia. This state of sleep inertia typically resolves shortly after awakening (i.e., approximately 5 to 20 minutes). Executive function control at this lowest tier typically is mediated nonconsciously in the form of a gradual return to wakefulness.

For some persons, however, it takes much longer to reach a state in which they feel "awake" and ready to function. When long periods of sleep inertia are experienced on a

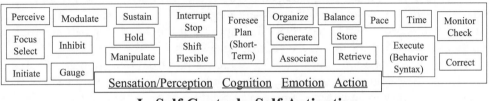

V. Trans-self Integration

| Sense of source, Cosmic consciousness |

IV. Self Generation

| Mind-Body Integration, Sense of Spirit |

III. Self Control:

Self Realization   Self Determination

| Self Awareness | Self Analysis | Goal Generation | Long-Term Foresight/Planning |

II. Self Control: Self Regulation

Perceive	Modulate	Sustain	Interrupt Stop	Foresee Plan (Short-Term)	Organize	Balance	Pace	Time	Monitor Check
Focus Select	Inhibit	Hold	Shift Flexible		Generate	Store		Execute (Behavior Syntax)	
Initiate	Gauge	Manipulate			Associate	Retrieve			Correct

| Sensation/Perception   Cognition   Emotion   Action |

I. Self Control: Self Activation

| Awaken, Attend |

Figure 9.1 The McCloskey Model of Executive Training. Copyright © 2007, George McCloskey, Ph.D. Reproduced with permission.

daily basis, the less than optimal direction of daily functioning that can result is likely to be viewed as a problem that needs to be addressed. When sleep inertia is problematic, some forms of habituated cueing can be activated to assist with the transition to a full waking state or to reduce the effects of prolonged sleep inertia.

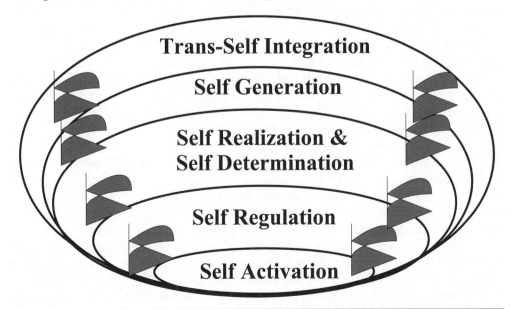

Figure 9.2 Holarchically Nested Levels of Executive Functions. Copyright © 2007, George McCloskey, Ph.D. Reproduced with permission.

Self-Regulation

Once self-activation has been achieved, access to the self-regulation tier is possible. The self-regulation tier is comprised of multiple executive functions capacities responsible for cueing, directing, and coordinating moment-to-moment functioning within the domains of sensation/perception, emotion, cognition, and action. Self-regulation executive functions can be activated either nonconsciously or through conscious effort. Whether nonconsciously or consciously activated, self-regulation executive functions are responsible for the self-regulated aspects of control that enable a person to direct day-to-day routines. The model of executive functions presented here identifies 24 self-regulation capacities that are used to varying degrees and in varying combinations to direct and cue perception, emotion, cognition, and action most of the time: Perceive, Focus/Select, Initiate, Sustain, Inhibit, Modulate, Gauge, Stop/Interrupt, Flexible/Shift, Hold, Manipulate, Store, Retrieve, Generate, Associate, Foresee/Plan, Organize, Choose/Decide, Balance, Pace, Time, Execute, Monitor, Correct. Brief descriptions of the 24 self-regulation executive functions specified in the model are provided in Table 9.1.

The 24 self-regulation executive functions are distinct from one another and are not uniform in their degree of control capacity; a person's effectiveness with each of these capacities can vary greatly; for example, a person might be very effective at using the Focus/Select cue to direct attention to a stimulus, but be very ineffective in the use of the Sustain cue when it would be advantageous to maintain attention to the stimulus for an extended period of time.

The diagram in Figure 9.3 shows four separate boxes for perception, emotion, cognition, and action. The distinct separation of the four domains is meant to highlight the fact that self-regulation, in the context of these domains, is not uniform, but rather is highly dissociable; the extent of control exerted by a specific self-regulation executive function capacity can vary greatly within each of the four domains (and within multiple subdomains within each domain). A person may be able to exert effective executive function control in one domain (or subdomain) but not in another. The result is a profile of self-regulation executive functions that varies individually by domain (and subdomain) of function. For example, a person might be very effective in cueing the inhibition of perceptions, emotions, and thoughts, but not actions, while at the same time being very effective at cueing a flexible shift in perceptions and actions but not emotions and thoughts. For any individual, a profile could be generated indicating the degree of effective use of each of the 24 self-regulation capacities within each of the four domains (and within multiple subdomains) of perception, emotion, cognition, and action.

Although the concept of variation of executive function capacity by domains of function helps to clarify the varied nature of many executive function difficulties, it cannot explain all of the variation that is observed in the daily use of self-regulation executive functions. An additional concept identified here as arenas of involvement represents a critical dimension for a fuller understanding of the range of variability in engagement of self-regulation capacities. Arenas of involvement reflect the behaviorally observable fact that executive function use can vary greatly depending on whether individuals are attempting to direct themselves in relation to their own internal states (i.e., self-regulation within the intrapersonal arena); to direct themselves in relation to others (i.e., self-regulation within the interpersonal arena); to direct themselves in relation to the environment around them (i.e., self-regulation in the environment arena); or to direct themselves in relation to engagement of culturally derived symbol systems that are used to process and share

Table 9.1 Brief Definitions of the 24 Self Regulation Executive Function Capacities

Perceive — The Perceive function cues the use of sensory and perception processes to take information in from the external environment or "inner awareness" to tune into perceptions, emotions, thoughts, or actions as they are occurring.

Initiate — The Initiate function cues the initial engagement of perceiving, feeling, thinking, or acting.

Modulate/Effort — The Modulate function cues the regulation of the amount and intensity of mental energy invested in perceiving, feeling, thinking, and acting.

Gauge — The Gauge function cues identification of the demands (perceptual, emotional, mental, physical) of a task or situation and cues the activation of the perceptions, emotions, thoughts, or actions needed to effectively engage the task or situation.

Focus/Select — The Focus/Select function cues the direction of attention to the most relevant specifics (perceptions, emotions, thoughts, and/or actions) of a given environment, situation, or content while downgrading or ignoring the less relevant elements.

Sustain — The Sustain function cues sustained engagement of the processes involved in perceiving, feeling, thinking, or acting.

Stop/Interrupt — The Stop/Interrupt function cues the sudden, immediate discontinuation of perceiving, feeling, thinking, or acting.

Inhibit — The Inhibit function cues resistance to, or suppression of, urges to perceive, feel, think, or act on first impulse.

Flexible/Shift — The Flexible/Shift function cues a change of focus or alteration of perceptions, emotions, thoughts, or actions in reaction to what is occurring in the internal or external environments.

Hold — The Hold function cues activation of the necessary cognitive processes required to maintain information in working memory and continues cueing these processes until the information is manipulated, stored, or acted on as desired.

Manipulate — The Manipulate function cues the use of working memory or other cognitive processes for the manipulation of perceptions, feelings, thoughts, or actions that are being held in mind or being accessed in the environment.

Organize — The Organize function cues the use of routines for sorting, sequencing, or otherwise arranging perceptions, feelings, thoughts, and/or actions, to enhance or improve the efficiency of experience, learning, or performance.

Foresee/Plan (Short-term) — Cues the anticipation of conditions or events in the very near future, such as the consequences of one's own actions, or cues the engagement of the capacities required to identify a series of perception, feelings, thoughts, and/or actions, and the likely or desired outcome that would result from carrying them out in the very near future.

Generate — The Generate function cues the realization that a novel solution is required for the current problem and cues the activation of the resources needed to carry out the required novel problem-solving.

Associate — The Associate function cues the realization that associations need to be made between the current problem situation and past problem situations and cues the activation of the resources needed to carry out the required associative problem-solving routines.

Choose/Decide — The Choose/Decide function cues the need to achieve closure, i.e., to make a choice among alternatives.

Balance — The Balance function cues the regulation of the trade-off between opposing processes or states (e.g., pattern vs detail; speed vs accuracy; humor vs seriousness) to enhance or improve experiencing, learning, or performing..

Store — The Store function cues the movement of information about perceptions, feelings, thoughts and actions from the mental processing environment of the present moment into "storage" for possible retrieval at a later time.

Retrieve — The Retrieve function cues the activation of cognitive processes responsible for finding and retrieving previously stored information about perceptions, feelings, thoughts, and actions. The more specific the demands or constraints placed on the retrieval task, the greater the requirements for precision of retrieval cues.

Pace — The Pace function cues the awareness of, and the regulation of, the rate at which perception, emotion, cognition, and action are experienced or performed.

Time — The Time function cues the monitoring of the passage of time (e.g., cueing the engagement of the mental functions that enable a person to have an internal sense of how long they have been working) or cues the use of time estimation routines (e.g., cueing the engagement of mental functions that enable a person to have an internal sense of how long something will take to complete, or how much time is still left in a specific period of time).

Execute — The Execute function cues the orchestrating of the proper syntax of a series of perceptions, feelings, thoughts, and/or actions, especially in cases where automated routines are being accessed or are initially being developed.

Monitor — The Monitor function cues the activation of appropriate routines for checking the accuracy of perceptions, emotions, thoughts, or actions.

Correct — The Correct function cues the use of appropriate routines for correcting errors of perception, emotion, thought, or action based on feedback from internal or external sources.

information (i.e., self-regulation in the symbol system arena). Brief descriptions of the nature of executive function involvement in each arena are provided below.

The Intrapersonal Arena   The intrapersonal arena refers to when a person is using self-regulation executive functions to cue and direct perceptions, feelings, thoughts, and actions in relation to oneself; that is, how a person perceives, feels, thinks, and acts toward him- or herself. Effective use of executive functions in the intrapersonal arena drives the daily engagement of purposeful, positive behavior, a positive sense of self, self-control, and self-discipline and enables a person to avoid self-destructive habits and patterns of perception, emotion, thought, and action that can reduce the quality of life.

The Interpersonal Arena   The interpersonal arena refers to when a person is using executive functions to cue and direct perceptions, feelings, thoughts, and actions in relation to the perceptions, feelings, thoughts, and actions of other persons. Effective engagement of executive functions in this arena enables a person to interact appropriately with others as circumstances dictate; to appreciate and deal with the perspectives of others; to generate a theory of mind that enables a person to understand, infer, and predict the motivations, needs, and desires of others; and to find ways to balance the needs of the self with the needs of others.

The Environment Arena   The environment arena refers to when a person is using self-regulation executive functions to cue and direct perceptions, feelings, thoughts, and actions in relation to the environment around them. Effective engagement of executive functions in this arena enables a person to interact with natural and man-made environs while anticipating the impact and consequences of one's own actions in and on the physical environment.

The Symbol System Arena   The symbol system arena refers to when a person uses self-regulation executive functions to cue and direct perceptions, feelings, thoughts, and actions in relation to the processing of information involving the use of human-made symbol systems. Effective engagement of executive functions in this arena enables a person to cue and direct the processes of reading, writing, and speaking one or more languages, mathematics, science, and other formal systems of thought and knowledge. Many persons who exhibit learning disabilities also demonstrate executive function difficulties in the symbol system arena, but the terms *learning disability* and *executive function difficulty* should not be thought of as being synonymous. As will be discussed later in more detail, executive function difficulties can impact the efficiency of new learning, but they are much more likely to impact attempts to demonstrate what has been learned.

As is the case with domains of functioning, arenas of involvement are dissociable; a person may experience executive function difficulties in one or more of the arenas while demonstrating very effective use of executive functions in one of more of the other arenas. Each of the 24 self-regulation executive functions is fully modular; each self-regulation executive function can have a varying level of effective use for each domain (and subdomain) of functioning and within each arena of involvement. For example, a person might effectively use one or more self-regulation executive functions to direct perception and cognition within the interpersonal arena while at the same time being very ineffective in the use of other self-regulation capacities to direct perception and cognition within that

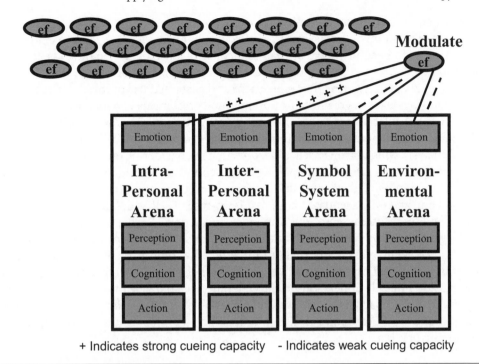

+ Indicates strong cueing capacity   - Indicates weak cueing capacity

Figure 9.3 Examples of variations in cueing capacity strength for the Inhibit self regulation executive function for the action of functioning within the four arenas of involvement.

same arena. Figure 9.3 demonstrates the full dissociable nature of executive functions, illustrating a possible combination of executive function strengths and weaknesses for a single self-regulation function (modulate) within a single domain of functioning (emotion) across the four arenas of involvement. The diagram shows a person who is able to cue the modulation of emotion very effectively when dealing with others and adequately when dealing with feelings about him or herself, but who has great difficulty directing the modulation of emotions relative to academic work (e.g., feelings of frustration with reading, writing, and math) as well as with situations that arise in the environment (e.g., feelings of anger about bad traffic conditions).

Self-Realization and Self-Determination

At the third tier of this model, self-control processes extend beyond the basic self-regulation capacities that govern day-to-day functioning. Executive functions at this tier are engaged in directing the development of a consistent self-image and goals and plans that extend beyond the immediate moment. The two subdomains distinguished at this level, self-realization and self-determination, are described below.

Self-Realization   Self-realization involves being able to direct, cue, and coordinate the use of self-regulation executive capacities, but does not require individuals to be consciously aware of what they are doing or how they are doing it. It is possible to nonconsciously make use of executive function capacities to self-regulate perceptions, feelings, thoughts, and actions without engaging in any conscious form of self-realization. The activation of separate neural circuits routed through specific portions of the frontal lobes is necessary for people to be aware of themselves in a reflective manner. Such self-reflective processes enable people to become aware of their nonconscious use or disuse of lower tier self-regulation executive functions and to take conscious control of these lower tier capacities (Johnson et al., 2002; Morin, 2004). Frequent and sustained use of these self-realization neural pathways leads to greater self-awareness and greater capacity for conscious control of the 24 self-regulation capacities that are typically accessed nonconsciously.

Frequent engagement of self-awareness capacities supports the emergence of a capacity for self-analysis, which involves self-reflection; that is, considering one's perceptions, emotions, thoughts, and actions, and making judgments about the adequacy or inadequacy of one's functioning in these domains. Such self-reflection and judgment create an idea of "who I am, and how adequate I am"; that is, a sense of self as defined by one's recollections of one's perceptions, emotions, thoughts, and actions. Such an increased awareness of self is distinct from, and can dissociate from, one's capacity for becoming aware of how others react to one's actions that presumably reflect one's perceptions, emotions, and thoughts. Self-reflection that takes into account other persons' perspectives on one's actions can add multiple dimensions to the generation of an image that defines "who I am." The self-analysis capacities accessed at this tier enable one to develop a sense of personal strengths and weaknesses and realize how they impact one's daily functioning and the functioning of others.

Self-Determination   Although day-to-day self-regulation executive functions can be consciously engaged, developing a broader sense of self-determination that extends beyond the immediate moment requires the engagement of specific neural circuits involving portions of the frontal lobes that enable goal setting and long-term planning (Luria, 1980). Effective use of these circuits makes it possible for a person to set goals and formulate plans that extend far beyond the capacity of the lower tier self-regulation executive function of Plan that cues the use of short-term planning routines lasting less than a few minutes.

It is important to recognize that no self-determined goal or self-desired outcome is necessary for effective use of lower-tier self-regulation executive functions, including the Plan cue. Consequently, it is possible for a person to engage self-regulation executive functions effectively on a day-to-day basis, responding only to fleeting inner urges or external demands imposed in the immediate moment without ever engaging higher tier self-determination capacities. Consistent with the holarchical conception of the model, however, the converse is also quite possible; that is, a person can engage higher tier self-determination capacities to generate long-term goals and formulate elaborate plans, but have little in the way of lower tier self-regulation executive function capacities to direct day-to-day perception, feeling, thought, and action in a manner consistent with the long-term goals and far-reaching plans generated at the higher tier.

Although self-determination executive functions can be greatly enhanced by the effective use of lower-tier self-regulation capacities, it is not necessary to have developed all 24 self-regulation executive functions to a high degree in order to successfully execute a self-determined plan or achieve a self-determined goal. The better developed a person's self-determination capacities the more likely it is that they will find ways to make the most of the self-regulation executive functions they might possess, whether great or few. Even in the case of exceptional self-determination capacities, however, it is possible that individuals can exhibit so many severe self-regulation executive function deficits as to make it highly unlikely that they will achieve the goals they envision or carry out the long-term plans that they are capable of devising unless the lower-tier self-regulation functions of others are enlisted to aid in the process. Conversely, a person can demonstrate a near complete lack of desire to generate personal goals or plans, instead following the goals and plans set out for them by others and doing so in a manner that leads to great success through the effective daily application of lower-tier self-regulation executive functions.

Self-Generation

The tiers discussed to this point have addressed how we can self-regulate perceptions, feelings, thoughts, and actions in our daily lives and how we can develop capacities for extending control beyond the immediate moment through self-reflection, foresight, goal-setting, and planning. At some point in life, however, a person may begin to pose questions about the nature of existence and the meaning of life. The propensity to ask such questions represents the emergence of the next tier of executive function control referred to in this model as the *self-generation* capacity. The pursuit of the answers to self-generation questions can lead to the development of a personal philosophy of life, or the need for the self-generation of a set of principles that can be used to guide perceptions, thoughts, feelings, and actions. Engagement of self-generation capacities takes the form of a spiritual path for many persons. It is at the self-generation tier that persons can become aware of and pursue the possibility of higher levels of executive function control that can exert influence over insights of self-realization, self-determined long-term goals and plans, and the daily self-regulation of perceptions, feelings, thoughts, and actions and bring them all in line with a personal philosophy of life to produce a greater depth of meaning and purpose. At this tier, it is possible to more fully realize the directive power of thought and the effects that directed intentions can have on all aspects of a person's life. Research has shown that posing self-generative questions and contemplating ethical dilemmas co-occur with the activation of neural circuits heavily dependent on specific areas of the frontal lobes (Greene, Nystrom, Engell, Darley, & Cohen, 2004; Greene, Sommerville, Nystrom, Darley, & Cohen, 2001; Newberg, Alavi, Baime, Mozley, et al., 1997; Newberg, Alavi, Baime, Pourdehnad, et al., 2001; Newberg, D'Aquili & Rause, 2001; Vaitl et al., 2005).

Like all other self-control executive functions in a holarchical model, self-generation capacities can emerge independently of the other executive function capacities and can be utilized to some degree regardless of the degree of development within the other tiers. A person might spend a great deal of time generating and contemplating a highly refined philosophy of life intended to guide daily functioning, but be unable to effectively guide self-regulation capacities in a manner that enables the realization of long-term goals or the production of consistent behavior patterns that are in keeping with the overarching philosophy that they have developed. Alternately, a person might be greatly invested in understanding the meaning of life or determining ethical principles for guiding human behavior but be lacking in awareness of how their own perceptions, feelings, thoughts, and actions affect others. Although activation at the self-generation tier might be viewed as an important advancement in personal development, a person might direct his or her life in a coherent and meaningful manner with a high level of personal awareness and with great success in achieving personal goals through the use of well-developed self-regulation executive functions, and yet never question the meaning of it all; that is, never activate neural circuits that are involved in the engagement of self-generation capacities.

Trans-Self-Integration

Beyond the posing of questions about the meaning or purpose of life and existence and the generation of higher levels of intention for self-direction lies the capacity to direct one toward contemplation of the interconnected nature of things. The desire to seek out experiences that would enable a person to transcend the limits of human perception and the sense of an individual self to experience a sense of "oneness" with everything is referred to in this model as trans-self-integration. These efforts to experience "ultimate truth" or the "reality beyond reality" often lead to what some mystic traditions refer to as unity consciousness. Engagement of trans-self-integration represents a desire to transcend all lower tiers of executive control; to see past the sense of self that is so central in the engagement of self-generation, self-realization, self-determination, and daily self-regulation.

As in the case of self-generation, there are compelling reasons for including trans-self-integration in a comprehensive model of executive functions. Neuroscience research has indicated that the ability to experience the phenomenological state of egolessness or unity consciousness is directly linked to neural circuits that are heavily dependent on areas of the frontal lobes (Benson, Malhotra, Goldman, Jacobs, & Hopkins, 1990; Herzog et al., 1990; Newberg, Alavi, Baime, Moxley, et al., 1997; Newberg, Alavi, Baime, Pourdehnad, et al., 2001; Newberg, D'Aquili, & Rause, 2001). As with *self-generation* capacities, engagement of trans-self-integration capacities can have a tremendous impact on how a person uses all lower tier executive capacities, serving as an ultimate source of intentional direction for many, or possibly all, aspects of the person's life. In educational therapy work with children and young adults, the likelihood of encountering an individual who has advanced their frontal lobe activation to this degree is quite low but certainly not impossible.

DEVELOPMENT OF EXECUTIVE FUNCTIONS

The tier structure shown in Figure 9.1 is not meant to represent a hierarchical tier-to-tier progression of neuropsychological development where one level is completed before advancement to the next level is possible. Rather, the model of executive functions presented here is conceived as a developmental holarchy similar to that described by Koestler (1964) and Wilber (1995) and depicted in Figure 9.2. In such a holarchical model, development unfolds in a fluid, dynamic manner; no rigid constraints are placed on movement between tiers. Development thus progresses from lower tier to higher tiers without the necessity of mastery of all of the capacities of a lower tier. Development at lower tiers can continue to progress at the same time as growth is occurring at one or more higher tiers.

In such a model, a person can be developing highly refined capacities at higher tiers while demonstrating substantial deficiencies in functioning at one or more of the lower tiers. For example, development of a sense of self and an awareness of what a person can and cannot do can be greatly enhanced by the effective use of self-regulation executive functions, but such higher level growth is not necessarily dependent on the effective development of any or all of the 24 specified self-regulation executive functions for its emergence or refinement; it is possible for a person to be very deficient in the use of one or more self-regulation executive functions and be painfully self-aware of these deficiencies.

It must be acknowledged, however, that some self-regulation deficiencies are more likely than others to make it extremely difficult, but not impossible, to develop self-awareness or to engage in self-reflection. For example, a person who is exceptionally poor at inhibiting impulsive perceiving, feeling, thinking, or acting, and who cannot sustain attention to perceptions, feelings, thoughts, or actions for more than a few seconds may find it extremely difficult to engage in a prolonged form of self-reflection or self-analysis.

Development of each executive function capacity is a slow, gradual, and relatively independent process; both inter- and intraindividual variation is common, especially among the executive functions of the self-regulation tier (Kinsbourne, 1973; Rubia, Overmeyer, Taylor, et al, 2000; Rubia, Smith, Woolley et al, 2006; Rubia, Smith, Taylor, & Brammer, 2007). Interindividually, although there tends to be a general age-related pattern of growth in executive function capacities, wide variations in development among individuals of the same age are observable. The development of any executive control capacity is a slow, gradual process over time that may be punctuated by occasional sudden growth spurts. Although each executive capacity follows a general timeline that is similar across all individuals, the developmental trajectories of specific individuals can vary greatly (Krain & Castellanos, 2006; Rubia et al., 2006; Shaw, Eckstrand, et al., 2007). Using the self-regulation capacity of Inhibit as an example, careful observation reveals that even 2-year-olds are capable of some degree of inhibition. How much inhibition can be demonstrated, however, can vary widely from one 2-year-old child to another. Furthermore, most 4-year-olds demonstrate greater proficiency at cueing the Inhibit function than most 2-year-olds. Likewise, 14-year-olds are more proficient than 4-year-olds and 24-year-olds are more proficient than 14-year-olds. With each passing year, however, the magnitude of difference in the capacity to inhibit becomes less obvious. The difference in capacity to inhibit between a 2-year-old and a 4-year-old is large and more easily recognizable than the difference between a 22-year-old and a 24-year-old or even that between a 24-year-old and a 44-year-old.

Intraindividually, a person's self-regulation capacities can be more or less developed at any given point in time. Having one or more well-developed self-regulation capacities does not guarantee that all of the other self-regulation executive functions will be developed to a similar level. For any given person, the specific profile of executive function strengths and weaknesses can show large variations at any point in time. A 14-year-old child, for example, might be able to cue inhibition as well as most other 14-year-olds and use the Focus/Select and Sustain cues better than most 14-year-olds while at the same time being much less effective than most 14-year-olds in the use of the Plan and Organize cues.

It is important to recognize that by early adulthood most individuals have developed some degree of facility with executive function capacities at the self-regulation tier, and a considerable proportion of individuals have developed some capacities at the self-realization tier. It is less common, however, for development to occur at the self-generation and trans-self-integration tiers, regardless of age. It is equally important to note that large shifts in the type and rate of executive function developmental processes are noticeable around adolescence, with the self-realization capacities involving self-awareness and self-determination typically showing considerable increases around this point in time. The pronounced increase in executive function capacities during adolescence has been a focus of popular media reporting on brain development. This media coverage, however, tends to give the inaccurate impression that adolescence represents a stage of development during which lower tier self-regulation executive function capacities initially emerge. This is clearly not the case; as noted earlier, self-regulation capacities begin to emerge shortly after birth and continue developing through the adolescent years and well into adulthood.

The wide variations in development of executive capacities among children of the same age are very similar in nature to the wide variations in physical development that are so obvious to any observer. Among a group of same age children, many will be very similar in general physical appearance. Some of the children, however, will stand out as appearing more similar to younger-aged children in physical appearance while others will clearly have the physical appearance of much older children. A similar range of developmental variability also is present in terms of these children's abilities to use specific executive function capacities, but this "mental" variability is not visible in the same obvious way as the physical variability. It is also critical to recognize that the external physical variability is not in lockstep with the internal mental maturity of executive function capacities. The youngest looking of these children may well have the best developed executive function capacities of the entire group, while the oldest looking of the group might have the least developed executive functions. For each person, physical development and mental development follow their own separate growth trajectories. In terms of mental development, there are numerous dimensions of development any of which can vary widely for the same person.

The fact that variations in the development of executive function capacities are neither physically apparent nor easy to observe seems to produce a perceptual barrier to the appreciation of the significant impact of these developmental variations, especially within school settings. Students the same age who vary widely in physical development are not expected to perform comparably in gym class (e.g., lift the same amount of weight, wrestle a much larger peer) in order to earn a passing grade. The accommodations made for obvious differences in rates of physical development when judging the adequacy of performance in physical education, however, typically are not afforded for the less obvious differences in executive function development when judging the adequacy of performance in mental education. To earn passing grades in academic areas, students often are expected to display the same degree of development of multiple executive functions bundled together under vague, poorly defined labels such as *self-responsibility* or *self-discipline*.

The perceptual barrier that obscures the recognition of variation in the development of executive function capacities is usually accompanied by the equally detrimental beliefs that physical development is out of the direct control of any child, but mental development, especially in the form of executive function capacities, is well within the direct control of all children. Children who do not demonstrate the appropriate degree of self-responsibility are regarded as simply choosing to do so. Such willful disobedience usually is attributed to poor parenting, poor schooling, the decline of societal value, a lack of internal motivation, or various combinations of these sources.

Often in school settings, and even in many homes, the inability to recognize natural developmental variations results in very rigid expectations for the demonstration of executive function capacities. The negative consequences applied to a child who is not measuring up to the expected standards can be severe, unreasonable, and often uncompromising in nature. Appreciation of the natural variations in maturation of executive functions is crucial for ensuring appropriate educational experiences for those children who are demonstrating nothing more than natural maturational delays in the development of these capacities. The fact that mental maturational lags cannot be identified as easily as physical maturational lags does not excuse away the need to identify them and to act in accordance with that knowledge.

It is important to note that educational systems in the United States and many other countries follow a rigid chronologically age-based structure. Children enter preschool, kindergarten, 1st grade, middle school, high school, and postsecondary institutions at predetermined chronological ages. Each transition from one level to the next within this system demands a greater degree of development of executive function capacities for success. The restricted age range for each of these transitions guarantees that some children will not be prepared to handle the executive function challenges of the more demanding newer environment. These children are at risk for failure to adapt quickly enough to the newly imposed conditions for no other reason than a lack of maturity of the necessary executive function capacities. For some of these children, the gap closes soon enough to enable them to recover from a rocky start and acclimate to the greater demands for increased executive function use. For others, the developmental lag is much greater and growth is much slower, resulting in adjustment difficulties that may persist throughout the entire time spent at that level. Given that a child's rate of development can change over time, some students experience a delay in readiness at one or more transitions while effectively navigating others.

In the case of some developmental syndromes such as ADHD, research findings indicate roughly a 30% time delay in the development of areas of the frontal cortex (Krain & Castellanos, 2006; Rubia et al., 2006 ; Shaw, Eckstrand, et al., 2007; Shaw, Lerch, et al., 2006). Chronologically, these findings indicate that a 6-year-old child with AD/HD is able to utilize specific self-regulation executive functions such as the Focus/Select, Sustain, Inhibit, and Modulate directive capacities about as well as the average 4-year-old. The same child at age 12 will demonstrate these capacities about as well as the average 8-year-old. At age 18, this child will demonstrate these capacities about as well as the average 12-year-old. It is not difficult for clinicians to realize the effects that such delays in maturation are likely to have on a child's educational experiences, especially in the performance of tasks involving those nebulous qualities of self-responsibility and self-discipline. Understanding the maturational delay aspect of the self-regulation problems exhibited by children in educational therapy will help clinicians appropriately conceptualize the nature of the child's difficulties and formulate appropriate interventions that reflect the need for great patience when faced with the slow progress that some of these children are apt to demonstrate.

EXECUTIVE FUNCTIONS AND CLINICAL DIAGNOSES

Considering the critical role that executive functions play in regulating perception, emotion, thought, and action in all four arenas of involvement, it is axiomatic that executive function maturational lags or deficits will impact on a person's academic, social, and emotional functioning. In the earlier discussion of executive function development, AD/HD was referred to as a disorder involving at least four specific self-regulation executive function deficits (i.e., inadequate use of the Focus/Select, Sustain, Inhibit, and Modulate cues). This reference raises questions regarding issues of impairment of executive functions and clinical diagnoses. Is there a specific clinical diagnostic category that identifies individuals who exhibit executive function difficulties? If persons diagnosed with AD/HD exhibit executive function difficulties, do all persons who exhibit executive function difficulties have AD/HD? While it would seem practical to have a specific diagnostic category with a name such as *executive dysfunction syndrome* or the like, the broad spectrum of difficulties that can result from inadequate use of executive functions will not fit easily into a single diagnostic category.

Terms such as *dysexecutive syndrome* (Wilson, Alderman, Burgess, Emslie, & Evans, 1996) are sometimes used to refer to individuals with executive function difficulties, but such terms currently do not relate to any widely accepted diagnostic schema. For example, the most recent version of the *Diagnostic and Statistical Manual of Mental Disorders* (American Psychiatric Association [DSM-IV-TR], 2000) offers no diagnostic category labeled *executive dysfunction* or *dysexecutive function syndrome*, although such a diagnostic category is likely being considered for inclusion in future editions of the DSM. Although there could be some merit in the development of a separate diagnostic category or educational classification for executive function difficulties, the greatest challenge to such an approach would be the fact that the diagnostic criteria of nearly all clinical conditions encompass difficulties with one or more of the executive capacities introduced earlier in description of the McCloskey model of executive functions. In a broad sense, the DSM-IV-TR can be thought of as "a *behavioral user's guide to all the things that can go wrong with the frontal lobes*" (McCloskey et al., 2009, p. 76). A number of researchers and clinicians have espoused similar perspectives (Arnsten & Robbins, 2002; Goldberg, 2001; Lichter & Cummings, 2001; Miller & Cummings, 2006; Pennington, Bennetto, McAleer, & Roberts, 1996; Stuss & Knight, 2002), especially when frontal lobe functions are operationally defined as all the executive function capacities defined here combined with working memory processes that also involve frontal lobe neural circuitry. For example, Arnsten and Robbins strongly articulated such a view, stating:

> Deficits in PFC [prefrontal cortex, aka frontal lobe] function are evident in every neuropsychiatric disorder (indeed, the term "psychiatric problem" seems synonymous with PFC dysfunction). Abilities carried out by the PFC can also become impaired in so-called "normal" individuals under conditions of uncontrollable stress, fatigue, and with advancing age. (p. 51)

It is important not to interpret statements such as this as implying that executive function difficulties are the sole cause of all disorders and syndromes listed in the DSM-IV-TR. Rather, these statements are meant to suggest that one or more executive function difficulties are associated in some way with nearly all of the DSM-IV-TR clinical syndromes. The observed executive function difficulties could be either the cause of, or the result of, the identified clinical status. Additionally, it cannot be inferred that executive function difficulties are only found in the presence of clinically identifiable disorders, as some individuals may demonstrate one of more executive difficulties without meeting the criteria of any specific diagnostic category.

Take as an example, generalized anxiety disorder (GAD), which is thought to involve neural circuits routed through a number of subcortical structures, such as the amygdala, that are classified as part of the limbic system (Krain, Gotiner, et al., 2008; Krain, Hefton, et al., 2006; Stein, Westenberg, & Liebowitz, 2002). When a person is experiencing a clinical level of anxiety, the disruption of neural circuits in subcortical areas can adversely impact frontal lobe portions of larger neural circuits that link the limbic system with areas of the frontal lobes. In a cascading effect, a person can lose the capacity to engage self-regulation executive functions to exert control over their anxiety symptoms. Concomitantly, the list of diagnostic criteria for GAD specifies difficulty controlling worry, difficulty concentrating, irritability, and sleep disturbance (APA, 2000). Although the cause of these symptoms might have originated in subcortical circuitry, all of these symptoms reflect difficulties with the engagement of various executive function capacities (e.g., difficulties with cueing the inhibition of, interruption of, or modulation of, perceptions, emotions, thoughts, or actions in relation to self, others, the environment, or symbol systems, or difficulties with cueing the focusing and sustaining of attention to important perceptions, feelings, thoughts, and actions that could be used to counter the anxious state). As will be discussed later in this chapter, the therapeutic techniques known as cognitive behavior therapy teaches clients how to engage executive function capacities to affect a positive change in the functioning of the subcortical neural circuits.

As noted earlier, the connection between clinical diagnosis and executive function difficulties is most obvious in the case of AD/HD. The DSM-IV-TR definition of AD/HD clearly specifies behavioral problems involving difficulties with the self-regulation cues of Inhibit, Modulate, Focus/Select, and Sustain. Consistent with the behavioral evidence, brain function studies of children and adults with and without AD/HD have identified the specific neural circuits affected by AD/HD that pass through regions of the frontal lobes, as well as other areas of the brain (Bunge, Ochsner, Desmond, Glover, & Gabrieli, 2001; Daw et al., 2005; Hill et al., 2003; MacMaster et al., 2003; Voeller, 2001; Zang et al., 2007). Although individuals accurately diagnosed with AD/HD demonstrate difficulties with the Inhibit, Modulate, Focus/Select, or Sustain cues, most of these individuals also demonstrate difficulties with the use of other self-regulation executive function difficulties (Barkley, 2006; Biederman et al., 2006; Pennington & Ozonoff, 1996; Rubia, Overmeyer, Taylor, et al., 2000; Rubia, Smith, Taylor, et al., 2007; Rubia, Smith, Woolley, et al., 2006; Seidman, Biederman, Faraone, Weber, & Ouellette, 1997). Barkley (1997/2005) suggests that most individuals diagnosed with AD/HD also experience difficulties with the Time and Foresee/Plan cues. Additionally, many individuals diagnosed with AD/HD are likely to demonstrate some degree of self-realization difficulties such as delayed development of self-awareness and self-analysis and long-term goal setting and foresight/planning.

Although individuals with AD/HD display multiple executive function deficiencies, the specific difficulties displayed beyond the common core of Inhibit, Modulate, Focus/Select, and Sustain and the total number and severity of the deficiencies demonstrated, will vary from individual to individual as well as intraindividually by age. This is one of the reasons why professional consensus on all aspects of AD/HD has been, and remains, difficult to achieve. Equally important to note here is the fact that there are many individuals who do not exhibit difficulties with the Inhibit, Modulate, Focus/Select, and Sustain cues, but who demonstrate many difficulties with other executive capacities within one or more tiers. These individuals do not meet the criteria for AD/HD; nor do they meet the criteria for any other disorder currently listed in the DSM-IV-TR, a problem that begs for a solution in future editions of the DSM.

In addition to the capacities articulated in the holarchical model of executive functions presented here, the concepts of domains of functioning and arenas of involvement are critical to understanding the complex nature of the association between executive function capacities and diagnostic categories. Consider, for example, the behavioral difficulties experienced by children diagnosed with oppositional defiant disorder (ODD) or conduct disorder (CD) as contrasted with autistic spectrum disorders (ASDs). ODD and CD clearly reflect multiple difficulties with self-regulation and self-realization executive function capacities; an important feature of both ODD and CD is that the deficits can affect all four domains of functioning (perception, emotion, cognition, action) but are manifested in a specific arena of involvement—the interpersonal arena. Thus, the control difficulties of children with accurate diagnoses of CD or ODD will be evident in the difficulties these children have with the cueing and direction of perceptions, emotions, thoughts, or actions when they are interacting with others. These self-regulation tier difficulties often are accompanied by self-analysis and self-awareness difficulties at the self-realization tier. Although difficulties may be exhibited at other tiers or in other arenas, they do not constitute the core difficulties represented in the DSM criteria for these disorders. The autism spectrum disorders (ASDs) include executive function deficiencies involving all four domains of functioning within the interpersonal arena as well as many difficulties within the intrapersonal arena. Additionally, these individuals exhibit severe, pervasive deficits with all capacities at the self-realization/self-determination tiers (self-analysis, self-awareness and awareness of others, long-term goal setting and long-term foresight/planning).

The discussion of clinical diagnoses and executive function difficulties provided here illustrates the need for revision of diagnostic schema to ensure that educational systems, mental health providers, and other professionals are able to provide the necessary assistance to individuals who exhibit executive function difficulties. Such a revision would need to address two separate problems apparent in the current diagnostic system. One of these problems involves the need to be able to diagnostically identify individuals who exhibit executive function difficulties but who do not meet the criteria for any of the existing diagnostic categories. The straightforward solution to this problem is to create an executive dysfunction diagnostic category with the necessary criteria for proper diagnosis.

The second problem involves the pervasive nature of executive function difficulties across almost all of the currently existing diagnostic categories. Simply including a new diagnostic category for executive function difficulties in future revisions of the DSM will likely result in the assignment of the executive dysfunction diagnosis as a secondary diagnosis for virtually all diagnostically classified individuals. Future editions of the DSM would have greater clinical utility if they were to incorporate a new axis, the executive function axis that could be used to identify the specific executive function difficulties exhibited by an individual in relation to the clinical diagnoses that are assigned. The use of the executive function axis therefore would ensure proper identification of executive function difficulties so that appropriate interventions that take these difficulties into account could be identified and implemented.

ENGAGING EXECUTIVE FUNCTIONS BY INTERNAL COMMAND VERSUS EXTERNAL DEMAND

How is it that some persons who exhibit effective executive function use when engrossed in activities of their own choosing can be so woefully inept when requested to perform the simplest of household chores, classroom tasks, or work assignments? This seeming paradox befuddles parents, teachers, work supervisors, and partners of persons who demonstrate executive function difficulties. Examples of such paradoxes could fill a book themselves. These are the "self-absorbed" persons, who for hours at a time with no breaks, can skateboard, text message, play videogames, read intently, practice musical instruments of their own choosing, or track down information about favorite subjects, but who seem unable to use one or more self-regulation capacities when a request is made from an outside source. Then there is the socially capable individual who becomes anxious to the point of physical sickness when required to speak to an audience. There are the meticulous builders of self-conceived designs who offer work products or school assignments that look as though they were assembled in the dark. Those who view these disparities often cannot help but think that these "sudden" incapacities are a matter of conscious choice—a convenient sham to avoid the hard work and effort that is being asked of them. In actuality, a large majority of these observed inadequacies are not a matter of conscious choice, but instead are the result of undeveloped, underutilized, or ineffectively engaged executive functions.

Explanation for these seeming paradoxes can be found in the concept of *locus of intentionality*. The term *locus of intentionality* as it is used here represents the important distinction that executive control can be engaged either by *internal command* or by *external demand* (Brown & Marsden, 1988; Freeman, 2000). The term *internal command* refers to the engagement of executive functions in relation to a person's own internal desires, drives, aspirations, plans, and proclivities. The term *external demand*, on the other hand, refers to the engagement of executive functions in an effort to respond to external sources, such as environmental conditions or the request of another person. Executive function engagement that arises from internal command utilizes specific neural networks routed through various areas of the brain including portions of the frontal lobes. These networks are distinct from, but not necessarily completely independent of, the neural networks of the frontal lobes and additional areas of the brain that must be activated when a person attempts to engage executive control in response to an external demand. The seeming paradox arises from the fact that executive control by internal command typically is much easier to engage because it flows naturally from the person's prevailing internal state. In contrast, activating executive function capacities in situations of external demand requires much greater mental effort and much greater facility with the use of executive function capacities.

In the case of internal control, a person is directing functioning in concert with internal desires and motivational states that are already activated and influencing functioning. In the case of externally demanded use of executive functions, a person must first engage the Stop/Interruptcue to disengage any internally commanded executive function capacities that are directing the current processing of perceptions, feelings, thoughts, and actions. Following the interruption of these ongoing processes, the person must take stock of the situation and determine what executive function capacities are needed to drive perception, emotion, cognition, or action in order to effectively respond to the external demand. For persons already functioning under strong internally generated self-determination and self-generation guidance routines, the external demand might need to be evaluated against these existing upper tier routines to reconcile or overcome any resistance to new demands due to possible conflicts of interest. After successful disengagement of internally commanded routines, a person now must bring on line the necessary executive functions and associated mental faculties required to comply with the external demand. All of these steps can be carried out either through conscious or nonconscious processing, but as is the case with most mental functioning, reactions to externally demanded executive control typically are carried out nonconsciously. In other words, all the steps described above typically occur without a person taking conscious control of the processes involved, although such conscious control over all of these steps is certainly possible.

Sports offer the best examples of the difficulties inherent in shifting executive function control from an internally commanded state to an externally demanded one. Examples abound of gifted athletes who fail to perform effectively in competition. Highly skilled, dedicated athletes spend a great deal of time training to perfect their skills in preparation for competition. In private, internally commanded practice sessions their performance is often flawless. Now faced with the external demands of the competition unfolding on the playing field, however, these highly skilled players sometimes find it difficult to effectively engage executive functions to match the precision of their internally commanded practice routines. Do dedicated athletes who perform poorly in competition all simply choose to fail? Was it simply that they did not want it bad enough? Do they all lack the desire to win? Were they not serious enough about their pursuit of excellence? After all, you have seen them perform much better than that many times before. How is it that when the demand is the highest, the performance is the poorest? In situations such as these, it is much easier to see that even the most capable of individuals can have difficulty directing and coordinating perceptions, feelings, thoughts, and actions under conditions of external demand. If handling external demands is an onerous task even for those who have attempted to perfect their executive control of specific perceptions, feelings, thoughts, and actions, it should not be hard to imagine what it must be like for persons who exhibit executive function difficulties when they are faced with sudden external demands and the expectations for immediate compliance that often accompany them. Parents, teachers, supervisors, and spouses, however, often fail to appreciate the plight of the person who has not mastered the fine art of instant obedience and flawless execution.

Figure 9.4 offers an example of the sometimes stunning disparity that can exist between what a person is able to accomplish in an externally demanded situation and what that person is able to accomplish in an internally commanded state of readiness. At the time of the evaluation when James was asked to draw the Rey Complex Figure shown in Figure 9.4, he remarked that he liked to draw and that he considered himself to be a good artist. Unfortunately, also at the time of the evaluation James was taking medication that had a detrimental effect on executive functions housed in the right frontal lobe. Imagine how stunned James was with his inability to command his drawing skills in his attempt

Production based on External Demand:

Model:

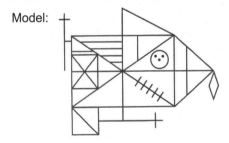

Production based on Internal Command:

Child's free-hand imaginative drawing:

Child's Attempt to Copy the Model:

Figure 9.4 An example of the contrast in performance between externally-demanded production and internally-commanded production for a child with executive function difficulties.

to provide an accurate copy of the design in front of him. Visibly shaken by his inept performance, James cried out in defense of his obviously subpar efforts: "But I *am* a good artist!" James' protest was certainly well-founded, as reflected in the free-hand sketch in Figure 9.4 that he completed on his own as a present for the lead author of this chapter after being off medication for more than a year.

Patience, a nonjudgmental attitude, and a realization of the effort and frontal lobe maturation required to adapt to external demands can go a long way in helping persons take a positive approach to efforts at developing greater on-demand executive function control of their faculties. And even under the best of conditions, consistent production might be a long, long time in coming. Conversely, attributing a person's lack of compliance with external demands to character flaws and negative personal traits or attitudes such as laziness, apathy, a sense of entitlement, or a desire to undermine authority will only serve to alienate the person, diminish any personal sense of connection, and often further reduce the likelihood of compliance with the demands.

EXECUTIVE FUNCTIONS IN LEARNING AND PRODUCING

Earlier in this chapter reference was made to the fact that some, but not all, persons with learning disabilities also exhibit executive function difficulties. Additionally, the issue of maturational lags in the development of executive functions and the potential impact of such lags on transitions in school settings were discussed. Understanding how executive functions are involved in learning and in demonstrating what has been learned is critical to working effectively with individuals who seek educational therapy services.

Learning can be viewed as a complex process involving the interplay of basic processes, abilities, skills, and lexicons (nexuses of stored knowledge) applied in the context of the active integration of multiple time-related frames of reference (accessing past experiences; registering immediate experiences; extending and manipulating immediate experience into the future through the use of working memory capacities). The 24 self-regulation executive functions play a critical role in the learning process because they are used to effectively coordinate the interplay of the basic processes, abilities, skills, and lexicons and cue the proper accessing of the necessary time-related frames of reference. Individuals who are able to apply age appropriate self-regulation executive functions have the capacity to become self-directed learners who require a minimal amount of input from other sources in order to learn effectively and effectively demonstrate what they have learned. Individuals who exhibit executive function difficulties require much more input from other sources to assist them in the learning process. Ideally, this additional input helps them to overcome their executive function difficulties so that they can make use of their adequately developed basic processes, abilities, skills, and lexicons. For example, a person who has difficulty with the Focus/Select and Sustain cues will benefit from teacher prompts that indicate on what or where to focus attention and prompts that indicate the need to sustain attention. When a person's executive function difficulties are effectively addressed, that person can learn effectively. Effective classroom teachers are masters at addressing the executive function difficulties of the students they teach. When good classroom instruction practices are used, students with executive function difficulties are able to use their processes, abilities, skills, and lexicons more efficiently, and learning occurs.

It is critical to note, however, that addressing executive function difficulties during instruction does not guarantee that adequate production will be obtained from those with executive function difficulties when new learning is assessed. When executive function difficulties are exhibited in the symbol system arena, inefficiencies in the learning process are manifested in inadequate forms of production; that is, inadequate responses to questions during instruction, failed tests, poorly completed or undone assignments and projects. If the individual learner has not been taught how to overcome their executive function difficulties, these difficulties are likely to impact efforts at demonstrating what is learned even though learning did take place. Because learning is judged, not on the process of learning, but rather on the product of that learning, students who demonstrate executive function difficulties can easily be mislabeled as having a learning disability when in fact they have what Martha Denckla (2007) has termed *producing disabilities*.

In other words, producing disabilities (or in their milder form, producing difficulties) are not the same thing as learning disabilities (or in their milder form learning difficulties). This distinction is critical to understanding the nature of the problem and how to address it. Learning disabilities involve the disruption of basic processes such that initial perceptions are not adequately prepared for mental representation. In broader models such as those proposed in RtI (Fletcher, Fuchs, Lyons, & Bryant, 2007), learning disabilities can also be the result of disruption of abilities that act on and manipulate mental representations. When learning disabilities are exhibited, a person is much less capable of learning new skills and building skill-based lexicons. Although demonstration of what has been learned will be poor for these individuals, the source of their poor production is the learning disability not a producing disability.

The best example of such a learning disability is developmental phonological dyslexia (Berninger & Richards, 2002; Shaywitz, 2003; Temple, 1997). A person's deficiencies with the basic auditory process of hearing subword sound units results in poor decoding skill development and poor overall reading achievement. When assessment of what has been learned involves reading on grade or age level, a person with developmental phonologic dyslexia is not likely to be able to demonstrate his or her learning. If a person with developmental phonologic dyslexia is identified at an early age and provided with appropriate remedial instruction, reading skills are much more likely to be at grade or age appropriate levels in later years. In the absence of any severe ability constraints or executive function difficulties, the remediated dyslexic is much more likely to perform adequately on assessments of new learning involving reading.

As noted earlier, the situation is different for the person who does not have a learning disability but who does have executive function difficulties. In the absence of a learning disability, the person will be able to learn effectively as long as the executive function difficulties are being addressed effectively during instruction or during periods of study. When assessment of what has been learned involves a degree of self-regulation beyond the person's existing capacities and no support is offered during the assessment, the person is at risk of not being able to demonstrate what they have learned; that is, they are at risk for demonstrating a producing disability rather than a learning disability.

Many very good teachers and clinicians who do a tremendous job of reducing the impact of executive functions during the learning process have a difficult time grasping the idea that if assessment is not guided in the same manner as instruction, or if the executive function demands of the assessment situation are not reduced or altered, some students are not likely to demonstrate effectively what they have learned. The objections to offering guidance during the assessment process usually center on the argument that assessment is not a fair and accurate estimate of what the student knows unless the student can perform without any form of assistance. The problem with this position is that it ignores the fact that unless some students are very effectively taught not just the content of the lessons, but also how to overcome executive function difficulties during assessment, a fair and accurate estimate of what these students know is not possible.

Students whose executive function development is lagging in one or more areas often have difficulty consistently producing at levels that effectively demonstrate what they have learned, especially during the initial period of a transition to the next level of schooling. When an educational transition occurs ahead of the development of the necessary executive function capacities, the student is underprepared for taking on the responsibilities of the new learning environment, and the result often is a lack of adequate production including failing grades. The lack of adequate production can be bewildering to the parents and the students alike, especially if no difficulties had been noted prior to this latest transition. Such "surprise" nose dives in academic production often occur during three specific education level transitions: from elementary to middle or junior high school; from middle or junior high school to senior high school; and from high school to a postsecondary setting such as a college or a technical school. There are many possible reasons for the sudden appearance of executive function difficulties during educational transitions. Abrupt shifts in teaching style; an increase in the number of teachers and teaching styles; increased complexity of learning and production demands; and increased expectations for self-direction of learning and producing all can have a negative impact on students who do not possess the executive function capacities needed to handle the changed conditions.

Whether a first-time occurrence or a chronic pattern, the results of a mismatch between a student's executive function development and the executive demands of a required educational transition can be very stressful and disconcerting for a student and their parents as well. For some students, as executive function development progresses their capabilities come to be more in line with the demands of the educational setting and adjustments can be made to bring production more in line with expectations. Because of the wide variation in rates of developmental progression, however, the timeline for making the necessary adjustments can vary greatly from one student to the next. Students experiencing more extreme developmental delays or medical conditions resulting in severe executive function deficits often are unable to produce work that is judged adequate by established standards, although many of these students have been able to learn new content and acquire academic skills. Whether the executive function difficulties are mild or severe, what these students have difficulty with is complying with the demands for production that demonstrate what they have learned. These students may struggle with one or more production formats such as recording their thoughts in writing, responding effectively to oral or written test questions, completing projects that are done within specified timelines and that contain all required elements or follow the required rubric, or remembering to do or hand in homework assignments, lab reports, or other required materials. The greater the number and severity of the executive function delays or deficits exhibited, the greater the problems from lack of production and the greater the risk of persistent failure in the school setting.

Exacerbating the challenges faced by students with executive function difficulties is the lack of a sanctioned diagnostic classification for executive function difficulties making it difficult if not impossible to obtain the educational services these students need to help them succeed in school. The distinction between learning and producing disabilities, or more generally between learning and producing difficulties, is an important one because it sheds light on why educational support services are, or are not, provided to children who are struggling in school. As mentioned earlier, it is certainly the case that a number of children demonstrate both learning problems due to processing deficits or ability constraints and production problems due to executive function difficulties. In fact, the clinical experiences of the authors suggest that children who have problems with both learning and producing are the most likely to be identified as learning disabled at a relatively young age. Figure 9.5 illustrates the three ways that learning and producing difficulties manifest. The center oval of the diagram represents those students who have both learning and producing difficulties. Typically, the lack of adequate production is what initially draws teachers' attention to the difficulties of these students. When a comprehensive assessment is undertaken with these students, the learning difficulties are also revealed. The dual nature of the problems exhibited by these students makes it easy for both teachers and parents to see the need for instructional modifications or specialized services to help these students succeed in school.

The upper nonoverlapping crescent portion of the diagram represents those students that demonstrate well-developed executive functions for their age but are hampered by specific learning difficulties. In the case of developmental phonological dyslexia described earlier, a student who has well-developed executive functions but limited decoding skills will find alternate ways to move new words from the status of unfamiliar and undecodable to the status of familiar and recognized by sight. When these students' word recognition skills are assessed, the extent of their word recognition skills masks the fact that they cannot decode unfamiliar words. Students with well-developed executive function capacities can be quite inventive in the strategies they develop to compensate for a learning disability. Those with exceptionally well-developed executive functions sometimes are able to maintain good academic production throughout all levels of schooling. At some point in the educational process, however, the production demands will become too much to handle for most students compensating for learning disabilities, and problems will persist until the students receive the assistance they need to manage the learning disability.

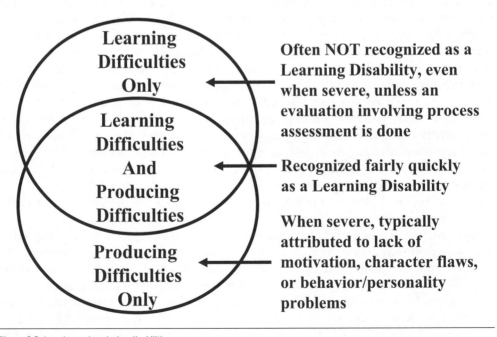

Figure 9.5 Learning and producing disabilities.

The fact that these students are able to produce adequately despite their learning disabilities makes it much less likely that their learning difficulties will be recognized by teachers or even parents, at least during the elementary school years. More often, the learning difficulties of these students surface in later school years when their executive capacities begin to be overtaxed in their efforts to compensate for the effects of the learning disability. At this point in time, parents are likely to be the first to see the struggles that the student is having in keeping up with coursework and to request assistance from school staff, who may be reticent in complying with parent requests at these later grades, especially if the student is earning passing grades. The problem here is that the school staff does not see the unusual compensatory strategies employed, the inordinate amount of time and effort required to complete school work, and the strain that these additional efforts are placing on the students at home. In the best case scenario here, perhaps through the assistance of an educational therapist, the parents succeed in convincing school staff that some kind of assistance is needed.

The lower nonoverlapping crescent portion of the diagram represents those students that do not exhibit any learning disabilities per se, but who are not demonstrating adequate production due to developmental delays or deficits in one or more executive function capacities. Like the students with both learning and producing difficulties, the lack of adequate production of these students leads to closer scrutiny by school staff and parents. In the case of some of these students, written expression production difficulties are noted, enabling them to be legally classified as learning disabled even though, had a thorough assessment been conducted, it would have been revealed that the lack of written production was not due to any basic process deficits or any lack of abilities that would constrain written production; that is, not really due to a learning disability, but rather due to an inability to cue and direct the coordination of all of the processes, abilities, skills, lexicons, and time frames needed for adequate production; that is, due to a producing disability. Although labeling a producing disability as a learning disability is inaccurate, it does provide a sanctioned administrative means for helping the student to improve his or her writing skills. For another subset of these students, competent assessment documenting their executive function difficulties, especially those related to poor cueing of inhibition and modulation and poor cueing of the focusing and sustaining of attention, and the impact these have had on academic production will lead to an appropriate classification of ADHD or ADD, making the student eligible for assistance through a 504 accommodation plan (i.e., section 504 of the 1973 Rehabilitation Act, the first civil rights law guaranteeing equal opportunity for more than 35 million Americans with disabilities).

For a larger percentage of these students, however, no specific learning difficulties are identified and ADHD is ruled out as the cause of their lack of production. Without the distinction of producing disabilities, their lack of production is attributed to any number of negative traits or character deficiencies such as laziness, apathy, lack of willingness to take responsibility for their own actions, lack of motivation, overt hostility, or lack of respect for authority. While attributing the difficulties of these students to such nefarious origins might ease the conscience of some parents and teachers or enable them to shift responsibility for dealing with the situation completely onto the poorly developed brain of the student, they typically do not solve the problems that have been created by the lack of production and certainly do not provide any guidance to these students' developing brains as to how to solve their problems. Conversely, these attributions often serve to exacerbate the situation, creating even more unwanted negative behavior, resulting in a larger rift between the student and those who hold expectations for production. Without appropriate identification of the source of the difficulties experienced by these students and proper assistance through interventions aimed at reducing executive function demands or improving the student's executive function capacities, this group of students faces the greatest risk of failing in school. The remainder of this chapter focuses on assessment techniques for identifying executive function difficulties and interventions for helping clients who demonstrate these difficulties.

ASSESSMENT OF EXECUTIVE FUNCTIONS

Knowledge of a client's executive function strengths and weaknesses is critical to the provision of effective educational therapy services. The state of the art in executive function assessment, however, makes the task of identifying client's executive function strengths and weaknesses somewhat problematic. Although a number of formal executive function measures are currently available for use, for example, the *Wisconsin Card Sorting Test* (WCST; Heaton et al., 1993), the NEPSY-II (Korkman, Kirk, & Kemp, 2007), the *Delis-Kaplan Executive Functions Scale* (D-KEFS; Delis, Kaplan, & Kramer, 2001), the *Behavioral Assessment of Dysexecutive Syndrome in Children* (BADS-C; Wilson et al., 1996), the *Rey Complex Figure* (RCF; Meyers & Meyers, 1995), their focus and scope are very limited in that they all:

1. Make use of norm-referenced, individually administered formats that only directly assess the child's use of a limited number of executive function capacities involved in the direction of a very limited number of tasks;
2. Focus assessment on executive function direction of specific information processing capacities only within three of the four domains of functioning: perception, cognition, and action; and
3. Focus only on the use of executive function capacities within a single arena of involvement: the *symbol system arena*.

Although the narrow focus on the symbol system arena is a good fit with the direct formal assessment methods that dominate clinical practice in school settings it has several drawbacks. The fact that executive functions assessments have focused almost exclusively on the role of executive functions in cueing and directing perception, cognition, and action only within the symbol system arena makes these tasks of little value in the assessment of executive function direction of perception, thought, and action in the intrapersonal, interpersonal, and environment arenas and in the assessment of executive direction of emotions within all four arenas.

The problems inherent in the current assessment offerings have not been readily acknowledged, primarily due to a lack of application of a comprehensive model of executive functions such as the one presented in this chapter. Without such a comprehensive model, researchers and clinicians alike have often made the incorrect assumption that the measures currently available assess executive functions in a very broad domain-general manner such that the results apply to the use of executive functions with all domains of functioning within all arenas of involvement. The incorrect assumption that executive function measures focused on perception, cognition, and action within the symbol system arena could be appropriate for effective identification of the executive function strengths and weaknesses of persons exhibiting difficulties with executive function control of emotions also has produced discordant results in the research literature. In the case of research on conduct disorder, for example, several studies have reported abnormal patterns of frontal lobe neural activation consistent with reported executive function difficulties in conduct disordered persons (Avila, Cuenca, Felix, & Pacet, 2004; Baving, Laucht, & Schmidt, 1999; Blake & Grafman, 2004; Clark, Prior, & Kinsella, 2000; Demakis, 2003; Oosterlaan, Scheres, & Sergeant, 2005), but psychometrically oriented research studies using symbol system measures of executive functions have failed to consistently identify executive function deficits in the test performances of individuals diagnosed with conduct disorder (Avila et al., 2004; Demakis, 2003; Feifer & Rattan, 2007; Oosterlaan et al., 2005).

This lack of consistency between neurocognitive and psychometric research findings is rooted in the use of assessments looking at executive function control of perceptions, thoughts, and actions only within the symbol system arena in order to identify executive function deficits in children and adults whose primary executive function problems involved executive function deficits related to emotional control deficits exhibited primarily in the interpersonal arena. In keeping with the comprehensive model of executive functions presented in this chapter, there is no reason to expect that individuals with self-regulation executive function difficulties in the interpersonal arena will also manifest such difficulties in the symbol system, environmental, or intrapersonal arenas, although overlap of difficulties in multiple arenas is certainly possible. In fact, the research studies cited here did report executive function deficits with symbol system content for some of the subjects in the studies, but these could be considered secondary to the reported intrapersonal arena executive function deficits that led to the diagnosis of conduct disorder in the first place (Avila et al., 2004).

An alternative to direct, individually administered measures of executive functions is available in the form of a series of behavior rating scales. These rating scales offer parents, teachers, and clients themselves the opportunity to offer their perceptions of the frequency of occurrence of behaviors thought to be indicative of executive function difficulties. Currently, the Behavior Rating Inventory of Executive Functions (BRIEF) is the only series of executive function rating scales that is appropriate for use with children as well as with adults (Gioia, Isquith, et al., 1996; BRIEF-Preschool Version, Gioia, et al., 1996; BRIEF-Adult Version, BRIEF-Self-Report Version, Guy, Isquith, & Gioia, 1996). These scales provide scores reflecting parent, teacher, and adult informant report ratings and child and adult self-report ratings of the frequency of ineffective use of executive capacities based on personal recollections of behavior during the most recent 6 month period.

The BRIEF rating scales offer norm-referenced documentation of parent, teacher, and self-appraisals of executive function deficits as they manifest within various self-regulation subcategories such as Inhibit, Shift, Emotional Control, Working Memory, Plan/Organize, Organization of Materials, and Monitor. Item content does reflect executive function difficulties across the four arenas of involvement, but not in a systematic manner resulting in uneven coverage of the four arenas of involvement within each executive function subcategory. A set of norm-referenced rating scales (McCloskey Executive Functions Scales [MEFS]) is currently in development that will enable clinicians to more effectively identify specific executive function strengths and weaknesses within the context of the comprehensive model of executive functions introduced earlier in this chapter (McCloskey, in press).

While individually administered norm-reference assessments and the BRIEF scales offer formal means for assessing some aspects of executive functions, a comprehensive view of executive functions necessitates a more in-depth multidimensional framework for assessment. Such a framework extends assessment beyond the focus of individually administered norm-referenced measures and parent, teacher and self-rating scales to ensure that a multifaceted perspective is taken when assessing a client's use, or disuse, of executive function capacities.

It is important for ETs to keep in mind that the purpose of the assessment of executive functions is not to determine whether a diagnostic label such as *executive dysfunction* should be assigned to a client. Rather, assessment should clearly identify the specific executive function problems being demonstrated by the client, specify any existing executive function strengths, and identify potential interventions that can draw on strengths to help with the remediation of specific problems and concerns. Discussing assessment of executive functions in this manner is consistent with the theoretical perspective offered in this chapter. The purpose for the elaboration of 24 distinct self-regulation executive functions shown in Table 9.1 is to define the capacity of self-regulation in enough detail to enable the development of intervention plans that can help clients overcome their educational difficulties by obtaining greater access to specific self-regulation capacities. The specification of the additional tiers of executive function development likewise enhances the clinician's ability to identify and address executive function difficulties at these tiers.

As explained in the comprehensive model presented in this chapter, executive function capacities can vary greatly depending on domains of functioning and arenas of involvement; the multiplicity of factors that can contribute to variability in the demonstration of executive functions necessitates a multidimensional, multimethod approach to assessment. The assessment methods employed should attempt to determine the effectiveness of executive functions for the cueing and directing of perceiving, feeling, thinking, and acting in relation to self (intrapersonal), others (interpersonal), the world (environmental), and the cultural tools of communication (symbol system).

The range of assessment approaches that can be applied in the assessment of executive function capacities in shown in Table 9.2. Although the assessments of each perspective x method category provide valuable information about a client's use of executive function capacities, collection of data only from a single category is not likely to produce an

Table 9.2 Executive Function Assessment Approaches

Assessment Perspective	Assessment Method	
	Formal Methods–	Informal Methods–
	Using interviews, records reviews, and observation and interpretation methods that make use of standards established through normative comparisons	Using interviews, records reviews, and observation and interpretation methods that do not make use of standards established through normative comparisons
Indirect Perspective– Collecting information in a manner that does not require direct contact with the client	Behavior Rating Scales Parent Behavior Rating Scales Teacher Behavior Rating Scales Self-Report Rating Scales (e.g., BRIEF or MEFS Parent, Teacher and Self Rating forms)	Interviews of Parents, Teachers (e.g., use of the EFSO) Review of School Records Process-oriented Interpretation of Parent and Teacher Ratings and Self Reports
Direct Perspective– Collecting information through direct interactions with the client or through direct observations of the client	Individually-Administered Standardized Tests (e.g., D-KEFS, NEPSY-II, WCST, BADS, BADS-C)	Child Interview Systematic and Nonsystematic Behavioral Observations (e.g., use of the EFSO and EFCO) Process-oriented Interpretation of Standardized Test Administrations and Classroom Work Samples

adequate assessment of executive functions. Ideally, a truly multidimensional assessment would gather data using one or more techniques in each category. Resources are available to assist clinicians with informal assessment approaches (McCloskey et al., 2009), such as the Executive Function Structured Interview (EFSI), the Executive Function Structured Interview for Children (EFSI-C), the Executive Function Student Observation Form (EFSO), and the Executive Function Classroom Observation Form (EFCO) (McCloskey et al., 2009).

ASSESSMENT OF EXECUTIVE FUNCTIONS RELATED TO ACADEMIC PERFORMANCE

The topic of assessment of executive functions in relation to academic performance requires a text of its own. However, readers interested in learning more about these topics are encouraged to read the scholarly publications of Virginia Berninger and her colleagues, especially the relatively recent summary of that work provided in the book *Brain Literacy for Educators and Psychologists* (Berninger & Richards, 2002). This topic also is discussed in much detail in the recently published volume *Assessment and Intervention for Executive Function Difficulties* (McCloskey et al., 2009) and *Essentials of Executive Function Assessment* (McCloskey, in press). Additional clinically oriented information can be obtained from *School Neuropsychology* (Hale & Fiorello, 2004), and discussion of theoretical perspectives on the role of executive functions in the school setting can be obtained from *Attention, Memory, and Executive Functions* edited by Lyon and Krasnegor (1996) and the more recent volume *Executive Function in Education: From Theory to Practice* edited by Lynn Meltzer (2007).

It is important for ETs to recognize that executive function difficulties involving the direction of perception, emotion, cognition, and action in the symbol system arena often have a significant impact on production in one or more academic area while having little or no impact on a person's learning of new material. In other words, many individuals who exhibit executive function difficulties that have a significant impact on their production on tests, classroom work, and course assignments do not exhibit difficulties in the learning of new skills or the intake and storage of new information. One of the reasons for this is that many good teachers deliver instruction in a manner that reduces the learner's need to self-regulate the learning process. The more a teacher offers guidelines and prompts for learning, the less likely it is that any self-regulation executive function difficulties that may be present will interfere with learning. In contrast, independent classroom work, test-taking, and completion of individual assignments and homework typically are not mediated by the teacher, but rather require the learner to use their self-regulation capacities to direct production effectively so that the final product accurately reflects what they have learned. In the case of homework and independent projects, many parents recognize the need for adult mediation of the activity and do their best in efforts to use their executive function capacities to help direct their children's efforts, or engage the assistance of others, such as educational therapists, to assist.

Consistent with the contrast between what an individual with executive functions can learn and what they can produce, it is often the case that individuals with executive function difficulties that impact classroom or work production and lead to failing grades or poor performance evaluations often are able to score quite well on various individually administered assessments such as tests of intellectual functioning, cognitive abilities, and achievement. The seeming paradox of good performance on individually administered tests and poor performance on classroom and work assignments has befuddled those who demonstrate such contrasts as well as their partners, parents, and professionals who work with them, leaving them all struggling to come up with an explanation for the disparities they are witnessing. As is the case with good teachers who mediate the classroom learning experience, the administrator of an individually administered test follows standardized procedures and uses cueing techniques that mediate the test-taking experience in a manner that enables many individual's with self-regulation executive function difficulties to perform very effectively. In many ways, good teachers and good test administrators are "frontal lobe substitutes" that take over self-regulation executive functions for learners and test-takers who exhibit executive function difficulties. Some individuals with executive function difficulties also can be quite adept at learning the procedures involved in standardized group testing. Keeping in mind that even group administered tests are mediated to some degree by a test proctor, these individuals earn much better scores on group administered tests than would be expected given their poor level of performance with independent class work and assignments that require the use of self-regulation executive functions without any form of teacher or proctor mediation.

In the elementary grades, the effects of executive function difficulties are most noticeable in the impact they have on a child's ability to consistently engage with nonmediated classroom routines and to consistently demonstrate mastery of written expression, reading, and mathematics skills. In the upper grades, executive function difficulties with basic skill production in reading, writing, and math calculation and problem solving often persist and are joined by difficulties with organization, planning, time management, and study skills that will affect test-taking and the completion of long-term projects and homework assignments, placing the student at risk of earning failing grades.

INTERVENTIONS FOR EXECUTIVE FUNCTION DIFFICULTIES

In the last section, we discussed how a comprehensive model of executive functions can be used to guide assessment of executive function difficulties. In a similar manner, the model can be used to guide intervention efforts with persons exhibiting executive function difficulties. The multiple tiers conception of the McCloskey model of executive functions can help to identify the nature of the executive function difficulties being exhibited. The tiers of the model also offer a general guideline for the kind of intervention techniques that are most likely to produce the desired results given the nature of the executive function difficulties that arise at each of the levels. What follows is a brief discussion of intervention related to each tier of the model. Readers interested in a more detailed treatment of intervention issues are encouraged to consult *Assessment and Intervention for Executive Function Difficulties* (McCloskey et al., 2009) as well as the various sources cited in the sections that follow.

Self-Activation

Many persons experience difficulties with self-activation capacities, finding it hard to awaken in the morning either for school or for work. Such self-activation difficulties can be greatly exacerbated when intrapersonal self-regulation problems exist. Mood disorders, excessive drug use, and sleep disturbances almost always have some impact on a person's self-activation capacities (APA, 2000). Given the frequency and severity of such difficulties, it is surprising that few intervention techniques for improving self-activation capacity have been proposed or researched (Millman, 2005).

The lead author of this chapter has had some success with stimulus-response conditioning to produce the engagement of automated, nonconsciously controlled behavior routines immediately upon awakening. Such routines enable a person to by-pass the "noise" produced by areas of the brain not directly involved in the awakening of frontal lobe self-regulation capacities (e.g., activation of internalized language processing responsible for "telling" you to go back to sleep when the alarm clock sounds) by nonconsciously engaging a set routine for accomplishing self-activation in a reasonable amount of time.

The concept of internal command versus external demand discussed earlier is critical to understanding inconsistencies in the demonstration of self-activation problems. Most persons have observed in themselves and others that it is much easier to awake when there is much positive anticipation of the day's activities. As noted earlier, the brain is primed for effective self-regulation when internal desires are guiding a person's functioning. In contrast, the self-activation routine is much more difficult to engage when awakening on time is being "demanded" in relation to less enticing external conditions such as the need to go to work or school for a person who does not find these activities very motivating. The more negatively viewed such activities are, the more likely it is that a person will experience some degree of self-activation difficulty or resistance.

In addition to the use of automatically conditioned wake-up routines, aligning external demands with internal desires also can impact the self-activation process in a positive manner. Although it may take a significant amount of belief restructuring for some persons, it is possible to find internally aligned reasons for positive anticipation of work or school, thereby decreasing the difficulties involved with self-activation. For some, all that might be required is to provide oneself with a reminder immediately before going to bed that awakening quickly and without difficulty is both possible and necessary in order to have the kind of day one desires. As will be discussed later, developing a greater capacity for conscious awareness and focused intention is an extremely effective means of effecting positive behavior change.

Self-Regulation

Individuals who have relatively little in the way of internal control over self-regulation executive function capacities require extensive assistance in the form of external control. Highly structured behavior modification techniques that impose external control are the most likely means for accomplishing treatment goals for such individuals (O'Neill et al., 1997). It must be acknowledged, however, that such external control techniques are not designed to help make a person aware of the specifics of the external control regimen that is being used, nor are they designed to make the person aware of the executive function capacities needed to self-regulate and self-correct problems with the direction of perceptions, feelings, thoughts, and actions. Rather, these techniques are designed to manage a person's behavior without the person being aware of the overall plan or purpose for management. Additionally, when such techniques are being applied there usually are no self-regulation goals in the behavior plans. Intervention goals tend to be focused on the desired behavior changes irrespective of the means by which those behavior changes are obtained. Educational therapists can provide a great service to these clients by helping them increase their awareness of the nature of the behavior management plans that are being implemented and by helping the clients to begin to learn ways to increase their capacity for self-regulation.

Pharmacological interventions are another form of external control that are similar to behavior modification techniques; that is, they are an external control source that can effect improvements in the regulation of perceptions, emotions, thoughts, and actions. When a person is extremely lacking in capacity for self-regulation, medications may well be the most effective form of treatment. As a more extreme form of external control, however, pharmacological interventions share many of the limitations of strict behavior modification techniques. The use of medication to reduce the impact of a lack of self-regulation does not necessarily make the person more aware of his self-regulation difficulties and does not teach the person how to increase the self-regulation capacities needed to begin to take control of the problems that led to the need to use medication. Although pharmacological interventions are not designed to increase a person's awareness of the self-regulation capacities needed to effectively cue and direct perceptions, emotions, thoughts, and actions, they sometimes can have exactly this effect on a person. The lead author of this chapter has observed cases in which a brief trial use of medication to treat ADHD symptoms "awakened" the person to what the mental state of increased self-regulation "feels like," consequently improving the person's capacity for using self-regulation executive functions without the continued use of the medication.

Individuals who are able to demonstrate some degree of internally generated self-control in one or more arenas are more likely to benefit from interventions that focus on teaching the client strategies for increasing self-regulation of perceptions, emotions, thoughts, and actions. The most widely researched of these types of therapeutic techniques are cognitive behavior therapy (Friedburg & McClure, 2002; Mennuti, Freeman, & Christner, 2006) and cognitive problem-solving models such as Myrna Shure's "I Can Problem Solve" program (Shure, 1992). These techniques can be applied with adult, adolescent, and even child clients. The younger the individual, however, the more likely it is that frequent prompts will need to be provided to cue the child to make use of the problem-solving strategies that they have learned.

Additional techniques that can be used to address some aspects of executive function self-regulation difficulties include motivational interviewing (Miller & Rollnick, 2002), social problem-solving therapy (Nezu & Perri, 1989) and social stories (Gray, 2002). Although the social stories approach was originally designed as an intervention to deal with the self-regulation deficits of children diagnosed with autism, variations of this approach could be used with nonautistic younger children who lack the developmentally appropriate level of "theory of mind" (realization of self and others) needed to size up situations in order to know how to respond appropriately.

From the educational and cognitive psychology literature, *metacognition* is a term that refers to how children think about thinking. The concept of metacognition overlaps greatly with the concept of executive functions. For example, metacognitive strategies for teaching skills such as reading comprehension (Allen & Hancock, 2008; Rosenshine & Meister, 1996) can be conceptualized as methods for teaching children how to use executive functions to guide thinking about what is being read. Additional instructional methods such as cognitive strategy training, instrumental enrichment, self-monitoring, and self-regulated learning have been documented as effective approaches for helping children develop the capacity to use self-direction cues to complete various routines that improve understanding and production of academic material (Althorp & Clark, 2007; Borkowski

& Muthukrishna, 1992; Case et al., 1992; Feuerstein, 1980; Gaskins & Elliott, 1991; Harris & Graham, 1996; Hartman 2001; Kurtz & Borkowski, 1987; Mastropieri & Scruggs, 1991; Miranda et al., 1997; Pressley & Woloshyn, 1995; Scheid, 1993; Schraw, 1998; Schunk, 1989; Scruggs & Mastropieri, 1992; Wood et al., 1995; Zimmerman, 1989, 1990).

While most of the previously mentioned sources discuss interventions for executive function difficulties without using the executive function nomenclature, Dawson and Guare (2004) and McCloskey et al. (2009) specifically address interventions for self-regulation executive function difficulties in the context of both the home and the classroom. Although the specific literature on executive function interventions is sparse, there are some indications that this may change in the future with the continued publication of articles such as those by Watson and Westby (2003) that addresses the executive function impairments of individuals prenatally exposed to alcohol and other drugs, and by Singer and Bashir (1999) that addresses the role of executive functions in language learning disabilities.

Self-Realization and Self-Determination

Research and discussion of successful therapeutic outcomes (Cozolino, 2002; Segal, Williams, & Teasdale, 2002; Siegel, 2007) have begun to emphasize the need to help clients develop greater self-awareness in order to effect longer-lasting positive alterations of perceptions, feelings, thoughts, and actions. Increased levels of conscious awareness and intention are achieved through the increased development and activation of self-realization and self-determination executive function capacities. Adolescent and adult clients who are developing, or who already possess greater self-realization and self-determination capacities are likely to be good candidates for the use of therapeutic techniques that emphasize the refinement of awareness to help deal with self-regulation difficulties. Such therapeutic techniques include mindfulness-based cognitive behavior therapy (CBT; Segal, Williams, & Teasdale, 2002; Singh et al., 2007; Wasserstein & Lynn, 2001). As with traditional CBT, mindfulness-based CBT techniques teach strategies for increasing self-control of perceptions, emotions, thoughts, and actions through the increased use of self-regulation executive functions. In addition to teaching strategies for increased use of self-regulation cues, however, mindfulness-based approaches also focus on increasing self-awareness; that is, increasing the client's capacity to carefully observe and reflect on his or her perceptions, emotions, thoughts, and actions. Mindfulness-based CBT recognizes that clients who are able to effectively engage self-awareness capacities are better able to monitor their perceptions, emotions, thoughts, and actions on a daily basis, thereby being more likely to realize when they need to make use of the CBT problem-solving routines that they have learned in order to improve their self-regulation capacities. Mindfulness-based CBT techniques therefore attempt to increase the clients' capacity to become self-aware of their own perceptions, emotions, thoughts, and actions, and aware of the strategies that can be used to alter perceptions, emotions, thoughts and actions that are hampering effective daily functioning.

It is important to note the parallel between mindfulness based techniques for improving self-awareness and the "spontaneous" enhancement of awareness alluded to in the case of individuals who use medication for very brief periods of time. Although both produce greater self-awareness, the benefits from brief exposure to medication are serendipitous and unintentional whereas in the case of mindfulness-based CBT, conscious awareness is intentionally generated through the therapeutic regimen. Educational therapists using techniques involving metacognition, self-monitoring, and cognitive strategy instruction are likely to find CBT-oriented approaches very useful when working with clients who have strong emotional reactions to their academic difficulties.

Self-Generation

Many adolescent and adult clients have the potential to activate neural networks involved with self-generation capacities. Clients who begin to engage in such neural processing spend time asking and pondering larger questions about the meaning of life. When such questions are posed, the answers that are generated are greatly influenced by the person's cognitive and social development, spiritual training and influences, and prevailing emotional state. Negative mood states associated with depression, anxiety, and other emotional problems can have a great impact on how a person perceives, feels, thinks, and acts regarding questions about the meaning and purpose of existence. Negative-mood-influenced nihilistic answers to such self-generation questions can result in a person believing that there really is no purpose or meaning to life, thereby releasing the individual from the need to be concerned for his or her well-being or the well-being of others. The negative perceptions, feelings, and thoughts associated with nihilistic answers to self-generation questions can lead to harmful actions that can be as extreme as suicide and murder. In some cases, the use of medications may be necessary to effectively treat severe depression, anxiety, and other mood disorders. Additionally, therapeutic techniques focused at the self-regulation and self-awareness levels may be used to externally control behaviors related to mood disorders or help the person learn to gain greater capacity for internal self-regulation. It is important to note, however, that pharmacologic and other therapeutic techniques aimed at dealing with lower levels of self-control will not address directly any associated problems at the self-generation level. At some point, a dialogue will need to be established to address the questions emanating from the person's accessing of self-generation capacities. While some choose to turn to religious doctrines to engage this dialogue, there are secular therapeutic approaches to dealing with these issues, such as Victor Frankl's *Logotherapy* (Frankl, 1984, 1988; Pattakos, 2008) and Roberto Assagioli's *Psychosynthesis* (1976). When a client begins to question the meaning of life and express negative views on this issue, it is important to recognize the risks involved and refer them to an appropriate source for treatment.

Conceptualizing Intervention Efforts

When working with clients exhibiting executive function difficulties, therapists need to have a sound conceptual grasp of the origin and nature of these difficulties in order to implement interventions effectively. It is important not to attribute the client's difficulties to character flaws or consciously chosen states of mind, such as laziness, lack of motivation, apathy, irresponsibility, or stubbornness. Rather, it must be understood that the observed difficulties reflect real deficits related to suboptimal brain functioning. In the absence of clear evidence that the client was born with severe brain damage or has suffered a severe traumatic brain injury since birth, it is best to approach intervention efforts thinking that a client possesses the capacity to alter how his or her brain is functioning. An optimistic stance related to change in brain function enables the clinician to conceptualize the ultimate goal of intervention to be that of helping the client learn how to effectively engage executive functions through self-generated internalized mechanisms rather than relying on externalized control strategies. If the executive function difficulties are the result of disuse of existing neural capacities, then an intervention plan focused on positive behavior change goals will be based on teaching the client how to activate these neural networks, either consciously or nonconsciously, to achieve the positive goals.

For clients who are seen on an intermittent basis, this conceptual stance is critical to intervention planning because of the limited amount of time spent with the client. While the therapist can apply external strategies to help the client improve production during the treatment session, the focus needs to be only developing the capacity to generalize that state of improved function through greater self-regulation across a broad range of settings. Time spent with the client should include work on assisting the client with becoming more internally self-regulated in addition to applying external strategies for immediate results. In more severe cases, intervention efforts need to start almost exclusively with external control techniques and only gradually move to teaching strategies that will lead to greater internal self-regulation. Unless the educational therapist has access to the client on a daily basis and can work directly with parents and teachers, however, they are not likely to be playing a major role in the implementation of intervention strategies for these more severely impaired clients.

Intervention Planning and Implementation

For the purposes of planning and implementing interventions that address executive function difficulties, the following general guidelines are offered:

- Help parents, teachers, spouses, and significant others to understand the need to provide the client with as rich an "executive function environment" as possible; that is, help them to see how they can model the effective use of executive functions in their interactions with the client; persons with executive function difficulties are not likely to spontaneously improve their functioning if there is a marked absence of positive modeling or the frequent presence of negative modeling.
- Adopt the perspective that the executive function difficulties the client exhibits are the result of nonconscious disuse of existing self-regulation capacities, and that the client can learn to consciously activate these self-regulation capacities through intervention efforts.
- Help the client to become aware of executive functions, most specifically, those needed to help the client increase effective self-regulation of perceptions, emotions, thoughts, and actions.
- Teach the client how and when to engage the needed executive function capacities with the ultimate goal being internalized self-activation of the self-regulation routines needed for effective functioning.
- Apply external control techniques as needed, but work with the client to help them understand the external control techniques that are being applied and how they are being applied.
- Explain to the client the need to move from your application of these techniques to the client's self-regulated use of strategies that replace the external control techniques.
- Maintain, model, and openly express attitudes of hope, perseverance, and patience throughout all intervention efforts.

- Help the client to see that change is possible through concerted effort across time. Record and share with the client observations related to positive changes over time, emphasizing the need for patience with the change process.
- Maintain, and foster in others, reasonable expectations for behavior change and the application of sensible and reasonable reactions to and consequences for problems that are the result of the client's executive function difficulties.

Intervention Strategies

Detailed discussions of specific intervention strategies for executive function difficulties are beyond the scope of this chapter. Readers interested in learning more about specific intervention strategies are referred to sources such as Dawson and Guare (2004), Friedburg and McClure (2002), R. W. Greene (2001), Greene and Albon (2006), McCloskey et al. (2009), Mennuti, Freeman, and Christner (2006), and Shure (1992). In general, intervention strategies can be ordered along a continuum from near-continual application of external control techniques by others to completely self-guided efforts to improve internalized self-regulation. A general overview of the kinds of strategies most frequently researched and applied for the purposes of increasing either internal or external control is shown in Table 9.3.

SUMMARY

The purpose of this chapter was to provide educational therapists with a broad overview of executive functions and their relevance to the practice of educational therapy. The chapter offered a comprehensive model of executive functions that offered a framework for discussing the role of executive functions in cueing and directing perceptions, emotions, cognitions, and actions within four arenas of involvement: intrapersonal, interpersonal, environment, and symbol system. Additional topics discussed were the development of executive functions across the life span, the important distinction between externally demanded and internally generated executive control capacities, the contrast between learning disabilities and producing disabilities, and the relationship between executive

Table 9.3 Internally- and Externally-Oriented Intervention Strategies for Executive Function Difficulties

Internally-oriented strategies for increasing self-control
    Increasing client's awareness of executive function difficulties and how to deal with them
    Modeling appropriate use of executive functions
    Teaching specific executive functions as skill routines
    Using and teaching verbal mediation
    Using and teaching verbal or nonverbal labeling
    Teaching the use of internal feedback
    Establishing self-administered rewards

Externally-oriented techniques for maintaining control
    Structuring of the environment
    Structuring time
    Externalizing cues for effective processing and improved production
    Providing feedback
    Providing rewards
    Aligning external demands with internal desires
    Pharmacological treatment

functions and clinical diagnoses. The chapter concluded with an overview of assessment methods for identifying executive function difficulties as well as an overview of approaches for helping clients deal with executive function difficulties.

REFERENCES

Allen, K. D., & Hancock, T. E. (2008). Reading comprehension improvement with individualized cognitive profiles and metacognition. *Literacy Research and Instruction, 47*(2), 124–139.

Althorp, H., & Clark, T. (2007). *Using strategy instruction to help struggling high schoolers understand what they read.* Washington, DC: Institute of Education Sciences.

American Psychiatric Association. (2000). *Diagnostic and statistical manual of mental disorders, Text revision* (4th ed.). Washington, DC: Author.

Arnsten, A. F. T., & Robbins, T. W. (2002). Neurochemical modulation of prefrontal cortical functioning in humans and animals. In D. T. Stuss & R. T. Knight (Eds.), *Principles of frontal lobe function* (pp. 31–50). New York: Oxford University Press.

Assagioli, R. (1976). *Psychosynthesis: A manual of principles and techniques.* New York: Penguin.

Avila, C., Cuenca, I., Felix, V., & Parcet, M. (2004). Measuring impulsivity in school-aged boys and examining its relationship with ADHD and ODD ratings. *Journal of Abnormal Child Psychology, 32*(3), 295–305.

Balkin, T. J., Braun, A. R., Wesensten, N. J., Jeffries, K., Varga, M., Baldwin, P., et al. (2002). The process of awakening: A PET study of regional brain activity patterns mediating the re-establishment of alertness and consciousness. *Brain, 125*(10), 2308–2319.

Barkley, R. A. (2005). *ADHD and the nature of self-control.* New York: Guilford Press. (Original work published 1997)

Barkley, R. A. (2006). *Attention-deficit hyperactivity disorder, third edition: A handbook for diagnosis and treatment.* New York: Guilford Press.

Baving, L., Laucht, M., & Schmidt, M. H. (1999). Atypical frontal brain activation in ADHD: Preschool and elementary school boys and girls. *Journal of the American Academy of Child and Adolescent Psychiatry, 38*(11), 1363–1371.

Benson, H., Malhotra M. S., Goldman, R. F., Jacobs, G. D., & Hopkins, P. J. (1990). Three case reports of the metabolic and electroencephalographic changes during advanced Buddhist meditation techniques. *Behavioral Medicine, 16,* 90–95.

Berninger, V. W., & Richards, T. L. (2002). *Brain literacy for educators and psychologists.* New York: Academic Press.

Biederman, J., Petty, C., Fried, R., Fontanella, J., Doyle, A., Seidman, L. J., & Faraone, S. V. (2006). Impact of psychometrically defined deficits of executive functioning in adults with attention deficit hyperactivity disorder. *The American Journal of Psychiatry, 163*(10), 1730–1738.

Blake, P., & Grafman, J. (2004). The neurobiology of aggression. *The Lancet, 364,* 12–14.

Borkowski, J. G. & Muthukrishna, N. (1992). Moving metacognition into the classroom: "Working models" and effective strategy teaching. In M. Pressley, K. R. Harris, & J. T. Guthrie, *Promoting academic competence and literacy in school* (pp. 477–501). San Diego, CA: Academic Press.

Brown, R. G., & Marsden, C. D. (1988). Internal versus external cues and the control of attention in Parkinson's disease. *Brain, 111*(2), 323–345.

Brown, T. E. (2006). Executive functions and attention deficit hyperactivity disorder: Implications of two conflicting views. *International Journal of Disability, Development and Education, 53*(1), 35–46.

Bunge, S. A., Ochsner, K. N., Desmond, J. E., Glover, G. H., & Gabrieli, J. D. E. (2001). Prefrontal regions involved in keeping information in and out of mind. *Brain, 124*(10), 2074–2086.

Case, L., Pericola, H., & Karen, R. (1992). Improving the mathematical problem-solving skills of students with learning disabilities: Self-regulated strategy development. *Journal of Special Education, 26,* 1–14.

Clark, C., Prior, M., & Kinsella, G. (2000). Do executive function deficits differentiate between adolescents with ADHD and oppositional defiant/conduct disorder? A neuropsychological study using the six elements tests and Hayling sentence completion test. *Journal of Abnormal Psychology, 28,* 403–415.

Cozolino, L. J. (2002). *The neuroscience of psychotherapy: Building and rebuilding the human brain.* New York: W. W. Norton & Co.

Daw, N. D., Niv, Y., & Dayan, P. (2005). Uncertainty-based competition between prefrontal and dorsolateral striatal systems for behavioral control. *Nature Neuroscience, 8*(12), 1704–1711.

Dawson, P., & Guare, R. (2004). *Executive skills in children and adolescents: A practical guide to assessment and intervention.* New York: Guilford Press.

Delis, D. C., Kaplan, E., & Kramer, J. H. (2001). *Delis–Kaplan executive function system*. San Antonio, TX: Psychological Corporation.

Demakis, G. J. (2003). A meta-analytic review of the sensitivity of the Wisconsin Card Sorting Test to frontal and lateralized frontal brain damage. *Neuropsychology, 17*(2), 255–264.

Denckla, M. B. (1996). A theory and model of executive function: A neuropsychological perspective. In G. R. Lyon & N. A. Krasnegor (Eds.), *Attention, memory, and executive Function* (pp. 263–278). Baltimore, MD: Brookes.

Denckla, M. B. (2007). Executive function: Building together the definitions of attention Deficit/hyperactivity disorder and learning disabilities. In L. Meltzer (Ed.), *Executive function in education* (pp. 5–18). New York: Guilford Press.

Feifer, S. G., & Rattan, G. (2007). Executive functioning skills in male students with social-emotional disorders. *International Journal of Neurosciences, 117*(11), 1565–1577.

Feuerstein, R. (1980). *Instrumental enrichment: An intervention program for cognitive modifiability*. Glenview, Il: Scott, Foresman and Company.

Fletcher, J. M., Lyon, G. R., Fuchs, L. S., & Barnes, M. A. (2007). *Learning disabilities: From identification to intervention*. New York: Guilford Press.

Frankl, V. E. (1984). *Man's search for meaning*. New York: Washington Square Press.

Frankl, V. E. (1988). *The will to meaning: Foundations and applications of logotherapy*. New York: Plume.

Freeman, W. J. (2000). *How brains make up their minds*. New York: Columbia University Press.

Friedburg, R. D., & McClure, J. M. (2002). *Clinical practice of cognitive therapy with children and adolescents: The nuts and bolts*. New York: Guilford Press.

Gaskins, I. W., & Elliott, T. T. (1991). *The Benchmark model for teaching thinking strategies: A manual for teachers*. Cambridge, MA: Brookline Books.

Gioia, G. A., Andrews Epsy, K., & Isquith, P. K. (1996). *Behavior rating inventory of executive function—Preschool version: Professional manual*. Lutz, FL: Psychological Assessment Resources.

Gioia, G. A., Isquith, P. K., & Guy, S. C. (2001). Assessment of executive functions in children with neurological impairment. In R. Simeonsson & S. L. Rosenthal (Eds.), *Psychological and developmental assessment: Children with disabilities and chronic conditions* (pp. 317–356). New York: Guilford Press.

Gioia, G. A., Isquith, P. K., Guy, S. C., & Kenworthy, L. (1996). *Behavior rating inventory of executive function: Professional manual*. Lutz, FL: Psychological Assessment Resources.

Goldberg, E. (2001). *The executive brain: Frontal lobes and the civilized mind*. New York: Oxford University Press.

Gray, C. (2002). *My social stories book*. London: Jessica Kingsley Publishers.

Greene, J. D., Nystrom, L. E., Engell, A. D., Darley, J. M., & Cohen, J. D. (2004). The neural bases of cognitive conflict and control in moral judgment. *Neuron, 44*(2), 389–400.

Greene, J. D., Sommerville, R. B., Nystrom, L. E., Darley, J. M., & Cohen, J. D. (2001). An fMRI investigation of emotional engagement in moral judgment. *Science, 293*, 2105–2108.

Greene, R. W. (2001). *The explosive child: A new approach for understanding and parenting easily frustrated, chronically inflexible children*. New York: Perennial.

Greene, R. W., & Albon, J. S. (2006). *Treating explosive kids: The collaborative problem-solving approach*. New York: Guilford Press.

Guy, S. C., Isquith, P. K., & Gioia, G. A. (1996). *Behavior rating inventory of executive function—Self-report version: Professional manual*. Lutz, FL: Psychological Assessment Resources.

Hale, J. B., & Fiorello, C. A. (2004). *School neuropsychology: A practitioner's handbook*. New York: Guilford Press.

Harris, K. R., & Graham, S. (1996). *Making the writing process work: Strategies for composition and self-regulation*. Cambridge, MA: Brookline Books.

Hartman, H. J. (2001). (Ed.). *Metacognition in learning and instruction: Theory, research, and practice*. Dorddrecht, the Netherlands: Kluwer.

Heaton, R. K., Chelune, G. J., Talley, J. L., Kay, G. G., & Curtiss, G. (1993). *Wisconsin card sorting test*. Lutz, FL: Psychological Assessment Resources.

Herzog, H., Lele, V. R., Kuwert, T., Langen, K. J., Kops, E. R., & Feinendegen, L. E. (1990). Changed pattern of regional glucose metabolism during Yoga meditative relaxation. *Neuropsychobiology, 23*, 182–187.

Hill, D. E., Yeo, R. A., Campbell, R. A., Hart, B., Vigil, J., & Brooks, W. (2003). Magnetic resonance imaging correlates of attention-deficit/hyperactivity disorder in children. *Neuropsychology, 17*(3), 496–506.

Johnson, S. C., Baxter, L. C., Wilder, L. S., Pipe, J. G., Heiserman, J. E., & Prigatano, G. P. (2002). Neural correlates of self-reflection. *Brain, 125*(8), 1808–1814.

Kinsbourne, M. (1973). Minimal brain dysfunction as a neurodevelopmental lag. *Annals of the New York Academy of Science, 205*, 268–273.

Koestler, (1964). *The act of creation*. New York: Dell.

Korkman, M., Kirk, U., & Kemp, S. (2007). *NEPSY* (2nd ed.). San Antonio, TX: Harcourt Assessment.

Krain, A. L., & Castellanos, F. X. (2006). Brain development and ADHD. *Clinical Psychology Review, 26*, 433–444.

Krain, A. L, Gotimer, K., Hefton, S., Ernst, M., Castellanos, F. X., Pine, D. S., et al. (2008). A functional magnetic resonance imaging investigation of uncertainty in adolescents with anxiety disorders. *Biological Psychiatry, 63*(6), 563–568.

Krain, A. L., Hefton, S., Ernst, M., Pine, D. S., Ernst, M., et al. (2006). A functional magnetic resonance imaging examination of developmental differences in the neural correlates of uncertainty and decision-making. *Journal of Child Psychology & Psychiatry, 47*(10), 1023–1030.

Kurtz, B. E., & Borkowski, J. G. (1987). Development of strategic skills in impulsive and reflective children: A longitudinal study of metacognition. *Journal of Experimental Child Psychology, 43*, 129–148.

Lichter, D. G., & Cummings, J. L. (Eds.). (2001). *Frontal-subcortical circuits in psychiatric and neurological disorders.* New York: Guilford Press.

Luria, A. R. (1980). *Higher cortical functions in man* (2nd ed.). New York: Basic Books.

Lyon, G. R., & Krasnegor, N. A. (Eds.). (1996). *Attention, memory, and executive function.* Baltimore: Paul H. Brookes.

MacMaster, F. P., Carrey, N., Sparkes, S., & Kusumakar, V. (2003). Proton spectroscopy in medication-free pediatric attention-deficit/hyperactivity disorder. *Biological Psychiatry, 53*(2), 184–187.

Maslow, A. H. (1962). *Towards a psychology of being.* Princeton, NJ: D. vanNostrand.

Maslow, A. H. (1970). *Motivation and personality.* New York: Harper & Row.

Mastropieri, M A., & Scruggs, T. E. (1991). *Teaching students ways to remember: Strategies for learning mnemonically.* Cambridge, MA: Brookline Books.

McCloskey, G. (2009). *McCloskey executive functions scales.* Unpublished manuscript.

McCloskey, G. (in press). *Essentials of executive function assessment.* New York: Wiley.

McCloskey, G., Perkins, L. A., & VanDivner, B. R. (2009). *Assessment and intervention for executive function difficulties.* New York: Routledge.

Meltzer, L. (Ed.). (2007). *Executive function in education: From theory to practice.* New York: Guilford Press.

Mennutti, R. B., Freeman, A., & Christner, R. W. (Eds.). (2006). *Cognitive-behavioral interventions in educational settings.* New York: Routledge.

Meyers, J. E., & Meyers, K. R. (1995). *Rey complex figure test and recognition trial.* San Antonio, TX: Harcourt Assessment.

Miller, B. L., & Cummings, J. L. (Eds.). (2006). *The human frontal lobes: Functions and disorders* (2nd ed.). (Science and Practice of Neuropsychology series). New York: Guilford Press.

Miller, E. K. (2001). An integrative theory of prefrontal cortex function. *Annual Review of Neuroscience, 24*, 167–202.

Miller, W. R., & Rollnick, S. (2002). *Motivational interviewing: Preparing people for change* (2nd ed.). New York: Guilford Press.

Millman, R. P. (2005). Excessive sleepiness in adolescents and young adults: Causes, consequences, and treatment strategies. *Pediatrics, 115*, 1774–1786.

Miranda, A., Villaescusa, M. I., & Vidal-Abarca, E. (1997). Is attribution retraining necessary? Use of self-regulation procedures for enhancing the reading comprehension strategies of children with learning disabilities. *Journal of Learning Disabilities, 30*, 503–513.

Morin, A. (2004). A neurocognitive and socioecological model of self-awareness. *Genetic, Social, and General Psychology Monographs, 130*(3), 197–223.

Newberg, A., Alavi, A., Baime, M., Mozley, P. D., & D'Aquili, E. (1997). The measurement of cerebral blood flow during the complex task of meditation using HMPAO-SPECT imaging. *Journal of Nuclear Medicine, 38*, 95.

Newberg A. B., Alavi, A., Baime, M., Pourdehnad, M., Santanna J., & D'Aquili E. G. (2001). The measurement of regional cerebral blood flow during the complex cognitive task of meditation: A preliminary SPECT study. *Psychiatry Research: Neuroimaging, 106*, 113–122.

Newberg, A., D'Aquili, E. G., & Rause, V. (2001). *Why God won't go away: Brain science and the biology of belief.* New York: Ballantine Books.

Nezu, A. M., & Perri, M. G. (1989). Social problem-solving therapy for unipolar depression: An initial dismantling investigation. *Journal of Consulting and Clinical Psychology, 57*(3), 408–413.

O'Neill, R. E., Horner, R. H., Albin, R.W., Sprague, J. R., Storey, K., & Newton, J. S.(1997). *Functional assessment and program development for problem behavior: A practical handbook* (2nd ed.). Pacific Grove, CA: Brooks/Cole.

Oosterlaan, J., Scheres, A., & Sergeant, J. A. (2005). Which executive functioning deficits are associated with AD/HD, ODD/CD, and comorbid AD/HD+ODD/CD? *Journal of Abnormal Child Psychology, 33*, 69–85.

Pattakos, A. (2008). *Prisoners of our thoughts: Victor Frankl's principles of discovering meaning in life and work.* New York: Berrett Koehler.

Pennington, B. F., Bennetto, L., McAleer, O., & Roberts, R. J. (1996). Executive functions and working memory: Theoretical and measurement issues. In G. R. Lyon & N. A. Krasnegor (Eds.), *Attention, memory, and executive function* (pp. 327–348). Baltimore, MD: Brookes.

Pennington, B. F., & Ozonoff, S. (1996). Executive functions and developmental psychopathology. *Journal of Child Psychology and Psychiatry, 37*(1), 51–87.

Pressley, M., & Woloshyn, V. (Eds.). (1995). *Cognitive strategy instruction that really improves children's academic performance.* Cambridge, MA: Brookline Books.

Rosenshine, B., & Meister, C. (1996). Teaching students to generate questions: A review of the intervention studies. *Review of Educational Research, 66*(2), 181.

Rubia, K., Overmeyer, S., Taylor, E., Brammer, M., Williams, S. C. R., Simmons, A., Andrew, C., & Bullmore, E. T. (2000). Functional frontalisation with age: Mapping neurodevelopmental trajectories with fMRI. *Neuroscience and Behavioral Reviews, 24,* 13–19.

Rubia, K., Smith, A.B., Taylor, E., & Brammer, M. (2007). Linear age-correlated functional development of right inferior fronto-striato-cerebellar networks during response inhibition and anterior cingulate during error-related processes. *Human Brain Mapping, 28,* 1163–1177.

Rubia, K., Smith, A. B., Woolley, J., Nosarti, C., Heyman, I., Taylor, E., & Brammer, M. (2006). Progressive increase of frontostriatal brain activation from childhood to adulthood during event related tasks of cognitive control. *Human Brain Mapping, 27,* 973–993.

Scheid, K. (1993). *Helping students become strategic learners: Guidelines for teaching.* Cambridge, MA: Brookline Books.

Schraw, G. (1998). Promoting general metacognitive awareness. *Instructional Science, 26,* 113–125.

Schunk, D. H. (1989). Social cognitive theory and self-regulated learning. In B. F. Zimmerman & D. H. Schunk (Eds.), *Self-regulated learning and academic achievement: Theory, research, and practice* (pp. 83–110). New York: Springer-Verlag.

Scruggs, T. E., & Mastropieri, M. A. (1992). *Teaching test-taking skills: Helping students show what they know.* Cambridge, MA: Brookline Books.

Segal, Z. V., Williams, J. M. G., & Teasdale, J. D. (2002). *Mindfulness-based cognitive therapy for depression: A new approach to preventing relapse.* New York: Guilford Press.

Seidman, L. J., Biederman, J., Faraone, S. V., Weber, W., & Ouellette, C. (1997). Toward defining a neuropsychology of attention deficit/hyperactivity disorder: performance of children and adolescents from a large clinically referred sample. *Journal of Consulting and Clinical Psychology, 65*(1), 150–160.

Shaw, P., Eckstrand, K., Sharp, W., Blumenthal, J., Lerch, J. P., Greenstein, D., et al. (2007). Attention-deficit/hyperactivity disorder is characterized by a delay in cortical maturation. *Proceedings of the National Academy of Sciences, 104*(49), 19649–19654.

Shaw, P., Lerch, J., Greenstein, D., Sharp, W., Clasen, L., Evans, A., et al. (2006). Longitudinal mapping of cortical thickness and clinical outcome in children and adolescents with attention-deficit/hyperactivity disorder. *Archives of General Psychiatry, 63,* 540–549.

Shaywitz, S. (2003). *Overcoming dyslexia.* New York: Knopf.

Shure, M. B. (1992). *Cognitive problem solving program.* Champaign, IL: Research Press.

Siegel, D. J. (2007). *The mindful brain: reflections and attunement in the cultivation of well-being.* New York: Norton.

Singer, B. D., & Bashir, A. S. (1999). What are executive functions and self-regulation and what do they have to do with language-learning disorders? *Language, Speech & Hearing Services in Schools, 30*(3), 265–274.

Singh, N. N., Lancioni, G. E., Winton, A. S., Adkins, A. D., Wahler, A. G., Sabaawi, M., et al. (2007). Individuals with mental illness can control their aggressive behavior through mindfulness training. *Behavior Modification, 31*(3), 313–328.

Stein, D. S., Westenberg, H. G. M., & Liebowitz, M. R. (2002). Social anxiety disorder a generalized anxiety disorder: Serotonergic and dopaminergic neurocircuitry. *Journal of Clinical Psychiatry, 63*(6), 12–19.

Stuss, D. T., & Alexander, M. P. (2000). Executive functions and the frontal lobes: A conceptual view. *Psychological Research, 63,* 289–298.

Stuss, D. T., & Knight, R. T. (Eds.). (2002). *Principles of frontal lobe function* (pp. 109–126). New York: Oxford University Press.

Temple, C. M. (1997). *Developmental cognitive neuropsychology.* Hove, England: Psychology Press.

Vaitl, D., Gruzelier, J., Jamieson, G. A., Lehmann, D., Ott, U., Sammer, G., et al. (2005). Psychobiology of altered states of consciousness. *Psychological Bulletin, 131,* 98–127.

Voeller, K. K. S. (2001). Attention-Deficit/Hyperactivity Disorder as a frontal-subcortical disorder. In D. G. Lichter & J. L. Cummings (Eds.), *Frontal-subcortical circuits in psychiatric and neurological disorders* (pp. 334–371). New York: Guilford Press.

Wasserstein, J., & Lynn, A. (2001, June). Metacognitive remediation in adult ADHD: Treating executive function deficits via executive functions. *Annals of the New York Academy of Science, 931,* 376–384.

Watson, S. M. R., & Westby, C. E. (2003). Strategies for addressing the executive function impairments of students prenatally exposed to alcohol and other drugs. *Communication Disorders Quarterly, 24*(4), 194–206.

Wilber, K. (1977). *Spectrum of consciousness.* Wheaton, IL: Quest Books.

Wilber, K. (1979). *No boundary: Eastern and western approaches to personal growth.* Boston: Shambhala.

Wilber, K. (1995). *Sex, ecology, spirituality: The spirit of evolution.* Boston: Shambhala.

Wilber, K. (2000). *Integral psychology.* Boston: Shambhala.

Wilson, B. A., Alderman, N., Burgess, P., Emslie, H., & Evans, J. J. (1996). *Behavioral assessment of the dysexecutive syndrome (BADS).* Lutz, FL: Psychological Assessment Resources.

Wood, E., Woloshyn, V. & Willoughby, T. (1995). *Cognitive strategy instruction for middle and high schools.* Cambridge, MA: Brookline Books.

Zang, Y. F., He, Y., Zhu, C. Z., Cao, Q. J., Sui, M.Q., Liang, M., et al. (2007). Altered baseline brain activity in children with ADHD revealed by resting-state functional MRI. *Brain Development, 29*(2), 83–91.

Zimmerman, B. J. (1989). A social cognitive view of self-regulated academic learning. *Journal of Educational Psychology, 81*(3), 1–23.

Zimmerman, B. J. (1990). Self-regulated learning and academic achievement: An overview. *Educational Psychologist, 25*, 3-17.

10

FROM ASSESSMENT TO INTERVENTION
IN EDUCATIONAL THERAPY

PHYLLIS KOPPELMAN

MEET JD

Deftly, JD removed the vent from the air conditioning shaft in the floor of my office. With only a few minutes left in his session, he had a mission to accomplish. After unseating the vent and peering down the shaft, he put his ear to the floor and reported hearing people talking. Spying a handheld mirror that I use for phonemic awareness instruction, JD positioned it so as to catch the light coming in from the window, causing it to bounce off the mirror and illuminate the world below.

Meet JD, age 13 years, an engaging, curious, inventive, and intelligent eighth grader. He was referred to me when he was 9 years old by a psychologist working with his family. His parents were worried about JD's struggles in learning to read, write, and master his math facts. They said that he became confused in noisy places, tended to daydream in school, and became easily discouraged. If he didn't think he could succeed at an activity, he would avoid it. Teachers at the local public school he attended reported that JD had a hard time following oral instructions in a group.

I met JD for his first session at my clinic when he was 9 years and 3 months old (date of birth, February 15, 1995) at the end of third grade. Small of stature, wiry, with a penetrating gaze, I found JD to be serious and reserved, yet curious about his surroundings. Early on, I discovered that his serious nature was punctuated by a whimsical sense of humor. Over the next 3 years, from May 2003 through August 2007, I was JD's educational therapist. He met with me twice a week for 50-minute sessions, except during holidays or when his family was on vacation. By the time JD entered seventh grade (he transferred to a small independent school when he entered sixth grade), his struggles and anxiety around math had increased significantly. When he perceived a math problem to be too difficult, such as open-ended investigations, he would shut down or insist, "Just tell me the answer." I arranged support twice a week at my clinic with a math specialist, an educational therapist, and a credentialed teacher working under my supervision. JD has continued to receive math support as an eighth grader.

The family psychologist, JD's parents, and I agreed that, based on the recommendations of a neuropsychological evaluation, educational therapy was an appropriate course of action for several reasons. The services of an ET are far more comprehensive than those of a tutor and more likely to help JD address some of his underlying struggles, such as his unwillingness to take risks in his learning. In addition, educational therapy considers and integrates the importance of the emotional connection to learning and functioning, especially in helping him develop strategies for managing and self-monitoring his anxiety. Educational therapy also considers the multiple arenas of school and home, in which JD learns and functions.

JD needed a more in-depth treatment plan, one that would help him develop perseverance and generalize strategies to meet the increasing complexity of academic demands. Findings indicated that JD had deficits in auditory processing, sensorimotor performance and integration, reading decoding, reading fluency, and a graphomotor disorder. Three months after the neuropsychological assessment, an audiologist diagnosed JD with auditory processing and integration deficits. A psychoeducational evaluation by the school district concluded that JD qualified for an individualized education plan (IEP; a 504 plan had been implemented in the fall of his second grade year), which his parents were anxious to see put into place, coupled with private educational therapy, beginning in the summer following third grade.

JD's multiple struggles, coupled with his anxiety had the effect of immobilizing him when he experienced cognitive overload. He would frequently shut down, or disengage from a task or discussion. Results of the multiple assessments and the vital connection between assessment and treatment will be explored in depth in this chapter. Please note that in using the case study of JD to discuss this connection, details and names have been changed in order to maintain client confidentiality.

BACKGROUND INFORMATION

JD is the only child of high-achieving, professional parents. He is in the care of a nanny Monday through Friday, typically from 7:30 a.m. to 8:30 p.m. or later. JD has often expressed fear of his father's criticism, "My dad will get mad if I don't finish my work." Although he would sometimes complain that he saw little of his parents during the week, he seemed somewhat resigned to the situation.

Intake information on JD and his family was obtained by questionnaire completed by his mother and returned to me, prior to my initial intake meeting with both parents at my office in the spring of his third grade year. JD's full-term birth and health history were unremarkable. Early developmental milestones were within the normal range. No illnesses, losses, deaths, or moves were reported. There was no history of recurring ear infections and results of a recent vision exam were normal. His mother noted that in preschool JD didn't gravitate to other children, and in a gymnastics class he would wander off at times. She described him as bright and inventive, empathic, and artistic.

When describing JD's academic experience, both parents voiced concern over their son, "giving up too easily," being "overly sensitive to criticism," and "not having much staying power when the going gets rough." JD's father summed up his fear, "The train's going to leave the station and JD won't be on it."

While he was adept at spinning tales, according to his parents and teachers, JD hated writing them down and he rarely picked up a book to read, unless he absolutely had to do so for school. He preferred to spend time making things out of clay or Legos or fixing things, such as broken faucets, around the house. In an effort to strengthen his phonemic awareness skills, as a second grader, JD had attended "Reading Revolution," a commercial program available at a local clinic. A year later, JD began work with a learning specialist at his public elementary school, twice a week for 30-minute sessions. Additional pull-out and push-in support was done on an "as-needed" basis. In addition, he received private tutoring in reading, spelling, and math facts twice weekly after school. JD's third grade teacher described him as a reluctant reader and writer, who had a hard time getting started, but once he "got going" he had creative ideas. Noting that he "responds better to one-on-one instruction," she described him as prone to "daydreaming" and sometimes "too social when he should be working." Confusion over directions, delays in getting started, unelaborated written output, and sensitivity to criticism have continued to be recurring themes expressed by JD's teachers over the course of treatment.

FORMAL ASSESSMENT

Formal evaluations were completed by a neuropsychologist, audiologist, occupational therapist, and the school district speech and language specialist. An auditory processing reevaluation was conducted after JD completed the first semester of seventh grade. Just prior to entering eighth grade, JD was reevaluated by the neuropsychologist.

A neuropsychological evaluation was first conducted when JD was 7 years and 10 months old. The purpose of the testing was to gain an understanding of his strengths and weaknesses in cognitive, neuropsychological, and academic performance in light of his academic difficulties. In addition to clinical interviews, parent and teacher checklists, record review, and consultation with school district personnel and a private educational therapist, were also part of the neuropsychological evaluation.

Cognitive test results revealed JD's superior IQ, based on The Wechsler Intelligence Scales for Children (WISC-III), with strong abilities in abstract Verbal Comprehension (97th percentile), reasoning, and expression. His WISC-III, Full Scale IQ (FSIQ) score was at the 91st percentile. IQ subtest scores for Vocabulary and Comprehension were at the 99th percentile. However, JD's scores were somewhat misleading because there was statistically significant intratest scatter, pointing to strengths and weaknesses or variations in response patterns in both verbal and nonverbal intelligence. The WISC-III organizes its subtests in thematic clusters called, "Index Scores." There were index discrepancies between JD's strong Verbal Comprehension and his weaknesses in the Freedom from Distractibility (Working Memory) Index (32nd percentile) and the Processing Speed Index (82nd percentile). Additional weaknesses were evident in executive functioning from tasks on the NEPSY. JD's visual memory was superior when there was no motor component involved.

In contrast to his strengths in cognition, JD's academic performance scores were at the low end of the average range in math, spelling, and reading. His academic scores on the Wechsler Individual Achievement Test, Second Edition (WIAT-II) reflected surprisingly strong reading comprehension (WIAT SS 104; 61st percentile), given his compromised reading fluency (WJ-III ACH SS 76; 5th percentile).

Acknowledging the challenge of teasing out attentional issues from auditory processing issues, the neuropsychologist concluded that JD had many symptoms and attributes that might suggest an inattentive type of attention deficit hyperactivity disorder, including restlessness, daydreaming, difficulties listening, and concentrating. The results of the Conners and Achenbach checklists completed by parents and teachers did not verify the presence of ADHD. The combination of clinical anxiety and auditory processing deficits can sometimes be confused with ADHD. Moreover, JD's overlay of avoidance and anxiety tended to confound the picture.

Three months later a mild auditory figure/ground problem for the right ear and a severe problem for the left ear were revealed through a diagnostic assessment. Consistent with the findings of the auditory processing evaluation and the neuropsychological evaluation, the speech and language assessment conducted early in the fall semester of JD's third grade year, indicated that JD had difficulty with auditory perceptual skills. The test battery profile was consistent with a positive finding of central auditory processing disorder (CAPD). The diagnosis of central auditory processing disorder had pointed to deficits in auditory integration, auditory decoding, auditory figure/ground, and short-term auditory memory.

It is important to understand that the term *central auditory processing disorder* has since been redefined as follows:

> Recognizing that disorders in processing may include both peripheral and central sites, the term, central auditory processing disorder, has been replaced with APD, which is broadly defined as a deficit in the auditory modality, characterized by problems with listening, understanding speech, language development and learning. (Young, 2001, p.1)

In an effort to better understand the nature of JD's graphomotor disorder and sensorimotor integration weaknesses he was evaluated by an occupational therapist at the end of the fourth grade, indicating that while gross motor skills were intact, JD would benefit from a structured hand-strengthening program with the goal to increase flexor muscle strength, increase isolated finger movements, as well as distal finger control, in order to allow for greater motor control, which would in turn, facilitate written output. She designed and monitored a home-based sensory integration and fine motor exercise program, implemented over the following several months.

WHY EDUCATIONAL THERAPY?

In spring of fourth grade, JD had presented with delays in academic performance, particularly in reading, spelling, writing, handwriting, and math. In addition, he lacked confidence and persistence with new tasks. He continued to have difficulty following group directions presented orally and tended to become disoriented in noisy places or among crowds. Both the auditory and the neuropsychological evaluations pointed to weaknesses in auditory processing and auditory memory. Additionally, the neuropsychological results indicated weakness in processing speed, working memory, executive functioning, visual-motor integration, and salience determination.

The neuropsychologist concluded that JD's academic performance was well below what appeared to be his IQ as a result of formal assessment, and that a diagnosis of a learning disorder not otherwise specified (currently listed in DSM-IV 315.9 as LD/NOS) accurately diagnosed his difficulties at that point in time (American Psychiatric Association, 2000).

Based on JD's assessments, an IEP was approved for him in April of his fourth grade year, concluding, "The IEP team finds there is a severe discrepancy between [JD's] intellectual ability and academic achievement in one or more of the following academic areas:

listening comprehension, written expression, mathematics calculation, and mathematics reasoning." JD's teachers and resource specialist recommended that JD's parents seek private educational therapy, in order to adequately meet his needs, given the limitations of the school district's resources.

JD's parents, neuropsychologist, audiology consultant, occupational therapist, family therapist, school district personnel, and I agreed that due to the complexity and depth of his learning profile that helping him to develop a metacognitive awareness and strategies for self-monitoring his anxiety comprised an appropriate course of action.

COORDINATING THE TEAM

In keeping with the recommendation by the neuropsychologist for regular communication among professionals, JD's parents and I agreed that as his son's educational therapist (meeting twice a week over a 3-year period), I would participate in IEP meetings and have quarterly phone consultations and e-mail communication as necessary, with his teachers, school learning specialist, audiologist, occupational therapist, and psychotherapist, in order to exchange observations and collaboratively implement the appropriate accommodations.

Since I began work as JD's educational therapist during the summer following third grade, my initial consult with his fourth grade teacher was not until the following October when school was in session. His fourth grade teacher voiced concern regarding JD's learned helplessness. "Too many adults are surrounding him and he needs to be the one to step up to the plate." She went on to say that if he wasn't able to finish his homework or was confused about instructions, then he needed to be able to communicate directly with her. Typically, JD took a long time getting started on class assignments. His written output wasn't "up to par" and he frequently resisted revising and editing his written work, and additionally, was sensitive to criticism. Confusion over directions, delays in getting started, unelaborated written output, and sensitivity to criticism continued to be recurring themes expressed by JD's teachers over the course of treatment.

In order to help JD engage in tasks requiring written output, one of the first interventions I used in my work with him involved writing a personal narrative, *All about Me*, using PowerPoint. I thought this approach might give him an opportunity to demonstrate his creativity and at the same time, risk trying something new.

As JD's educational therapist, I noticed that he seemed to be more successful when he utilized his own internal processing, rather than rely on an externally generated format. If he did not understand the format or did not feel comfortable with it, his performance was adversely affected. In our work together, JD demonstrated his affinity with technology and he found keyboarding far easier than writing by hand, given his graphomotor disorder. Writing a minimum amount of text (one or two sentences) per screen would also help him manage his cognitive overload.

JD began sharing stories about himself, including his inventions, his pets, and how his parents marveled at his ability to fix things around the house. He went on to describe one of his favorite pastimes, ice hockey. JD was in charge of his own "show"; he was director, producer, and screen-writer. PowerPoint was like clay in his hands. I facilitated the process mainly by asking clarifying questions and responding to technical questions, such as "How do you add … photos … music … sound effects … graphics and animation?" We also figured out together (he liked the idea that I was learning too) how to incorporate his own original drawings, which were whimsical and expressive. Observing JD at work gave me an opportunity to watch him fully engaged, telling his own story on his terms. Getting a glimpse into his thinking and writing process and "voice" gave me much pause to think about how to leverage his strengths over the course of our work together, in order to help him develop the basic writing skills he needed.

JD met with the family psychotherapist every 2 weeks during the first year and a half of our work together. During the course of JD's treatment, the psychologist and I had telephone consultations monthly, often more frequently if needed. The psychologist was instrumental in shedding light on a number of issues, including JD's attachment issues, sleep disturbances, and anxiety.

I consulted twice a year with the audiologist in order to better understand JD's APD and to monitor his progress. She explained that the integration between his hemispheres was weak. As a result, JD would often have temporal gaps and miss salient information, ending up with an "incomplete puzzle." I also spoke with the occupational therapist semi-annually, in order to better monitor the recommended regimen of sensory integration exercises, As a result, we incorporated sensory integration exercises into our sessions, using theraputty and a large thera-ball.

In order to help address the issue of JD missing salient information, quite by accident I discovered a useful intervention. Previously, I used graphic organizer software with JD to map an experience or a paragraph as part of the prewriting process. However, much to JD's surprise it was an effective preplanning and organizational activity as well as an aid in helping him to distinguish the main ideas from the details. We used a school-based assignment, a description he had already written on the snowy owl of the Arctic, entitled, "King of the Sky." First, we made a list of subtopics about the owl, creating a "bubble," for each one. Our list included "what it looks like," "where it lives," "how it hunts," and "what it eats." We added details in separate bubbles under each category, such as "what it looks like: sharp talons, broad wing-span, camouflage, and thick feathers." I helped him color-code main ideas in one color and details in another color. I asked JD to experiment with the order by moving the "bubbles" around the screen. We talked about what difference the order of topics and details made. For instance, I asked him whether it would be important to know about the owl's sharp talons before or after describing how it captured its prey. We had created a simple "postplanning" visual map together, using visual mapping software. Since JD loved "taking things apart," deconstructing his story *after* writing it, rather than before, turned out to be gratifying.

THE LINK BETWEEN ASSESSMENT AND INTERVENTION

Data from the multiple assessments previously discussed, directly clarified and informed the design of the educational therapy treatment plan in several ways. First, the treatment plan needed to help JD leverage his intellectual strengths, especially his strong verbal comprehension, reasoning, and oral expression, in order to effectively address his weaknesses. Leveraging his strengths could potentially help him develop a greater sense of competence and confidence. Given his strong reasoning abilities, JD was a candidate for developing metacognitive strategies. Learning strategies of this caliber might also help him feel more in control and perhaps indirectly help him manage his anxiety and take more risks if he felt more in charge. Second, deficits in auditory integration and auditory memory needed to be addressed. Recommendations based on the auditory processing evaluation, included the utilization of software to strengthen auditory processing, thereby enhancing interhemispheric connections and the further development of phonological processing. Third, educational therapy would address academic skill deficits in reading fluency, written expression, and math. Fourth, the treatment plan needed to target weaknesses in executive functioning and attention, which included processing speed and working memory.

Several questions lingered in my mind, as I designed JD's treatment plan. Did JD really have separate attentional issues or were they intertwined with his executive functioning issues? Were they part of his auditory processing disorder? Was one difficulty masked by another? Or, were executive functioning skills underlying many of his symptoms and behaviors? JD's visual-motor and sensorimotor weaknesses also needed to be addressed. The occupational therapist designed and monitored the progress of a home program to increase visual-motor and sensorimotor exercises. In light of the multiple diagnoses the treatment plan needed to be comprehensive in its recommendations for interventions based on careful assessment.

Consistent with the recommendations of the neuropsychologist and audiologist, I needed to consider environmental modifications and classroom accommodations, maintaining an awareness of where JD and I were standing or seated in relation to one another. If I sat to JD's right (next to his "mild" ear), I would not be able to see his paper easily as he worked, since he was right-handed, so I would need to sit to his left or directly across the rectangular table, where we worked. We collaborated on what we could change in order to make our sessions easier. For instance, I hung a decorative 9 × 12 foot rug on one wall of my clinic, strategically placed in order to buffer any extraneous noise. I worked with JD's teachers, most of whom were receptive to implementing the following environmental modifications, based mainly on the auditory processing evaluation:

- Reduce extraneous background noise.
- Use preferential seating, with right ear (stronger in processing) toward teacher, in order to maximize visual and auditory cues.
- Avoid seating next to door with competing noise, open window, or heating or air conditioning vent.

In view of the misunderstandings that can sometimes occur in working with students with auditory processing disorders, easy-to-follow charts have been developed for teachers and administrators, with staff development meetings and quarterly team meetings. With input from educational therapists, teachers, and JD's parents, we developed a manual for teachers with frequently asked questions about auditory processing disorder and how it affects JD. The following is an excerpt from the manual:

What Is It Like to Have Auditory Processing Disorder (APD)? How Can I Understand JD's Experience?

Imagine having a phone conversation with a weak connection. The caller says four sentences to you. You hear and understand the entire first sentence. But you miss a couple of words in the second sentence, several words in the third, and all of the fourth. It's challenging—and irritating. Wouldn't you want to hang up?

How Do I Know It's Not Just Laziness or Stubbornness?

Cognitive and auditory test results confirm that JD processes auditory information less effectively and more slowly. He has other learning issues, too: though verbally quick, he processes more slowly than most and has weaknesses in active working memory (his ability to hold and manipulate information). As a result, he is behind in basic skills and works more slowly than his peers.

JD responds to his difficulties with feelings of confusion, frustration, embarrassment, discouragement, fatigue, anxiety, and helplessness; he sometimes copes in unproductive and inappropriate ways. His fatigue or resistance can often be addressed by using humor, giving him a break, shifting your approach, or allowing him some choice.

The *Guide to Accommodations for JD* was designed to provide guidelines for helping teachers understand JD's needs, communicate with him more effectively, and implement specific accommodations. JD's parents and I met with his teachers, the learning specialist, and school psychologist, introducing them to the chart. His teachers offered feedback, progress, and questions by e-mail and phone.

As described in the neuropsychological evaluation, managing cognitive overload was going to be important in JD's treatment plan, in order to help him manage and self-monitor his anxiety. During the first year of our work together, JD tended to "shut down" when he became frustrated by a task he was working on, such as a 5-minute "quick-write." In an effort to assist him with his mounting anxiety he agreed to utilize a frustration scale, consisting of increments of one to five, five being the maximum level of frustration. This process helped him to concretely identify his present level of functioning, which allowed us to then transition to a problem-solving strategy. Together, we broke the task into more manageable segments. For instance, instead of writing sentences for his quick-write, he

Table 10.1 Guide to Accommodations for JD

What You Might See	What May Be Happening	What You Can Do in Advance	What You Can Do in the Moment
JD seems to be ignoring teacher or speaker. JD is looking down or away for extended periods of time (not making eye contact with speaker, not taking notes, not following along in book) during class discussion or activity.	JD's greatest challenge is in processing symbols when relying solely on auditory channel in isolation. When he reaches overload, he may "check-out." JD becomes anxious and his anxiety exacerbates overload of the auditory channel. JD may feel discouraged and may have given up.	Explain all tasks up front (or preview them with JD), clarifying what he will do and how he will do it, and show what the finished product will look like. Use a visual outline of "big picture" concepts on the board: List "key terms" to know on the board: "Make sure you understand:…" Provide an outline or graphic organizer for notes.	Use non-verbal cues to help JD re-direct attention and reactivate his auditory channel. Incorporate short (2- to 5-minute) breaks into the work session. Have JD write or diagram steps as a recipe for future reference. Reengage JD with a task he can do with ease. Ask JD to try a task while you watch; then give explicit feedback.
JD is off task (sitting quietly, disengaged, or chatting about other things) during small group activity.	JD can be overloaded or confused by background noises, causing him to have difficulty selecting salient information. JD has auditory discrimination and integration issues; information from each ear does not always lead to a meaningful whole unit.	Provide a written list of steps, prompts or questions. Provide a written template, outline, or study guide. Have JD add details to support key points on an outline or template. Plan to incorporate kinesthetic modality (e.g. cutting, drawing, manipulating) with auditory input.	Have JD highlight key words on outline or study guide. (He may need specific directions to guide his highlighting.) Repeat spoken directions, using the same wording (not rephrasing).

(continued)

Table 10.1 Continued

What You Might See	What May Be Happening	What You Can Do in Advance	What You Can Do in the Moment
JD is sitting quietly, disengaged, or chatting about other things during individual work time.	JD's greatest challenge is in processing symbols when relying solely on auditory channel in isolation.	Provide a written list of steps. Plan to include kinesthetic modality simultaneously with auditory input.	Ask JD to rephrase directions to you (rather than asking if he understands).
JD seems to be confusing words that sound similar. JD seems to be having difficulty following multi-step directions. JD seems to be having difficulty knowing how to respond and appears confused by others' reactions.	JD experiences sound distortion and sound sequencing difficulty. JD has inefficient short-term auditory memory and working memory. JD has inefficient auditory integration, leading to an "incomplete picture."	Provide a note-taker and/or recording device. Provide JD with discussion questions in advance.	Use signal words ("These next three steps are important" or "First... Next... Finally...") to alert JD to steps or important points. Provide JD with extra time to respond orally. Give one sensory cue at a time, asking JD to look THEN listen rather than look AND listen.
JD appears "shut down" (silent, avoiding eye contact, turned away, fidgety and agitated or still).	JD's processing may be overloaded, contributing to a shutdown.	Plan to give JD options (instead of asking, "What would help you?") Establish a signal you can use to tell JD to take a break.	Prompt JD with a question or direction to reactivate processing. Offer two choices, as in, "Should we try again or leave it for now and come back to it?". Offer appropriate kinesthetic activity (e.g., squeeze ball or "fidget toy").
JD says, "What...what?" and/or looks at adult blankly or quizzically. JD seems to be interpreting words too literally. JD seems to be overreacting to background sounds. JD seems to be missing sounds or important information.	JD has difficulty attending to important sounds when there is background noise ("figure-ground" distortion). It's hard for JD to integrate information from each ear. JD may miss word parts, words, or word meanings (auditory integration weakness). Voices tend to "disappear." JD has difficulty figuring out where sounds are coming from and which are important to attend to (weak noise suppression and sound localization).	Plan to provide a quieter area of the room for him to move to if necessary. Provide a written list of steps, key ideas, prompts or questions to aid comprehension. Establish in advance a non-verbal cue you can use (e.g., tap on his shoulder) to redirect JD's focus.	Have JD watch speaker's face. Suggest that JD move to a quieter area of room. Have JD read back important information. Repeat exact directions, rather than rephrasing.

wrote a list of words, sometimes using a category prompt such as "things that glow in the dark."

Examples of Tasks and Exercises in Educational Therapy Sessions with JD

Auditory Integration Software   In order to strengthen auditory processing and integration, JD and I used the auditory integration software recommended by the audiologist. We set aside 10 to 15 minutes per session for auditory processing exercises. Interestingly, as the task became more challenging, as long as JD understood what was expected of him, his time on task and his level of engagement increased. For example, in the auditory integration software game "Memory Matrix," as the background noise increases in volume and distraction, the task of selecting words ending in the same sounds, becomes increasingly difficult. "Memory Matrix," targets auditory attention, auditory sequential memory, and auditory performance with competing sounds, short-term auditory memory, and following oral directions, all skill deficits identified by the neuropsychologist and the audiologist. The rationale for using "Memory Matrix" is that, as the player's ability to remember sounds and words improves, his comprehension will improve. This turned out to be the case for JD. Use of progress charts enabled JD to see tangible results of his efforts, and he found the explicit feedback satisfying.

Auditory Discrimination Puzzles   In addition to using auditory processing and integration software to strengthen JD's auditory processing and integration skills, I used exercises from Landmark School in Prides Crossing, MA (unpublished), including auditory discrimination puzzles which involved listening to and following a sequence of oral instructions. These visual-motor tasks required adding, deleting, and replacing letters and words in sentences. JD was enthralled by the mystery of solving these "riddles," particularly since the content was astronomy, which I knew he loved. I modeled the steps in small, manageable chunks, in order to avoid cognitive overload. We tackled the riddles together, using a visual hand-out for JD to refer to as needed. I encouraged him to create his own symbols in order to help him remember each step (a precursor to note taking). For example, if the directions said to find the second vowel in the alphabet in the third word, he used the symbol "V2" to represent "second vowel." I asked JD to tell me when he needed to hear the instructions again, in order to get an idea of how much he understood as well as to provide practice in self-advocacy, or asking for what he needed. I practiced single cuing in a single modality at a time. I would *repeat* the instructions and *then* show him the written directions. JD learned to listen for signal words, such as *first, next,* or *finally*, to highlight that important information would follow. Gradually, I scaffolded the process, so that he could grapple with the steps himself. Within the first eight months, JD progressed from solving a four-step sequence to a six- to eight-step sequence. In addition to strengthening auditory processing, practice with auditory discrimination puzzles also increased JD's time on task from 6 to 8 minutes initially, to 10 to 15 minutes and enhanced his visual-motor integration and working memory.

Sentence Expansion   Since JD loved telling stories, but hated writing them down, we began with oral work at the word level and progressed to phrases and sentences during the first 6 months of our work. We took turns tossing the ball to each other as we expanded sentence kernels, in order to strengthen auditory memory, retrieval, and working memory. For example, we started with the kernel *snakes*. We took turns being student and teacher, each repeating the entire sentence with each turn.

"Add what kind of snakes." "Slimy snakes." "Add to what." "Slimy snakes slither." "Add where." "Slimy snakes slither at Safeway." "Add when."?"Slimy snakes slither at Safeway when they're ravenous," and so on. Whoever had the ball chose the kind of word to add. Over time, we incorporated use of a whiteboard, Post-Its, storyboarding, and the software "Inspiration" as planning tools. In follow-up work, JD would write the kernel sentences we had practiced orally. I later used his expanded kernel sentences to teach JD syntax and parts of speech.

Effective Graphic Organizer Software   Use of a graphic organizer or mapping software was targeted to help JD leverage his visual memory, a major strength noted by the neuropsychologist. A planning tool for writing, the mapping software offers the flexibility of creating a visual graphic organizer or "bubble map," which can be converted to a conventional outline format in a single keystroke. Although in educational therapy JD initially resisted using a graphic organizer, approaching it in small, bite-sized chunks helped to minimize "cognitive overload." We began by making a four-bubble map, and later added color-coded main ideas and supporting detail. Of note, is that JD found it more effective to build his own template for mapping main ideas and supporting evidence, rather than using one of the commercial software templates in various domains (such as language arts, social studies, science, thinking). JD's process was consistent with the way he processed information visually, working from part to whole, until he uncovered the gestalt, drawing from his own internal landscape instead of using an external overlay.

Task Management   JD also used mapping software in order to help him anchor information and make long-term projects more manageable, such as his "year-long" sixth grade research project on atoms. Working backwards on the calendar from the final deadline, we divided the project into bite-sized tasks and assigned an interim deadline for each task. Still resistant to using his assignment planner, we used a 16 × 20" dry erase 30-day calendar, plotting interim steps, using action verbs. JD color-coded tasks and deadlines. It took a full year for JD to experience the value of using graphic organizer software as a planning tool, amidst his protests, "I just want to get it done," or "This is a total waste of time." After creating his own visual map, however, he referred back to it constantly, checking off each section as he completed it and commenting on how cool it was, that at the touch of a button, he could transform a visual "bubble map" into a conventional outline. While using the mapping software and the large dry erase calendar for his research project helped him with time management and anxiety, his efforts were punctuated by "overwhelm" and "cognitive overload." Weary of working on the project, he would occasionally "forget" to bring in note cards, books, or articles he needed. Several times he shut down completely, voice barely audible as we tried to find a section on quantum mechanics that he had worked hard on and couldn't access. Later, he realized that it was on his home computer, where he had completed the section in question.

Revising and Editing   During the course of our work together, JD brought in rough drafts of his stories and compositions from school, written slowly and painfully, every error noted boldly in red. Often feeling frustrated and defeated, he would announce that he wasn't about to change a word. In response, I would make two photocopies of his dog-eared, red-lined draft, one to crumple up and recycle immediately, saying, "Okay, let's get rid of it!" and the other, for us to get to work on, after diffusing his anxiety with my acknowledgment. I suggested that he e-mail his cultural studies teacher, with my help, in order to communicate strategies that might help make the revising and editing process easier, such as tackling a single category of error at a time. Resistant at first, JD's relief was palpable. At the same time, he had an opportunity to practice his skills at self-advocacy. I followed up by scheduling a phone appointment with his teacher, who was receptive to finding ways to help JD make the work more manageable.

NEUROPSYCHOLOGICAL REASSESSMENT: NEW FINDINGS

In an effort to better understand JD's current academic struggles, determine appropriate high school placement, and update accommodations, JD was reassessed as he embarked on the fall semester of eighth grade by the same neuropsychologist who administered the original evaluation 5 years earlier. Results of cognitive ability test scores were stable and consistent with the previous evaluation in revealing intelligence scores in the Very Superior Range, with significant intratest scatter. Full scale IQ was 122, two points higher than previously.

JD's learning issues, as well as reports of anxiety and depression, masked his attentional issues when he was first assessed. The most striking finding of the second neuropsychological assessment was the diagnosis of attention deficit hyperactivity disorder (ADHD), combined type. The new diagnosis of ADHD was based on DSM-IV criteria, parent and teacher Conners attention checklists, Levine ANSER checklists completed by parents, teachers, and educational therapists, observations of JD, and patterns of test results based on scores on the NEPSY-II (Attention and Executives subtests), and the Dellis-Kaplan Executive Function Systems (DKEFS) tests. JD's scores on the attention and executive function tests indicated that he had difficulties with cognitive flexibility, inhibiting previously learned responses, consistent performance of many tasks, attention maintenance, and impulse control, all of which suggested attention deficits. Thus, it is not surprising that it has been particularly challenging in the classroom setting for JD to stay focused, shift between tasks, and simultaneously manage auditory and visual information. Add to the attentional and executive functioning challenges, JD's graphomotor and processing speed deficits, and difficulties following directions and taking notes become more readily understandable.

Also exacerbating JD's attentional struggles have been his relatively weak working memory (WISC-IV Working Memory Index, 55th percentile), auditory processing scores, and weak recall of information and orienting to a new verbal learning task (Children's Memory Scales [CMS], composite Standard Score of 97; 42nd percentile). According to the neuropsychologist, JD understood the procedure of some of the subtests and developed strategies; whereas, an individual with a pronounced language processing disability would not have been able to perform as well.

Acknowledging that JD has had a history of functional difficulties with processing new verbal information, based on observations of parents and teachers and auditory processing assessments, the neuropsychologist concluded that, while JD does have some indications of weakness in auditory processing, in fact, they are secondary to his ADHD. The recent reassessment also concluded that JD does not have a language processing problem—he obtained strong scores on both expressive and receptive language test on the WIAT-II.

THE LINK BETWEEN NEW FINDINGS AND INTERVENTION: PAUSING AND PIVOTING

Results of the neuropsychological reassessment call for changes in JD's treatment plan going forward. Prior to our recent Student Study Team (SST; JD's parents, school learning specialist, and educational therapists, including myself) meeting at JD's independent middle school, JD demonstrated his emerging self-advocacy skills by submitting the following list of concerns for discussion:

Help me understand my homework.

I feel like I'm in the right math group, but the math homework is very hard.

I want to take notes on my own this year.

I'm trying to use my planner and write things down this year.

I want to know the limit of how many problems or the amount of time I should be spending on homework. I'm not sure if I'm doing too much or too little.

I'm worried about when homework builds up and getting it all done.

The SST met to discuss the findings and implications of the reevaluation with the neuropsychologist. Both goals of the treatment plan, as well as implementation and accommodations needed to be reviewed in the light of the recent data. Clearly, functionally, the auditory processing deficits continue to be a significant struggle for JD. However, according to the neuropsychologist, the cause is more attentional and the auditory processing and anxiety are secondary, due in part to the various learning disabilities and weak executive functioning. He has the inattentive type of ADHD which causes deficits in organization and study skills and wide variations in his effective ability to process auditory information in the classroom.

In light of JD's increasing math anxiety, I recommended to his parents that JD begin working with one of my clinicians twice a week, an educational therapist and credentialed math teacher. Since my own specialization as an educational therapist has been in reading, written expression, executive functioning, and helping to facilitate metacognitive awareness, I felt that it was now time to shift the focus of JD's support to math. I continue to be involved in a mentoring role for the educational therapist now working with JD and in a consulting capacity for JD's parents and teachers.

Based on this new diagnosis, we plan to review and update the resources developed for teachers in order to assist in the implementation of these ideas in the classroom. These include the *Guide to Accommodations for JD*, a detailed chart for teachers which highlight the following categories: "What you might see," "What may be happening," "What you can do in advance," and "What you can do in the moment."

Following a medical and neuropsychological evaluation JD is currently embarking on stimulant medication trials. Potential side effects, including insomnia and depressed appetite, need to be monitored, since they can impact JD's learning and classroom behavior. Auditory processing is still a problem in the classroom as well as outside the school setting.

Because of the recent diagnosis of ADHD, the educational therapist, who has been focusing on math with JD over the past year, has shifted her work with him in several ways. First, since JD has wanted to get his math homework "over with" and "off his plate," finding ways to engage him more deeply in math tasks has been challenging. When faced with a daunting task, his response has been, "Don't explain how to do it, just tell me what I need to know, so I can get it over with."

The cognitive overload he experiences is palpable. He continues to avoid new tasks, making it difficult for his educational therapist to identify precisely where he is stuck. Historically, when JD has shut down, he has become immobilized and unresponsive to direct questions. Recently, the discovery of a "teaching moment" happened quite by accident in the middle of a shutdown. The educational therapist tried to explain a new concept related to tables and graphs. Resistant, JD, discovered a graphing calculator on his iPhone. Intrigued, he showed her, offering to download it onto her cell phone so they could both make use of it. His body language and tone of voice revealed full engagement in the task at hand. Now in a "teaching" role, he was back in the driver's seat and fully engaged.

Similarly, in working on reading, note taking, and written expression, the implications for treatment are significant. First and foremost, facilitating a deeper level of engagement continues to be essential to the success of his treatment plan. The most successful sessions leverage his strong verbal skills and the ability to teach. For instance, in order to teach JD the skills involved in note taking, I used a two-column organizational system, breaking the procedure out into a series of steps. Before reading text, we practiced first by taking turns being the "professor." One person would give the lecture, while the other took notes. The "professor" would then critique the notes, making sure that main ideas were listed accurately in one column and supporting details were listed in the other column. JD "lectured" on one of his favorite pastimes, rock-climbing. Since he was doing the talking and he was passionate about the topic, it was easy for him to stay engaged. He was truly the expert. Using a whiteboard, he drew pictures of the basics of rock-climbing, explaining the process with a dramatic flair. Afterwards, he took great care to critique my notes, wanting to be sure that I "got it all."

After practicing introductory note-taking skills for several weeks, we shifted to reading an article on "Teen Peer Juries," taking turns, reading aloud. I modeled how to highlight key ideas and phrases in the first two paragraphs and then asked JD to try the third paragraph to make sure he understood salience in reading text. We summarized the main points together orally. Next, I modeled highlighting supporting details, using the same procedure, but highlighting key details, using a different color highlighter. I used a scaffolding technique in the process, having JD demonstrate mastery by identifying details (Vygotsky cited by Wertsch, 1985, p. 148). We continued working through the text, only this time, JD and I each color-coded main ideas and supporting evidence on our own separate copies, comparing our results afterwards. Even with a great deal of practice during sessions, generalizing the skill of note taking has been a struggle for JD. Listening to a teacher, especially with the introduction of new material, copying from the board or figuring out what is most important to include in his notes (salience determination) has been challenging. Using his laptop for note taking has required a juggling act. For instance, he may be in the process of thinking about what to write down next, while the teacher has already leaped ahead to the next point. Use of signal words by the teacher has helped, as in, "This *next* point is *very important*." Visual hand-outs with outlines, where he fills in supporting details and evidence, have been an effective accommodation in helping JD to organize and anchor information.

In addition to facilitating a deeper level of engagement, another key ingredient has been helping JD become more aware of the need to self-monitor his focus and staying power, taking short breaks (5 minutes) every 20 minutes or so. Since his occupational therapist stressed that "heavy work" was most effective in facilitating focus, we have incorporated exercises using weighted wrist and ankle bands as well as hand-held weights. Occasionally, JD has been so anxious or stressed, as evidenced by his extreme hyperactivity or shutdown, that it has been difficult for him to sustain focus, even with breaks. For just such moments, I have kept a stash of odds and ends and tools on hand in my clinic.

JD relishes the times when he can fix a broken, detached doorknob or tinker with the broken motor in a plastic robot I have picked up from a local Salvation Army store. He is increasingly aware of how the deep level of engagement in working with such "treasures" soothes him and makes whatever tasks that follow less daunting. I recall one such session where JD was clearly on overload; staying on task seemed near impossible. I brought out a large, empty cardboard box and shipping material I had on hand, having just taken delivery of a new computer that morning. JD went to work immediately, with intense resolve. He created what he called his private "retreat," complete with windows and a door that opened and closed. Crawling inside, he proposed that I leave his retreat in place for other students to use. He even added written instructions for admitting visitors. As a result of creating a "protected" space for himself, JD was then able to emerge and tackle his work with new-found triumph. We used the metaphor of his "refuge" to explore ways JD might create an emotional safe haven from which to take risks and meet unforeseen challenges.

As we have seen, JD's strong cognitive abilities combined with his own increasing self-insights continue to inform his dynamic treatment plan. We explored the link between the assessments—neuropsychological, auditory processing, and occupational therapy—and intervention, continually pausing to reexamine and refine our goals, methodology, and outcomes. JD continues to leverage his strong abstract reasoning, verbal comprehension and expression in an effort to manage his struggles, including attentional issues, anxiety, auditory attention, and graphomotor deficits. As we understand more about how to connect assessment to intervention and apply our insights in working with other clients, the image of JD creating a safe haven or figuring out how to access the world below the air conditioning vent is a humbling reminder that at the heart of our work is the unique genius of each child, guiding us in our efforts.

REFERENCES

American Psychiatric Association. (2000). *Diagnostic and statistical manual of mental disorders* (4th ed., text rev.). Washington, DC: Author.

Wertsch, J. V. (1985). *Cultural, communication, and cognition: Vygotskian perspectives*. Cambridge, England: Cambridge University Press.

Young, M. L. (2001, November 1). New directions in auditory processing. Retrieved from http://audiology.advanceweb.com/Editorial/Content

11

STORY LINKS

Using Therapeutic Storywriting with Parents and Pupils
Who Are at Risk of Exclusion

PATRICIA WATERS

This chapter will explore how the Story Links model of intervention can engage parents in supporting pupils at risk of exclusion because of behaviors related to attachment anxiety. A pilot 3-day Story Links training was delivered (Story Links, n.d.), with the support of the South-East Region Special Educational Needs Partnership (SERSEN), to 12 educational professionals drawn from four local authorities (LAs) in the South of England. As originator of the model I have also been involved in piloting the model in five schools in the south of England in order to refine and develop the training program. This paper will draw on my work with a parent and 8-year old pupil, who for the purpose of this paper I will call Owen. I will first explore some of the general theoretical underpinnings of the Story Links model and then use the case study to further illustrate these theoretical points. Parental consent has been given for the use of material included and all names have been changed to protect confidentiality.

INTRODUCTION AND BACKGROUND TO THE MODEL

Story Links uses the principles of therapeutic storywriting (Waters, 2004a) to engage parents in supporting children who are at risk of exclusion from school because of their behavior. While it is the child's behavior that will trigger school exclusion, these pupils often also have severe underlying emotional difficulties. Therapeutic Storywriting uses story metaphor to address emotional issues that might be overwhelming for the child, and possibly for the parent, if addressed directly.

The intervention particularly targets primary age pupils exhibiting behaviors associated with attachment anxiety and who also have below average reading skills. The emotional preoccupation of pupils with poor attachment experience means that they are often unable to engage with educational tasks, with the consequence that they are likely to have not only behavioral, emotional, and social difficulties (BESDs) but also poor literacy skills.

The Story Links program therefore addresses the needs of some of the most vulnerable students in our primary schools. By including parents in sessions, Story Links aims to nurture more positive attachment patterns between parent and child while engaged in the twofold task of (1) developing the child's reading skills and (2) improving the his or her behavior in school. Working with the parents of these vulnerable children can itself present challenges, given that they often have a poor history of positive engagement with the school. Thus, the model has been developed to be both nonthreatening and emotionally containing for parents who may themselves feel vulnerable within the school environment.

DEVELOPMENT OF STORY LINKS AS A WAVE 3 INTERVENTION

Story Links grew out of the now established Therapeutic Storywriting Groups (Waters, 2004a), also developed by the author with the support of SERSEN, which were designed for small groups of pupils and which have now been introduced into many schools in England. The groups are a wave 2 intervention and target pupils who are typically at School Action (SA) or School Action Plus (SA+), on the Special Educational Needs (SEN) register because of BESDs that require more support than can be provided in the whole class group. The evaluation study, *Writing Stories with Feeling* (Waters, 2004b), which was commissioned by SERSEN, showed that Therapeutic Storywriting Groups develop students' emotional literacy and social skills as well as increasing their motivation to write.

The Story Links model to be discussed here, however, is a wave 3 intervention in that it provides support for those individual pupils whose BESDs are giving the school particularly serious cause for concern both in terms of the children's inclusion in the classroom and their progress in learning. These pupils will be on the SEN register at either SA+ or statement level for BESDs, indicating that their needs require a more specialist support than is normally provided by the school. As parental participation is central to the Story Links model, the curriculum area chosen as the context for the intervention is not writing, as in the Therapeutic Storywriting Groups, but reading because this is an area of learning in which most parents traditionally expect to play a role.

A THERAPEUTIC TEACHING APPROACH

Story Links is a therapeutic teaching model that uses the educational curriculum as a therapeutic context. It does not require educational professionals to become therapists but rather to bring psychological mindedness to their work in supporting pupils with severe behavioral, emotional, and social difficulties. By focusing on this interface between education and mental health, Story Links is very much in line with the current UK SEN policy outlined in *Every Child Matters* (DfES, 2003) and *Removing Barriers to Achievement* (DfES, 2004); both of these documents stress the need for educational professionals to become more aware of pupils' mental health issues and to explore new ways of using the curriculum to support emotional literacy.

The model draws on psychodynamic thinking and in particular the concepts of attachment, emotional containment, and creating a "potential space" (Winnicott, 1971/1999) where parent and child can meet in a mutually enjoyable activity. It also aims to integrate this psychodynamic perspective of behavior with the positive behavioral perspective which usually informs schools' behavior policies and practice.

THEORETICAL UNDERPINNING

Attachment Theory, Behavior, and Learning

Attachment theory was developed by Bowlby (1988/1997) in the 1950s and highlights the central importance of the parent–child relationship for the child's healthy psychological development, particularly in the first 2 to 3 years of life. While this is now taken for granted by most child professionals, it was a radical departure from the then established developmental models, most of which considered developmental stages as being entirely located within the child. What Bowlby did was to emphasize that a child's development can only be considered within the context of his or her relationship with a primary carer. When Ainsworth (1979) published the results of her Strange Situation clinical experiment, showing that healthy attachment patterns along with three anxious forms of attachment— avoidant, ambivalent, and confused—can be identified at one year of age, attachment theory began to receive widespread acceptance and even to change social policy particularly in relation to parental contact for hospitalized children.

While attachment theory has informed health policy for many years, it seems, however, that it has had a much lower profile in relation to educational policy. True, it is beginning to inform practice in the early years (Elfer, 2002), particularly within the UK Sure Start initiative, but at primary school level and beyond, while attachment anxiety is beginning to appear on pupils' individualized education plans (IEPs), there are few educational professionals who have an understanding of attachment theory. This is so despite a growing body of research evidence that poor attachment patterns have a strong correlation not only with BESDS but with poor educational achievement (Sroufe, Egeland, & Weinfeld, 2000).

Children bring into school behavioral patterns from the relational dynamic established with their primary carer and these will affect the quality of their relationships with both peers and adults. Behaviors associated with poor attachment patterns that are exhibited in the classroom may include: poor concentration, constant talking, ignoring instructions in class, getting into trouble between classes, refusing to be helped with work, presenting explosive reactions, exhibiting a sudden deterioration in behavior when making mistakes (Geddes, 2006). These are clearly behaviors that can seriously challenge a class teacher and it is easy to see why these pupils are often at risk of exclusion.

THE CHALLENGE OF PARENTAL INVOLVEMENT

The view that the quality of the child–parent relationship affects educational achievement throughout the primary phase of schooling is supported by the findings of the influential Desforges and Abouchaar report (2003) which reviewed the latest international research on the effects of parental involvement on pupil achievement (see Table 11.1).

Table 11.1 from Sacker et al. (2002, cited by Desforges & Abouchaar, 2003) shows that right up to the age of 11 years, parents continue to have more influence on their child's achievement than does the school. Therefore, in addressing the needs of poorly performing pupils with BESDs, parental involvement is crucial.

However, parents of pupils at risk of exclusion are often the group of parents who are hardest to engage in school partnership. This can be due to the defensiveness engendered by having to continually come into the school to hear about their child's poor behavior, by the triggering of uncomfortable memories of their own schooling, or it may be due to the fact that they are themselves under stress and struggling to cope with day-to-day matters.

Table 11.1 The Challenge of Parental Involvement

The view that the quality of the child-parent relationship affects educational achievement throughout the primary phase of schooling is supported by the findings of the influential Desforges and Abouchaar report (2003) which reviewed the latest international research on the effects of parental involvement on pupil achievement.

	Effect of Parent on Pupil Achievement	Effect of School on Pupil Achievement
Age 7	0.29	0.05
Age 11	0.27	0.21
Age 16	0.14	0.51

From Sacker et al., 2002, cited in Desforges and Abouchaar, 2003.

So how do we go about engaging such parents in school? The Story Links program uses a solution-focused approach by inviting them to come into school to support their child's reading rather than asking them to come in to discuss behavior difficulties. Parents of pupils at risk of exclusion may be defensive, disengaged, and even aggressive toward the school but in my experience they always want their children to learn to read. So here is an assured point of mutual interest where parent and school can meet.

OUTLINE OF A STORY LINKS SESSION

The Story Links program runs over 10 weeks and is led by an educational professional who has attended a 3-day training course. The facilitating professional can be a special educational needs coordinator (SENCO), SEN support teacher, educational counselor, learning mentor, or inclusion manager (for ease of writing, the term *teacher* will be used to refer to this group of professionals). Sessions with the parent and child last 30 minutes with a further 30 minutes required by the teacher for writing up, printing, and distributing the story. A teaching assistant (TA), ideally one attached to the pupil's class, also joins in the sessions and implements two 20 minute school-based follow-up sessions using the written text to develop the child's reading skills during the week. As the model has an open systemic structure other professionals such as a learning mentor, home–school liaison officer, or a social worker engaged in supporting the child can also be invited to attend sessions. There is an initial session with the parent and child to tell them about the program, deal with any concerns, and ensure commitment to the program of 10 sessions.

The main sessions begin with the teacher having a few minutes with the parent to review how things have been at home with their child during the week and in particular to ask about the success or otherwise of joint reading activities. They are then joined by the TA and the pupil who will bring some feedback from his or her classroom teacher on the child's behavior during the week in class which is shared with the parent. There follows a "feelings check-in" during which the teacher uses active listening skills (empathic verbal reflection) to reflect and contain the feelings expressed by the parent and pupil. The child then reads the previous week's story to the group with support from the teacher or the parent. This then leads into the central activity of joint story making. The teacher gives the story opening, which will have emerged from the discussion with the parent about the child's current emotional issues. For instance, if the parent says the child has had angry outbursts it might be, "Leslie the lion roared. He was furious." Beginning with the child and followed by the parent, each person present then takes a turn to continue the story, with the teacher making notes. The teacher takes responsibility for completing each week's story and then retells the newly created story to the group. The child leaves the room with the TA and the teacher encourages the parent to reflect on the metaphor/imagery in the newly created story and to think about what metaphors might be included in the next week's story. Once the parent has left, the teacher types up the story at the appropriate reading level for the child. This is not done as a verbatim report but the core story line is maintained with an effort made to include the actual phrases used by the parent and child. A copy then goes home with the child to be read with the parent at home and a copy goes to the teaching assistant for work on the two 20 minute reading skills sessions during the week.

USE OF STORY AS AN ATTACHMENT OBJECT

Attachment anxiety occurs when the primary carer has been unable to provide appropriate emotional containment for the child, so the Story Links model is based on the premise that for such pupils, attachment anxieties in school may be reduced if a way can be found to bring the parent into a positive relationship with the child within the educational environment.

Healthy attachment occurs when the parent and child are engaged in a mutually enjoyable activity. When the parent of an infant engages in games such as peek-a-boo he or she is not thinking "I'd better do this so that I form a good bond with my child"; they are doing it because they're enjoying it; because it gives them, as well as the baby, pleasure. By engaging the parent in the creative process of spontaneous story making, Story Links sessions aim to provide a mutually enjoyable educational activity. The idea is that the cocreated story can become a positive attachment object for the child by enabling him or her to hold a reminder of the parent while the child is in school and a reminder of a positive shared school-based experience while the child is home.

In discussing the home learning program the parent is encouraged to reflect on whether the reading activity was something that they also enjoyed. Parents and children can easily become embattled over homework activities, particularly with this group of children. So at the beginning of each session the teacher asks the parent open questions about the home reading activity: Was it a relaxing time for them? Was their child relaxed? Where did they sit? Were they snuggled up together on the sofa or under a duvet? Did they both enjoy it?

A CASE STUDY

Identifying Attachment Anxiety

Owen was an 8-year-old boy who had initially been referred to a Therapeutic Storywriting Group that I was running in a school where I was modeling the intervention for a group of staff I was training. The school was in the local authority's most socially deprived area and there were concerns about both the school's poor attainment levels and the high number of exclusions.

Although the least able in the group, with his writing and reading still at level 1, Owen worked well in the group sessions when he was present. However, he was often absent due to the fact that he was excluded on four separate occasions during the school term when the Therapeutic Storywriting group was running, with one of his exclusions being for 5 days. The reasons for his exclusion were challenging behaviors that included running out of class, violent outbursts in class, and in particular, physically attacking other children. According to his classroom teacher, while he often seemed to "kick off" for no apparent reason, his anger could also be easily triggered by some of the other children making a disparaging comment about his mother. He had been referred for diagnosis of ADHD but this had not been confirmed.

The head teacher described Owen as one of the most troubled and troubling pupils in the school. He also said that Owen's mother usually came "gunning" for him on a daily basis; he then added, "and often not once but twice a day." It seemed that Owen's mother was as much of a concern to the school as Owen himself! In fact when I spoke to a number of staff about how we might best support Owen, I was told by more than one person that his problems came from his home situation. When I suggested that we might invite his mother to participate in a Story Links program I was told, again by more than one member of staff, that she was unreliable and that she was unlikely to attend sessions. Despite Owen's challenging behavior, all of the staff who had contact with him appeared to also have a soft spot for him—they particularly mentioned his honesty as a redemptive characteristic (i.e., he always admitted what he had done). There was a feeling that he somehow couldn't help himself when he "kicked off" and blame was generally placed on the mother's parenting rather than on Owen.

I spoke to the SENCO and found out a bit more about Owen. She told me that he, along with his younger brother, had been taken into care for 2 years when he was 3 years old because of child protection concerns. Certainly, Owen's behavior seemed consistent with a child with confused attachment: hyperactivity, rescuing the parent, "kicking off" for no apparent reason (Barrett & Trevitt, 1991; Geddes, 2006). This hypothesis was confirmed by a short piece of writing he had produced in the Therapeutic Storywriting Group.

I had given the group the opening "Dino the dragon lay outside his cave. Never before had he felt so lonely...." I wrote this opening in Owen's book to help him get started. After 10 minutes of concentrated effort he managed to write "because he didn't have anyone who wanted to play with him. So he burnt his Mum's plants" (spelling corrected).

I then used active listening skills and reflected back to Owen, "I imagine Dino was upset because he didn't have any friends, but I wonder why he burned his Mum's plants?"

He then replied, that Dino "wanted to tell his Mum how miserable he felt and he had called her 17 times but she didn't come. So Dino just walked off into the dark shadows." I typed out his story, including his reply, in italic and pasted it into his book.

Engaging the Parent

Owen's mother was invited in to meet me by the SENCO at the school. When she arrived she accepted my offer of a cup of coffee, and I then explained the outline of the Story Links program, focusing first on the school's concern over Owen's poor reading skills and pointing out that as the most important person in his life it might make a difference to his achievement if we could work together to support his reading for a period of time. I also said that we would use the stories to address emotional issues that Owen might be having difficulty with in order to help him feel happier in school.

Mother listened but seemed rather noncommittal until I showed her Owen's book from the group. I took what felt like a calculated emotional risk and read her Owen's story about Dino's mum not coming despite his calling her 17 times. Owen's mother then seemed to become engaged for the first time in our meeting. She looked me directly in the eye and asked, "Do you think children just write stories or are they writing about themselves?" Using my best active listening skills I replied, "What do you think?" She then said, "I think this story is about him. I think it's because I don't give him any time. I give all my attention to his younger brother who's still my baby even though he's only a year younger than Owen." She then said that she thought she should come into the sessions in order to give some time to her older son. She mentioned how she found his behavior hard to manage at times though she also mentioned how he seemed to think he was "the man of the house" and would "have a go" at his younger brother if his brother was "horrible" to her.

Owen's mother then spoke about how the children had been taken into care but that they had been returned to her 3 years ago and that she was now trying to get her life back on track . She also asked if her trusted social worker would be able to come along to sessions with her. As the Story Links sessions have an open systemic format I said this would be no problem. I later contacted the social worker who was pleased to have a chance to be involved with a school-based project. Mother was also concerned about her own poor literacy skills and described herself as being dyslexic. I reassured her that this wouldn't be a problem. With the support of the social worker, Owen's mother managed to attend 8 out of the 10 sessions, with one missed because of a hospital appointment and one missed without any explanation.

The Stories

In all of the spontaneously created stories, most of the story elements introduced by Owen related to dangerous and fear-provoking situations; these included a boy being imprisoned in a jar; the badger's hillside being burned; fox cubs not being fed by their family; two little monkeys being attacked by a snake; and two hound-dogs being attacked by wasps. My role as the facilitator in all of these stories was to aid the exploration of feelings that were pertinent for Owen and also to contain the fearful emotions within the structure of the story by bringing each story to some point of resolution. For as Bettelheim points out: "For a story to truly hold the child's attention, it must … be attuned to his anxieties and aspirations; give full recognition to his difficulties, while at the same time suggesting solutions to the problems which perturb him" (Bettelheim, 1991, p. 5).

I will now share a story created in the sixth week of the course of sessions to illustrate the process.

The Wasps and the Two Hound-Dogs
Owen: One day there was a wasps' nest and two hound-dogs. But the wasps weren't just any wasps—they were dangerous wasps and the hound-dogs were stung by them.
Mum: The wasps' nest was really close to a children's playground and the children kept getting stung by the wasps.
TA: So somebody reported the wasps' nest to the council.
Social worker: The men from the council came in their protective suits and took the whole nest away.
Jo: But the two hound-dogs saw one wasp that had got away and was up in a tree.
TA: So the hound-dogs hid in some bushes at the end of the garden.
Mum: The wasp met another normal wasp and got married.
Jo: But the normal wasp then turned poisonous and they had lots of baby wasps who had extra long stings that could go through protective suits.

Social Worker: So the men at the council got some extra thick protective suits and came again. They took the wasps away.

TA: This time they took all the stings out of the wasps and then let the wasps go free.

Me: The wasps never stung anybody again. The two hound-dogs came out of their hiding place and played in the garden. The End.

Owen: There's one more thing: The two hound-dogs both had a prickle on their nose to remind them of the wasps.

DISCUSSION OF SESSIONS IN THE LIGHT OF UNDERPINNING THEORY

Story Imagery as an Expression of the Unconscious

The process of creative story-making involves the use of imagery which often arises out of the unconscious as do images that arise in art or play therapy. In the above story, 8-year-old Owen certainly did not consciously plan, nor do I think his mother did, that we would make up a story about child protection issues, as one might interpret that this story is about. The spontaneous nature of the story-making activity precluded the possibility of such a conscious approach to the story line. Bruner describes this as the "narrative mode of thinking" which is associated with right-brain activity, and he emphasizes that this is different from the more analytical logical mode of thinking but equally valid in conveying meaning.

Story as a Medium for Attachment

Schore (2000), whose work bridges the fields of neuroscience and psychology, discusses the role of dyadic engagement in right-brain activity as fostering attachment relationships. This was evident in the sessions particularly with respect to Owen's mother whose body language would often reflect a depressive and isolationist state of mind. However, each week her face lit up as we began the story. She listened attentively, particularly to her son, and she appeared enlivened as she made her contribution. There was often laughter in the group as the story lines emerged, which provided a joint experience of attachment-promoting fun for parent and child.

By taking the story home with them, Owen and his mother were reminded of this positive shared experience that had taken place in school. And in working with the story in school with the TA, Owen had a reminder of his mother's presence in a supportive context. The TA mentioned that he was always interested to point out which part of the story was his contribution and which was his mother's. Thus, the actual story text could be considered as a positive attachment object linking mother, child, and the school.

Close physical proximity and comfort is important in fostering attachment, so Owen was seated next to his mother and encouraged to give his mother a hug at the beginning and end of each session, which he did. His mother was also encouraged to think about how the reading activity at home could be a time for the two of them to be close. This required some thought as she said that the younger brother would often push Owen away if he snuggled up with her at home. We talked this through, and she decided to make some time for Owen after his younger brother was in bed. She had difficulty keeping to a regular schedule but mostly managed this once or twice a week.

Interpretation of the Story Metaphor and Encouraging Parental Reflection

While the above story can be interpreted as reflecting Owen and his brother's experience of feeling unsafe and of the central role that social services has had in providing child protection, it is not the place of the facilitator to make these interpretations to the mother or to other professionals. A key point made in the training course is that any interpretations by the teacher should be held tentatively and reflective comments kept within the context of the story. This is a key distinction between implementing therapeutic teaching and therapy as such. Hence, at no time did I attempt to give an analysis of the above story to the parent or other professionals.

However, key to the intervention is to involve the mother in reflecting on the story herself and to encourage her to think about what might be useful to include in future stories. Using the medium of story gives parents the opportunity to think about their child's internal world and to express empathy within the emotional safety of the story metaphor. That Owen's mother was capable of doing this was reflected in her comment on the initial Dino the dragon story. There is also an attempt by the mother within the above story to provide some normality for the two hound-dogs when she says: "The wasp met another normal wasp and got married."

It was clear from Owen's behavior in defending his mother both at home and school that he was acting at times as the parentified child. As mentioned above, this is typical of children with confused attachment where there has been inconsistent care giving.

According to Piaget and Inhelder (1969/1979), it is only around the time of adolescence that children begin to develop the capacity for abstract or metacognitive thinking. The interpretation of metaphor, the meaning of which is to transfer something from one level or place to another, is itself a metacognitive skill. This is why a child will accept a story at face value, operating as he does at what Piaget calls the "concrete-operational level," while as adults we have the ability to intuitively read it on another level. The basic activity of thinking in the metaphor is an adult skill. Thus by supporting Owen's mother to reflect on the stories and imagery that might be used in future stories, she was encouraged to take on the parent/adult position in relation to her son.

Empowering the Parent to Support the Child's Learning

The sessions were also used to encourage the mother to support her son's reading. Although she described herself as dyslexic, it turned out that she could easily recognize high frequency words and could certainly read better than her son. In the first couple of sessions, myself or the TA would support Owen when he read last week's story at the beginning of the session—helping him to sound out the letters and recognize familiar patterns. In the third week his mother began to join in supporting his reading of the text. The TA and I now stepped out of the supporting role as Owen sat closer to his mother, looking to her for help. Occasionally when Owen's mother would give an inappropriate reading clue (e.g. asking him to think what color the sky was in order to decode the word *blue*), I would mention afterwards when Owen had returned to class that it might be helpful to get him to sound out and blend the first two letters so that he could then use this strategy with other words. As the weeks went on mother became increasingly confident in supporting Owen with his reading in the sessions, again enabling her to be in the position of enabling parent and Owen to be the young child that he was.

Interestingly mother mentioned her own parents on more than one occasion in the sessions. A couple of stories had been shared with the paternal grandparents at home and in one story the main character finds safety in the grandparents' actual garden. Adult attachment interview research (Main & Goldwyn, 1995) shows 70 to 80% correspondence between parents' early experience and their own parenting style. Mother was clearly proud of the work she was doing in supporting Owen and was keen to show this to her own parents. It seemed that her own inner child was being put into the appropriate relational context (i.e., with her own parents), as she stepped into a more adult role with her own son.

This also reminded me of the importance of the whole family network in supporting the child's learning and emotional well-being. In Story Links sessions with other parents and pupils, the story has sometimes been taken by the child to read to the parent who has left the family home, thus providing a link between members of the extended or separated family.

Therapeutic Storywriting as a Process-Oriented Activity

While it is useful for the parent to begin to reflect on the story metaphor in relation to her child's internal world, the story making process itself provides an opportunity for parent and child to process unresolved emotional issues. To quote Bettelheim (1976/1991) who spent much of his life using stories to support children with severe emotional difficulties,

> When unconscious material is to some degree permitted to come to awareness and worked through in imagination, its potential for causing harm—to ourselves or others—is much reduced; some of its forces can then be made to serve positive purposes. (p. 7)

It is not about getting a clever or the "right" interpretation but rather about providing a safe or potential space where unresolved issues can be explored, played with, and re-storied within the world of the imaginary. It is this process that is so engaging for the parent and child, particularly as their jointly created story will contain images projected from their own internal imaginary worlds. It is this resonance with their internal worlds that gives parent and child ownership of the jointly created stories and the reason why Owen and his mother were so very proud of them; Owen asked his teacher to read them to his classmates and mother shared them with her own parents.

Providing Emotional Containment in Order for Thinking to Take Place

Bion (1963/1984) made extensive clinical observations of mother–child interactions and focused particularly on the relationship between cognitive and emotional development. The theory of thinking that he developed states that containment of emotional anxiety is required for thinking to take place. Owen clearly was far too emotionally preoccupied to focus on educational tasks in the classroom and it seemed from the family history that mother was also too emotionally preoccupied with her worries to provide sufficient emotional containment for her children. It was of utmost importance, therefore, that the sessions would be emotionally containing (i.e., that both parent and pupil experienced the room and session as a safe place and that the activity did not leave them feeling emotionally vulnerable at the end of the session). This was achieved by attending to beginnings and endings both of individual sessions and the whole course; by ensuring time boundaries were kept; giving time for everyone to share how they were feeling; keeping a consistent session structure; using the same room with a set seating arrangement; and by employing active listening skills. Thus the session provided parent and child with what Winnicott (1971/1999) terms a *potential space*; that is, an emotionally containing place where there is the possibility for the parent and child to engage in a relaxed manner in shared playful activity.

Maintaining Time Boundaries

Maintaining time boundaries was a challenge at first with Owen's mother as she would often turn up 10 or 15 minutes late and then want to keep talking about other issues at the end of the session. I responded to this by ensuring a cup of coffee was ready at the time the session was due to start and saying before we began when I would need to finish. I tried not to get drawn into tangential discussions on other matters to do with school by referring her on to other professionals in the school. Fortunately her social worker was able to pick up issues related to health and housing. As mother became more familiar with the routine structure of the sessions the time boundaries were tested less.

Reframing the Parental Thinking about Behavior

Occasionally, behavioral incidents would be mentioned by the mother in the few minutes before Owen joined the session. One time near the beginning of the term mother referred to an incident in the previous term when Owen had hit a child who had said something rude about her. Mother's response was supportive of Owen saying that "Of course he's going to hit out—I don't expect him to just take that sitting down." There was a few minutes discussion with myself and the social worker pointing out that the outcome to Owen's response was often exclusion which then created problems for him and her. Clearly mother thought about this because a couple of weeks later when Owen mentioned a conflict incident with another child in the feelings check-in she said, "You remember what your uncle said: 'It's a bigger man who can walk away.'" This felt like a significant shift in her thinking and the messages that she gave to Owen about how he should respond in a conflict situation.

Linking to the School's Behavior Policy

The school's behavior policy used a point system for rewarding pupil effort in relation to both behavior and learning. The weekly sessions were a valuable point of contact between the school and home, and I arranged with the classroom teacher that he would give Owen a score out of 10 for meeting a set behavior target chosen by the teacher as the behavior that would most support his learning. The teacher decided this should be that Owen did not hit any other children in the classroom. Rather than provide a reward in the classroom I suggested that Owen's mother could reward him if he met his target. Each week Owen brought his score, drew it on a bar chart, set his target for the coming week, and negotiated a reward with his mother. I facilitated this negotiation to ensure that mother was not bamboozled by Owen's demands and that she felt confident about delivering the reward, which I stressed need not involve expense. The first reward negotiated was to go lizard hunting together—something that turned out to be of interest to both Owen and his mother and thus functioned as an attachment-promoting activity. I discouraged discussion of events that had influenced any loss points but the bar chart gave the parent a visual picture of how her son had done over the week. This seemed reassuring for her because she had complained in the past that it was only when she was informed that Owen was to be excluded that she was told that things were not going well for him in school. This bar chart also meant that Owen's classroom teacher although not present was able to input into the sessions.

A Convergent Personalized Systemic Approach

It is very easy for the support networks put in place to support vulnerable pupils to mirror the fragmentation that has occurred in the child's home life where there may have been, as in Owen's case, lack of contact with a parent, separation, frequent house moves, and general inconsistency. While a multiagency approach is essential, care needs to be taken to ensure that support does not get divergent and distant from the child when assessments are made and reports are written. Story Links sessions have a systemic structure in that they can include different professionals while engaging in a task with the child and parent. While there can be several adults in the room with the child, and in Owen's case there were four, sessions are democratic in that everyone present has a chance to initially share how he or she is feeling and then contribute to the story, thus avoiding the child feeling overwhelmed by too much attention. However, all of the adults will be holding the individual child's particular needs in mind, thus providing an intervention that is focused or convergent on the child and one that is personalized to meet the child's needs at the time.

OUTCOMES OF STORY LINKS COURSE

The Story Links program was evaluated using pre- and post-semi-structured interviews with Owen, his mother, Owen's classroom teacher, and the school principal. The TA who supported Owen was also asked to evaluate the work she had done with Owen at the end of the course. Owen was not excluded once during the term when the Story Links program ran, compared to his four exclusions in the previous term. The school principal also reported that his mother's attitude toward the school had dramatically changed and that she had even mentioned running a stall with books made by children for the Xmas fair. In reality this didn't happen but it was interesting to note how her attitude had changed. The TA reported that Owen, who she had supported before the course of Story Links, was now generally keener to read than he had been before. Owen himself thought his reading had improved and also said, "It's good when my mum's there—it makes me feel more supported and it helps me to calm down."

The social worker who attended the sessions mentioned how it was a new experience for her to work collaboratively in the school situation and found the structure of the sessions provided a good framework for her contact with the family.

Owen's mother gave a positive evaluation of the program in relation to Owen's behavior and his reading. She said that, "He does walk away from conflict sometimes now—he has more patience even with his brother at home." She also said that Owen was now looking at writing in shops and added: "I thought it was going to be difficult but it has helped me to realize a few things, especially about O. It's taught me how to help Owen with reading and also helped me with my reading."

While the evaluation showed that Owen's engagement with reading had improved the study did not include a standardized assessment of his reading progress. It is planned to build this into future case study evaluations. One issue that had arisen over the term, however, was that Owen's younger brother had started to present more challenging behavior at school and also at home and this was proving to be a concern.

CONCLUSION

The above case study illustrates the positive effect that the engagement of a parent in creative story-making with her child had in reducing his risk of exclusion. The pupil who had been excluded four times in the previous term had no exclusions during the term the parent engaged in the Story Links program. The emotional containment provided by the regularity of the sessions, the use of active listening, and the structure of the stories themselves created a potential space where a parent with a previously hostile attitude to the school could begin to collaborate with the school in supporting her son's learning. The sense of fun and shared laughter meant that the parent and child found mutual enjoyment in the shared story-making activity, an essential factor in promoting more positive attachment patterns.

By supporting the parent to think about her child within the story metaphor and to become more confident about her ability to support him in developing his reading skills, she was able to take a more authoritative parental position, hence alleviating the child's need to parent his mother.

While largely drawing on psychodynamic theory, the Story Links program was also integrated with the school's positive behavioral policy and the educational curriculum. Sessions incorporated feedback from the teacher on the pupil's behavior during the week and the finished stories were used by the TA in the classroom to support the child develop his reading skills. The created stories became a positive reminder for the child of the voice of his mother and when using the stories as his reading text in his work with his classroom TA, he became eager to read whereas before he had been a very reluctant reader.

IMPLICATIONS FOR FUTURE WORK

While the above case study is very positive in its outcomes, it would be useful to evaluate the outcomes of Story Links programs implemented by other professionals who have completed the 3-day training, given that the facilitator in this case is also the author of the model. It would also be helpful to engage an expert in the field of evaluation in future research to ensure that any issues relating to bias are addressed. In order to assess the impact of the program on the pupil's learning more precisely, future evaluation would benefit from the inclusion of a standardized testing of pupils' reading skills before and after the intervention.

The above points were included in a proposal for further research into the impact of Story Links in supporting pupils at risk of exclusion and submitted to the Esmee Fairbairn Foundation and the UK Teaching and Development Agency for Schools, both of which have kindly agreed to support the project. The results of this wider research evaluation will be available in December 2009 (Waters, 2010).

REFERENCES

Ainsworth, M. (1979). *Patterns of attachment: A psychological study of the strange situation.* Hillsdale, NJ: Erlbaum.

Barrett, M., & Trevitt, J. (1991). *Attachment behavior and the schoolchild.* New York: Routledge.

Bettelheim B. (1991). *The uses of enchantment.* London: Penguin Books. (Original work published 1976)

Bion, W. F. (1984). *Learning from experience.* London: Maresfield. (Original work published 1963)

Bowlby J. (1997). *A secure base. Parent-child attachment and healthy human development.* London: Routledge. (Original work published 1988)

Bruner, J. (1986). *Actual minds, possible worlds.* Cambridge, MA: Harvard University Press.

Desforges, C., & Abouchaar, A. (2003). *The impact of parental involvement, parental support and family education on pupil achievement and adjustment: A literature review.* Nottingham, England: DfES.

DfES. (2003). *Every child matters* [Green paper]. London: The Stationery Office.

DfES. (2004). *Removing barriers to achievement: The government's strategy for SEN.* Nottingham, England: DfES.

Elfer, P. (2002). Attachment and the key person role. Retrieved from http://www.surestart.gov.uk

Geddes, H. (2006). *Attachment in the classroom.* London: Worth.

Main, M., & Goldwyn, S. (1995). Interview based adult attachment classification: Related to infant–mother and infant–father attachment. *Developmental Psychology, 19,* 227–239.

Piaget, J., & Inhelder, B. (1979). *The psychology of the child.* London: Routledge & Kegan Paul. (Original work published 1969)

Schore A. (2000, March). *Attachment, the developing brain, and psychotherapy.* Lecture to the Bowlby Conference, Tavistock Clinic, London.

Sroufe, A., Egeland, B., & Weinfeld, S. (2000). Attachment from infancy to early adulthood in a high-risk sample: Continuity, discontinuity and their correlates. *Child Development, 71*(93), 695–702.

Story Links. (n.d.).Training. Retrieved from http://www.TherapeuticStorywriting.com

Waters, T. (2004a). *Therapeutic storywriting.* London: David Fulton.

Waters, T. (2004b). *Evaluation report: Writing stories with feeling.* London: South-East Region SEN Partnership, SERSEN, Surrey.

Waters, T. (2010). *Story links programme evaluation: The impact of a parent partnership intervention that uses therapeutic storywriting to support pupils at risk of exclusion.* Available from Teacher Training Resource Bank, http://www.ttrb.ac.uk

Winnicott, D. (1999). *Playing and reality.* London: Routledge. (Original work published 1971)

12

THE EDUCATIONAL THERAPIST IN PRACTICE

Explicit, Systematic Strategies for Teaching Reading:
Why to Teach Them,
How to Teach Them

NANCY CUSHEN WHITE

INTRODUCTION

Academic self-image is shaped between the ages of 3 and 10. Children who take an early dislike to schoolwork or have doubts about their academic worth face disadvantage in all future learning.

(New York Times, 1996)

I cannot imagine a life without reading. Reading was my refuge as a child in times of crisis. Growing up in a small town, reading gave me options for adventures I might not have imagined on my own. My younger brother, who did not learn to read easily, was appalled at my proclivity for spending time with books. One summer evening when he was 8 and I was 12, Billy arrived home with evidence to indicate he had been in a fight. "What happened?" we all asked. "Somebody called Nancy a bookworm!" he announced with disdain. "But Billy, that's okay. I am a bookworm," I explained. "Nobody calls my sister a bookworm and gets away with it!" he proclaimed.

In my small town with a population of 700, reading was taught in the same way to all: "Class," our teacher said as she held up a flashcard, "This word is *mother*. Read the word." In unison, we repeated the word. That was it. Our teacher had "taught" it. We had "learned" it—or so she hoped. I was lucky; that worked relatively well for me. Along came my younger brother in the same school with the same teachers and the same way of teaching reading. That method did not work for Billy who was very bright and extremely innovative in devising other ways to use his time—since reading was not an option. I believe his teacher, Miss Ethel Taylor (perhaps St. Ethel would be more appropriate), taught him to read in self-defense: She kept him after school every day using an explicit, phonics approach—and she taught Billy how to read. She recognized both his need and his potential for success, and she addressed both. He never forgot the incredible gift she had given him.

I loved reading and I loved books before I became a teacher. My zeal for words and the structure of language was launched much later—in the midst of my search for effective instructional approaches. I desperately needed to know how to teach those students who could not learn to read until I figured out how to teach them the way they needed to learn.

When I became an elementary classroom teacher in a large urban school district, my students were bright, eager, and willing to work very hard, but they were not learning to read. I could motivate them to come to school, to behave once there, and to try their best to learn. Still, given how hard they were trying to learn and how hard I was trying to teach them, the rate at which they were progressing would never allow them to catch up to their peers—or even to attain the most basic level of literacy. I realized, despite teaching credentials in three states indicating that I should be able to teach reading to students in grades one through eight that my education had equipped me to teach reading only to those students who were able to learn to read in spite of my teaching—not because of it. Humbling indeed!

It was this humbling realization that prompted me to begin my quest for instructional approaches in reading that would work—whoever my students might be. I took many courses designed to "teach" teachers to teach reading more effectively. I learned something from every such course and each resulted in some new ideas to try that made my instruction slightly more engaging or somewhat more effective. There were organic approaches that suggested asking students to choose the words they wanted to learn to read. There were programmed reading series and a method designed to develop visual perception that promised transfer to reading ability. There were kits and games supposed to teach everything from eye–hand coordination to auditory sequential memory to visual discrimination to vocabulary. With all of that and more, however, I had not learned to teach the struggling students who most needed me to teach them to read.

After several years as a classroom teacher, I was asked to move from the regular classroom into special education to teach a "learning disability group (LDG)." I explained that I was not a good choice for teaching students with learning disabilities because I had not yet even figured out how to teach struggling students in my regular classroom how to read. "But you like those students," replied the Director of Special Education. "Yes, I like them, but I don't know how to teach them. I don't even have a special ed credential," I explained. "No problem," she replied. "There isn't a credential yet for teaching students with learning disabilities. Besides, with smaller groups of students, you will figure it out." I was convinced to give it a try—but with justified trepidation. Smaller groups allowed me to accomplish more than I had in the past—but still not enough to ensure that my students would "catch up" to their peers and certainly not enough for most of them to reach their true potential which was often far above average.

Near the end of that year, my principal suggested that I attend a teaching demo after school. The serious-looking white-haired demonstration teacher was wearing dark-rimmed glasses. She taught a group of junior high school boys—students she was meeting for the first time and all at least a foot taller than she was. She taught with confidence at a quick pace—but never faster than her students could follow. Her explanations were clear. She modeled and verbalized each procedure. When it was an individual student's turn to demonstrate, she provided only as much guidance as each one needed. She held each individual to high standards but demanded no more from her students than she delivered to them. The structure she provided built the foundation for their success.

Based on what I had observed, I signed up to take a month-long intensive multisensory structured language education course the following summer—a classroom adaptation (Slingerland, 1971, 2008) of the Orton-Gillingham approach for teaching students with dyslexia (Gillingham & Stillman, 1960, 1997). Although designed as a preventive classroom approach, it is also used successfully to teach small groups and individual students from kindergarten through adult levels.

Despite my observation of that impressive demo lesson, I had developed a hefty cynicism about reading instruction after 5 years of searching for efficacy, so I was somewhat dubious as to what effect this new approach would have on my inner city students. "These students are from the suburbs. What about my students in the city?" I had so many questions that I am certain my instructors would have liked to put a huge sock in my mouth to quiet me. I returned to my district and found, to my delight, that some of the same students I had previously taught began to make progress at a remarkably more rapid pace than before—and still, I only knew a tiny little bit about this new world of multisensory structured language instruction (MSLI). For the first time, however, I finally had an instructional roadmap that guided my lesson planning as well as my teaching. There were two other very important pieces of the puzzle that I was beginning to understand: (1) the many skills and abilities that are reading and written expression, and the necessity for integrating all of them; (2) the complexity of understanding language structure—and why that understanding is the key to unlocking language for students who struggle.

Priscilla Vail (1991), a master teacher of children and teachers, once defined language during a presentation at an IDA conference as: beauty in texture; and, dependability in structure. Struggling readers are robbed of the opportunity to appreciate the beauty in the texture of their language when they do not understand the structure sufficiently to be able to depend on it to light their way. During that introductory course, I learned enough to know "what to do" during the subsequent school year. I also learned enough to know how much more I needed to learn. I completed all levels of the course to become certified at the Instructor of Teaching level and continued to train teachers in multisensory structured language instruction. I haven't had a summer vacation since, but I am so lucky to have landed in a profession that is this much fun! It's fun because:

- There will always be more to learn.
- Nothing can beat watching a student discovering for the first time that he or she "gets it." Teaching reinforces learning and leads to automaticity, deep understanding, and confidence. Teaching is both an art and a science. Honing the art of the relationships is just as crucial as acquiring new knowledge to support the science.
- Working with other professionals who share a passion for teaching and learning creates camaraderie.

My experience includes teaching students in first grade through high school and adults—in the classroom, in small groups, and individually as an educational therapist. I have taught in public schools, independent schools, and in private practice; in general education classrooms, in special education pull-out programs and special day classes, and for mentor court pretrial diversion programs. Explicit, thoughtfully planned instruction—informed by both formal and informal assessment—is most critical for the students who are most dependent on quality instruction to attain literacy. Without it, students who have not had access to high quality instruction, students who have not had the benefit of rich language experiences during the critical periods for acquisition of early language skills, students who are English language learners, or students with learning disabilities will not survive with their academic self-image intact. My little brother was beginning to dislike school as he questioned his ability to succeed because he was forging a path that would have led to academic failure—if he had not been fortunate enough to have a teacher like Miss Ethel Taylor to save his future.

The story of Arthur encompasses many critical aspects of my never-ending journey toward becoming an effective teacher. This journey has led me along two converging paths: (1) development of background knowledge in language structure and learning-teaching strategies; and (2) development of ways to deliver effective instruction to struggling learners with precision and respect for individual differences.

THE STORY OF ARTHUR

> The potential possibilities of any child are the most intriguing and stimulating in all creation.
>
> (Ray L. Wilbur, 2007, p. 195)

I began working with Arthur when he was nearly 8 years old and could not recognize the word *the*. His passage comprehension score (Figure 12.1), before beginning educational therapy, earned a standard score of 64—in the severely below average range. In stark contrast, his listening comprehension performance earned a standard score of 140—in the very superior range. The 76-point discrepancy between these two scores is equal to more than five entire standard deviations. Arthur did not have a language comprehension problem; he could not read the words. As Joseph Torgesen, a pioneer in the research of phonological processing and reading disabilities, said in his keynote address to the 2003 Annual Conference of The International Dyslexia Association, "No comprehension strategy is powerful enough to compensate for the inability to read the words."

When Arthur entered my office for the first time, he looked around and announced, "This place is pandemonium!" "Indeed it is," I had to agree. "I hope you like pandemonium because it is not likely to change in the near future." We stepped into the teaching room, and I asked him to tell me his birthday. He enthusiastically announced the month and day of his birth and then said, "I can never remember the year—only the month and day." I explained to him that his birth date, including the year, was a *palindrome*: 8-9-98. He was delighted with both the mnemonic for remembering his birth date and the new entry in his very rich oral vocabulary. That was the auspicious beginning of a 6-year teaching–learning relationship. Step-by-step, he was taught the structure of his language as he learned to encode (spell) and decode words. He learned phonology, phonemic awareness, phonics, morphology, and etymology. He learned to chunk words into meaningful phrases so that he could read connected text fluently, with prosody, and with comprehension. He learned grammar and syntax to strengthen his reading comprehension—especially of academic language—and to instill confidence in his competence for written expression. Arthur's educational therapy lessons were planned with multiple goals and purposes:

- To integrate Arthur's need for remediation, use of compensatory strategies, and accommodations;
- To provide him with direct instruction in learning strategies for improvement of discrete skills;

- To provide instruction and guided practice in learning strategies for application of skills at increasingly higher levels of functional use;
- To ensure that Arthur developed expertise in knowing his own unique pattern of learning strengths and challenges:
  - How to use his strengths to compensate for his weaknesses;
  - Which strategies to use in which situations;
  - How much time he needed for which tasks—and why.

Figure 12.1 shows Arthur's progress (Woodcock, 1997) during the first 9 months—72 hours of educational therapy, and Figure 12.2 shows growth (Wechsler, 2002) during the following school year—80 hours of educational therapy.

Arthur's skills, and his application of skills for functional use, improved significantly in every aspect of reading. He learned to segment spoken syllables into their component sounds (phoneme segmentation-phoneme analysis/whole-to-parts/inductive reasoning), and he learned to blend sounds together into spoken syllables (phoneme synthesis-sound blending/parts-to-whole/deductive reasoning). He learned to encode words by associating each sound within a syllable with the grapheme (letter or letters that spell a phoneme) that represented it. Then he learned to use explicit, systematic decoding strategies to identify familiar and unfamiliar words with predictable orthographic (spelling) patterns; he learned to apply these strategies functionally when reading text. He practiced reading unpredictable words—and he knew precisely which parts were unpredictable and why. He learned to self-monitor so that he read text at his own individual "ideal speed"; he read as fast as he could read accurately—which allowed him to comprehend—but as slowly

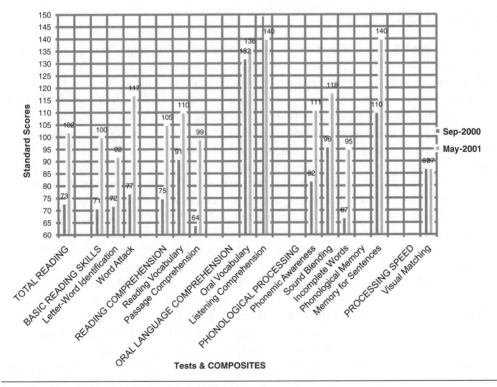

Figure 12.1 Arthur-WDRB standard score growth 72 hours of educational therapy.

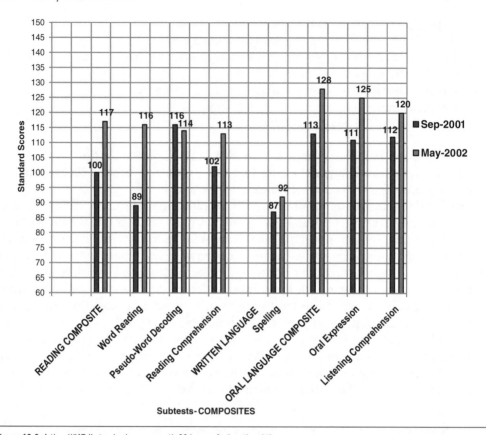

Figure 12.2 Arthur-WIAT-II standard score growth 80 hours of educational therapy.

as necessary to allow for use of newly learned decoding strategies that guaranteed his accuracy. As he read text, he learned to monitor his comprehension by chunking words into meaningful phrases; as a result, he read with prosody. His listening vocabulary and speaking vocabulary were extraordinary—which provided a foundation of background knowledge for his reading comprehension and his acquisition of new knowledge of the logic and structure of English. Over the course of that first year of educational therapy, Arthur's already remarkable listening comprehension continued to be a strength. His phonemic awareness skills, the basis for understanding and using phonics, improved dramatically. His phonological memory for meaningful information, just above average at the beginning, jumped to the very superior range. He learned to chunk words into meaningful phrases as he read connected text, which helped him to recall longer and longer strings of spoken language. Still, his processing speed was below average. He read slightly faster at the end of the first year than he could read at the beginning of that year, but his peers were increasing their reading speed at a far greater rate. He was learning to read accurately and to comprehend all that he read. He read fluently—accurately, and at a consistent rate, his ideal speed—and with prosody; as a consequence, he comprehended all that he read. If pushed to read faster than his ideal speed, he read inaccurately, was forced to guess from context, and reverted back to word-by-word reading; consequently, his comprehension would have been compromised if forced to read faster.

Arthur's confidence in his academic worth soared. He learned to know himself as a learner. He knew his strengths as well as his weaknesses. He understood that he read slower than his peers, but he also understood that he could read with accuracy and comprehension at levels far above age and grade expectations—as long as he read no faster than his own individual ideal speed. He knew that he was in control of his own academic performance; he had learned to "figure out" what he had been previously unsuccessful in memorizing by rote without understanding or strategies.

As a fourth grader, Arthur loved to read so much that he hid a flashlight and his books under the covers so he could read after "lights out." As a fifth grader on a panel of students discussing their learning disabilities for an auditorium full of prospective teachers, he was asked if he perceived any advantages to his difficulty with learning to read and spell:

> In third grade, every week my teacher gave us a test on words we had misspelled in our writing. She called our practice with these words "have a go." Every week I hated those tests because I just can't memorize words. At the end of the year, she surprised the class with a test on all those words. I was the student who spelled the most of those words correctly! Why? I can spell words because I know how the words work. I know syllables and vowel patterns and suffixes and prefixes and roots. I know how to figure out how to spell. I don't need to memorize words—which is a good thing since I couldn't anyway. The amazing part was that by the time of the end-of-year test my classmates had forgotten how to spell words they had "memorized."

YOUNG ADULTS—PRETRIAL DIVERSION

> We either make ourselves miserable, or we make ourselves strong. The amount of work is the same.
>
> **(Carlos Castaneda, 1972, p. 184)**

Another rewarding educational therapy experience has been the privilege of teaching literacy skills to young adults in the Pre-Trial Diversion Project through the Mentor Court Program of San Francisco Superior Court. These young men and women were victims of an educational system that has left them functionally illiterate. No teacher ever had a more motivated group of students than those motivated and intelligent young adults. They were eager and enthusiastic learners. They were thinkers who enjoyed solving problems and figuring out how to use new information. At the beginning, most of them were reading and spelling only words they had previously memorized. Consequently, they could not use information about one word to figure out another one—for reading, spelling, or meaning. They quickly began to make connections and to use new knowledge in conjunction with their good thinking skills to explore language. They were very respectful to each other and supported each other in learning and a variety of other ways.

Ilana had memorized a substantial sight vocabulary, but she had no sense of how her language works. More importantly, she did not trust herself to figure things out. She thought the only way she could be successful was to memorize everything. It was very difficult for her to begin to trust herself to break things down into parts. She found it difficult not to blurt out answers when it was another student's turn because she believed she was helping the other person by telling the answer. Eventually, she began to trust herself more and was able to take her time to use the decoding and encoding strategies she was learning to figure out words she may have never seen before. She was very pleased with her accomplishments.

Demetrio was very motivated once he arrived in class; unfortunately, he came late almost every week because he had to travel across town by bus from his job. He was especially excited about the grammar he learned. He also enjoyed structured reading (studying of text) and vocabulary study. He learned rapidly and he retained all that he learned. He has great potential for continued success if given the opportunity to continue instruction.

James was enthusiastic no matter what we were learning. It was sometimes difficult to figure out exactly how he arrived at some of his responses because he would often say things that did not seem to make sense in the context of what we were discussing. With encouragement and guidance, he began to express his ideas more clearly. He was always helpful and very considerate of the other students. He knows a lot and he has learned to organize what he knows into usable "files."

David took some time to get himself focused, but was usually the first student to arrive and was always ready to work. He made connections, used what he learned, and asked pertinent questions. He commented to the class about the usefulness of his new skills in the rest of his life.

Lawrence had an amazing memory for details and was the star of the class in remembering the meanings of various Latin and Greek prefixes, suffixes, and roots. He thrived on structure and fell apart when instruction was not patterned the way he expected. He needed to know what to expect. He learned effectively when he knew the steps of a process and was given sufficient guided practice in how to use the steps to solve problems. He never forgot what he had truly learned. He was willing to practice and to work hard to learn what was important to him.

Mary was the quiet member of the group. She watched and she listened and she learned. She always spoke in a soft voice, but she had the respect of the group, and fellow students worked hard to hear what she had to say. She gained confidence as the class progressed. She did not often ask questions, but she demonstrated that she was learning by her responses and her written work.

Donald was a serious student. He appreciated the opportunity he was given to "begin again," and he practiced without prodding. He became a role model for other students and volunteered as an assistant teacher in a summer school program the following year. Later, he began taking courses in an early childhood education program at City College.

When first assessed, their skills in word identification and spelling were so meager that their percentile rankings were only a fraction. A graph illustrating progress in reading and spelling is shown in Figure 12.3. These students thrived on the structure inherent in the strategies they learned for word identification, spelling, reading comprehension, and written expression.

In order to teach these young men and women the skills they needed to become readers and writers, it was necessary to begin at the most basic level. I needed to ask them to learn to use and practice using strategies they might consider appropriate only for much younger students. I needed to convince them to invest themselves fully in a process they would instinctively want to reject wholly. I chose to give them explanations of neurology, language acquisition, and multisensory structured language instruction that were the basis for my choice of instructional strategies. I gave them rationales for what I would be asking them to do. I acknowledged that I would be asking them to do activities and to use strategies they might not like. I explained that while I understood why they might not want to do certain things, I expected them to do them nevertheless. I concluded by asking them to ponder one last thought, "I must *really* believe all these things are extremely important or I wouldn't have the nerve to ask you to do them." They thought that made sense, so I pushed a little further by asking them to give their best effort to all that I asked of them for 2 weeks without complaining. Then, at the end of the 2 weeks, we would assess their progress and discuss any lingering complaints. At the end of the two weeks, they had little to complain about because they were so pleased with what they were learning.

Only 2 hours per week were designated for this instruction—based on the needs of these students it was far less than indicated. Still, note the rate of their progress in Figure 12.3 (bar graph of pre- and posttest scores for reading and spelling).

DONALD: AGE 23, 1 TO 9 MONTHS

With determination, conviction, tenacity, humility, humor, and effective instructional strategies, we can teach students of all ages to read, spell, and express themselves in writing. Effective teaching is both an art and a science. To do the job well, educational therapists

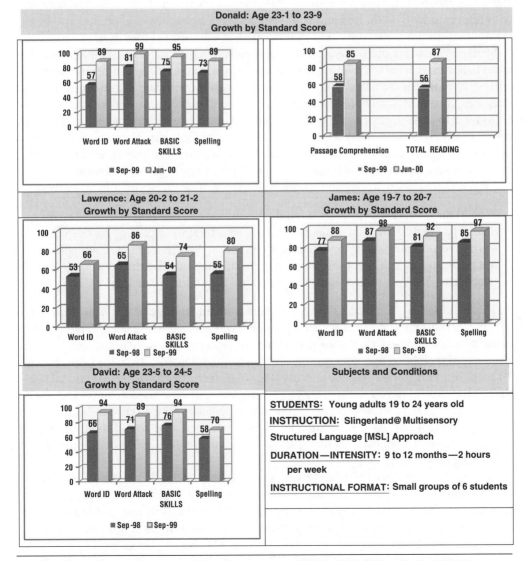

Figure 12.3 San Francisco pre-trial diversion mentor court project progress in Reading (*WRMT-R/NU*) and Spelling (*WRAT-3*).

need to be constantly honing their techniques, continually devouring knowledge of the science as it evolves, and above all tenaciously keeping the individual student as the focus. Mutual respect between educational therapist and student, in conjunction with careful preservation of dignity, will pave the way to a productive working relationship.

Teaching and learning about language structure is one of the joys of my life. It does not matter how old or how young my students might be, where they live, what school they attend, or how many years they have been struggling readers. When their eyes light up with the realization that they finally "get it" and know they possess the tools to figure out what they were unsuccessful in learning previously, I feel the exhilaration that someone else might experience upon reaching the peak of Mount Everest—well perhaps only Mount Tamalpais. Discovering effective instructional strategies for teaching literacy has been a long and arduous search, but well worth the time and effort. It is a quest that will never end for there will always be something more to learn. Every time I teach a different student, a group of students, or a group of teachers, I learn something new that may help with future students—children and adolescents as well as teachers and prospective teachers. It is within this framework that I function as an educational therapist.

Struggling readers and writers need to be involved in the process of their education in order to become part of the solution to their educational dilemma. Results of any diagnostic testing, formal or informal, should be discussed with the individual student in terms of strengths, weaknesses, and proposed strategies for remediation and accommodation. Students need to be told why certain tasks are difficult and how they can be made easier. The results of any assessment must be the basis for informing the instructional plan. Awareness of strengths and weaknesses is of little value without a plan for improvement. Knowledge of *how* a student learns is a formidable weapon in the armory for self-advocacy.

Regina Cicci (1989), a wise and wonderful teacher of children and adults, warned:

> A good diagnosis is essential for a child with dyslexia or any other kind of learning disability. By its definition a diagnosis leads to a treatment plan or an evaluation leads to recommendations for teaching intervention. Whether or not diagnosticians use the term dyslexia is not the purpose of this discussion. The children exist. Their problems exist. Whatever we call the problems, the children need our help. (p. 6)

Through the years, I have had the privilege of watching many children transform from frightened, resistant students, discouraged from years of failure, to eager learners, confident of their competence. All they needed to attain this success was explicit instruction in the structure of their language, consistently and logically presented with many opportunities for modeling and guided practice at every stage of learning from skills to functional use—based on a clear understanding of their learning strengths and weaknesses—and always with the goal of independent reading and writing. Maintaining a sense of humor along the way always helps! As their academic competence increased so did their confidence and self-esteem. An educational therapist has both the privilege and the responsibility of facilitating this journey.

To reap the benefits of their hard work, readers must comprehend what they read. To comprehend, it is necessary—but not sufficient—to be able to accurately identify words—familiar as well as unfamiliar. Sadly, having the ability to read does not enable a person to teach someone else to read—especially someone who needs to be taught. In a statement to the Committee on Labor and Human Resources, U.S. Senate, Dr. G. Reid Lyon (1998), Chief of Child Development and Behavior Branch of National Institutes of Health offered some sobering statistics:

- 5% will learn to read on their own.
- 20–30% will learn to read relatively easily once exposed to formal instruction; most methods will be effective.
- 30–50% will find learning to read to be difficult without direct systematic explicit instruction.
- 30–50% will find learning to read to be the most difficult challenge they will ever face.

Students with reading problems often have other academic problems—and diminished feelings of self-worth as well. The more intelligent they are they more aware they are of their weaknesses. Often these students are their own worst critics. Low self-esteem, due to repeated failure in school, may lead to behavior problems secondary to the learning issues—but equally detrimental to school and social success.

Many children who are significantly below average in reading in third to fifth grade can be brought up to grade level if they are given intensive, linguistically informed teaching for up to 2 hours per day (Torgesen, 2003). Several methods (Foorman & Torgesen, 2001) seem to be equally effective, but all that have been proven effective included these components:

- Direct teaching of language structure with an emphasis on decoding fluently and accurately;
- Ample practice with skill application in meaningful contexts.

There are multiple levels of language organization and structure from below the word level to above the word level:

Phonology—sound structure of a language; rules for the combination of sounds (phonemes)
Orthography—spelling patterns (graphemes)
Morphology—units of meaning within words (morphemes)
Syntax—phrase and sentence structure
Semantics—word, phrase, and sentence meaning
Pragmatics—word choice and use of language in context
Text Structure—organization of connected text (sentences to paragraphs)

One of the challenges of teaching students with language weaknesses about language and how to use language is that the language itself is the medium for learning and teaching.

It has been established by many studies that phoneme awareness—the ability to identify the individual sounds within words—and phonics—the ability to represent those sounds with letters—are essential for skilled reading (Adams, 1990; Ehri, 1996).

Ehri (1994) has studied the sequence in development of word recognition. The first words most people read are context dependent and based on visual cues. For example, when young children recognize "McDonald's," it is the golden arches they recognize; few are associating the letters in the word with the sounds they represent. Likewise, when a young child reads his name on a puzzle, he knows it spells his name, and he is recognizing his name puzzle—not the letters. The students who will learn to read "in spite of instruction, not because of it," will soon begin to notice the letters at the beginnings and ends of words and the sounds they represent; they will begin to generalize what they learn to other

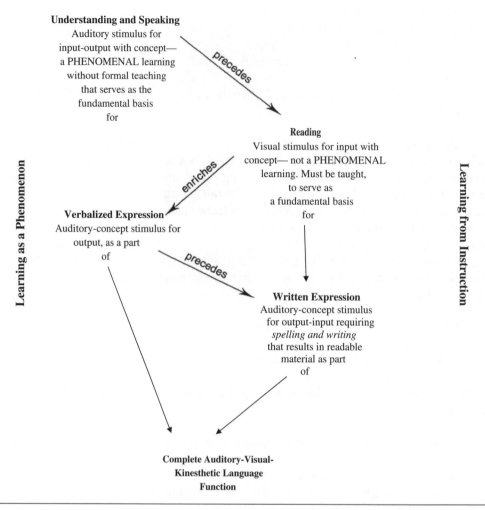

Figure 12.4 Global development of normally acquired language function. From Slingerland, 2008. Reproduced with permsiion.

words. They begin to learn the names of letters and to develop rudimentary phoneme awareness. As they learn the names of the letters, they will attempt to use the sounds they hear in the letter names to spell, and they will begin to develop the ability to blend and segment individual sounds (blending and segmenting).

Wagner, Torgesen, and Rashotte (1999) organizes phonological processing into three categories: phonological memory, phonological awareness, and naming speed. Phonemic awareness is a subset of phonological processing and includes those skills needed at a rudimentary level in order for phonics to make sense to students. Marilyn Jager Adams (1990) defines phonemic awareness:

It is not working knowledge of phonemes that is so important but conscious, analytic knowledge. It is neither the ability to hear the difference between two phonemes nor the ability to distinctly produce them that is significant. What is important is the awareness that they exist as abstract components of the language that can be manipulated. Developmentally, this awareness seems to depend upon the student's inclination or encouragement to lend conscious attention to the sounds (as distinct from the meanings) of words. (p. 65)

Children who are not naturally "inclined" to lend this conscious attention to the sounds of their language must be encouraged—relentlessly encouraged—because these are the students at risk for difficulty with learning to read and spell. Most 4-year-olds enjoy rhyming games and can easily generate words that rhyme. I overheard a group of kindergartners playing a rhyming game:

Annie = *mat* Eddie = *rat* Jean = *cat* Fred =*dog*.

Fred supplied a word related to *cat*, but he had not "noticed" the parameters of the game his classmates were playing—the sounds that made up the words. Fred needed to be taught to notice the sound structure of words, and he needed instruction and guided practice to ensure that he had learned. In order to benefit from phonics instruction, students need to have <u>rudimentary</u> knowledge and understanding of the following phonemic awareness skills and they should be able to perform these types of tasks:

Phoneme Blending (Phonemic Synthesis—skill needed for decoding)

/sh/ + /e/ + /l/ = /shell//m/ + /a/ + /t/ = /mat/

Phoneme Segmentation (Phonemic Analysis—skill needed for encoding)

/scratch/ = /s/ + /k/ + /r/ + /a/ + /ch//blink/ = /b/ + /l/ + /i/ + /ng/ + /k/

Phoneme Manipulation/Phoneme Substitution

Change the /b/ in *beam* to /t/.

Change the /p/ in *trip* to /k/.

Change the /m/ in *smash* to /l/s

Phoneme Deletion

Say /*meat*/ without the /*m*/

Say /*sleet*/ without the /*l*/.

A phoneme is a single speech sound, a distinctive linguistic unit. A single phoneme change creates a word with an entirely different meaning:

house, mouse, louse

street, straight, strut

sheaf, beef, **thief**

street, stream, streak

Individual phonemes can be difficult to isolate or identify, especially when they are changing in subtle ways caused by co-articulation (other sounds/phonemes that surround them). Pronounce each of the words below and consider both the sound and the oral-motor movement (location and manner of articulation) in your mouth as you pronounce each /p/:

post spark stop lisp sipp**ed** /**sipt**/

Adams (1990) explains why phoneme awareness is at the same time both vital and challenging:

- People must know about phonemes at some level in order to produce or understand speech. (p. 65)
- Adults can consciously access the presence of a phoneme only through the time-consuming and retrospective process of taking apart the syllable that has already been perceived. (p. 66)
- The deep and automatic encoding of phonemes is the product of the fact that we know them so well that we have overlearned them even at a very young age. Does it become an unconscious skill? (p. 66)

Adams (1990) explains that it is "because we have so thoroughly automated, so thoroughly mechanized and sublimated, our processing of phonemes that we have attention and capacity for the higher-order meaning and nuances of spoken language" (p. 66). As a consequence, to learn an alphabetic script, we must learn to pay attention to what we have learned not to notice as we learned to speak and understand spoken language with little effort (Adams, 1990). In his turn-of-the-century classic on reading, Edmund B. Huey (1898) stated, "Repetition progressively frees the mind from attention to details, makes facile the total act, shortens the time, and reduces the extent to which consciousness must concern itself with the processes" (p. 104).

> Continuous effort—not strength or intelligence—is the key to unlocking our potential. (Black Elk, ASCD *SmartBrief*, January 28, 2005, SmartQuote)

HIGH SCHOOL STUDENTS AND ADULTS

Even high school students and adults who have not acquired automaticity with the processing of phonemes can benefit from instruction. Adolescents and adults often bring issues of low self-esteem and frustration. Before effective instruction can occur, it is critical to establish a milieu of mutual respect and trust. I sometimes teach a month-long intensive summer school class to high school students who are in need of instruction in the basic written language skills of reading, spelling, and written expression. One summer, the mother of one of the prospective high school students asked if she could join the class as a student. As we were discussing the results of her son's screening assessment, she realized that the issues her son was experiencing were very similar to her own experiences in school. I told her it was fine with me for her to join our class as long as it was acceptable to her son. Laney was a wonderful addition to our class. Her work ethic and tenacity were noticed and admired by the high school students in the class. At the end of the month, she gave me the following excerpt (Day 2) from the journal she had kept throughout the class:

> Each day as I proceed on my path of learning how to learn, many emotions seem to block my path forward. I have an image come to mind. I am in a large birdcage. In my youth, someone outside is calling to me, encouraging me and cursing me at the same time. There is the idea that I could, I should fly free, if I would just come out of the cage. But I can't find my way out, so I am cursed as stupid. Don't you know the

difference between the b and the d, left and right? Can't you see the way out? I don't see. Eventually the birdcage becomes real. No one expects me to find my way out of the cage. Instead, I sing wildly within my walls and play on the swing provided, eat a minimal diet of information, and suppress the now almost vague image of freedom. Many call me a creative bird, but I am not. That portion of creative thought which gets expressed in my simple songs is miniscule compared to what is unexpressed. One day I hear a voice from the outside. It says, here is a key that might unlock the door. It is the sound of the short vowels, a, e, i, o, u. There are five sounds. At first I hear only one sound. Voices in my head are reminded of long ago. You're stupid, can't you spell, don't you hear what I am saying. The emotions are immense and jar the door shut. I cry softly. Imitating the person on the outside, I pull on my ear, /eh/, then /ahh/. Two sounds. An excited expectant hope starts to boil within.

Laney was an intelligent, competent, and very creative adult. Still, the lack of a basic understanding of the structure of her language had diminished her self-esteem and blocked her path throughout life. Major benefits of that one month of intensive instruction were her newly gained confidence and insight into how her language works.

Recent research by neuroscientists and cognitive scientists has provided ample data to support a speech to print approach to teaching beginning reading. These studies point to the fact that the *foundation of reading is speech* and that the organization of new reading skills in the brain must be built on this foundation (Herron, 2008). We are born with hardwiring for speech and listening comprehension. Herron discusses the power of the speech connection to sound—the oral-motor connection, or auditory-kinesthetic integration:

- Phonemes are not processed by the auditory system alone; they are *articulated* sounds. (p. 78)
- The powerful motor system of speech sequences and remembers phonemes. (p. 78)
- Letters represent articulated sounds.
- Text is a way of making speech visible.
- The process of learning to read should start by turning <u>spoken</u> words into <u>visible</u> words.

Following are examples of phonological errors in speaking and listening:

- My mother uses a *valid* when she votes. (*ballot)
- After decoding the word *refreshment*, the teacher asked Matthew if he knew the meaning. He replied, "Yes, it's the first year of high school."
- When first graders were asked what a *phrase* is, Sally raised her hand enthusiastically. "Phrase God from whom all blessings flow," she said proudly.

Phonemic awareness supports reading and writing the alphabetic code, but it will not automatically generalize to word recognition, fluency, comprehension, or spelling. For most people, reading and spelling skills must be taught.

English is both an alphabetic-phonic system and a morpho-phonemic system. Students must learn the names of the letters of the alphabet to complete automaticity. Priscilla Vail (1996), a master language teacher, said, "Words are tags that lead to concepts." Adams

(1990) discusses the importance of "a distinctive and uniform label for a concept—especially concepts that vary across occurrences." The name of a letter is its most stable property. The shape of a letter may change (e.g., upper-lower case forms, cursive-manuscript). The speech sound represented by a letter may change (e.g., long or short vowel sound, hard or soft *c* or *g*).

Letters are the data that make reading possible; all readers visually process every letter (Adams, 1990). Novice readers who automatically recognize individual letters are ready to learn orthographic patterns (familiar letter sequences—spelling), an essential step toward becoming a good reader (Ehri, 1998). Knowing letter names provides a springboard for learning and remembering letter-sound relationships (Ehri, 1983). Students must associate the name of a letter, a *constant*, with the *variable* properties of letters, such as sound and shape (Cox, 1992).

"Skillful readers visually process virtually every individual letter of every word as they read, and this is true whether they are reading isolated words or meaningful, connected text" (Adams, 1990, p. 409). Although this processing may not be perceived consciously, studies show that readers unconsciously detect misprints of even very familiar words. When the letters *tqe* (for *the*) were embedded in a sentence, the amount of eye fixation time increased (Adams, 1990)—even though many of the adult readers were not consciously aware of the misspelling.

The reader recognizes letters, associates them with speech sounds, and attaches meaning based on the context (e.g., *row* as a line of things or people or to propel a boat with oars; *crane* as a lifting machine or a long-legged bird or to stretch the neck; *bat* as a flying mammal or a club used in sports or to hit with a bat or to quickly open and close one's eyes). Reading words over and over leads to the learning and reinforcement of letter sequences-orthographic patterns—pattern recognition. For fluent reading to develop, a student must learn to recognize frequently occurring orthographic (spelling) patterns in words. Eventually, readers seem to recognize words as wholes because they have acquired a deep, richly interconnected, and ready knowledge of their spellings, sounds, and meanings, but skillful readers automatically and quite thoroughly process the component letters of text because their visual knowledge of words is from memories of the sequences of letters of which the words are comprised (Adams, 1998).

Liberman and Liberman (1990) explained how we move from spoken language to the written code, "The reader must have awareness that all words are specified by an internal phonological structure, the shortest elements of which are the phonemes that the letters of the alphabet represent" (p. 60). Beginning readers must come to the same conclusion that the inventors of the alphabet made in their discovery: spoken words differ not holistically "but only in the particulars of their internal structure" (p. 61). English has a less-than-perfect sound–symbol match (26 letters to spell 44+ phonemes) partly because it is a language that consists of "a river of words formed from many tributaries of different languages" (Gillingham & Stillman, 1960). Knowledge of letter names can help students identify and spell unknown words because the phoneme represented by a grapheme (letter or letters that spell it) is often embedded in the letter's name and can be inferred by students (Ehri, 1983). Below are examples of first graders' use of letter names to spell familiar words:

> *trtl* for *turtle jal* for *jail ets* for *eats biet* for *bite koped* for *copied yel* for *will*

Letter names provide a foundation for learning the alphabetic principle (Ehri, 1987).

These examples illustrate a beginning understanding of the alphabetic principle in which a grapheme represents a phoneme.

Reading research has firmly established that word reading ability is influenced primarily by phonological processing skills (Adams, 1990; Stanovich & Seigel, 1994; Vellutino, 1991). There is also evidence that reading accuracy and fluency are influenced by orthographic recognition—the ability to recognize a letter or letter cluster (Olson, Forsberg, & Wise, 1994); and rapid naming skill (Neuhaus, Foorman, Francis, & Carlson, 2001; Torgesen, Wagner, Rashotte, Burgess, & Hecht, 1997; Wolf & Bowers, 2000).

Tests of rapid automatized naming (*RAN*) are well-established as tasks that robustly predict word reading and reading comprehension over time (Neuhaus, Foorman, Francis, & Carlson, 2001; Wolf, Bally, & Morris, 1986). The *RAN* has been used recently to determine why rapid naming is related to word reading (Denckla & Rudel, 1974; Wolf, 2007).

Early oral language development is established as the foundation for later language development before a child enters kindergarten. Preschool oral language development is enriched by abundant talking, labeling, and reading with children.

General oral language is supported by verbal (phonological) memory. Verbal memory also supports the storage and retrieval of specific verbal labels—letter names and sounds assigned to the letters needed for reading.

Practice with naming letters should continue even after students have begun to read words. Letter familiarity is connected to both faster articulation and faster cognitive processing (Neuhaus & Swank, 2002). Letters are the building blocks of words, and automatic letter recognition is the key to automatic word recognition. Children do not learn about letters and words at the same rate; at-risk students were found to need over 20 times the amount of literacy practice needed by children who were not at-risk (Berninger, 2000). Letter-naming fluency is dependent upon familiarity with the orthographic *and* phonological properties of letters. Letter shapes must be associated with letter names *and* sounds. These associations must be overlearned in order to support rapid fluent letter reading that leads to word reading accuracy, word reading fluency, and reading comprehension (Neuhaus & Swank, 2002).

Orthographic memory is the memory for *patterns* of written language—graphemes (letter or letter sequences that spell a single phoneme), syllables, and morphemes (prefixes, base elements and suffixes). We can see graphemes. Syllables are linguistic units; we speak and hear syllables, but we do not see them. The ease and automaticity with which a skilled reader is able to read individual words is known as instant word recognition. Instant word recognition is achieved by repeated encounters with words and by overlearning (i.e., learning to automaticity) the orthographic and phonological patterns of the language. Explicit use of the visual, auditory, and kinesthetic-motor (speech *and* writing) channels for learning help to reinforce learning and consolidation of learning into long-term memory. Automatic word recognition depends on repeated encounters with words in connected text, knowledge of orthographic patterns, and understanding of word origins (etymology).

Phonics is the association of a single sound (phoneme) with the letter or letters (grapheme) that represent that sound in print. This pairing is called symbol–sound, letter–sound, or grapheme–phoneme correspondence. There are various ways of teaching phonics. Phonics instruction found most effective for beginning readers, poor readers, or at risk readers is explicit phonics instruction—systematic, not random—that incorporates the following:

- Sequence of skills (informed by assessment and needs of students)
- Progression from simple to complex
- Introduction of high-utility, high-frequency, generalizable sounds and letters first
- Separation of easily-confused graphemes and phonemes
- Visually similar—*b-d g-q n-u* Auditorily similar—/b/ /p/ /ch/ /sh/ /t/ /d/
- Systematic introduction of one vowel grapheme (spelling pattern) at a time with ample practice before introduction of another.

The six basic *syllable types* were regularized by Samuel Webster to justify his 1806 dictionary's division of syllables (Moats, 2004; *LETRS*-Module 3). Knowledge of syllable types (determined by vowel pattern/grapheme) helps students read longer words because it allows them to systematically divide them into "chunks" instead of attempting to read them letter by letter. Learning to identify the six syllable types/vowel patterns is useful for students because it helps them determine how to pronounce the sounds of the vowels in unfamiliar words. It also helps students to know when to double consonants when spelling unfamiliar words. Spoken language syllable divisions often do not coincide with the conventions for dividing written syllables. As you pronounce the word /wĭggle/, you may naturally divide the spoken syllables between /wĭ/ and /gle/. However, the first syllable /wĭg/ is a closed syllable: It ends in a consonant—and the vowel–consonant grapheme spells its short vowel sound. In the word /būgle/, you may naturally divide the spoken syllables between /bū/, and /gle/. The first syllable, /bū/, is an open syllable because the syllable ends with a vowel sound. The vowel sound in this open syllable is long because the open syllable is accented. The result of the syllable combining process requires a double "g" in wiggle to complete the closed syllable/short vowel sound spelling—but only a single g in bugle. These spelling conventions—closed and open syllables—were invented to help readers decide how to pronounce a word. These conventions also help a student to know how to spell words—although knowledge of syllables alone is not sufficient for being a good speller. Explicit, systematic instruction includes the following steps:

- Teacher models/demonstrates and verbalizes steps of strategy.
- Individual student practices and explains steps of strategy verbally.
- Individual student practices with teacher guidance, verbalizing each step.
- Teacher observes student during guided practice and verbalization; gives corrective feedback.
- Teacher uses individual student performance during guided practice to inform planning of subsequent lessons and additional practice opportunities.
- Teacher includes both skills instruction and instruction in application of skills in every lesson.

At the beginning, more time will be spent on skills instruction because students have learned very few letters and sounds; more time will be spent in instruction in application of skills to functional use activities as students acquire fluency and automatic use of the phonemes and graphemes taught. Teachers should keep two examples of sage advice in mind:

Go as fast as you can, but as slow as you must. (Margaret Byrd Rawson)

We can never teach them all they need to know, but we can teach them to think. (Beth Slingerland)

As educational therapists, we don't always know how far-reaching the effects of our efforts may be. I have been very fortunate because so many of my students have continued to keep me posted on their adventures. When Trav, one of my former students, was a senior in high school, he sent me a copy of the essay he had written as part of his college applications. This young man had been my student from second grade through seventh grade. He was a gifted athlete, and arrived for his twice-weekly educational therapy sessions at 7:00 p.m. after a full day at school and sports practice (soccer, basketball, baseball—depending on the season). He never failed to appear with a smile and a positive attitude. I will always treasure his words during our last educational therapy session. I complimented him for his accurate and fluent reading of a favorite Greek myth, and he replied, "Well you know, Ms. White, once you know those prepositions, you can see 'em coming." What a wonderful farewell gift to his teacher! But that was just the beginning. It never occurred to me that he might be making a connection between his exceptional athletic talent and his struggles with learning to read and express himself in writing—until I read his college application essay.

> The midday shadows began to creep across the dirt as I stood on the mound. A hundred thoughts were running through my mind but I knew I had to focus. My team was winning by one run in the bottom of the seventh; the game was in my hands. I had two outs and I was facing the last batter between a championship or a defeat. I could either fold under the pressure or rise to the challenge. I wiped the sweat off my brow and looked into the catcher for the sign. As I came set, I began to visualize myself throwing the perfect pitch. I fastened a fast ball grip in my glove and went into my windup. I delivered the pitch with all my heart and soul, hoping the batter would not end the game with one swing. The batter waved at the pitch and hit a weak grounder back to me. I pounced on the ball, gathered myself, and fired a bullet to the first baseman. My team won the championship. The mental skill that I used to pitch that day, I learned when I was 7....
>
> One day, my mom picked me up from school and told me I had a doctor's appointment. It was a typical foggy San Francisco Day. When we pulled up to the doctor's office, I was surprised to see that it was a house. I got out of the car and walked up the driveway and up some old creaky steps. I was hesitant to enter, but finally gathered the courage to open the door. Inside was one of the most inviting rooms I had ever seen. The door closed shut, blocking the fog and all my doubts. The room was filled with pictures and poems and in the corner was a green couch covered with stuffed animals. The room had only one lamp that lit the warm room. I was at Nancy's office.
>
> We began to talk and she explained to me that I had dyslexia, a learning disorder. I did not understand what she was telling me because a part of me did not want to believe her. I did not want to be different than my peers. She told me this disorder was affecting my English skills. My thoughts were clear, but when I tried to put them on paper, I often misspelled words and left words out of sentences. I had difficulty applying language rules because I had a memorization problem making foreign language very challenging. After we finished talking, we walked into the back room and began the first of many sessions where I started the long process of learning the basics of the English language. For the next four years, I worked with her every week refining my English skills and finding new ways to comprehend material to fit my learning style. Whenever I step onto a baseball mound, I try to emulate the

skills to beat my opponent that I learned in that room. Just as I broke down words into parts to read them, I break down my motion to get the maximum power behind every pitch. I survey the field before every throw to make sure my team is ready. As I raise my leg, break my hands, I drive off the mound to deliver the pitch. When I write an essay, I follow the same process. I gather my information, and then break it into paragraphs, each paragraph essential to the meaning of the paper. I try to make every word count, just as I try to pitch without any wasted motion. The foundation of my paper, the grammar and structure, have to be strong, just as my fundamental baseball skills have to be strong. However, athletics and academics are not the only areas to which I apply my learning skills.

I have learned that the visualization of a picture is a key skill in photography. Whenever I go to the beach and look at a sunset, I try to capture that feeling and convey it in a photograph. The position of the sun over the sparkling water surrounded by the layers of rich colors blend together to form an indescribable sight. Without the sun, the sparkling water, or the clouds, the entire photograph has no meaning. These elements of the photograph remind me of how Nancy taught me to read. I would not only divide words into parts, but I would also slowly balance the sounds of each vowel and consonant. Every time I was able to decipher a difficult word, I would remember how essential each sound was to the process. Just as every sound in a word is important in conveying its meaning, each part of a photograph is imperative in portraying the feeling of the picture.

The skills that I have used throughout my life have taught me that if I patiently put forth my best effort, I will be rewarded by the quality of my work and the feeling of achievement.

I was sitting on that green couch covered with stuffed animals when I read Trav's essay just after it arrived in my mailbox. As I read the first paragraph, I was thinking about his fine writing skill and how difficult written expression had once been for him. When I began to read the fourth paragraph where he discussed how he "breaks down his pitches" the way he learned to decode words, I was completely speechless. I needed to reread that paragraph more than once before I believed that he was actually making such an astonishing analogy.

Trav's essay illustrates the beauty of incorporating both the art and the science of teaching and relationships into educational therapy:

- Giving our students what they need—even if it is not what they might want;
- Acknowledging their effort—especially when they are doing what they do not want to do but need to do;
- Valuing their efforts to think and solve problems—even when it leads to a flawed result;
- Celebrating their successes—no matter how small or great;
- Offering support and camaraderie—when they are discouraged or when they fail.

The relationship between educational therapist and student becomes so much more than the sum of its parts, and we never know just how far-reaching the effects of this relationship may be.

REFERENCES

Adams, M. (1990). *Beginning to read: Thinking and learning about print*. Cambridge, MA: MIT Press.

Adams, M. J. (1998). The three-cueing system. In J. Osborn & F. Lehr, F. (Eds.), *Literacy for all: issues in teaching and learning* (pp. 73–99). New York: Guilford Press.

Berninger, V. B. (2000). *Language based reading and writing intervention: Findings of the University of Washington Multidisciplinary Center*. Paper presented at the meeting of the International Dyslexia Association, Washington, DC.

Castaneda, C. (1972). *Journey to Ixtlan*. New York: Simon & Schuster.

Cicci, R. (1989, Fall). Diagnosis of dyslexia. *Perspectives, 15*(4), 6. Baltimore, MD: International Dyslexia Association.

Cox, A. R. (1992). *Foundations for literacy: Structures and techniques for multisensory teaching of basic written English language skills*. Cambridge, MA: Educators Publishing Service.

Denckla, M. B., & Rudel, R. (1974). Rapid "automatized" naming of pictured objects, colors, and letters, and numbers by normal children. *Cortex, 10*, 186–202.

Ehri, L. C. (1983). Summaries and a critique of five studies related to letter-name knowledge and learning to read. In L. Gentile, M. Kamil, & J. Blanchard (Eds.), *Reading research revisited* (pp. 131–153). Columbus, OH: C. E. Merrill.

Ehri, L. C. (1987). Learning to read and spell words. *Journal of Reading Behavior, 19*, 5–31.

Ehri, L. C. (1994). Development of the ability to read words: Update. In R. Ruddell, M. Ruddell, & H. Singer (Eds.), *Theoretical models and processes of reading* (4th ed., pp. 323–358). Newark, DE: International Reading Association.

Ehri, L. C. (1996). Development of the ability to read words. In R. Barr, M. Kamil, P. Mosenthal, & P. D. Pearson (Eds.), *Handbook of reading research* (Vol. 2, pp. 383–417). New York: Longman.

Ehri, L. C. (1998). Grapheme-phoneme knowledge is essential for learning to read words in English. In J. L. Metsala & L. C. Ehri (Eds.), *Word recognition in beginning literacy* (pp. 3–40). Mahwah, NJ: Erlbaum.

Foorman, B. R., & Torgesen, J. K. (2001). Critical elements of classroom and small-group instruction promote reading success in all children. *Learning Disabilities Research & Practice, 16*, 203–212.

Gillingham, A., & Stillman, B. W. (1960). *Remedial training for children with specific disability in reading, spelling, and penmanship*. Cambridge, MA: Educators Publishing Service.

Gillingham, A., & Stillman, B. W. (1997). *The Gillingham manual: Remedial training for students with specific disability in reading, spelling, and penmanship* (8th ed.). Cambridge, MA: Educators Publishing Service.

Herron, J. (September 2008). Why phonics teaching must change. *Educational Leadership, 66*(1), 77–81.

Huey, E. B. (1898). Preliminary experiments in the physiology and psychology of reading. *American Journal of Psychology, 9*(4), 575–586.

International Dyslexia Association. (1998, February). *Understanding your Dyxlexia* (Fact Sheet #5). Just the Facts. Baltimore, MD: Author.

Liberman, I. Y., & Liberman, A. M. (1990). Whole language vs. code emphasis: Underlying assumptions and their implications for reading instruction. *Annals of Dyslexia, 40*, 51–76.

Lyon, G. R. (1998, April 28). Statement to the Committee on Labor and Human Resources, U.S. Senate, National Institute of Child Health and Human Development, National Institutes of Health. Washington, DC.

Moats, L. C. (2000). *Speech to print: Language essentials for teachers*. Baltimore, MD: Brookes.

Moats, L. C. (2004). Module 3—Spellography for teachers: How English spelling works. In *Language essentials for teachers of reading and spelling (LETRS)* (pp. 47–64). Longmont, CO: Sopris West Educational Services.

Neuhaus, G. F., Foorman, B. R., Francis, D. J., & Carlson, C. (2001). Measures of information processing in rapid automatized naming (RAN) and their relation to reading. *Journal of Experimental Child Psychology, 78*(4), 359–373.

Neuhaus, G. F., & Swank, P. R. (2002). Understanding the relations between RAN letters subtest components and word reading in first grade students. *Journal of Learning Disabilities, 35*(2), 158–174.

Olson, R., Forsberg, H., & Wise, B. (1994). Genes, environment, and the development of orthographic skills. In V. B. Berninger (Ed.), *The varieties of orthographic knowledge: Vol. 1. Theoretical and developmental issues* (pp. 27–71). Dordrecht, The Netherlands: Kluwer Academic.

Rawson, M. (1992). *The many faces of dyslexia*. Baltimore, MD: Orton Dyslexia Society.

Slingerland, B. H. (1971). *A multi-sensory approach to language arts for specific language disability children: A guide for primary teachers*. Cambridge, MA: Educators Publishing Service.

Slingerland, B. H. (2008). *A practical guide to teaching reading, writing and spelling*. Bellevue, WA: Slingerland Institute for Literacy.

Stanovich, K. E., & Seigel, L. (1994). The phenotypic performance profile of reading-disabled children: A regression based test of the phonological-core variable difference model. *Journal of Educational Psychology, 86*, 24–53.

Torgesen, J. K. (2003, November 13). *Closing the gap through intensive instruction: New hope from research.* Keynote address for 54th Annual Conference of The International Dyslexia Association. San Diego, CA

Torgesen, J. K., Wagner, R. K., Rashotte, C. A., Burgess, S., & Hecht. S. (1997). Contributions of phonological awareness and rapid automatic naming ability to the growth of word-reading skills in second to fifth grade children. *Scientific Studies of Reading, 1*(2), 161–185.

Vail, P. L. (1991). *Common ground: Whole language and phonics working together.* Rosemont, NJ: Modern Learning Press.

Vail, P. L. (1996). *Words fail me: How language works and what happens when it doesn't.* Rosemont, NJ: Modern Learning Press.

Vellutino, F. R. (1991). Introduction to three studies on reading acquisition: Convergent findings on theoretical foundations of code-oriented versus whole-language approaches to reading instruction. *Journal of Educational Psychology, 83*, 473–443.

Wagner, R. K., Torgesen, J. K., & Rashotte, C. A. (1999). *Examiner's manual for comprehensive test of phonological processing.* Austin, TX: PRO-ED.

Wechsler, D. (2002). *Wechsler individual achievement test* (WIAT-II) (2nd ed.). San Antonio, TX: Psychological Corporation.

Wolf, M. (2007). *Proust and the squid.* New York: HarperCollins.

Wolf, M., Bally, H., & Morris, R. (1986). Automaticity, retrieval processes, and reading: A longitudinal study in average and impaired readers. *Child Development, 57*, 998–1000.

Wolf, M., & Bowers, P. G. (July/August 2000). Naming-speed processes and developmental reading disabilities: an introduction to the special issue on the double-deficit hypothesis. *Journal of Learning Disabilities, 33*, 322–324.

Woodcock, R. W. (1997). *Woodcock diagnostic reading battery* (WDRB). Rolling Meadows, IL: Riverside.

Woodcock, R. W. (1998). *Woodcock reading mastery test-revised[NU]* (WRMT-R[NU]). Circle Pines, MN: American Guidance Service.

IV

Case Management and Navigating Multisystems

13

THE MANAGEMENT OF A PRIVATE PRACTICE IN EDUCATIONAL THERAPY

ANN KAGANOFF

INTRODUCTION

Being an educational therapist in private practice might seem to be the very definition of the American Dream. You are a highly trained professional. You are self-employed. You have complete control of your working hours. You own your own business. You make all the decisions about where to locate, which clients to accept, how to treat your clients, what materials to use, how to market your services, and when to take a vacation. You are, in short, your own boss. If managed effectively, a private practice may indeed reflect the American Dream. However, it must be noted that this form of work exceeds the American Dream in one important sense: We do what we do in order to help others learn. It is a remarkable form of work that is of equal benefit to both giver and receiver.

The purpose of this chapter is to offer a structured framework for the effective management of a private practice that will result in positive outcomes for both the educational therapist and his or her clients. The recommendations made here are based upon the writer's own experiences with a home office, as well as many observations of the private practices of my colleagues. It is my hope that my own observations and experiences will offer practical guidance and will alert you to some of the pitfalls that can be avoided. I hope that my reflections about private practice will convey a sense that many of us share, namely, that thanks to the complex nature of the client–therapist relationship the private practice of educational therapy is a fascinating combination of the unexpected, the humorous, and the challenging. We have the opportunity to engage in problem solving that calls upon our highest levels of critical thinking and the constant application of what we know. I often remark that every day I use everything I know, and every day brings new learning. And every day, I have the opportunity to make a significant difference in my clients' lives.

DEFINITION: WHAT CONSTITUTES A "PRIVATE PRACTICE"

According to the tax accountant consulted by this writer, the term *private practice* is not a legal definition. Rather, it is defined, in practical terms as a business operation run by a sole practitioner in either a commercial location, such as an office building, or a home office. Many ETs work within centers as part of a larger group of providers of related services, such as speech and language specialists, where the financial arrangements may involve a salary. However, even in a commercial location, where the private practice ET may be part of a group that shares a common waiting room or receptionist, she is still working for herself as opposed to being paid a salary. An alternative private practice arrangement is the home office, where the ET again is working solely for herself and is not paid a salary.

BUSINESS LICENSE

Most cities have requirements regarding business licenses. You need to consult the regulations governing the operation of a sole proprietorship business operation in your local area where your business is located, particularly as they apply to a home office business. A call or visit to City Hall will help you get the required forms, and keep you in compliance with city regulations.

BEGINNING A NEW PRIVATE PRACTICE

An ET may decide to work within the private practice framework for a number of reasons. A private practice may emerge as an alternative to being connected to a center or a group of allied professionals; for example, a center or group may change its philosophy or management. An ET may be transitioning from, or supplementing, a related career in the educational system, and may wish to give private practice a trial on a small scale before committing to it as a full time job. Or private practice may simply be the preferred model for operating because it may appear to offer an ET the greatest number of professional options.

Both private practice and an affiliation with a center or group offer significant benefits that must be considered when a decision is to be made about whether to set up a private practice. A group affiliation is particularly attractive if the members of the group share similar goals, philosophies, and work ethics. It offers the opportunity to share ideas with like-minded professionals in a shared work environment, and to take advantage of complementary or supplementary skills. An ET will have the benefits of being connected to a referral network, whether the group is comprised of allied professionals or other ETs.

The private practice, on the other hand, offers the ET sole control over working conditions, hours of operation, and client privacy. Access to allied professionals or colleagues may take a little more effort, but with the use of the phone and e-mail, consultations can be arranged as needed. Private practice eliminates the need to negotiate over shared resources such as a copier, waiting room, or receptionist.

Once the decision is made to enter private practice, the ET must decide whether to locate in commercial office space or set up a home office. Commercial spaces have the obvious constraints associated with building access, parking, and monthly cost. For some, the impersonality of a commercial space is a negative; however, for others the use of home space represents an infringement upon one's private life.

There are a number of general considerations to setting up an office space, whether in the home or in a commercial space. The nature and age of the client group often determines the type and size of office space that is needed, particularly if the ET specializes in one age group, such as young elementary children or adolescents. The type of furniture and materials required by younger children and the amount of space they will need to move around in will differ from adolescents' space requirements. An ET may have a specific method of instruction, for example, that requires many manipulative materials, access to water or a kitchen. The relative amount of floor space needed will depend upon the needs of the clients, as well as the amount and type of instructional material to be utilized. Storage space for records and materials is a major consideration. Computers, fax machines, and copiers are regarded by ETs as essential to their practice.

In addition to these within-office considerations, you must consider location of the office, relative to the majority of clients who will be served. In urban and suburban areas, spending time on freeways and in traffic may cause added to stress for the client family, but may be inevitable. Educational therapists often counsel families to seek an ET in a geographic area that is as close as possible to home to reduce the stress associated with travel to and from sessions. Access to the office, parking space, and waiting areas are important considerations for parents or students.

The waiting area in either the commercial office or the home office deserves special mention here, because for many families privacy is a serious issue that must be managed by the ET. Most ETs see clients on an hourly basis, with one student departing as another arrives. In small communities, or in locations where potential clients attend the same schools, there is often a chance that families will know each other. In most cases this is not a problem, and there may even be possibilities for car pooling. However, you must consider the possibility that a family may not wish for others to know that a child is receiving educational therapy. In some locations, clients may come from "high profile" families who wish to maintain a high level of privacy. Thus the individual therapist's method of transitioning from one session to another, and preferred method for drop-off and pick-up of students, must be fully discussed at the outset. It is often very reassuring to students to learn that someone they may actually know is also seeing the ET, but this may also lead to a whole new set of ethical and privacy issues as a child may express curiosity about another child's sessions.

It is important to anticipate the kinds of ethical issues you may need to handle in terms of client privacy. In my particular case, with a home office in a suburban neighborhood, I have had to pay particular attention to how I manage the moments of drop-off and pick-up. A child may arrive in acute distress, refusing to get out of the car, or yelling very publicly at the parent. Such situations need to be quickly and skillfully defused because there is usually another client being retrieved at the same time. I try to keep a balance between sparing the parents embarrassment, and enabling the distressed child to begin a productive session with dignity, making the best use of the time available. These problems are more easily handled once you have developed a good relationship with the client. You may also find there are unexpected benefits, as happened recently when one of my older students was switched to a different session time, and suddenly discovered I had other high school age students. She was not the only high school student on the planet who needed extra support!

The overall ambiance of your office will reflect your own temperament and priorities. In all cases the office should have a welcoming feeling of openness, friendliness, and safety for all clients, regardless of age. Because many of our clients are highly distractible, many ETs seek to reduce the amount of distracting material in the office. Most offices have at least one spot, such as a cozy couch or chair, which offers the client a place to deal with momentary anxiety or stress. On the other hand, the office needs to have a highly professional feel to it, with a visible supply of reference materials such as dictionaries, globes, and encyclopedias, an in-office library of both fiction and nonfiction books, and other sorts of learning materials. I have found it very useful to have items of interest to students, such as my rock and shell collections, for those times when a client needs to take a "walk-around" break.

The personal nature of the home office merits specific discussion. Not all homes offer a suitable space without some modification to the existing building, such as a separate entry (though a good many practices have been initially begun at the kitchen table). A home office may impinge on the privacy of other family members. An ET with his or her own young children will need child care arrangements. You may feel that you never get away from work. Finally, for both men and women ETs, personal safety is an issue. If the practice includes clients who may be emotionally unstable, particularly if they are adolescent or older, the ET needs to have a strong sense of when not to see the client. This is ideally determined at the period of client intake, when you may decide that the client needs the services of a clinical psychologist or psychiatrist before educational therapy can be effectively undertaken. You must be willing and able to make a strong determination if there is any indication that the client cannot be successfully managed with just your own immediate resources.

On the positive side, a home setting can offer a great deal more comfort to clients than the more impersonal commercial office, which the client may associate with other, negative "office" experiences. A more informal tone can be established. Field trips can be made to the kitchen or the back garden as needed. Your clients may find it helpful to know that you have children or grandchildren, interests in art, music, or science, and a life outside of work that contributes to your ability to be a good educational therapist. Finally, from a practical point of view, there are tax advantages in the form of deductions for a home business, depending on the tax laws of the state of residence. A home office can permit the well organized ET to maximize the use of time in the absence of a need to commute to work.

MARKETING YOUR SERVICES

Educational therapists tend to enter a practice from a wide variety of routes and backgrounds. Most of us have had experience with the educational or allied professional community, and many of us transition to educational therapy from a related profession such as special education, speech and language, or social work. However, some of us begin new practices in new geographic locations, where we must build complete new networks among the allied professions. This section will consider these two avenues separately.

If you are transitioning from a related profession and are doing additional training in educational therapy through a training program, you are likely to be a member of the Association of Educational Therapists (AET). If you already have contacts in a community through previous work, such as with a school district or a clinical practice, it is recommended that you contact the various professional organizations through a colleague who might facilitate entrée to an appropriate meeting. Such groups often wish to hear a brief presentation on educational therapists and the services we offer. Study groups often have lists of recommended allied professionals who can be contacted through a letter or brochure. School principals often will permit an ET to speak at a school staff meeting. Many an educational therapist has made herself known in a community through her work in her children's classroom, or through her children's pediatrician. It is also suggested that the beginning ET call a few private schools in the area and request a visit with the administrator. Educational therapists frequently are asked to suggest alternative placements for clients at both the elementary and high school levels, and with this knowledge the administrator will recognize that the ET has something to offer the school, as well as asking for referrals from the school.

Setting up a practice in an entirely new community requires careful and patient work to lay a foundation of contacts and referrals. You must do your homework. You must first find out about the allied professionals in your area and be prepared to contact them and get to know them. You must find out about whether they hold professional meetings on a monthly or semimonthly basis, and ask if you might be given a few minutes of meeting time to introduce yourself and discuss the services you offer. Often one strong contact will lead to another. If you are hesitant about making "cold calls" to strangers, it is helpful to remember that many of the people you contact will be extremely happy to know that you are setting up a practice. They have often been looking for someone exactly like you.

BEING A SOLE PRACTITIONER

It has been noted above that working as a sole practitioner requires extra effort in several respects. Centers typically offer ongoing and immediate contact with allied professionals or other ETs. As a private practice ET, on the other hand, you may sometimes feel alone and isolated. Educational therapy sessions can be extremely intense, particularly when, as so often happens, you are dealing with clients in severe distress. Decisions have to be made as to how best to use the session time, often with incomplete data and insufficient time to reflect. You may wish that you could just visit across the hall to ask another ET how he or she would handle a given situation. Few of us have encountered all the possible variations of what clients can bring in the door, and few of us can completely anticipate how a given situation will affect us. Thus we must pay close attention to our own needs for time and space and reflection. We must learn to trust our own experience and intuitions. We must remember that in most cases we will have a chance to return to the problematic situation, often after consulting with a colleague meanwhile.

Those of us who have been in practice over time have learned that educational therapists are a collaborative group. We have learned that our professional ties are invaluable in many ways, whether through workshops and conferences, through study groups, or through close partnering with a valued colleague. A single set of eyes is rarely enough, given the complex nature of what we do. For the newcomer to private practice, there is a vast wealth of experience and knowledge available from other educational therapists. The section on "Reflections" will present some more philosophic reflections on what we can learn from ourselves.

MAINTAINING AN ONGOING PRACTICE

Intake

It is important to note at the outset that "intake" has a meaning to the new educational therapist that differs from its meaning for the experienced ET with a full practice and a waiting list. This section will address those two cases separately, though they share common features, and will also review specific intake steps that apply to most practices.

Every ET must have an efficient intake procedure that provides the gateway to a successful practice. Before the days of the Internet, referrals tended to come from known referral sources and therefore came with something of a personal connection. We now are likely to receive calls or e-mails from people who used the Internet to find us and with whom we may have no previous connection at all. Many ETs take calls as they come in, while others use voicemail to record incoming calls so that they can be screened and returned at a time chosen specifically for that purpose. There is a clear advantage to the latter procedure, especially for the ET in a home office. Since the initial call may be a client's first contact with you, it is very important that you make it at a time when you can give the client your full attention, preferably with a note pad in hand to take notes.

What information should we glean from that first contact? Let us first consider the ET in a new practice, responding to a call from an unknown client. If you are building a practice, there is of course the need to have clients, and thus there is the temptation to take any and all callers. It is important to be clear in your own mind what kinds of clients are best suited to your present skill set, your knowledge of the different profiles of learning disabilities, and of course your background experience with clients of different ages. You may feel the pressure of financial need, along with the pressure exerted by an anxious parent. Experienced ETs know that we learn a good deal from our clients, and as our skill grows, we learn much from our clients as to how they need to be taught. This process of learning from the client cannot substitute, however, for good judgment at intake. It is extremely important not to overestimate one's own capacity to learn on the job, particularly in cases that present with obvious complexity. It is advisable to err on the side of caution, to avoid finding 2 months into the relationship that this is not a client you can work with successfully.

The experienced ET with a waiting list may have another set of considerations, such as availability of an appropriate time slot or the complexity of the case. Before you take on a new client it is suggested that you evaluate the impact on the balance in your practice. This means keeping a balance between the clients who you can predict will be very needy, complicated, and demanding, with those who will more readily benefit by working with you, the "garden variety" clients. With experience you will often be able to determine which category a prospective client belongs in just from talking to parents. Be careful not to overload your capacity to handle the seriously involved cases; they take more time and energy (even if they seem particularly interesting and challenging).

The initial call from a client may be preceded by either a call or an e-mail from the referral source, giving critical information or urging you to take the client. Since the referral source is all important, consideration of the source helps us maintain our relationships with allied professionals who refer clients to us. You may be able to quickly identify some cases as clearly inappropriate. The reasons may be as simple as a client located too far away geographically, requiring too much travel time. At the other extreme, the case may require skills outside the boundaries of educational therapy such as client involvement with drugs, a client with significant behavioral problems, or client involvement with the juvenile justice system.

Most ETs will want to know the following at the very beginning of an intake conversation:

- Referral source (if the source is unknown to you, ask a further question)
- Age and grade level of client
- Prior test data
- Location of family; name of school or school district
- Immediate concerns, reasons for calling

Most of us use the above questions to make a quick determination. However, in most cases much more information is needed. Both new and experienced ETs generally have some form they wish the new client to fill out, and most of us then schedule an intake interview to help determine the suitability of the client. If you are sure the client is not a good fit, say so and have a name handy for referral. You may already have enough information to know which colleague may best suit the caller. If you are uncertain, be clear at the outset that the initial intake consultation will help both you and the parent to decide. New ETs may decide to do the initial consultation without charge. This is probably a good public relations decision when you are first setting up a practice. It is also a bit of insurance against having to refuse the case, yet charging for the consultation.

How then do we decide which clients to take? With experience we learn to listen to the client with what Dorothy Ungerleider, the founder of the Association of Educational Therapists calls "the third ear." If we assume that the majority of our callers are families in distress because of a struggling learner, we learn to listen for particular cues. A parent with a long, rambling, and somewhat confused presentation may have a limited understanding of the client's problems, and may indeed have some of the same issues as the child. At the other extreme is the parent who has done extensive homework or who has had the client seen by multiple specialists. This parent may use a good many labels and may in fact be looking for a particular type of intervention that in the view of the ET may or may not be appropriate. Most cases fall somewhere in between. If the caller seems to be a good prospect and fits well with my other clients, I then send out my background information form so that I can set up a file on the client.

Initial Intake Interview

If I have space available that works for the family, I set up a meeting with the parents for an interview. The initial consultation is an opportunity to meet the parent or parents (or sometimes a grandparent) without the child, and to get a sense of whether the relationship will work. It is also a time for them to see me in my office and to assess whether they feel the child will connect with me. I try to meet with both parents together, even if they are divorced. If only one is available, I ask how the results of our meeting will be communicated to the other parent. I prefer to see both parents because they are both a part of the client's life, and I am interested in the interaction between the parents.

Prior to the initial meeting I have asked to have any test reports that have already been done on the child, the individualized education plan (IEP) if there is one, grade reports, standardized test scores from school, in addition to the form I have sent out. The background information I expect to receive is similar to the information that would form the basis of a good case study. It would include family members, IQ scores, standardized test scores, information on general health history and medications, previous diagnoses such as ADD, dyslexia, Asperger's, history of schooling, information about vision and hearing (including early ear infections), speech and language assessments if any. I go carefully over this data to see what is there, and what is missing. I formulate a list of questions that I wish to have answered. For example, if it is indicated that the child has seen a vision specialist and has been prescribed glasses, I ask the simple question, "Does she wear them?" The answers are often not what I would expect.

The above items constitute the more formal sources of information. However, the initial consultation is also the source of information that is more dependent upon listening with "the third ear" (Field, Kaufman, & Saltzman, 1993). Since I can reasonably anticipate that the relationship may continue over an extended period of time, it is important to get a sense of the family. A significant first question for me is, "How do these parents feel about the child?" Many of our clients severely test the parenting skills of the parents. How well are the parents coping with these stresses? Have they managed to continue to let the child know that he or she is loved regardless of the challenges? Are they searching for someone to "fix" a broken child, or are they realistic enough to be seeking strategies that help them cope productively and positively? What are the parent expectations, and are they realistic?

In addition to these questions, it is necessary to know what other interventions have already been tried, and to determine the parents' estimation of their effectiveness. If you find you are yet another in a long string of interventions, you must consider carefully what role you must play in dealing with their previous disappointments and their expectations. If you are well established in your community, you may be familiar with local practices or practitioners whom you consider either unethical or ineffective because of their extreme promises or their heavy sales pressure tactics. It is important to be very careful about how you communicate a negative opinion. It may be sufficient to just say that you have had other families who have been less than satisfied with the particular operation.

The initial interview is also a good time to get a sense of the client's personality and temperament. I specifically ask what they value about the child. Parents under stress have often lost sight of their child's strengths, and may be hard pressed to come up with examples of the positives. If they give only minimal examples, I now have a window into the world of a child who is a "disappointment" to parents and family. I may also get a sense that this is a client who is hard to like, and may be a challenge to me as well.

It is important to find out about a client's interests, as specific interests provide a powerful foundation for intervention. Educational therapists often develop knowledge in unexpected areas in order to share at some level in the interests of a client. Even the nonsports minded can hold onto data about the local professional basketball team. For the ET who sees clients with a wide range of age levels in widely differing school settings, the day's topics may range from turtles to Turgenev! Educational therapists who see adult clients will need data on school and work histories, as well as information about previous interventions, if any. The ET who works with adults will find that a specific interest form for adult backgrounds is imperative.

The initial intake interview is also a time for me to evaluate how well I think I can communicate with and serve the needs of this family. In turn, the parents must decide if they want a relationship with me. They need to know specifically how I operate, how I approach my teaching, what materials I would typically use, how I would propose to help their child. They will need to know how I interface with school projects and homework assignments. Frequency of sessions or time of day may depend on what time slots are available. Do I expect homework for my sessions in addition to what is expected at school? Do I contact the teacher or teachers? Do I make a classroom observation? Do I participate in IEP meetings? How do I measure progress, and how do I communicate progress with the parents? What are my fees, and how do I collect payment?

Parent Communication

Communication with parents is a major responsibility of the ET, and effective parent communication is one foundation of a successful practice. There are many ways to maintain communication, especially in the age of e-mails. Some ETs do a formal periodic parent conference. Some use the 5 minutes at the end of a session when the student returns to the parent to update both the parent and student on progress. This moment of transfer is rich in diagnostic data as you can watch the parent's response to both the good news and the not-so-good news about the session. It is a time for you to recap and label, in the presence of the student, the strategies that were developed, the concepts that were mastered, and the areas yet to be practiced and mastered. If there are issues to be shared only with the parent, this can be done in a follow-up phone call or a face-to-face meeting for more serious matters. It is unwise to use e-mail for the more serious issues, as written messages can go astray.

A particularly effective practice that I use is to invite the parent to sit in on a session. I try to plan this ahead of time, though it may also be spontaneous, depending upon the signals I get at the beginning of a session (which I refer to as "storm clouds" and try to handle immediately). The teaching table should have a specific chair for this purpose. I discuss the purpose of the visit with both the student and the parent ahead of time (or at the time). I use the time to discuss with both parent and child the purpose of each teaching activity, and to give a bit of the history of its effectiveness. I may pull from the folder previous dated work samples in writing or other exercises (see section on "Record Keeping") as a demonstration of progress or need. I use the session to demonstrate to the parent how I give feedback to the child. I make recommendations about how the parent and child might work together, depending on the age of the student.

These parent–child sessions are revealing in many ways. I can observe how well the parent listens to the child. Does the parent speak for the child when the child is asked a question? Does the parent seem genuinely interested in what goes on in a session? Does the parent take notes or ask questions, which indicates to me that there will be follow-up at home? The parent is observing the child responding to tasks that are generally out of the domain of ongoing family activities, and the tasks often reveal sides of the child that the parent has not had the opportunity to see first hand. Often the most touching moments occur when a parent says, "I had no idea she couldn't do that!" or alternatively, "I had no idea she *could* do that!"

Decision Making within the Session

The wide variety of teaching and therapeutic techniques used in educational therapy is addressed elsewhere in this volume. A successful and effective practice involves decision making in every phase of the practice, and good decision making takes careful planning. It has already been noted that you must plan for a balanced practice starting with intake, and planning must continue through the life of the practice.

Is there a generic lesson plan that applies to most educational therapy sessions? There probably isn't such a plan given the wide differences in client ages and needs. However, successful interventions are based upon a combination of careful planning for the expected, and the ability to anticipate and deal with the unexpected. Session time is generally limited by client availability and client resources, and therefore each instructional minute is precious. Session time will be allocated depending upon the needs of the client, and the goals of your intervention.

I start each session with a written plan that is based upon the previous session and that was written immediately following that session. I generally overplan each session because each one tends to have unexpected events. Since all of my clients are engaged in some form of schooling, I can reasonably anticipate that each session must begin with a discussion of school issues. My clients understand that I will always have "our lesson plan," but that our plan may be put aside if an assignment is due or a study strategy is needed for a test the next day. If the latter is the case, the student understands that we will focus not only on the immediate need for help, but that we will use the specific lesson to develop strategies that apply to long term learning.

I use the idea of "time management" within a session to teach time management in the broader sense. We utilize every aspect of task analysis as we break the task into components, estimate the amount of time required, determine the sequence of specific elements, and make a plan for completing the task. I make all of these operations explicit by voicing and explaining my own decision making steps as we go along. As the student becomes more familiar with the process, I will often begin by saying, "What is your plan for doing this assignment?" This question signals my assumption that the student is capable of having a plan, and gives us the opportunity to then work collaboratively to fine-tune the plan. If the student has no plan, it is a good time to confront the reason why not.

The experienced ET knows that no matter how carefully we plan, we also have to be prepared to abandon our plan when the student comes in with a level of distress that precludes learning. Responses to this kind of situation will vary depending upon the experience background of the ET, the needs of the client, and how such issues have been handled previously. However, it is important for the student to understand that the sessions will always involve the development of strategies and models for problem solving that extend well beyond the immediate situation. These long term strategies must be reviewed and revisited no matter what transpires during the individual session.

Postsession Planning and Record Keeping

A successful practice owes much to careful planning immediately after the session. It is essential to keep progress notes in a timely and systematic manner. In my own practice, I initially kept progress notes mainly to track the specifics of the session, so that I could refer back in the folder to what was done and when. However, as I gained experience, my notes took on a more important and deeper function. Instead of being a mere record of what happened during a session, the note writing itself became a vehicle for reflection and deeper understanding of the dynamic of intervention. I found that the note writing provided insights and perspective into the nature of the client and the intervention that might not have occurred if I had not spent the time on the notes. I found that the act of writing helped me shape the "story" of the client as I went beyond the immediate details to sense the larger trajectory of our work together. Sometimes there will be an "Aha" that is so dramatic that I get on the phone immediately (depending upon how late it is) to share an insight with a parent.

Managing client records can be time consuming, but careful record-keeping is essential to a well-managed practice, and is therefore worth doing well. There are as many ways to keep records as there are individual ETs, so I will offer my own system as one example. In my practice each client has a two-part folder for tracking the ongoing sessions. Each client also has a second folder with permanent records of grade summaries, evaluation reports, IEP documents, and other relevant material. On the left side of the session folder is a session summary form on which I record such essentials as date of birth, grade level, and dates of assessment and initial session. This sheet contains a table which allows tracking of attendance, with date and length of session. Beside each date is a line for a brief summary of tasks accomplished. This provides a handy reference for the entire history of our work together. For my long term students, the sheets may go back over several years, and are never archived out of the folder. Abbreviations keep the information load manageable. Parents are often extremely grateful that I have this information, in cases of IEP negotiations or court cases.

On the right side of the session folder I keep each dated lesson plan sheet on which I record a more complete summary (progress notes) of each task undertaken and its results, along with comments about the general tone of the session, any specific problems noted, follow-up actions needed. This sheet forms the basis of the next lesson plan, which is made as soon as possible following the session. It is also the record of the progress notes referred to earlier in this section, which have come to form the basis of much of my own learning about how to do educational therapy. In addition, the right side of the folder houses specific materials connected to the work of the session, including relevant writing samples, copies of assignment outlines, and partially completed work. This side of the folder can get very full over time; work is taken out periodically and is archived in the garage (or other storage area).

There are a number of benefits to this high level of record keeping. Most importantly, the presence of the client folder is a signal to the client that everything we do is important and is recorded. The record can be consulted to remind us of when specific strategies, topics, or tasks were introduced. I review the folder immediately before the session to keep my session plan firmly in mind and to help shape the direction of the session. This helps me keep on top of the student's ongoing work and assures the student that I do not forget what needs to be done! The folder is invaluable in parent conferences or school conferences as a demonstration of what the sessions have entailed. The folders have often saved the lives of the students who somehow lost their own notes from the session or did not realize they needed certain records from a specific assignment. They often value the folder as much as I do, though for different reasons.

WORKLOAD MANAGEMENT

A significant benefit of being in private practice is the ability to create a schedule that meets the needs of both the clients and the ET. This benefit can be the source of great flexibility, in that we can choose when to work. It can also result in very long days. Our schedules are frequently determined by our clients' school schedule. During the school year, with a few exceptions, students are available primarily after school hours. Some ETs see students during the school day, at the school site (this generally applies only to private schools, and only in locations where an on-site space is available). Some older adolescents and college students with flexible schedules can come to our offices during the daytime hours. Some ETs see students in the morning, before school starts.

Another important benefit of being in private practice is the ability to determine the overall workload, by deciding how many and which clients to add to our case load. From a personal point of view, we need to determine our capacity for work that is not only highly rewarding, but also very intense and involving by its very nature. To the ET starting a new practice, the prospect of "burn-out" may seem unlikely, when the most pressing task is to develop any case load at all. To the experienced ET, the prospect of "burn-out" is relevant when we have begun to take on some of the distress of our clients. However, if the practice is our source of income, then from a business point of view we need to determine how to keep sufficient work in the pipeline, so that if a client drops out unexpectedly, we are still able to survive financially. It can be a delicate balance.

The typical private practice revolves around the ongoing sessions with clients. Additionally, a practice will require other activities that support our work, such as school site meetings, classroom observations, conferences with parents and teachers, and IEP meetings. The weekly session schedule needs to be set up with these extra demands in mind. There are other life demands that have to be accommodated because they impact the billable hours, such as care of our own children, doctors' appointments, and jury duty. And during the course of a calendar year, we need to anticipate the times when school is not in session, such as the various holiday periods, when students may either not be available at all, or may want to make up extra sessions. Some ETs take summers off, while others view summer sessions as a critical element in successful intervention. The summer is a time that offers the possibility of a "summer intensive," when a student may be seen daily for 6 to 8 weeks or more. In my experience, the summer intensive can be one of the most productive experiences I can offer, especially for students who need significant remediation.

MATERIALS

Regardless of the nature of your practice, a sizable investment must be made in materials of instruction. Most ETs work with the literacy skills in some way, which requires a library of reference materials such as dictionaries, encyclopedias, and atlases. Depending upon the age levels you teach, you will also need a personal library of fiction, nonfiction, and poetry books. A good personal library will contain a selection of Newberry award books, as well as other well recognized beginning reader and chapter books. You will need to be familiar with the books that are typically assigned for English and literature classes at whatever level you teach. If you are unfamiliar with a given book, you will need to read it. We can benefit from the study guides and chapter questions received from the English teachers. Having an extensive library makes it possible, first, to assist students in appropriate book selection, and second, to insure that the student leaves with a book in hand from the "lending library."

In the nonfiction area, it is helpful to have a selection of the textbooks that are in use at the grade levels you teach. You need to be familiar with school curricula and state standards across age levels; even if you are not qualified to teach science or social studies directly, you need to be able to demonstrate the appropriate study strategies such as previewing and learning vocabulary terms. In social studies particularly it is helpful to be able to place the current topic of study in the overall context of history, especially when certain themes or concepts are repeated each year, such as the influence of geography on culture. I can remind my fourth graders when they first encounter the term *agriculture* that they will need to know this word in fifth grade, in sixth grade, and the year after that, so they might as well learn it now. I also keep a selection of trade books that deal with science topics. Students who struggle with the demands of fiction (the heavy inference load, the difficulty of tracking dialogue) are often very motivated and successful when reading books about animals, scientists, interesting places, or the fascinating world of nature.

Instructional materials may well include kits of various types that teach such skills as phonics and spelling. There is no shortage of choices in this area, and many are well marketed and well distributed. Parents may request that you teach a certain methodology based on these materials. Your decisions in this area will be based upon such considerations as storage space and cost of product, but primarily upon the flexibility and applicability of the material. A material with a single application that might be used infrequently, no matter how attractively packaged, is not a good choice. Parents may ask for advice about what to purchase or ask the school to provide. A well informed ET should be able to evaluate materials from packaged programs in terms of their strengths and limitations in order to advise both parents and IEP teams. Keep a list of questions parents should ask regarding these programs. Finally, you need to be familiar with sources of high quality educational materials provided by well recognized companies such as EPS, Curriculum Associates, and LinguiSystems.

EVALUATING CLIENT PROGRESS

Client evaluation at all stages of the intervention is discussed elsewhere in this volume. Progress evaluation is especially relevant to a section on managing a practice, however. For clients receiving educational therapy, there will be multiple indicators of progress relative not only to the particular types of learning issues, but also to the total life context of the client. Dorothy Ungerleider (personal communication, 1991) often remarks of educational therapists, "We are never out of the oven." The same may be said of our clients. We therefore owe it to our students to keep an eye on several key relationships: degree of achievements relative to ever-changing goals, personal accomplishments relative to external demands, parent expectations relative to client expectations, and most importantly, a client's own expectations.

In some areas of intervention, periodic retesting using standardized instruments will be used. For some, school grades are a meaningful marker. In other cases, a more descriptive measure is more relevant, such as the progress notes. Student self-evaluation is useful, as is parent feedback. Being "out of the oven," even when it does happen, is itself a relative state, as a student's remarkable leap forward may be eclipsed by the sudden escalation of school expectations. As the therapy continues, our clients need to be shown systematic steps in self-evaluation, so they become more independent in determining how well they measure up. Self-evaluation and self-advocacy go hand in hand.

Many ETs engage in systematic goal setting by the client, and the goals themselves are used to help measure progress. This may be a somewhat oversimplified idea of progress evaluation, as goals themselves are generally complex and subject to shifting and changing, and progress is rarely linear. How, then, are we to say that progress is made? The idea of "progress" connects closely to one of the most important elements of the relationship between client and ET. The ongoing job of the ET is to be a careful observer and a trusted witness. We are in the unique position of truly knowing the client, knowing what skills they arrived with, knowing the history of the work, knowing (and documenting) the steps of the journey. We are the ones who witness the struggles and the courage first hand, and who bear testimony to the achievements. We are the ones who give the feedback that matters, because it is specific and based upon real time events. In many cases we are there to cheer; in some cases, the breakthroughs come when we are not present in person, but our gifts to our students have kept on giving.

TERMINATING A CLIENT

Client termination takes many forms and happens for many reasons. Educational therapists are accountable to many stakeholders in a practice, including our clients, their families, the schools and workplaces, and ourselves, and therefore many points of view must be considered. Sometimes circumstances will decide: a parent's job loss, a move to another town, a divorce in the family. Sometimes the student will decide that she is ready to try things on her own. Sometimes the therapist believes the course of therapy has accomplished all reasonable goals, though the parent may be reluctant to part with the support. The therapist may feel that he or she can no longer effectively serve the client, and may refer the family to another therapist. The therapist may find that there are other more urgent needs that must be met before educational therapy can be effective, such as psychological or family counseling. Sometimes the parting is abrupt and unannounced; sometimes it takes place at a time that has been planned in advance. Most ETs try to get a final session to review goals and achievements, and often leave the door open for subsequent sessions on an as-needed basis. We all must recognize that some of the work will remain unfinished.

THE FINANCIAL ASPECTS OF A PRACTICE

A private practice is a business, and the educational therapist's best friend is a good accountant. There are a number of issues on which the accountant can advise you. If you are just setting up your business, you may benefit from advice as to a business plan. You will need to establish a goal for the number of clients you need in order to be financially viable. You will need to determine how many hours per week you will need to work. You will need to decide your weekly rate, which is often based upon the rates charged by other ETs in your area, rates charged by tutors, and rates charged by comparable professionals. It is certainly the case that some areas of the country have populations of clients who are more financially able to provide educational therapy for their children than other areas. At the time of this writing, there are relatively few insurance plans that pay for educational therapy, and that seems unlikely to change in the near term.

Your record keeping set-up needs to include ways of tracking the number of sessions you teach per week. It may be advisable to have multiple means of tracking, such as your attendance records in individual client's folders plus a central tracking sheet that lists all your clients. Some ETs may utilize automated (computer-based) billing programs, while others may do billing using self-designed forms to create invoices, and a spread sheet to track payments as they come in. It is important in your monthly planning to allow time each month for preparation of invoices, unless you pay someone else to do this. Time spent per month should not exceed 4 to 6 hours. Your accountant can advise you as to a method of tracking income so that your taxes can be paid on a quarterly basis. Choose an accountant who is familiar with methods used by the self-employed to track income and pay taxes.

Some ETs use very formal contracts with their clients, in which agreements are signed as to number of sessions to be held per week or month. Some expect payment per session, while others bill at the end of the month. Some ask for payment at the beginning of the month as opposed to the end of the month. All ETs should have a written policy statement regarding cancellations, late cancels, and no shows that is given to the parent or responsible party at the very beginning of the relationship. Most ETs charge for late cancels and "no shows," as would any other professional who keeps booked appointments. Most ETs develop flexible policies for families that temporarily cannot meet payments, such as sliding scales, especially when the sessions are urgently needed by the client to preserve momentum. In all cases, the process of billing and collecting fees needs to be kept at the highest professional level. The ET who asks for cash payments at the door does not look like a true professional.

LINKS BETWEEN PRIVATE PRACTICE AND THE ALLIED PROFESSIONAL COMMUNITY

Interface with Allied Professionals

The practice of educational therapy is necessarily enhanced by and dependent upon the input and expertise of allied professionals. These experts include the developmental pediatrician, the clinical or educational psychologist, the neuro-psychologist, the pediatric optometrist/ophthalmologist, the psychiatrist, the occupational therapist, the physical therapist, the speech and language specialist, the resource or special education teacher, and the classroom teacher. Each of these experts brings important diagnostic and treatment information to our work. We often see students who have already been seen by multiple specialists, whose reports on our clients we must be familiar with and of whose reputations in the community we need to be aware. We receive referrals from them, and we collaborate with them in developing appropriate treatment plans.

As part of managing a successful practice in educational therapy, it is important to become known to these professionals in the community (see the section above on "Marketing Your Services") as a necessary first step. Additionally, ETs in different parts of the United States where educational therapy is uncommon or even unknown will need to be able to communicate about both the work of the ET and our perspective relative to the other specialties. We need to communicate the boundaries of our practice such that it is clear where our work interfaces with and complements the work of other specialists. We need to be perceived as collaborators, not as competitors. One educational psychologist in my community, who does assessments only in the mornings, is very clear about how she regards our ongoing work with patients and clients: "Ed therapists are the real heroes. You get them [the clients] after school when they are exhausted and cranky, and you still know how to help them learn!" As an ET who sees adolescents often as late as 8:00 at night, I felt very validated by her recognition.

However, it is important to note that as educational therapists, we are often confronted by specific ethical issues, such as what to do when we disagree with the recommendations, or even the basic diagnoses of an allied professional. It is important that we not only understand the nature of the work of these specialists, to include all terminology relevant to the client's diagnosis, but that we also are able to anticipate and deal with any areas of question, confusion, or disagreement. Rich and positive relationships within the allied professional community benefit all concerned.

Relations with the Schools

Almost all educational therapists connect with the school system in some way. Therefore it is your responsibility to become familiar with your community schools, which will include both public and private schools. All of us need to be familiar with the academic demands our clients face (see section on "Materials"). For this reason, many of us do classroom observations as a part of assessment and treatment to gather contextual data about the client. Knowing what goes on in a client's classroom gives our own lessons great validity: "Your teacher will want you to...." Having direct relationships with the schools, including the classroom teachers, the resource or special education specialist, and the IEP team, promotes good communication and better integration of goals. Teachers need to know that the student is receiving specialized help, and to know that the family is providing this extra support.

Part of our job may be to lead the teacher to understand a client's special needs. We may need to intervene if the school expectations are unrealistic and inappropriate for the child. If when we can meet with teachers we can show good knowledge of the child, and can validate what the teacher is doing in the social learning setting, we can promote the kind of ongoing communication that will benefit all parties. Knowing the school setting can help us navigate such matters as interpreting a school assignment that is not clearly specified in the school materials sent home. A timely call to the teacher can prevent misunderstanding or misinterpretation of assignments. The ET must often address such problems as what to do if the teacher or school is in an adversarial relationship with the family, or when the classroom teacher is threatened by the presence of the educational therapist. We often provide essential perspective among conflicting parties when we remind everyone that we must do "what is in the best interests of the child."

THE ROLE OF REFLECTION FOR AN EDUCATIONAL THERAPIST

It is a truism of educational therapy that we learn from our clients. Careful and systematic reflection after a session contributes much to a deeper understanding of each individual I work with. In the quiet moments after the client leaves, or during the process of writing progress notes, I always see indicators that guide subsequent work. In addition, patient and wise observation during the session allows me to question, ask, discuss, explore, and in various ways work out a collaborative plan for helping each individual learner. When students are given the kind of attention that truly elicits self-reflection on their part, they are often extremely wise about their own learning. When students feel that they are being listened to by a responsive teacher who truly knows them, they are often stunningly insightful and honest about themselves. I call this process "acknowledgment," in which I recognize, moment by moment, not only the struggles, but also the courage and achievements of the students I work with. This acknowledgment is reassuring to the student, and a source of ongoing development of my own skills.

KEEPING A BALANCE OF DIFFERENT TYPES OF CLIENTS

It then follows that I benefit professionally by keeping a balance in my own practice of the kinds and relative complexity of the clients I take. In the section on "Intake" I noted the importance of balancing the relative difficulty of clients, such that I do not overwhelm my own resources with the more demanding cases. To be fair to myself and to my overall practice, I must safeguard my ability to respond to client needs appropriately. Therefore I must be able to estimate the level of energy, effort, research, and preparation any given client may require, in order to give the very best treatment that each one needs and deserves.

USING THE LESSONS OF ONE CLIENT TO INFORM MY TEACHING OF OTHERS

A good educational therapy practice can be regarded as a laboratory in which ongoing research in teaching and learning is conducted. Thanks to having a wide diversity of ages and types of learners, I am able to introduce a specific learning strategy to a range of individual learners and thus to observe the commonalities and the differences in their responses. In this way I build a basis of what to look for as I work with students at the different ages. A good example of this is my approach to teaching the critical thinking skill of inference in reading. All readers need to be able to make inferences, but will do so depending on their capabilities, and their linguistic and cognitive development. A specific inference lesson I use starting at fourth grade will elicit different responses from students at different ages (including my adult students). I am able to place the individual student's response in the developmental framework across ages, and thus tailor my expectations and my instruction appropriately.

Another example is the use of a particular material that is used to teach a targeted skill. The material might be appropriate for students at several age levels, yet will produce different responses depending on the student's ability and maturity. Having observed many students respond to the specific passage or exercise, I am able to interpret the response within that broad framework of past responses, and may even be able to predict it ahead of time. This is, of course, what all experienced teachers do as they develop lessons over time. But it is particularly valuable and intriguing in educational therapy lessons because we may work with clients who on the surface appear to be widely divergent as learners, but who have important underlying commonalities. As a result, we can become more efficient in diagnosis and treatment.

Students with learning disabilities can present with very different individual profiles, yet share common needs as learners. The effective ET uses an awareness of these common needs to help the student develop a balanced repertoire of strategies to use in learning. To draw from the reading example once more, many struggling readers who experience decoding difficulties begin to define reading as primarily a decoding process. But if we overfocus on decoding, we fail to meet the student's overall needs in the critical thinking skills that are required by good readers. As teachers we must always keep an eye on the underlying learning strategies required for all learning.

In a similar manner, if we are able to gain experience with students at different age levels, we have an added strength as teachers. We can offer an ongoing perspective to our learners. The skills we teach a fourth grader can be presented in terms of how that skill will be useful in fifth grade and in seventh grade and in ninth grade. As Jane Holmes Bernstein (1997) has commented, "We are not trying to create the world's best 3rd grader. We are trying to create a comfortable, competent 25 year old" (p. 1). My students are much more impressed with a lesson or skill exercise when I tell them, "You are going to be ready for this when it comes up next year." This of course assumes that we are all very familiar with curricular requirements across the grade levels, as well as the current state standards that students must meet. These are usually available in written form from state departments of education.

GIVING "INFORMATIVE FEEDBACK"

Few parts of the interaction with students are as important as how we give feedback. Much has been written about the effectiveness of positive feedback, but merely repeating "Good job, Johnny" throughout a lesson misses a far more important function of feedback. The educational therapy session offers a unique opportunity to do careful observation of a student's performance and to respond to it in a way that shapes the student's perception not only of him- or herself as a learner, but also of the perception of the very nature of learning. I am often struck when I do a classroom observation by how much of student learning goes unremarked by the available adults, who of course are outnumbered by the students and are occupied with furthering the teaching agenda. It is relatively rare that the significant moments of student insight, recognition, solution, and triumph are witnessed and celebrated. It is rare indeed that a student is told explicitly, "You are good at linking our reading work with what you have learned in social studies," because the available adults may not be able to focus on such matters.

In the educational therapy session we present the student with a problem to solve, and then we are there to acknowledge, to scaffold, to shape, and to comment. We can skillfully use our own language to label what the student has done: "You have found the right category label for that group of words." "You have included a nice paraphrase in your answer." "You have just written a good example paragraph. You would not have been able to do that six months ago." "You just applied a vocabulary word from last week." "You are choosing good synonyms now." And so on. The "teacher talk" of the educational therapist is a skillful combination of the level needed for student understanding along with careful modeling of the more difficult terminology coming up in the next lesson or the next grade.

In addition to a focus on student effort and attainment, my use of feedback often also includes articulation of the method I am using and its goal: "I am going to model a good alternative topic sentence for this paragraph so you will know how to do more than one." "I am showing you how to use a subordinate clause to start your sentence." "I am giving you a paragraph to read that has a very good example of a generalization. Can you find it?" "I am going to stop this part of the lesson to give you time to think more about the idea we just discussed." When I speak directly to the student about some (but not all) of the decisions I am making during the course of an instructional session, I am introducing a more metacognitive and collaborative note to the session. I am still in charge, but I am enlisting student cooperation in the planning and implementation of the lesson by sharing my thought process. I am modeling how the analytic process works in teaching and learning. This is often effective with the resistant student. It also makes teaching much more dynamic and interesting for me.

I often speak of feedback as one of the key "gifts" we give our students. Feedback involves being there to witness the struggles and to acknowledge or label the nature of the struggle. Feedback may take the form of recognizing the extreme courage it often takes for our clients to just keep going in spite of tremendous obstacles. It may be the shared moment when I can communicate that I "know who you are and can appreciate what it must be like to be you." It also works in the teacher's direction when I can reinforce my own directive to a student by rolling my eyes and saying, "You know what I expect here!"

ETHICAL ISSUES IN EDUCATIONAL THERAPY

All educational therapists will confront ethical issues. We deal with real-life families meeting real-life problems, many of them intractable and tragic. Ethical issues test our experience, our wisdom, our resolve, our patience, and our resilience. It is not the purpose of this chapter to enumerate all the categories of ethical issues, nor to list their possible solutions. However, it is extremely important to recognize this aspect of a private practice so that when it happens, you are not unaware or unprepared. There is no substitute for experience in this area, but fortunately we all benefit from our collective experiences, from knowing what issues might arise, and from observing how they have been handled in the past by our professional colleagues. A code of ethics, such as *The Association of Educational Therapists Code of Ethics*, is a useful guide (www.AETonline.org).

LEARNING FROM FAILED CASES AND AVOIDING BURN-OUT

Failed cases are variously defined, depending on the circumstances. It may be the client who we never were able to like or the client who chose to leave before treatment had a chance to take hold. It may be the client whose behavior we were unable to control or who made us feel threatened. There is the client whose work with us was sabotaged by a parent or teacher and the one who failed to engage in spite of our most creative and committed efforts. And then there is the client whose premature departure made us feel relieved. If our personal standard for ourselves includes being successful with every student, we may need to think about how that same student might have fared, had we not been there. Most of us would agree that our failed cases have been among our best learning experiences. While the failure was not especially enjoyable at the time, we benefited from the introspection, analysis, and sorrow, to become more aware, more mindful, and more sensitive with the next client.

I recall one of the earliest workshops I attended when I first started my practice. The term *burn-out* was mentioned, and I marveled that anyone could even think of such a word in connection with doing this kind of work. How could one burn out when doing work that is so challenging, so interesting, and so much fun? Educational therapists as a group are mindful of this issue. Our colleagues are frequently the source of advice and support when we feel overwhelmed. We often function for each other as we function for our clients: provide perspective, ask the critical questions, and suggest solutions. The lines of communication are varied, and often operate across distances. I once commented to a friend, at a time of personal stress, that I was very lucky to have so many therapist friends!

USING SELF-REFLECTION TO ATTAIN MASTERY

In educational therapy, as in other complex professions, there is no substitute for experience. Each client we deal with, each set of problems we solve, each crisis we navigate will contribute to a wiser response the next time. At the beginning of my practice I felt frequently blind-sided by the unexpected. My lesson plan did not go as expected. The student did not respond to my obvious skill and careful planning. The parent was not thrilled with the progress. The teacher did not hop on my astute suggestions. Over time, I have been blessed with access to nearby colleagues with whom I could discuss problems, as well as with the professional workshops, study groups, and conferences from which to learn. But I have also learned to learn from myself. This is the creative and reflective side of educational therapy, and to me it is at least as rewarding as the big and little successes I have with my clients.

Purposeful reflection must be an integral part of our professional growth. The life of the wise ET must be an examined life. This purposeful reflection can take many forms. For some of us it is a natural consequence of the problem solving we do constantly with and for our clients as we do our daily documentation and planning. For others it comes when we prepare case studies for study groups, when we retest, or when we prepare for an IEP meeting. Some of us may set professional goals as a result of our continuing education. We may target specific types of student treatments or specific areas of instruction in which we wish to become more skilled. Some of us may prepare presentations at workshops and conferences, or engage in training programs for new ETs. Some may write professional articles in which we articulate our ideas and experiences, and thus add to the growing body of knowledge in educational therapy. Some may contribute to a textbook.

It is true that at this writing there are too few people who are trained to provide educational therapy. It is true that our services are often desperately needed. It could be argued that each of us has a special mission to educate the public about educational therapy. We must recognize that in addition to helping our individual clients, a well run practice is an asset to the allied professionals with whom we work. It is an asset to other educational therapists among whom we make referrals. Finally, it is an asset to the entire community as they become aware of the nature of educational therapy and begin to expect these high quality services for all struggling learners.

THE EDUCATIONAL THERAPIST'S SENSE OF HUMOR

I have yet to meet one educational therapist without a sense of humor. If you are that one, you must quickly begin to associate with your colleagues and shortly a sense of humor will emerge. There is an immensely powerful effect from recognizing the humor in a learning situation. I frequently laugh heartily at a novel and surprising response, and my students like to make me laugh. It is understood that laughing is a part of our learning, and a session without a good laugh is rare indeed. At a deeper level, the laughter reflects my strong conviction that these clients, these struggling learners, can become overwhelmed by the sadness of the struggle. If I can give them the gift of lightness and humor, when things look their darkest, I have modeled a tool for them to use independently. I often comment that "learning is a messy business," at the same time I freely share my own enthusiasm for learning and the light that learning can bring into all our lives.

REFERENCES

Association of Educational Therapists. (1999, August). *Association of educational therapists code of ethics.* Los Angeles, CA: Author.

Bernstein, J. H. (1997, November). *A neuropsychologist's view: Going beyond diagnosis to strategies, tactics, tools, and techniques.* AET Annual Conference, San Francisco, CA.

Field, K., Kaufman, E., & Saltzman, C. (1993). *Learning and emotions reconsidered: An international perspective.* New York: Gardner Press.

14

ETHICS AND ETIQUETTE IN EDUCATIONAL THERAPY

Recurrent Ethical Issues in Professional Practice

SUSAN FOGELSON AND ELLEN OPELL

Everyday matters requiring solutions by educational therapists (ETs) do not present themselves in black or white. Rather, there are many recurrent ethical situations that come in shades of gray. It is therefore crucial that all ETs not only have an understanding of what ethical practice is, but also the standards of practice that need be followed on a wider range of ethical issues.

Educational therapy is an interdisciplinary field, thereby requiring that ETs, as case managers, wear many hats and interact with many people. Aside from their individual clients, they communicate with parents and other family members, school personnel, and a variety of allied professionals including psychologists, psychiatrists, neurologists, pediatricians, speech and language therapists, occupational therapists, and others who might be helpful in dealing with their clients' educational difficulties. Educational therapists may work with ages that range from preschool children to adults, and their practices may be in settings that vary from private offices, schools, clinics, and learning centers to hospitals, public agencies, and businesses. The clients that ETs work with may have issues that range from learning disabilities, attention deficit disorder, and processing deficits to problems with executive function, motivation, school anxiety, organization, and study skills. This wide spectrum of ages, settings, and educational issues makes it impossible to anticipate every ethical issue that might arise in the practice of educational therapy. However, it is possible to create a road map to help practitioners first recognize and then navigate more successfully through ethically challenging situations. It should be noted that not all ETs handle these situations in exactly the same manner. Rather, the important thing is for ETs to be made aware of the need to question themselves and have good rationales for why they take the positions they do. Self-awareness, active listening, tact, and diplomacy are crucial components of the "etiquette" of educational therapy. Educational therapists are encouraged to seek the counsel of other experienced ETs when difficult problems arise and they are not certain how best to proceed, akin to a medical, psychiatric, or even business model which utilizes and values the expertise of colleagues.

BUSINESS PRACTICES

Many ETs are expected to be skilled in both formal and informal assessment. However, in the area of assessment, there is no uniformity among states as to which professionals can administer which evaluative tests. Therefore, it is incumbent upon the ET to investigate his or her own state to discover the restrictions, if there are any. Not all ETs do formal testing, but all (need) to be knowledgeable about interpreting psychoeducational evaluations. Some clients arrive with a full file of test results while others have never been evaluated. There are also those whose evaluations are incomplete. Questions arise as to whether a complete battery of formal tests is always necessary and if so, should the referral be to the local school or to an allied professional. Whatever the decision about formal testing, all ETs administer informal clinical evaluations throughout the course of their work with clients. Additionally, the field of educational therapy overlaps to some extent with that of other professionals such as speech and language therapists. Since ETs come into this field from a variety of backgrounds, it is essential that they know which issues they are trained to deal with and which they refer out to allied professionals. "Know thyself" is a crucial mantra of anyone in the field of educational therapy. For example, ETs routinely work with students having difficulty with reading comprehension, poor vocabulary, and written expression and some of these students might be better served by seeing a speech and language therapist instead of, or in addition to, the ET. There are many decisions ETs are required to make about the nature of their practices. Obviously, there are business decisions such as office settings (home or away, clinic, school, or learning center, to name a few), what fees to charge, the length of their sessions, and whether they bill at the beginning or end of each month or receive payment at the end of each session. There is no right or wrong for any of these, but ethical situations could arise as a result of these choices. For example, if the ET bills at the beginning of the month, clients are prepaying for services. If there are cancellations during the month, there is the question of scheduling makeup sessions. What happens if the client and the ET cannot find a mutually agreeable time for the makeup? If the ET receives payment per session and sessions are canceled without appropriate notice, how does the ET bill for these missed appointments? On the other hand, if the ET bills at the end of the month for services already received, there is the possibility of parents being delinquent. How does the ET deal with this? The ET considers these scenarios when formulating billing policies, knowing that these problems are possible. Other business decisions also have ethical components. When ETs begin working with new clients, they have parents sign a Release of Information form and provide a clear policy statement including such items as the length of a session, the fee per session, billing practices, cancelation policy, what the procedure is when the client falls ill and cannot come to a session, and whether there is a makeup policy. Along with providing all this information, it is also *incumbent upon the educational therapist not to promise a cure*. When working with a client and his or her family, the ET is very clear about this. Parents are seeking answers and hope for a child who is struggling and to give them false or unrealistic expectations is unethical.

There are many extenuating circumstances which might inhibit the work ETs do. For example, in K's family there was little follow-through on the plan we created to help with his learning problems. K's parents promised to read with him every night and then life interfered. It was difficult for his parents to work with him without causing arguments and ill feelings. In another family, P did not want to take notes, make flashcards with pictures as cues for spelling words, or help her study for tests. On the other hand, R's parents were too busy to oversee that her homework was placed in her backpack the night before school. The reality is that currently not only are there no cures for learning disabilities, but also ETs work within the world that is, rather than the world they would like. As a result, they teach clients strategies for strengthening their areas of weakness, capitalizing on their areas of strength, understanding their learning styles, coping with their problems, and becoming effective self-advocates. There is no "fairy dust" or quick fix for many of their issues, although understandably many families would like there to be.

Most ETs do not come from business backgrounds, and since they are in a helping profession, they are sometimes uncomfortable charging for the comprehensiveness of their services. This can become an ethical issue if they feel resentful that families are taking advantage of them. ETs need to think through their policies and make sure they explain them clearly to the families they see. Do they charge for telephone time with parents, schools, and the allied professionals they communicate with on behalf of their clients? Are they comfortable taking on low-fee clients? What do they do if parents are constantly late with payments? How do they deal with last minute cancelations? These and similar issues are best dealt with in advance so that the ET/client relationship is not undermined.

I faced this type of situation in my work with M who came to see me when she was in seventh grade. She had problems with executive functioning, impulsivity, time management, and study skills. M did not always hand in her homework, and she rarely spent the necessary time to study for tests. Her parents were not interested in an evaluation for ADD, since they said they had no intention of putting her on medication. As we worked together, it became clear that M's family set few rules for her and acted more like her friends than her parents. I explained to them that it would be helpful if there were some behavioral consequences for her lack of participation in school, suggesting that she could earn the TV, phone, and Internet connection that she already had in her room by doing such things as handing in her homework or completing projects in a timely manner. Unfortunately, they were not willing to have her get mad at them. Although I had a good relationship with M, I found myself getting frustrated because one session a week of educational therapy was meaningless if there was no follow-through at home. To make matters worse, M's parents were constantly late paying my bill. I frequently had to call them to ask for reimbursement, and sometimes they were 2 or 3 months late. I realized that the situation was not conducive to effective work, and I did not want my frustration to turn into resentment of M. I called her parents and told them that if I were to continue working with M, I needed to be paid at the time of service. They agreed to the new financial conditions, but then started randomly canceling appointments. It was clear that they were not committed to the educational therapy, and we mutually decided to terminate.

My experience with T and his family was totally different. When I first started working with T, he was still in elementary school. He was severely dyslexic and had great difficulty with gross motor skills. He was embarrassed about his deficits and received a lot of teasing at school. We were able to qualify him for an individualized education plan (IEP), and he came to me for educational therapy. T was very conscientious; his parents were extremely supportive; and he made good progress.

However, it was clear that he would need educational therapy for the long haul. When T started middle school, his father lost his job. His parents felt that they could no longer afford to bring him to me, but I made the decision to keep seeing him pro bono. It was an informed decision, and I never regretted it because T was such a hard worker and grateful to be able to continue his work with me. When the family's economic condition improved, they again began paying for my services.

The difference in attitudes of these two families helped me come to my decisions about how to proceed. In the first case, the family neither valued my work enough to follow through with suggested interventions nor were they fiscally responsible. I found myself getting resentful and knew I could not continue to work effectively in this situation. In the second case, it was clear that my client and his family were anxious for my support and were willing to do their part to make the educational therapy successful. Although I was not receiving monetary payment from them while they were facing financial problems, I was paid by their gratitude. I was in a place where I could afford to do community service for a deserving family.

Ethical questions also arise when ETs are asked to work with friends' or relatives' children, or with the siblings of their current clients. As a general rule, it is never a good idea to work with the children of friends or relatives. It is too difficult to maintain a purely professional relationship in these instances, and therefore the educational therapy is bound to be comprised. On the other hand, while not highly recommended, it may be possible in some instances to work with the sibling of a client.

However, the ET investigates whether the original client has qualms about "sharing" or fears a potential conflict of interest. That being said, it is probably better for the family to get a different ET to work with the sibling.

SETTING BOUNDARIES

While it is essential for ETs to be both caring and supportive and to foster trust and honesty with their clients and families, it is also crucial that ETs set up professional boundaries for these relationships. The *Code of Ethics* for ETs does not describe rigid guidelines for these boundaries (Association of Educational Therapists, 1999). There are no hard and fast rules prohibiting ETs from sharing information about their own lives, accepting gifts, or attending special functions such as graduations. However, it is imperative that ETs recognize that relationships which become too personal can undermine or contaminate their primary missions with their clients.

Some ETs feel most comfortable adhering to the psychotherapeutic model of keeping very strict personal and professional boundaries. This model is similar to the practice of educational therapy in the United Kingdom, which has been renamed as the practice of *educational psychotherapy*. Others find that accepting small gifts and attending important milestone celebrations when invited do not jeopardize their professionalism. Ethically, the ET considers whether he or she can continue to be objective, remembering always the need to act in the best interest of the client.

I was once asked to join a client's family on their vacation, not in my role as an ET, but rather as an expression of their appreciation for the work I had been doing with their son. Although the invitation was sincere, I knew that this certainly stepped over the boundary of maintaining a professional relationship. I thanked them, but made it clear that this would impact my work, since spending time in this social situation would change the dynamics of our roles.

Early in my career, I made the mistake of working with the child of a close family friend. The educational therapy component of our work together was successful, but the parents were delinquent in paying my final bill and after addressing it with them once, I was not comfortable in pursuing it. I made the decision that the friendship was more important than the money. However, I learned never again to work with friends or family; adding a personal component to the educational therapy relationship can result in sticky situations. There is no question that ETs must be wary of allowing their relationships with parents and other family members to become, or even seem to become, anything less than professional.

SCHOOL

Educational therapists work with clients in a multitude of settings. While they usually see their clients one on one, they do not work in a vacuum. This speaks to the ecocultural aspect of the work (Keogh, 2004) and the person-in-context approach that is central to the work of ETs with children and adolescents in school. School-age clients spend most of their days in classrooms. Therefore, it is important for ETs to forge good relationships with school personnel and the various teachers who are a part of their students' lives. Educational therapists try their best to work cooperatively with everyone at the schools their clients attend and to be seen as allies rather than as adversaries. When ETs contact teachers to let them know they are working with students, most teachers are pleased that there is someone to support what they are doing. However, some feel threatened and concerned that parents do not feel they are doing their jobs adequately. While maintaining good communication and building positive relationships with school personnel are essential for ETs to help their clients receive the best services possible, sometimes tact and diplomacy can only take one so far.

A number of years ago I worked with a client who came to me with severe reading problems. B was in the third grade in his local public school, one that I had not worked with before. Psychoeducational testing confirmed his learning disabilities, and I attended his IEP with his parents. We had no difficulty getting B approved for the IEP, and he was put into a Resource Specialist Program (RSP) class 5 days a week for reading and language arts. After getting a release from B's parents, I called his RSP teacher to introduce myself and let her know that I was seeing B for educational therapy.

I reported the areas that he and I were working on and asked her to keep my phone number in her file. I told her that she should call me with any concerns, and that I would be happy to support her in any way that I could. Usually, when I make this type of phone call, I get warm thanks and assurances of mutual cooperation. This time, however, my call was met with an icy acknowledgment. The RSP teacher sounded very defensive, and I feared that this did not bode well for our ongoing relationship. Unfortunately, I was correct. The next day B's mother telephoned. She told me that she had gotten a call from B's RSP teacher, who questioned why the mother thought she needed to pay for educational therapy while he was in her RSP class. The teacher went on to say that she thought it was a waste of time and money, and that she could recommend a friend of hers who was a good tutor if she felt B needed any additional help. His mother was astonished and told me that she had no intention of stopping educational therapy.

Needless to say, I had a problem. It was clear that no matter how I might try to ingratiate myself with B's RSP teacher, it was not going to help and might only make matters worse. She was the only RSP teacher for grades one through three at that school, and I did not think the problem would improve if I complained to the administration about her behavior. I decided that my best option would be to try an "end run" around the situation. Whenever I felt that something needed to be communicated to the RSP teacher, I would explain to B's mother what to say, and she would in turn speak to the teacher. Obviously this was far from ideal, but it worked well enough, and B had a productive year. I did attend B's next IEP, and since he was starting fourth grade, he was given a different RSP teacher. Fortunately she was much more receptive to collaboration, and I could return to my more traditional role of communicating.

One of the roles that ETs play in the school setting is accompanying parents to IEPs and 504s. Educational therapists serve as advocates with a lower case "a" for families, helping them navigate the system, understand their rights, and interpret test results, as well as making recommendations to the school team for appropriate modifications or accommodations. The better the relationship the ET has established with the school, the more smoothly the process is likely to go. Educational therapists who walk into these meetings expecting confrontations are more likely to have them. However, there are times when it is clear that no matter how cordial or respected the ET is, the IEP process is vulnerable to becoming adversarial. In these cases, it is ethically incumbent upon the ET to recommend that parents find an experienced advocate to represent them. Not only do professional advocates have a better chance of getting the disputed services, but also their involvement helps the ET stay apart from the fray and therefore to preserve a good working relationship with the school in question.

An ethical dilemma can arise when an ET believes that a client is eligible for a 504 designation, but because of all the outside support the client is receiving from the circle of treatment providers, the grades may not indicate that the client meets the mandated qualifications. Does this mean the ET has to recommend to the parents that support should be withdrawn in order for the client to fail and then qualify for appropriate accommodations? Another problem can occur when a client who does qualify for RSP does not want to be pulled from classes and be embarrassed about receiving special services. What does the ET recommend? There is not a "one size fits all" answer to these questions.

INAPPROPRIATE PLACEMENTS

Another role that ETs play regarding schools is in helping parents find the most appropriate placements for their children. The Association of Educational Therapists' *Code of Ethics* states that ETs should "Promote corrective action by school administrators and colleagues when educational resources and placements appear to be inadequate or inappropriate for clients" (AET, 1999, p. 6, Section Two, 3. D.). In order to do this, ETs educate themselves about the schools their clients attend, which requires a certain amount of extra time researching specific issues and the variety of settings in which the client lives and learns. This includes getting information about such things as the school's philosophy, curriculum, student body, faculty, and resources. When a client is struggling, a change in teacher or course level might be warranted to help him or her become more successful. In other cases, the school itself may not be a match for the student.

A number of years ago I worked with a family which was very committed to the highly academic private school their children attended. The two children had been students at this K-12 school since the first grade, and their mother was a member of the school's board. Their son J was referred to me when he started doing poorly in the ninth grade. The older of two brothers, he had done fairly well in elementary and middle school, but he was struggling with the increased difficulty of the academic load in high school. He was very anxious about his low grades, had become quite depressed, and was having problems not only completing his work, but also showing up at school on days he was due to take tests. J was already in psychotherapy, and psychoeducational testing did not show any specific learning disabilities.

As I worked with J, it became clear to me that the pace and demands of his high school program made this school a mismatch. The high school prided itself on frequently using college level novels and texts even in the non-Advanced Placement classes, and J was completely overwhelmed. However, when I broached the possibility of his transferring to a less pressured environment, J's parents were adamantly opposed to the suggestion, and J himself was worried about having to leave his friends at school.

Ethically, I had a dilemma. I needed to respect the wishes of J's parents, even though I disagreed with their decision. But it was also necessary to try to do what was best for J. I told his parents that I would do whatever I could to help him succeed where he was, but that I wasn't comfortable with the expectation that educational therapy alone would solve his problem. We worked together on time management, study skills, and test taking strategies, and he certainly made some progress. I kept in frequent touch with J's psychologist and teachers, and I was able to get him a few accommodations such as being allowed to spread out his tests over the week by going in early or staying late to take them instead of having to face two or three tests in the same day. However, it was far from an ideal situation, and J had little time for doing anything other than spending long hours every day and weekend on school related work.

Over time, J and I developed a close relationship, and he knew I was not only supportive and encouraging, but also that I was honest about how difficult school was for him. As the end of 10th grade approached, J asked me if I would talk to his parents again about changing schools. He did not want to disappoint them, but he was tired of working so hard to just get Cs and not being able to spend time with his friends or participate in extracurricular activities. I suggested that we speak to them together, which we did. I reassured them that J would be able to apply to 4-year colleges even if he attended his local public high school and they were impressed with J's ability to explain his reasons for wanting to transfer. They agreed to look at other schools for him, and J was able to make the change for 11th grade. We continued to work together regularly for a little while to ease his transition, but he was soon able "graduate" to educational therapy on an "as needed" basis. He knew I would always be available for him, but he was in an environment where he could do well on his own.

CRITICAL ISSUES

Ethical questions frequently arise concerning what to do when clients come to sessions wanting to do homework or talk about "burning issues." When ETs first meet with parents, they take comprehensive educational, social, emotional, and medical histories of their clients, and they discuss the presenting problems that have brought these families to seek help. The ET then develops strategies to help remediate these problems, setting short term and long term goals along the way. But as noted before, ETs do not see students in a vacuum. They are not teaching a specific program with iron-clad guidelines that determine the nature and sequence of each session. Rather, they are sensitive to the psychoeducational needs of their students, and this may mean dealing with burning issues that were not on the original lesson plan. The ET makes certain that parents understand this important aspect of educational therapy.

When clients walk into my office, the first thing I do is ask about their day/week and how things have been going. While we are talking, I also look through their backpacks, notebooks, and binders, a process which has been agreed upon at the very first session.

This is a little like a doctor taking a patient's vital signs at the beginning of an examination. The conversation not only sets a supportive mood, but it also lets me know how productive it will be to try to go right into the prepared agenda for our session. If clients are anxious about tests coming up or papers that need to be turned in the next day, it is going to be very difficult to have them concentrate on the planned lessons. Therefore, we first spend time addressing their immediate problems, which may well make them more available for other learning. Sometimes clients will come in with social or emotional issues which are not in the domain of educational therapy. A little time to vent may be all they need, but if things are more serious or take up a lot of time in ensuing sessions, I try to guide them (and their families) to seek more appropriate assistance with allied professionals.

WORKING WITH ALLIED PROFESSIONALS

It is imperative for ETs to recognize their boundaries. Establishing a network of trusted allied professionals provides an important consultation and referral base. It is germane that ETs "Recognize and acknowledge the competencies and expertise of members representing other disciplines as well as those members of their own discipline" (AET, 1999, p. 7, Section Three, 2. A). Mutual respect is crucial when ETs work as members of an interdisciplinary team. This collaborative approach is most often beneficial for the welfare of the client. However, ethical issues can sometimes arise when professionals disagree about the best course of treatment for a client.

This situation arose when N, a student in middle school, was referred to me. The ET he had been working with was moving, and she gave his parents my name. N had been in speech and language therapy, psychotherapy, and educational therapy since the third grade. He had had an IEP in elementary school for language processing difficulties which had been changed to a 504 when he started middle school. N had terminated his sessions with his speech and language therapist by the time I started working with him, but still had great difficulty with reading comprehension, higher level critical thinking skills, and writing.

After several months went by, I began to suspect that in addition to his identified issues, N might also have attention deficit disorder without hyperactivity (ADD). I had a consent form to speak to his psychotherapist whom I did not know. I called her to voice my concerns. I understood that I was the "new kid on the block" and tried my best not to make her feel defensive or that there was something she might have missed, but N's therapist was not open to even considering the possibility that he might have ADD. I did not want to antagonize her, but I felt that ethically it was my responsibility to discuss the issue with N's parents, which I did. I acknowledged to them that I certainly didn't know whether N had ADD, and that his therapist and I had different points of view, but I needed to make them aware of my observations. They were grateful for my concern, but chose not to pursue an evaluation at that time. Sometimes an ET can only sow the seeds and hope they might germinate in the future.

We try to give our best advice, understanding that it may not be followed. N and I continued to work together, and we paid special attention to developing strategies to improve his organizational skills, executive functioning, and active reading capabilities. When N graduated from high school, he went to an out-of-town college, but kept in touch from time to time. After his first year away, he called to tell me that he had made the decision to get an evaluation for attention deficit issues, since concentrating during long lectures and focusing on complicated novels that did not have Spark Notes was making life too difficult for him. He had started taking medication and reported that it was helping.

From time to time, families ask their ETs for their opinions about some of the alternative therapies that do promise cures for their children. It is important that ETs answer with caution. On the one hand, ETs frequently refer parents to reputable allied professionals when they think they can be of benefit to their clients. Similarly, they try to stay as up-to-date as possible with promising new research in the field that may prove valuable. On the other hand, some therapies come onto the market making claims for success that ETs may feel are unsubstantiated or questionable. The dilemma is that while an ET tries to guide the family as honestly as possible, he or she must be careful not to make comments that can lead to lawsuits for restraint of trade. Teaching families to be educated consumers and to know what questions to ask is probably the best way to deal with these situations.

CONFIDENTIALITY

The initial call from a client or his or her family to an ET is a call for help. It is a public admission that someone in the family has a problem. Establishing trust is essential in achieving a successful outcome of educational therapy. Confidentiality is a key component necessary in reaching this goal. Although ETs are not licensed, they do have a responsibility to report any evidence of suspected child abuse. In all other cases, a signed release to receive and give information to other professionals working with the client is imperative. If family members other than the parents are paying for the educational therapy, parents still need to give permission for them to receive information about the client. Educational therapy is a multidisciplinary profession, and consultations with school personnel and allied professionals to collect background information or share concerns about a client are frequently required in order to provide the best services possible. Educational therapists explain to clients their commitment to confidentiality as well as the benefit of appropriate consultations. However, it is the right of the client to determine whether and when this information is shared. One very frustrating experience for me happened when I was working with L, a 10th grader. He was very tenacious and worked extremely hard, putting in long hours and was rewarded with good grades. However, when it came time to take the SATs, he did not perform as well as he had hoped and his mother requested extra time of the SAT Board. This might not have been a problem, but because his mother was adamant about the fact the school should not know that her son had a diagnosed reading processing problem, I was never able to ask the school to give him the appropriate accommodations. I had a very good relationship with the school and was frustrated that I did not have permission to share L's diagnosis with them. There were appropriate accommodations which could have been made so that L did not have to devote the long hours to getting his work done. Because this did not happen, there was no paper trail to use as evidence for the SAT Board. In this case, keeping confidentiality backfired for the client and L did not receive the accommodations he well deserved. Nevertheless, I had to respect my client's wishes regarding confidentiality.

There are times when ETs meet other professionals—educational therapists, speech and language pathologists, psychotherapists, and pediatricians, to name a few—either at social gatherings, professional meetings, or schools, where conversation turns to clients. It is recommended that identifying details or names not be used in these informal settings. We live in a very small world and we never know who knows whom. Sometimes a client may question whether or not a schoolmate also comes to the office. The ET answers that no information is given about any other client. Breaking the code of confidentiality is a breach of ethical conduct, and there can be no indulgence in gossip. This is true when students attend the same school, the same grade or class and when parents know each other. If parents or students choose to talk to each other about their educational therapy, that is their prerogative, and not the right nor option of the ET who is the treatment provider. The ET, as a treatment provider, adheres to the same concept of confidentiality as do professionals in the fields of medicine and psychology. Confidentiality is an ethical concern, not to be confused with the legal concept of "privilege."

Confidentiality when working with teenagers can be especially sensitive. My teenage clients know that what is said in our sessions is confidential *unless* they are doing harm to themselves or others. When one client, who I had been seeing for a long time, shared the fact that he had been doing some very harmful things to his body and that this had been going on for a while, there was no doubt that I had to alert his parents. This was made very clear at our very first session. While it was important that I maintain T's confidence in our relationship, I told him that I would be calling his parents. I asked if he wanted to be part of the conversation. At first he did not want anything to do with it, but as we talked, he rethought his position and agreed that it might be a good idea after all. Since there was a sense of urgency, we were able to schedule a meeting for the next day. Being in the position of an advocate for T, I was able to provide him with the confidence and support he needed when we told his parents what was happening. Needless to say, his parents were very upset and bewildered that they had missed any cues. It was agreed that they would seek counsel from a psychotherapist as quickly as possible. While T was not happy, he understood that this was the way it had to be and was perhaps a bit grateful that he was receiving my support at this difficult time in his life. Not only was the issue of confidentiality at hand, but also the issue of knowing our own professional boundaries. I could be supportive to my client and his family, but it was beyond my training to give him the psychological help he required at this time.

Ethical questions can also arise when an ET is working with a client who is technically an adult (over 18), but whose parents are paying for the therapy. S was a young woman in her middle 20s. I had previously worked with her when she was in high school, but we had not been in touch for more than 5 years. Apparently S had briefly attended junior college after graduation from high school, but she had dropped out after a year and had been working at a succession of low paying retail jobs. She had recently decided that she wanted to go back to school to become an early education school teacher and was concerned about passing the math requirements for her certificate. S's parents had agreed to pay for her educational therapy to help her through her program. We arranged that I would bill her parents at the end of each month and we started working together again.

At first S was very enthusiastic about our sessions together. She came promptly, was well prepared, and seemed quite motivated. She was also doing well in her classes. However, after a few months she became less consistent. At first she would call in advance to cancel sessions, knowing that I have a 24-hour cancelation policy. But then S began to skip sessions without calling. I realized that I faced a dilemma over confidentiality. How could I charge S's parents for missed sessions without letting them know what was happening? And yet, did that compromise my client's confidentiality? I spoke to S about my predicament, and she acknowledged that she was ambivalent about being back in school. We decided together that she probably wasn't ready to make the commitment necessary and that she needed to let her parents know what was happening. We talked about the possibility of her getting some psychotherapy, and I also gave her a referral to a vocational counselor who might help her with some career guidance. Finally, I assured S that I would be happy to work with her again in the future if she needed my assistance.

PARENT ISSUES

Although the primary work is with clients, ETs can spend many hours talking to, calming, and advising parents. Developing trust and maintaining effective communication with parents is vitally important to the successful treatment of their children. The hour or two a week that ETs work with clients is time spent in learning new methods and strategies for dealing with their problems. Implementing these strategies can be another matter though. It is extremely helpful if parents can be and are willing to participate in this journey. If they can be supportive without being antagonistic or punitive, it is possible that progress can be achieved more quickly. On the other hand, there are situations when parents' involvement can be problematic. Sometimes parents are angry, anxious, in denial, sabotaging, or disorganized. They may have a lack of understanding or appreciation of the learning differences and styles of their children which can cause upset and perhaps hostility in the household. The ET wants parents to be knowledgeable about goals and the plan to achieve them, but is cognizant that sometimes appropriate help may not be provided at home. There are parents who would rather drop off and pick up their children and not be personally involved. They have a "*you* fix it" mind-set. My client J had such parents. Not only did they drop her off, but they honked the horn when it was time for her to leave. I tried to call and inform them of our progress, but there was little interest. I tried to arrange a conference time when we could discuss what was happening, but there was never the right time. After a while, I gave up trying to involve her parents and acknowledged to myself that J and I both knew we were making strides which were evidenced in better school grades. I felt bad for J because it also reflected an attitude at home, but there was not much I could do about it and continued to encourage her and tell her how proud I was of her success. I did, however, make sure that there was one scheduled meeting to evaluate our progress at the end of each year.

The other side of the coin is the parent who has boundary issues. He or she feels comfortable calling daily. This is the way V's mom behaved. She called almost every day to discuss problems that happened in the classroom, concerns about the teacher, the fact that there was too much homework and V had to stay up too late, the work was too hard, and anything else she could remember. I began to resent her phone calls and became concerned that this was influencing my attitude toward V. I discussed this with my peer review group and decided on a plan. I asked V's mom to keep a journal and write down whatever concerned her instead of calling me. Then we made an appointment after 5 days to discuss her entries. This was very helpful and after a relatively short period of time, she waited a week and then 2 weeks before she felt the need to call and share this information with me. It was important for V's mom to have a way to express herself and begin to prioritize her issues. She learned a coping strategy and was better able to step back and give her daughter the opportunity to grow and become more independent. Thus, not only did my feelings toward my work with V improve, but as V watched her mother recede into the background, she became more confident which showed in her attitude toward school.

DIVORCE

Dealing with families who have either gone through or are in the throes of a divorce can present difficult scenarios and challenges to the ET. It is important that the ET "Recognize that the relationship of home and community environmental conditions affect the behavior and outlook of the client" (AET, 1999, p. 5, Section Two, 2. E). This is particularly important in cases where clients are dealing with the effects of their parents' divorces. There are instances when, while both parents may believe the interests of their child is paramount, their own inability to communicate with each other can cause extremely stressful situations. Joint parent meetings with the ET may or may not occur. It is possible that separate meetings may be necessary with the understanding that each parent is being given the same information. It can also happen that the parents have very different perspectives concerning their child and educational therapy. The ET needs to be aware not to "choose sides" regardless of personal feelings because the ET's prime allegiance is to the child and has to remain objective. An example of this occurred, when due to a joint custody arrangement, E spent parts of each week with each parent. Feelings were so volatile between the parents that a driver was hired to take E from one house to another in order to prevent face-to-face meetings between the mother and father. E's mother was not so sure that there was enough progress being made in our educational therapy sessions, while his father was very encouraged and supportive. It was important for me to have communication with both parents, even though I found it difficult to speak with his mother. Because E spent more school days at Dad's house, I would receive phone calls from his father asking if I would please tell E's mother that there was a book report to be written or a portion of a project to be completed on "her" weekend. Dad felt as if he was always the task master and Mom's home was the place for fun. I became the intermediary, helping E learn how to manage his world, understand his parents' limitations, and take more responsibility for himself.

Ideally, it is extremely valuable when divorced mothers and fathers understand the importance of parental cooperation. In the case of S, knowing that his parents were in agreement and would follow the same routine eliminated confusion and provided structure. There were two sets of books in case one was forgotten at the other house, and both parents were aware of S's activities and projects at school, determining with each other who was responsible for which part. Both parents arrived at our conferences so there was no confusion. They were both aware of their roles and were equally pleased when S showed progress and more responsibility.

Although divorces are difficult in the best of circumstances, when parents fight over child custody, it becomes even more toxic for the children. Sometimes the parents try to pull the ET into the middle of the battle, which creates ethical issues for the therapist. When R first came to me for educational therapy, he was basically a nonreader entering second grade. He had tremendous anxiety about school and also showed definite signs of poor attention, impulsiveness, and distractibility. I referred R for a psychoeducational evaluation, which confirmed that he was dyslexic and had ADHD. The parents, who were still married at the time, had very different attitudes about how best to respond to R's problems. His mother accepted my recommendations that we try to get an IEP for R, and that he see a psychiatrist to evaluate the possibility of going onto medication. His father was not happy with either suggestion, stating that in his opinion R was just lazy, needed to work harder, and would probably feel worse about himself if he was treated "differently" from the "normal" kids at school. I did my best to assuage the father's fears, and when he reluctantly agreed to the treatment plan, R began to make progress at school.

When R was in the sixth grade, his mother called to inform me that she and her husband were getting a divorce, and it was clear that it was going to be a very acrimonious one. They had already started to live separately, and their methods of parenting were totally different. According to Mom, she was the disciplinarian who made sure that R took his medication, did his homework, went to bed at a reasonable time, and generally followed her house rules. She reported that Dad was happy for R to skip his medication and paid little attention to making sure that R stayed up to date with his school work. Dad, in turn, felt that Mom was too strict and that R didn't need medication anyway. Both parents were applying for physical custody of R, and the mother wanted me to testify in her behalf at the hearing.

Ethically, I had some problems. I had an opinion about which home environment would be better for R, but it was important that I not alienate his father, who only grudgingly accepted the need for educational therapy at all. I wanted to have open lines of communication with both parents, and hoped that over time I might be able to help modify Dad's position. I told the mother that I could only testify as to what type of home environment would best meet R's educational needs, but that I could not talk specifically about which parent he should live with. She was satisfied with that explanation, and I did receive a phone call from a representative of the court and gave my recommendations.

Ultimately, R's parents were awarded joint physical custody. Although this was far from ideal for an ADHD student, since traveling back and forth between houses meant that he frequently didn't have the right materials in the right places, but R gradually learned to adjust to his situation. As he got older, he was able to become more of a self-advocate, and since he enjoyed getting good grades, he learned to be responsible for his own medication when he was at his father's house.

TERMINATION

There are no hard and fast rules about the ideal time for termination of educational therapy services. This transitional stage should be based on criteria established mutually between client/parent and therapist. Some of the clients ETs work with may need just a year or two of educational therapy before they no longer need support. Others may stop for a while and then return when they move on to the next level, from elementary to middle school or middle to high school. Still others will probably need services for as long as they are in a school environment. In an ideal termination, the ET and family are both satisfied that the client has met the agreed upon goals, but leave the door open for returning in the future if necessary. However, ethical issues can arise when the termination is less than ideal.

Sometimes the ET may feel that a client is ready for termination, but the parents are not ready to let go. In these cases, the ET tries to explain the reasons why ending therapy is deemed to be appropriate. But if parents remain overanxious about stopping, it may be best for the ET to continue for a while, since the parents' anxiety may create too much pressure on clients and undermine their self-confidence. Gradually cutting back on sessions and eventually going onto an "as needed" basis is a way to ease the transition. When families understand that the ET is not deserting them, they may feel more reassured.

In other instances, although continued educational therapy may be advisable, a client may need the services of one or more allied professionals as well. While ETs often work in collaboration with other professionals, parents may have limited financial resources. There is also the issue of time. As younger clients get older, they are often confronted with many more commitments such as attending religious school and participating in sports. Sports particularly are areas where clients may be able to perform better than they do in the classroom, thus raising their self-esteem. As a result, all of these activities compete for the few hours available after school. The ET's role is important in helping the family to prioritize and pursue treatment for the most pressing issues first. If educational therapy was stopped prematurely, the client can return to in the future.

Termination may be necessary if the educational therapy is just not working. This may be due to a mismatch between the ET and client, in which case a referral to another ET is appropriate. It may be necessary if an ambivalent family sabotages the educational therapy with frequent canceled sessions, late arrivals, and the like. In this case, the ET needs to confront the parents and speak frankly about the problem to see if the relationship can be salvaged. Finally, termination may be warranted if a client (typically a teenager) does not want to be in educational therapy at all and is being forced to attend by his or her parents. It may be possible for the ET to gradually break through this resistance, but if it continues over time, it may be best to acknowledge that it would be a waste of time and money to continue.

I had this type of problem with M, who was brought to me the summer after he failed his junior year of high school English. Testing showed no evidence of specific learning disabilities, but although M was bright, he did have difficulties with reading comprehension, written expression, and poor vocabulary that prevented him from doing as well as he might. His solution to his frustration with school had been to do as little work as possible. He did not study for tests, turn in his homework regularly, or make any effort on his papers, thus earning him a trip to summer school and my office. When M came for his first session with me, he looked sullen and annoyed because he had to humor his parents by showing up or else he would lose his car keys. I chose to be very straight with him and told him what I could and could not do to help teach him strategies to deal with his learning problems. I also informed him that if after a few sessions it seemed like I was working harder than he was, I would tell his parents that it was not worth our continuing. M was quite taken aback by my comments, but it did shake him out of his "attitude." We worked together successfully over the summer, but he was not anxious to continue our sessions in the fall. I counseled both M and his parents that perhaps a less rigorous senior year schedule with an eye toward junior college would probably be most effective for him, not because he did not have ability, but because he did not yet have the motivation necessary to work up to his potential. I frequently see junior college students in my practice who are joys to work with, but who admit that they would not have taken advantage of educational therapy if parents had forced them to attend when they were in high school.

Occasionally, parents will decide to terminate when the ET does not think it is advisable. In such cases, the ET tries to find out their reasons for wanting to leave. If there is a financial problem, perhaps some arrangement could be worked out. If they are unhappy with their child's progress, perhaps they have unrealistic expectations. The ET can offer to make referrals to other ETs and try to schedule a final session with the client to have some closure if possible. It is important for ETs to realize that no matter how hard they try, not every case will end successfully. Acting professionally at all times and keeping their clients' best interests at heart is the ethical thing to do.

CRITICAL ISSUES FOR EDUCATIONAL THERAPISTS

Self-awareness is crucial to the ethical practice of educational therapy. It is helpful for ETs to "seek assistance, including the services of other professionals, in instances where personal problems threaten to interfere with their job performance" (AET, 1999, p. 3, Section One, 2. F). Educational therapists are in the profession of helping others, which is admirable. However, it is important for them to acknowledge that they are human and, as such, sometimes face their own personal issues which may have a negative impact on their work. In these cases, ETs can best help their clients by getting help themselves. Peer supervision and consultations with appropriate professionals can be of great benefit in ensuring that these difficulties do not sabotage their professional effectiveness.

Just as ETs teach their clients strategies to optimize performance, using coping strategies themselves is important. Overscheduling and poor time management can lead to therapist burn-out. There can be instances where an ET and client might be a bad fit, even though the ET is trained to work with the client's age group and learning problem. Honest introspection at times like these encourages the therapist to refer to a colleague who would be a better match. Some ETs prefer to work exclusively with younger or older clients, while others enjoy working across a broad spectrum of age groups. Educational therapists benefit from an awareness of the client hours they can successfully manage without creating an overload of work for themselves, taking into consideration the additional time necessary for phone calls, meetings, and preparation before sessions. There is no one right way to organize a practice. Rather, it is most important that ETs are both competent and comfortable with the range of ages and types of learning issues they chose to deal with.

CONCLUSION

The field of educational therapy works in the domain of education; however, ETs are not tutors or just teachers. Sessions not only address the client's learning differences and styles, but also the learning environment. As case managers, ETs not only work with their clients and families, but also with schools and other professionals that impact their lives. Discovering why clients are experiencing problems in the psychoeducational arena and deciding on how best to help them is what makes the field so complex. The AET *Code of Ethics* provides an important guide to the ethical practice of educational therapy. However, ETs also need to be prepared to cope with the ethical dilemmas that do not have black or white solutions. Because of these gray areas, it is important even for veteran ETs to seek peer supervision when confronted with difficult ethical situations. Additionally, attending conferences, workshops, courses, and study groups for continuing education is essential for keeping up with current research, both in educational therapy and in related fields. In this way, ETs can best adhere to the principles of "protecting and enhancing the fundamental dignity of every person seeking their services," and "developing the highest educational potential of their clients" (AET, 1999, p. 2, Principles, I).

REFERENCES

Association of Educational Therapists (AET). (1999, August). *Code of ethics.* Los Angeles, CA: Author.

Keogh, B. (2004, October 22). *Different perspectives on "differences."* Paper presented at the AET 27th Annual National Conference, San Francisco, CA.

15

THE COLLABORATION BETWEEN EDUCATIONAL THERAPY AND MENTAL HEALTH PROFESSIONALS

Case Study Analyses

BEVERLY METCALF, MICKEY KIRAR ASHMUN, AND NATALIE O'BYRNE

INTRODUCTION

Each new developmental period within the lifespan provides the opportunity to master situations never before encountered. To the unfolding child, each new challenge may feel temporarily like a crisis; however, from these experiences a new piece of the self emerges, new coping mechanisms develop, and new skills are mastered. In each new period, with its opportunities and challenges, children use skills acquired while progressing through earlier developmental periods in an epigenetic fashion. Each stage leads to changes and a new slate of abilities. The child can cope with just enough information and experiences to master appropriate new skills and to move on to the external and internal demands of the ensuing stage. At the same time, the sheer pleasure of learning drives the child on through these learning cycles.

The authors propose that learning occurs in a neurologically and psychologically predictable manner affected by inner developmental stages as well as environmental stimulation. No matter what is presented at each developmental level, the challenge initially is met with confusion simply because the situation has never been experienced before. At this point, the child needs to reorganize and develop new coping skills. These new abilities, in turn, lead to effective learning. This releases new energy for approaching the next challenge level. Each stage is thus met with a sense of mastery propelling the child forward to continued learning.

However, when confronted with the confusion accompanying new learning, some children experience a sense of helplessness that may develop into a sense of hopelessness with its accompanying symptoms. Educational therapists work with these children because of their learning problems, but these children will need additional support to face and conquer their anxieties and fears about learning. An ET intervention usually revolves around setting limits on the confusion by using a specially designed remedial program and by providing the structure needed. What the ET does is design a set of parameters that serve to decrease the anxiety and despair so that the child can remain accessible to new learning. All children want to master, it is as innate a need as nurturance, and, once the presented material has been mastered, the child will experience new energy which can be applied to the challenges of a subsequent developmental level.

An emotional component to a child's learning process always exists, if only because the child is using undeveloped or inadequate skills to organize the world at the same time this real world is creating challenges. Children with learning disabilities—or psychological issues that impede the use of otherwise natural skills—are particularly susceptible to suffering setbacks in their regular progress from confusion to integration. Nevertheless, emotional factors, though ever present, are rarely the prime factor we deal with in an educational therapy practice. Even though children have had frustrated learning experiences, we educational therapists have an armamentarium of techniques to help our students over the hurdles of shame and guilt that may have led to their referrals in the first place.

We make use of basic psychological principles such as Maslow's motivation theory and Vygotsky's scaffolding process, where we determine and then provide the needed steps to conquer a task, and control, where we provide a therapeutic amount of authoritative direction while still helping the clients see the sessions as their own (Miller, 2001). We determine what is possible and start from there, making the students leaders in their own remediation. We demonstrate how students can do the required work a different way, their way, so they can feel the competency and mastery they need to spur on their growth and development. The bulk of our case load is comprised of willing children, longing to succeed, easily relating, and trusting us to be of help. Effective remediation relies on proper evaluation of needs, the sound planning for a remedial program, and the involvement of those others in the child's life who command some place in the decision-making process; usually this is simply the parents and the school.

At times, however, an ET must work in a more complicated setting, where the given child's drive to persist and to learn is thwarted. A child's resistance to learning is a "red flag" that something is askew within that child's world and that it is necessary to assess where the trouble lies. Most often, the identification process begins with the school. Three vignettes to follow are examples of children with whom all three authors worked. The children initially were identified by their schools and then referred for outside assessment and support.

THE CASE OF ANDREW

The ET at Andrew's school was asked to evaluate him in kindergarten because, in spite of efforts to engage him, he was persistent in his behavior of turning his back on the class and on all challenging activities. Because so many variables appeared to be interfering with his learning, the school appraisal was followed by an outside assessment completed by a child therapist, child psychologist, learning specialist/ET, neurologist, and speech/language specialist. All saw Andrew's school problem as an inability to overcome his personal fears in order to join his teacher and peers and persist at necessary school routines. The child psychologist and the child therapist were troubled by Andrew's very harsh and crippling judgment of himself, most likely associated with that of his very harsh "perfectionist" mother (her word). The speech/language specialist, neurologist, and ET pointed to Andrew's slow use of his sensory skills when needed in combination for the integrated work required in school. (Although his visual/motor integration was fine, he had difficulty with the auditory/visual integration that would be required to deal with the alphabet, reading, and spelling.) All of these points of view were valid, and this meant that Andrew would need help to stay on task and to master assignments, and that this help was needed in school, in play therapy, and in educational therapy.

Although a regular case management plan was not established because at the time of evaluation each professional's part in the arrangement was determined, with permission and encouragement from Andrew's parents, communication remained excellent among the team serving Andrew. Scheduled meetings were less valuable than quick phone calls when something unusual occurred, each call motivated by need for communication rather than by an established schedule. Otherwise, as arranged by school personnel, the team reviewed Andrew's intervention plan at the end each school year. It is important to note that this group of professionals had worked together before and with the school and a working, trusting relationship already existed, essential if such a complex, long-term intervention is to succeed.

Both private sessions with Andrew and the pull-out program at the school were slow in their progress. The one thing all the work had in common was Andrew's clear reluctance to make mistakes. He didn't learn from them; they depleted him. Throughout the sessions he seemed constantly fearful, testing whether, if he made errors, he could count on others to be there for him. Early on, this was observed in his attempts to flee the room while at the same time making minimal efforts to escape one's restraints. Whether it was a physical or mental "escape," the attachment cry of, "If you love me, you will control me, and you will help me learn" was evident to all those who worked with him.

Andrew always seemed torn between his need to protect himself from the danger of failing and his wish to find comfort in a learning setting made accessible with the aid of scaffolding, which provided a way that he could perform successfully and a place for him to do so; this could be modified as his needs changed. For example, in his educational therapy hours the ET encouraged him to process classroom material through the involvement of his phenomenal sketching and cartooning abilities. Gradually, over the years, although maintaining this talent, he also dared to do the standard classroom work as assigned. He became able to mount a second effort after difficulties and, later on, to do so on his own. In spite of doubts and frustrations, he proceeded to perform to the point that his schoolwork became acceptable in his highly challenging school and led to acceptance into the best high schools in the area.

Sometimes the resistance that flags the school's attention is interpreted as antisocial behavior. In George's case, the referral for an evaluation turned things completely around.

THE CASE OF GEORGE

George had been an A and B student in his school until the big shift into sixth grade where he began to earn Cs along with dreadful comments about his behavior. George's performance and school behavior continued to worsen through sixth and seventh grade. Because George was uncooperative and not admitting to his erratic performance, the school felt that George might have some underlying psychological concerns and they referred the parents for consultation with an expert in emotional development of adolescents. That mental health specialist, in turn, recommended a full evaluation that would include educational testing, neurological evaluation, and psychological assessment.

Again, the three authors were working together and were fascinated to learn how these evaluations complemented each other: George had impressive verbal skills, average visual understanding, but a great deal of difficulty with visual/motor tasks that required memory and organization. In spite of his good verbal skills, his written expression was scant and disorganized in the educational testing. He earned low scores in the psychologist's visual/motor tasks: the WISC-III's Coding subtest (also involving speed), and Object Assembly (also involving organization). His work on the Bender Gestalt, which combined the need for visual/motor and organization skills, was very slow.

Although prior to sixth grade his school performance had been excellent, handwriting, written expression, lengthy term reports, and homework requiring planning and organization, all common challenges in middle school, were far beyond George's skill level. It was clear there was a neurological basis for George's frustration and resistance, and that this would in turn affect his psychological state. It is important to note that many bright, highly verbal children like George, who handle the challenges of their early school years so easily, are overwhelmed when they enter this new developmental stage where executive function tasks are assigned and orderly work required, and they now find themselves failing.

In addition to the other findings, the fact that George was not antisocial was evidenced in his responses to the psychologist's projective tests and in his very cooperative manner in both educational and neurological testing and mental health evaluation sessions. This was a boy who cared dearly about what others thought of him. Because of his fear of failure, he avoided doing certain types of work. This meant that George's behavior had quite different motivation from that of an antisocial adolescent's and should be handled differently.

George needed psychotherapy and educational therapy but for a brief time only. Both interventions involved helping George understand his learning style and his strengths as well as weaknesses, so that he could feel self-respect again. In the educational therapy, he was helped to improve his keyboarding skills and to learn to use tools to aid planning and organization. With no strong reasons to resist, George quickly achieved the needed skills that had not developed automatically because of his learning differences. This bright boy became very adept at using strategies taught to him in his educational therapy work and he gloried in his successes and his mastery. At this age he took great pleasure in his real skills and achievements, and this all contributed to his emotional and ideological individuation. In this brief period, George went from being an eighth grade student about to be expelled from a school he had attended all his school life to being a strong, happy, contributing academician, well liked by his peers and teachers. Note that in order to understand him and know what kinds of interventions George required (other than expulsion!) the school needed the points of view of four outside professionals.

In the situations with Andrew and George, school referrals for evaluation eventuated in the parents' acceptance of all recommended interventions (educational therapy and psychotherapy). Caroline is another child whose needs (though less apparent) were assessed psychologically, neurologically, and academically. She and her parents then saw the psychiatrist in counseling and therapy, and Caroline saw an ET for 5 years:

THE CASE OF CAROLINE

Caroline was a second grade student when she was tested and began remediation. She was a worried, vigilant child, extremely alert to the wishes of others and to whatever she interpreted as signs of approval or disapproval. She was confused by new visual material such as the meaning of placement of numbers for math and the nonverbal routines of her second grade classroom. Her educational therapy sessions aimed at helping Caroline to learn to use words (her strength) to understand otherwise daunting visually presented tasks.

During her early sessions Caroline spent an inordinate amount of time seeking ways to make the ET happy (e.g., massaging her shoulders, bringing her flowers picked outside, etc.). This is sometimes a signal that the child feels a need to care for others because of insecure support at home, and, indeed, Caroline had a depressed, needy mother whose interactions with her daughter led to a reversal in caretaker roles. Although this vigilance meant that she learned a great deal in her first year in order to please the ET, there were serious concerns of her ever being able to learn for her own sake. Her emotions were not on the surface. Instead of anger or resistance, the ET was the recipient of a level of sweetness that was seriously questionable and discomforting.

It was not until the second year in educational therapy that Caroline began to understand and accept the fact that she needed help and could count on the ET to give this to her. Words like, "You know I am here to help you. Let's talk about what we can do together that might help with schoolwork" were used to make it clear that the ET understood Caroline's needs even if Caroline failed to recognize/acknowledge them herself. Note that the ET's words were delivered as statements, not questions, so that no response was required; if questioned, Caroline might have felt she needed to deny what the ET was saying. The ET always followed such words with suggestions of work to do, and later on, as she changed in her ability to trust and accept help, Caroline eagerly came to sessions with a list of things to accomplish. Even later, with no prompting from the ET, Caroline prioritized tasks in regard to time.

About this time Caroline's school was planning for the fourth grade; they had a policy of providing extra school support for their academic struggling students during the period most students took a foreign language. When Caroline adamantly insisted she wanted to take French and get her help from the ET after school, it was clear that she had become self-motivated learner. At a conference, the school personnel, the ET, the child therapist, and the parents agreed to support this arrangement, and all were pleased about Caroline's newfound sense of self-worth, a necessary step for true learning. (Incidentally, Caroline was very successful with spoken French and later spent her college sophomore year in Paris.)

Caroline's subtle resistance was not a consciously chosen way to minimize the combination of neurological and psychological issues causing her learning problems. She simply had found a way to please and propitiate and to appear to be an uninhibited learner. Yet, when so much of her time was spent in concern for the ET's comfort, she could not actively invest in her own learning. It was apparent that Caroline was not using these interpersonal techniques to deliberately avoid the remedial work; she was behaving in a way that she felt would ensure her relationship with the ET. In contrast, the ET's goal was to make Caroline comfortable and secure about her own performance, enough so that she could learn for herself and not for the ET. One would usually find such beginnings of autonomy and individuation around age 2, but because of Caroline's precarious relationship with her mother, she had remained overdependent on the opinions of others. If she was to progress, it wasn't better grades she needed but a more self-directed and fulfilling approach toward her own learning.

In our three vignettes thus far, the work of the ET has not been solitary. From the beginning, cooperation between the school, the mental health practitioner, and the ET provided a sound foundation. In Andrew's case his resistance was extreme and resembled panic, but all of the professionals worked together to deal with it. In George's case what initially appeared to his school as antisocial behavior was his means of avoiding the overwhelming school tasks, and fortunately the team was able to determine George's real needs. In Caroline's case her resistance was motivated by a need to find approval for her own worth, and suggested past disruptions in her individuation process.

In the preponderance of cases, the authors maintain that the professional skills of the ET alone are adequate to deal with the learning difficulties and also to deal with the school, the parents, and the inevitable resistance to change found everywhere. However, the cases of Andrew, George, and Caroline are examples where a team of professionals was necessary. The following two vignettes are examples of resistance that threatened the success of the educational therapy, and the ET was forced to work alone. Such cases develop in complexity, yet begin so subtly that the ETs are "trapped" before they have barely assessed the problem. At that point, it is difficult to set up a team.

THE CASE OF JEROME

Jerome was a slender, freckle-faced first grader referred by his school for a full evaluation because of inattention and learning issues. The family had followed through with a single assessment by a psychologist and in turn had brought Jerome for educational therapy, ignoring both the psychologist's recommendation for counseling and a school request for an evaluation of ADHD by a pediatric specialist. When ETs accept a case like this, they must be alert to the resistance already there. This doesn't mean immediate confrontation is called for, but it does point out that some form of resistance can be expected in the future and that successful educational therapy will probably require some understanding of the parents' reluctance.

The psychologist's report supported the fact that Jerome was having trouble with the beginnings of reading and writing complicated by an impulsive style, evidence of anxiety and depression, and the tendency to externalize his anger. The school interpreted this as a problem of both perception and attention. In addition Jerome's mother shared with the ET that she herself had faced early school difficulties and that she was not happy with the way Jerome's learning challenges were being addressed at school. She added that she thought the classroom teacher was being insensitive. All of this information suggested this was more than a reading and writing issue.

In the first and second educational therapy sessions Jerome separated rather easily from his mother. However, by the third session he began to fight the separation. His mother was invited to stay a short while and then leave; the ET saw this as an opportunity to demonstrate those academic tasks she might follow through with at home. However, during each ensuing session Jerome demanded his mother remain a longer time and this escalated to where he was unwilling to work unless she remained present throughout the full session.

Concurrent with the educational therapy sessions, the ET helped the parents locate a pediatric specialist who evaluated ADHD and whose costs would be covered by medical insurance. The parents remained ambivalent about the need for counseling in spite of the ET's efforts to encourage it. At a school conference arranged by the parents, the pediatric specialist recommended a trial of medication. It was also learned that Jerome was cooperating in the small structured group in the resource room but doing little except wandering in the regular classroom; and that even though he loved baseball he was having conflicts with his baseball coach.

Around this time, when arriving for the educational therapy sessions, Jerome frequently refused to get out of the car, so this became the new place for negotiation. The end of the school year was approaching. It was agreed Jerome would have two more sessions. Jerome's father told Jerome if he cooperated fully in these sessions they would attend a major league baseball game together. However, when brought by his mother for the next session, Jerome refused to get out of the car. Reminded that he would forfeit his ball game, he responded, "No I won't. He'll take me anyway."

The last session was a meeting with Jerome, his father, and the ET. Jerome was compliant and on task. The ET demonstrated summertime reading materials, and both father and son agreed to tackle these. However, at the end of the summer Jerome's mother returned the obviously unused materials. The ET facilitated locating another ET closer to home, but later it was learned that when the new arrangement was attempted Jerome refused to get out of the car, so the contract was terminated.

"If you love me you will control me." Jerome had not found that he could trust the guidance and limits set by his parents; instead, he created a partial sense of safety by arranging the learning situation for himself. The limits Jerome set may have felt emotionally necessary to him, but at the same time they produced even more anxiety and sabotaged something else he desperately wanted and needed in order to move forward in his development: mastery of academic skills.

Educational therapists do work with such children and parents and at times can furnish the support needed to keep such a child on task. However, until parents such as Jerome's are ready to examine their own ambivalence, an ET can set rules for the child but compliance constantly will be undermined by the child's own concerns and anxieties. The parents needed to follow through on the psychologist's recommendation for counseling. Alternatively, the pediatric specialist, in addition to beginning a trial of ADHD drug therapy, could have addressed the connection between Jerome's behavior issues and the parents' inconsistent limit setting. Finally, the ET might have insisted earlier on in the year's work that the parents needed to find a way to help Jerome accept the educational therapy. This was not just one year in Jerome's life; it was a very important developmental period in which a child becomes conscious of the difference between industry and inferiority. Although Jerome wished to avoid ridicule and embarrassment, he could have benefited from the relationship with an empathic ET helping him to persist at overcoming obstacles.

Sometimes it is particularly necessary for an ET to be aware of how the relationship with a child is confusing the needed progress. The following work with Judy introduced feelings, questions, and doubts that made it necessary for the ET to reevaluate her contract and think of ways to correct an ineffective work plan. This is an example of the ongoing planning and replanning that must take place when encountering resistance.

THE CASE OF JUDY

Judy was a 13-year-old middle school girl almost ready for high school but with a learning difficulty that compromised her math and science performance. She was referred for help in learning how to use her strong verbal skills to approach nonverbal subject matter instead of allowing her initial visual confusion to overwhelm her. From the beginning of their sessions the ET accepted Judy's reluctant presence because the ET understood that much behavior at this age is conflictual, driven by the need to individuate but compromised by the need for support. The ET felt over time Judy would come to trust the ET's sincerity and to understand that these sessions were designed to point out Judy's many strengths and to offer ways to use them for achievement in school, something Judy herself wished for.

Nevertheless, Judy's passive presence was a distinct red flag that she was fighting the work. She would behave as though no one had been talking to her, showing her something, or expecting a response from her. The ET's reaction, that of believing/hoping Judy just needed to give it a little more time, was typical, and time passed with the ET pondering the issue of how long she would find herself talking to Judy rather than with Judy. Was this helpful, a means of demonstrating empathy, to continue to put up with her obstinacy? Or was it more important to be direct and specific, to face Judy with the necessity to look at the behavior interfering with the remediation of her math and science confusion?

To begin with, the ET might remind herself that the time spent just sitting with Judy, understanding the resistance, can be an important therapeutic intervention. No words are needed except those used to encourage the student back to work, but the melody of the words needs to be empathic. Change is difficult, even worthwhile change. New challenge brings initial confusion and at this point may lead to helplessness and even hopelessness. However, through a relationship with a supportive figure such as the ET, the child can be helped to integrate a new experience and develop a new skill. This is a major part of the ET's work: to be there when needed and eventually to have the student, not the ET, be the one to manage confusion. The self-doubters like Judy, who present with such a false adolescent bravado and disdain, long for a modicum of effective support as they face daunting challenges of learning while becoming their own person. The experienced ET sees through the facade to the neediness and realizes that even at this age the cry is, "If you love me you will help me learn...and you will also help me individuate."

When no other developmental information is available, an ET might formulate an understanding of how important it is for a client Judy's age to find real achievement. For this reason, she may not need just support, but also a new involvement. The ET might need to find the "right" time, when both the ET and Judy seemed ready, to discuss a new contract, one in which Judy took more responsibility for her behavior during the sessions and for her own learning. Meanwhile, there is a healing quality to sitting with someone who is in conflict.

At times we work with students who have a good deal of supportive help during the early developmental stages so that they appear quite capable of progressing in the academic world. Nevertheless, the ET can often be the quiet listener to stories of past difficulties that remain in the person's emotional world from long before, in another developmental period. The cognitive skills of the formal operations stage do not negate the leftover fears of ridicule and embarrassment of the 6-year-old. One author recalls a husky football player from a high school team bursting into tears when telling of having to repeat second grade (something his parents had said he handled with no apparent concern at the time). Another ET reports her experience of a talented college student whose recollections of elementary school still could lead to his total disintegration. Margo is an example of a learning disabled child who, in spite of her wonderful progress, continued to need all of the skills of an ET.

THE CASE OF MARGO

Margo's auditory processing and expressive language difficulties were identified in kindergarten. During elementary school, she received both intensive computer-based interventions and remedial help from a speech/language specialist. In addition, she received academic support through middle school from a reading specialist.

Socially, Margo remembers those years as painful. "I didn't have any friends." However, an only child, she was close to her parents and part of a busy, active extended family. Her parents, both psychologists, understood the plasticity of the growing brain. They also knew that at this time in her life Margo's attachment needs included "love me, control me, and help me learn."

When Margo graduated from middle school, she and her parents located an alternative high school in the same county. Margo was an artist and particularly a photographer. In this independent high school, arts were more integrated into daily work than in traditional high schools. The high school also routinely accommodated its students by encouraging the use of a laptop computer and providing extended time on tests. Margo did well, both socially and academically. Her parents' one major concern was that she may not be developing study skills required to be effective in more traditional, "language-loaded" upper level classes; for example, taking in and thoroughly processing lecture and text information in a way that prepared her for tests.

Margo entered educational therapy the second half of her junior year. Margo's goals were knowledge and self-advocacy about her own learning style and also appropriate academic skills and strategies; for example, note taking. It was immediately apparent that Margo was in that wonderful developmental period Piaget called "formal operations" in which her frontal lobes had developed and, as Margaret Mahler would have pointed out, she was becoming strong both in emotional and ideological terms. Although if overloaded by only partially processed language she still could be vulnerable, she also could radiate pleasure in a realistic sense of self and in her achievement. While working together with the ET on assignments, she regularly sought her own "voice," often quirky, playful, but always grounded in a desire to accomplish the task.

Margo seemed a "dream student" to the ET not because she learned particularly easily, but because she put up almost no resistance to breaking down tasks and to incorporating sometimes time-consuming strategies. In addition, she was able to be vulnerable, sharing memories such as her sense of isolation and lack of friendship in elementary and middle school. Margo trusted the adults in her life, including the ET, to function supportively and collaboratively. Simply stating to the ET a painful memory of her latency years, for example, "I had no friends," became a therapeutic experience for Margo; the ET needed only to acknowledge those feelings to be of help. Meanwhile, confronting learning challenges, recognizing strengths, and empowering oneself with techniques for moving forward are equally therapeutic. Within such a setting, Margo continued to progress.

So far, the vignettes of this chapter have attested to the wide range of situations with which ETs deal. These include team work with other professionals (Andrew, George, and Caroline), a case where one author worked alone and had to deal with parents' resistance (Jeremy), a case where the ET had doubts about the work with a "disdainful" teenager (Judy) to a case where a student, although relatively autonomous and realistic in the present, still was affected by difficulties of the past (Margo). Educational therapists speak with pride about their successful collaboration with other professionals or of how they sometimes convince a school to change its opinion of a student's prospects, or even its school rules, for the best interest of the student, and the authors have done so here as well. However, the most essential and basic collaboration that ETs have to foster is that with parents.

Working with parents requires a strong sense of our profession of educational therapy.

Parents *always* feel intimidated when dealing with their children's difficulties. Therefore, from our initial meeting on, ETs should expect to encounter very worried, threatened individuals with whom we are striving to establish a working relationship. Sometimes we too can feel intimidated by what appear to be very powerful parents, but we must keep their needs in mind, not ours. The following vignettes illustrate multiple issues that can make collaboration either a challenge or a success.

IMPOSING PARENTS

The ET knew of the background of these parents she was about to meet: a divorced couple, both remarried and sharing custody. In this case the mother and stepfather and father and stepmother all chose to meet together because they felt it was the most efficient way to plan for their daughter. The ET knew that the two fathers were high-powered lawyers in opposing law firms, and felt concern about the initial meeting, wondering whether she could keep it at a positive, productive level.

From the outset, managing this meeting was intimidating in the ET's mind. She knew, first, she had to determine what she planned to ask the parents to do, and ask herself whether they actually could do it. She also needed to be aware that intimidation was a parallel process: the intimidation she felt to some degree the parents also were feeling because they had far stronger fears and sense of responsibility for their child's learning.

All parents were on time for the meeting. In walked the two "mothers," then the father and stepfather, each holding his ostentatious leather briefcase. On seeing them, what flashed in the ET's mind was the image of the fathers holding their security blankets, worried, vulnerable, very much in need of empathy and support. Once the ET's concerns became about the parents' needs, not her own, there was no difficulty giving the needed aid, direction, and perspective. It was a very successful meeting.

As they learn slowly about their child's circumstances and mourn the loss of a carefree, happy-go-lucky child they might have envisioned, sometimes it seems the most work to be done is with the parents.

THE CASE OF CARL

Carl's parents were referred directly to the ET by his new school. The referral came with a good deal of valuable background information. Carl had entered his school in the third grade after leaving one he had attended for 3 years. Carl's parents reported that he was not yet reading, although he was interested in being read to. He had had no extra help with reading from his previous school, and this was the source of the parents' complaints and eventual move.

Carl had been accepted into his new school on the condition that, as this school also had no remedial reading program, he would receive outside help. Carl had been tested when he was 7. This evaluation had demonstrated poor integration skills and strong visual but weak verbal/auditory processing. Because integration was a weakness, Carl had been placed in an extracurricular multisensory reading program. However, it hadn't helped; even when that material was presented within a relatively structured routine, he didn't yet have the ability to integrate two kinds of sensory information. By third grade Carl was embarrassed about his inability to read and spell and he began to withdraw from learning, even from math which had been such fun for him. It was hoped that in the new school Carl would get a fresh start.

The ET contract began with an interview with the parents. Here they spoke of family history, of father's early learning difficulties and their prayers that Carl would escape the same early problems. Although the psychological testing furnished no information about Carl's emotional status, the parents were very helpful in providing examples of how he gradually was becoming more and more stressed after a bad day at school. They were convinced something needed to be done. The ET arranged with the parents that they continue to read to Carl every night before bedtime and, if they were comfortable with it, help him complete his math homework at home. They agreed for now the ET would be in charge of all reading homework. The parents were quite obviously relieved. They were happy to give their consent for collaboration between the ET and the school. It was then arranged with the school that the ET would direct the reading program and that they were not to hold themselves responsible should Carl fail at this task. (It is remarkable how this contract with a school can ease the environment.)

As expected, progress was very slow. Carl wasn't ready for some of the remedial reading tasks and, in addition, he had very serious memories of countless failures. Instead of moving into a multisensory program right away, the ET used a visual sight-reading approach to prove to Carl he "could read." All initial auditory work was done in isolation and did not require any sound/symbol knowledge. Gradually auditory skills became strong to the point that some of the protective scaffolding was taken down and Carl gradually learned to read "regular books" (chosen for their familiar sight vocabulary). Here his performance was accurate but slow; all sound/symbol integration took effort.

Significant adults were thrilled with Carl's progress, yet at the same time they all knew he continued to have learning difficulties that complicated school progress. The ET worked with Carl for 2 years. Each year, his father especially needed help accepting that although Carl was getting only very average grades nevertheless this demonstrated steady neurological growth and increasing resilience. Carl's father, perhaps as a result of his own painful school experiences, constantly hoped for a "cure." However, although Carl had not been "cured," he did move forward. In fifth grade, with the assistance of the ET, he entered a school specially designed to handle the academic issues that plague a bright dyslexic child.

Both Carl and his parents needed information and intervention. The benefit of working with a family early on in the developmental phase is twofold. The ET can introduce remedial skills that ensure children such as Carl will not be acquiring maladaptive compensations while trying to meet the challenge of schoolwork. Like every child engaged in an unfolding developmental process, he needed to discover and to employ his own learning style. In addition, the ET could use this time to help the parents understand the nature of their child's difficulties and get a perspective as to the seriousness of the problem. There was time for discussions, both practical (e.g., schools) and philosophical (e.g., child's future "success or failure").

Parents will be ever present in our work. They are the ones who pay for our services, and they need to be kept informed as to what they are paying for. Confidentiality with teenagers not withstanding, parents have a right and need to know our overall goals and how we incrementally plan to meet them. The goals need to be specific and concrete. Most ETs know this and establish some form of ongoing communication to accomplish this. They recognize that through collaboration and consulting we are best able to affect changes in our students' lives.

We are the professionals. We know what to look for at different developmental stages. We understand the learning process. We have a perspective about learning differences/disabilities that frightened parents couldn't possibly have on their own. When we communicate with parents, it helps to apply the basic learning cycle to these interactions in the same way we do with their child. We are the supportive figures who make it possible for them to move beyond confusion, helplessness, and even hopelessness to a mastery of emotions and to the planning for a sensible future for their child. Finally, we know that, similar to our students, parents need to be presented with information repeatedly and in various ways in order to assimilate it. This is a task implicit in our work if we intend to deal with the total child.

REFERENCE

Miller, P. H. (2001). *Theories of developmental psychology* (4th ed.). New York: Worth.

V

Future Perspectives and Research
in Educational Therapy

16

WORKPLACE ISSUES OF COLLEGE-EDUCATED ADULTS WITH LEARNING DISABILITIES

DIANE GOSS

Adults with learning difficulties/attention deficit disorder (LD/ADD) are often confronted with workplace issues arising from the nature of their learning differences. Many of these individuals suffer damage to self-esteem and emotional stress related to the workplace. On the other hand, there is ample evidence that individuals who learn differently can thrive and excel in the right field with the right strategies and support (Vogel & Adelman, 1999). This chapter presents personal perspectives of adults with learning disabilities on issues encountered in the workplace, and examines strategies employed by these adults to cope with the challenges they face.

RELEVANCE TO THE FIELD OF EDUCATIONAL THERAPY

Many adults cite problems in the workplace or desire for advancement in the workplace among their reasons for seeking the assistance of an educational therapist. Workplace challenges often trigger a reemergence of issues experienced during their earlier school years, and compel many of them to pursue a clearer understanding of these issues from their present perspective. Adult participants in educational therapy often share workplace dilemmas and the emotions evoked by them with the therapist. Educational therapy sessions with adult clients frequently involve clarifying workplace problems and helping the clients find effective solutions. Even when educational therapy is focused on helping adult students reach academic goals, there is often a parallel focus on the world of work. For adults, the academic and the vocational converge. Concerns about their present work situations as well as their future options are interwoven with their academic goals, problems, and issues. They are also interwoven with their personal growth and sense of self.

The insights gained through this research can help educational therapists to recognize the challenges their adult clients face and determine effective interventions. These insights can also benefit therapists who work with a younger population because issues that later contribute to the quality of an individual's workplace experience can often be addressed earlier in life, preventing or mitigating some of the difficulties that might otherwise be encountered in adulthood.

There is a notable lack of research on work-related issues of adults with learning disabilities (Gerber & Price, 2003), especially on those who have graduated from postsecondary institutions (Madaus, 2006). This study, using qualitative methodology, was designed to explore a particular aspect of this topic, specifically addressing the questions of how college educated adults with learning disabilities perceive the difficulties they face in the workplace and how they cope with the challenges they face.

METHOD

The researcher conducted a qualitative study exploring the workplace experiences of 14 college-educated adults with learning disabilities or attention deficit disorders.

Participants

Purposive sampling was employed to select a group of participants that reflected the range of variations among the population of students who had participated in a support program for college students with learning disabilities at Curry College in Milton, Massachusetts. Fourteen college-educated adults, seven men and seven women, diagnosed with learning disabilities and/or attention deficit disorder were interviewed. All participants had college degrees at the time of their interviews. One had earned an associate's degree and was within 12 credits of completing her bachelor's degree. All of the others had earned a minimum of a bachelor's degree. Two were currently enrolled in graduate programs, and five had earned master's degrees. One had earned a certificate of advanced graduate study (CAGS). The average age of the participants was 39.8 with a range from 25 to 52.

All participants had previously submitted psychoeducational evaluations documenting their learning disabilities to the support program for adults at Curry College. Participant data on file indicated that all of the subjects were of average to above average intelligence. Wechsler Adult Intelligence Scale (WAIS-III) Full Scale IQ scores ranged from 92 to 116 with a mean IQ score of 103.5. Verbal IQ scores ranged from 93 to 122 with a mean Verbal IQ score of 105.3. Performance IQ scores ranged from 80 to 122 with a mean Performance IQ score of 102.1. The average age of participants was 39.8 with participants ranging from 25 to 52 years of age.

The participants were employed in a variety of professions and included two teachers, two school counselors, a social worker, a nurse, a college librarian, an accountant, a sales associate, a vice president of a financial management company, a consultant/trainer, and a fundraiser/program developer. Two participants were currently unemployed at the time of the interview. One was a former teacher who had left the profession and was not seeking employment outside the home because she was devoting herself to raising her children. The other had been in technical support until downsized from a high technology company and was seeking employment while also raising his two young children. All of the others were employed full-time, working in a variety of settings including educational institutions (early childhood center, junior high, middle school, high school, and college), nonprofit human service agencies, a hospital, and businesses.

PROCEDURES

In-depth interviews, approximately 2 hours in length, were conducted with each of the study participants. The interviews focused on exploring the participants' personal perceptions of workplace challenges related to their learning disabilities and their own efforts to cope with these challenges. An interview protocol with predetermined questions was developed and used during the interviews, but in the spirit of qualitative research, participants were also allowed to pursue related topics that they raised. Similarly, the interviewer used follow-up questions to pursue topics suggested by individuals' responses. Interview questions explored work history, satisfactions and achievements, problems encountered, coping mechanisms and compensatory strategies, disclosure, and accommodations. Demographic data including age, gender, work history, current employment status, and level of educational attainment were also collected during the interviews.

Data Analysis

Interviews were recorded, transcribed, analyzed, and coded to identify major themes that emerged. Consistent with a qualitative approach, participants' own voices were valued and are reported through direct quotations in the presentation of results. Several themes emerged from the interviews. The major themes that will be discussed here include workplace challenges and frustrations related to LD/ADD, and strategies utilized to compensate for difficulties. This article will also discuss the relevance of the findings to the field of educational therapy. The issue of disclosure is discussed more fully in a separate article (Goss, 2008).

WORKPLACE CHALLENGES AND FRUSTRATIONS

Participants reported a variety of workplace problems that they attributed to their learning disabilities. Perhaps the most striking finding regarding this area is the relative rarity of an isolated problem specific to a particular learning disability. Almost always, issues and problems were complex and multifaceted, and involved both cognitive and emotional components. For example, time management, organization, and writing difficulties often coexisted and frequently were exacerbated by the anxiety evoked by the situation as well as by low self-esteem and lack of confidence. It was also clear that more generalized difficulties in various areas of executive functioning (e.g., initiating, shifting, planning, organizing, pacing, executing, and others) contributed to many of the specific problems cited by the participants.

Writing Problems

Difficulties in writing were noted by virtually every participant, including those whose learning disabilities were not language-based. For the majority of participants, tasks involving writing triggered feelings of incompetence and resurrected old failures. A social worker sighed heavily as she described her fear of tackling aspects of her job that required writing. "I've got to the point where I don't dare to write anything up. I'm absolutely terrified, stopped in my tracks. I get frustrated when things are more of a challenge for me and take me so long. I'm always feeling like it's going to take me the whole day to write one sentence, and I don't have the time, and how's anyone going to believe that it would take me that long." A counselor had left her previous position and called herself a failure because she was unable to keep up with the required writing.

Even small writing tasks trigger anxiety and bring up past failures. The former teacher recalled her difficulties with a routine writing task. "In my first job, we would have to write up little behavior programs, and even [for] those, just 3 or 5 sentences, I remember feeling just awful and thinking, 'I know this doesn't sound right and doesn't make sense, and I'm going to be given a hard time for it.'" Her eyes filling with tears, she also connected her anxiety to her childhood difficulties in school and said, "I was mortified because I just knew it was another, like, 'there's the dummy.' Anything that had to do with writing was mortifying … I couldn't put my thoughts down on paper in a logical way that made sense and sounded good."

Another participant, also a teacher, described the same aversion and the feelings of incompetence reinforced each time she struggled with writing. "Whatever writing I had to do, I just avoided it. And every time I had to write and it didn't work out, it became another validation of [the idea that] I'm not smart. I'm stupid. I can't write. And it just kind of perpetuated itself … I'm thinking, here I've got a master's degree and somehow I managed that, but the writing piece always made me feel stupid."

Even after gaining competence and confidence in one area of writing, participants continued to find new areas of challenge as workplace demands changed. The consultant/trainer noted that when he was promoted to a position training other social workers, he discovered new issues with his writing. "One of the things I have trouble with is shifting my writing style," he stated, noting that his various roles as clinician, trainer, and consultant all required very particular and different ways of communicating in writing. "That made some of those positions harder for me."

Sometimes difficulties in writing can interfere with the expression of the individual's strengths. In spite of her creativity and exceptionally good oral presentation skills, the fundraiser noted her frustration at putting her ideas for publicity campaigns into writing. "My mind goes a hundred miles an hour. I have it all in my head, but by the time I put it down, I lose that momentum. I can't get it all down on paper because my mind goes too fast and I get overwhelmed. I have my ideas, and I'm always adding things, and I'm, 'My gosh, where am I going to put all these ideas?' My pen has just got point one and I'm already at Z. I need to stop myself. I need to learn how to transfer my ideas onto paper. That to me is an obstacle. I have a lot up here, but I can't get it on paper."

Even comparatively simple writing tasks that people without learning disabilities give little thought to can be intimidating to individuals with learning disabilities. The very accomplished vice president of a financial management firm noted that even "the day-to-day tasks that people take for granted, like writing somebody an e-mail, take longer for me." He went on to note the stressfulness of having to check and double check for errors in everything he wrote.

These participants make it clear that in professional positions, a variety of writing demands present challenges to individuals with dyslexia, organizational problems, and attention deficits. Challenges may be expected to appear and reappear throughout the individual's professional life as new responsibilities present different demands. For individuals with learning disabilities, writing adds significant additional stress to the workday and impacts on their sense of competence in roles in which they are otherwise quite capable.

Time Management Difficulties

Managing time constraints was another almost universally cited area of challenge, one tied closely to problems in executive functioning. The librarian stated that he has difficulty in "any task that requires time management." He went on to talk about a long-range project he had been putting off in spite of his awareness of his time management problems and recognition that the deadline was fast approaching. "I'm going to get in trouble with that in the end. I haven't done enough. And I hope I have enough social capital to take the hit on that. I'm aware that I have to do this thing. I'm not disciplined enough to say I'm going to do this every day because a lot of times other things come up and I get overwhelmed emotionally. I feel guilty about it because I know that's part of who I am."

This participant recognized the emotional component at work, noting that time management difficulties were a source of great anxiety for him. He had worked on these difficulties in his college support program and was currently working on them with his therapist, yet he had been unable to overcome them.

Time management issues are complicated by the fact that they are often related to other types of deficits. For example, the participant quoted above noted at another point in the interview that he couldn't keep up with clerical work because of his poor visual-motor skills. Other participants recognized that attention deficits were at the root of their time management problems.

Many of the time management problems noted by participants seem to be part of a broader difficulty with organization and general executive functioning. One participant told of leaving his first teaching job after college. "Because of my organizational difficulties, I really couldn't keep up. It was too hard for me to organize and read, and gather all this material and learn it fast enough." A social worker said, "I do better if I have something concrete, like paperwork to do. Otherwise, I waste time organizing myself to get somewhere, and then the whole day is over." This woman was still struggling to understand the root of her time management problems after many years of grappling with the issue. "I'm not sure what that's about yet. I'm trying to figure it out. I have to go through A, B, C, D, before I can settle in on what I'm supposed to do. It feels like I get sidetracked a lot. And I make sure I do all the routine stuff before I get to the project stuff." This participant also recognized her difficulty in knowing when to initiate a task and when to shift to another task. "The problem I have in trying to manage my own time is realizing that it's OK to work on a project and not do the everyday stuff. But then I miss the everyday stuff, and someone criticizes me. I say I was working on a project, and they say, 'Well, you shouldn't have.' It's that kind of gray area that I have trouble with."

Many participants reported difficulties with the pace at which they could perform various job-related functions. Several stated that many tasks take longer for them to accomplish than for others. The participant who had been a customer support specialist for a technology company described his frustration. "[My learning disability] has made it harder to learn things. Many times I was required to learn something in a short period of time and then help customers learn it. This was difficult because I felt bad not having a good grasp of the product before I was on the phones with customers. My frustration has been not being able to learn things fast enough." A very experienced and successful early childhood teacher who has few workplace issues also acknowledged difficulties with pace. "There is a problem that I do have at times. People sometimes move mentally or physically faster than I do and then they take over situations [in which] I have just as much knowledge."

The accountant who had always struggled with time management issues found it particularly difficult in his position because he was "constantly being pulled in 14 different directions." He expressed frustration with the fact that his to-do list would never be completed because he'd be interrupted by other demands. He noted, "It's up to the project managers, and you jump when they say jump. They want it done now.... What I'm finding out now is you really need to prioritize."

Difficulty meeting time management demands in the workplace can be related to a variety of specific learning disabilities from executive functioning and organizational disorders to language-based or memory deficits that require the individual to take more time accomplishing particular tasks. Perhaps that accounts for the universality of time management problems and for the stubbornness with which time management difficulties persist in spite of the desire and the efforts of the individuals to overcome these difficulties.

Organization

Organizational problems which were not related to time management emerged less frequently in the interviews, although strategies for organization (discussed later in this chapter) were often cited and described as essential for almost all of the participants. Some of the organizational issues reported by participants are related to sequencing and working memory issues. "I get impatient with too many steps. I can't hold a bunch of steps. I can't hold all that in my head while I work through it." Several participants noted that the external physical environment exacerbates their organizational difficulties. One participant appeared visibly distraught as she described her current working conditions and her frustration during a renovation that relocated her office and disrupted her organizational structures. "I need to be where everything is in its place. I don't have my own desk. I don't have my own phone. To me that's a horrible situation. I need to know everything is in that one place." Though she had expressed her needs to her supervisor, the woman had not taken her concerns seriously. She felt frustrated, helpless, and unheard in the situation. "Every single time I foresee some problem or I experience something, it's downplayed."

Some have worked hard at it and developed good organizational skills, but recognize that they have to expend a significant amount of energy on their organizing efforts. An early childhood teacher noted that though she maintained her organization at school, at home she had "these piles that I never get to." She explained that she was too tired when she got home to tackle the task again there. Other participants recognized that they overcompensate in this area. A school counselor said that her main difficulty at work involved organization and noted that "Because of [my difficulties in] the spatial piece, I can get too overly organized to the point of disorganization at times. I'm always reorganizing, trying to make it better." A nurse recognized that her language-based learning disability had contributed to her developing rigid organizational patterns. These patterns had helped her to succeed, but also had a downside. She described her rather compulsive organizational habits as being a

> catch-22 that's a positive and a negative. I don't cut myself slack in one area of my life, not one. That's where my fault is. I'm a friend that way. I'm a daughter that way. I save money that way. My closet's organized that way. My car is cleaned that way. I clean my house that way. I get up in the middle of the night when the dishwasher stops; I've got to empty it right then. My lunch is made every night before I go to bed. Things have to be structured and organized. I think as a young kid that was the only thing I was able to control.

It is clear that, like time management problems, organizational issues faced by the participants are complicated and stem from a variety of neurological, cognitive, environmental, and emotional sources.

Attention Difficulties

Although approximately one third of the participants had diagnosed attention deficits, few reported attentional difficulties experienced in the workplace. The issues that were raised were mainly related to environmental factors rather than to internal distractions. A social worker diagnosed with ADHD noted the impact of environmental factors on her ability to function well. "I just moved into an office with seven people. It's like an open sardine can." She went on to explain that she finds the situation difficult, not only because she is distracted by hearing other people, but also because she has been told by others that she is too loud and is distracting them. "You forget you're in a room where you're not alone because you're on the phone yourself, and I'm excitable. I just don't know how I'm going to function. It's getting worse." During her interview, this woman reported having difficulties not only with attention, but also with many other aspects of executive functioning including working memory, initiating, organizing, modulating, shifting, and inhibiting behavior.

A teacher who has ADD reported a difference in her reactions to various types of distractions. "I find it distracting at times. It depends. If it's productive distractions, I'm OK, but if it's people being loud, making too much noise, or walking in and out of the classroom, that bothers me and it interferes with the children's learning." This participant recognizes that she is neurologically very sensitive and has a heightened response to sensory stimulation.

This woman was also worried about the impact of some of her ADD-related behaviors on her colleagues. She noted that she found it difficult to "slow down the motor that's racing inside of me" and was concerned that those she worked with might think she was bored with them and find it insulting.

Most of the participants, including those who had struggled with attention deficits in the classroom, did not express difficulty with attention at work. For some, it is possible that the workplace environment offers more flexibility and variety than the classroom and that the attentional demands in the workplace are not as difficult for them to manage. It is also likely that attention deficits are contributing to some of the writing, organizational, and time management difficulties described above, but were not identified explicitly by participants as playing a role. In addition, since many of the participants were diagnosed over 10 years ago, it is possible that some of them may have been diagnosed with attention deficit disorders for want of a better diagnostic category. They may actually have executive functioning disorders or other conditions that were not identified.

Memory Difficulties

About one fourth of the participants noted memory deficits as problematic on the job. One participant stated, "I forget things, and I used to beat myself up about that. Somebody would tell me something, and they'd get frustrated with me because I couldn't remember." Another said, "If I haven't written it down, it's up here, and then I'll forget it." A third noted, "The only problem I have with my manager is that everything is not written down.

Most things are [only stated orally] and I have to memorize them, unfortunately. He tells me what to do, and if I forget, oh boy!"

One participant realized the solution to his problem, but hasn't yet implemented it. "I want to take notes when people tell me things so I actually remember what they told me and I'm not asking them again. It might be a procedure we do once a month. And at that time, you just ask and you're just kind of rushing. And then the following month, I'm asking the same question. And honestly, I should have wrote [sic] it down, but I'm sort of lax on doing it."

Difficulties with Expressive Language

Challenges in oral expressive language present obstacles and were reported as a source of frustration for a small group of the participants. A school counselor related her frustration at meetings. "I need a lead time before I say something. I like to make sure I'm not just rambling or just spouting off. And people don't allow it. They jump in and then it looks like I'm not competent. And that leads to frustration." A social worker encounters similar frustration at meetings.

"Sometimes I have the ideas and I can't organize them to present them." A teacher told of trying to resolve a conflict between her view of a classroom situation and that of another teacher. "I could not express myself well enough to be able to get my point across, and I broke down in tears. I was trying to get her to understand my point of view.... It was expressive language and confidence." It was clear that for these participants, expressive language difficulties are highly frustrating and are related to issues of competence and confidence. They realize that they may be judged unfavorably or underestimated because they can't express their ideas fluently.

Self-Esteem and Self-Confidence Issues

Like the previous participant, all of the other participants in one way or another allude to issues of confidence and self-esteem. Vogel, Murray, Wren, and Adelman (2007) also found issues of confidence and low self-esteem in many of the professionals they studied. This theme arose universally in all of the interviews in the current study. The teacher who had left the profession recognized the role played by low self-esteem in her difficulties in the classroom. "I would say 99% of my difficulties were due to lack of confidence and self-esteem. The learning disability had a little bit to do with it, but then it snowballed. When I was teaching, I had no self-esteem, no self-worth."

Lack of confidence related to having a learning disability often heightens the fear of failure and enhances sensitivity to criticism. A woman just beginning her career as a nurse described the impact of her earlier school experiences on her confidence.

Everyone tells me don't worry about it, you know. You're going to get a variety of patients and you'll learn as you go, but I'm thinking, "They're smarter than me and they learn better than me." Even in a hands-on environment where I usually thrive, I'm still scared. At a very young age where there was a critical period, where a lot of learning happens, I struggled with reading and math. I said, "Forget it. I'm afraid to try because I'm afraid to fail." And those are the feelings that I have even now.

A participant in her 50s linked her feelings of inadequacy and fear of criticism to her school failures and status as an outsider in school as a child.

I think part of it is me wanting to make sure I've thought of every aspect [of a task] so that I'm not criticized. By procrastinating, I have an excuse in case I forget something—I was in a hurry. This is just reinforcing my low self-esteem. People look at me as inadequate, failure, what's wrong with you.... And I don't handle it well because of my history and always feeling on the outside anyway.

Heightened sensitivity to failure and criticism was also clearly linked to prior history by another participant. "My self-esteem definitely has been affected by my LD, negatively.... Any embarrassment which happens is huge. I have emotions about learning that other people don't have, so if they don't achieve something that they wanted to, it's not as big of a blow."

A participant who was considering a job change recognized the way his fears were influencing his decisions about future prospects. "I worry about the job a lot of the time. Sometimes I'm really self-conscious about making mistakes. I think that's why there's been reluctance for me to move on. If I go somewhere else, will they be as accepting? Am I going to be able to thrive somewhere else? Do I want to have to open up again? That's a hard thing."

The successful trainer/consultant, who exudes an air of quiet assurance also noted the impact of confidence issues on his willingness to take advantage of new opportunities.

When you're under stress or when you're thinking about making a change, the little words in the back of your head kick in that say, "Come on, can you really do this?" I remember when I began graduate school thinking I didn't want to invest $20,000 and then find out I couldn't do it. The reality is I got straight As. Going in, there was the intellectual part in the front of my brain that said, "You can do this." And then there was that more sort of reptilian, emotional side that would go, "Can you really though?" Because you don't know if you can. And I know this goes back to the same anxiety I felt in the high school English class where I had to read *Oedipus Rex*.

Another participant who also gives the appearance of confident self-assuredness described the difficult process of recovering from a mistake that others might simply shrug off.

When I'm on a high and I'm doing fantastic, it's great. And then that one thing comes up and I crumble. I just lose my momentum. It's insecurity. And then I spend a whole bunch of time, it may be 2 or 3 weeks, building myself back up there and trying to recuperate. When I miss something, it crushes me completely. I always have to show that I'm good. I'm always proving myself at the workplace, and I need the affirmation that I did a good job. I know I can do it, and I want to do it, but the disability is saying, "Maybe you can only do so much." Other people make mistakes too, but they don't have that [reaction], "Omigosh, here it comes again. Here's my old friend insecurity," where he tends to knock you down.

There is no doubt that these adults have suffered long-term injury to their self-esteem and self-confidence. As a result of painful childhood experiences related to their learning disabilities, they suffer anxiety and emotional pain in spite of their resilience, courage, and successes. All of the participants in this study are very aware of the damage inflicted on their self-esteem and many philosophically accept the idea that having a learning disability leaves a wound that will never be completely healed. One says, "It's like falling off your bike. You're gonna have that scar forever ... things get embedded in you." Another participant, though successful today stated, "It's kind of like this scabbed over wound emotionally and it ties into my self."

COPING MECHANISMS AND STRATEGIES

The adults in this study have used their creativity, experience, and intelligence to discover inventive ways of dealing with the challenges they've faced. Most of them are actively working at becoming more skillful in coping and adapting. Several strategies that contributed to their success emerged in the interviews.

Finding a Good Fit

One of the most important actions taken by participants was finding the right job to accommodate their learning disabilities and utilize their strengths. This is not always easy, and several spoke of walking a difficult path to a good career fit. One participant, in particular, exemplifies the challenge of finding the right match. In spite of having a very high level of intelligence, he floundered in several positions before becoming successful. His first job out of college was teaching at a private school for students with learning disabilities. "Because of my organizational difficulties, I really couldn't keep up. It was too hard for me to organize and read, and gather all this material and learn it. Also, [the students] were doing stuff that I probably needed remediation in myself." He left that position feeling discouraged and shaken and took a clerical job that he again found to be a poor fit. "It's hard for me to process a lot of information and organize," he explained. By then he was deeply discouraged and turned to the state office of vocational rehabilitation for help. He received counseling and training and was placed in a new job, working with a team of people converting records. Once again, his organizing and processing deficits interfered with his success. "All that detail and sequencing! I have a very hard time holding onto a lot of sequencing information, so it was not the best place to be." After leaving this job, he found a position with a data processing firm. "I was put in customer service and I was having a hard time. Again it was a bad fit." He transferred to another department doing "simpler clerical stuff," but hated it. "This stuff was killing me," he groaned, shaking his head at the memory. "I was really discouraged by the whole thing because I didn't know what I could do really. And this work that I was doing was completely boring and tedious. I was just a monkey."

By this time, he noted, "my self-esteem was uuugh." He began working with a social worker who specialized in helping individuals with learning disabilities find the right career. During this time, as he grappled with the issue of what he might do well, he found something that sounded good to him. "By chance I picked up some book on super searchers that I thought was really interesting. And I thought, oh yeah, maybe I'll look into this library stuff because it uses computers which I've always used as a tool and was always good with. I might like to work in a library and use some of these electronic tools, and I like finding information." The social worker encouraged him to pursue this path because he had also noted his client's curiosity and inquisitiveness. The man went back to school to earn a master's in library science and did several internships that allowed him to make additional discoveries regarding the right setting for him. He noted, "Even within the profession, I realized there are differences. What you're really selling as a librarian is the timeliness, the degree to which you can get the information in a timely fashion." He interned in a business library, and found the pace too fast. "They needed new information daily by a certain deadline. Can you imagine how much pressure that is?" At another internship, he discovered he was excellent at working at a reference desk in a college library. "That was the easiest thing for me to do because I can talk and get through issues rather quickly and am good with computers." He noted that "I realized an academic library was a better fit for me." He is currently successful and happy as a research and instruction librarian in a college library and has become an expert in research-related technology as well as in assistive technology. A combination of honest self-assessment, outside support, and serendipity had finally brought him to the place where he belonged.

Finding the right fit requires a habit of metacognitive self-reflection that allows individuals to recognize both their strengths and their weaknesses and to identify ways to meet the challenges inherent in particular positions. In his model of executive function capacities, McCloskey identifies self-realization as having an important place in the hierarchy of these functions (McCloskey, Perkins, & Van Diviner, 2008). The ability to cognitively engage in analysis of, awareness of, and reflection on self is essential to the development of higher levels of executive function. It is also extremely important to workplace success. The participants in this study had all participated in the learning disabilities support program at Curry College, which has a strong emphasis on developing metacognitive knowledge and strategies. Their metacognitive awareness and use of metacognitive knowledge in the workplace was clear in all of their interviews.

One participant described how she deals with failure by acknowledging it and then finding a way to go forward. She had made a transition from pursuing a career in government to working in a human service position after she asked herself, "Do I really want to do this and get defeated, or do I want to concentrate on something that I can succeed in?" Another talked about constantly reflecting on her performance and workplace behaviors, and asking herself, "What do I need to change?" She described herself as "so reflective, so very reflective, without even wanting to be."

Another participant described his efforts to increase his awareness of his performance on the job. "In the last couple of positions, I've tried to have, like once a week, a meeting with my boss. I might not have anything in particular to discuss that week, but I told her even if it's constructive criticism, whatever it is, tell me. Maybe you think I did this wrong, or have a little problem [with what I've done]. Try to explain it to me." The honesty and willingness to assess both one's strengths and one's weaknesses demands courage, but contributed greatly to the success of the participants in this study.

Assertiveness in Explaining One's Challenges and Needs

Metacognitive knowledge is also important in another strategy employed by some of the participants in this study; that is, being assertive about letting others know what they needed to succeed. The school counselor with wonderful ideas who struggled with expressive language problems learned to speak up and say, "Could I just please have my wait time, just give me a second to formulate what I want to say so it's meaningful." Her colleagues acknowledged her request, and she reported that recently a teacher at a core evaluation meeting spoke up and said, in a friendly effort to support her, "Hold on: Martha's wait time." Another participant stated, "I explain to my colleagues, I love working with you, but there are times you talk very fast, and I get overwhelmed. I'm not ignoring you. Just slow down if you need to talk to me. And they're fine with that. As long as I explain, they're good."

While many participants informally discussed their challenges with colleagues or supervisors, they did not necessarily disclose that these challenges were related to a learning disability. A few did follow a policy of open disclosure, frankly discussing their learning disabilities with others. The majority, however, were highly selective in disclosing their learning disability in the workplace, sharing the information only with those they trusted. Another group were vehement about never disclosing, fearing it would put them in a vulnerable position (see discussion in Goss, 2008). None of the participants in this study requested formal accommodations for their learning disabilities, preferring to find informal ways to accommodate themselves. This finding is consistent with that of Price, Gerber, and Mulligan (2003) who found that none of the 25 adults they interviewed had requested accommodations in the workplace.

Writing Strategies

Not surprisingly, most of the participants noted strategies they employed to help them deal with the challenge of writing. One of the teachers used voice-to-text software for some writing tasks. When reading students' papers, instead of writing comments on the papers, he would dictate his comments using Naturally Speaking and attach these comments to the students' papers. Among participants in this study, he was one of only two who used this type of writing software. Two others used presentation software like PowerPoint in giving presentations. All of the participants, however, used word processing software and found spell check very helpful. "Thank God for spell check," the nurse exclaimed. The fundraiser stated, "I use spell check all the time, even in my e-mails. The first thing I do is make sure spell check is clicked on before I send out anything."

Most found they had to develop a habit of editing their work diligently. The highly successful vice president of an investment firm described his efforts.

> I have to reread [my e-mail message] numerous times. A lot of times if I need to respond to something quickly and concisely, I'll text message somebody with just abbreviations because people are more forgiving [of that]. When it's something that warrants more detail, like an e-mail that has to go to our president or our largest customer, and it has to look and read well, I'll write it, take a break and come back to it. Every single time I come back to it, I'll change something—I don't like what I've done, or it doesn't make sense. If I like a sentence, I'll highlight it in blue and then go on to the next sentence until I'm a hundred percent sure of that sentence. I actually have sent e-mails to people [other than the intended recipient]—a nonjudgmental eye, to say, "Read this," to get them checked. The tendency in the business world is to respond quickly, but quickly doesn't work well for me.

Several other participants also asked others to check important documents for them, not just for spelling, but for grammar and content. One said, "If it needs to be sent to the board or [an important organization], I e-mail it to my boss first to see what she thinks, and if I need to change anything, she'll make recommendations." Others asked trusted colleagues, friends, or spouses for editing and proofreading help.

One of the most common writing strategies among the participants in this study involved developing a template or model to use repetitively. The trainer/consultant in social work used this strategy for a variety of writing tasks. "I learn how to write the way a particular role requires, and then I replicate it over and over again. Like for my clinical notes, I have bullet points already laid out. If I'm working with a particular treatment modality, there are things I always say about how to do that. You can retrieve my plans, and they say exactly the same thing as the one before." A teacher noted that in spite of her writing problems, "I could write a good IEP because I followed a certain format and plugged in specific things." Another teacher noted his use of teaching resources on the Internet to find generic statements that were helpful to him in writing the many progress reports he needed to produce each semester. From these, he constructed his own database of comments and goals, from which he selected appropriate statements to paste into his reports. Like the trainer above, he further simplified the process of writing reports by using bullet form for the comments. He also used teacher resources that came with the textbooks to help him create quizzes, handouts, and other written products. He noted that he adapted these to his purpose. "You can't just plug them. You have to do your own research. You have to stay on top of that. But I go through them and pick the questions I like and cut and paste them to make my own quizzes."

Replicating Successful Formats

Many participants stated that replicating successful formats helped them not only in writing, but in many other workplace tasks as well. One participant described an Excel spreadsheet she had created at another job to figure out the return on investments. "I've taken that to every job. I'm not going to invent the whole wheel again when it's already been done for me." A participant who is in sales talked about having a structured routine for multistep tasks. "Repetition. Everything in a structured routine. It makes me be sure to keep track of what I'm doing."

Many of the participants talked about implementing replication strategies for making presentations. The fund-raiser described her structure for presentations using a slide show, cognitive maps, and other visual representations. "I have to do a lot of presentations to board members. I usually break it down visually. Because of this, I'm able to have confidence in myself. I know what to do, I know how to get there, so let's walk it through. Let's do the steps to be able to get to the end product. I use the visual so I can see how to tell the story. I need it in front of me."

Another participant says, "I have to have my bullet points. If I'm doing a presentation, I'll give you a succinct presentation with all my bullet points organized … [without the bullet points] I'll just talk from associating. There'll be a thread there, but I'll just go off."

An executive who makes many business presentations stated, "One of the best things to do if your job entails presentations is come up with a format that is comfortable for you. Come up with a format that makes sense. [If you have the format] no matter what information is plugged into that, you know the organization of your presentation." He continued to describe his strategy of using flip charts and creating cognitive maps with participants, drawing out their ideas and organizing them visually. "I turn presentations into meetings," he concluded, thereby engaging the participants and presenting himself as a consultant rather than a "sales guy."

Organizational and Time Management Strategies

All of the participants brought up time management and organizational strategies they use. These strategies were used to compensate for other deficits as well as for weaknesses in organization itself. A teacher talked about using a carefully structured documentation and grading system, using a folder for each student's work, and having a place for everything. The librarian, who struggles with organization, uses his computer to keep organized and stated, "The less paper I have, the better. It's just more for me to lose." The fundraiser attributed much of her success to, "Organization, organization, organization. Thinking things through from start to finish." She described her strategy of using large sheets of paper and big display boards to list all of the steps in a project from beginning to end. She also uses a huge wall calendar marked with dry erase pens to plan the many events she runs so she can see and make entries on several months at a time. She even takes it down, rolls it up, and brings it to meetings with her. Another participant says, "I have a 'to do' list every day of what I'm supposed to be doing. I have a calendar that is insanely well laid out. I have to be that way in order to get things done." Even though he usually didn't accomplish everything on his to do list, another participant noted, "If I didn't write a to do list, certain things would be forgotten." Another participant took out his laptop and showed the interviewer how he uses a calendar that connects his Palm Pilot and e-mail with a calendar on a server shared by all members of his department. "I was always good at technology. The interface, the visual interface, helps me remember. And the structure. It acts as a visual memory structure for me to follow a sequence."

Others prefer a less technical aid. "I don't keep a Palm Pilot. I have one but rarely use it. I need to see the time lines in front of me. I have the black teacher's planner (though she is not a teacher) because I need to see the whole week in front of me."

In spite of using strategies for more efficient use of time, most of the participants in this study, like those in other studies (Vogel et al., 2007) noted that they simply had to put more time in to compensate for their difficulties. A counselor expressed her awareness that her dedication and the extra time she puts in are related to her need to compensate.

It goes back to, you know, compensating. For the past month I've been reflecting back on this. I'm at work late last night because I need to organize, I need to get rid of, I need to do other things, and other people are gone. It's just who I am and what I do. I think you overcompensate, and people see you as probably one of the best workers ever because you are doing 10 times more.

Another participant recognized this relationship as well.

I take my work home with me so that I can slowly figure it out. In the office, it's busy and you really can't get to do that. What takes a quote, unquote normal person one day to do, it takes me two or three. You can see this as both a positive and a negative because I'm not as quick as other people, but I put more time and concentration into my work, and I use time management skills. It takes me longer to do something, but I bring a commitment to the job. I wrap my arms around a project and I really get into it and dedicate the time I need to make it good.

Several participants describe their strategy of coming in early or staying late at the office. An executive stated, "A lot of times I was still at work at midnight. I had to put more time in." Another participant said, "I come in first thing in the morning, like 7:30, and it's just quieter. And I work a little later. I'm certainly there if I know I've got to get something done." Taking more time to complete tasks has also been noted as one of the most common compensatory strategies in other studies (Vogel et al., 2007).

Strategies for Improving Focus and Concentration

Working earlier or later was also a strategy participants used to improve concentration and minimize distraction. One said, "I wait till other people are gone so I'm not interrupted. If I'm interrupted all the time, it interrupts my train of thought, and I can't do it." Another said, "I actually changed my schedule so that I'd stay later. I find it's quieter." Others come in before their colleagues arrive in the morning or go to work on days when others are not there to accomplish tasks that require much concentration. "I go in to the office when nobody's going to be there just to have thoughts to myself and to be quiet."

Several people mentioned taking work home with them so they could focus better. The social worker stated, "Sometimes I work from home because I don't get anything done in the office." The participants who talked about bringing work home conveyed a willingness to do so. One participant expressed the acceptance common to several others, "So I take my work home with me. I just accept that."

None of the participants complained about having to adjust their schedules and put in more hours than their coworkers. They accepted this necessity and expressed willingness to do so in order to complete their work and feel satisfied with their performance. This willingness to work hard was also found by Reiff and Ginsberg (1995).

A woman who found it difficult to slow down her racing thoughts found physical exercise, tai chi, and meditation helped her to "pull in the reins." Finding a distraction-free environment was also a strategy she and others found helpful. "To help you focus, find a place that will keep you focused. I go to the library ... if you find the right environment for what you have to do, that helps a lot."

Collaboration and Delegation

Collaboration with others was frequently noted by participants as essential to their success. Most of the participants described ways in which they utilized their strengths while also relying on abilities of others to accomplish goals in the workplace. A high-level executive noted his facility in building teams that allow him to be effective and efficient in tasks he finds challenging.

> What I do [to accomplish a major task like writing a proposal] is take teams, people with diverse backgrounds, and come up with a team to respond to this. I delegate certain things and then bring them all together. I know conceptually this is the way we need to respond, but I rely on others to get the detail. And when I'm responsible for hiring people within our organization, I'm asking detailed questions about what their pluses are. They don't realize their pluses are going to help my minuses. I'm good at identifying what other people are good at, realizing what tasks are needed to do the job.

He also used his leadership abilities to motivate others without revealing his own deficits. "What I do is put it under the guise of 'Let's do this as a team,' rather than, 'I can't write this. I'm going to freeze because it has to be done in 2 hours.' I'll come up with the concepts and talk to someone about it, and say, 'You know what I'm talking about. You write up the language. I have to move on.' I know conceptually this is the way we need to respond, but I rely on others to get the detail. I'm not a detail guy."

He also reflected on the ethics of his strategy.

> Is it up front and honest? No, but the business world is a very unforgiving environment, so I overcome difficulties by using my ability to get people motivated and excited about things. I roll that into teamwork and it's proven successful. And they feel part of it. What they don't realize is that you're asking them to help with whatever your deficiency is under the guise of teamwork. And it allows people, some

people younger than I, to have experiences they wouldn't normally have had. And they look at me as an incredible manager-team player to relinquish that kind of responsibility to them.

Another participant described trading his expertise for help from others in areas in which he was weak. He was taking a work-related course that involved math, an area of great difficulty for him. He talked with the head of the math department, and helped her get a computer and set it up for her. Then he told her about his problem with math and asked her for some help that she was happy to provide.

Reiff and Ginsberg (1995) use the term *social ecologies* to describe the interdependent relationships that provide support in the workplace for many of the adults with LD that they interviewed. These relationships are mutual, not dependent, and allow individuals with learning disabilities to rely on their strengths while compensating for their weaknesses.

Reframing

One of the more common coping strategies described by participants involved reframing their view of their learning disabilities. Reframing appears to be essential in overcoming the negative effects of having a learning disability. Gerber, Reiff, and Ginsberg (1996) note that, "A lack of reframing in the developmental process can keep individuals from deriving productive meaning and experience from their learning disabilities in adulthood" (p. 98). It was clear from the interviews that most of the participants had engaged in reframing, changing the way they made meaning of their disabilities and acquiring more positive perceptions of them. They were able to put their difficulties into perspective and to see their learning difficulties as a smaller part of the larger picture. Though he had encountered difficulties, the accountant stated, "I think I've been very lucky at work. For the most part I've had really positive experiences. In relation to my learning disability, I haven't had a lot of difficulty."

The social work consultant compared his own struggles with those of his clients to help him put his problems into perspective. "I work with so many kids that deal with such incredible stuff that I think, this [my learning disability] is nothing. I've got nothing to complain about. These kids have got it way harder than I do, and have a learning disability on top of something else really terrible that happened to them. So that's helped me to realize I have no excuses."

Through the process of reframing, all of the interviewees had come to some level of acceptance of their learning disabilities and made peace with their past struggles. The nurse recognized that she had to let go of the pain she had experienced in the past as a result of her learning disability and needed to focus on her current and future achievements.

It can be annoying, you achieve so much, but then you still say, "Wow, this problem is still there. It's never going to go away, and that's just the way it is." So finally, I'm learning to deal with it and I'm OK with it. There's only so much you can go back and change, and after that you just have to try to let it go because it's there and it's almost permanent. There's only so much unweaving you can do because then you're living in the past and you lose the future. It's always going to be there. You're always going to remember it. Some people think they have to work at it and work at it until they look back and they don't care anymore. That's never going to happen. Not with something like this. The damage already has been done and you have to move forward. The past is already gone, you know.

Then she added, "I have an LD. It's not the norm. It's not in the box, but sometimes outside the box is actually better. The grass isn't always greener inside."

A middle-school teacher philosophically demonstrated the self-acceptance that is a critical aspect of reframing.

The hardest part of having a learning disability in the workplace is just being comfortable with yourself. I know that some of my stuff's not too good, but I make up for it in other areas. I can take a hundred English classes, but it's still going to be like this. I'm 41 now, and I'm never going to learn how to spell well. There's certain ways I have to do things. I have to work very hard. I'm very dyslexic, and this is what I've got to do.

He paused and then said resolutely, "Acceptance."

Other participants reframed their perceptions of their learning disability by emphasizing its positive impact on them and their satisfaction with the person they have become. "I think it's definitely been a struggle, but as much as there's been many times when I wished I didn't have to deal with this, I wouldn't be the person I am strength-wise and goal-wise. I wouldn't have as much independence. Because [of my struggles with my learning disability] I know what it's like to go out and get something and work hard for it." Reiff, Gerber, and Ginsberg (1994) observed similar types of reframing among successful adults with LD and see it as a critical component of their model of employment success.

IMPLICATIONS FOR EDUCATIONAL THERAPISTS

It is clear from the experiences of these adults that learning disabilities persist into adulthood and continue to present challenges long after the individuals have left the classroom behind and enter the vocational arena. In addition to the common workplace challenges faced by any worker, adults with learning disabilities bear the burden of finding ways to cope with, compensate for, and overcome difficulties related to their learning disabilities.

It is also clear, however, that individuals with learning disabilities can and do utilize their considerable strengths, coping mechanisms, compensatory strategies, and problem-solving techniques to meet the challenges they face. They draw on inner strength and resiliency, commitment, creativity, and other personal gifts to overcome obstacles, solve problems, face fears, and bounce back. In spite of the difficulties encountered in the workplace, the overwhelming majority of the participants in this study were successful in their positions, happy in the fields they had chosen, and content with their situation. In their study of college-educated adults with learning disabilities, Madaus, Ruban, and Zhao (2005) also found that, in general, the participants reported favorable employment outcomes and satisfaction with their jobs. A learning disability is not a predictor of workplace failure. In fact, the attitudes and behaviors acquired by many individuals with learning disabilities may actually contribute to their success in the workplace.

The experiences and insights of the participants in this study can help educational therapists to better understand the roles they might play in supporting their clients' efforts to achieve and maintain success in the world of work.

Helping Clients Find the Right Fit

One of the most important insights provided by the participants and identified in many other studies is the importance of finding a position that is a good fit for the individual (Reiff & Ginsberg, 1995). Finding such a position requires self-understanding as well as knowledge of the various types of work available.

Career counseling and support for individuals with learning disabilities should be provided throughout college, and should continue during the period of transition to the workplace after graduation. Educational therapists working with college students should pay particular attention to helping students choose majors that are consistent with their strengths and that will prepare them for careers for which they are well-suited. Gerber and Price (2003) note that: "A good 'job fit' can mitigate the challenging effects of learning disabilities." Informal observation, activities, and discussion as well as more formal inventories that help students to identify their skills, talents, values, and career goals should be used. Volunteer positions, internships, field placements, and other types of experiential learning can be invaluable in helping students to explore various types of work and discover whether particular positions are a good match for them. By encouraging their clients to engage in such opportunities and guiding them in reflecting on their experiences, educational therapists can facilitate the development of self-awareness and self-analysis, important executive function capacities critical to vocational success.

Hitchings, Luzzo, Ristow, and Horvath (2001) assert the critical importance of specialized career development services for college students with learning disabilities. They recommend that in addition to traditional career development activities, such services include helping students consider the impact their learning disabilities may have on various career choices and ensuring that they have the self-advocacy skills that may be essential to their success. Unfortunately, many career service professionals have little background in learning disabilities. Career counselors providing assistance in acquiring career-related skills such as choosing a career, job searching, and interviewing may not always understand the specialized needs of students with learning disabilities. Educational therapists can be a vital part of the web of collaboration that includes the career services and LD support components of the college. The educational therapist can provide clients with specialized, individualized assistance based on a thorough understanding of issues related to their learning disabilities. Teachers in LD support programs, career services personnel, and educational therapists working with individuals prior to their graduation from college can address and help college students develop attitudes, strategies, and skills that successful individuals have found helpful in the workplace. Acquisition of these abilities will likely contribute to the students' academic success as well as to their future success in the workplace.

Supporting the Transition from School to Work

Provision of transition support for graduates is also of critical importance. While colleges give their graduates access to the general career services of their schools, those with learning disabilities may need specialized support in career planning, job finding, and transitional coaching/counseling to facilitate adjustment to the workplace. Such specialized support should acknowledge the particular challenges faced by the individual with a learning disability, but at the same time must avoid the erroneous presumption that the individual has less potential than students not similarly challenged. Educational therapists may be uniquely able to capitalize on the uniqueness and special gifts of the individual and provide help in identifying and applying these gifts to his or her career. The transition period may also resurrect past struggles and feelings of inadequacy. An educational therapist, being well aware of the earlier struggles most adults with learning disabilities have endured, can help clients to understand the emotional dynamics of the situation, assist them in coping with threats to fragile self-esteem, and foster self-acceptance and resiliency.

Supporting Adults with Learning Disabilities at Critical Points in Their Career Path

The services of an educational therapist may also be needed at other times in the career of the individual challenged by learning disabilities. Job advancement, ongoing training/continuing education, career shifts, and changing workplace demands may necessitate support at various turning points in the individual's work life. Since learning disabilities do persist through adulthood, support services may be needed across the lifespan (Raskind, Goldberg, Higgins, & Herman, 1999). Many individuals in this study noted difficulties that arose when they advanced to more demanding roles, when they considered changing jobs or taking advantage of new opportunities, when they needed to pursue further career-related education and training, and when restructuring or other changes in the workplace presented new challenges.

Fostering Metacognitive Processing

Educational therapists can contribute greatly to the success of adults in the workplace by engaging them in metacognitive processing of workplace issues. Like the adults in this study, clients with learning disabilities will benefit from being able to engage in metacognitive analysis of themselves and their workplace situations. Metacognitive support provided by educational therapists may involve helping clients recognize the strengths they can utilize in the situation; supporting them in identifying cognitive, emotional, and behavioral patterns they need to change; helping them understand the roots of these patterns in the neurobiology of their brains and in their past experiences; assisting them to explore more productive attitudes, beliefs, and behaviors; and encouraging them to analyze problems and generate possible solutions.

Metacognitive processing is especially important for helping clients recognize the role of various executive functions in the workplace and their own levels of proficiency in them. Helping clients acquire higher levels of executive functioning and guiding them as they advance through various stages from self-actualization and self-regulation to self-realization and self-determination, and even beyond to self-generation and trans-self-integration requires a high level of sensitivity on the part of the therapist. McCloskey et al. (2008) assert that framing executive function problems properly is crucial to successful intervention. Individuals with executive function difficulties have often been blamed for their problems, and their failings have frequently been attributed to negative personality traits such as laziness, irresponsibility, apathy, or stubbornness. An effective intervention will identify the problem in terms of the specific behavior that is interfering with the client's success and will help the client to find ways to change the behavior. McCloskey et al. (2008) note that the cognitive coach can function as an external substitute for an executive function that is underdeveloped in a client. In taking on this role, the coach or educational therapist increases the client's awareness of the function and provides a model of how to operationalize it. They also recommend verbal mediation in which the coach or therapist guides the client's thinking process by using strategic verbal cues and questions and provides the client with a vocabulary that will allow them to label and better understand various aspects of executive functioning. In addition, McCloskey et al. recommend strategies of cognitive behavioral therapy as well as mindfulness-based approaches that can help client's develop greater awareness.

Many techniques of transformative adult education also lend themselves to metacognitive analysis of workplace issues. By using a critical incident technique (Brookfield, 1990), therapists can help individuals assess a specific situation, the task itself, the other players, and their own role. Through this technique educational therapists may help clients to recognize behaviors that may be counterproductive, identify possible sources of support, and determine future actions. The therapist can help the client to make an action plan and can function as a coach as, over time, the client takes the steps necessary to bring about positive change. Other techniques of transformative adult education can be used in similar ways, such as journal writing, metaphors representing clients' experiences, case studies, role plays and simulations, and self-assessment activities (Cranton, 1994).

Through the strategies described above, therapists can assist their clients in the metacognitive work necessary to reframing. One of the most important roles of the educational therapist is to support individuals in reframing their views of their learning disabilities. This process of reframing was demonstrated by many of the adults in this study and has been shown to be essential to success in the workplace for individuals with learning disabilities (Gerber et al., 1996).

Developing Specific Workplace Strategies

Educational therapists can also teach their clients a large repertoire of specific strategies from which they can select. They can work collaboratively with the individual to select, adapt, create and assess the effectiveness of various strategies. They can build confidence by helping clients improve skills in particular areas (e.g., writing reports, giving presentations), whenever possible using actual workplace tasks for which the client is responsible. Helping clients acquire organizational and time management skills and working with them to create templates and other formats they can replicate, as many of the participants in this study did, can also be helpful. Also important is encouraging development of skills in collaboration and cooperation in the workplace. While this comes naturally to some, clients who have social skill deficits may need intensive support in this area.

Providing Emotional Support

Provision of emotional support is another important role for educational therapists. Many adults with learning disabilities feel alone in the workplace, fear rejection, and are unable to share their dilemmas with others who may not understand. Educational therapists can provide an understanding heart, validation and encouragement when clients are discouraged. It is often helpful to offer role models of other individuals with learning disabilities who have struggled and then succeeded. This may be accomplished by introducing clients to successful adults with LD or providing articles that highlight the achievements of such individuals. Therapists many also offer groups in which adults discuss workplace problems and strategies, engage in collaborative problem solving, and share their feelings in a nonjudgmental setting.

All of the adults in this study reported deep-seated and sometimes painful emotions related to their learning disability and its impact on them in the workplace. The majority recognized the connection between the difficult experiences of their school years and the emotional challenges they still faced. Educational therapists are uniquely suited to providing the combination of emotional support and practical strategies that will help adults with learning disabilities to face and overcome their workplace challenges.

Promoting Stress Management

Most adults experience some level of stress and anxiety in the workplace. Many adults with learning disabilities, however, suffer from the added stress of managing their learning disabilities, the fear of failure, and the anxiety of being criticized or disdained. They bear the scars of past failures and mistreatment that may make them more vulnerable. Teaching them stress management techniques like meditation, visualization, breathing exercises, and others can help them to reduce their anxiety. Discussions about nutrition, exercise, and other aspects of a healthy lifestyle can be part of an educational therapy session as can cognitive-behavioral strategies to set goals and measure and track progress.

Enhancing Clients' Understanding of Their Disabilities and Their Rights

The adults in this study had opportunities during their college years, through the help of their support program, to come to an understanding of their learning disabilities, and were able to articulate this understanding. Gerber and Price (2003) note that because learning disabilities are invisible, it is very important for employees to be able to clearly explain their disabilities and their impact in the workplace. Though requesting accommodations is a very personal choice, and one that appears to be seldom chosen by college educated adults with LD, they should be aware of their rights under The Americans with Disabilities Act and should be able to self-advocate and clearly explain their disabilities to their employer should they decide to do so. Educational therapists can facilitate the development of their clients' self-advocacy skills and analysis of the pros and cons of disclosure or of requesting accommodations in particular workplace situations.

Training in the Use of Adaptive Technology

Assistive technology is rapidly developing. Adults with LD who have been out of school for several years may be unaware of innovations that might be helpful to them. Educational therapists can help them to become aware of such technology, provide opportunities to experiment with it, and help them to learn how to use it effectively in the workplace. Text-to-speech and speech-to-text programs have proven invaluable to some adults with dyslexia or dysgraphia. These programs can help people with difficulty in reading or writing to keep up with their workload, save time, and produce better products. Again, a metacognitive approach is best, encouraging clients to explore and reflect on the usefulness of such technology in their personal situation. In this study, only two participants used assistive technology (though all used word processing and spell check), but those who did found it very helpful.

Significance of the Learning Conversation

The benefits of simply talking about the issues faced by employees with LD should not be underestimated. One of the participants in this study stated, "There's something really therapeutic about just talking about yourself. It allows you to hear yourself say things I [sic] don't like. When you're talking, sometimes you say, 'Ohmigod, I don't like that. But you come up with a plan when you're talking." Educational therapists provide an important service in engaging with their clients in conversation about their work lives. The wonderful interweaving of the theoretical and the practical, the educational and the personal, the emotional and the intellectual in educational therapy makes it remarkably well-suited to serving the needs of adults with learning disabilities in the workplace.

The participants in this study provide valuable insights into the dilemmas and challenges faced in the workplace by college-educated adults with learning disabilities. Their honesty, perceptiveness, and willingness to share their experience with others is highly valued by the researcher. Their circumstances and the courageous, creative, and resilient ways in which they have dealt with them can help those of us in the field of educational therapy to better understand the needs of this population and our role in supporting them in achieving the wonderful potential they have. It is to be hoped that future practitioner research by educational therapists in various areas of practice will provide a window into the experience of other groups of adults and young people with learning challenges. The more we understand, the more able we will be to provide the support and challenge our clients need and the better we can guide them in the path of development.

REFERENCES

Brookfield, S. (1990). Using critical incidents to explore learners' assumptions. In J. Mezirow (Ed.), *Fostering critical reflection in adulthood: A guide to transformative and emancipatory learning* (pp. 177–193). San Francisco, CA: Jossey-Bass.

Cranton, P. (1994). *Understanding and promoting transformative learning: A guide for educators of adults.* San Francisco, CA: Jossey-Bass.

Gerber, P. J., & Price, L. A. (2003). Persons with learning disabilities in the workplace: What we know so far in the Americans with Disabilities Act era. *Learning Disabilities Research and Practice, 18*(2), 132–136.

Gerber, P. J., Reiff, H. B., & Ginsberg, R. (1996). Reframing the learning disabilities experience. *Journal of learning disabilities, 29*(1), 98–101.

Goss, D. (2008). To tell or not to tell: The workplace disclosure dilemma for college-educated adults with learning disabilities. *The Educational Therapist, 29*(2),16–21.

Hitchings, W. E., Luzzo, D. A., Ristow, R., & Horvath, M. (2001). The career development needs of college students with learning disabilities: In their own words. *Learning Disabilities Research and Practice, 16*(1), 8–17.

Madaus, J. W. (2006). Employment outcomes of university graduates with learning disabilities. *Learning Disability Quarterly, 29*(1), 19–31.

Madaus, J. W., Ruban, L., & Zhao, J. (2005). *Factors contributing to the employment satisfaction of university graduates with learning disabilities.* Storrs, CT: Center on Postsecondary Education and Disability.

McCloskey, G., Perkins, L. A., & Van Diviner, B. (2008). *Assessment and intervention for executive function difficulties.* New York: Routledge.

Price, L., Gerber, P. J., & Mulligan, R. (2003). The Americans with Disabilities Act and adults with learning disabilities as employees: The realities of the workplace. *Remedial and Special Education, 24*(6), 350–358.

Raskind, M. H., Goldberg, R. J., Higgins, E. L., & Herman, K. L. (1999). *Learning Disabilities Research and Practice, 14*(1), 35–49.

Reiff, H. B., Gerber, P. J., & Ginsberg, R. (1994). Instructional strategies for long-term success. *Annals of Dyslexia, 44,* 270–288.

Reiff, H. B., & Ginsberg, R. (1995). New perspectives on teaching from successful adults with learning disabilities. *Remedial and Special Education, 16*(1), 29–37.

Vogel, S. A., & Adelman, P. B. (1999). Adults with learning disabilities 8-15 years after college. *Learning Disabilities, 10*(3), 165–182.

Vogel, S. A., Murray, C., Wren, C., & Adelman, P.B. (2007). An exploratory analysis of employment-related experiences of educators with learning disabilities. *Educational Considerations, 34*(2), 15–20.

17

THE EFFICACY OF EDUCATIONAL THERAPY
Research Analysis

PHYLLIS MASLOW AND DOROTHY UNGERLEIDER

*The following article is an abridged description of the first formal study to examine the ef-
ficacy of educational therapy, a 28-year-old interdisciplinary profession in the United States,
created by a group of committed professionals of the Association of Educational Therapists
(AET), to serve the comprehensive needs of children, adolescents, and adults with suspected
and diagnosed learning difficulties (Kaganoff, 2001; Werbach, 2002; Ungerleider, 2005).
The developmental roots of educational therapy emerged in Vienna through the efforts of
Auguste Aichorn (1965).*

*This chapter is reproduced with permission from the Association of Educational Therapists (AET).
Ungerleider, D. and Maslow, P. (2005). "The Efficacy of Educational Therapy, Part II." In* Survey of
Treatment Effectiveness 2005. *Los Angeles: Association of Education Therapists.*

INTRODUCTION

The Association of Educational Therapists (AET) is a national professional organization
first formed in California in 1979, with current membership now existing nationwide
as well as in 11 different countries. The purpose of AET was and is to meet the needs of
a subgroup of special educators whose work integrates the clinical with the educational
models of intervention. This clinical teaching model, brought to America from Europe in
the 1940s by pioneers like Marianne Frostig, Katrina DeHirsch, and others, was inspired
by the work, called *heilpedagogie*, of August Aichorn in Vienna (Aichorn, 1965), who attempted to address the issues of adolescents whose learning experiences were challenged
as a result of their life circumstances. Many of these practitioners, in preparing for this
unique pedagogy, independently trained themselves from the course offerings of two or
more disciplines, from fields such as special education, psychology, speech/language, and
child development.

Because of the lack of specific training for this profession which would necessitate a
unique, multidisciplinary curriculum in college and university programs offering this sort

of multidisciplinary curriculum, AET was established as a professional organization to formally define educational therapy for the public and to establish principles of practice, standards, and ethics in order to define its professional boundaries for academic and clinical training.

Trained educational therapists are expected to have skills in the following psychoeducational therapeutic processes: 1) formal and informal educational assessment; 2) synthesis of information from other specialists; 3) understanding the client's psychosocial context of family/school/-community/culture; 4) development and implementation of appropriate remedial programs for school-related learning and behavior problems; 5) strategy training for addressing social and emotional as well as academic aspects of learning problems; 6) formation of supportive relationships with the individual and with those involved in his educational development; 7) facilitation of communication between the individual, the family, the school, and involved professionals (Ungerleider & Maslow, 2001).

THE STUDY

The research team in this study consisted of Phyllis Maslow and Dorothy Ungerleider, in collaboration with other professionals in AET who understood the mission and goal of this research. The over arching question posited in this study was: Is educational therapy effective? This study sought answers to this question in order 1. To demonstrate the level of perceived accountability professionals in the field of educational therapy had in relation to their clients; and 2. To provide useful information for the continued growth of the AET's specialized training programs, master's and post-master's level certificate programs, workshops, seminars, and conferences. The research team identified two major concerns:

1. The actual subjects who were part of the study were clients of Board Certified Educational Therapists (BCETs).* They wished to maintain anonymity in order to be able to speak freely about the BCET, and because many did not wish to disclose that their children had received educational therapy.
2. The importance of being able to articulate how "efficacy" is defined within the context of educational therapy for the respondent, the client, the BCET, and the research team was challenging.

Methodology

A survey form was collaboratively developed by the research team and AET board members, as well as from feedback that was reported by practitioners in the field. Dorothy Ungerleider and Phyllis Maslow drafted the initial version of the survey, and in 2002–03 board members administered it as a pilot survey with their clients.

The pilot survey yielded results that led to the present study. The survey used in this study is divided into five sections: 1. Background Information (gender, medication, parent or guardian occupation and education, language spoken in home, and reasons educational therapy was initiated); 2. Client History (children and adolescents); 3. Educational Therapy Services and Outcomes; 4. Parental Perspectives on Implementation (requesting ratings on a five-point Likert scale); and 5. General Questions (overall ratings; reasons for ending educational therapy; and comments). "Efficacy" as a result of educational therapy was considered to be: 1. The client's satisfactory and independent progress in school; and 2. Favorable evaluations by the clients' parents of the interventions employed by practitioners.

The procedures for contacting clients for the study were designed to maintain confidentiality. A list of BCETs dating back to November 2005 was used as the pool of educational therapists (ETs) who would ultimately provide data for the study. From the original pool of BCETs, 112 were selected. The criteria that determined eligibility for each BCET to participate in the study included: 1. Having clients who had terminated within the last two years; and 2. Having clients with whom the BCET had worked for at least nine months (but not presently).

With the assistance of the AET office staff, 33 eligible BCETs (29.5% of the original pool of potential contributors) were issued packets that included: 1. The survey; 2. A letter for each client; and 3. Self-addressed stamped envelopes for the return of the survey to the AET office. With one exception, all BCETs selected for the study resided or conducted their educational therapy practices in urban or suburban areas of Southern or Northern California. They requested 236 survey forms to send to clients. The number of surveys requested by individual BCETs ranged from 1 to 28; the average number was 7.

The packets were mailed between November 2005 and June 2006. By July 1, 2006, 70 clients had returned the survey, a return rate of 29.7%.

Characteristics of Clients

Sixty-eight of the clients were between the ages of 9 and 20, with a mean of 13.6 years at the time the surveys were completed. One client was an adult. Since all but one of the BCETs who treated the clients were from California, it can be assumed that the majority of clients were from urban and suburban areas of that state. Sixty-nine of the surveys were completed by parents, providing the following data.

Sources of Referrals

Referrals to educational therapy were made by the following: friends and colleagues, 21; teachers and schools, 19; school counselors, learning specialists, educational therapists, and tutors, 12; speech therapists, 10; pediatricians, 6; psychologists, 3; occupational therapists, l; and others who reported other sources of referrals, with some who reported more than one source.

Gender Breakdown
   The study included 36 males and 34 females.
Home/Primary Language
   English was reported as the primary language in the homes of all respondents. One family also spoke Cantonese in the home; one, Farsi; and one, French.
Adoption
   Four children (5.7%) were adopted, all at birth.
Ethnicity
   Ethnicity was predominantly Anglo-European (40, or 57.1%). Twenty (20) respondents declined to answer (28.6%). The remainder of the respondents consisted of: 1. African-Americans; 2. Asian-Americans; 3 Hispanic-Americans; and 4. Middle Eastern-Americans.

Concomitant Prescribed Medication

During educational therapy, 17 clients (24.3%) were taking prescribed medication for ADHD/ADD, 3 for asthma, 1 for allergies, and 1 for depression. The majority (48, or 68.6%) were not on any medication.

Parental Educational and Career Data

The parents of the clients were predominantly college educated. Forty-five (64.3%) of the fathers were professionals or business executives, and 23 (32.9%) were in the arts, middle management, or were skilled workers.

- Twenty-four (34.3%) of the mothers were professionals or business executives, and 15 (21.4%) were in the arts, middle management, or were skilled workers.
- Eighteen (25.7%) of the mothers were homemakers.
- Eleven (15.7%) of the mothers, but none of the fathers, described themselves as educators.
- Two of the fathers graduated from high school, two declined to answer, and the remainder completed some college. Thirty-five (50%) earned graduate degrees. Four of the mothers graduated from high school, and the remainder of mothers completed some college. Twenty-seven (38.6%) of the mothers earned graduate degrees.
- The one adult client earned a clinical graduate degree, and three of the clients were in college at the time of the study.

PROVISION OF EDUCATIONAL THERAPY

Reasons for Seeking Educational Therapy

Respondents were asked to check all reasons that applied for why educational therapy was initiated (see Table 17.1).

In the academic domain, respondents gave a total of 98 replies concerning the components of reading (reading words, fluency, and comprehension). Writing (mechanics, quality, and structure) received a total of 108 replies. Mathematics (calculation, reasoning, and applied life math) received a total of 26 replies. "Low grades" were cited 16 times as one of the reasons educational therapy was initiated.

Eighteen (18) or more of the respondents were concerned about all the processing and strategies skills listed, with the exception of spatial skills. The greatest number of respondents checked study strategies (30), organizational problems (29), sequencing and ordering (28), and time management (26).

Attention to task, homework issues, self-confidence, and procrastination were checked by 20 or more respondents under the "Behavioral and Social" category.

Grade Level at Initiation of Educational Therapy

Educational therapy was first initiated in grades ranging from pre-kindergarten to tenth, with 4.3% beginning in kindergarten or pre-kindergarten, 78.8% beginning in elementary school (grades 1–6), 11.4% in junior high school (grades 7, 8, 9), and only 1.4% in high school. Two respondents did not answer this question. Over half (51.4%) began in pre-kindergarten, kindergarten, and grades 1, 2, and 3.

Table 17.1 Reasons Why Educational Therapy was Initiated; by Category (N = 70)

Reason	N	Reason	N
		Academic Needs	
Writing mechanics	43	• Low grades	16
Reading comprehension	39	• Verbal expression	14
Writing structure	38	• Math calculation	1
Reading pace/fluency	30	• Math reasoning	11
Reading words	29	• Oral comprehension	9
Writing quality	27	• Applied life math	4
Vocabulary development	18	• Other	2
Processing/Strategies		**Behavioral/Social**	
Study strategies	30	• Attention to task	26
Organizational problems	29	• Homework issues	26
Sequencing and ordering	28	• Self-confidence	20
Time management	26	• Procrastination	20
Following directions	23	• School-related anxiety	14
Listening skills	21	• Social skills	12
Memory skills	20	• Motivation	10
Note taking	20	• Responsibility	9
Visual processing	19	• Attitude toward school	8
Test-taking strategies	18	• School behavior	6
Spatial skills	7		

Duration

The average length of time spent in educational therapy was 3.8 years. Six clients spent 9 to 10 years in educational therapy. Twenty-one spent 2 years, and 10 clients spent 1 year.

Other Services

Educational therapy was the only ancillary service in addition to regular schooling provided to 18 (25.7%) clients. Subject matter tutoring was the most common service in addition to educational therapy provided to the clients. Twenty (28.6%) respondents reported that tutoring was conducted concurrently, and another 8 (11.4%) reported that tutoring occurred before and during, during and after, and before, during, and after educational therapy services. Fifteen (21.4%) received speech and language therapy at the same time as educational therapy. Fourteen (20.0%) received psychotherapy concurrently with educational therapy; 11 (15.7%) received occupational therapy. Fourteen (20.0%) received help from resource specialists in school during educational therapy, and one client was a student in a privately funded clinical school.

Services Provided by the Educational Therapist

Two survey questions were asked relating to specific services provided by the educational therapist. Table 17.2 reports the results of school-related or other services provided by the educational therapist. The most frequent contact the educational therapist had with a

Table 17.2   Services Provided by the Educational Therapist (ET)

The ET interacted with the school to arrange and/or attend the following:		
	N	**%**
Teacher telephone contacts	30	42.8
Teacher conferences	26	37.1
Parent/Teacher conference	21	30.0
Individual Educational Plan (IEP) meeting	12	17.1
Classroom observations	11	15.7
Student Support Team (SST) meeting	7	10.0
Workplace observations	2	2.9
Other helping services provided by the ET:		
	N	**%**
Explained options for accommodations	30	42.9
Provided support in stressful situations	27	38.6
Served as spokesperson/facilitator	24	34.3
Ensured agreement in writing education plane	19	27.1
Facilitated professional referral as needed	18	25.7
Prepared questions/requested services	15	21.4

school was through telephone conversations with a teacher (42.9%), followed by attending a conference with a teacher (37.1%) or a parent/teacher conference (30%).

Parent Perspectives

Parents responded positively to the provision of services provided to their children by the educational therapist. As reported in Table 17.3, 80% or more strongly agreed or agreed that the educational therapist provided a supportive setting, honored their input into goal setting, discussed and clarified assessments, assisted in building confidence and a sense of self-competency in their child, and helped them understand the strengths and challenges of their children. The educational therapist helped parents learn alternative methods for teaching their child, and the parents tended to agree that the findings of the educational therapist were consistent with their own perceptions of their child. Although 72.9% of parents felt they learned what accommodations their children needed to acquire, it remains a concern that more than 25% of these parents often are not aware of how to incorporate these accommodations for the benefit of their children.

Almost two-thirds of the parents agreed that "The duration of the educational therapy was discussed," and "A plan was made for future meetings to evaluate, refine, and revise goals." For the others, these issues may not have been discussed either because they were unknown or considered implicit. The two services that a quarter of the parents did not feel applied to them, or to which they did not respond, related to whether the educational therapist "addressed personal and social crises that interfered with academic tasks and goals" and made referrals "to appropriate allied professionals as needed." This suggests that these areas did not arise or were not indicated as necessary during educational therapy, an implication of the study that requires deeper investigation, considering the interdisciplinary nature of the profession.

Table 17.3 Number and Percentages of Parents' Perspectives of Services

		SA/A	N	SD/D	NA
The ET provided a supportive setting in which to talk, share, and learn	n	62	5	2	1
		88.6%	7.1%	2.9%	1.4%
My input was honored in setting goals for the educational therapy	n	61	4	3	2
		87.1%	5.3%	4.3%	2.9%
The formal and informal assessments were discussed and clarified in understandable language	n	61	5	2	1
		87.1%	7.1%	2.9%	1.4%
The findings of the ET's assessment were consistent with my perceptions of my child	n	60	3	4	2
		85.7%	4.3%	5.3%	2.9%
I learned about my child's areas of strengths and weaknesses	n	56	9	2	2
		80.0%	12.9%	2.9%	2.9%
The duration of the educational therapy was discussed	n	45	13	7	4
		64.3%	18.6%	10.0%	5.3%
The ET's intervention plans were consistent with my goals	n	59	6	2	3'
		84.3%	8.6%	2.9%	4.1%
The ET helped build confidence and a sense of self-competency in my child	n	58	4	7	1
		82.9%	5.3%	10.0%	1.4%
I learned how skills/competencies could be taught to my child through alternative methods	n	54	7	4	5
		77.1%	10.0%	5.3%	7.1%
I learned what accommodations my child needed to acquire skills and competencies (e.g., extra time, books on tape, tape recording)	n	51	6	7	6
		72.9%	8.6%	10.0%	8.6%
A plan was made for future meetings to evaluate, refine, and revise goals	n	43	15	6	6
		61.4%	21.4%	8.6%	9.6%
The ET referred us to appropriate allied professionals as needed for specialized problems that surfaced during sessions	n	34	6	3	27
		48.6%	8.6%	4.3%	38.6%
The ET addressed personal and social crises that interfered with academic tasks and goals	n	32	12	7	19
		45.1%	17.1%	10.0%	27.1%

SA/A = Strongly Agree/Agree; N = Neutral: Sd/D = Strongly Disagree/Disagree; NA = Not Applicable/ No Answer.

Parent Evaluation of Educational Therapy

In general, educational therapy was considered successful in meeting the academic, behavioral, and social needs of clients. Half to two-thirds of the respondents believed educational therapy helped improve grades and reading skills.

More specifically, for two-thirds of the clients, educational therapy was helpful in word decoding, fluency, and comprehension. Further, slightly more than half of the parents perceived that educational therapy not only helped to improve grades in school, but also helped develop efficient reading techniques and improve the quality and organization of ideas in writing. 67.1% of the parents saw improvements in writing mechanics. Almost one-third improved in math, but over half the respondents gave "Not Applicable or No Answer" responses, implying that math skills were not targeted and addressed as an issue needing remediation, an implication supported by Table 17.1.

Approximately half of clients improved in their study habits, test-taking, time management, and ability to generalize. Less than one-third improved in note-taking.

Almost half (47.1%) of the respondents reported that the client fulfilled homework demands with less resistance and turned in work on time, and learned to express feelings and anxieties related to learning processes and the demands of school. Over a third (38.6%) of the respondents felt that educational therapy helped the clients use knowledge of strengths in developing plans for the future. While 31.4% of respondents felt that educational therapy had helped them develop and maintain social relationships, 54.3% either did not respond or felt that this behavior was "Not Applicable." Slightly more than a quarter of the respondents (28.6%) felt that the clients had been helped to develop stress management techniques, with 45.7% not responding or saying this was "Not Applicable."

Overall Evaluation

Sixty-three or 90.0% of the respondents reported that educational therapy had provided them with needed support, and 62 (88.6%) of the respondents felt that educational therapy helped their children function more effectively. Not only did educational therapy help clients function more effectively at school, behaviorally and socially, but almost three quarters (74.2%) of respondents perceived it as also helping families function more effectively.

All respondents paid privately for the educational therapy. Although it is encouraging to note that 39 (55.7%) of the respondents were able to terminate because the client was progressing satisfactorily in school, 4 respondents left because the client was not making progress. Financial concerns were mentioned by 17.1% of the respondents.

DISCUSSION

"Success" in educational therapy was defined in this survey by the authors as (1) satisfactory independent progress in school, and (2) favorable evaluations of the interventions by the clients' parents. Success defined in this way may not be attributed solely to the interventions by the educational therapist; the efforts of the parents and school personnel, as well as the increasing maturity of the clients, play a significant role as well. All people involved in the life of the child play a role in the ultimate success of any intervention.

The data presented indicates that the majority of the parents perceived educational therapy as being successful. Written comments from the parents buttress this conclusion; e.g., "Educational therapy made a huge, positive difference in his life and in his school experience. I don't know where and how he would have ended up without it." Certain responses highlight areas that require more intensive and focused attention in the professional training of educational therapists.

A very common question asked by parents was the expected duration of educational therapy services. It depends, of course, on the child's strengths and weaknesses, the rate at which the child progresses, and the plan, program, and expectations of the parents, educational therapist, and the school. The average length of educational therapy reported by respondents in this survey was 3.8 years, although 31 (44.3%) spent one to two years. Comments made by parents indicate that those who were in educational therapy longer had more pervasive and/or more severe difficulties in academic skills. Further research with a larger pool of respondents would increase the validity of the data, allowing a more in depth analysis of age, gender, socio-economic status, language preference and skills, and residence (rural, suburban, urban) in each case. Are those clients who began educational therapy in pre-kindergarten or kindergarten those whose problems were more severe (thus resulting in earlier intervention)? Are these the same clients who remained longer in therapy? Did certain indications for educational therapy arise only in higher grades? Is there some procedure for operationalizing severity of learning difficulties?

The number of clients who received tutoring as well as educational therapy is somewhat puzzling, even though tutoring and educational therapy serve different and often overlapping functions. Did parents who wanted to keep their children in public school pay for both educational therapy and tutoring to help ensure that their children kept up with their peers? Older clients who need help in advanced subjects, such as calculus, are often referred to tutors who are experts in a particular field and continue to receive help from the educational therapist in processing and strategic areas. In this survey, however, the parents responded that clients received tutoring in elementary and junior high schools. A therefore clearer distinction between educational therapy and tutoring needs to be articulated, and included in future research, presenting the ET with an opportunity to clearly address this distinction at the outset of educational therapy with a client.

The relatively low number of responses to the listing of educational therapist and school interactions indicate that educational therapists may need specific training in how and when to collaborate with school personnel. It should be noted that some parents expressly prohibit the educational therapist from contacting the school. It may also be that parents checked only one service on the survey instead of all that might have been relevant to the client. Referrals to educational therapists come predominantly from school personnel, a strong reason to more fully investigate how this critical professional alliance may be improved upon. Additionally, it may be helpful to have school personnel address educational therapists in training through in-service workshops, thereby establishing the boundaries of how ET's may be helpful to clients, and to the school as well.

A similar issue is the relatively low number of other services for the client reported by the parent. Further research can determine whether parents believe that their input is perceived as important in determining how the goals of educational therapy may be realized.

Almost three-quarters (72.9%) of the parents felt that they learned what accommodations their child needed to acquire skills and competencies. Learning difficulties persevere across the life span, although perhaps manifest themselves in different ways, depending upon the stage of human development. Most parents continue to help in seeking appropriate accommodations in work, school, and social settings, advocating their children's needs when required, and teaching their children to self-advocate.

Difficulty in writing (mechanics, quality, and structure) was checked more than any other subject as the reason for initiating educational therapy. Average improvement in these areas was 60.5%. Writing is a very complex skill, as is the teaching of writing skills, and one that can be included in the professional training of educational therapists.

Over half of the respondents agreed or strongly agreed that educational therapy had positively impacted their child's self-confidence, behaviors and attitudes toward school, and in the learning and acquisition of appropriate strategies. Although parents rated stress management, social relationships, and planning for the future less positively, a high percentage of parents also did not respond or felt that these areas were "Not Applicable" for their child. This is yet another indication that a clear distinction must be articulated between tutoring and educational therapy, as some parents may be depending upon the ET to provide only skill-based assistance, or monitor the progress of assignments in school. Further study in this area will also help the ET determine how and if a therapeutic approach is present in the client-ET relationship.

In some instances the client was perhaps too young to merit serious concern for the future. Because children with learning difficulties experience stress frequently, and because high levels of stress interfere with learning, ET's can provide clients with training in behavioral methods of lowering stress. For extreme cases that are not responsive to simple stress reduction techniques, referrals to other professional interventions may be indicated, yet another indication of further study.

Fifty percent (50%) or more of the parents responded positively, and 10% or more responded negatively to the following items, indicating the need for further attention: improvement in study habits, test-taking, time management, note-taking, ability to generalize, attitude toward school, "stick-to-it-tive-ness," taking increased responsibility for academic outcomes, and learning to use knowledge of strengths in developing plans for the future. These qualities may be considered "how to learn in academia and life," and are qualities specifically in the domain of educational therapy.

This is another implication for further study and for additional professional training for ETs.

It must be emphasized that efficacy of educational therapy as explored in this survey has been assessed only for clients from English-speaking, higher income families. The question of its efficacy for clients from more diverse backgrounds has not been studied, and cannot be until educational therapy is more affordable for everyone who may benefit from these specialized services.

RECOMMENDATIONS AS A RESULT OF THE STUDY

1. A further study of the family and environmental perspectives of the treatment is needed, with an increased awareness of the importance of collaboration among parents, teachers, and all other family members and professionals concerned with the academic, social, and emotional development of the client.

2. An ongoing and reflective assessment of the practice of educational therapy will help to establish short- and long-term goals in collaboration with the client and family. Collaboration and reflection will enable both the ET and the client to develop methods for the cultivation of knowledge and skills, or learning *how* to learn in school and in life situations.

3. Efforts to make educational therapy affordable will offer a larger pool of clients the benefits of receiving the unique services offered by an ET. The respondents to this survey mentioned the time and expense the family expended on the services of an ET. A comment from a parent illustrates the issue: "The only problem with educational therapy is the cost. Our child needed so much of it that the cost was very hard on us and would be to most families." The AET must continue to address this problem of affordable services. At the same time the organization is committed to training more professionals for the field to ensure a wider range of available services. The desirability of setting fees on a sliding scale can be endorsed during training, in journal articles, and in study group discussions. The organization must also do whatever it can to make educational therapy available to children in the public schools as well as through private practice, which may or may not be covered by insurance.

4. Further training for professionals can be enhanced through follow-up studies, using the original survey form adjusted to suit the needs of the group(s) being targeted for analysis.

5. Further studies, based on the results of this study, can be designed through the assistance of grants and donations from public and private sources.
6. The study indicates a need for more clearly articulated and defined boundaries in regard to distinguishing between the roles of the ET and a tutor, or a psychotherapist; and, more specifically, explaining what is the therapeutic aspect of educational therapy. Defining the role and the ability of an ET is necessary in order to be able to establish for the public how these services are unique and useful, and how and why they might better serve the needs of an individual with suspected or diagnosed learning difficulties across the life span.

REFERENCES

Aichorn, A. (1965). *Wayward youth.* New York: The Viking Press.

American Psychological Association (APA): Success. (n.d.). Dictionary.com Unabridged (v 1.1). Retrieved July 26, 2007, from Dictionary.com website: http://dictionary.reference.com/browse/success

Frostig, M., & Maslow, P. (1969). Treatment methods and their evaluation in educational therapy. In J. Hellmuth (Ed.), *Educational therapy, 2* (pp. 413–432). Seattle: Special Child Publications.

Hirsch, K. (1977). Interactions between educational therapist and child. *Bulletin of the Orton Society, XXVII,* 88–101.

Kaganoff, A. (2005). Educational therapy defined. *The Educational Therapist, 22*(1); Los Angeles: The Association of Educational Therapists.

Keogh, B. K., & Ungerleider, D. (2005). A different perspective on differences. *The Educational Therapist, 26*(2).

Ungerleider, D. (2005). You're an educational therapist, but what do you do in that job? *The Educational Therapist, 26*(1).

Ungerleider, D., & Maslow, P. (2001). Edited excerpt from Association of Educational Therapists: Position paper on the SAT. *Journal of Learning Disabilities, 34,* 311–314

Werbach, G. (2002). Psychoeducational perspectives. *The Educational Therapist, 23*(1).

ASSOCIATION OF EDUCATIONAL THERAPISTS
SURVEY OF TREATMENT EFFECTIVENESS 2005

PURPOSE: To assess the efficacy of educational therapy (ET) on academic, strategic, and social/behavioral outcomes.

Survey completed by: ☐ **PARENT** ☐ **ADULT CLIENT**

Referral to Educational Therapy Made By:

☐ Friend/colleague   ☐ Pediatrician   ☐ Psychologist
☐ Teacher   ☐ Psychiatrist   ☐ Speech Therapist
☐ Other (describe) _____

Section One. Client Background Information

☐ Male   ☐ Female   Current age _____
Ethnicity, eg., African-American, Asian, Anglo/European, Hispanic, Middle Eastern, etc.
(optional): _____
(Requested to help us assess the diversity of clients seeking educational therapy)

Language spoken in home:

☐ English   ☐ Other (describe) _____

Adopted:

☐ No   ☐ Yes   If yes, age at adoption _____

Was the client on medication for the following conditions during educational therapy?

☐ ADHD/ADD   ☐ Depression   ☐ Allergies   ☐ Asthma
☐ Seizures   ☐ Other, please specify condition _____

Parent or Guardian Occupation and Education:

Father's occupation _____
Father's highest level of schooling: ☐ grades 1–8, ☐ some high school, ☐ high school diploma,
☐ some college, ☐ college degree (A.A., B.A. or B.S), ☐ graduate degree (circle M.A., M.S., Ph.D.
Ed.D, other _____)

Mother's occupation _____
Mother's highest level of schooling: ☐ grades 1-8, ☐ some high school, ☐ high school diploma,
☐ some college, ☐ college degree (A.A., B.A. or B.S), ☐ graduate degree (circle M.A., M.S., Ph.D.
Ed.D, other _____)

Adult Client Occupation and Education:

Occupation (or current schooling) _____

Highest level of schooling: ☐ grades 1-8, ☐ some high school, ☐ high school diploma, ☐ some college, ☐ college degree (A.A., B.A. or B.S), ☐ graduate degree (circle M.A., M.S., Ph.D., Ed.D, other _____)

Reason Educational Therapy Was Initiated (Check all that apply)

Problems noted in:

ACADEMIC NEEDS	PROCESSING AND STRATEGIES	BEHAVIORAL AND SOCIAL
☐ reading words	☐ listening skills	☐ school behavior
☐ reading pace (fluency)	☐ visual processing	☐ attitude toward school
☐ reading comprehension	☐ memory skills	☐ school-related anxiety
☐ writing/mechanics (spelling, grammar, etc.)	☐ spatial skills	☐ motivation
☐ writing/ quality of ideas	☐ following directions	☐ attention to task
☐ writing/structure	☐ sequencing and ordering	☐ social skills
☐ math calculation	☐ study strategies	☐ self-confidence
☐ math reasoning and problem solving	☐ test-taking strategies	☐ homework issues
☐ applied life math	☐ time management	☐ responsibility
☐ verbal expression	☐ organizational problems	☐ procrastination
☐ comprehension of spoken language	☐ note-taking strategies	
☐ vocabulary development		
☐ low grades		
☐ Other (describe)		
☐_____		

Section Two. Client History

History of Seeking Help:

Age when problems were first suspected: _____

When client was professionally identified as having a learning problem/learning disability:

    Age _____   Grade _____

When client first got special help for the problems:

    Age _____   Grade _____

When was the educational therapy initiated?

    Age _____   Grade _____

Special Services for Client:

NOTE: If services were interrupted and restarted at different times, indicate. Example: 1st to 3rd; 6th & 7th; record services even if they were prior to or concurrent with educational therapy.

1. Educational Therapy
   During what grades? _____

2. Tutoring
   During what grades? _____

3. Resource Specialist Program (RSP), Special Services at school
   During what grades? _____

4. Special Day Class (SDC) or special school
   During what grades? _____

5. Special Education non-public school
   During what grades? _____

6. College special services
   Describe types _____

   _____

7. Speech/language therapy
   During what grades? _____

8. Psychotherapy
   During what grades? _____

9. Occupational therapy
   During what grades? _____

10. Other (describe) _____

    _____

    During what grades? _____

Section Three. Educational Therapy Services and Outcomes

Did the educational therapist interact with the school to arrange and/or attend the following?
(Check all that apply.)

☐ Student Study Team (SST)   ☐ Teacher Phone Contacts
☐ Individual Educational Plan (IEP   ☐ Parent/teacher Conferences
☐ Class Observations   ☐ Workplace Observations
☐ Teacher Conferences   ☐ ADHD Coaching

Did the educational therapist provide other helping services?
(Check all that apply)

☐ Prepared questions and requests for services
☐ Explained options for accommodations
☐ Provided support in stressful situations, such as school conferences
☐ Served as spokesperson or facilitator if requested

PARENT'S / ADULT CLIENT'S PERSPECTIVE ON IMPLEMENTATION:

The educational therapy resulted in the following:
(Rate level of agreement or disagreement from 1 to 5. Circle NA if Not Applicable to you)

strongly disagree	disagree	neutral	agree	strongly agree	not applicable
①	②	③	④	⑤	NA

①②③④⑤NA   The ET provided a supportive setting in which to talk, share, and learn.
①②③④⑤NA   My input was honored in setting goals for the educational therapy.
①②③④⑤NA   The formal and informal assessments were discussed and clarified in understandable language.
①②③④⑤NA   The findings of the ET's assessment was consistent with my perceptions of [myself/my child].
①②③④⑤NA   I learned about [my child's/my own] areas of strengths and weaknesses.
①②③④⑤NA   The duration of the educational therapy was discussed.
①②③④⑤NA   The ET's intervention plans were consistent with my goals.
①②③④⑤NA   A plan was made for future meetings to evaluate, refine, and revise goals.
①②③④⑤NA   I learned how skills/competencies could be taught to [my child/me] through alternative methods.
①②③④⑤NA   I learned what accommodations [my child/I] needed to acquire skills and competencies (e.g., extra time, books on tape, keyboarding, tape recorders, etc.).

①②③④⑤NA   The ET addressed personal and social crises that interfered with academic tasks and goals.

①②③④⑤NA   The ET helped build confidence and a sense of self-competency in [my child/myself].

①②③④⑤NA   The ET referred [me/my family] to appropriate allied professionals as needed for specialized problems that surfaced during sessions.

Outcomes of the Educational Therapy:

The educational therapy resulted in the following:
(Rate level of agreement or disagreement from 1 to 5. Circle NA if Not Applicable to you)

strongly disagree	disagree	neutral	agree	strongly agree	not applicable
①	②	③	④	⑤	NA

①②③④⑤NA   The client improved in word decoding.

①②③④⑤NA   The client improved in reading fluency (pace and smoothness).

①②③④⑤NA   The client improved in reading comprehension.

①②③④⑤NA   The client developed efficient reading techniques, such as surveying textbooks, questioning, summarizing, paraphrasing, etc. ("active reading" skills).

①②③④⑤NA   The client improved in the mechanics (spelling, grammar, punctuation) of written composition.

①②③④⑤NA   The client improved in written expression (quality and organization of ideas).

①②③④⑤NA   The client improved in brainstorming and outlining for writing assignments.

①②③④⑤NA   The client improved in math calculation skills.

①②③④⑤NA   The client improved in math application, reasoning, and solution of word problems.

①②③④⑤NA   The client fulfilled homework demands with less resistance and turned in work on time.

①②③④⑤NA   The client's grades improved.

①②③④⑤NA   The client's study habits improved.

①②③④⑤NA   The client improved in test-taking by developing strategies to help memory, etc.

①②③④⑤NA   The client improved in time management, including use of organizers, lists, charts, etc.

①②③④⑤NA   The client developed efficient note-taking techniques.

①②③④⑤NA   The client was able to generalize (apply) newly learned skills to other settings.

①②③④⑤NA   The client improved in attitude toward school.

①②③④⑤NA   The client's school-related anxiety and frustration level decreased.

①②③④⑤NA   The client developed greater awareness of and self-confidence about his/her abilities.

①②③④⑤NA   The client showed increased "stick-to-it-ive-ness," even on unpleasant tasks.

①②③④⑤NA   The client developed stress management techniques.

①②③④⑤NA   The client became more active in developing and maintaining social relationships.

①②③④⑤**NA**   The client took increased personal responsibility for academic outcomes.

①②③④⑤**NA**   The client developed the ability to describe his/her strengths and weaknesses.

①②③④⑤**NA**   The client learned to use knowledge of strengths in developing plans for the future.

①②③④⑤**NA**   The client learned to express feelings and anxieties related to learning processes and school demands.

Section Four. General Questions

1. Overall, do you feel the Educational Therapy helped [you/your child] function more effectively?

   ☐ Yes ☐ Generally ☐ Sometimes ☐ No

2. Did Educational Therapy help the family function more effective?

   ☐ Yes ☐ Generally ☐ Sometimes ☐ No

3. Did you get the kinds of support you needed from the educational therapist?

   ☐ Yes ☐ Generally ☐ Sometimes ☐ No

4. Did you pay for the educational therapy?

   ☐ Privately ☐ Through insurance ☐ School district

5. When was the major course of educational therapy ended?

   (Disregard occasional follow-up visits)

   ☐ Age _____ ☐ Grade _____

6. Why was the educational therapy ended?

   ☐ Client progressing satisfactorily in school

   ☐ Financial reasons

   ☐ Family moved away

   ☐ Client not making progress

18

THE VOICE OF EDUCATIONAL THERAPY
FOR THE FUTURE
An Integrative Analysis

JANE UTLEY ADELIZZI, MARCY DANN, AND MAXINE FICKSMAN

CHANGING OUR BRAINS FOR SURVIVAL

Jane Utley Adelizzi

> *It's not what if, it's what now.*
> (Author unknown)

When many people decided to take the plunge into The Genographic Project (www.nationalgeographic.com/genographic), their curiosity was in all probability peaked by the media, one of the most relied-upon sources of information in the Western world. While those of us who took the journey felt a sense of connectedness with our ancient roots, there were some people who hoped to uncover vital clues that might lead to a deeper understanding of themselves and the people who passed their unique genomic imprints from one generation to the next. What we did experience as a result of the Genographic Project were some of the common migratory patterns, leading to a treasure trove of implications and projects suitable for many disciplines and across the lifespan, akin to the ancestral and migratory patterns of educational therapy. In 2007 Chicago public schools joined forces with Genographic/Silk Road Partnership, and using the DNA of 1,000 students embarked upon research that focused on a core and sometimes haunting question: Who Am I? What a rich, multicontextual project to undertake.

Should we ruminate about whether or not people who migrated through Asia or Africa and then into more Western European areas experienced a shift in brain development? They did, after all, have to cope and adapt to different climates, possible blends in cultures, and develop new skills in order to survive. Would that thinking then lead us to wonder how brain development impacts learning and functioning in our work as educational therapists? Anthropological and neurobiological considerations may take shape in our thinking, letting us rest on the work of Maryanne Wolf's *Proust and the Squid* (2007) as she led us to the reading brain, or possibly tracing the research on dyslexia by Norman Geshwind and Albert Galaburda for our consideration. We might then stop to listen to Piers Anthony (1995) in *Shame of Man*, as he explored the implications of left-handedness, beyond what most of us know about brain laterality and into the finer details which manifest themselves in the daily lives of people. According to his research, left-handed people are not only still experiencing discrimination in our world, but they are also at a higher mortality risk than their right-handed peers. Do we accommodate left-handedness today when administering assessments to individuals? Are their assessment scores impacted by their ability to copy numbers and symbols as quickly as their right-handed peers? Is their processing speed at a disadvantage when employing paper and pencil skills, working from left to right as the timer ticks away the seconds? As educational therapists (ETs), can we find ways to make what is perceived by many of us as minutiae tasks, more manageable, or just simply fairer? It is fair to answer a resounding "yes" to the above questions.

As we unconsciously continue to ignore what is unfair in our world, do we inadvertently contribute to the increased number of suicides in our society by consistently overlooking the potential for, and the existence of depression in individuals across the lifespan with learning and attentional disorders who are at a greater risk for mood disorders than their peers who do not struggle with these conditions and issues? As ETs, we move and shift our work, and the treatment alliance we have developed with individuals from the clinical setting of our offices to schools and classrooms, to IEP meetings, to home visits, to the workplace, and sometimes to the courtroom. We sit in a privileged position that informs us of the multi-contexts in which our clients suffer indignities to their human spirit, directly influencing how they behave and respond to others. They may be repeatedly humiliated when their shortcomings are exposed to the world as "examples," and when they spend twice the amount of time and energy than their peers finishing a task … on time. Is it any wonder that some individuals who experienced the unrelenting pressure of "keeping up" become depressed as children and adolescents? Is it a surprise that they are often depressed as adults after the mental and emotional equivalent of climbing Mount Everest on a daily basis? The answer of course is "no."

It's not a secret that depression is a leading cause of suicide in the United States. In October 2008 our fellow researchers in Canada reported that there is an abnormal distribution of the neurotransmitter, GABA, in individuals who are depressed. The presence of GABA in the frontopolar cortex of the brain is located in an area responsible for the ability to mentally retain and manage a goal, while simultaneously managing smaller and connected goals, a process we might refer to as cognitive multi-tasking, much like what we and our younger clients engage in as part of daily life: text messaging while shopping, doing homework, or listening to a teacher talk about Shakespeare. The prefrontal cortex is the home of executive functioning, an area in which multi-level communications take place, contributing to evidence-based decision-making; to the experiencing and demonstration of emotional responses to a variety of external stimuli; and, to the ability to remember where we are going, why we are going, and what we need to bring with us.

The scatter of GABA, or its unavailability for the purposes of feeling good, can be ameliorated or assisted to some degree with pharmaceuticals, mindful meditation, yoga, or similar practices (Wenner, 2009). Laughter promotes an increase of endorphins and GABA invites good feelings to the forefront, sending unpleasant feelings on a hasty retreat to the background, even if just temporarily. As these good feelings take center stage in our lives, they are simultaneously playing a role in changing brain chemistry. It is with the unconscious process of engaging in activities that increase endorphins and the subsequent role of GABA, that our clients, as well as ourselves as ETs, are able to function in a more satisfactory manner. We are then able to move forward in a less inhibitory manner, feeling not quite as skittish about looming tasks which pose the potential threat of becoming fears, or new triggers for old responses. Many people with comorbid diagnoses that impact learning and functioning become consciously aware of this cycle, which tends to become repetitive, eventually impacting the willingness to engage in what is perceived as a threatening undertaking. Fear and avoidance then become the task-masters in daily life, which leads to making oneself invisible in the classroom or in the workplace.

A molecule called methyl is often attached to a GABA-A receptor, inhibiting the opportunity for increased growth of that amino acid, thereby decreasing opportunities for good feelings (Wenner, 2009). The occurrence of this phenomenon in victims of abuse, which encompasses a wide range of situations and events, takes place in the hippocampus, the location for short-term memory. This is no surprise to most of us when we think about how our levels of anxiety impact how fast we think on our feet, or rather how slowly we retrieve important information when we're fighting for control over our emotions. If we accept the notion of classroom trauma (Adelizzi, 1998, 2003; Adelizzi & Goss, 1995, 2001), then this phenomenon is not surprising considering the repeated kinds of psychological abuse some children and adolescents endure during their educational histories, nor is it surprising that this theory is understandable in adults who were educated in systems and cultures that used corporeal punishment as well as public humiliation. With the anticipation of another unpleasant event that is unavoidable (e.g., being called on in class), the individual may become disoriented, panicked, lose the ability to recall recently acquired information, and be unable to retrieve language that appropriately addresses the situation. Or, does this provide the educational therapist with food for thought regarding the self-imposed persona of the class comedian, a clever, albeit unconscious way to generate the good feelings that come from GABA, while simultaneously deflecting criticism? We underestimate the skills and resilience of some of our students who bear the diagnosis of being learning disabled. They cope and adapt brilliantly.

However difficult some children and adolescents find the educational system, specifically the daily survival of the classroom and playground, some of these individuals demonstrate more resiliency than others, and make the journey into adulthood with their dignity more intact than in other cases where individuals retreat further and further into themselves, their psychoeducational profiles eventually leading to psychiatric diagnoses. Individual profiles are greatly impacted by environmental factors which are certainly key factors in either success or failure in life's many contexts. However, genetic patterns cannot be underestimated and can claim anywhere from 40% to 60% of susceptibility to mood and anxiety disorders (Canli, 2008). We do not pay enough attention to the multi-layered contributing factors with a client's repeated stumbling blocks, nor to the mysterious and surprising success on a previously failed task.

A decade ago Bridget Murray, a reporter for the *Monitor on Psychology*, informed readers that neuroscientists were learning more about how brain imaging research potentiates the identification of learning disabilities as well as instruction in the classroom. This might lead to the revelation of effective intervention and instruction with the use of pre- and post-brain imaging. What a seemingly amazing and simple approach to what remains today as a head-scratching puzzlement for many professionals who endeavor to design and implement individualized instruction for children and adolescents with a range of learning disabilities, each profile as uniquely mystifying as the next. Bringing education and neuroscience together to address these specific needs will steadily nudge scientific research forward, providing teachers with individualized instruction plans that are based on empirically sound feedback. The ET, in this case, will take on the role similar to that of a compounding chemist, considering the diagnosis and prescription issued by the medical profession, based on pre- and post-brain imaging results. She may then work from her generic template for intervention, adding components that are sensitivity-free, keeping only that which is compatible to the diagnosis which is directly linked to the research. Each one of these compatible interventions that make up each client's educational treatment plan, is a technological click away, helping to create a highly sophisticated educational therapy treatment plan comprised of empirically based research in conjunction with information regarding the client's ecocultural background as it relates to learning and functioning.

As ETs we might look forward to the day when the disciplines of education and psychology join forces to integrate research and practice in order to develop a comprehensive profile of an individual which includes not only the most recent progress report in school, but also a snapshot at least of how that student copes with stress and disappointment when academic expectations seem overwhelming. Will we collaborate to assess how the underpinnings of executive functioning skills relate to every aspect of human interaction, ranging from negotiating the expectations of family life, to the demands of a classroom, to visual-spatial and perceptual prowess on the soccer field, as well as to the incrementally acquired skills necessary for social relationships in a variety of contexts? How comforting it would be to have our lives, and the lives of our children and grandchildren, regarded as fluidly "whole" and not merely a collection of parts, each of which speaks to a set of tasks which are relegated to an academic discipline, indicating that we shift our behaviors and responses in robotic and predictable ways.

The Reinstitution and the Purpose of Play

When we consider the role of endorphins and GABA in the process of developing a sense of ease with oneself, we might also look at how over the centuries and decades the construct and evolution of "play" has shifted the way in which parents, teachers, and society view what is acceptable and beneficial to children and adolescents. Unstructured play comes with no specific rules unless there are environmental factors that threaten the well being of a participant. It's a natural, ancient, and beneficial practice that allows children to learn how to engage in relationships, share their toys, mimic their parents, and favorite characters in books and on TV. Through the natural predilection of social learning theory, scripting and scaffolding provided by a more experienced playmate such as a sibling or parent (Miller, 2002; Pellegrini & Smith, 2005), lights the pathway for understanding what kinds of behaviors and guidelines are acceptable in order to experience a sense of belonging in a variety of social contexts. Some children engage in more physically aggressive play, which is not always an indication of a budding psychopath, but rather a demonstration of "practice" for protecting oneself against others, and exercising the ability to balance, touch, feel, and gain a sense of self in space, or in relation to other people and the objects that comprise any given area or context. During the earlier stages of unstructured play we may recognize that:

Pretend play often involves object substitution. A wooden block becomes a cake for a picnic, a stick or piece of lego becomes a gun for war play, a cardboard box becomes a boat. Thus, the presence of play props can facilitate play; for younger children it helps if the real object bears some similarity to the pretend object. For older children, greater dissimilarity can be accommodated—a process called decontextualization. A further stage of this development is to imagine the object. (Pellegrini & Smith, 2005, p. 181)

At the stage where we begin to see children either be able or unable to imagine an object, or even imagine what someone else might be feeling or anticipating, may be when we see how the development of empathy unfolds. As the nature of play matures by including more sophisticated scenarios and the incorporation of language in relation to negotiation, and competitiveness in the acquisition and exhibition of skills, the benefit of practice is accruing in preparation for the navigation of life's joys, challenges, and societal expectations.

Free play is a release valve for adolescents as well as for children. It's time to shut the bedroom door after school, turn on the tunes and dance wildly, with a flailing of arms and legs either in sync with the music's rhythm, or simply as a response to incoming stimuli that promotes "feeling good." Teddy bears may be reinstated as a part of free play, often as dance partners, or as the recipients of the news of the day. This is spontaneous play, free-flowing thought and response to the environment, and a release of tension from a day filled with structure.

All too often we tamper with the natural development of play during the various stages of child and adolescent development, the changes arriving as a result of necessity when the management of a home and family requires more than one salary. Family life in the 1960s began to change, and through the 70s, 80s, 90s, and into a new century experienced major changes in how family life was organized and realized. Day care centers were established by the drove, not just for mothers who were single parents and required assistance with childcare, but also for mothers who made the decision to return to work to contribute financially to household obligations, or because women were feeling encouraged to compete in the professional world, experiencing a sense of wholeness that comes with inclusion. After-school programs were established as a way to keep children safe and busy until a family member could pick them up at supper time. Organized sports lost their status of being a sought-after option and became a mandated activity for some youngsters, another way to keep children and adolescents busy and safe for a portion of the day. With the addition of structured play that grew from structured programs and games, came the ghostly presence of past unstructured play, the time when twirling around until you were dizzy was okay; the time when laying on the ground to study cloud formations for boundless periods of time was acceptable because no one was expecting that you do anything other than what you were doing at that moment … except possibly your homework.

It is during these periods of change in our society that ETs can step in and help to reinstate the *practice* time that is invaluable in preparation for life, much as an apprentice-ship or a re-learning of a lost art. As we read the accounts of ETs, we know how clinically valuable it is to engage in dialogue, to joke, to play, to lose or win a game of Candyland Bingo or Scrabble, to draw pictures that have no rules, and to create a climate that forgives mistakes and encourages risks … just for the fun of it sometimes.

As endorphins dance wildly and GABA opens the door a crack to view slivers of the underpinnings of executive functioning in a less anxious way, we can see the importance of reinstating the irreplaceable practice of free play in our lives in order to keep our keyboards and soccer rules in their place. The shaping of our brains as individuals, and as a culture of human beings who learn and function, can occur not only with the institution of technology and structured activities, but also from the scripts we write in our heads, the dialogue we share with our best friends, and the time we spend with our imaginary friends....

THE FUTURE OF TECHNOLOGY IS ALREADY HERE

Marcy Dann

Technology will never replace the human interaction that is crucial to the treatment alliance between the ET and her client. The trend towards computer-based learning will continue to grow, enabling students to engage in learning that is individualized for content, format, and pacing. As the use of technology becomes more prevalent in classrooms, often beginning in the first grade, the clients who seek educational therapy may encounter academic, social, and emotional difficulties as they endeavor to navigate the complex systems that have evolved over recent decades. An ET will seek professional training to keep updated with applicable computer programs for her clientele, and with technological skills that enable her to organize, remediate, coach, and conduct research within the scope of her practice.

The general population of ETs can be regarded in two general sub-groups in relation to technology: (1) those who are regarded as technologically savvy, and (2) those who are regarded as less proficient in their skills. Some experienced ETs can recall times when low-tech assistance was relied upon in classrooms and offices. For example, damp paper copies on a mimeograph machine whose circular arm movement sent an acrid aroma of purple ink through the air was commonplace and considered reasonably advanced. Carbon paper was pushed between sheets to produce a hand-written or typed copy. Teachers learned to "let their fingers do the walking in the Yellow Pages," as they searched the cumbersome hardcopy directory for contact information.

Today, multiple copies are a click away on the keyboard, and online directories provide easy access to information that feels vitally important in an immediate way. In contrast, ETs who are younger and new to the practice cannot imagine life in the classroom or office without high tech tools and the multiple gadgets that have become necessities in life such as cell phones, lap top computers, and hand-held music devices. Their fingers don't do any walking because they touch, click, cut, paste, and drag important information from one location to another in seconds. There has been asynchronous development of technological skills among practitioners, depending upon the type of clientele with whom an ET typically works. While some ETs will continue to eagerly build their skills, keeping abreast of new technology as part of their repertoire, some will choose to pursue this kind of training slowly, carefully choosing what can be comfortably incorporated into practice. The burning question is whether or not ETs are prepared for the future, considering the girth of knowledge that clients are expected to master in their academic lives.

Understanding that our educational system and our home lives have been forever changed with the use of technology is alternately exhilarating and anxiety provoking. The field of special education researched the use of technology and provided resources, products, and services to professionals in their field. Yet, educational therapists have, by comparison, had less exposure and training in these areas, and must pursue training independently to provide updated services for clients.

The landscape of assistive technology in education is augmented by instructional software and the introduction of universal design. Assistive technology is a term that commonly refers to "any device, piece of equipment, or system that helps bypass, work around or compensate for an individual's specific learning deficits" (Raskind & Stanberry, 2006), and ranges from "no tech" to "high tech." Examples of high tech are computer applications that translate speech to text like Dragon Naturally Speaking or iSpeak, or that scan text that can be read aloud like Kurzweil. Part of an ETs independently sought training includes knowing how and when to utilize specific technology with clients, depending upon the type and severity of disability with which they struggle.

When considering the use of assistive technology for a client in educational therapy, the question becomes: Would this technology aim to remediate the client's specific skills deficit, or would the technology be chosen as a compensatory approach that would bypass the deficit? If a client has difficulty learning to read, would instructional software be chosen to teach phonemic awareness, or to expand reading vocabulary? Would an audio E-book or CD be assigned so a client could hear the text, or would the choice be a wireless delivery in an audio-visual format? Dr. Marshall H. Raskind, a researcher in the field of learning disabilities and assistive technology, emphasizes that a client may benefit by both a remedial and compensatory approach. "There is overlap between these two categories with compensatory technologies sometimes having a remedial function. For example, there is evidence that students who use speech recognition systems that convert spoken language to text on a computer screen, may also improve their reading comprehension and word recognition skills through the use of the system" (2009).

Lists of assistive technology tools are available online to help parents of students who struggle with listening, math, organization and memory, reading, and writing (Raskind & Stanberry, 2006), as well as worksheets to help select assistive technology tools. For example, software programs like Microsoft Word afford writers with fluency and legibility during the writing process. Spell check answers our most fervent wishes, especially for students who are orthographically challenged. Using a calculator and a keyboard allow for automaticity. Alphasmart, a portable desktop word processor, allows students to use a lightweight keyboard in class, and although the viewing window is limited, the content can then be uploaded into a desk or laptop computer. The Writer Learning Systems created Fusion, a keyboard that translates text to speech and offers word predictability. Graphic organizer programs like Inspiration aid students who need assistance with the generation, organization, and planning of written language. There are organizations such as Recording for the Blind and Dyslexic that provide audio recordings of books that can be listened to while reading, in lieu of, or along with reading the text. Trained educational therapists are able to assess the needs of a client in order to identify and recommend the best assistive technology tools while taking into consideration the "dynamic interaction between the individual, technology, task and context" to bypass difficulty in specific academic skill areas (Raskind & Stanberry, 2006).

As with learning any new skill, there must be time built in for training, and time built in for assessing progress, and within this process there are "four components to be considered: (1) the individual who needs the technology and their specific strengths, limitations, skill sets, knowledge, and interests; (2) the specific tasks or function the assistive technology is expected to perform (such as comprehension for a reading, writing, or memory problem);

(3) the setting where the assistive technology will be used (school, home, workplace); (4) the device itself including considerations such as ease of operation, reliability, portability and cost." (Raskind, 2009). Assistive technology is designed to enable a client to work at a level commensurate with his cognitive ability, so that his interest and motivation are not compromised.

Additional technology includes the philosophy of Universal Design in Learning (UDL). According to Anne Meyer at the Center for Applied Special Technology (CAST), UDL mirrors universal design movement in architecture and product development. "Think of speaker phones, close-caption television, and curb cuts all universally designed to accommodate a wide variety of users, including those with disabilities. The same features that are built-in to help those with disabilities benefit everyone" (CAST, 2007). Since students with individualized learning profiles are learning at different levels and function at varying paces within classrooms, having the curriculum support access to technology sounds wonderful were we learning and living in an ideal world. This philosophy is aligned with educational therapy as ETs are trained to consider the "whole child" whose learning needs are diverse and personally unique. Consider the stages of the clinical model of educational therapy in order to assess the training, expertise, and intervention ETs require for the future:

1. Willingness of the ET to equip her office with updated computer technology.
2. Willingness of the ET to commit to ongoing and updated training in order to make technology available during sessions, and transfer these skills to clientele.
3. Integrating the topic of technology as part of an initial intake session with the parents and/or clients.
4. Considering assistive technology as part of a formal or informal assessment plan.
5. Including psycho-educational goals that reflect the assessment findings in the integrated use of technology in sessions.
6. Collaborating with parents and school personnel regarding accessibility, operability, organization, engagability, and ease of use of assistive and/or instructional technology in the home and in school.

For an ET to consider including the above list in her practice, she will need to assess current technology tools to choose those best suited to her clientele. As the ET often aligns her psycho-educational goals with what is currently happening in the public school systems, she will need to consider the prevalence of computers in education for the future. The National Association of Independent Schools conducted a study in 2007, which investigated the integration of technology into the curriculum, professional development for the faculty, established policies for the use of technology in schools and classrooms, and current criteria for staffing and systems (Booth, 2009). The use of educational software, word processing, the Internet, and other digital sources for the purposes of research and reading instruction are introduced in primary grades. These skills increase as students progress to middle and high school. The ET is in an ideal position to design a treatment plan, which integrates the use of technology, and which, in collaboration with her own ideas, are those contributed by members of the treatment alliance. The treatment plan is enhanced by her willingness to stay updated with district requirements by visiting the classrooms to observe how technology is used in classroom instruction and in computer labs.

The concept of global connectivity often takes the ET beyond her practice and into the schools which are part of the treatment alliance, as well as into other environments where technology dominates the entertainment and social networking in the lives of clients. The Internet, Web 2.0, has dramatically impacted the environment in which our clients navigate. Clients of all ages, as well as our adult peers, enjoy the interactive nature of the Internet and could easily spend hours surfing the web if physical needs such as sleep and hunger did not interfere (although a common parental complaint is that their child tends to stay up too late sitting at a computer screen and often skipping meals). The future may see students of all ages creating blogs of their own, offering new information and insight to their peers, and finding a forum in which to vent opinions and emotional responses to a variety of issues relevant to their worlds. The future will recognize advances in the concept and functioning of MySpace, Facebook, and LinkedIn, online communities in which members post profile information, submit status updates, and communicate with each other. Social media tools such YouTube and Twitter will likely experience similar growth. It seems that everyone has an email account, but we still can think of a few colleagues who choose their phones as a chief means of communication. As we move into the future these colleagues will become cyber-savvy, joining the ranks of others who will depend on technology for both their personal and professional lives. While problems with the ability to regulate time and energy on the Internet could pose problems for clients with weak skills in that area, the opportunity to interface with other people via technology can be extremely beneficial. Activities of this nature can potentially be assisted by an ET in order to encourage the articulation of thoughts and ideas in language, while simultaneously enhancing social interaction.

Today, books and articles can be downloaded in a click, and Ezines can be sent to our email boxes daily. Will the future see school assignments and agendas automatically downloaded on a student's email account each morning? Will the continuing explosion in technology have implications for the future of distance education? If so, then curricula will be made available to students who experience school phobia, to home-schoolers who will be able to join a group online for discussion, and to the bedside of students who cannot attend school. The potentiality of ETs developing a treatment alliance with more advanced technology than we presently experience is a reality that can encompass the collaboration of experts in specific fields from all over the world, and be available to students in entire districts, states, and even countries, bridging cultural gaps that were otherwise difficult to overcome.

While many adults today can remember the either welcoming or threatening intrusion of technology into their lives, or have at least heard about these experiences from their parents, most school aged children cannot fathom a time when these affordances were not at the fingertips of the general public. The future will recognize history books that outline the evolution of technology, tracing its roots-in-motion from a home or office desktop to the current iPod, which serves as a way to hear one's favorite music, to an expedient way to develop, rehearse, and execute a power point presentation to a lecture hall full of students as well as to thousands who gather online, listening, watching, contributing to this new wave in education.

Students with cell phones often text each other between classes in a short hand language that looks like re-invented spelling. Will the future see our students transferring their thoughts to a screen for the purposes of documentation and communication? This may sound far-fetched, but considering the rapidity of the development of very complex technological systems … it's worth thinking about. If we advance our technology in education to this point, students will be able to check their electronic calendars, chat online, surf the web, play a game, and in the narrow spaces in between these tasks may speak or think their thoughts to another device that will save the process as a means of documenting the meta-analysis of functioning to be reflected upon at a later date … if there's time. What will be sacrificed as this explosion continues to change the lives of individuals across the life span?

The ET of the future will require and employ the same level of sophistication in her technology as the public school system does, and if she is working with clients with suspected or diagnosed learning disabilities she will need to consistently explore updated software and other technological tools that address the needs of this population of learners. She will need to have updated software that allows her an ease of communication with schools, organizations, and professionals whose expertise can contribute to the development of an educational therapy treatment plan. Additionally, her skills in technology will be germane to her ability to administer and score formal assessments, while continuing to provide comprehensive and meaningful written reports for clients and their families. The quality and breadth of service that an ET can deliver will grow as does the field of technology in education. With assistance from an ET, students with learning disabilities will be able to review material, practice skills, learn new vocabulary, develop essays, and rehearse social banter to engage confidently in social exchanges. If students today require repeated instruction or clarification of directions, they can often seek teachers' web pages for information ranging from assignments to due dates to links for educational sites that are relevant to their work. The future will provide ETs, as well as teachers and other members of the treatment alliance, the opportunity to put the client in touch with in-person-information, offered worldwide, and most likely in an on-screen face-to-face format. Will this be another step closer to hybrid models of education in public schools? Will the ET's role shift accordingly, creating another niche for her skills with the student who finds it extraordinarily difficult to learn new concepts through a system of delivery that eliminates the need for an in-person relationship?

Today, private schools, public school districts, and universities are seeking technological solutions to provide immediate communication and effective programming to a wide range of students. Grades are currently monitored online through a variety of programs such as Powerschool or Aeries. Assignments, quizzes, and exams can be posted, taken online, and graded by teachers using a program called WebCT or Moodle. Some teachers post their email addresses as well as their phone extensions on their school's website. Students may be allowed to make arrangements with their teachers to send emails to request additional information. Other students may be allowed to email assignments as attachments or to a teacher's website rather than hand in assignments, so that the assignments are not misplaced or late. Are these more recent changes in education yet another step closer to eliminating what some visionary critics might consider the more extraneous commodities in a school building? If the answer is yes, then this builds a stronger case for the development of distance learning at all levels of education, requiring fewer teachers, although requiring more expanded services from each remaining teacher as she re-considers her notion of praxis. The concept of best practices in teaching will shift as student outcomes become documented, reconsidered, and analyzed through distance learning.

With all the convenience that comes with information and communication arriving in an immediate way, a great deal of foresight is required to plan the use of technology so that it empowers rather than jeopardizes our lives and the lives of students. For ETs in clinical practice, this means examining the balance between what can be gained by using technology and what might be lost. Will the future see ETs meeting with clients in cyberspace? With existing technology, the ET today may sit at her desk in front of the computer screen and watch and listen to a client in a different location read a passage from his paper. The ET and her client are both capable of reading the same document on a shared whiteboard while discussing and making changes to the document. Given these scenarios, consider how the interactivity of the Internet might impact the ET-client alliance and the range of service provided. For which clients might this be ideal? Which clients might still require the live, off-line, in-person relationship with an ET, benefiting from the reciprocity of emotional responses?

As I ponder the ramifications of forming judgments about which clients might benefit from more or less human contact, I'm reminded of reading Ray Bradbury's short story, "There Will Come Soft Rains" (1989), about a family who perished in 2026, leaving a technologically automated house to continue carrying on the daily tasks necessary for human survival. It's hard to believe that the science fiction I read as a child has become a possibility in my lifetime. As mentioned previously, the technological future is already here!

TRAINING EDUCATIONAL THERAPISTS FOR THE FUTURE

Maxine Ficksman

> Education is not the filling of a pail, but the lighting of a fire.
> **(William Butler Yeats, quoted in Litky & Grabelle, 2004, p. 3)**

The future implications for training in educational therapy are limitless and profound; limitless in the capacity to provide worldwide training; and, profound in the potential impact this limitless training has on ETs and their clients for future generations. Currently, ETs work both in the public and private sector, serving children and adults with learning difficulties that may be related to anxiety, trauma, ADHD, executive function, and other comorbid issues. While there has been some advancement in reaching out to students through nonprofit clinics and public agencies, many students and families cannot afford to pay for private clinical educational therapy services. Since there is no licensure for the profession in any state or country, few medical insurance policies cover this expense. Thus far, the Association of Educational Therapists (AET) is the professional certifying body providing standards and ethics of practice, membership requirements for training and continuing education, and board certification in educational therapy, conceived after much consideration by the pioneering ETs in California, and following the recommendation of Dr. Albert Galaburda to fashion the certification after a medical model.

In California and other states, funding for educational therapy services through individualized education programs (IEPs) has been greatly reduced due to budget issues. The National Institute for Learning and Development (NILD) has been successful in receiving grants from state and federal agencies to fund a limited but growing population of identified at-risk students. The AET continues to identify funding sources to assist this population of students. While educational therapy services will reach some students through these grants and agencies, only a very small percentage of students will benefit from a profession that has the potential to make a tremendous impact on those who experience difficulty in learning. The educational therapy model addresses the needs of individuals with learning disabilities, yet its components of empathy, resilience, self-advocacy, and the love and curiosity of learning can be adopted by all educational institutions for the general population. As public schools identify the benefits of educational therapy services for their students, a greater number of ETs will be hired. The increase in demand for educational therapy services will likewise stimulate the demand for more graduate level training programs and opportunities for jobs in the field of educational therapy.

In Los Angeles, California, institutions such as Kayne-Eras Center—Exceptional Children's Foundation, Watts Counseling and Learning Center, and the Frostig Center in Pasadena, continue to serve at-risk students who need, but cannot afford, educational therapy services. However, in order to serve a broader population, it is critical that clinical training in educational therapy be made available to a wider audience. California State University Northridge (CSUN) and Holy Names University in Oakland will serve as models for universities that seek to provide on-site educational therapy internship opportunities to serve communities without adequate resources. The AET will continue to partner with the National Joint Council on Learning Disabilities (NJCLD) and NILD to influence educational policy and to reach out to at-risk students in these communities. In the future, as the numbers of ETs expand, states will license and recognize educational therapy as a necessary service in public education. Educational therapists will be enlisted to train regular and special education teachers and to assist in developing national, state, and local educational policy based on the principles of educational therapy, hallmarks of the practice and the graduate curriculum. Nancy Burstein, Chair of the Special Education Department at California State University at Northridge (2008), suggests,

> … Educational therapists play a significant and expanding role in providing support and intervention in a variety of settings including public schools, private schools, clinical settings and research institutions. Like other professions, I envision that educational therapists in the future should have state certification, with rigorous standards developed that all training programs would need to meet. Only individuals who complete certification programs would be qualified to provide services as educational therapists.

"Educational Therapy's Ancestry and Migration" by Werbach, Kornblau, and Slucki in chapter 3 of this text provides a comprehensive history of educational therapy training programs throughout the United States and Great Britain. Currently, educational therapy programs in California include California State University, Northridge (CSUN; master's and post-master's certificate), Holy Names in Oakland (master's and graduate certificate), University of California at Santa Cruz Extension (graduate certificate), and University of California at Riverside Extension (graduate certificate). The Massachusetts School of Professional Psychology in Boston is scheduled to offer the first doctoral level course in educational therapy in 2010, an elective for students seeking the credential of doctor of psychology in school psychology, with Jane Adelizzi as the instructor. On March 25, 2009, Professor Jose Cordoves Aviles reported he received approval from the Inter American University of Puerto Rico to develop a master's degree program in special education. The AET will work with the university to integrate the certificate in educational therapy into the new graduate program. Following final approval of these courses for graduate credit and developing an online ET program in Spanish, Professor Aviles hopes the courses will train Hispanic ETs all over the world. When asked what he envisions as the future training of educational therapists, he reported:

The diagnosis of children with every kind of disability is dramatically increasing in Puerto Rico. Educational therapy is what these children need, offering the difference between failure and success in school. Also, it is imperative to raise the consciousness in the government to include educational therapy in the list of funded related services for children with disabilities. The presence of AET in Puerto Rico would be a very important step in this direction.

In the next few years, international clinical educational therapy training opportunities, based on competencies established by AET, will be burgeoning. In February 2009, Marion Marshall, Coordinator of the Holy Names University Graduate Educational Therapy program predicted,

> Training programs need to keep pace with changes in the dynamic field … and reflect that cases are becoming more complex. Classes should be taught by highly experienced ETs and allied professionals who balance history, theory and best practices … each specific case must be viewed holistically within the larger context of the school setting, curricular expectations and family milieu, while keeping in mind the student's cognitive profile.

How do graduate programs in special education differ from educational therapy training programs? Most master's degree programs in special education train teachers who work primarily in the public schools. These courses are prerequisites to graduate programs in educational therapy, providing an essential foundation for the clinical educational therapy curriculum. For example, in a special education assessment course, students learn how to administer and interpret standardized tests required for IEP evaluations and to write an assessment report that includes academic goals and activities based on the assessment results. An advanced assessment course in educational therapy teaches students how to develop a client's learning profile by selecting, administering, and interpreting informal and formal assessment tools from an educational therapy perspective, which considers a client's socio-cultural, behavioral, and emotional background. A course of this nature will assist ETs in learning how to write a psychoeducational report, without the vernacular commonly used by some allied professionals, so that it can be understood by parents and school staff members. Graduate level training in educational therapy will also address the interpretation of cognitive testing and neuropsychological instruments. Other distinct aspects of the course will include the ET learning how to collect, identify, and evaluate the client's specific contextual, or sociocultural, information. This new knowledge helps the ET learn how to develop a treatment plan, which encompasses the creation of a trusting alliance with the client and family and developing and prioritizing specific psychoeducational long and short term goals based on the client's learning profile. Additionally, this course will provide the ET with skills for effective case management, collaboration with all team members, and communication. As in all educational therapy courses, ETs will learn more about how ethical and clinical boundaries relate to their work.

Future programs in educational therapy will be designed to meet three different levels of expertise: the novice with a master's degree in special education or a related field; the novice with experience unrelated to special education (such as law and business); and, the experienced educational therapist. While some allied professionals with training in speech therapy, psychology, occupational therapy, and regular education have expertise in specific areas and will contribute significantly to this multidimensional field, these aspiring

ETs will need additional coursework in order to meet AET's standards for training. For example, as part of the defined standards of training, ETs need to demonstrate evidence of the satisfactory completion of special education coursework that includes techniques in teaching reading and the administering and interpreting of informal and formal assessments. Educational psychologists may have extensive knowledge of assessment but not the teaching of reading; regular education teachers may have extensive knowledge of teaching reading, but not of teaching remedial reading or administering and interpreting assessments to create a treatment plan for children with learning disabilities.

As the number of educational therapists increase, there will be professionals among them who are experienced in, or who aspire to work with specialized client groups such as preschool children, adults in colleges, universities, and vocational settings, in correctional education programs, as well as in mental health programs. Working with literate adults who experience difficulty with written expression, and adolescents and adults whose second language is English and who have the additional struggle of a language based learning disability, requires a different skill set than working with preschool aged children. The future of graduate level training for ETs may include elective coursework in order to meet the needs of the professionals who choose to work with unique client populations.

As technology advances and new devices are utilized in the schools and at home by the students and teachers, the training of ETs will address how to tailor specific devices for a client. For example, students with problems in reading production can download books onto their handheld Kindle and it will read the text for them. Imagine the relief for the student and his parent who spent hours reading the text together so the student could complete his assignment on time. While the level of complexity and sophistication of future learning devices remains unknown, we proceed with the knowledge that our flexibility and curiosity will help us to appropriately revise coursework so that technological advances can be incorporated to meet the learning challenges of our clients. For example, as e-books of different forms become favored over paper books, modifications and techniques to match these technological advances will be developed and addressed in the techniques courses.

Educational therapy coursework and training will be provided through varied channels including online programs at colleges, universities, and extension programs. These professional training and development opportunities can also be available through AET's Educational Therapy Institute (ETI), and conferences and workshops through programs designed by organizations such as AET, NILD, and the Tavistock Clinic in London. For example, students in Britain may take classes offered in the United States, and U.S. students may take classes offered through the Caspari Foundation in London. Providing opportunities for ETs to learn and appreciate the international diversity of methods, approaches, and theories will enhance the experience, knowledge, and skills of all ETs. Students and ETs will be offered a range of training sites ranging from the typical university classroom to their home office. Some classes will be held at specified times in virtual classrooms, while others may be located online 24 hours a day. Students from different cities, counties, and countries will have opportunities to view, share, and critique educational therapy sessions that were prepared as podcasts. Additionally, courses can be offered through the traditional university setting as well as though hybrid models. Training programs may reach into the smallest corners of the world, and be offered in a wide range of languages.

Training opportunities will increase the visibility of the profession to the general public as well as to the professional communities. An increase in graduate programs and training will encourage more cutting edge research and professional writing in the field, addressing the best practices in educational therapy. Educational therapists will publish textbooks, workbooks, and children's books to illustrate to the general public, allied professionals, and parents the unique niche that practitioners fill in a variety of settings. As research informs the public of the positive outcomes of educational therapy for individuals with learning disabilities, schools will include educational therapy as part of their intervention services, leading the practice and profession a step closer to state and national licensure. Both regular and special education teachers will be trained in the utilization of the rudiments of educational therapy with students in their classrooms, collaborating as well with ETs. School administrators will become aware of educational therapy principles, integrating those elements into the curriculum, and informing staff, students, and parents of their importance and usefulness.

As educational therapy training programs expand internationally, the practice of educational therapy will reflect the cultural diversity of the world and as a result more ETs will better understand the distinctiveness of their clients' cultures. Texts such as the present work will be translated into various languages for those in different countries who do not speak English or Spanish as a first language. Parents will be able to seek ETs who may better understand the impact of cultural diversity on learning and academic survival, possibly strengthening relationships in the treatment alliance.

With the potential for an increase in graduate level educational therapy programs throughout the world, the demand for qualified professors and trainers will increase as well. Some graduate professors in related fields such as educational psychology, child development, special education, and speech and language may be recruited and trained in the principles of educational therapy. Additionally, some educational therapists already teaching at the university level and those interested in pursuing a career in teaching at the graduate level would be excellent prospective candidates. While a partial need for this large pool of trainers in educational therapy may be eliminated by piggybacking online courses and programs that are all over the world, training graduate studies' professors in the principles of educational therapy will remain a priority in the near future.

The core principles of educational therapy provide a compatible framework for to-day's educational systems. At the very least, these principles are applicable to courses and workshops that may be provided to educators as part of professional development institutes. Experienced teachers who love their profession and yearn to work one-to-one with students may find educational therapy to be a solution for their retirement years; and, younger teachers may find this a valid route to pursue for part time work which allows them to specialize in unique populations. Counselors and social workers who find themselves working with populations who face struggles with learning and functioning may find educational therapy courses and workshops a stimulus to their practice, broadening their understanding of individuals who benefit from a treatment plan and alliance that addresses these issues. No matter what genre of education, psychology, or social work in which ETs are likely to be found, the core principles maintain a presence.

REFERENCES

Adelizzi, J. (1998). *Shades of trauma*. Plymouth, MA: Jones River Press.
Adelizzi, J. (2003). Posttraumatic stress in women with ADHD. In K. Nadeau & P. Quinn (Eds.), *Gender issues and AD/HD: Research, diagnosis and treatment*. Silver Spring, MD: Advantage Books.

Adelizzi, J., & Goss, D. (Eds.). (1995). *A closer look: Perspectives & reflections on college students with learning disabilities.* Milton, MA: Curry College

Adelizzi, J., & Goss, D. (2001). *Parenting children with learning disabilities.* Westport CT: Bergin & Garvey.

Anthony, P. (1995). *Shame of man.* New York: Tor Fantasy.

Booth, S. (2009). Technology use in independent schools. *Independent School, 68*(2), 70–79.

Bradbury, R. (1989). *There will come soft rains* (Tale Blazers). Logan, IL: Perfection Learning.

Canli, T. (2008, January 31). The character code. Scientific American. Retrieved from http://www.sclam.com/article. cfm?id=the=character=code

CAST, Inc. (2007). Retrieved from http://lessonbuilder.cast.org/window.php?src=videos

Galaburda, A. M. (2005, March). Neurology of learning disabilities: What will the future bring? The answer comes from the successes of the recent past. *Learning Disability Quarterly, 28*(2), 107.

Ingram, J. C. L. (2007). *Neurolinguistics: An introduction to spoken language processing and its disorders.* New York: Cambridge University Press.

Litky, D., & Grabelle, S. (2004). *Education is everyone's business.* Alexandria, VA: ASCD.

Miller, P. H. (2002). *Theories of developmental psychology* (4th ed.). New York: Worth Publishers.

Murray, B. (2000, March). From brain scan to lesson plan. *Monitor on Psychology, 31*(3).

Pellegrini, A., & Smith, P. (2005). *The nature of play: Great apes and humans.* New York: Guilford.

Raskind, M. (2009). Retrieved from http://www.ncld.org/at-school/general-topics/assistive-technology/choosing-an-assistive-technology

Raskind, M., & Stanberry. (2006). http://www.greatschools.net/LD/assistive-technology/parents-guide-to-assistive-technology.gs?content=784ScienceDaily.Retrievedfrom http://74.125.47.132/search?q=cache:BEWzyf_jORMJ:www.sciencedaily.com /releases/2006/11/061101151341.htm+statistics+of+suicide+and+learning+disabilities&hl=en&ct=clnk&cd=1&gl=us

Wake Forest University Baptist Medical Center. (2006, November 3). Reading disabilities put students at risk for suicidal thoughts and behavior and dropping out of school.

Wenner, M. (2009, February/March). The suicidal brain. *Scientific American Mind, 11.*

Wolf, M. (2007). *Proust and the squid: The story and science of the reading brain.* New York: Harper.

EDITORS

Maxine Ficksman, MA, MA, BCET, FAET earned her BS in secondary education/social sciences, from Boston University, MA from Adelphi University in secondary education, and a second MA in reading with distinction plus a special education credential from CSUN. In 1969, she joined Volunteers in Service to America (VISTA), working with underachieving readers and continued working in the field of education as a reading specialist, learning specialist, and consultant. For the past 20 years, Maxine has worked in private practice as a board certified educational therapist. Additionally, Maxine has been employed as a graduate part-time instructor for three educational therapy post master's training programs. For her work in community service, coordinating and providing educational therapy services for students involved in the Juvenile Justice Connection Project, Maxine was recognized by the city and county of Los Angeles. During her AET presidency (1994-1996), Maxine spearheaded the formation of several training programs in California and subsequently developed and coordinated the UCLAX graduate level educational therapy certificate program. In 1998, Maxine co-wrote with Ann Kaganoff, "The AET Graphic Model of Educational Therapy", published in the *The Educational Therapist*. The model was the first published visual paradigm for the field of educational therapy. In 2007, as Chair of Graduate Education for AET, Maxine developed and coordinated the AET Educational Therapy Institute (ETI). Maxine currently serves as a consultant to the CSUN educational therapy master's and post master's certificate programs.

Jane Utley Adelizzi, PhD, BCET, FAET earned her doctoral degree in educational studies at Lesley University in 1996, her dissertation focusing on the impact of psychological trauma on learning and functioning in women with learning disabilities. She is a board certified educational therapist, registered art therapist, and a certified Canadian counselor. Jane is Professor Emeritus at Curry College, where in 1985 she completed her M.Ed. degree, the concentration of which addressed tailoring techniques and structures that provided frameworks to enhance the academic performance of students with diagnosed learning disabilities. Jane's publishing career began in 1994 in the article, "The Unconscious Processes in the Teacher-Student Relationship", for the journal, *The Educational Therapist*. Throughout her professional career she has continued to publish magazine and journal articles; be interviewed by the *Monitor on Psychology* in 2003 on her contribution to the book, *Gender Issues and ADHD* (2002); be interviewed by CN8 journalist, Barry Nolan, on her co-authorship of *Parenting Children with Learning Disabilities* (2001); authored *Shades of Trauma* (1998); and, co-edited *A Closer Look: Perspectives & Reflections on College*

Students with Learning Disabilities (1995). During her academic and publishing career she introduced the concept of "classroom trauma", the symptomatology of which relates to anxiety and mood disorders, and in more severe cases to posttraumatic stress symptoms. Presently, the focus of her work is a culmination of her former research and publications, and focuses on the overlap of symptomatology in mood and anxiety disorders, learning disabilities, and attentional disorders.

CONTRIBUTORS

In Tribute:
    Beverly Metcalf, an exemplary clinical educational therapist and kind friend.

Roslyn Arnold, MBA (HEM) (UnivLond.) PhD, MA, MEd (UnivSyd), DipEd is an Honorary Professor in the Faculty of Education at the University of Sydney where she has spent most of her career. She has been a professor, Dean of Education, and Head of School at the University of Tasmania and Pro-Dean and Head of School at the University of Sydney. Her research interests include writing development, arts education, teacher education, leadership development, and empathic intelligence, a theory of teaching and learning which conceptualizes the qualities of exceptional educators. She has delivered keynote addresses on her research interests in Australia, the United States, England, Canada, and Singapore. Her books include *Writing Development: Magic in the Brain* (Open University, 1992), *Empathic Intelligence: Teaching, Learning, Relating* (UNSW Press, 2005), and a collection of her poems, *Mirror the Wind* (St Clair Press, 1997). She has received a University of Sydney Teaching Excellence Award.

Mickey Kirar Ashmun, MS, BCET earned her master of science degree in special education at the University of Wisconsin. Her first job was with special needs children in Waianae, Hawaii, and for 2 years she taught children in the Peace Corps in Nepal. For over 35 years, she has worked in Northern California as a special education teacher, learning specialist, and currently as an educational therapist in private practice. Her own work was enriched through collaboration with Dr. Natalie O'Byrne, a psychiatrist in the area, and Beverly Metcalf, a fellow educational therapist. She joined AET in the early 1980s and is a board certified educational therapist (BCET).

Marcy Dann, MA, BCET has been in clinical practice in educational therapy for over 22 years. Marcy has also served as a part-time instructor for the educational therapy certificate and master's courses at UCLA Extension, the Educational Therapy Institute (ETI), and CSUN. Currently, she is the coordinator of the master's and post-master's certificate programs in educational therapy at California State University, Northridge (CSUN) and a consultant at Bridges Academy, a school for twice-exceptional students. Marcy is President-Elect of the Association of Educational Therapists (AET).

Susan Fogelson, MA, BCET, FAET has been an educational therapist in private practice working with children and adults in the Los Angeles area for over 30 years. She received her bachelor's degree in psychology at Barnard College, Columbia University, and her master's in learning and reading disorders at California State University Northridge. A founding member and past president of the Association of Educational Therapists, she continues to work with AET on the Certification Board. Additionally, she has organized and moderated the Ethics Panels presented at AET's National Conferences for the past 8 years.

Diane Goss, EdD is a professor in the Program for the Advancement of Learning at Curry College in Milton, MA, the first U.S. postsecondary support program for students with learning disabilities. She also administers psychoeducational assessments for the college's Educational Diagnostic Center. Diane earned her doctorate in adult education at Teachers College, Columbia University, and has over 30 years experience working with students who struggle with learning. She has also provided consultation and training for the Massachusetts Department of Education and for alternative schools and adult education programs. Diane's publications include *Parenting Children with Learning Disabilities* (Bergin & Garvey, 2001); *A Closer Look: Perspectives and Reflections on College Students with Learning Disabilities* (Curry College, 1995); "To Tell or Not to Tell: The Workplace Disclosure Dilemma for College-Educated Adults with Learning Disabilities" (*The Educational Therapist*, Summer/Fall 2008).

Ann Kaganoff, PhD, BCET, FAET is a past president of AET. She received her doctorate in reading and language development from the University of California, Santa Barbara, Graduate School of Education in 1981. She has worked in education for over 50 years, teaching students ranging from preschool to graduate school. She served on the faculty of the University of California at both Santa Barbara and Irvine campuses in the capacity of clinical practice and teacher training. Ann was Acting Assistant Director of Teacher Education at UC Irvine, and the founder and director of the UC Irvine Reading and Neurolinguistic Clinic from 1984 to 1992. She is currently in private practice as an educational therapist in Irvine, California, and specializes in all aspects of literacy skills, including reading, writing, and critical thinking for learners of all ages.

Karen A. Kass, PhD, MFCC, BCET, FAET received her master's degree in special education from New York University, and a doctorate in psychology and special education from Yeshiva University. She taught students in special education in Spanish Harlem and developed special educational materials for classroom teachers. A board certified educational therapist and licensed marriage and family therapist, Karen has been in private practice in West Los Angeles for over 20 years. Karen served as Senior Educational Specialist of the Dubnoff Center for Child Development and Educational Therapy and Dean of the College of the Center for Early Education in Los Angeles. As Dean, she, in collaboration with AET, developed the first graduate certificate program in educational therapy in Los Angeles. Karen is currently a part-time instructor in the graduate programs in educational therapy at California State University, Northridge and the Educational Therapy Institute (ETI).

Phyllis Koppelman, MEd, BCET is a graduate of UCLA in English/speech. She earned her MEd in special education from UC Berkeley. She is an educational therapist, founder, and mentor for Strategies for Learning, a private clinic in Oakland, California. For over 25 years, Phyllis served as an elementary and secondary classroom teacher, mentor teacher, reading specialist, curriculum designer, staff developer, and school administrator in both public schools as well as independent schools. She coedited an anthology (with L. Reese and J. Wilkinson), *I'm on My Way Running: Women Speak on Coming of Age* (Avon Books, 1985).

Barbara Kornblau, EdD, BCET, FAET has practiced educational therapy in Southern California for over 25 years. A founding member of AET, she served as its second president from 1982 to 1984. Barbara was Assistant Headmaster and Director of Support Services (K-12) at the Oakwood School, in North Hollywood, California. She taught special education courses at various universities and coauthored the chapter, "Teacher's Perceptions and Educational Decisions" with Barbara Keogh, PhD in *New Directions for Exceptional Children*, edited by J. J. Galagher (Jossey-Bass, 1980).

Linda Clow Lawton, BA, ET/P earned a bachelor's degree in communication and public policy from the University of California, Berkeley. She holds a California single subject teaching credential and a certificate in middle level studies from San Francisco State University. Linda received her certificate in educational therapy from UC Berkeley Extension and completed a residency in assessment at the New Learning Clinic in Berkeley. For 20 years Linda has taught nearly every grade level, and currently works with adult clients. For the past 5 years, Linda has maintained her educational therapy private practice in the Berkeley area.

Lori Lennon, PsyD is a certified school psychologist who has worked in Pennsylvania within the Central Bucks School District since 2000. She currently serves as an adjunct instructor in the School Psychology Program at Philadelphia College of Osteopathic Medicine. Lori is certified as a school psychologist by the Pennsylvania Department of Education and the National School Psychology Certification Board. She earned her master of science degree and certification in school psychology from Millersville University and completed her doctoral studies at Philadelphia College of Osteopathic Medicine. In her current role as a practicing school psychologist, Lori serves as a district coordinator and trainer for the implementation of the response to intervention (RTI) model within the district's 15 elementary schools, and as a member of the district's RTI Program and Review Committee. Her professional interest is in applied school-based neuropsychological assessments, including the assessment and intervention of learning disabilities and executive functioning.

Phyllis Maslow, PhD, FAET received her master's degree from the University of Chicago and her doctorate from the University of Southern California. She was an associate of Marianne Frostig from 1959 to 1987, and together they coauthored the textbook *Learning Problems in the Classroom*. She also published several articles as well as a monograph, *The Developmental Test of Visual Perception*. She taught at California State University from 1976 to 1988. She retired as Professor Emerita in 1990 after 2 years as Associate Dean at the College of Education at CSU Long Beach. She has been a long-time professional member, advisory board member, and fellow (FAET) of the AET.

George McCloskey, PhD, is a professor and director of school psychology research in the Psychology Department of the Philadelphia College of Osteopathic Medicine. He frequently presents at national, regional, and state meetings on cognitive and neuropsychological assessment topics. George is the lead author of the text *Assessment and Intervention for Executive Function Difficulties* and *Essentials of Executive Function Assessment* (2009). He has been involved in test development and publishing activities for more than 25 years. He directed the development of the WISC-IV Integrated and was a senior research director and clinical advisor to the Wechsler Test Development Group for The Psychological Corporation (Harcourt Assessment) as well as the associate director of test development for AGS.

Beverly Metcalf, MS, BCET, FAET originally worked as a social worker and received a master of science degree in learning disabilities in 1978. She began her work at the University of California, San Francisco Department of Psychiatry, and in her private practice. In 1984 she was involved in the establishment of the AET in the San Francisco Bay area and has served that organization as president and advisory board chair. Beverly also has served on school boards, as lecturer, and as a consultant when both psychological and educational issues need to be addressed. She has worked on multidisciplinary teams in educational therapy, often including Mickey Kirar Ashmun and Dr. Natalie O'Byrne.

Patricia Mytkowicz, EdD holds an undergraduate degree in English and secondary education, a master of education in special education/learning disabilities, and a doctorate in higher education and curriculum. Her research interests include second language speakers with learning disabilities as well as computer-assisted language learning (CALL) for English language learners. Publications include (2004) "Digital Portfolios for Diverse Learners," *Essential Teacher, 5*(1) and (2009) coauthor of "Multilingual College students with Learning Disabilities," in *Changing Lives Through Metacognitive Relationships: LD/ADHD and College Success.* In her 15 years at Curry College, she has combined her expertise in English education and background in learning disabilities as a learning specialist in the Program for Advancement of Learning (PAL), an internationally renowned support program for college students with learning disabilities. Since 2004, Pat has served as Coordinator of PML for Multilingual Students.

Natalie O'Byrne, MD was originally a pediatrician specializing in adolescents, and returned to postdoctoral training to become a psychiatrist and child psychiatrist. She was an associate professor in the department of psychiatry at the University of California, San Francisco, and has had a private practice which frequently involved working with allied professionals such as educational therapists and psychologists in the schools. In this capacity she has kept a long term collaboration with Beverly Metcalf and Mickey Ashmun. Natalie has led workshops emphasizing the overlap of psychological and educational issues and has been a strong proponent of a developmental approach to understanding children.

Ellen Opell, MA, BCET, FAET received her bachelor's degree in psychology from William Smith College, Geneva, NY and her master's in special education, learning and reading disorders, from CSUN. Ellen has worked as an educational therapist for more than 25 years serving clients of all ages in the Los Angeles area. In addition to her private practice, she has worked in regular and special education as a teacher's assistant, teacher, and supervisor. She also supervises novice educational therapists. Ellen is a frequent member of the Ethics Panel at the Association of Educational Therapist annual conference. She is a past president and a fellow of AET.

Carole Slucki, MS, BCET, FAET received her bachelor's degree in general elementary education from the University of California at Los Angeles (UCLA) and her MS in special education from the University of Southern California. She was a teacher for the Santa Monica Unified School District and concurrently served as a training teacher supervising student teachers from UCLA. Subsequently, she taught elementary school children with learning differences in a small group setting for the Los Angeles Unified School District. For the last 30 years she has maintained a private practice as an educational therapist in Los Angeles. Carole has been a member of AET since 1979 and served as its president from 1988 to 1990. Carole coauthored an article with Susan Fogelson and Gail Werbach, "Educational Therapy Defined" (*The Educational Therapist*, 1986, AET).

Dorothy Ungerleider, MA, BCET, FAET is an educational therapist in private practice in Encino, California and the founding president of the AET. She helped to develop and teach university training programs in educational therapy, and currently mentors public school teachers by implementing Dr. Mel Levine's "Schools Attuned" program. As a faculty lecturer for the National Council of Juvenile and Family Court Judges, she provided workshops for juvenile court judges and probation officers, contributing to a Bench Book for screening delinquent youth. She spearheaded a pro bono community service project for two Los Angeles agencies: the Juvenile Justice Connection Project and New Directions for Youth, bringing remedial and advocacy services to delinquent and high risk youth. She is the author of *Reading, Writing, and Rage* (Jalmar Press, 1996) and *Psychoeducational Perspectives* (AET Publications, 1991).

Patricia Waters, BSc (hons), MA(Ed), Dip. Psych is a senior lecturer in Special Educational Needs at the University of Chichester (UK), where she teaches in the MA(Ed) program. She is also director of the UK Centre for Therapeutic Storywriting which provides training in educational therapy. Following her master's research in therapeutic interventions in schools, Trisha was funded by the Department for Education and Skills (UK) to develop training courses for teachers working with pupils with emotional and behavioral difficulties. Since then she has led a number of research and development projects in the field of educational therapy. She is currently working, in conjunction with the Training and Development Agency for Schools (UK), to promote parent partnership with pupils at risk of exclusion. Her commitment is to developing training models that enhance educational professionals' understanding of the psychological aspects of pupils' learning. Trisha is author of *Therapeutic Storywriting* (David Fulton, 2004). She has presented at many conferences, both in the UK and Europe.

Gail Werbach, MA, BCET, FAET has practiced educational therapy in private practice for over 35 years in the Los Angeles area. She is a founding member and fellow of AET and served as president from 1984 to 1986. Gail has a bachelor's degree in French from UCLA (1967), Certificat d'Etudes: Université de Bordeaux, France, 1964, postgraduate work in education at UCLA (1966), a master's in special education, learning, and reading disorders at CSUN 1979, and was a trainee in educational therapy at Thalians Mental

Health Center, Cedars-Sinai, Los Angeles, 1972. Professional work includes Chairman, Foreign Language Department, Oxon Hill High School, Maryland, 1968 to1969 and Director, Department of Educational Therapy, Ross-Loos Medical Group, 1976 to 1982. She participated in the development of the AET Certification Program (1979–1981) and facilitated the presentation of workshops for training. Gail published "Educational Interventions" in the *Handbook of Child and Adolescent Psychiatry* (Vol. 6, 1998).

Nancy Cushen White, EdD, BCET is Associate Clinical Professor in Adolescent Medicine at UC San Francisco, and she has served as a classroom teacher, special education teacher, and special education program specialist for San Francisco Unified School District. Currently, she is an educational therapist in private practice, and continues to coordinate and teach in the Slingerland Teacher Training Course and Summer School for Students in grades 1–9 at the Dyslexia Evaluation and Remediation Clinic. She is a past member of the International Dyslexia Association Board of Directors, a current representative for the National Joint Committee on Learning Disabilities, and the 2007 recipient of the Margaret Byrd Rawson Lifetime Achievement Award from IDA.

INDEX

Page numbers in italic refer to figures or tables.